VICTIMHOOD NATIONALISM

COLUMBIA STUDIES IN INTERNATIONAL AND
GLOBAL HISTORY

COLUMBIA STUDIES IN INTERNATIONAL AND
GLOBAL HISTORY

Cemil Aydin, Timothy Nunan, and Dominic Sachsenmaier, Series Editors

This series presents some of the finest and most innovative work coming out of the current landscapes of international and global historical scholarship. Grounded in empirical research, these titles transcend the usual area boundaries and address how history can help us understand contemporary problems, including poverty, inequality, power, political violence, and accountability beyond the nation-state. The series covers processes of flows, exchanges, and entanglements—and moments of blockage, friction, and fracture—not only between "the West" and "the Rest" but also among parts of what has variously been dubbed the "Third World" or the "Global South." Scholarship in international and global history remains indispensable for a better sense of current complex regional and global economic transformations. Such approaches are vital in understanding the making of our present world.

Hale Eroğlu, *Muslim Transnationalism in Modern China: Debates on Hui Identity and Islamic Reform*

Sandrine Kott, *A World More Equal: An Internationalist Perspective on the Cold War*

Julia Hauser, *A Taste for Purity: An Entangled History of Vegetarianism*

Hayrettin Yücesoy, *Disenchanting the Caliphate: The Secular Discipline of Power in Abbasid Political Thought*

Anne Irfan, *Refuge and Resistance: Palestinians and the International Refugee System*

Michael Francis Laffan, *Under Empire: Muslim Lives and Loyalties Across the Indian Ocean World, 1775–1945*

Eva-Maria Muschik, *Building States: The United Nations, Development, and Decolonization, 1945–1965*

Jessica Namakkal, *Unsettling Utopia: The Making and Unmaking of French India*

Michael Christopher Low, *Imperial Mecca: Ottoman Arabia and the Indian Ocean Hajj*

Nicole CuUnjieng Aboitiz, *Asian Place, Filipino Nation: A Global Intellectual History of the Philippine Revolution, 1887–1912*

Mona L. Siegel, *Peace on Our Terms: The Global Battle for Women's Rights After the First World War*

Raja Adal, *Beauty in the Age of Empire: Japan, Egypt, and the Global History of Aesthetic Education*

Ulbe Bosma, *The Making of a Periphery: How Island Southeast Asia Became a Mass Exporter of Labor*

Perrin Selcer, *The Postwar Origins of the Global Environment: How the United Nations Built Spaceship Earth*

Dominic Sachsenmaier, *Global Entanglements of a Man Who Never Traveled: A Seventeenth-Century Chinese Christian and His Conflicted Worlds*

For a complete list of books in the series, please see the Columbia University Press website.

VICTIMHOOD NATIONALISM

HISTORY AND MEMORY IN A GLOBAL AGE

JIE-HYUN LIM

TRANSLATED BY
MEGAN SUNGYOON

Columbia University Press
New York

Columbia University Press
Publishers Since 1893
New York   Chichester, West Sussex

Translation copyright © 2025 Columbia University Press
희생자의식 민족주의 © 임지현, 2021. Original Korean edition published by
Humanist Publishing Group Inc.
All rights reserved

Library of Congress Cataloging-in-Publication Data
Names: Im, Chi-hyŏn, 1959– author. | Megan Sungyoon, translator.
Title: Victimhood nationalism : history and memory in a global age /
Jie-Hyun Lim ; translated by Megan Sungyoon.
Other titles: Hŭisaengja ŭisik minjokchuŭi. English
Description: New York : Columbia University Press, 2025. |
Series: Columbia studies in international and global history |
Includes bibliographical references and index.
Identifiers: LCCN 2024024941 (print) | LCCN 2024024942 (ebook) |
ISBN 9780231216890 (hardback) | ISBN 9780231216883 (trade paperback) |
ISBN 9780231561396 (ebook)
Subjects: LCSH: Nationalism. | Collective memory. |
History, Modern—20th century—Historiography.
Classification: LCC JC311 .I49513 (print) | LCC JC311 (ebook) |
DDC 909.82—dc23/eng/20240820

Cover design: Chang Jae Lee
Cover image: © Ishiuchi Miyako, ひろしま/hiroshima#88, donor: Okimoto
Shigeo. Photograph courtesy of the J. Paul Getty Museum, Los Angeles.

GPSR Authorized Representative: Easy Access System Europe, Mustamäe tee 50,
10621 Tallinn, Estonia, gpsr.requests@easproject.com

> *In the past, the Jews were envied for their money, qualifications, positions, and international connections—today, they are envied for the very crematoria in which they were incinerated.*
>
> —WITOLD KULA (1970)

CONTENTS

Preface ix

1. MNEMOHISTORY 1
2. GENEALOGY 21
3. SUBLIMATION 50
4. GLOBALIZATION 77
5. NATIONALIZATION 111
6. DEHISTORICIZATION 142
7. OVERHISTORICIZATION 178
8. JUXTAPOSITION 214
9. DENIAL 244
10. FORGIVENESS 276

CODA: BEYOND MNEMONIC EUROCENTRISM 304

Notes 317
Bibliography 385
Index 419

PREFACE

On January 18, 2007, I sensed something odd while reading the morning newspapers. All the dailies delivered to me that morning published a scathing review of *So Far from the Bamboo Grove*, an autobiographical novella by Yoko Kawashima Watkins, as the headline of their cultural sections. The book did not seem like a grand masterpiece, but the articles were huge. I checked other major daily news outlets online and realized they also published similarly critical reviews of the book on that same day. The essence of the critique was that *So Far from the Bamboo Grove*, a novella about the suffering of the Japanese colonial settlers in Korea during their return journey from northern Korea to Japan, maliciously revised history by depicting Koreans as evil perpetrators and the Japanese as innocent victims. Such unanimous consent from all the Korean media under the culture war was truly exceptional.

According to the *Boston Globe*, on January 16, local time, the Korean Consulate General in Boston sent a letter of complaint to the Massachusetts Department of Elementary and Secondary Education. Considering the time difference between South Korea and the East Coast of the United States, the consulate general sent the letter and the South Korean press published the critical articles almost simultaneously. Something felt off to consider this to be a mere coincidence. The acute criticisms by the Korean press might have been an expression of unease provoked by the book's potential infliction of damage on the dichotomous generalization of Korean victims versus Japanese perpetrators. The worry that the depiction of Koreans who threaten and rape Japanese refugee women would absolve Japan's colonial guilt and prompt historical revisionism was palpable between the lines. Witnessing the Korean media's categorization of victims and perpetrators by national belonging, I was reminded of Hannah Arendt's critique of collective guilt and collective innocence.

What made the debate even more interesting was that it blew up across the ocean in the United States. It began in September 2006, when Korean American parents in Boston and New York filed a complaint against listing the book on the recommended reading list for students in sixth to eighth grades. The complaint addressed their concern regarding the book's historical revisionism that depicted Koreans, the colonized, as perpetrators and Japanese, the colonizers, as victims. This complaint seems reasonable in the U.S. context, where average students with little background knowledge of East Asian history could absorb the information uncritically and paint Koreans as evil perpetrators and the Japanese as innocent victims. *So Far from the Bamboo Grove* only highlights the suffering of Japanese refugees while silencing the history of Japanese colonialism that prompted the Japanese to settle in Manchuria and the Korean peninsula. The historical context in which such a large Japanese population was transplanted in those regions and expelled after the war is absent from the book's narrative.

That said, a snap judgment on Yoko's memory as "historical denialism," as opposed to the "accurate history" accounted by "us-Koreans," is too simplistic to reflect the historical complexities. Although the book's narrative is problematic for its reconstruction of a young girl's tragic experience out of historical context, calling it "fake" is also an overstatement. The complaint from the Korean American community should have been accompanied by a critique of the Eurocentric or "patriotic" education in world history in the United States. U.S. history education and memory culture are riddled with problems because they focus on European history. In contrast to the emphasis on educating about the

Holocaust and other Nazi atrocities, history education in the United States has remained oblivious to East Asian history. Even the Vietnam War was peripheralized, marginalized, and silenced, though it was a deep memory among veterans and bereaved families of the war dead in the United States. Unexpectedly, however, the history debate in the United States over Watkins's book fueled the memory war in East Asia.

As the conflict over *So Far from the Bamboo Grove* crossed the Pacific Ocean, I was reminded of the memory war that involved Germany, Poland, and Israel, and I was suddenly struck by the concept of "victimhood nationalism." I first introduced this concept to analyze the East Asian memory war in my column on the politics of history published in the *Korea Herald*, an English-language Korean newspaper, on April 29, 2007. After its publication, I began receiving angry emails from the Korean American community, the epicenter of the conflict. The contents of these emails varied, from an explosive charge from an "Ivy League Ph.D." who could not believe how a charlatan like me could teach history at a Korean university, to an emotional appeal from a parent whose child came home in tears and said he was bullied for being Korean after reading *So Far from the Bamboo Grove* in class. By reading these heated reactions, I came to believe that victimhood nationalism carries an unavoidable truth that people so desired to deny.

It was extraordinary to witness the process in which the diasporic nationalism of Korean Americans was reimported to stimulate the victimhood nationalism on the Korean peninsula. The mainland Korean media burnt the diaspora nationalism of Korean Americans to heat Korean nationalism, reaffirming the transnational nature of nationalism. If the "long-distance trade" drove world capitalism, "long-distance nationalism" characterized transnational nationalism. As a participatory observer of the debate, I realized that victimhood nationalism could capture the transmorphosis of nationalism in the twenty-first century. The shift of the nationalist discourse from heroes to victims seemed crucial. While investigating sources to delve into this hypothesis, I also encountered the bizarre phenomenon where the memory cultures of Germany, Italy, and Japan—the perpetrator nations of the Holocaust and colonial genocide—preempted the position of victims. When the perpetrators played victims in the global memory space, the collective memories of Poland, Israel, and Korea began to arm themselves with hereditary victimhood to reclaim the victim status stolen by the perpetrators. The countless memory wars unfolding within today's global memory formation share this structure.

Since then, I have developed and refined the concept of victimhood nationalism from the perspective of global history and memory. I have spent the past fifteen years brainstorming, collecting data, and outlining victimhood nationalism globally, with the European memory space centering on Poland, Germany, and Israel as one pillar and the East Asian memory space consisting of the United States, Japan, and Korea as another. The ideas central to this book were first published around 2010 as thesis papers in Germany, the United Kingdom, Poland, Korea, and Japan, although this compiled edition has only now materialized. In the meantime, I spoke on victimhood nationalism at universities and institutes in more than a dozen countries. I could develop and refine my ideas thanks to these diverse audiences. I still vividly remember the impassioned expression of empathy, especially from the audiences in Poland, Serbia, Slovenia, Finland, Peru, Ukraine, etc., which had been considered at the margin of global modernity. The audiences from the "margin" also gave me the most poignant counterarguments. Mostly, they felt their ontological security of victimhood identities shattered when I revealed the political instrumentalization of victimhood nationalism. One attendee in Berlin surprised me by talking about my "surprising talent" for making all involved parties uncomfortable.

As empirical research, this book is a product of more than a decade of collecting, analyzing, and studying English, Polish, German, Japanese, and Korean materials from online and offline multinational archives and public spheres. I strove to peruse the primary sources ranging from the official diplomatic documents to public debates in academia and media, testimonies, newspaper and magazine articles, documentaries, films, cartoons, novels, television shows, grassroots popular culture, and social media to observe the process of how the narratives of victimhood nationalism are produced, distributed, and consumed. Instead of remaining complacent with the hierarchical academic division of labor where the West proposes theories and the East provides empirical data to support them, this book aims to theorize the experience of the margins of global modernity, especially Eastern Europe and East Asia, into victimhood nationalism. Observing the materials makes clear that victimhood nationalism is not fragments of memories confined within state borders but a transnationally entangled memory through traveling, migration, juxtaposition, metonymies, cross-referencing, etc. I can confidently say that nationalism, including victimhood nationalism, cannot be understood from a single national history perspective.

The epistemological focus of this book lies in the "mnemohistory" that constructs and represents victimhood nationalism via the interaction of history and memory. Memory is not an empirical substitute for documentation but a vital apparatus for epistemological politics representing the past and constructing history. From the perspective of the phenomenology of memory, this book examines the global history and memory of victimhood nationalism. As a praxis, this book tries to engage critically with the memory regime in the "Global Easts." Traversing between Seoul and Warsaw since the 1990s, I have worked on global history and memory with a regional focus on Eastern Europe and East Asia. I consider the memory regime change as urgent as the political regime change in both regions. Any political regime change without changing memory regimes in the Global Easts has proved superficial. Now is the time we reassess the issues about the memory regime that penetrates Global Easts as the knowledge power to produce and structuralize the truth. This book is expected to contribute to a memory regime change in Global Easts by sacrificing victimhood nationalism in the global memory space.

The history of this book begins in 2007, when I first conceived the concept of victimhood nationalism. As a participant observer of memory politics and history reconciliation of the Global Easts, I have since navigated global memory space and developed the initial concept into a comprehensive history and theory that I am grateful to share in this book. It seems only appropriate for me to take this opportunity to express my sincere thanks to the individuals and institutions whose support, feedback, and solidarity I am lucky to have received. I thank Columbia

University, Hitotsubashi University, Leibniz-Institut für Geschichte und Kultur des östlichen Europa, Sogang University, Warsaw University, the Wisseschaftskolleg zu Berlin, and Nichibunken for their generous support to stay and study, and National Research Foundation of Korea for the long-term funding of the distinguished scholar project.

I extend my thanks also to the colleagues who helped me develop the ideas by engaging and organizing the stimulating forum in the past: Ien Ang, Aleida Assmann, Stefan Berger, Zuzanna Bogumił, Sebastian Conrad, Fabrice d'Almeida, Alain Delissen, Edem Eldem, Takashi Fujitani, Michael Geyer, Carol Gluck, Małgorzata Głowacka-Grajper, Frank Hadler, Pertti Happala, Nobuya Hashimoto, Minoru Iwasaki, Sang-Hyun Kim, Jürgen Kocka, Satoshi Koyama, Marcin Kula, Namhee Lee, Youjae Lee, Joyce C. H. Liu, Ping-Chen Hsiung, Alf Lüdtke, Matthias Middell, Dirk Moses, Katja Naumann, Nagao Nishikawa, Yukie Osa, Tetiana Pastushenko, Karen Petrone, Jan Piskorski, Eve Rosenhaft, Michael Rothberg, Dominic Sachsenmaier, Naoki Sakai, Katsumi Sawada, Andre Schmid, Michael Schoenhals, Franziska Seraphim, Michał Śliwa, Naoyuki Umemori, Tanja Vaitulevich, Joanna Wawrzyniak, Michael Wildt, and numerous others whom I could not mention. Megan Sungyoon made an excellent draft of the English translation by navigating several alien languages. I have ultimate responsibility for the finished text, but this book would not have been possible without Sungyoon's translation work. Heeyun Cheong and Kyudong Lee lent their hands in tidying the bibliography. As before, Caelyn Cobb shepherded the production process expertly and with a masterly touch.

In return for their invaluable support, I will continue to sacrifice victimhood nationalism globally to rescue the dignity of innocent victims from posthumous political instrumentalization.

VICTIMHOOD NATIONALISM

1

MNEMOHISTORY

TRANSNATIONAL NATIONALISM

The most common misunderstanding about nationalism is that it is, by nature, national. In reality, nationalism has been transnational. As our imagination became unshackled from the nation with the globalization of the late twentieth century, it began to question methodological nationalism to bestow the nation with a natural law–like legitimacy.¹ Once we broke away from the tunnel vision of methodological nationalism, the transnational and global nature of nationalism appeared more pronounced. The widespread notion that a nation emerges endogenously over the course of domestic historical development was a delusion created by nationalism. Historically, the causal order was the opposite: transnational comparisons among nations were a prerequisite to the nationalist imagination of one's own peculiarity. Nationalism could not have been formed and understood within the horizons of a single nation. The essentialist notion of national peculiarity was a nationalist mirage constructed only through transnational cofiguration and comparison.² Nation as a permanent reality passed down from time immemorial was an illusion on the premise of transnational imagination.

The spread of the term "international" predates the appearance of the term "nationalism."³ From the Peace of Westphalia (Westfälischer

Friede) of 1648 that heralded the birth of a modern nation-state with sovereignty and territory; Latin American Creole nationalism in 1760–1820; U.S. anticolonial nationalism of 1776 against the British Empire; French Jacobins' Gallic male nationalism in 1789; Haitian Jacobins' Black nationalism against the white nationalism in 1791; Romantic nationalism that swept Central-Eastern Europe during the 1848 revolutions; popular nationalist movements of the Young Italy (La Giovine Italia), Young Ireland (Éire Óg), and Young Turks (Genç Türkler) throughout the nineteenth century; national self-determination of Lenin and Woodrow Wilson around the First World War; anticolonial resistance nationalism of the "Third World" and the Bandung regime of 1955; Trumpism and Brexit nationalism of the postcolonial melancholy in the Anglo-Saxon democracies; to Japan's *hikikomori* nationalism, nationalism has always been a byproduct of international politics and globalization.[4] The point of departure for this book is that nationalism cannot be but transnational. Victimhood nationalism is no exception.

Victimhood nationalism is a narrative template to grant moral superiority and political legitimacy to a present nation of "hereditary victimhood," which inherited the legacy of ancestral victimhood in history and memory.[5] The nation of hereditary victimhood is thought to be ontologically justified as its national suffering is sublimated into the universal cause of humanity in the global memory space. It requires a perpetrator nation as a matching collective—just as it is difficult to imagine a victim without a perpetrator, a victimized nation without the other perpetrating nation is unthinkable. The epistemological frame of "negative symbiosis" functions as a chain link, with which victims and perpetrators collectively constitute the global history and memory of victimhood nationalism. Distinctively, Germans and Jews have each constructed their national identities within this frame.[6] Later, this very frame regulating the German-Israel nexus was reproduced in Israel-Palestine relations.[7] This chain link also regulated the entangled history and memory of Germany and Poland. One can find a similarity in failed historical reconciliations between imperial Japan's and colonial Korea's victimhood nationalism. Japan's collective memory of being victimized by American imperialism since the arrival of Commodore

Perry in 1853 shares a code with the collective memory of Korea being invaded by Japan since the *Un'yō* incident in 1875. Likewise, British colonialism and India's anticolonial nationalism were "the intimate enemy."[8]

The global history of victimhood nationalism is composed of the chain of negative symbiosis between victims and perpetrators. The epistemological collusion between perpetrators and victims, imperialism and nationalism, colonizers and colonized, West and East is rendered more transparent when juxtaposed in the transnational discursive space. The complicity between Germany's Orientalism, in which Polish studies was entitled *Ostforschung* (Eastern studies), and Poland's Occidentalism, in which German Studies was called *Studia Zachodnie* (Western studies), seems more apparent when the two are cofigured.[9] Similarly, imperial Japan's *Toyoshi* (Eastern history) orientalized the history of Asian neighbors China and Korea. At the same time, it promoted *Kuksa* (National history) in postcolonial Korea as an antithesis to Japanese Orientalism.[10] Despite the asymmetry in power-knowledge relations, Orientalism and Occidentalism epistemologically colluded to essentialize the East and West through configuration. The narrative of victimhood nationalism also requires a cofiguration of collective victims and perpetrators. Victimhood nationalism operates at this mnemonic junction where the empire and the nation, collective guilt and innocence, globalization and nationalization, criticism and advocacy, forgiveness and reconciliation intersect. Inevitable is the entangled history of victimhood nationalism, cofiguring the national units of perpetrators and victims on the same page.

This book was initially conceived to analyze victimhood nationalism within the binational relations between Korea and Japan, Poland and Germany, Germany and Israel, and Poland and Israel. A closer look, however, shows that victimhood nationalism extends beyond the transnational binary of a perpetrator nation and a victim nation. By tracing globally how victimhood nationalism unfurled after World War II, I realized that it was imperative to seek a multilateral interaction that surpasses the perpetrator-victim binary. To understand East Asia's victimhood nationalism, not only the regional state actors like Korea,

Japan, and China but also global state actors of the United States, Russia, and the other European colonizers must be considered. The same is true for the victimhood nationalism of Germany-Poland-Israel—other than these three countries, the United States, the Soviet Union, NATO, Warsaw Pact countries, and even African and Arab countries were important state actors. The colonial race between Western imperialism and the Axis powers, mnemonic interactions of the Holocaust, Stalinist red terror, and colonial genocides, the global Cold War and post–Cold War, and tensions between postcolonial and postcommunist memories are all intricately entangled with the progression of victimhood nationalism. It becomes more complicated when historical actors include not only the nation-states but even the diverse memory activists of global networks, regional, national, and local NGOs, top-down and grassroots organizations, and individuals with different political and moral agendas. Victimhood nationalism in such a global entanglement makes it more challenging to map its trajectories.

As I read through the sources for this book, my initial plan to write a transnational history of victimhood nationalism had to be expanded into a global history beyond the national dichotomy of perpetrators and victims. The global memory culture focusing on victims has dawned on us as an undeniable reality with the entangled memories of African American slavery, the colonialist genocide of indigenous people including the Herero and Namas in German Namibia, the Armenian genocide, the Holocaust, the Vietnam War, Algerian colonial war, the Rwandan genocide, ethnic cleansing in the Balkans, Japanese military "Comfort Women," forced sexual labor in the Nazi concentration camps, gendered violence during the Yugoslav Wars, the Stalinist Gulag regime, the political genocide of the communist and developmental dictatorships in the global Cold War era, etc.[11] Once entangled, compared, cross-referenced, and contested, the victimhood competition in the global memory space has become interactive globally, which becomes a hotbed for nourishing victimhood nationalism. Traces of victimhood nationalism under the globalization of memory in the twenty-first century are globally stretched more than nation to nation. A global, more than transnational, approach to victimhood nationalism is now inevitable for a more balanced understanding of the globally entangled history of victimhood nationalisms.[12]

GLOBAL MEMORY FORMATION

Globalism of the twenty-first century has shifted its focus from imagination to memory.[13] The era of global memory has dawned. "Traveling memories" heralded it. When the war refugees were massively evacuated, expelled, resettled, and displaced across borders after 1945, their memories traveled with their luggage. Diverse memories of migrants inadvertently encountered and interacted with one another in a transcultural migratory context.[14] When the Cold War ended, the globalization of memory picked up speed. Freed from the Cold War constraints, the global mnemoscape showed an exceedingly dynamic move—the Holocaust became a reminder of the transatlantic slave trade and colonial genocide, and the memory of colonial violence reciprocally evoked the Holocaust and other genocides. The issue of Japanese military "Comfort Women" catalyzed the memory of sexual violence at the Nazi concentration camps. Also, the systemic sexual assaults against Muslim Bosnian women during the Yugoslav Wars reinforced global awareness of the "Comfort Women" issue. The globalization of memory also allowed memory studies to break away from Eurocentrism. The postcolonial memory regime challenged the mnemonic Eurocentrism with a rich catalog of memories of the slave trade, colonial violence, ethnocide, and gendered violence in tricontinents Asia, Africa, and Latin America. The competition, conflicts, compromises, and solidarity among memories of various victims are constantly on the move in the twenty-first century.

The globalization of memory in the twenty-first century engendered "global memory formation."[15] I propose "memory formation" as a metaphoric parallel to Marxian "social formation." If "social formation" is an ensemble of political, economic, social, and cultural relations, "memory formation" is the aggregate of individual, vernacular, collective, and metamemories. It is processual more than fixed. Depending on how political, social, economic, cultural, linguistic, and religious relations are combined, a memory formation is a net of composite cognition that reflects the contradictions between reality and perception, fact and truth, history and memory, past and present, individual and collective, society and state. Memory formation embodies material power in that memory, for its affective nature, wields more performative influence over other discourse.[16] The performative power of affective memory was extensively demonstrated by the memory war revolving around the issues of Japanese military "Comfort Women" in East Asia, the dispute over the Holocaust and Stalinist terror in Eastern Europe, and the debates on colonial genocide and antisemitism that connect Germany, Israel, Namibia, and South Africa.[17] Sparked by the Black Lives Matter movement of 2020, the series of protests to decommemorate the colonialist commemoration of slavery and colonialism in the United States and Western Europe again reminded us of the affective power of memory that instantaneously intensifies public sentiment.

Memory is fundamentally a cognitive process not of passive learning that reaffirms a fixed past but of capturing an instant from the constant flow of the past. If the past is being remembered now, memory is the history of the concurrent present. Here, Paul Ricoeur's proposal for the "phenomenology of memory" to replace "what to remember" with "who remembers" warrants attention.[18] Memory is an active cognition that recreates the past rather than a simple reflection of it. The past differs, depending on by whom and in which frame it is perceived and remembered. The old Soviet joke that one can predict the future but not the past poignantly demonstrates the phenomenology of memory. The past is in constant flux and is subject to change. The globalization of memory in the twenty-first century was crucial in rescuing memory from the Nation. The nation-state's monopoly of collective memory has dwindled significantly—a change brought about by the dynamic globalization of memory through which multifarious memories clash, compete, check, reconcile, coordinate, and negotiate across national borders. On the epistemological level, the advent of the global paradigm has disturbed and deconstructed the privileges of a nation-state as a repository, curator, and destination of memory. Yet this was not an either-or change where global memory replaced national memory. It was the beginning of multivocality in global memory formation rather than the birth of a homogeneous global memory to unite hitherto discrepant memories that had clashed at regional, national, and global levels.[19]

The globalization of memory is not a sudden phenomenal shift of the twenty-first century but a gradual process that began at the end of World War II. As forced migrants, the displaced, fugitives, refugees, exiles, and immigrants relocated and resettled in alien lands on an unprecedentedly large scale after the war, their memories of the Holocaust, colonial genocide, Stalinism, and other atrocities migrated along with them. Global memory formation develops as diverse memories are mimicked, evoked, appropriated, referenced, and entangled in the global memory space.[20] Those entangled memories had never crossed paths in actual courses of history before. As people began to reflect on their own past through what happened on the other side of the planet, they became aware of how tightly the world was interwoven. The global memory formation called for people's realization of "history that can happen to me too, though it has not happened to me yet." Moreover, it was a moral wake-up call that reminded people of the possibilities of atrocities that "I did not perpetrate, but I may as well in the future." The realization that any one of us can be, if placed in a particular situation, not only an innocent victim but also a devil perpetrator of the Holocaust-like was an apocalyptic prophecy and ethical imperative.[21] The Holocaust memory as a global civil religion was founded on such desperation to prevent the apocalyptic prophecy from becoming fulfilled. Holocaust memory, for its exterritoriality of cosmopolitan memory, promulgates universal ethical and political guidelines despite all arbitrary appropriations and mnemonic abuse.[22]

That said, the global memory formation is also a web of hegemony where power-knowledge regulates theory and praxis. The political regime change would not guarantee a fundamental transformation without the memory regime change. The strategy to transform international politics while keeping the territorialized memory culture intact has already declared historical bankruptcy. The memory wars, elevating significantly in East Asia and Eastern Europe today, make it desperate to deterritorialize the cultural memories as the hegemony generator. It is naïve to hope international conflicts over the past will be consequentially resolved once historical facts are illuminated and truths revealed. As the aporia of Auschwitz indicates, often the problem is not historical facts but memories of the past.[23] Even if it is possible to gather "accurate" facts about the past on which everyone could agree, it would still be challenging to come up with an objective interpretation that all interested parties would accept. With this point in mind, this book aims to investigate the issues of memory politics of victimhood nationalism beyond the positivist truth battle. Each country's coming to terms with the past has mostly been a history-rebuilding process to project the nation's past into the designated future, and memory has often been evoked to mobilize the people through the emotional interaction between official history and grassroots memory.

Victimhood nationalism cannot be hegemonic if it stops at the official memory imposed from the top down. When the official memory of the state, vernacular memories of the civil society, and personal memories of individuals are resonant, victimhood nationalism becomes a material power beyond the abstract idea. It is impossible to rank these tridimensional memories in a linear order. They are relational categories that comprise an ensemble of memory culture, constantly negotiating one's level of importance.[24] The dynamics of victimhood nationalism stem from the collusive tension created as the official and grassroots memories get meshed interactively. Victimhood nationalism becomes increasingly persuasive when the top-down memory politics meet the vernacular and individual memories. Then, it becomes a key to the nation's ontological security.[25] Official memories do not always contradict vernacular memories, and neither are vernacular memories always more democratic and subversive than official memories. The hegemonic effect of victimhood nationalism blurs the distinctions between domination and collusion, coercion and consent, and subordination and resistance in memory politics. Also, it is crucial to understand how victimhood nationalism is part and parcel of the affective memory culture and what hegemonic effects it induces. The emotional appeal of victimhood nationalism is so enormous that memories of sacrifice reverberate through the heart and move people's minds.[26]

The global deployment of the Cold War was also crucial in constructing victimhood nationalism in the postwar mnemoscape. Under its ideological imposition, memory was selective—anything reminded of the allies' wrongdoings was taboo, and crimes against humanity were commemorated only when they were perpetrated by "enemies." The "Western" NATO countries welcomed West Germany as an anticommunist ally with their eyes closed to Nazi crimes. In contrast, the "Eastern" Warsaw Pact countries obliterated vernacular memories of the Red Army's atrocities. Where the "West" highlighted Stalin's antisemitism to play down the Holocaust of West Germany, the "East" reduced the Holocaust to the crime of Western capitalism. In the McCarthy-era United States, the anticommunist popular media willfully erased the memories of the Holocaust in exchange for the celebration of German soldiers. Supposedly, their heroic sacrifices and superhuman bravery saved the Western culture from the Asiatic savagery of Bolshevism.[27] For Jewish Americans after the Rosenberg spy case, clearing themselves of the charge of communism was a more urgent task than remembering the Holocaust. The official memory of the communist bloc countries also expunged the Jewish identity from the Holocaust victims by labeling them only as Soviet patriots, communist partisans, or Polish citizens.[28] Proletarian internationalism covered up the antisemitism of national communists who downplayed the Jewish Holocaust victims under the internationalist banner. Until the fall of the Berlin Wall in 1989 and the dissolution of the Soviet Union in 1991, memories of World War II had thus remained ideologically instrumentalized.

The collapse of the Cold War catalyzed the globalization of memory, opening the road to global memory formation. The post–Cold War mnemoscape is most notably marked by entangled memories of the Holocaust, colonial genocide, and Stalinist terror.[29] The Memorial Island in the Bergen County Justice Center, New Jersey, symbolizes the emergence of global memory formation differently. As Bergen County erected the "Comfort Women" memorial plaque as part of the World Women's Day celebration on March 8, 2013, now the Memorial Island houses the monuments to the victims of American slavery, Irish famine, Armenian Genocide, the Holocaust, and the "Japanese sexual slavery."[30] The Memorial Island represents the memories of global immigrants to the United States. The various immigrants' grievous memories got entangled and hung together in the United States. Through the mnemonic interaction in a host country, the memories of immigrants once dispersed throughout the world came together to constitute a part of the global memory. This mnemonic interaction shows how global memory formation was developed as distant memories met, competed, reconciled, cross-referenced, and affirmed one another globally. It was more than a merely physical aggregation of territorialized national memories. A key to understanding this new phenomenon is not "entangled history" but "entangled memory."[31] As national memories became entangled in global memory formation, the algorithm of victimhood nationalism has become even more complicated.

Global memory formation went in parallel with "internal globalization,"[32] which provided momentum to develop our empathy toward the suffering of the distant other. The global civic virtue of human rights is based on compassion, the ability to share the other's suffering of injustice. In a new memory culture of "moral remembrance," empathizing with victims became even more critical and righteous an ideal.[33] Based on the heightened sensitivity of human rights, global memory formation raised moral standards in our remembrance. The UN Report of the Special Rapporteur on Cultural Rights (2014) promulgated that "memorialization should be a means of combating injustice and promoting reconciliation." It emphasized that it is "geared not only towards the past (recalling events, recognizing and honoring victims and enabling stories to be related), but equally to the present (healing processes and rebuilding of trust between communities) and the future (preventing further violence through education and awareness-raising)."[34] The discussions of the Holocaust within the contexts of "global memory space," "transnational memory culture," "cosmopolitan memory," and "multidirectional memory" show the way of how to globalize the national memories in resonance with the human rights regime.

The advent of the human rights regime accelerated a shift in the nationalist discourse from heroism to victimhood. It is not heroes but victims who bear the moral asset of nationalism. Global memory formation is filled with transnational solidarity among victims and nationalist victimhood contests. The Holocaust as a memory template also holds the twofold nature of de- and reterritorialization. One can frequently witness the dark side of the cosmopolitanization of the Holocaust that diverse nationalist groups stimulate their victimhood by standardizing their narratives to fit the Holocaust. Thus began the "distasteful competition over whose nation suffered the most," and the competition became cutthroat.[35] The fear that global memory triggers memory war by intensifying victimhood competition has already become a reality. The tyranny of memory gives birth to a certain exclusivism, the epistemological belief that only victims have the right and ability to remember and assess the past correctly. More often than not, it is used as a sacralized weapon that safeguards the exclusivity of victimhood nationalism by blocking all external criticisms. Global memory formation has ultimately become an incubator for the nascent victimhood nationalism. The group communications between Israel and Palestine tell us that the expansion of human rights sensitivity instead reinforces each nation's in-group unity and solidifies racial borders rather than promoting actions toward transnational solidarity of human rights.[36]

At times, human rights were an ideological instrument of liberal conservatism to dilute the public demand for social justice; at other times, they operated with the logic of imperialism that justified external interventions. The assessment that human rights have become incorporated into the power structure has a point.[37] Global concern about human rights violations within a sovereign nation is not necessarily imperialist intervention or racist attacks, however. By transposing universal human rights into national rights, the postcolonial states have covered up their internal colonialism and domestic oppression with the vocabulary of victimhood nationalism.[38] Also, the advent of the human rights regime contributed to democratizing memories to elevate our empathy for the subalterns whose misery and distress have been largely ignored. Accordingly, personal memories became increasingly more crucial, which opened the "era of witnesses." Testimonies were instrumental in resurrecting and remembering subaltern victims whose past was never recorded. Personal narratives-cum-testimonies put human faces back into historiography. The global audience who listened attentively became the secondary witnesses for human rights violations.[39] The advent of victim-centered memory could have been unimaginable without the epistemological shift from written documents to oral testimony. The analyses and descriptions in this book would also reach beyond the "traditional" written history toward the realm of memory studies that focus on personal experience and testimonies.

MNEMOHISTORY AS METHODOLOGY

This book is an attempt at a mnemohistory of victimhood nationalism. Mnemohistory is concerned with the past. Mnemohistory of victimhood nationalism traces the trajectory of the remembered pasts in change. This book investigates the history of cultural memory of victimhood nationalism more than history per se. It owes much to many preceding methodologies and studies, including Maurice Halwachs's "collective memory" and Jan Assmann's "cultural memory" and "mnemohistory." Both are synthesized into the umbrella concept of mnemohistory in this book.[40] Halwachs's collective memory, which explains that individuals understand the past via structural channels like family, local community, academic institution, and nation-state, provides a valuable methodological frame. Though *Victimhood Nationalism* keeps its reservation on his dichotomous distinction between individual and collective memory, Halwachs's insight left a foundational impact on the writing of this book. Traces of collective memory in flux amount to a history of memory. Assmann claims that cultural contents like texts, rituals, and memorials, along with the systemized communication that implements such contents, establish sustainable "figures of memory" that construct cultural memories systemic in a society or state. According to Jan Assmann, cultural memory takes its course, often severed from personal memories, to convey society's self-image.[41] Assmann's concept of cultural memory and Halwachs's collective memory have been conceptual pillars in recognizing the "narrative template" of victimhood nationalism. The primary goal of this book is to investigate the victimhood nationalism as a cultural memory.

However, I must figure out to what extent collective and personal memories can be distinguished. Often mutually exclusive, personal memories of individuals, vernacular memories of civil society groups, and official memories of the state also not infrequently infiltrate one another. Some personal memories are processed and morphed to correspond to the official memory of the state, while some grassroots memories, in conflict with the official memory, retreat to privacy and eventually disappear. At times, nationalist hegemony manifests even more blatantly in grassroots than official memories. The collective and individual memory dichotomy does not correctly answer how a society's hegemonic memory constitutes victimhood nationalism. Investing the mnemohistory of victimhood nationalism, this book works closely with Carol Gluck's meticulous categorization of mnemonic topography: the official memory of the state, vernacular memory of civil society, individual's memories of more private and intimate, and epistemological metamemory.[42] However, these four categories of memory will not be treated with mechanical equality, which is neither possible nor desirable. This book primarily traces the mnemohistory of victimhood nationalism that has regulated, systemized, and driven the memory culture, where memories of all four categories are intricately interwoven and interact.

Writing the mnemohistory of victimhood nationalism begins from the premise that memory is a social construction more than positivistic evidence. Memories in all terrains, from the state to the individual, fluctuate per changes in social norms and hegemonic narratives. That is why the phenomenology of memory is the critical focus throughout this book, which goes beyond the factuality of memory, a simple fact-checking on whether a specific memory is "correct" or "wrong." The imminent task of this book is to question why, how, where, when, and by whom the victimhood nationalism as a memory template came to a rise and to investigate the political impact of such memories at events, conjunctures, and longue-durée of history. Vis-à-vis positivistic attacks from more traditional historians, victimhood nationalism responds beyond the passive defense, such as "a memory is also a part of the truth and no less accurate reflection of the past than History." It actively reassesses memory as a vehicle of history-politics that reenacts the past to make History at present.[43] It is not the primary concern of this book whether memory can represent the past just as factually as History. The book questions power relations and political implications under the code of memory culture operating at the state, civil society, and individual levels. Also, I will investigate how the nation produces, delivers, consumes, and appropriates memory culture.

Methodological highlights in this book are as follows: First, it takes the stance of transdisciplinary memory studies. Anything can fall into its interest regardless of the genre as long as it contributes to the production, circulation, and consumption of cultural memories: history, literature, cinema, art, theatre, communication, gender studies, media studies, cultural studies, psychoanalysis, etc. Of course, it is exhausting and almost impossible to cover all the cultural phenomena that configure memory politics; therefore, I intend not to go into details about every single rendition but to capture victimhood nationalism as a hegemonic narrative template that dominates and regulates a nation's cultural memory.[44] Even oral testimonies among victims are not mere substitutes for official records but personal memories in constant negotiation with cultural memory. The cultural memory overwrites the historical narrative not unilaterally in a top-down fashion but through negotiations with grassroots memories. I will examine texts across genres, from the state's official history to intimate personal memories that contribute to building victimhood nationalism as the canon in all terrains of memory.

Second, while sailing the sea of memory studies, this book considers entangled memories as another methodological point. Adopting the perspective and critiques of entangled history to memory studies gives a critical gaze at the methodological nationalism of memory studies, which keeps entangled global memories fragmented within the national container. Entangled memories of victimhood nationalism would reveal the transnationality of nationally fragmented memories and thus deconstruct victimhood nationalism by depriving it of its epistemological basis to categorize victims and perpetrators by national belonging. Of course, entangled memories do not necessarily entail the deterritorialization of national memories. Victimhood nationalism is a new trend in the twenty-first century, which implies that global memory formation can be fertile soil for the reterritorialization of memory. The perspective of "entangled memory" will shed light on which victimhood nationalisms compete and struggle for global recognition to establish the nation's ontological bridgehead. Memories are entangled, not only between national perpetrators and victims but also between global perpetrators or victims.

Third, the book attempts a global history of victimhood nationalism. A global perspective is appropriate and inevitable when delving into victimhood nationalism. Nationally fragmented memories compete, conflict, negotiate, and compromise across borders in the global mnemoscape. Even in the era of "postmemory," where the later generations inherit the ancestral victims' memories, the knots in memory entanglement are pulled tighter to increasingly diversify, enlarge, and solidify the ensemble of memories, which I call global memory formation. These memories that constitute the global memory formation are now entangled more tightly than ever through multidirectional interactions, such as critical juxtaposition, cross-referencing, exculpatory relativization, and critical relativization. Initially, Michael Rothberg used the term "multidirectional memory" to catch how the long-distance memories of the Holocaust and decolonization movements galvanized each other to deterritorialize national memories.[45] The global trajectory of victimhood nationalism is full of multidirectional memories, too. It is undeniable, however, that the multidirectionality of victimhood nationalism often works for the reterritorialization of memories by strengthening victimhood contests globally.

The approaches to victimhood nationalism from the perspectives of global history and memory decidedly influenced the selection of materials. From history textbooks and academic publications to films, historical fiction, television series, museums and galleries, comics, video games, social media, and online reviews, everyday cultural activities that intervene with the production, distribution, and consumption of memory culture are under scrutiny in this book. As print capitalism of newspapers and fiction brought a national unity among distant readers who never met each other, digital capitalism provided a sense of connectedness among users across the nation and globe. To show how memory culture materializes through interactions between memories of the official, vernacular, and personal, I will discuss relevant materials that constitute a memory culture. The criterion by which I select references from the vast sea of sources is whether they apply to the production and consumption of victimhood nationalism as the hegemonic narrative template. Victimhood nationalism is a memory regime more than ideology—it is a dense cultural web that keeps the hegemonic position of nationalism in the age of global memory. Victimhood nationalism as a memory regime demands a multifarious understanding of memory culture, from the state's official narrative to the emotional labor of memory activists.

Unfolding the global history of victimhood nationalism from the perspective of memory studies, this book's narration has obvious temporal and spatial limits. Temporally, it will mainly cover the period from 1945 to the present. A particular focus is put on the post–Cold War era because the triple victimhood of colonial genocide, the Holocaust, and Stalinist terror began to be entangled in the global memory space after the fall of the Berlin Wall. As the ideological "wall" that had obstructed the free flow of memories was demolished, global memory formation emerged without delay. In Eastern Europe, memories of the Holocaust and Stalinist terror suppressed by the Communist Parties had resurfaced to flare up the East European version of *Historikerstreit* (historians' dispute). In Western Europe, repressed memories of colonial atrocities and forgotten genocide haunted the postimperial memory space as the ideological cause of fighting global communism faded away. The dissolution of the global Cold War was a breakthrough for the memory regime in East Asia, where the anticommunist alliance suppressed grassroots memories of Western colonialism and Japanese aggression. The former colonies no longer needed former colonizers as Western allies to fight the communist enemy as the Soviet Union collapsed. This book will examine how the global memory space has become a battleground for victimhood nationalism in the post–Cold War era.[46]

Spatially, this book will focus on the intricate relations among Poland, Germany, Israel, Korea, and Japan in analyzing how the memories of colonialism, the Holocaust, and Stalinism have converged and intertwined in the global memory space. The memory cultures of these countries were greatly agitated after the fall of the Cold War regime; During the Cold War, the memory of the Holocaust was used to legitimatize the "liberal democracy" of the West more than to demonize the Nazis.[47] The *Sonderweg* (particular path) thesis of German history fetishized Western modernity by attributing the problems of Nazism to the "peculiar" semifeudal premodernity of Germany.[48] In this metahistory level, Western modernity and liberal democracy were once again justified compared to "Asiatic Bolshevism." There were also attempts to connect the memories of colonialism with those of the Holocaust. The postcolonial perspective viewed both colonialism and the Holocaust as consequences of Western modernity.[49] Nazi occupation of Eastern Europe was understood as an extension of the colonial practice of the imperial Germany. For German colonialists and Nazi ideologues, Eastern Europe was the Germany's "East," a symbol of periphery and underdevelopment.[50] With its spatial focus, this book illustrates the global history of victimhood nationalism as the entangled memories of triple victimhood: colonialism, the Holocaust, and Stalinism.

This book problematizes victimhood nationalism as a "memory regime." By memory regime, I mean the ensemble of all levels of memory regulating a hegemonic operational mechanism. As an intellectual with everyday life rooted in a nook of East Asia, I perceive the change of the memory regime to be no less, or even more, urgent than the political regime change. The memory regime in East Asia symbolizes a failed liberation, and failed liberation is aligned with failed memories. The relationship between failed liberation and failed memories is not linearly causal but reciprocal. A transwar history of East Asia shows that political transformation without a memory regime change has proved defunct.[51] The memory regime, as the constituent power, dictates that the future of East Asia is beyond the true or false questions about the shared past. I believe the critical historicization of victimhood nationalism is to problematize the present memory regime in East Asia. It would mark one step forward to the memory regime change in East Asia if this book successfully sacrifices victimhood nationalism globally.

MAPPING

Victimhood Nationalism comprises ten chapters. Following this introductory chapter, chapter 2, "Genealogy," traces the formation of victimhood nationalism as a concept, starting from Zygmunt Bauman's hereditary victimhood in Israel and Poland to the long-distance nationalism in the transpacific memory space. I could forge the victimhood nationalism as a conceptual tool to capture contemporary nationalism globally while, as a participatory observer, tracing the memory wars in Global Easts-Eastern Europe and East Asia. Chapter 3, "Sublimation," argues that victimhood nationalism emerges in the sublime transition of "passive" victims into "active" martyrs. Victimhood nationalism was made possible by the rituals of the political religion sublimating immortal patriotism as the sacralized object of the belief. National priests of political religion democratized and nationalized all the dead for the nation. There was no discrimination among the dead. The chapter explains how and why victimhood nationalism has contributed to making a self-mobilization system through national commemorations of the patriotic dead. Beyond the top-down official nationalism, victimhood nationalism functions as a hegemonic memory because its affective power of religious rituals touches directly on grassroots sentiment.

Chapter 4, "Globalization," configures 2000 CE as Year Zero of the global memory formation. The Year Zero commenced with the Stockholm Declaration in January, which sublimated the Holocaust memory into the global civic virtue and ended with the Women's International

War Crimes Tribunal on Japan's Military Sexual Slavery in Tokyo in December. It marked the evolution of territorialized national memories into deterritorialized global memories. Chapter 5, "Nationalization," opens with a description of the Hiroshima-Auschwitz Peace March of 1962–1963. The Japanese peace activists' good intentions toward the associative memory of Hiroshima-Auschwitz ended up being utilized in the nationalization of memory in both Japan and Poland. The chapter revolves around the tension between the ethics of deterritorializing national memory and the practices of reterritorializing global memory.

Chapter 6, "Dehistoricization," investigates how the perpetrators and accomplices of Germany and Japan unreservedly registered their memories as victims after losing the war. They dared to compare their misery embracing the defeat with even the Holocaust. Dehistoricization of suffering was at the center of those inverted memories. They spread the misconception that highlighting the memory of our nation's suffering would cancel out our own perpetration against others. Chapter 7, "Overhistoricization," looks at how the individual perpetrators in Poland, Korea, and Israel represent themselves as victims by inheriting the position of ancestral victims. "Collective innocence" grants individual perpetrators an indulgence for being a victimized nation member. Self-exculpatory memories of overhistoricizing one's national identity display the moral complacency of victimhood nationalism. One cannot but fail to spot the mnemonic collusion between the overhistoricization by the victim nations and dehistoricization by the perpetrator nations.

Chapter 8 contains a critical inquiry about the "juxtaposition" of memories resulting from a meticulous political calculation. Subtly constituting cultural memories and stimulating emotions, juxtaposition is also used as an instrument to justify victimhood nationalism. The chapter focuses on how postwar Japanese memory culture juxtaposed the Polish Catholic martyrdom in Auschwitz with the atomic bombing of Nagasaki in an exculpatory way. Juxtaposition is a double-edged method promoting deterritorialization and reterritorialization simultaneously. Chapter 9, "Denial," looks at how the diverse forms of denialism imitate and reference each other in global memory formation. The metalanguage of denialism that justifies and incites genocide is a form of verbal abuse, as it is often called "the last step toward genocide." I critique positivistic denialism by leveraging the epistemology of empathy like "intellectual memory," "deep memory," "factual truth," and "narrative truth" and review the epistemological questions and political connotations cast on the field of history and memory studies by the past represented by witnesses.

Chapter 10, "Forgiveness," reexamines the letter of reconciliation of the Polish bishops to the German bishops in 1965 in the context of East Asia's memory war and historical reconciliation. Known for its declaration, "We forgive and ask for forgiveness," this document was a wise combination of the political logic of reconciliation and the Christian ethics of forgiveness. This chapter will reveal that forgiveness is a double-edged sword that can destroy or justify victimhood nationalism. Finally, the epilogue imagines mnemonic solidarity through the provocative hypothesis that the loud cacophony of East Asian memory war and postcolonial debates on the Holocaust in Germany, Israel, and Eastern Europe is better than radio silence. It raises a concern about mnemonic Eurocentrism. Mnemonic solidarity begins from maintaining a sound tension among cacophonous memories of the Holocaust in the European dark continent and colonial genocides in non-European tricontinents. Overcoming Eurocentrism will remain one of the most challenging tasks in the future of memory studies.

By sacrificing victimhood nationalism that absolutizes "our" nation's suffering while subordinating others' pain, we will become able to tread the first step to mnemonic solidarity.

2

GENEALOGY

SIN AND CRIME

On January 17, 1987, the Polish literary critic Jan Błoński published an essay titled "Biedni Polacy patrzą na getto" (The poor Poles look at the Ghetto) in *Tygodnik Powszechny* (The common weekly), the Kraków-based liberal Catholic weekly.[1] Briefly shut down for refusing to publish Stalin's obituary in 1953, the weekly enjoyed trust not only among Catholics but also among critical intellectuals at large. Secular dissidents around Komitet Obrony Robotników (Committee to Protect Workers) and Solidarność (Solidarity) were regular contributors and readers. Błoński's essay critically reflected on the actions and attitudes of Poles toward neighboring Jewish victims during the Holocaust, which triggered sharp polemics. Recalling the overwhelming volume of angry letters from irritated readers, the magazine's editor at the time, Jerzy Turowicz, recounts that no piece of writing had ever caused so much controversy in the magazine's history since 1945.[2] Allegedly, no other individual's short essay published since the end of World War II had as much impact in Poland's public sphere as Błoński's essay.[3] As if to unlock the Pandora's box of the agonistic memories of the Nazi occupation and the Holocaust, Błoński's moral adventure aroused the guilty conscience of Poles who helplessly witnessed their Jewish neighbors being massacred by the Nazi's overwhelmingly violent devil force.

Like many controversial works, Błoński's essay became a historical "event." Błoński's self-criticism of Poles, negligent of the massacre and sufferings of their Jewish neighbors, uprooted the complacent collective memory immersed in the victimhood of the Polish nation. Collective memory in communist Poland consisted of the government's official memory of the Nazis' biggest victims and the civil society's grassroots memory of Stalin's and Hitler's worst victims—hence the Polish nation, placed on the evil intersection of Nazism and Stalinism, was the most tragic victim of World War II along. The shocking reminder that Poles were also bystanders and accomplices of the Holocaust questioned Polish victimhood as the source of ontological security for the Polish nation. The essay marked the point of no return for Poland's collective memory. Many Poles felt the shift of the position from victims to bystanders was a moral degeneration. The bystanders were not legally indictable for the Nazi crimes against humanity, yet their sins should be pardoned through forgiveness.[4] What Błoński emphasized was also not "crime" but "sin." Original sin ingrained in Polish Catholic culture was perhaps another element that elevated the Błoński debate from a historical to an ethical-ontological one. Many liberal Catholic intellectuals felt themselves as Cain in the Bible, who protested God by saying, "Am I my brother's keeper?" to hide that he murdered his brother Abel. Also noteworthy is that the English translation of Błoński's essay and related debates was published with the title *My Brother's Keeper*.

The vehement reaction to Błoński's essay across the political spectrum can be understood as an extension of the shock brought to Polish intellectual society by *Shoah*, Claude Lanzmann's documentary film released in 1985. The documentary drew attention and applause from film critics globally. A film review in the *New York Times* called it "an epic film about the greatest evil of modern times." Film critic Roger Ebert raved that it was "one of the noblest films ever made [that is] not documentary, not journalism, not propaganda, not political," and "an act of witness."[5] Also, *Shoah* immediately became an issue in world politics. Headed by then president of France François Mitterand, the public figures who attended the film's screenings included Mikhail Gorbachev and Václav Havel. In international politics, still under the shadow of the Cold War, the political leaders of the United States, France, Czechoslovakia, and the Soviet Union unanimously praised the same film, which was unforeseen.

The official reaction of communist Poland, led by the Polish United Workers' Party (Polska Zjednoczona Partia Robotnicza, PZPR), was adverse—or bewildered, perhaps. The state media and the party propaganda machine accused the film of proliferating the stereotype of antisemitic Poles and the incorrect impression of Poles as the only collaborators of the Holocaust.[6] In the documentary, the peasants who lived near the "death camps," like Sobibór and Treblinka, are brought forth as witnesses, and they reveal their naked antisemitism with nonchalance and sarcasm.[7] On-screen, the Polish women do not hide their hostility toward "attractive" Jewish women, and Polish men openly accuse Jews of exploiting the Poles. At times, their antisemitic view goes further to claim that Poland as a whole is in the hands of greedy Jews.[8] These grassroots antisemites show their twisted fondness toward their Jewish neighbors only when they talk about the "exotic" sexuality of Jewish women. *Shoah* was banned in Poland.

The Jewish witnesses in the film also do not hide their grudges against the Polish neighbors. Abraham Bomba, the documentary's important witness who worked as a barber in Treblinka, testifies that 99 percent of Poles happily laughed when they saw the train full of Jews entering the extermination camp.[9] The faces and voices of the Polish peasants, caught in Lanzmann's lens, eloquently witnessed that antisemitism is still alive and well, deeply rooted in their everyday lives. The camera exposed the deep-seated prejudices among the Poles in the countryside, even without the help of translation. Ultimately, it seems the film tries to say the Poles were the Nazis' collaborators during the Holocaust. Grassroots antisemitism was not the peculiarity of Polish peasants; the Jewish witnesses who were forced to migrate from Corfu, Greece, also testified on Lanzmann's camera about their Greek neighbors' antisemitism and apathy toward the Jewish suffering.[10] Other Europeans' attempts to cover up their own antisemitism by relegating antisemitism to Poland's historical exceptionalism should be criticized. However, ubiquitous antisemitism does not exonerate Poles from its charge of antisemitism. Grassroots antisemitism, which confuses their memory of being Nazis' most prominent victims, was an uncomfortable, unpalatable reality for many Poles.

The image of the Holocaust collaborators depicted in *Shoah* collided directly with the official memory of the communist regime in Poland.[11] Party historians in People's Poland (Polska Ludowa) penned the state's official past following the grammar of nationalism. Proletarian Internationalism was merely a fancy gown on the body of nationalism. With General Mieczysław Moczar in the vanguard, the nationalist faction organized a comprehensive antisemitic campaign in 1968 with the banner of anti-Zionism.[12] The hypocrisy of ideology was rendered apparent as the ruling nomenklatura that proclaimed Proletarian Internationalism launched an antisemitic campaign at the very site of the Holocaust. Behind the colorful rhetoric that emphasized the socialist virtue of Proletarian Internationalism and Universalism, the communist regime regressed frequently into primitive nationalism. The socialist ideals, which stressed the ethical-political unity of the people, fortified the primordial perspective that views a nation as an organic community.[13] The *nomenklatura* (ruling elites) of the Communist Party desperately attempted to overcome the regime crisis by instigating emotional nationalism to counter noble internationalism, and antisemitism was the most convenient agent in promoting ethnic nationalism in Poland. Nationalism was the last word of communism.[14]

However, the dominant memory of postwar Poland as the most victimized nation of World War II was not unfounded. According to Polish War Reparations Bureau (Biuro Odszkodowań Wojennych) statistics from 1947, a total of 6,028,000 Poles were killed during the war. This number has been engraved in the official memory in communist Poland, though it is arguably a result of a quick fabrication rather than an actual count. The first draft of this report estimated the number of Polish civilian victims to be around 4,800,000. Still, Jakub Berman, then chief of the Department of Security (Urząd Bezpieczeństwa), insisted on the figure of six million, which assured equal counts between

Jewish and ethnic Polish victims, with three million each.[15] The total of 4,800,000 victims carried a risk of a backlash as it connoted 3 million Jewish Poles and 1.8 million ethnic Poles. It seems even Berman, a veteran Jewish Communist and older brother of the Zionist left Adolf Berman, could not disregard victimhood as the source of the ontological security in postwar Poland.[16] Disagreements on the statistics were present even among state organizations. A report in 1951 by the Polish Ministry of Finance presents a different number, estimating the death toll at 5,085,000, with 1,706,700 ethnic Poles and 3,378,000 Jews. That report shows 940,000 fewer deaths than the Polish War Reparations Bureau report of 1947, which accounts for the missing people who were included in the death toll but returned home later.[17]

The Ministry of Finance report presented its number as the most up-to-date data, inclusive of the number of returnees from concentration camps and forced labor, prisoners of war, and the integrated border population. However, the Party remained firm on the figure of six million victims that ensured an equal three million for both Jewish and ethnic Polish victims. Open discussion on the political motives and the accuracy of the numbers became possible only after the fall of communism in 1989. For the national communists of Poland, which could not rest unless the number of ethnic Polish victims matched that of Jewish victims, Proletarian Internationalism was an ideological oxymoron. Since the fall of the Berlin Wall, estimates have been provided by the Institute of National Remembrance (IPN), Tadeusz Piotrowski, Czesław Łuczak, and others. The IPN statistics indicate 5.47–5.67 million casualties in the Nazi-occupied territory (around 2.7–2.9 million Jews and 2.77 million ethnic Poles), in addition to approximately 150,000 in the Soviet-occupied area, totaling 5.6–5.8 million victims.[18] Piotrowski estimates a total of 5.6 million victims: 3 million Jews, 2 million ethnic Poles, and 600,000 Ukrainian, Belarussian, and other nationals. The number of victims decreased to 5.2–5.3 million according to Łuczak's estimation, which suggests 1.4 million ethnic Polish victims.

The controversy surrounding the Polish death toll exhibits the politics of numbers characteristic of victimhood nationalism. Every single unreasonable individual death warrants just as much grievance and sorrow as any other. The different numbers—whether 6 million or 5.2 million—never proportionately indicate the size of pain and suffering. In the intimate memories of individual victims and families, the exact size of the collective death is the last thing to be concerned with; of far greater importance is *how* my family and friend suffered and died. On the other hand, the politics of numbers prioritize statistics, a crucial element of victimhood nationalism that competes over who the "bigger victim" is and, thus, whose nation deserves more empathy and moral justice. The politics of numbers is engaged when casting an illusion of scientific reasoning over the distasteful debate on whose side suffered more deaths, hence more significant sacrifice, by pretending that more victims account for greater moral legitimacy. At times, even boastful of the more considerable number of "our" deaths that had accrued, the illusion of statistics backed by authority became a stern reality. Despite the inevitability of statistics in understanding the past, the political instrumentalization of numbers calls for closer attention.

Accounting for the statistical error, the death toll as a percentage of the total population at the time in Poland is estimated to be 24 percent at the highest and 20 percent at the lowest. Poland's casualty rate was undeniably the highest in Europe, beyond comparison with France and Belgium (1.2 percent of the population) or the Netherlands (2.4 percent), and with only the Soviet Union being a close second (12.4 percent). During World War II, Warsaw lost 720,000 people. Some 98 percent of its Jewish citizens and 25 percent of non-Jewish citizens were killed. Of the prewar Warsaw population of 1.2 million, 60 percent were sacrificed during the war, exclusive of those injured or missing. In Warsaw alone, almost seven times as many had died as the entire civilian casualties in France (100,000, including 78,000 Jews). The highest estimate of deaths by the atomic bombing of Hiroshima amounts to 160,000, about 45 percent of the city's population at the time. The death toll of the Dresden raids is estimated at 25,000 among the city's total population of 640,000. Even by these quick comparisons with the two most notable cases of mass civilian deaths in Asia and Europe, one can infer the gravity of damage Warsaw suffered during World War II. Thus, it is not an exaggeration to say that Poles were the biggest victims of World War II, based on deaths per capita.[19] Quantitative and qualitative damage was considerable to the Polish society; those who received higher education, hence intellectuals and elites, were significantly affected. According to a report by Polish War Reparations Bureau from 1947, the casualty rate increased exponentially by education level: by the Nazi actions against Polish intelligentsia, 56.9 percent of lawyers, 38.7 percent of doctors, and 27 percent of Catholic priests, including five bishops, were murdered, as were 5.1 percent of primary school teachers, 13.1 percent of secondary school teachers, and 28.5 percent of college professors. As most of the victims had received higher education, about one-third of people who had a college degree were killed.[20]

The Korean casualties during the Asia-Pacific War are estimated at 70,000, according to the Report of the Working Group for Asia and the Far East at the United Nations Economic and Social Council. The organizing committee for the "Commemoration of the Koreans Deceased in War Catastrophe" held in Seoul in 1946 provided the same estimate.[21] Based on this estimate, Korean casualties per 23,913,063—the entire population of colonial Joseon at the time of the Japanese surprise attack on Pearl Harbor in 1941—would be 0.29 percent, which is seventy to eighty times less than the Polish casualties during World War II. Those statistics are at odds with the Korean collective memory portraying themselves as the most victimized nation by the most brutal Japanese imperialism. In Asia, China (over 10 million casualties), Indonesia (3–4 million deaths due to famine and disease), and Vietnam (1–2 million deaths by starvation) come close to Poland in terms of death toll. Still, the Poles vastly outnumber these most victimized Asian countries in the per capita death rate.[22] Poland also suffered immense financial damage, which amounted to US$49.2 billion in 1939—more than seven countries' economic damages combined, namely, France (21.1 billion), Yugoslavia (9.1 billion), the Netherlands (4.4 billion), Czechoslovakia (4.2 billion), Greece (2.5 billion) Belgium (2.3 billion), and Norway (1.3 billion—all amounts in 1939 USD).[23] Only the Soviet Union surpassed Poland in material damage.

Thus, it is not surprising that the Poles were livid at *Shoah*'s portrayal of them, for it insinuated that they, the biggest victims of World War II, colluded with the Nazis in the Holocaust. The Communist Party's ban on *Shoah* seems predictable, too. The party had striven to clear itself of the Żydokomuna (Jewish commies) stereotype that linked communism to Jews and the common suspicion that the party championed Jews.[24] Even after the ban was lifted due to international pressures, Polish society remained in shock because the century-long victimhood, the pillar of Poland's cultural memory since Partition in 1795, was shaken. In postwar Poland, victimhood of "the crucified nation" in terms of Adam Mickiewicz remained as the narrative touchstone that dominated the nation's historical consciousness and cultural memories.[25] For this reason, *Shoah* appalled even the anticommunist Catholic intellectuals, albeit in a way different from what it did for the Communist Party and bureaucrats—they denounced the film for being biased. They expressed strong disapproval of Lanzmann's critical gaze on the Poles, who were, after all, the biggest victims of World War II. Even the Social and Cultural Association of Jews in Poland wrote a letter of petition to the Embassy of France in Warsaw to protest the French government, which sponsored the production of *Shoah*.[26] However, Lanzmann's camera caught in close-up the ordinary antisemitism wandering about the very sites of the Holocaust. The myth of the Polish nation who fought a relentless, uncompromising battle against the Nazis turned out to be a "screen memory" to suppress the antisemitic past of sympathizing or collaborating with the Nazis. That discovery must have been a painful experience for many Polish intellectuals. The more the Cainian fear of God swept over the Polish society, the thicker the defensiveness of their collective memory had become.

After World War II, the ruling communist party of Poland advertised the establishment of the first homogenous nation-state as its achievement. What was left unsaid was that they had lost three million Jews, which was 90 percent of the entire Jewish population in Poland at the time, by the Holocaust, and that they forced displacement of Ukrainians, Belarussians, and Germans. Many ethnic Poles were also complacent about "Poland without Jews," however tacitly. When the few Holocaust survivors returned home, the reactions of the Polish were, "Are you still alive?" It was as if they did not want the survivors, the rightful owners of the homes they took, to come back. Such viciously greed-motivated antipathy toward the returned Jewish Holocaust survivors was found not only in Poland but also widely in Austria, France, the Netherlands, and other Western countries. Lacking popularity and support from below, the PZPR tried to avoid conflicts with the masses who dispossessed Jewish properties, including factories, houses, and land. Therefore, there had been a silent but widespread collusion between the people and the party.[27] The cruelest among the cruelties of the Nazis was their dehumanizing and demoralizing campaign against the vulnerable before victimizing them. Poland had to suffer also from severe moral degeneration that lasted for a considerable time after the war. During the Kielce Pogrom in July 1946, the communist leaders met with backlash from the workers who were disinclined to condemn the pogrom. The party secretary of Kielce Province even withdrew from addressing the crowd galvanized by antisemitic instigations, afraid that the party might be seen as being supportive of the Jews.[28]

PRIDE AND SHAME

January 1987, when Błoński's essay "Poor Poles Look at the Ghetto" was published, was a tipping point to demolish the communist regime's official memory in Poland. The title of this groundbreaking essay is a parody of "A Poor Christian Looks at the Ghetto," a poem composed by Czesław Miłosz. To the Polish society, the article penned by a famed literary critic at Jagiellonian University in Kraków—the cradle of Polish culture—that prodded the guilty conscience of the Poles by citing the Polish Nobel laureate came with far greater poignancy than did the critique from Lanzmann, an alien French Jew.[29] The poem was written immediately after the Nazis closed the Warsaw ghetto and deported its Jewish residents to Auschwitz in 1943. Miłosz depicts the horrible reality of the Holocaust with grotesque images in the first two stanzas: red liver; black bone; the breaking of glass, copper, violin strings, and trumpets; phosphorescent fire engulfing animal and human hair; white bone; torn paper; snakeskin; the roof and the wall collapsing in flame; and a leafless tree on the sandy, trodden-down earth. However, "a guardian mole" suddenly appears in the third stanza, "with a small red lamp fastened to his forehead." Rummaging through corpses and ashes to count the dead, the mole is a guardian of the underworld. What is curious is that the first-person speaker of the poem writes, "I am afraid, so afraid of the guardian mole." Why would he be afraid of this guardian mole, with swollen eyelids like those of a patriarch reading in the light of candles the great book?

What is grotesque is not the poetic diction but an inevitable realization stemming from it. In the final stanza, such a realization is manifested as the fear of the second coming of Jesus, who will count all (Polish) Christians among the helpers of death (of Jews). Christians were, at the same time, "Jews of the New Testament" who awaited the coming of Jesus and "the helpers of death" for actual Jews.[30] Here, through the poem's apocalyptic diction, Miłosz holds not only the Nazis but also Christian Poles morally accountable for the death of Jewish neighbors. In Błoński's essay, Miłosz's quiet poetry is retold in Błoński's voice—as the guardian mole from the underworld asks us: "Oh, yes, and you too, have you been assisting at the death? And you, too, have you helped to kill?" Or, at the very least: "Have you looked with acquiescence at the death of the Jews?"[31] Those thorny questions would be the reason Poles are not comfortable talking about their past regarding the Holocaust.

Another poem by Miłosz quoted in Błoński's essay, "Campo di Fiori," is more straightforward. At the beginning of the poem, Miłosz describes the Romans who enjoyed their cheerful day in February 1600 while Renaissance humanist Giordano Bruno, accused of heresy, was being burned alive at the stake in Campo di Fiori of Rome. The citizens of Rome, who mindlessly watched Bruno dying on the burning stake, returned to the taverns even "before the flames had died." In the third stanza, the scenery of Campo di Fiori, where "baskets of olives and lemons" are "again on the vendors' shoulders," suddenly overlaps with the Krasiński Square in the Aryan side of Warsaw, where people rode the sky-carousel on a beautiful Sunday. It was impossible for the citizens of Warsaw not to know what was happening that day when the flames from the ghetto reddened the entire sky of Warsaw.[32] The Warsaw citizens who rode the sky carousel amid the smoke and the sounds of gunfire and uproar were bystanders, just as the Renaissance Romans were. The poem is a mournful collage of the images of Giordano Bruno and the Jews behind the ghetto wall:

> In Rome on the Campo di Fiori
> baskets of olives and lemons,
> cobbles spattered with wine
> and the wreckage of flowers.
> Vendors cover the trestles
> with rose-pink fish;
> armfuls of dark grapes
> heaped on peach-down.
>
> On this same square
> they burned Giordano Bruno.
> Henchmen kindled the pyre
> close-pressed by the mob.
> Before the flames had died
> the taverns were full again,
> baskets of olives and lemons
> again on the vendors' shoulders.
>
> I thought of the Campo di Fiori
> in Warsaw by the sky-carousel
> one clear spring evening
> to the strains of a carnival tune.
> The bright melody drowned
> the salvos from the ghetto wall,
> and couples were flying
> high in the cloudless sky.
>
> At times, wind from the burning
> would drift dark kites along

and riders on the carousel
caught petals in midair.
That same hot wind
blew open the skirts of the girls
and the crowds were laughing
on that beautiful Warsaw Sunday.

. . .

But that day, I thought only
of the loneliness of the dying,
of how, when Giordano
climbed to his burning
he could not find
in any human tongue
words for humankind,
humankind who live on.[33]

"Campo di Fiori" was written on Easter day of 1943, when the Warsaw ghetto uprising was at its peak. On May 1 Simha Rotem, the courier for the ghetto uprising, escaped the ghetto through a secret underground tunnel below Bonifraterska Street to meet with Antek (Yitzhak Zuckerman), who was in the "Aryan side" of Warsaw to contact the Polish resistance.[34] To Rotem, who had just come out of the dark underground tunnel, the bright streets of Warsaw in the early morning seemed like an entirely new world. He later recalled that it felt like he came from another planet as the life in Warsaw, with open doors to the cafés, restaurants, theater, buses, and streetcars rolling on the street, was surprisingly normal, as if nothing happened.[35] Ewa Berberyusz recalls that on that very Easter day in 1943, she was walking with her father on Orła Street when he suddenly let go of her hand and froze at the sight of black smoke rising from the ghetto. What Berberyusz saw from her father being powerless in the face of tragedy was quite different from the heroic image of the resistance she learned from school.[36]

As Miłosz admitted, the formal rendering of "Campo di Fiori" is somewhat simple: Giordano Bruno at stake with the ghetto fighters and the Renaissance Romans with the people of Warsaw seems to be an easy juxtaposition. The poet called the piece "highly immoral" and accused himself of illustrating the death of Jews from the perspective of someone watching with his arms crossed. Yet, Błoński has a different take on the poem—he argues in the essay that Miłosz saved the dignity of Polish poetry by writing "Campo di Fiori" on that gruesome Easter day.[37] Błoński explains that the poet's intention hidden between the lines is that the Poles must, albeit painfully, confront their deplorable past and understand their moral accountability instead of making a series of self-exculpatory questions such as "What could we possibly do? What more could we Poles do under such extenuating circumstances? We might not have always been the best neighbors, but we have long been living together with Jews. Yes, there have been moments when the relationship between Poles and Jews was somewhat shaky, but who can blame it solely on us, Poles? Who dares to point the finger at the Polish nation, the biggest victims of the Nazis?"[38] Błoński's essay marked a shift of the Polish memory culture from complacent "tea culpa" to critical "mea culpa."

The guilty conscience of the Poles about the Holocaust that had been suppressed after World War II resurfaced through the debate triggered by Błoński's essay. To the stormy discussion, in which defense and accusation, repentance and penance, pride and shame, anger and grievance were mixed, the Poles' reactions were twofold: self-justificatory and self-reflective. The former blamed misrepresentation by the "Western" media—that the biased media and press of the West had made extreme generalizations about the antisemitism of "a few greedy peasants and jealous petit bourgeois" to incite negative sentiments toward the Polish nation. The self-justificatory group argued that the United States, the United Kingdom, or the governments of other Allied or neutral countries could have intervened to save the Jews much more proactively than Poland under the brutal Nazi occupation. However, the international media unfairly condemned Poland while remaining silent about the inaction of the West.[39] According to them, the Holocaust was not something about which the Poles should be ashamed, and no other country in Europe could depreciate the Poles' heroic resistance against the Nazi perpetrators; the Polish nation had done all they could do in the face of an overwhelming power of the unprecedented evil. Some even opined that the Poles could not help the Jews who did not help themselves and passively followed the Nazi rules without protest. Władysław Siła-Nowicki justified the self-exculpatory memory by stating that what the Polish nation had done during the Nazi occupation was not a reason to be ashamed, as Błoński claims, but rather a noble act.[40]

Even those on the self-reflective criticism admitted that there was not much the Poles could do to save the Jews. In its estimation of the dreadful situation of Poles under the Nazi occupation, the self-reflective critics did not veer much from that of the self-exculpatory side. Nevertheless, these critics paid attention to the moral responsibility of the Poles who left their Jewish neighbors to be murdered in isolation. As one journalist expressed, the question was not whether the Poles could stop the Holocaust but whether their neglect had let the Jews die alone.[41] This self-reflection also resonated with the question of whether the lack of empathy for the fate of Jews had spurred the Holocaust.[42] Without antisemitism, the Poles could not have saved the Jews but would have at least had a different attitude toward the Nazi atrocities happening on their soil.[43] The point was whether Poles were empathetic enough to share the suffering of Jews, at least emotionally.[44] That no one could point the finger at the Poles for having been bystanders did not mean they were free of moral culpability. It is why Błoński highlights "sin" (*grzech*) rooted in religious conscience and not legal "guilt" (*wina*). What is imperative, therefore, is questioning oneself about whether one tried one's best for the Jewish neighbors suffering the unprecedented plight rather than self-exculpation that rationalizes the extenuating circumstances under which one could not act differently. No call for moral conscience can remake the past of the Holocaust, as it already happened; still, the self-reflective questions to oneself would nevertheless be conducive to the reconstruction of Holocaust memories for the future.

The story of Jerzy Jastrzębowski's family seems very telling at this juncture of the Błoński debate. The family had a Jewish friend, Elijasz Parzyński, whom little Jerzy and the family called "Grandpa Eli," as he was their grandmother's friend. One day in 1941 or 1942, the year when the Warsaw ghetto was being packed to capacity and deporting all Jews to the extermination camps became clearer, Grandpa Eli came to this family and asked if they could shelter him and his sisters. At the risk of having the entire family face execution, they decided to hide him. However, they could not extend the invitation to his sisters who came with him—the sisters spoke with a thick Yiddish accent, and one of them even wore a blond wig to cover her dark hair. There was only a slim chance of staying unnoticed with all four of them, and if they were found, everyone—the Jastrzębowski family, Grandpa Eli, and his sisters—was going to be executed. The family's decision may be morally questionable, even though it was a "rational" choice to save their friends and the family.[45] Still, the Jastrzębowski family could never see Grandpa Eli again. Although the murder of Grandpa Eli and his sisters could not be blamed on the Jastrzębowski family, not to mention that their decision to hide Grandpa Eli was a very courageous one, their last encounter remained a painful memory, which the family had to bury deep in their minds even after the war. What can heal the trauma of Grandpa Eli and his sisters, who could not but turn around and face death together, and of the Jastrzębowskis, who had to ask them to part at the doorstep that divided life and death?

The Jastrzębowski family could never be free from the guilty conscience, even though their decision was a rational one. Should we view their decision as practical and necessary, we would be making an inhumane, morally abominable assessment of the situation; if we profess that they, for the sake of human dignity, should have chosen the option to have everyone executed, that would be an imposition of extremely absolutist morality. However, something was omitted here. Jastrzębowski alludes to a Polish cardinal, Bolesław Kominek, preaching that "omission is the most common sin in the life of humankind," which suggests his thick answer.[46] In the extraordinarily inhumane world under the Nazi occupation, reason was the enemy of morality. Rationality collided with humanity, as the Nazis forged the rules of the game to irrationalize what makes one human—morality, for example—vis-à-vis rationality inherent in survival instinct. "Rational" thinking insisted on compliance with the Nazi atrocities and turned a blind eye to the neighbors' death.[47] It is within this context that Zygmunt Bauman stressed the liberating effect of shame in driving out the evil of the Holocaust. The core of the problem was not about choosing between the justificatory national pride in the heroic resistance and the reflective shame of being unable to save more. According to Bauman, it was a question of choosing between pride, from feeling shame that would lead to moral restoration, and shame, from having indulged in pride that entails moral degradation.[48]

"BROTHER'S KEEPER"

Jan Gross's *Neighbors* (*Sąsiedzi*) has exposed that the relationship between the Poles and the Holocaust was more than a collusion on the levels of morality, conscience, and shame, but in actual crimes like murder and pillage. Published first in Polish on May 19, 2000, *Neighbors* covers the Jedwabne pogrom in which about 1,600 Jews were murdered in a small eastern town of 3,000 people.[49] What brought attention to the pogrom was not its scale but the faces of the murderers. Throwing Polish society into yet another colossal shock, *Neighbors* disclosed detailed accounts of the Polish villagers who were not just collaborators but even leading perpetrators of the Holocaust in a small village called Jedwabne. What Gross excavated from the judicial records of and the survivors' testimonies from the trials held at the Łomża district court in May 1949 and November 1953 was the rediscovery of the heinous crime—involving indiscriminately men and women, young and old. Gross's description of the massacre paints macabre scenes, together with the fact that the murderers were longtime neighbors of the victims. The brutal massacre of July 10, 1941, in which not the faceless Nazis but the familiar neighbors slaughtered other neighbors, is represented in graphic detail in Gross's book. As a reader, one cannot help but be appalled at the historical irony where only a few Jews who were drafted for forced labor at a municipal Nazi police office could save their lives. Agnieszka Arnold, who made a documentary film about the Jedwabne pogrom titled it *Where Is My Elder Son Cain* (*Gdzie Mój Starszy Syn Kain*), connoting the Poles, metaphoric Cain, that stoned the Jews, Abel, to death.[50]

On November 24, 2000, the Institute of History at the Polish Academy of Sciences hosted a colloquium on *Neighbors*. More than a hundred historians and journalists crowded the room, where their furious shouts and irritated cries, mixed with quiet sobs, overwhelmed the discussion.[51] Anna Bikont, one of the journalists at the meeting, remarked that the five-hour-long colloquium was a kind of group therapy session.[52] The issue at stake seemed even graver once the immediate revulsion inflamed by such a grotesque massacre cooled off. The very structure and premise of the collective victimhood inherent in the Polish historiography were to be uprooted, as the ordinary Poles in the small village were rediscovered as brutal perpetrators of the Holocaust. The justificatory memory prevalent in the Polish memory culture, which had framed the Poles and Jews equally as victims of the Nazis and World War II, as well as the reflective memory of the Holocaust, which had categorized the Poles as bystanders in the tripartite structure of perpetrator–victim–bystander, had to be changed. In light of unambiguous crimes excavated by Gross's *Neighbors*, Błoński's question of shame about the Polish bystanders became a moral extravagance. The point of discussion shifted from the level of moral sin to that of judicial crime. As the ugly truth about the Jedwabne pogrom was revealed, the historical position of the Poles shifted from the victims of the Nazis to complicit perpetrators.

The deprivation of the morally comfortable status of the victim called forth a painful shift in Polish memory culture. What the Jedwabne pogrom shows is the impossibility of understanding the complexity of historical reality by using the perpetrator-victim binary. It brought to light a case in which historical actors were at once victims and perpetrators. If Błoński's essay (1987) and Lanzman's *Shoah* (1985) formed a compelling text-film ensemble, Paweł Pawlikowski's *Ida* (2013) would be the cinematic counterpart of Gross's *Neighbors* (2000). A kind of road movie, *Ida* follows the protagonist "Ida," a young nun raised in a convent after neighboring Polish peasants murdered her parents during the Nazi occupation, as she travels with her aunt to her hometown and the graves of her parents. With its restrained direction and subdued black-and-white images exposing the crimes of the Polish neighbors, *Ida* received numerous awards, including the Polish Academy Award for Best Film of 2013, the European Film Award for Best Film, and the 87th Academy Award for Best Foreign Language Film, yet it endured harsh criticism from Polish nationalists. The critiques that accused the film of proliferating the stereotype of Poles as antisemites and exaggerating the negative aspect of the Polish nation out of animosity were in many ways reminiscent of the hostile reception of *Neighbors*.[53]

Until the end of the twentieth century, the professional historiography of academia, history education at elementary and secondary schools, and both the official and vernacular memories in Poland were all morally complacent in the perception that simply equated the Polish nation with the collective victims. They were oblivious to the complex historical reality of the Holocaust. It was self-righteousness sprouted from the hereditary victimhood that hampered critical self-reflection. The uncomfortable postwar history, such as the state-led antisemitism of 1968 and "antisemitism without Jews" after the fall of the Berlin Wall, was related to their cultural memory based on hereditary victimhood. The claim that the historical debate revolving around *Neighbors* started a true "moral revolution" alarming the entire society tells the gravity of the discussion.[54] Nothing is more dangerous than collective moral righteousness without individual self-reflection. As Agnieszka Arnold, the director of documentary films on the Jedwabne pogrom, recalled in an interview with radio channel TOK FM in 2017, the Polish society's reaction to the debate was that it was "their" fault, not "ours." The war had shown them the fragility of humans confronting the temptation of evil, and the moral degradation and fear pushed to the brink had resulted in the genocidal tragedy in Jedwabne.[55]

In postcommunist Poland of the 1990s, one of the most prominent historical discourses was that the international community had not sufficiently acknowledged the suffering of the Poles who were doubly victimized by the Nazis' brown terror and the Stalinist red terror.[56] As the postwar experience of communist crimes was still recent and its memory vivid, the main issue in coming to terms with the past was Stalinism. The Poles' historical accountability for or guilty conscience about the Holocaust remained on the margins and were overwhelmed by the memories of the Stalinist oppression. As long as the memory of being victims of the Stalinist terror dominated the mnemoscape, there was not much room for the memory of the complicity in the Holocaust.[57] Hence emerged counterclaims, such as that the Jedwabne pogrom was against the people's will as the Poles were coerced and terrorized by the Nazis' killing task forces, or that the violence was not done by the Polish villagers in Jebwabne but by criminal gangs who were brought from outside—suggesting that the slaughterers were not "ordinary Poles" but "thugs" hired by the Nazis, a group of "professional criminals" who would readily forfeit their human dignity in exchange for a fraction of financial gain.[58] Another claim that it was done solely by the Nazis surfaced as bullets that belonged to the German military were discovered in the barn where the Jewish victims were locked in and burned. However, it was soon debunked as the bullets were confirmed to be from a different period. Behind all these claims stood the premise that no "ordinary Pole" would commit such a horrific crime. Also seething under the counterclaims was the irrepressible resentment against the claim that the Poles, the biggest victims of World War II, could also be perpetrators.

The most extreme faction of self-justificatory memories has gone even further to claim that Jews victimized Poles. These anticommunist nationalists define the period between 1939, when the Soviet Army occupied Poland according to the German-Soviet Pact, and 1941, the year the Nazis invaded the Soviet Union, as the era of Soviet-Jewish Occupation, a designation to highlight that the Jewish neighbors collaborated with Russian Stalinists to oppress patriotic Catholic Poles. According to their claim, the "Jewish commies" (Żydokomuna) were at the forefront of deporting Poland's anticommunist, anti-Russian patriots to Central Asia or Siberia by betraying them to the NKWD, Soviet secret police. This claim, therefore, supports that the victims were not Jews but Poles and that the violence against certain Jews was history's retribution for their betrayal.[59] For the advocates of this claim, Jan Gross, the author of *Neighbors*, and Aleksander Kwaśniewski, the then president of Poland who publicly issued an apology on behalf of the Polish people at the sixtieth anniversary of the Jedwabne pogrom, are no different from Stalin's secret police who hated and oppressed the Polish nation. This faction, which is linked to far-right Catholics like Radio Maryja, insists to this day that Nazi Germany alone was responsible for the genocide of Jews and that the antisemitism of Poles was a well-earned punishment for the "Jewish commies."[60]

Both the Błoński debate in 1987 and the Jedwabne debate in 2000 occasioned the reemergence of victimhood rooted deeply in the collective memory of postwar Polish society. The Polish sociologist Zygmunt Bauman elaborated on the Polish memory of victimhood through the concept of "hereditary victimhood" based on his experience in Israel, where he stayed for a short time in political exile.[61] A devout socialist, Bauman was exiled to Israel when he was targeted for the anti-Zionist campaign launched by the nationalist-communist partisans of Poland in 1968. In Israel, Bauman witnessed the Zionists who wielded Holocaust victimhood as their political weapon for self-justification. At the psychological root of how the Israeli soldiers justified their bloody suppression of the Palestinian youths' resistance, Bauman excavated hereditary victimhood as the cultural memory that dominated and framed the postwar generations' remembrance of Poland and Israel. Inheriting ancestral victimhood in the form of postmemory, the postwar generations could consider themselves as the victims of World War II and the Holocaust.[62] Based on Bauman's personal experiences in postwar Poland and Israel, hereditary victimhood is also a valuable framework for understanding the memory culture of postcolonial societies.

At the fourth workshop of the East Asia History Forum for Criticism and Solidarity in April 2003, I examined the applicability of this frame in the context of Korea through my presentation of "Hereditary Victimhood and Postcolonial Historiography."[63] The main point was that we must escape hereditary victimhood and institute self-reflective critical memory. Otherwise, we would close our eyes to the possibility that any of us, even those who were formerly colonized, can be perpetrators of colonial violence. Insofar as a nation confines itself in the frame of hereditary victimhood, internal criticism of latent colonialism within the nation becomes unlikely. At the base of hereditary victimhood, one can find the desperate desire to avoid being victimized again. Such eagerness does not fundamentally reject the colonialist structure of oppression. Under the surface of hereditary victimhood is remorse for the history of being colonized and not colonizers. This logic problematizes not colonialism but the fact that a nation failed to build an empire and become colonized. Albeit its ostensibly anticolonial message, hereditary victimhood thus hinders postcolonial thinking. Koreans' aggressive neocolonialism toward Southeast Asian, Mongol, and Central Asian countries was appearing on the scene.

LONG-DISTANCE NATIONALISM

From the afternoon through the evening of January 17, 2007, articles critical of the novella *So Far from the Bamboo Grove* were uploaded on the websites of all major daily newspapers of South Korea, from left to right, to be published on January 18.[64] In the world of the Korean press, where progressives and conservatives acutely conflict over every issue, such coordination between left and right was a scarce sight. *So Far from the Bamboo Grove* is an autobiographical coming-of-age novel by the Japanese writer Yoko Kawashima Watkins as an eleven-year-old girl. She depicts the author's experience of surviving with her family on their return journey to Japan from Ranam, a municipal district in what is now North Korea, amid life-threatening terror, hunger, and sexual assault. Written in a realistic yet easily comprehensible language for pre- to early teens, *So Far from the Bamboo Grove* might have appealed even more to young American readers for its straightforward narrative structure centered on a protagonist who suffers through a series of challenges in the return and resettlement processes, eventually to be rewarded by growing up and overcoming the pains.

First published in the United States in 1986, the novella was translated and published in Korean with the title 요코이야기 (Yoko's story) in April 2005. The book did not seem to bring about any controversy at its publication. A reviewer in *Yonhap News* on May 13, 2005, writes that the book is "an autobiographical novella from the perspective of a little girl whose family had to go through a difficult journey back to Japan from Ranam after the defeat of Japan in 1945." A book review by *Chosun Ilbo* on May 6, 2005, reads: "If we can briefly ignore the author's nationality, the book is an earnest *Bildungsroman* that illustrates how war pushes a family's life into agony." The initial reviews like these indicate that *So Far from the Bamboo Grove* was received as one of many, perhaps not so distinctive, books.[65] In January 2007, however, Watkins's book was suddenly under the spotlight of most major news outlets in South Korea. As attested by the scandalous headlines, such as "Gullible South Korea Publishes *So Far from the Bamboo Grove*, the Novel Dismissed Even in Japan," "A Phony Memoir on Joseon-Korea Written by Daughter of Japanese War Criminal," "The Japanese Version of the Diary of Anne Frank Deceived Even American Readers," and "*So Far from the Bamboo Grove* Full of Lies," the point of argument shared by all news articles, regardless of each platform's political leaning, was that the book was faking history.

Before the competitive reporting of the South Korean media, the controversy surrounding Watkins's book was already in flames in the United States. In September 2006 a group of Korean American parents in Boston and New York complained about including *So Far from the Bamboo Grove* in the reading list for sixth-to-eighth-grade students. One student of Korean descent boycotted a school for teaching *So Far* in class, followed by a collective action by Korean American parents in the greater Boston area to demand that the local board of education stop using *So Far* as course material. The crux of the issue raised by the Korean Americans was that the book depicted Koreans, the victims of colonialism and war, as perpetrators and the Japanese, the actual perpetrators, as victims. The criticism that the book could wrongly characterize Koreans as ruthless criminals and the Japanese as innocent victims for young American students who were not familiar with the history of East Asia seemed like a sound one in the context of the United States. Indeed, any mention of crimes and atrocities perpetrated by the Japanese Army or of the historical/moral injustice of colonialism is undoubtedly missing in this book. Its only acknowledgment of colonialism is in passing:

"Koreans were part of the Japanese empire and hated the Japanese people."

The most notable shortcoming of *So Far from the Bamboo Grove* is its decontextualization of the bleak past, the history of Japanese colonialism. As can be seen from the campaigns of the Japanese Society of History Textbook Reform, a group dedicated to constructing Japan's image as the victim of Korean and Chinese nationalism, historical decontextualization is equal to the political instrumentalization of history and the ignorance of difficult heritage. Japan's history of justifying its invasion of China by blaming it on aggressive Chinese nationalism and Western imperialism is a good example of the threat of decontextualization. Decontextualized from the Japanese colonialist past in the Asia-Pacific, the self-justificatory memory culture in Japan gives the impression that the Japanese empire was a victim rather than a perpetrator. Even Nazis tried to justify its invasion of Eastern Europe by citing the human rights of the German ethnic minorities (*Volksdeutsche*) under the national oppression. Historical decontextualization is often the indulgence to exonerate the perpetrators from their historical crimes. Thus, it is entirely possible to criticize the oversimplified and decontextualized memory of *So Far from the Bamboo Grove*, narrated by a young girl who sees the world through the black-and-white dichotomy. All that being said, the book cannot be accused of fabricating the history of the Japanese repatriates in misery. There is a difference between falsified history and decontextualized history.

According to the official documents published by the Japanese Ministry of Health, Labor, and Welfare, the number of Japanese nationals residing outside the Japanese archipelago by the war's end in August 1945 totaled about 6.9 million, with 3.2 million civilians and 3.7 million soldiers. Among them, 720,100 civilians and 336,000 troops, the army and navy combined, were on the Korean peninsula, and 1,550,000 civilians and 664,000 army troops were in Manchukuo.[66] The number of *hikiagesha* (Japanese repatriated after the war) returned by 1976 is estimated at 6,290,000. This ministry report shows a lesser number because it does not count missing people as nonreturned, as the "Nonreturned Act" implemented in 1959 allowed the families of missing people to report them dead.[67] The return of Japanese nationals from colonial Korea, Taiwan, and mainland China began in October 1945 but involved primarily military troops and their families at first. The civilians in colonial Korea were detained on the Korean peninsula for more than three years after the end of the war. They were not released until the U.S.-USSR agreement was signed. In Manchuria, Japanese residents were strongly advised against returning due to food and housing shortages in Japan. Return was impossible from Southern Manchuria, including Fengtian, and coastal cities like Dairen, as the Soviet Union invaded those regions. Under these circumstances, the evacuation of the Manchu pioneer settlers and their families began in May 1946. It lasted until November 1946, sending back to Japan about 109,000 out of 225,000 settlers, of which 82,000 were dead or missing, and the Soviet Army detained 34,000. The number of deaths among Japanese repatriates in Manchuria is estimated to be around 110,000, which was increased by famine and disease.[68]

Since the end of the war, the Japanese detainees on the Korean peninsula had all their accumulated wealth confiscated by Koreans, as well as U.S. and Soviet military forces. They were exposed to retaliation, famine, and the cold without shelter. During this period of a maximum of three years, approximately eighteen thousand Japanese nationals died on the Korean peninsula—many of them elders, women, and children. The financial damage was also significant in Manchukuo and colonial Korea. About 95 percent of the total economic loss of overseas Japanese were the assets left in China and on the Korean peninsula.[69] Amid the postwar chaos, the safety of Japanese civilians in Manchuria and on the Korean peninsula was not the primary interest of the local governments or the U.S. and Soviet military. Suffering the aftermath of the defeat, even the Japanese society did not wish for their immediate return, wary of them worsening the chaos. The Japanese civilians living overseas were one of the groups that were most vulnerable to violence at the tail end of the war. *So Far from the Bamboo Grove* recollects the shared experience of many *hikiagesha* who were on their way back to Japan from the Korean peninsula, marked by the dread upon the surrender of Japan, the sudden decline of status from colonizers to war criminals, the forced labor in the Soviet POW camp, the Red Army's occupation and sexual violence, the revenge attacks by the Chinese in Manchuria and colonial Koreans, and extreme malnutrition and disease.

The recently discovered memoir by Narihara Akira, a *hikiagesha* from Ranam, Hamgyeong Province, illustrates an experience that is surprisingly similar to that in *So Far from the Bamboo Grove*. Similar to Yoko's, Narihara's experience spans crossing the 38th parallel north on a train and boarding a ship to Japan from the port of Busan after a series of struggles against air raids, retaliation from Joseon Koreans, sexual assault by the Soviet military in the refugee camp, typhus and other diseases, and malnutrition.[70] What cast doubt on the integrity of *So Far from the Bamboo Grove* should have been its almost stereotypical plotline. The book is not to be read as a personal experience of a single protagonist but a general outline of collective suffering. Yoko Kawashima Watkins's remembrance was not free from the cultural memory of *hikiagesha* framed in postwar Japan. However, the criticism from the Korean American community tended to focus on the "fakeness" of this autofiction—which, according to the complaint, promulgated the false idea of evil Korean perpetrators versus innocent Japanese victims, when in the colonial reality, the perpetrator-victim relation was the opposite. The logic of such criticism displays nationalist thinking that categorizes individuals by nation while remaining willfully oblivious to each individual's action and consequence within a specific historical context. To the supporters of this logic, with their unwavering belief in the collective guilt of the Japanese, the phrase "Japanese victim" must have felt like an oxymoron. The Voluntary Agency Network of Korea (VANK), a nationalist NGO in South Korea, holds a similar stance—that Yoko Kawashima Watkins disguised herself, a child of Imperial Japan, as "the Japanese Anne Frank" to vandalize the reputation of the Korean nation whom the Japanese had already victimized through murder and rape, such as the case of "Comfort Women."[71]

The rage of the Korean community in the United States against *So Far from the Bamboo Grove* was amplified as it traveled across the Pacific and reached the Korean peninsula. Completely different from the relatively positive, albeit lukewarm, reviews of the book in 2005, a uniformly hostile reception dominated the public discourse. On either side of the political spectrum, Korean society's reading of Watkins's painful recollection seemed to negate even the very possibility of the suffering of individual Japanese. In addition to the malicious rumor that Watkins's father was a high-ranking officer of Unit 731, the division of the Imperial Japanese Army notorious for its disturbing biological and chemical experiments on human bodies, allegedly scrupulous fact-checking was used to disprove the authenticity of Watkins's experience depicted in *So Far from the Bamboo Grove*: that bamboos cannot grow in Ranam, as it is too cold for the species; that the B-29 raid did not even happen; and that the communist army was yet to be formed at the time of Yoko's evacuation. Under the cover of such fact-checking was the failure to accept the unstable boundary between "Japanese perpetrator" and "Korean victim"--their discomfort and resentment with the depiction of Koreans as perpetrators in Watkins's novella, which interfered with their morally comfortable victimhood nationalism. Thus, the hostile reception was an expression of the mnemonic insecurity coming from shattered position of morally safe victims.[72] The overemphasis on Yoko's standing as a colonial oppressor, by discrediting the narrative because it is "a personal experience recalled and reconstructed by a little girl" and spreading rumors about her family background, reflected the anxiety of the shattered memory.

The cartoon book published by VANK exemplifies Koreans' anxiety about mnemonic security. Made for anyone with an elementary–middle school level of reading skills, this "educational" cartoon reinforces the stereotypes of the Japanese as "bad guys" through unequivocal visual elements, such as an image of slant-eyed Yoko Kawashima Watkins wearing a kimono. Toward the end, the book assigns its young readers various thought exercises. The first is to find out the lies in *So Far from the Bamboo Grove*, in the order of the bamboo grove, the air raid, and the communist army—along with an extra-credit activity, which is to spot similarities and differences between *The Diary of Anne Frank* and *So Far from the Bamboo Grove*. The second exercise, "Report the Japanese Atrocities!," includes the stories of the "Comfort Women" and Unit 731, "the most heinous and brutal criminals in human history." Following the battle to refute false war stories, this exercise is designed with a visible intention to offset the suffering of civilian evacuees against military atrocities. The third exercise is a call to action titled "Stop American Schools from Using *So Far from the Bamboo Grove* in Class!," which encourages readers to write letters of petition to the U.S. Department of Education and individual schools for removal of the book from the course material, to the publisher for suspension of publication, and to the author for an official apology. The fourth exercise is to "Find New Information About *So Far from the Bamboo Grove*!" The final one is to "Illuminate the Truth About *So Far from the Bamboo Grove*." At the end of some of these exercises, a template for a petition letter, an example of a newspaper clipping, and blank manuscript papers were enclosed to streamline readers' engagement.[73]

Such an overreaction prompted by the victimhood nationalism of Korea had an unexpected effect—a nationalist publisher in Japan published a Japanese translation of *So Far from the Bamboo Grove* eight years after it was published in South Korea. The Japanese translation (with the localized title *So Far from the Bamboo Grove: A Japanese Girl Yoko's Wartime Memoir*) has garnered much attention since its publication in 2013, ranked as the second most popular book among war memoirs.[74] On January 22, 2022, the number of reviews for this book on Amazon Japan amounted to 342, more than twenty times the number of reviews for Tei Fujiwara's *Tei: A Memoir of the End of War and Beginning of Peace*, a long-time classic in the genre of *hikiage* memoirs. The star rating averages 4.5, while reviews like "Reality is more dramatic than fiction," "Recommend to everyone," "A must-read masterpiece," "It's a mystery why this isn't taught in schools in Japan," and "A book to resolve any questions left about the post-war period" flood the website. Some even opine that it is a shame the Korean American community boycotted such a great book, and anyone who thinks this is an anti-Korean or anti-Chinese book is hiding an ulterior motive.[75] What is more interesting is the list of books also bought by those who purchased *So Far*, including *The Future of the World Depends on Japan: Stop the Chinese Invasion*, *Senkaku: The Last Ditch*, *China's Lightning Attack*, and other Sinophobic titles, along with books denying the "Comfort Women." On the list were also the Total War era textbooks that might rekindle nostalgia for the educational ideology that "fostered Japanese pride and military spirit." It seemed the victimhood nationalism in Korea provoked the far-right readership of Japan and unintentionally increased the presence of a book that used to receive only minor attention. Operative in East Asia's memory space, the antagonistic complicity between Korean and Japanese nationalists secretly emerged from the shadows.

Amid the turmoil, I wrote a column in English for the *Korea Herald* titled "Victimhood Nationalism: Compelling or Competing?" to assess nationalism in Northeast Asia.[76] In this short piece, for the first time, I proposed the idea of victimhood nationalism as a conceptual frame to explain the postwar memory culture, in which different nations battle for the victim status to secure moral legitimacy over other nations in the transnational memory space. Following publication of the column, I started receiving emails of complaints from Korean Americans who had caused the controversy surrounding *So Far from the Bamboo Grove*, accusing me of warping the colonial history by claiming that the Japanese evacuees were the victims of vengeful Koreans in my column. Sometimes, when describing themselves as someone educated in an elite university, my critics admonished me that someone like me should not teach history to college students of their motherland. They were unpleasant, but I also enjoyed these criticisms—the aggressive emails and complaints, marked by resentment, seemed to prove the explanatory power of victimhood nationalism vis-à-vis the reality it indicates. People tend to be angered by truth more than falsehood because they fear inconvenient truth more than lies about themselves. What intrigued me even more was that this uproar started in the United States and traveled across the Pacific to activate victimhood nationalism in the Korean peninsula.

The long-distance nationalism of Asian Americans manifested in the transpacific memory space is undoubtedly distinct from Latin America's "Creole nationalism" in the transatlantic memory space of the nineteenth century. The driving force of the Central and South American revolutions, Creole nationalism was a movement among the European colonial settlers in the Americas who were alienated and marginalized by the elites of the "center." Creole nationalists tried to establish an independent state divorced from "the mainland."[77] In contrast, victimhood nationalism rekindles nationalism of the "mainland" rather than opposes it, as the collective memory of the nation becomes repatriated. Taxidermized in the old yet more stubborn spirit of nationalism immigrants held at the moment of immigration, long-distance nationalism tends to be more rigid and essentialized than the "mainland," which has gone through constant sociocultural changes. The Korean Americans' long-distance nationalism was no exception. I could confirm yet again that nationalism is a transnational phenomenon through this experience of witnessing how the nationalist memory culture of Korea got reinforced by importing back the Korean American's long-distance nationalism, which had been intensified in the racist yet multicultural environment of the United States.

At this juncture, it is logical that the research of victimhood nationalism requires the perspective of transnational history surpassing that of national history—moreover, this book calls for global history beyond transnational history. To understand victimhood nationalism merely regarding the interrelations between Korea and Japan, Japan and the United States, Poland and Germany, Germany and Israel, and Poland and Israel, the lens of transnational history may suffice. However, the memories of and about victims reach far beyond national or continental borders via imitating, juxtaposing, and cross-referencing. The memory culture of East Asia that remembers both the Japanese war crimes and the atomic bombs benchmarks the memory of the Holocaust, and vice versa—as the memory of "Comfort Women" awakens Europe's memories of its wartime sexual violence and enforced prostitution. Once victimhood nationalism connects the transpacific and transatlantic memory spaces, its memories become interwoven into a global memory formation. The complicated aspect of global memory formation, constructed by the alliance and dissolution of the memories of the Holocaust, colonial genocide, and Stalinist terror, demands the perspective of global history stretching beyond the level of transnational history shackled by the binary opposition between victim and perpetrator. It is for this reason that this book maintains the perspective of global history on the victimhood nationalism of Korea, Japan, Germany, Poland, and Israel.

3

SUBLIMATION

SACRALIZATION OF VICTIMS

How are "victim," "sacrifice," and "martyr" different from one another? How appropriate is it to differentiate passive victims from active martyrs, innocent victims from sublime sacrifices, and unfortunate casualties from heroic war dead? Toward which is victimhood nationalism leaning—victims, sacrifices, or martyrs? If I may cut to the chase, it is difficult to restrict victimhood nationalism to any frame of victims, sacrifices, or martyrs. Victimhood nationalism is processual, coming onto the scene through the cumulatively commemorative sublimation of sacralizing passive victims into self-motivated sacrifices or martyrs. When the unfortunate victims who died unjustly transform into righteous martyrs who voluntarily sacrificed themselves for the just cause, the gate to victimhood nationalism opens. When innocent victims are sacralized as righteous self-sacrifices in martyrdom, victimhood nationalism wears fatalistic transcendence. Secular ideologies dreaming of the eternal fatherland, powerful nation-states, heroic revolutions, filial communes, and futuristic societies are then elevated to ontological fate through the sublimation of sacrifice.

From a semantical point of view, victimhood nationalism takes a different approach in its sublimation of victims by language. First, there is almost no distinction between victim and sacrifice in German and Polish: The German word *Opfer* and the Polish word *ofiara* have both victim and sacrifice meanings. Thus, depending on the context, the same word can describe a pitiful victim or a noble sacrifice. Both *Opfer* and *ofiara* connote sacrifice: *Opfertod* (a compound noun of *Opfer* and *Tod*, the latter meaning death) means "sacrificial death," and *ofiara całopalna* (the latter word meaning complete burn) indicates "holocaust" in the sense of "burnt offering" in the Old Testament. In everyday usage, however, *Opfer* and *ofiara* usually mean "victim." In both German and Polish, the word for "martyr" more accurately delivers the sense of someone who sacrificed their life for a more significant cause, as opposed to a passive victim—such as *Märtyrer* in German and *męczennik* in Polish, both of which originated from the ancient Greek word *mártyr*, which means someone willing to sacrifice their own life for their belief.[1]

In English, "victim" and "sacrifice" are more distinct. There are times when the two words intersect. Still, in general, the definition of "victim" is adjacent to a passive sufferer, whereas "sacrifice" often means an active volunteer committed to a more significant cause. Thus, one might question my decision to translate victimhood nationalism as 희생자의식 민족주의 (*huisaengjauisik minjokjuui*) in Korean despite the fact that the English equivalent of the Korean term 희생자 (*huisaengja*) is "sacrifice." Semantically, victimhood nationalism is activated in the sublimation process where an innocent victim of war, colonialism, and genocide is converted into a sublime sacrifice for a secular entity like the nation, fatherland, independence, revolution, peace, human rights, or democracy in postwar memory culture. A "victim" is a raw material to be sublimated into a "sacrifice" in the repository of victimhood nationalism. The sublimation rites of death that transform pointless death into predestined sacrifice share the same code with the nationalist sacralization of death for immortality. When inscribed as sacrifices for the national cause, meaningless deaths become sublimated into immortal deaths that perpetually revitalize the nation.[2]

A compound noun made of 犧 (meaning untainted, single-colored lambs or cows) and 牲 (a cow that is sacrificed alive at a ritual), 犧牲 (*huisaeng* in Korean pronunciation) is an indicative term shared in the

Sinographic cultural sphere for animals sacrificed at religious ceremonies. Interestingly, it is almost identical to the Latin *sacer*, from which the English word "sacrifice" originated. In the East Asian languages based on Sinograph, the passive suffering of the victimized and the active forgoing of one's life in sacrifice are differentiated. It is not to say there is no connotation of unreasonable death in the word for "sacrifice." Still, it is used far more dominantly as a term for an active, determinant, and voluntary commitment, either to save someone else's life or to keep one's dignity. The Sinographic phrase 犧牲者意識 民族主義 (victimhood nationalism) would resonate similarly among East Asian readers. The reasons I insisted on adding 意識 (consciousness) to the word 犧牲者 (the victim) were, first, to capture the generative process of memory that sublimates a victim into a sacrifice, as I thought emphasizing consciousness—hence "victim*hood*"—would be more effective in explaining the politics of rhetoric that paints a victim with the sublime aesthetic of a sacrifice; and second, to expand on "hereditary victimhood," the historical consciousness of the postmemory generation who inherited the ancestral position of victims and thus pretend to be victims rather than the actual victims themselves.

"Victim" and "sacrifice" are often grouped into one word, as in German and Polish, or treated as two unequivocally distinct signifiers, as in English and, more apparently, in Sinographic languages. A signifier can signify differently depending on the context, and two different signifiers can often mean the same. In contrast to the inconsistent lexical relation between "victim" and "sacrifice," "martyr" has an almost uniform meaning across languages. In European languages like English, German, and Slavic languages, as well as in Sinographic languages, "martyrdom" means an act of enduring torture and risking one's life for a religious or political belief, reflecting the history of religious persecution and inquisition. Especially in the Christian imagination, there is no meaningless pain—ultimately, any suffering leads to martyrdom.[3] Tied to a fatalistic religion that promises resurrection in the afterlife for those who dedicate their present lives, martyrdom embraces the dialectic of sacrifice and victory. Sacrifice then equals victory. At this juncture, the attempt to explain the "suicide terrorism" of Jihadists or the "suicide attack" of Palestinian fighters with the altruistic suicide paradigm seems plausible.[4] Søren Kierkegaard wrote, "The tyrant dies, and his rule is over; the martyr dies, and his rule begins."[5] The tyrant enforces subordination by power, but the martyr secures authority by dying.

When the rule of martyrdom begins, victimhood nationalism is also activated. For martyr worship to develop into victimhood nationalism, however, the selected few martyrs must multiply into collective martyrs in large numbers—it requires nationalization or massification of martyrdom. When not only the chosen few but the entire nation become martyrs, victimhood nationalism surpasses being an abstract ideology to be a materiality. Now, it is "our" martyrdom. The democratization of death, through which massive nameless heroes replace the hero of great eminence, manifests itself, especially in adoration of unknown soldiers, which requires the format of traditional religion deeply rooted in the everyday lives of ordinary citizens. "We are holy from now on!" wrote a military volunteer upon being blessed in a church before leaving for the battlefield during World War I.[6] It was as if he was prepared for death. The myth of a "manly" soldier who sacrificed himself for a noble cause dates back to the Greek War of Independence (1821–1830). The poet of "tempestuous passion and tragic fate," Byron idolized the fallen and created myths. When the tale of the fallen who died bravely and will resurrect is established, the horrible war experience is turned into a happy ending that transcends death.[7]

Jo Jihun, the Korean poet known for his involvement in the Blue Deer school of lyric poetry, evidently depicts the rhetoric of transcendental sublimation in his lyrics for "Song of Memorial Day": "As you fought to the end, made last stands for our nation, / That sincerity protects the fatherland now and for good / Oh, nature in my homeland, / Please lay warriors to rest / But our hearts are where all loyal souls exist / You are symbolic of our unwavering national spirit."[8] Composed in 1957 by Im Won-sik, "Song of Memorial Day" was popularized under the mass dictatorship of the 1970s, when all "industrial warriors" were mobilized to the "modernization of fatherland." It was selected as a "patriot folk song" mandated to be included as the final track of every pop music album, along with other patriotic folk songs like "Song of Constitution Day" that reaffirm that the Republic of Korea could secure its "land for a trillion years" today because the patriots had thrown their lives to save the homeland.[9] Together with the national anthem, the patriotic ceremonial songs with austere melodies and lyrics about sublime sacrifices were often sung at various events and ceremonies. Despite the hackneyed lyrics and boring tunes, people who sang these songs would feel a kind of sentimental unity. When strangers sing the same song together, an imaginative community manifests in echoes.[10]

The dispute over the singing of "Marching for Our Beloved" at the May 18 Gwangju Uprising commemoration started in 2009 during the presidency of Lee Myung-bak and can be understood in a similar vein—the organizers of the commemorative event intended to secure a sense of unity by singing the song together. In contrast, the conservative politicians preferred the professional choir's performance because of concern that the audience would bodily connect to the memory of the people's uprising in Gwangju in 1980 and find solidarity with each other. Only a few activities are as conducive to sentimentally connecting strangers and creating imaginary communities as the tunes of anthems and songs of revolution and resistance. Compared to on- or off-stage performances by professional choirs, the performativity of singing by a crowd of thousands in unison is much more audience-friendly and directly affective on a personal level. Be it of the nation or revolution, the cultural memory of an imagined, immortal community is deeply rooted in the vernacular memory realm through its performativity.[11]

Making grand spectacles all over the country at a designated time, dramatic rituals of a nation-state expand the performativity of victimhood nationalism and implant a sense of shared history among the nation at the same time-space. At this juncture, victimhood nationalism achieves material power beyond abstract conceptuality of victimhood. Nationalism maximizes emotional attachment among the people by calling forth the memory of shared suffering. As Ernest Renan aptly points out, "suffering in common unifies more than joy does. Where national memories are concerned, griefs are of more value than triumphs."[12] Victimhood nationalism fits perfectly with the definition of political religion, which consecrates and worships the secular reality or values like nation, ethnicity, race, empire, state, history, revolution, and freedom.[13] The memory of collective sacrifice becomes an even better ingredient for political religion than any secular values because it transforms unreasonable deaths into ones that were inevitable to immortalize the community through the sublimation of sacrifice. Therefore, the myth of sacrifice was optimal material for *Wiederzauberung* (re-enchantment) of political religion, which filled in the gaps caused by *Entzauberung* (disenchantment) of traditional popular religions.

NATIONALIZATION OF THE DEAD

Rituals to console and commemorate the dead are not necessarily unique to modern nation-states and can also be found in premodern societies. A mourning ceremony is one aspect of human life that transcends time. However, there is a qualitative difference between the premodern rites to solace the souls of the dead and the national rituals of modern states to honor the war dead. For example, the funeral rites of premodern East Asia were founded on the belief that the unresolved souls could cause natural disasters or spread diseases—thus, the objective of such rites was to prevent a catastrophe by consoling the vengeful and embittered dead (冤魂, 怨靈, 冤鬼), who would otherwise remain resentful of their inexplicable and wrongful deaths and avenge one's grudge on the living. At the foundation of the premodern rituals was the fear of the vengeful and forlorn wandering spirits of the war dead who would retaliate against the living unless consoled—in short, the war dead were treated as wicked ghosts that needed to be lulled to peace.[14] The traditional mourning rituals were thus characteristically different from the sublimation of the war dead in the modern era.[15]

The birth of the modern subject goes hand in hand with the sublimation of war dead in the official commemoration to unify and control the diverse, unorganized masses under one political agenda. The objective of war dead sublimation is reflected in the homogenization process of the modern subject, namely, the nationalization of the masses.[16] The formation of the modern subject dates back to the French Revolution. The idea emerged in 1750s France when Neoclassicism idealized the civic republic of ancient Greece and Rome. The three elements of an ideal community the neoclassicists imagined were a community based on communal will, citizens with equal rights and responsibilities, and citizens' devotion to the community.[17] Preceding the French neoclassicists, the Whigs of seventeenth-century England also equated themselves with the citizens of the ancient republics, which the Whigs understood as "patriotic communities formed by associations of equal citizens."[18] The Enlightenment interpretation, which appropriated ancient Greco-Roman civic republics as the Western tradition, coincided with the paradigm shift that erased the traces of African and Semitic cultures and replaced the ancient model with the Arian model.[19] Within this frame of modern nation-state, the commemorative tradition of the "West" met the pacifying tradition of the "East." The two practices merged into the national ceremony.

With the introduction of national ceremonies of modern nation-states to East Asia, the unidentified spirits of those who died pointlessly amid war began to be converted into the fallen heroes who sacrificed themselves for the greater good. The classical nationalism and patriotism of the French Revolution, and later fascism in the 1930s, developed the symbolism of death and funeral rites that sanctify national death. It was reaching beyond logical persuasion and attaining emotional exaltation of secularized religious beliefs. The symbolic rituals of modern death nationalized death by determining eligibility for the national funeral based not on the place of birth or privilege but on the dead's service to the country.[20] The secular objects become sanctified through martyrdom, continuously demanding sacrifices. The concept of martyrdom formulates the dialectic of victory and sacrifice via its apocalyptic intervention in history, warranting the emergence of the potent victim, not a helpless sufferer but a warrior of liberation that subverts the preexisting power structure.[21] The heroes and the victims in the nationalist discourse may seem contradictory to each other but are interpenetrated in national memories through images of martyrdom. When the discourses of heroism and victimhood transfuse, personal or collective suffering becomes the source of national pride. The war dead acquire immortality by persisting in national memories.

Victimhood nationalism differs from heroic nationalism as the former sublimates not only the war dead who threw themselves into battles for the fatherland but also all innocent victims who died unreasonable and wrongful deaths. It means that death has been democratized—when the notion of human rights replaces the elitist discourse about martyrdom, victimhood nationalism gains more traction.[22] Where the war dead commemoration democratized the deaths of all who died in battles, victimhood nationalism unsettled the hierarchy of death that distinguished civilian victims from the war dead. Through the lens of human rights, the war dead and civilian victims are equal in that their most basic human rights were violated. Slavoj Žižek's argument that the Holocaust cannot even be a tragedy becomes unconvincing when seen from the perspective of the democratization of death. Žižek's interpretation that, unlike tragic heroes who keep their dignity by death, the Holocaust victims had been denied even their dignity is based on the traditional plotline of tragedy that sublimates the protagonist's death.[23] The deaths of the Holocaust victims who were slaughtered "like lambs" at the Einsatzgruppen's gunpoint or in the gas chamber seem to be far from the heroic deaths in classical tragedies. Victimhood nationalism is one up on heroic nationalism in that it sublimates even the "inglorious" deaths. Centering victims' human rights rather than heroes' courage is a righteous political standpoint that is difficult to refute in global memory formation.

When the cultural memory of the dead shifts from martyrdom to human rights globally, the innocent victims get their ontological morality acknowledged in the newly created global memory space and the heightened sensitivity toward human rights. As the distance between a hero and a victim closed, survival itself began to be understood as an expression of spiritual strength and ontological resistance, especially under extreme circumstances such as the Holocaust.[24] Even at the time of the Holocaust, Rabbi Isaac Nissenbaum of the Warsaw ghetto had already characterized the act of survival as religious and transcendental. Resistance lacks its significance as living itself is already an act of resistance. Under those extreme circumstances, victims become the courageous heroes of everyday life, with their internal pride growing as big as the shame externally insisted on them. The tragedy focuses on everyday resistance and becomes ever more vulgar, while the melodrama with a victim as the protagonist gets popular. The audience has no reason to feel reluctant about identifying themselves with the victims who refused to become pawns in history and attempted everyday resistance as attractive historical actors. However, this comes at a price—the audience identifies with the present victors who were victims in the past at the expense of empathy with the current Others under oppression.[25]

With the advent of victimhood nationalism, which pushed the suffering of victims from the margin to the center of national memories, victims began to share the status that national heroes of the past had enjoyed. An innocent victim was now turned into a moral hero because of the very violence s/he had to suffer. The sublimation process in victimhood nationalism diverges significantly from that of heroic nationalism. The domain of secular religion that garners support for victimhood nationalism has been enlarged by erasing the distinction between martyrs and victims to democratize death further. In that sense, victimhood nationalism promoted the democratization, popularization, and nationalization of death. The reverse side of the democratization of death is that it contributed to the victimhood competition among nations over who suffered the most. The more extensive and gruesome a nation's suffering has been, the more deserving the nation is thought to be of a greater moral righteousness and ontological primacy.[26] There indeed is a certain truth in the claim that the new paradigm of memory that emphasizes the suffering of victims justifies liberal democracy and neoliberalism in transitive societies in southeastern Europe, South Africa, Latin America, and elsewhere.[27] On the other hand, the crux of my criticism is that victim-centered cultural memory provides a moral foundation for victimhood nationalism to ultimately reconstruct nationalism, which is adaptive to the globalization of memory in the twenty-first century.[28]

Since World War I, the crucified Christ has epitomized the metaphors for the war dead. On a postcard by a German soldier from the battlefront was a picture of Jesus Christ stroking a dead soldier. Through the fallen, the state was related to the suffering of Christ, and the soldiers in trenches were praised as the group that best realized His sacrifice. The metaphor of the war dead as martyrs provided immortal nationalist beliefs to overcome the fear of dying and accomplish patriotic vocation even as dead. Hung in the main hall of the Fogliano Redipuglia War Memorial is a painting titled *The Apotheosis of the Fallen*, in which a dead soldier is held in the arms of Jesus Christ.[29] This is an excellent example of how a modern nation-state places the fallen within the familiar composition of Christianity with martyrdom and resurrection. The experience of sacralizing the lives and death of soldiers through the symbolism and rituals of Christianity was what made the Christians' conversion to the religion called Fatherland more conducive.[30] The memory of World War I was an essential stepping stone to victimhood nationalism.

CIVIL RELIGION

Nationalism as a civil religion was not born out of thin air during World War I. Its origin can be traced back to Jean-Jacques Rousseau, who advised the Polish nation in peril to establish a civil religion.[31] Though Rousseau's advice might have arrived late for Poles, the Jacobin regime turned Rousseau's "general will" into a civil religion through various political customs, ceremonies, myths, and symbolism.[32] If fascism was "a new political model based on the idea of popular sovereignty that emerged in the 18th century," the cult of the fallen soldiers was made possible by the volunteer soldiers who were committed to "the noble cause" during the French Revolution. The cult of the fallen soldiers stemmed from the rituals to commemorate members of the bourgeoisie who died in war. Unlike mercenaries of the Middle Ages consisting of alien professionals, criminals, vagrants, and paupers, the volunteer soldiers were somebody's sons, brothers, neighbors, and, therefore, valid members of the local society and the state. The bourgeois soldiers mythologized and circulated their experience of war, and the deaths of a husband, friend, and son were glorified as sacrifices for the state and the national cause. The redesign plan for the central cemetery in Paris in 1792 proposed that the ashes of soldiers be mixed with those of France's great men inside a pyramid.[33] However grotesque the idea of a pyramid for the ashes of fallen soldiers may sound, the democratization of death implies a posthumous national integration. The Jacobin revolutionaries also turned the Panthéon into the monumental temple of the national heroes martyred for the homeland. The royal church of the Bourbon dynasty turned into the national temple of war heroes. The Panthéon was the birthplace of civil religion that appropriated traditional religion.

The cult of the fallen soldiers provided martyrs for the secular religion adoring the nation-state, and the last haven for the dead became the temple for national reverence. Details regarding the construction and maintenance of the cemetery, such as burial and memorial, and which symbolism was to be projected on the monument became more elaborated and systematized through World War I. Passed through the circuit board of the memory culture about World War I built around the cult of the war dead, the Christian tradition of martyrdom was transformed into a patriotic tradition of dying for one's country. The cult of the fallen soldiers began to reflect the shape of the political religion of modern nation-states as the Catholic principle *pro domino mori* (dying for God) was converted to *pro patria mori* (dying for the country).[34] When religious martyrdom transposes to patriotic martyrdom, "national heroes" replace "martyred saints," and privates who risked their lives to remain loyal to their country are honored as highly as generals, the domination of patriotic martyrs commences, and the political religion that worships the nation ascends. *A Tribute to the Army and Navy*, the funeral oration for the German soldiers, written in 1920, said that the war dead will return "to rejuvenate the *Volk*" and that "from out of their death the *Volk* will be restored."[35] As Benedict Anderson aptly stated, "No more arresting emblems of the modern culture of nationalism exist than cenotaphs and tombs of Unknown Soldiers."[36]

Anxious about life's contingent and finite nature, people tend to wish for a particular connection to the immortal, absolute being. It gave rise to nationalism, which advanced as a secular religion to replace traditional religion. Perpetuated by individual death, the myth of nation emerged as a secular religion. It satisfied the human desire for transcendence as traditional beliefs declined in the process of disenchantment in the modern era.[37] Disenchantment of conventional religions also meant re-enchantment of the political religion. Modern progressive ideologies such as Marxism and liberalism tend not to take a great interest in topics like death or immortality and answer rather unclearly to fatalistic questions regarding contingency and the perpetuity of life. In contrast, nationalism asserts that it connects the already dead and yet-to-be-born through the fantasy of the continuous life of the nation. The religious imagination of nationalism is more profound and potent than any other secular ideology. The national narrative of a collective life that perpetuates from the immemorial past to the infinite future filled the mythical vacuum left by the disenchantment by converting each individual's finite life into the immortal life of the nation.[38]

The advent of victimhood nationalism is also related to religious imagination. Believing that a nation is "a community of fate perpetuated since the immemorial past," nationalism reaffirms such a belief through the rituals to commemorate the war dead. For a nation as a ritual community, the cult of the fallen soldiers has secured its position as the transnational principle of all nation-states across borders, from the empire to colonies, from dictatorship to democracy, and from socialism to capitalism. The more people die for their fatherland and the bigger the national tragedy is, the stronger the bond is among the members of the ritual community. "National history"—as well as "national literature"—is the memorial the state addresses as a ritual community. A national historian is Oedipus, à la Jules Michelet, who teaches the dead the meaning of their death, of which they were unaware. With the teachings of historians, whether the dead understood the meaning of their sacrifice matters no longer.[39] Because the already dead cannot protest, they are sacrificed once again for the national memory. Through the words of national history, the dead resurrect as heroic spirits and position themselves as martyrs who perpetuate the nation's life. The cult of the fallen soldiers is the source of the mythical power of nationalism, and it aims for the "politics of salvation" through death.[40]

The moment the dead are called heroic spirits and their sacrifice is celebrated, death permeates the perpetual life of the nation and earns immortal status. The plotline where the dead return home to see if their death was to any effect was not rare in art genres like movies and novels after World War I. Reality often shows that death is futile. As Abel Gance's film *J'accuse* shows, the returned ghost faced his hometown's lazy, worn-out everyday life. The neighbor who stole his business and his wife who deceived him were unfaltering proof that his sublime sacrifice was in vain.[41] Though the families' requests to bury the dead in their hometowns were often impeded by bureaucracy, finding and returning the bodies of the war dead to their families was a lucrative governmental project. Sometimes, the state and the Catholic Church clashed over issues regarding who was the social subject to mourn the dead and in which manner the funerals should be held.[42] What is essential in religious mourning is not the perspective of the dead but that of the living. The subject of mourning is not the dead but the living. The sublimation of the dead into the holy sacrifice, who ultimately becomes a savior, is not to soothe the soul of the deceased. It is the living who sing the requiem. Through the act of mourning, the living identify themselves with those sacrificed and cleanse themselves of survivor's guilt. The dead are called on to serve the living mourners, while the living strive to be rid of their guilty conscience by mourning the dead.[43] It is not that the living mourn the dead but that the dead console the living.

By conferring sanctity on the dead through mourning, survivors seek to wash away their sins committed in war. When combined with the religious spirit of Christianity, the cult of the fallen soldiers efficiently surpasses mourning and reaches the level of sublimation. Especially as the hegemony of "moral capital" becomes solidified in the modern disenchantment process, which, having lost the vision of secular progress, regresses to the religious enchantment of the past, the official memory pursued by the state relies increasingly on religious symbolism.[44] Good examples would be the cult of the fallen soldiers and the political religion first developed in Italy and Germany during the interwar period. "Victimhood," in particular, tended to make the interpenetration and paradoxical combination of the sacred and secular more conducive through its conceptual flexibility. Ultimately, the collective memory of war determines the moral layer of historical policies created and propagated by the state. The protagonist of the official memory composed by the state was not the dread of war but its glory, not the victim but the hero. After World War I, the war memory composed of sacred experiences provided the nation with unprecedented religiosity and projected the traditional belief in martyrdom and resurrection on the all-encompassing civil religion that was the state. It is no surprise to see the Pietà as a motif in remembering the war dead. The serene image of "our" soldier enjoying the beauty of nature around the battlefield was in sharp contrast with the demonized stereotype of the enemy soldiers casually perpetrating sodomy, pillage, and murder.

With the cult of the fallen soldiers, political religion that sacralizes the nation and state was a unique politico-cultural phenomenon that dominated the era of fascism in the 1930s. Fascist Italy formed a model for secular religion through various nationalist rituals implemented in schools, military, governmental organizations, political parties, national funerals and commemorations, and even sports and community clubs. Nazi Germany and Bolshevik Russia were also eager to create "the people" who would willingly sacrifice themselves for the state. Still, nationalism as a political religion, which cleansed the society with the bloodshed in war and restored the nation through struggle and sacrifice, thrived in Italy.[45] Having inherited the tradition of Risorgimento with the slogan of *religione della patria* (religion of the fatherland), fascism was virtually the declaration of sacralized politics.[46] Italian fascism was essentially a pseudo-religion in that it was not satisfied with seizing power and attempted to control the inner workings of individuals by converting all Italians to fascism.[47] The fascists saw themselves as the Italian crusaders and the prophets of patriotic civil religion, punishing socialism for blasphemy against the nation.[48]

YASUKUNI SHRINE WITHIN US

The cult of fallen soldiers and political religion were not restricted to Europe. Yasukuni Shrine shares the code of civil religion in cultivating the cult of war dead. Japan's State Shinto, which reveres those who threw themselves for the state as the gods in Yasukuni, has proven itself to be an epitome of the cult of the fallen soldiers, not any less in its intensity than that of European Christianity.[49] Thanks to the religious characteristics of State Shinto, Japan's political religion can be more thorough and practical in sacralizing secular/political realities like the state and nation.[50] Deifying fallen soldiers as "the war gods of national defense" in Japan was also a privilege unimaginable in monotheistic cultures that proscribe any challenge to the singularity of God. The sacralization of politics, which made the secular realities the object of religious worship, was the core of political religion that has often been in competition with the traditional religion for loyalty in Europe—the French republican-secularist principle of *laïcité* conflicts with the tradition of Catholicism, for example. However, the Japanese Shinto deifies the state and the war dead and, therefore, does not pose a threat to the political religion. Unlike Christianity, which demands exclusive worship of the one and only God, the tradition of Shinto is not against the state becoming the object of worship.

Even for the fascists in Italy, where Europe's political religion originated, Japan was the ideal model of political religion. According to Enrico Corradini, one of the most well-known theorists of fascism, Japan could win the Russo-Japanese War because of Shinto, which unified the Japanese by sacralizing the fatherland and elaborating on the absolute worship rituals. Corradini was very impressed that the god of Japan was none other than Japan.[51] To borrow the words of Kawakami Hajime, "All Japanese . . . consider the state as the god, an absolute being, that they think sacrificing their lives by order of the state is what's expected of them. Then those who died for the state get worshipped in Yasukuni."[52] Compared to Europe's nation-states that had to compete with Christianity for the people's loyalty, Japan, with the tradition of State Shinto, preempted a more advantageous position in developing a political religion. In the case of Shinto, where the state was sacralized to replace the god, the secular state did not need to compete with the god.⁵³ Especially in 1937–1938, after the outbreak of the Sino-Japanese War, terminologies like "the spirit of national defense" and "the war gods of national defense" began to appear in commemorative rituals, advancing the war dead to the rank of gods. Thus, the political religion of Japan was more suitable for the cult of war dead than the monotheistic traditions of Christianity and Islam, which prohibited deifying the war dead. In East Asian societies, with the tradition of worshipping their ancestors, the war dead after the national rites could be sublimated into "the ancestral gods of the nation and the state."⁵⁴

The political religion of Japan was developed as the modern state system was reorganized after the Meiji Restoration. June 4, 1879, when a shrine called Shokonsha (招魂寺, temple to evoke spirits) was renamed Yasukuni Shrine, was a special day in the history of modern political religion. After the visit of the Meiji emperor on January 27, 1874, and 192 soldiers who died fighting samurais who were against the modern reformation of the country were buried in February of the same year, the shrine gradually became the first site of Meiji Japan's necropolitics. The military that strongly demanded state-hosted rituals for the war dead also had a significant impact.⁵⁵ In the official ceremonies at Yasukuni, the war dead from the Russo-Japanese War were called "heroic spirits" (英靈) to remember their devotion to the state, and the act of remembering them was called "illuminating" (顯彰), rather than "mourning" (追悼) or "consoling the spirits" (慰靈), as the intention was to discover and praise achievements of the fallen. Yasukuni Circus, the "spectacle" and a popular amusement park during the Edo period was transformed into Yasukuni Shrine, the "sanctum" that remembers and worships the war dead through the wars with China and Russia. When the war ended, the war dead, who were renamed "honorable spirits," became the gods of Yasukuni Shrine.⁵⁶

If Yasukuni were the temple of political religion, its secular priests would be national historians. The father of the Rankean school, a positivist approach to Japanese history, Kuroita Katsumi actively participated in making Yasukuni Shrine the political religion site after visiting Europe on a research trip. Impressed by Europe's national monuments and patriotic celebrations, Kuroita suggested building a holy space for national festivities in a shape resembling the ancient Greek stadium of Olympia near Yasukuni Shrine.[57] Ironically, regarding his reputation as the founder of Japanese historical positivism, Kuroita was not concerned himself with the factuality of a nationalist myth as long as it enriched the people's love and commitment to the nation and state; the "scientific, empirical historian" was willing to turn a myth into history. As long as the national myth of Wilhelm Tell promoted the people's love and commitment to the nation and state in Switzerland, it could be enlisted as a part of national history.[58] When people start to believe a myth is factual, the myth is already a reality. History is where an imagined or perceived reality has more power than reality. Behind its backdrop is the political religion. The war dead were not the object of mourning and grief but the source of pride and joy in the necropolitics unfolded in the "sanctum" Yasukuni Shrine. Calling forth the dead required a rite that was much more meticulous than what was needed to mobilize the living.

The funeral rites standardized by the Japanese military during the Asia-Pacific War exemplify the extent to which details were configured. An aspect of it can be read in the detailed documentation of the funeral of Kurokawa Umekichi, a soldier who died on the battlefield of Manchukuo in 1934. Collected immediately after his death, Kurokawa's body was first moved to the nearest Japanese Buddhist temple and cremated through the official regimental rite to be partially buried in the local cemetery. The rest of his ashes were put in a wooden urn shrouded in a white cloth and sent to his home in Japan. The urn boarded a ship in Dalian and arrived at the port of Kobe. From Kobe, it was taken on a train to make about ten stops and go through solemn rites on different scales, each organized by the Veterans' Association, the Association of Women for National Salvation, the Patriotic Women's Association, and others until it finally reached Kanagawa prefecture, Kurokawa's hometown.[59] As soon as the train stopped at the Kamakura station, Kurokawa's parents and the mayor of Kamakura picked up the urn for a grand Buddhist funeral hosted by the city in place of the summer festival. The funeral lasted at least three days; the guests paid weekly visits. The local paper that reported his death published an article titled, "Father Tomizo, Tears Full of Emotions: I dedicated my son's death to His Majesty." The cult of the fallen soldiers, as these anecdotes attest, was an apparatus that attributed the highest glory to the war dead and families to make an older man at the memorial service feel the death of his only son was worth it, and dying on the battlefield the happiest task one could undertake.[60]

The most dramatic example of the cult of the war dead can be seen in the memorial service for soldiers sacrificed for the Kamikaze attacks. As one commanding officer of the Special Attack Units said, "The purpose of the special attack is not accomplishment but death." Those sacrificed in the mission of suicide attack prompted an image of the purest form of death, untainted and full of love for their country.[61] Taking a step further from the concept of "noble death" that enabled "the noble foundation of peace and democratic development of postwar Japan," the Kamikaze Special Attack Unit provided an appropriate element for projecting the beauty of death. The "pure" death of Kamikaze agents, most of whom were too young to have married, had children, or left any trace of their physical selves, was a fitting element to become sublimated into a national narrative of mourning stemmed from "the spiritual combination of the dead and yet-to-be-born." The collective sorrow for the premature deaths of the young Kamikaze volunteers implanted the affective memory of victimhood nationalism in the cult of the fallen soldiers. The militarization of aesthetics was a part of victimhood nationalism in Japanese war memory.[62]

The rituals of the cult of the fallen soldiers and the political religion of Imperial Japan persisted in postcolonial Korea. In the Seoul National Cemetery, a bridge named *Jungkook* (靖国) was pronounced *Yasukuni* in Japanese. The term *jungkook* can be traced back to *Zuozhuan*, where the term was used to mean "steadying the country." Yasukunis in postcolonial East Asia evidence the afterlives of the Japanese imperial formation. As can be seen from the oft-used titles for national rituals, such as "the heroic spirits," "the war gods of national defense," and "the guardian angels of the homeland," the tendency to glorify the war dead strengthened in postcolonial Korea. The war dead, who "protect the achievement of the nation's wish by becoming the righteous spirit for national defense," obtained "eternal life" through "sacred death" and "noble sacrifice."[63] In 1956 the South Korean government designated Memorial Day as a national holiday to promote and standardize the rituals for the war dead. Continual efforts were made to establish a mnemonic community through commemorating rituals in the nationally synchronized time and space, such as simultaneous silent tributes to the war dead, national flags at half-staff, the building of memorial towers and arches, singing of memorial songs, memorial flights, and medal conferment ceremonies.

Just as the rituals at Yasukuni Shrine did, the commemoration of the fallen soldiers held at the Seoul National Cemetery included special attention to and accommodation for the families of the dead. The representatives of the bereaved families addressed the visitors as a part of the official ceremony and sat near the president and other dignitaries. The family members were also given complimentary transportation and lodging, an exclusive information booth, various programs to ease the consolation process, and a round-table meeting with high-ranking government officials. Instead of the condolence money issued by the emperor during the Japanese colonial rule, the families received the nationwide collected "voluntary" donations and a separate present from the Korean government. Buddhist and Christian aesthetics replaced that of State Shinto in the commemorative rituals of newly independent South Korea. However, they could essentially be traced back to the politico-religious rituals of Imperial Japan.[64] What was most notably different between the rituals of postindependence Korea and those of the colonial era was the subject of remembrance.

While the war dead commemorations in colonial Joseon were designated for Korean soldiers and army civilians who died in the Asia-Pacific War, the rituals of the Republic of Korea did not pay attention to the colonial Korean soldiers who died in the wars of Imperial Japan. They were "the abandoned soldiers," and their deaths were "the forgotten deaths."[65] Although the memorial service for the Korean War dead of the Asia-Pacific War was held at Gyunggi Middle School on January 18,

1946, it was an unofficial ceremony organized by a private organization. A memorial ceremony for the victims of forced labor who died on their return home was also neglected by the public. The Pacific Comrades Association, a group that was formed by the survivors of colonial conscription and forced labor, and the Joseon National Maritime Youth Corps, organized by navy veterans of the Japanese empire, co-organized a communal memorial ceremony for all Korean soldiers, army civilians, forced laborers, and "Comfort Women." Still, they faced practical difficulties amid indifference and neglect from the government and society. The subjects of this ceremony were called "the unreturned," "vengeful lonely spirits," "ghosts of the Pacific," and "compatriots who were forced to perish for our enemy Japan" rather than treated as the objects of worship and reverence.[66]

It was in the twenty-first century, as victimhood nationalism dominated the cultural memory of South Korea, that the war dead in the service of the Japanese imperial army were viewed no longer as colonial collaborators but as sublime sacrifices. "Forced mobilization" was now divided into the subcategories of forced labor, military conscription, and mobilization of women labor. Therefore, the victims could all be recategorized as the victims of forced mobilization. The government-sponsored Foundation for the Victims of Forced Mobilization Under the Japanese Occupation has launched different projects of "demanding returns of the remains of the unreturned war dead," the "commemorative tour and consolation ceremony at the sites of the Asia-Pacific War," and the "welfare support for the victims and their bereaved families." That implies that colonial Korean soldiers in the Japanese Imperial Army have become reintroduced as victims of colonial violence in South Korea's official memory.[67] In the mnemoscape of Korean society, such historical rehabilitation of victims was possible mainly because of two factors: the globalization of memory and the democratization of politics. As the Holocaust emerged as the civil religion of Europe, victims' moral and ontological righteousness was highlighted across borders. The democratization of politics enabled the remembering of the marginalized, peripheralized, and silenced victims by raising awareness of human rights. It is also true that the restoration of the victim status was a part of the political instrumentalization of the memory, which ultimately manifested itself in victimhood nationalism.

In the early period of the Republic of Korea, the "heroic anticommunist spirits" replaced the war dead of the Asia-Pacific War as the object of worship and reverence. From the victims of the Sinuiju Student Protest against the Red Army, the police officers, military personnel, railroad workers, and volunteer firefighters sacrificed by the leftist rebels to fighters of anticommunist organizations were all made the center of the commemorative rituals. The promotion of "the anticommunist war dead" peaked with the funeral of "the ten suicide warriors" who died in the skirmish of Kaesŏng in 1949. Unlike "the three suicide bombers" of the Japanese empire, who were supposedly "a suicide squad that followed the order of the state," the ten suicide warriors of South Korea were mythologized as "voluntary sacrifices." The ceremonial rituals for the anticommunist war dead, who were "the war gods of the homeland" and "the immortal flame of justice," continually advanced through rituals like "the joint memorial ceremony for our fallen soldiers" during the Korean War. Exalted as much as independence fighters and martyrs, the soldiers were now labeled "patriots" and "patriotic martyrs." Ironically, the actual patriotic martyrs—those who were killed in armed struggles against the colonizers—were gradually being forgotten by the state and the society.[68]

The democratization of death—in other words, the ideals of the political religion that painted ordinary citizens with the image of a martyr—was often let down in the face of reality. A news anchor at NHK who covered live the memorial ceremony at Yasukuni Shrine vividly remembers the moment when he struggled to keep the voices of the families screaming "murderers" and "give me my child back" off the air—even the notorious military police could not drive out the furious and heartrending complaints of the families who lost their husbands and children.[69] The soldiers were hardly in a better state: the naval aviators drafted for the Kamikaze strikes testified that they were "not gods but humans, so how is receiving a command to come back dead supposed to help with the morale?," claiming that the Kamikaze order boosted the morale of the naval aviation units was a blatant lie.[70] It would be an overestimation of the impact of ideology to interpret the parents of a deserter passively watching in shame their son's corpse trodden on by the Japanese military police as "imbued in the totalitarian ethics of the Emperor system that infiltrated deep into families." The logic of forced mobilization in imperial Japan—either the narrow definition of nationalism as worshiping "the state and the emperor" or the universalism that promulgated "the liberation of Asia"— did not convince many Japanese, aside from the nationalist intellectuals pushing for the theory of overcoming modernity.

DESERTERS AND COUNTERMEMORY

On the opposite side of a brave soldier who gets praised posthumously as the "war god" stands a deserter. The sheer number of Nazi deserters— approximately fifty thousand—is indeed astonishing; more shocking is the number of German deserters who were executed, totaling about thirty-three thousand.[71] Günter Grass's memoir, about the corpses of deserters, hung on street posts as examples of the consequence of military trials toward the end of World War II, provides an ample illustration of how severely the state power oppressed those who denied the civil religion. The image of the deserters' dead bodies reminds one of medieval heretics burned at the stake. Comprising seasoned soldiers with three years of combat experience and the Iron Cross second class, the Feldjägerkorps, also known as the "front-line hunting squad," was in charge of returning or executing Nazi deserters. Under the Führer's command, they seized not only deserters but also men aged fifteen to seventy who ran away to avoid conscription. Near the end of the war, the deserter hysteria was at such a peak that in Berlin, a minuscule suspicion could lead to a summary execution. When the Allies advanced on the city, Berlin's trees, street posts, and barricades were dotted with the executed bodies. A thousand were executed over the final three months of the war in Berlin only. It was only in 2002 that the German parliament officially overturned the guilty verdict on Nazi deserters.

Compared to that in the Soviet Union, the number of deserters in Nazi Germany looks like a drop in the bucket. A whopping 158,000

Soviet soldiers were sentenced to death for desertion, treason, and cowardice during the war. Stalin's Order No. 227 organized the "penal battalions" consisting of convicts, including deserters, to be sent to the front during advance and the rear during withdrawal. In the armored units, they were assigned to T-34 tanks with a meager survival rate when hit by enemy shells, and in the air force as machine gunners of bombers easily targeted by enemy fighters. The high death rate of the penal battalions—which amounts to 34 percent—indicates the fate of Soviet deserters. Among 500,000 soldiers who served in the penal battalions, about 170,000 deserters were expended as cannon fodders. The agents being trained for suicide missions in today's Palestine, albeit with much stronger ideological loyalty than that of an average draftee during World War II, also show a remarkable disparity between the ideology and reality when seen up close: according to studies that interviewed these martyrs-in-training, many of them were preoccupied with skepticism about the suicide attack rather than a passion for martyrdom; some even gave up on the mission due to extreme fear and aversion.[72]

The projects to convert an individual to the civil religion, which demands dedication to the fatherland, such as *Homo Sovieticus*, *Homo Fascistus*, or the "war god" of Yasukuni, exhibited apparent characteristics of mythology. By erasing the tragedy of deserters from social memory, the postwar German, Soviet, and Japanese societies could maintain the myth of civil martyrs who saved the nation from their enemies. The deserters, who "betrayed their comrades and fatherlands," remained forgotten for long. The Austrian deserter Richard Wadani's recollection of the white handkerchief his mother gave him the day before his enlistment denotes that the parent would rather have her son return alive, even if that meant he surrendered to the enemy, than be made proud of his death for the country.[73] Making one "feel that the happiest thing one could do was to die on the battlefield" by crediting the highest glory to the deceased and their families was merely a wet dream of those in power. Though the political religion that worships the fatherland rose on the basis of the absurd death, its limitations were also due to the fear of death. The nationalization of death, in which all people voluntarily martyrize themselves, was not the reality but the doctrine of political religion. The political religion worshipping the nation would lose its power as the new ideal of patriotism, which had shifted from reckless death to survival and resistance to war, spread among lower-ranking soldiers.

The most notable example of antihegemonic memory culture against the cult of war dead would be the monuments to deserters. The memorial to Wehrmacht deserters in Vienna, inaugurated on October 24, 2014, is one of them—with its surface engraved with "All Alone," an equivocal two-word poem by the Scottish poet Ian Hamilton Finlay, this X-shaped monument to deserters was built in Ballhausplatz.[74] The X shape on top of the three foundations connotes the determination to put forgotten deserters at the crux of memory culture.[75] Also suggestive is that Ballhausplatz is located just a hop away from Heldenplatz, where about 250,000 Viennese passionately welcomed Adolph Hitler declaring the annexation of Austria in 1938. Especially because Heldenplatz is home to the monuments to unknown soldiers, the war dead of the Habsburg Empire, and victims of the Nazis, the deserter monument in Ballhausplatz feels like a silent protest. It carries a critical message against the cultural memory of Austria, which remembers the country as "the first victim of Hitler" despite its passionate support for the Nazis. What is interesting is that the Austrian soldiers in the German Armed forces were often considered by their fellow Austrians as loyally fulfilling responsibility, as the inscription on the memorial reads "*Opfer in Erfüllung der Pflicht*" (sacrifice in fulfillment of duty), or even as heroic. On the other hand, the Nazi deserters were deemed as the "betrayers of comrades." In an interview with BBC, some Austrian Veterans' Association members openly complained about confusing the "comrade-betraying" deserters with "the resistance fighters."

The story of a deserter in the correspondence between Günter Grass and Oe Kenzaburo, coordinated by the *Asahi Shimbun* to commemorate the fiftieth anniversary of the end of World War II in 1995, is also telling. In his letter, Grass remembered corpses of German deserters hanging on the street poles after the summary execution on the Western Front. Unable to wash off such a gruesome memory, he writes that "they were not cowards but the true heroes of World War II who refused to commit war crimes." Oe Kenzaburo's account of Japanese deserters is even more appalling: his was a story of a couple who just stood watching their son's body, executed for desertion, being trodden under the boots of the Japanese military police. He explains that the parents were ashamed of their deserter son "because the totalitarian ethics represented by the monarchy had deeply infiltrated into families."[76] On the other hand, there is an image of a mother shedding tears of joy in front of her son's "heroic spirit" enshrined in Yasukuni Shrine. The shame incurred by looking at the deserter-son's dead body and the pride felt at the enshrined spirit of the son killed in war are head and tail of the same coin. When the shame or pride overshadows the sorrow of losing a child, personal memories correspond to the official memory of the war dead.

The correspondence between Günter Grass and Oe Kenzaburo carries strong protest against the official memories of the war dead kept in the state's repository. Their correspondence questions the memory of patriots who bravely sacrificed themselves for the country and challenged the memory culture that inseminates the cult of fallen soldiers. From the perspective of antiwar memory, the deserter monument is more precious than war memorials like the Tombs of the Unknown Soldiers. Memorializing deserters is not a brand new idea—as early as in 1943, in World War II, one antifascist partisan in Venice, Italy, suggested destroying "the ridiculous monuments to those who died for the fatherland" and replacing them with monuments to deserters. He reasoned that even those who died on the battlefield must have loathed the war and envied deserters at the instance of death. According to him, "resistance is born out of desertion."[77] Before this partisan, there was Kurt Tucholsky, the German peace activist, journalist, and writer who criticized the cult of the fallen soldiers. Enraged by the sight of World War I monuments in construction, he suggested a memorial to deserters. He composed the deserter's epitaph in 1925: "Here lived a man who refused to kill his fellow men. Honor his memory!"[78] The commemoration of "unknown deserters" instead of "unknown soldiers" contributes to a countermemory against victimhood nationalism.

Tucholsky's suggestion of a deserter monument was not realized for long. The demand for justice for deserters was driven out by the agony of German POWs who returned from the Soviet prison camps, and deserters were completely marginalized in Germany's postwar memory culture. The autobiographical fiction about the experience of desertion during World War II by Heinrich Böll and Alfred Andersch suffered hostile reviews and vehement criticisms. German deserters were not able to receive the just acknowledgment that their desertion was to resist Hitler. They were also excluded from the reparations law, as it was complicated for them to be verified as victims of Nazi military courts. While members of Waffen-SS and their families were compensated for wartime injuries and losses, deserters were ineligible for such compensation unless they could prove that their desertion was politically motivated. The memories of deserters were revisited when the issues regarding restitution for the Sinti and Roma peoples, homosexuals, forced laborers, and victims of sterilization and euthanasia programs were raised.[79] Starting from the "Unknown Deserter" sculpture installed in Karlsruhe in 1983, more than twenty-five monuments were built all over Germany to commemorate the deserters, including in Bremen (1986), Kassel (1987), Ulm (1989), Erfurt (1995), Potsdam (1999), and Stuttgart (2007). Following Germany's example, the UK also became home to a deserter monument in 2001 to remember the 306 deserters of the UK and Commonwealth who were executed for desertion and cowardice during World War I, thanks to the continuous effort of Shot at Dawn, a group of memory activists, for the amnesty of deserters over many years.[80]

The politico-religious psyche of the cult of the fallen soldiers did not budge an inch in postcolonial countries where nation-building was the primary goal. It is not surprising that both postcolonial Korea in North and South deliberately appropriated the Japanese imperial legacy of political religion. The Pledge of Allegiance to the Korean flag, frequently recited in South Korea even today, is a flat imitation of the Oath of the Japanese Imperial Subjects that used to be recited every Monday morning in schools and even at weddings. Only the oath subject has changed from "imperial subjects" to "Korean citizens," and their object of allegiance from the Japanese emperor to the Republic of Korea; most formalities remained unchanged. The cult of Kim Il-sung, the national leader revered as the "sun of the nation" and the immortal spirit, and the North Korean aspiration for the family state can also be understood in the continuity of the Japanese emperor worship.[81] If I may risk oversimplification, the political religion of imperial Japan, which flourished under the total war system, is still the code that dominates postcolonial East Asia. George Mosse's conclusion that political religion had not disappeared after the fall of fascism and Nazism is alive and well in the present.[82]

Mosse's insight penetrates into today's East Asia, too. Political religion is still a living text in the region. The fantasy of martyrdom is even more deeply rooted among those who have never experienced the war than those who did. The resistance to martyrdom is stronger among soldiers, who witnessed death and feared it to the core. In a way, surviving the war was an act of resistance. Instead of expecting from victims boiling passion for martyrdom, the global memory formation now allows survivors who overcame the deplorable life a transcendental meaning. When the complex interiority of a victim is restructured, what used to be viewed as humiliating survival through subordination to the oppressor becomes an everyday resistance to preserve the dignity of one's life.[83] As Tzvetan Todorov poignantly points out, a wise decision is required at every moment to survive extreme circumstances like war or concentration camps. Enduring the abject state of everyday life is, if not a heroic death or magnificent martyrdom, itself resistance and sacrifice.[84] Perhaps those who strongly argued for heroic death and against cowardly survival did not dare to face the difficulty of living. Such an aspect further complicates victimhood nationalism as the new nationalist discourse to replace heroic nationalism—victimhood nationalism can exist in vastly different forms depending on how the difficult task of sublimating those unjustly sacrificed and unhonored survivors into the abstract subjects of worship and transcendence is undertaken. This unfolds the global history of victims, which at times is paired with hero nationalism and other times opposes it, in which the historical places of perpetrators and victims and winners and losers are reversed, where perpetrators disappear. Everyone claims to be the actual victim.

4

GLOBALIZATION

2000, YEAR ZERO

If 1945 was the "year zero" to Ian Buruma in that it was the year of birth of the global modern world,[1] 2000 was the year zero of global memory to me because it was the year of the rise of global memory formation. In 2000, self-reflective memories resonated loudly across borders to rattle the global memory space. The emergence of a global memory culture, which criticized the territorialized memory of one nation and empathized with the suffering of other nations, including "enemy" countries, signaled the deterritorialization of memory. Even before the buzz of excitement about the first year of the third millennium went away, a summit conference titled the "Stockholm International Forum on the Holocaust" took place from January 26 to 28, 2000, in the capital city of Sweden. The grand scale of the summit meeting, which gathered political leaders of forty-six countries, including heads of twenty-three states and fourteen deputy heads, was unprecedented. What grabbed people's attention was the topic, "Holocaust Education, Remembrance, and Research." Holocaust memories and education had been raised before in smaller-scale, more intimate summits, but a focused discussion and a joint declaration by heads and representatives of forty-six countries had a different level of significance. The conference left a message that the globalization of memory is a new consideration in international politics. Released on January 28 at the end of the meeting, the "Declaration of the Stockholm International Forum on the Holocaust" indicates that the Holocaust holds "universal meaning" and "must be forever seared in our collective memory." The first four articles included these statements:

1. The Holocaust (Shoah) fundamentally challenged the foundations of civilization. The unprecedented character of the Holocaust will always hold universal meaning.
2. The magnitude of the Holocaust, planned and carried out by the Nazis, must be forever seared in our collective memory.
3. With humanity still scarred by genocide, ethnic cleansing, racism, antisemitism, and xenophobia, the international community shares a solemn responsibility to fight those evils. Together, we must uphold the terrible truth of the Holocaust against those who deny it.
4. We pledge to strengthen our efforts to promote education, remembrance, and research about the Holocaust.[2]

Articles 5 to 8 reemphasize the importance of memory that carries empathy with the victims, the commitment to promote education and research on the Holocaust in the public sphere, and the encouragement of appropriate forms of remembrance and commemoration for the victims. As article 8 states, remembering the victims while empathizing with and respecting the survivors was also a process to reaffirm "humanity's common aspiration for mutual understanding and justice."[3] If the Declaration of the Rights of Man and of the Citizen granted the French Revolution universal historical significance, the Stockholm Declaration set the remembrance of the Holocaust as "the transnational civic virtue."[4]

The Stockholm Declaration evidenced that global memory formation had become an unavoidable reality. Memory diplomacy has become crucial in international relations. Even before the year zero, Holocaust memory and education had been included in the negotiation of memory diplomacy. The first instance of such negotiation was at a conference in December 1997 regarding a "pile of gold" stored in vaults at the

Bank of England. The gold was looted by the Nazis from the occupied regions, presumably from Jews on the run who carried monetary gold. After the defeat of the Nazis, the gold ended up in the Bank of England vaults for unfathomable reasons instead of being returned to its rightful owners. Granted, it must have been almost impossible to find the owners as most of them were murdered during the Holocaust. As the looted gold garnered the attention of international media, discussions followed regarding what to do with the "ownerless" gold, valued at about £46,000,000 at the time. Thus, a Conference on Nazi Gold was held in London in December 1997 with representatives from Europe, Israel, and the United States to address the disposition of this pile of looted gold. The conference decided to monetize the remaining gold as soon as possible to secure funds for various projects commemorating the Holocaust.[5]

In 1998, just a year after the Conference on Nazi Gold, an international conference on postwar restitution was held in Washington, D.C., hosted by the U.S. Department of State and the Holocaust Memorial Museum. This large-scale conference convened representatives from more than forty states and interested parties, one being the World Jewish Congress. During the conference, the representatives of Germany, Israel, Sweden, the United Kingdom, and the United States formed the "task force for international cooperation on holocaust education, remembrance, and research," which implored "parents, teachers, activists, political and spiritual leaders" of all participating states to strive for education on, remembrance of, and research on the Holocaust, along with issuing a statement that highlights the opening of all archives and democratic access to documents on the Holocaust.[6] The first draft of the Stockholm Declaration (2000) reaffirms "the opening of archives in order to ensure that all documents bearing on the Holocaust are available to researchers," targeting the East European archives with documents regarding the Holocaust and World War II that remained shut due to the communist-era bureaucratic secrecy. For the former communist countries in Eastern Europe that needed financial support and collective security from the West, agreeing to the Stockholm Declaration was a prerequisite for joining NATO.[7]

The historical significance of the Stockholm Declaration lies in the endorsement of universal human rights as the modus operandi of global memory politics. The topic of memory, education, and research on the Holocaust for a meeting where the heads of forty-six states gathered at the threshold of the third millennium envisioned the twenty-first century's memory politics, which accelerated the globalization of memory. Remembering the Holocaust has now become the civil religion of global memory formation beyond the Israeli state and the diasporic Jewish community.[8] I have reservations, however, about the argument that the memory of the Holocaust now functions as the foundation of modern Europe, symbolically replacing the French Revolution, the point of continuous return for Western civilization to reconfirm its humanistic values.[9] Considering that the Holocaust was a child of Western modernity, which pioneered genocidal crime in colonies, it is a Eurocentric oxymoron to remember the Holocaust to reconfirm the humanistic values of Western civilization. Critical engagement with that mnemonic Eurocentrism was to evoke the memories of "forgotten victims," including the Roma and Sinti, homosexuals, Germans of African descent, Jehovah's Witnesses, people with disabilities, Soviet prisoners of war, and so on. Thus, the Holocaust has been expanded from the tragedy of Jewish people and the identity of Europe into the global memory space that reminds humanity of universal suffering. That explains why the postcolonial debates on the Holocaust are the crux of global memory formation now.

Not even four months had passed since the Stockholm Declaration when *Neighbors* was published on May 19, 2000, which perturbed the memory culture of Poland and Eastern Europe. Written by Jan Gross, the Polish sociologist-historian who lived in exile in the United States after being involved in the student protests of 1968, *Neighbors* caused a seismic shift in Polish memory culture. It revealed that the Jedwabne pogrom of July 10, 1941, was perpetrated not by the Nazis but by local Polish neighbors. The publication of *Neighbors* agitated and subverted the memory culture of Poland at the levels of epistemology, ontology, and ethics. By encountering history to expose the unpleasant truth that ordinary Poles were active perpetrators of the Holocaust, the national image of Poland as "the crucified nation" was irrevocably damaged. It shook the global memory formation beyond Poland. Long before this uproar, Leszek Kołakowski insisted in 1992 that *Historikerstreit* would be most necessary for Eastern Europe in coming to terms with the communist past. Kołakowski warned about how the cultural memory of Eastern Europe tended to avoid its own accountability for the Holocaust by hiding behind the victimhood memories.[10] His insight was indeed ahead of its time.

On August 2, 2000, the German Bundestag passed a law concerning reparations for foreign nationals who were drafted for forced labor under the Nazis. When the German Foundation Act, which ensured that the German state and economy were politically and morally accountable for the forced laborers exploited by the Nazi state, was passed, forced laborers from Poland, Ukraine, Russia, Belarus, Lithuania, Latvia, Estonia, Moldova, the Czech Republic, and other Eastern European countries, as well as Jewish and other prisoners of the camps and POWs from the Soviet Union, France, Serbia, and Italy, were able to receive reparations. The act that launched the Remembrance, Responsibility and Future Foundation to establish a compensation program took effect on August 12, 2000. By 2009, 13 million victims, including approximately 8,435,000 foreign workers and 4,585,000 POWs, who were previously excluded from Germany's reconciliation and reparation policies, had acquired mnemonic citizenship in Germany.[11] Despite complaints from various sources regarding the amount and eligibility, the Foundation Act holds significance in that it obliged large German corporations like Deutsche Bank, Allianz, Daimler-Benz, Bayer, BMW, and Volkswagen to admit their accountability for the forced labor, list themselves as partners, and capitalize the funds for the reparations program.

Compared to the previous stance of the government and the business world of Germany that the London Agreement on German External Debts of 1953 had settled all postwar reparations, the establishment of the Remembrance, Responsibility and Future Foundation was a sign of significant progress. The German government's shift in stance was due to the nullification of the article in the London Agreement that deferred the settlement of reparations until a peace treaty was signed. The Treaty on the Final Settlement concerning Germany (Zwei-plus-Vier-Vertrag), signed by East and West Germany, the United States, the United Kingdom, France, and the Soviet Union in 1990, was enough to be regarded as a peace treaty. On the opposite end of this were the class-action lawsuits filed by Jewish victims in U.S. courts against German companies that used slave labor in concentration camps and forced labor in their factories and fields during World War II.[12] Afraid of sanctions within the United States for involvement in crimes against humanity, the German companies might have become more serious about reparations issues. The hypothesis that companies that were more dependent on the U.S. market would have paid more than those who exploited more forced laborers during World War II seems plausible.[13] The change of collective memory about the forced laborers in Eastern Europe from national traitors and Nazi collaborators to innocent victims of the war also pressed the German government and corporations for apologies and reparations. Such a change could have become possible as the memory culture of Eastern Europe was released from the ideological strain of the Cold War.

The news about the reparations program for forced laborers in Germany left a considerable impact globally. Especially responsive and excited was the South Korean press, which estimated the total number of Korean forced laborers in the Japanese empire to be 7,827,355.[14] Headlines read: "The World Acclaims Germany's Nazi Reparation and Repentance," "German Corporate World Welcomes the Foundation for Nazi Labor Reparation," "Seven Countries to Sign an International Agreement on the Restitution to the Victims of Forced Labor Under the Nazi," and "Germany—Compensates 1.5 Million Nazi Laborers, up to 8 Million Won per Person." As can be seen in these headlines, the Korean press was more welcoming of the news than the press in Eastern Europe, who were quite unsatisfied with the reparations.[15] *Kyunghyang Shinmun*'s headline on June 12, 2007, "Reparations for Nazi Past Finalized—At Odds with Japan," demonstrates that the focus of the Korean press was on pushing the Japanese government and corporations to pay reparations to the Korean forced laborers under the colonial rule. Notably, *Kyunghyang Shinmun*'s report on the seven-year reparations process by the

Remembrance, Responsibility and Future Foundation that paid 5.84 billion to 1.67 million victims of forced labor under the Nazis quotes the *Jerusalem Post*, among many other international news outlets.[16]

In 2000 the Friedrich Ebert Foundation in Seoul published an interesting report on Germany's reparations for forced laborers by two Korean scholars of German history. With the ending remark of the lawsuit brought in California by Chinese forced laborers against Japanese corporations like Mitsui and Mitsubishi, the report shows what inspired the interest in Germany's reparations program among Koreans.[17] The news from Eastern Europe gave rise to the reconsideration of conscripted Korean soldiers, forced laborers, and "Comfort Women" as the victims of forced mobilization who had been suppressed in the memory culture of Korea. After independence in 1945, Korean society viewed the victims as those "who surrendered their precious lives for the enemy Japan." The developmental dictatorship regime had viewed the issue of reparations as settled by the Treaty on Basic Relations Between Japan and the Republic of Korea in 1965 and suppressed the dissenting voice of victims. Then, reparations for each individual became a pressing issue in the historical reconciliation between Korea and Japan. The development of global memory formation and the rise of victimhood nationalism prompted the reconstruction of the victims as those sacrificed by forced mobilization under the Japanese empire. The democratization of South Korea was also crucial in reviving the forced labor issue because the suppressed victims became vociferous in their opposition to forced silence.

COMFORT WOMEN AND SEXUAL VIOLENCE

The issue that marked the final page of 2000, year zero of global memory formation, was the Women's International War Crimes Tribunal on Japan's Military Sexual Slavery (WIWCT) held in Tokyo on December 8–12. Modeled after the Russell Tribunal in the anti–Vietnam War movement of the 1960s, the WIWCT was not legally binding but still left a huge political impact on the global memory culture. Memory activists from all over the world gathered to file a lawsuit against the ten leading Japanese political and military figures, including the Japanese emperor Hirohito, for crimes against humanity. The judges selected the testimonies and recorded interviews of the thirty-five surviving "Comfort Women" as credible evidence. The court established that the government of the Japanese empire and its military institutionalized the sexual slavery system, based on the words of survivors whose deep scars and obvious suffering further attested to the validity and integrity of the testimonies, which were supported by circumstantial evidence contained in the admissions from former soldiers and officers, admissions by the state of Japan, testimony from experts, reports from the UN Special Rapporteur on Sexual Slavery, and background evidence contained in the International Military Tribunal for the Far East's records.[18] As a result, the WIWCT found the defendant guilty of crimes against humanity for rape and sexual slavery committed under the "Comfort Women" system.

After stating the Japanese government's responsibility and appropriate repentance, apology, and reparations, the final written judgment concludes as follows:

> In conclusion, through this Judgement, the judges wish to acknowledge all the women victimized by Japan's military sexual slavery system. We also recognize the great fortitude and dignity of the survivors who have reconstructed their lives and testified before us. The crimes committed against the survivors remain one of the tremendous unremedied injustices of the Second World War. There are no museums, no graves for the unknown comfort woman, no education of future generations, and no judgement days, for the victims of Japan's military sexual slavery. Many of the women who have come forward to fight for justice have died unsung heroes. While the names inscribed in history's page are often those of the men who commit the crimes, rather than the women who suffer them, this Judgement bears the names of the survivors that took the stage to tell their stories, and thereby, for four days at least, put wrong on the scaffold and truth on the throne.[19]

Even though the judgment was not legally binding to enforce the Japanese government's official acknowledgment of its responsibility and reparations for individual victims, the landmark of the WIWCT in global memory formation cannot be stressed enough. The tribunal was a proclamation that the issue of remembering the sexual violence perpetrated by the Japanese military during the Asia-Pacific War had been elevated to the point of human rights. From the time Kim Hak-soon broke the silence about her experience as a "comfort woman" in 1991 until the WIWCT in 2000, the world witnessed two civil wars in Rwanda and Yugoslavia. The Rwandan genocide of 1994 had shown that rape was not only a war crime but a weapon of genocide. The scale of violence that assaulted most of the Tutsi women age twelve and over and the cruelty that recruited HIV-infected Hutu men for the "rape squads" prove the genocidal impact of sexual violence in Rwanda. The horrors of it were made apparent in the statistics that report that a large number of newborns of rape victims were murdered by their birth mothers. The report that most of the "war babies" of Bosnia were abandoned or murdered between 1992 and 1995 also attests that the result of racist sexual violence is analogous to that of genocide. Thousands of babies were born after the Rape of Nanjing. However, no woman acknowledged that she was raising the child of a Japanese soldier. Infanticides by women who gave birth after the Nanjing Massacre were also reported to have been widely committed.[20]

The world was aghast at the horrors of Rwanda and Yugoslavia broadcast on TV screens across the globe. The appeal of moving images was much more potent than abstract concepts like women's rights. The sexual violence in Rwanda and Yugoslavia that broke the universal moral code inspired compassion all over the world for the pains women had to suffer for being women in wartime. What the global audience witnessed on television was too intentional and cruel to be lumped into "collateral damage." The rage against the inhumane violence expanded into a consensual understanding of sexual assault as an issue of inalienable, unnegotiable human rights, and the International Criminal Tribunal for Rwanda (ICTR) and the former Yugoslavia (ICTY) ruled that wartime rape is a crime against humanity. The list of lawyers who participated in the WIWCT exemplifies how the rage of global society against the sexual violence of Yugoslavia and Rwanda had extended into the recognition of the Japanese military "Comfort Women" system as a crime against humanity. Among those were Gabrielle Kirk McDonald, who served as the presiding judge of the ICTY, and Patricia Viseur-Seller, the special advisor for gender for the Office of the Prosecutor of the ICTY and ICTR.[21] Their participation implies that the "Comfort Women" system during the Asia-Pacific War and the systemized sexual violence during the civil wars in Rwanda and Yugoslavia are grouped into the same category of crimes against humanity at the International Criminal Court.

In 1989–1991, when the liberal West was complacent with its optimistic triumphalism after the collapse of the Soviet Union and the communist East, the genocide and systemized rape in Rwanda and Yugoslavia were a chilling reminder that this era we are living in is not the end of history but a repetition of it. The genocidal mass rape of Muslim women during the Bosnian War reminded the world of the Japanese military "Comfort Women" system. In reverse, the ICT referred to the "Comfort Women" issue in its deliberation of the systematized rape in Rwanda and Yugoslavia. The International Labor Organization also viewed the "Comfort Women" case as a violation of the Forced Labor Convention of 1930.[22] Following the World Conference on Human Rights in Vienna in 1993, which stressed that women's rights are a human rights issue, the United Nations General Assembly adopted the Declaration on the Elimination of Violence against Women in December. The Rome Statute of the International Criminal Court prescribes "rape, sexual slavery, enforced prostitution" as not only "war crimes" but "crimes against humanity." Now, the "Comfort Women" issue is a human rights issue—the emergence of the "Comfort Women" as a global issue significantly contributed to the acknowledgment of wartime sexual violence as a crime against humanity. To borrow the words of Carol Gluck, "just as the Holocaust became a global example of genocide, so did the Comfort Women become a touchstone for new international law relating to the violence against women in war. And so rape, a violation as old as warfare itself, became a crime against humanity in international law."[23]

Indeed, sexual violence is the most primitive and effective means of control, and it puts not only women victims but also men in shame and humiliation. As of the twentieth century, sexual violence, including gang rape, has become one of the primary weapons of genocide. Combined with the genocidal strategies that regulate the biological reproduction of victims, sexual violence has become ever more systematic and complicated. In ethnocentric patriarchal societies where having a child of a different ethnicity is considered an improper reproduction of lineage, rape is an incredibly potent means of genocide. The patriarchal tradition that represents the national body through women's bodies results in sexual genocide that aims for the sterilization of women in a targeted minority group.[24] A conviction for sexual violence is also a conviction for genocide. While the punishment for genocide gets delayed, the victims who can no longer represent the body of the nation have to suffer from attacks not only from the alien perpetrators but also from the patriarchal guardian nationalists. However, the indictment and punishment for sexual violence were peripheralized at the Nuremberg Trials and the Tokyo Trials, which prioritized the issues of the Holocaust, the Nanjing Massacre, and the torture and assault on POWs.

It was not until the twenty-first century that wartime sexual violence became a crime against humanity. The moral sensitivity toward the hitherto marginalized victims of sexual violence was greatly improved along with the emergence of global memory formation.[25] After the ICTY convicted the Serbian nationalist militia of sexual slavery for the collective rape and sexual violence of Muslim women in Bosnia, the International Criminal Court investigated the cases of women who were abducted and raped through the forced marriage system and charged Germain Katanga and Mathieu Ngudjolo Chui with sexual enslavement. The first court ruling that acknowledged forced marriage as a crime against humanity was the appeal judgment in the Charles Taylor case by the Special Court for Sierra Leone in 2012. Involving even the UN Peacekeeping Forces, the demand for prosecuting forced prostitution as a crime against humanity could be understood as an attempt to overcome the limitation in prosecuting sexual violence at the ICC, which focuses primarily on rape cases.[26] With the call for criminalizing homosexual violence getting louder than ever, the expansion of the scope of sexual violence as crimes against humanity is an irreversible trend.[27]

The process in which the Japanese military "Comfort Women" have been elevated to a global issue is also remarkable from the perspective of transnational memory activism. The NGOs in South Korea and Japan have brought the "Comfort Women" as a grave case of human rights violation to the attention of the UN Human Rights Council. The diasporic Korean women in North America played an important role in making the "Comfort Women" a global issue. Perhaps the bitter experiences of female Asian migrants, who were underprivileged doubly as women and national minorities, might deepen their empathy for "Comfort Women."[28] The work of Nikkei for the Civil Rights and Redress (NCRR), a Japanese-American NGO, also draws attention. Organized for rehabilitation of and reparations for the Japanese Americans who were falsely accused of espionage and imprisoned in the internment camps during World War II, the NCRR not only advocated erecting the "comfort woman" statue in Glendale, California, but also demanded the Japanese government's official apology along with due reparations to and rehabilitation of the victims.[29] It also released a stern critique of the "Comfort Women" agreement jointly issued by Japan and South Korea on December 28, 2015, and participated in the candlelight vigil at the statue in Glendale on January 15, 2016. The NCRR is notably different from Japanese nationalists who have denied the "Comfort Women" and pushed the White House, Congress, and municipal governments for the removal of the statue and monuments.[30] It has continually collaborated with the Muslim Public Affairs Council to protest against Islamophobia in the United States, aggravated since 9/11.[31]

In global memory formation, the debate on the Japanese military "Comfort Women" is restructured as the conflict between Japan's historical denialism and international human rights norms, not Japan and Korea.[32] At this juncture, it is significant that two groups of memory activists, one for the remembrance of the Armenian Genocide and the other for justice for the Japanese military "Comfort Women," have demonstrated solidarity. Zareh Sinanyan, a member of the Glendale City

Council, advocated for the statue in Glendale against the Japanese government's powerful lobbying. He explained his move in the opening statement for the statue's unveiling. The NCRR's newspaper *Rafu Shimpo* reports that, as a grandson of the Armenian genocide survivor, Sinanyan said that he understood the pain and horror the victims had suffered: "The best way to heal wounds . . . is to acknowledge them. . . . My people, my grandfather, were subjected to a horrible, horrible crime. . . . To this day, because no apology has come, no proper acknowledgment has come. . . . The wound is deep, it is festering, and there can be no moving forward without it."[33] The family memory of the Armenian genocide must have evoked an emotional empathy toward the "Comfort Women" victims. The fact that Glendale is home to the largest Armenian community in the United States answers the question, "Why Glendale?" The memory of "Comfort Women" crossed the Pacific Ocean to meet with the memory of the Armenian genocide in California, culminating in global mnemonic solidarity.

ReflectSpace, an art gallery inside Glendale Central Library, which is just a stone's throw away from the "comfort woman" statue, draws attention too. The gallery's inaugural exhibition in May 2017, *Landscape of Memory*, was dedicated to the relationship between the official memory and survivors' testimony of the Armenian genocide. This theme seems natural for the city's large Armenian population. What is intriguing is the exhibition that followed, *Do the Right Thing: (dis)Comfort Women*, which is an artistic reflection "on the silence and dialogue by and about the women who were forced to become sex slaves by the Japanese Imperial Army before and during World War II."[34] The exhibition curators also bear significance: Jun Hyeyeon Monica, a Korean curator, and Ara and Anahid Oshagan, an Armenian American couple, cocurated the exhibition. ReflectSpace has been consistent in its pursuit of remembrance and representation of tragic history by organizing a series of exhibitions with themes ranging from the legacy of slavery in today's American society (*Wake: The Afterlife of Slavery*) through the multifaceted narratives of the Holocaust depicted in rare and contemporary photographs (*i am: Narratives of the Holocaust*), to *Nonlinear Histories: Transgenerational Memory of Trauma*. According to the Oshagans, what held these exhibitions together was "the tension between the inability to speak about personal trauma and the deep human urge to tell," common in all victim-survivors of genocide.[35] ReflectSpace is an excellent testament to global memory formation, in which distinct memories of the victims of American slavery, the Armenian genocide, the Holocaust, and the Japanese military "Comfort Women" are in communication with each other through artistic representation.

Women's rights as a universal value allow the mnemonic solidarity for the "Comfort Women" across the Pacific, from the civil society organizations in South Korea, Japan, China, the Philippines, Taiwan, and Indonesia to the women's organizations in the Americas. The transpacific women's solidarity is also observed in the Japanese feminists' effort to fuel their domestic #MeToo movement with the memory of the "Comfort Women." Muta Kazue's short film implies the potential for solidarity between the #MeToo movement in Japan and the international memory activism of the "Comfort Women." In the film, Muta positions the "Comfort Women" victims who broke the silence to testify publicly as the pioneers of the #MeToo movement. The "Comfort Women" became the symbol of feminist solidarity.[36] On the opposite side, the denialism of the Japanese military's "Comfort Women" signifies solidarity among the oppressive ideologies, as the intersection of the fascistic patriarchy of imperial Japan, male-chauvinist misogyny, and the ethnic nationalism in postwar Japan.[37] In Japan's national mnemoscape, "Comfort Women" denialism is closely linked to the androcentric contempt for the #MeToo movement. Muta's argument resonates more deeply in today's Japan, where sexual violence continues to be overlooked and tolerated despite the #MeToo movement.[38] The memory of the "Comfort Women" has shifted its focus "from women's shame to men's crime."[39] It is now frequently recalled as a reference in discussions on the violations of women's rights revolving around the issues of the sexual slavery of the Islamic State and Boko Haram, human trafficking, and forced marriage.[40]

The exhibition held at the Mauthausen Memorial in 2005 on the Nazi concentration camps and forced sexual labor occasioned a full-fledged public discussion about the issue of forced prostitution within the camps.

In September 2007 the Ravensbrück Summer University discussed "Comfort Women," the mass rape of Muslim women by Serbian nationalists in Grbavica, and the forced prostitution at Nazi concentration camps in close relation to one another. That summer school explored the entangled memories of the sexual violence in the Asia-Pacific War, the Nazi Holocaust, and the Yugoslav wars. Separately from the problematization of the "Comfort Women" in East Asia, Christa Paul in Germany was leading the research on forced prostitution under the Nazis. Paul published an essay in the feminist magazine *Emma* in 1992 based on the interview in 1990 of Maria W, a survivor of the Auschwitz brothel, and then a full-length book on her research in 1994.[41] There is no way of confirming that the "Comfort Women" memory activism in South Korea sparked interest and research within German academia, as some South Korean media outlets claim.[42] It is noteworthy that memories of Japanese "Comfort Women" and the Nazis' forced prostitution met in the global memory space and were developed in tandem with the issues of women's rights. Both memories formed mnemonic solidarity despite having never crossed paths with each other in the current of history. Global memory formation began to take shape as memories of history traveled globally and as transnational memory activists strove for mnemonic solidarity.

BLACK ATLANTIC AND THE HOLOCAUST

The significance of 2000 as year zero of global memory formation is now well addressed. However, global memory formation was not born out of thin air in 2000 CE. The global solidarity among victims traces back further than one might imagine. It has been a long time since the first American slavery met the Holocaust in the global memory space. A good example is "The Negro and the Warsaw Ghetto," a short essay by W. E. B. Du Bois. Du Bois was the first Black person to receive a doctoral degree from Harvard University and a radical sociologist who poignantly observed the paradox of American society where class conflicts overlap with racial conflicts. On April 16, 1952, the progressive Jewish monthly *Jewish Life* asked Du Bois to speak for fifteen minutes on "the significance of the ghetto fight for the Negro people in the United States today" on the ninth anniversary of the Warsaw ghetto uprising. The letter written by Louis Harap, editor-in-chief of the magazine, clearly indicates the purpose of the speech by requesting an address on the historical significance of the Warsaw ghetto uprising from the perspective of the joint struggle of Jews and Blacks in America.[43]

In his essay, Du Bois recounts anecdotes from the early 1890s when he gained new insights into racism. He traveled to European countries, including Switzerland, Hungary, Austria, Czechoslovakia, and Poland, during his graduate studies in Berlin. When he stopped at a small village in Polish Galicja, the coachman who drove the carriage to his lodging observed Du Bois for some time and asked "whether he would like to sleep among the Jews (Unter den Juden)."[44] Confused, Du Bois said yes, and the coachman drove the carriage to a small Jewish hotel at the far end of the village. The coachman, who had never seen a Black person before, assumed Du Bois to be Jewish. At that time, Polish Galicja was called "India in Eastern Europe."[45] The following anecdote is set at a social gathering in a small town in Germany. When the party suddenly cooled, Du Bois thought his presence as a Black person was making the crowd uncomfortable, just as in the United States. However, a German friend sitting next to him whispered, "They think I may be a Jew. It is not you they object to; it is me." Du Bois was surprised to learn through antisemitism in Germany that "any exhibition of race prejudice could be anything but color prejudice." On his way home from Moscow after attending the International Sociological Association in 1949, he visited the ruins of the Warsaw ghetto. There, he imagined hearing the screams and gunshots of the Atlanta Race Riot and saw the hallucination of the marching Ku Klux Klan. To borrow his own words, Du Bois could get a "more complete understanding of the Negro problem" through three visits to Poland, particularly the Warsaw ghetto in 1949.[46]

Du Bois's anecdote is not the first transatlantic encounter between African American and Jewish memories. The descendants of enslaved

African Americans have kept the communal dignity of the African diaspora by looking at themselves through the lens of Jews who left Egypt in the Exodus.[47] Reciprocally, Jewish immigrants have expressed empathy toward the suffering of enslaved African Americans. The Black-Jewish relationship strengthened as Eastern European Jewish immigrants in the southern United States often boarded at the houses of the African Americans they visited to sell goods. In 1868 a Yiddish translation of *Uncle Tom's Cabin* was published in Vilnius as *Di shklaveray oder di laybeygnshaft* (Slavery or serfdom) by Ayzik-Meyer Dik, who was inspired by the rebellious Russian intelligentsia.[48] Later, the radical Yiddish newspaper *Forverts* in New York actively promoted the movie *Uncle Tom's Cabin* when it was first screened in 1927. The Yiddish-language papers and magazines showed deep empathy with race issues and openly pursued Black-Jewish solidarity. Despite Toni Morrison's poignant observation that *Uncle Tom's Cabin* was not written for Black Americans to read,[49] the novel unexpectedly enjoyed an empathetic readership among the Haskalah Jews in the United States and Russia.

When the Convention on the Prevention and Punishment of the Crime of Genocide (hereafter "the Genocide Convention"), which Raphael Lemkin—a Polish Jewish lawyer from Polish Galicja—drafted, was adopted by the newly founded UN General Assembly in 1948, the community that welcomed it first and most passionately was radical Black Americans. After the Genocide Convention, they submitted a petition titled "We Charge Genocide" to the UN in 1951 to point out the commonality between the Nazi Holocaust and racial discrimination in the United States. The petition aimed to have American slavery acknowledged as genocide by the United Nations. The petitioners even contacted Lemkin to ask for his support, but Lemkin turned down the request. His original draft of the Genocide Convention was already torn to pieces due to the Cold War power politics. The Western superpowers guilty of colonialism, including but not limited to the United States, the United Kingdom, and France, pressed to remove the article on cultural genocide, such as the extermination of indigenous culture. Also excluded was the article on political genocide, at the objection of the Soviet Union. With the Western colonial genocide and the Stalinist political genocide crossed out, there remained only the Holocaust. For Lemkin, who was desperate for the ratification of the Genocide Convention, it must have been difficult to stand by the radical Black Americans, as confronting the U.S. government could mean a complete revocation of his proposal.[50]

As early as the 1930s, Aboriginal Australian political activists had lent a hand to the Jews under Nazi oppression. On December 6, 1938, the political leader of Yorta descent William Cooper organized a protest in front of the Nazi German Consulate in Melbourne to condemn *Kristallnacht*, an incident on November 9, 1938, in which Nazi paramilitary storm troopers looted and vandalized Jewish stores and synagogues. Cooper intended to deliver a petition that condemned the "cruel persecution of the Jewish people by the Nazi government," yet the consulate remained shut. This letter was finally delivered to the German Consulate seventy-four years later when Alfred Turner, Cooper's grandson, reenacted the protest. He handed the letter to the German Consulate to the applause of the Jewish and Aboriginal audience.[51] Cooper's demonstration in 1938 was impressive, given the country's post–World War II immigration policy known as the "white Australia policy," which issued visas for light-skinned Ashkenazi Jews but not for darker-skinned Sephardi Jews. Also, it was only in the twenty-first century that Yad Vashem belatedly created and dedicated the position of the "Chair for the Study of Resistance During the Holocaust" to Cooper to honor his righteousness in December 2010. According to the press release, "the Chair, part of the International Institute for Holocaust Research at Yad Vashem, will support the study of the phenomena of resistance against Nazi Germany and its collaborators during the Holocaust."[52]

The *Diary of a Young Girl*, by Anne Frank, was popular among the anti-Apartheid activists of the African National Congress, and it also tells about the proto-globalization of memories. The Prison of Robben Island, the infamous political prison during Apartheid, exhibits the inmates' notes, including the notebook of Ahmed Kathrada, which carries eighteen years' worth of quotes collected from books and newspapers smuggled into the prison. In Kathrada's notebook, Anne Frank is one of the four most frequently quoted people, alongside Sophocles, Confucius, and Joan of Arc. For those battling against Apartheid and its outdated racism, the memory of Anne Frank, who was a victim of yet another extreme racist crime, was a valuable memory asset. Nelson Mandela, the lifetime anti-Apartheid activist and first president of democratic South Africa, also reminisced how Anne Frank's diary strengthened his spirit and convinced him of eventual victory. Even in the early 1940s, the anti-Apartheid activists in South Africa aimed to gain international support by connecting Apartheid to Nazis' extremely violent antisemitism. The comparison of the Apartheid regime with Nazism remained an oft-repeated topic for discussion surrounding justice and reconciliation regarding Apartheid and its victims' memory and reparations, even in the 1990s after South Africa's democratization.[53]

For the European activists who highlighted the anti-Apartheid front as the most critical moral battle after the fall of the Nazis, *The Diary of a Young Girl* was also a key text bridging the memory of the Holocaust and Apartheid under the rubric of the crimes against humanity. The special exhibitions on *Nazism in South Africa* held in Amsterdam's Anne Frank House for three years in the 1970s are a good example. The first exhibition, in summer 1971, was to display the direct correlations between the Nuremberg Laws and the Apartheid judiciary, the ghettos, and Bantustans (designated territories in South Africa for black Africans to segregate them from the white population). According to the exhibition curator, there was no need to show the exact quotation from the Nazis as anyone who saw the exhibition could link Nazism and Apartheid. Perhaps due to the specificity of the venue, the exhibition drew many visitors. Starting from the second floor, where the Frank family had lived in secrecy, the visitors were to stroll down to the first floor and finish viewing by the gallery entrance. Everyone had to walk under the banner that read "Nazism=Apartheid" to exit the gallery. In the second exhibition, in summer 1972, a life-size papier-mâché figure of then prime minister of South Africa Balthazar J. Vorster holding the Nazi Hakenkreuz greeted the visitors, along with posters of racist remarks by various Apartheid politicians hung on the walls. The second exhibition was also a great hit.

The third exhibition, in 1973, drew attention because its guest book survived the time—many thousands of visitors from Europe, the United

States, Central and South America, Japan, Australia, Israel, South Africa, and elsewhere left vastly diverse responses. Many wrote that they were convinced by the comparison between Nazism and Apartheid and felt the need to fight against racism. However, most Israeli visitors showed indifference, and visitors from South Africa complained vehemently. Though many South African visitors accused it of being a biased, frenzied censure against their country, some argued that the exhibition's portrayal of South Africa would stay the same as long as Apartheid continued. There was a disparity in opinions even among the exhibition's organizers. For instance, Otto Frank, Anne Frank's father, who had been supportive of using Anne's legacies for the battle against Apartheid, also expressed his disapproval of the simplified equation between Nazism and Apartheid. Others stressed the accountability of colonizers not for Nazism but for Apartheid. Still, activists in South Africa continued to compare Apartheid to Nazism. Equating the white supremacy of South Africa to the Nazi concept of "master race" (*Herrenvolk*), Mandela often used phrases like the "Hitler-like" National Party and "future Gestapo" and warned that "the specter of Belsen and Buchenwald concentration camps are wandering in South Africa." In the end, Anne Frank House and the South Africa–Netherlands activist group split after the 1973 exhibition.[54]

The "Black Germans," those who immigrated from the colonies in Africa to Germany during the 1920s, and their children suffered intense discrimination at school and work, bullying in the local community, and forced sterilization. Had Germany won World War II, their fate would not have been that different from that of the Jews and Roma. *The Book of Harlan* (2016), a novel by Bernice McFadden, depicts African American Jazz musicians Harlan and Lizard as victims of the Holocaust. Based on the true story of Harlan McFadden, the author's grandfather, the novel was criticized for its inaccurate portrayal of the Buchenwald concentration camp, unhistorical character settings of Karl Otto and Ilse Koch, and highlighting of African Americans as the victims of the Holocaust over African Germans or Blacks in Europe.[55] In contrast, British filmmakers of African descent, John Sealey and Amma Asante, made their protagonists a Black Senegalese POW in the French colonial legion and a "Rhineland Mongrel" in the movies *The Great Escape* and *Where Hands Touch*. The films successfully expanded the mnemonic landscape of the Holocaust into colonial Africa. Black victims of the Holocaust became feasible by recounting the "human zoo" (*Völkerschau*) and sterilization enforced on the "Rhineland Mongrels."[56] The memory of African European Holocaust victims warrants attention as a guideline for "multidirectional" memories of the Holocaust and American slavery without privileging one victim group over another. Also, the excavation of August Agbola O'Brown, a Nigerian Polish jazz musician, from the memory archive of Armia Krajowa (AK) during the Warsaw Uprising in 1944 is a moment to deterritorialize the ethno-nationalist memory of the resistance in Poland.[57]

Still, when the Holocaust and colonialist genocidal memories face each other, the competition for "who is the bigger victim" does not seem to be eased. The global memory formation is dotted with tensions about which memory should achieve the position of "narrative template." The ongoing Mbembe debate that heated Germany was exemplary. Achille Mbembe, an African postcolonial thinker, was invited to give an opening speech for the Ruhr Triennial Arts Festival in August 2020. Upon hearing the news, Felix Klein, the federal government commissioner for Jewish life in Germany and the fight against antisemitism, demanded to cancel the invitation. The reason was that Mbembe relativized the Holocaust by equating the state of Israel to the Apartheid regime of South Africa. Klein and other critics indicated that Mbembe's stance breached the long-standing German policy to defend the *raison d'etat* of Israel. Mbembe countered by calling Klein racist, and a group of Jewish German and Israeli memory activists came forward in solidarity with Mbembe.[58] What caused this controversy was an excerpt from Mbembe's book *Politik der Feindschaft* (Politics of enmity), in which Mbembe "compares" the Holocaust and Apartheid without "equating" the two. Mbembe made clear that the two occurred in different historical contexts. Nowhere in the book does he "equate" or "relativize" them, as his critics argued.[59]

In Natan Sznaider's view, the Holocaust message of "Never Again!" brought about mainly two strains of interpretation: one, as represented by the UN's Universal Declaration of Human Rights, the discourse in support of the universal human rights to prevent genocide, dictatorship, colonialism, Apartheid, and other inhuman acts; and two, the restriction of the meaning of the Holocaust to the crime against Jews with an emphasis on the state of Israel as a safe haven for the Jewish people, supported by the Israeli Declaration of Independence.[60] In the cultural memory of Germany, which admits the nation's exclusively "collective guilt," there has been a concern that comparing the Holocaust to other crimes might alleviate the uniqueness of the Nazi crime or attenuate the national accountability of Germans.[61] The specter of *Historikerstreit* of 1986–87 still haunts the memory culture in Germany—the concern over comparison stemmed from vigilance against self-exoneration by Ernst Nolte and other revisionists who argued that Nazism was a reaction to Stalinism and saved the Christian civilization of Europe from the Asiatic Bolshevik's barbarism. To them, Holocaust was an "Asiatic act" the Nazis adopted from Stalin. Under the frame of the "European civil war" between Nazism and Stalinism, they tried to sanitize Nazism by blaming Bolshevism for Nazi crimes.[62]

Indeed, critical intellectuals who spearhead the post-1968 memory culture in Germany have had an emotional resistance to "relativization." However, denying the possibility of comparison with other historical tragedies absolutized the Holocaust. Then, the Holocaust as "absolute evil" became a fossilized moral code. The pointed criticism of Mbembe was an expression of the stance to disallow non-European memories of Apartheid, slavery, and colonial genocide from being parallel with the Holocaust. However, Germany, which had colonized Namibia, is historically implicated in today's racism, a colonial legacy. Also, as the current Israeli-Palestinian conflict is the aftermath of the Holocaust, German society is required to build a responsible memory of the current issue in Palestine. The "multidirectional memory," in which the memory of the Holocaust communicates rather than competes with memories of other genocide, or "critical relativization" of the Holocaust to evoke the West's colonial genocide and Stalinist political genocide, would be a methodological foundation for embracing simultaneously the singularity and multidirectionality of the Holocaust.[63] I cannot help but point out that the oblivion of the criminal colonial past in Namibia and the moralist absolutization of the Holocaust have paired up in the memory culture of postwar Germany.

For example, Namibia was not registered as a site of German-responsible genocide. German colonialists' public discussion of genocide as a "utilitarian" solution for the Nama and Herero peoples' uprising in 1904–1908 leaves a lot to think about. It seems that the unilateral emphasis on the Holocaust memory screens the colonial past in Germany's memory culture. With the colonial past in oblivion, Germans' self-definition of "colonialism without colony" and "the first postcolonial state" excused Germany from the colonial guilt. It is in stark contrast with Jan Józef Lipski, a leading Polish leftist dissident intellectual in communist Poland, who criticized the "extermination of Hereros" as an integral part of European civilization in 1980.[64] Indeed, the East European perspective sheds light on Germany's forgotten colonial past. Should the Nazi attacks on the neighboring Slavic states in Eastern Europe be interpreted as an extension of the colonialist project, the oblivion of colonialism in Germany's memory culture calls for grave concern.[65] The colonial ignorance shows how the hegemonic status of the Holocaust has obscured the colonial genocide in coming to terms with the Nazi past in Germany. The Holocaust memory became a screen memory when any comparison with Apartheid or colonial genocide is denounced, and even the sound criticism of Israel's *E'tatism* is labeled antisemitic. When the Holocaust and the Nazis' colonial rule of the Slavic East are critically disentangled from the postcolonial perspective, the German memory culture will move from the parochial to the global.

CIVIL RIGHTS MOVEMENT AND THE POSTCOLONIAL

The horizontal entanglement of the memories of the Black Atlantic, European colonialism, the Holocaust, and the Nazis' colonizing project in Eastern Europe aptly reveals the deterritorialized cross-section of the global memory formation. Undoubtedly, the U.S. civil rights movement in the 1960s was historical grounds for promoting deterritorialized mnemonic solidarity. Joined by the worldwide antiwar movement against the U.S.-led Vietnam War, the civil rights movement in the United States contributed to the development of global memory formation. Many Jewish American students engaged in the civil rights movement were reminded of the Holocaust by the U.S. military's racist massacre in Vietnam. Echoing the antiwar protest, the U.S. prosecutor at the Nuremberg Trials, Telford Taylor, wrote *Nuremberg and Vietnam: An American Tragedy*, in which he draws a parallel between the U.S. military atrocities in Vietnam and the Nazi crimes during World War II.[66] Bertrand Russell organized the "Russell Tribunal," modeled after the Nuremberg Trials, to criticize the massacre and war atrocities by the U.S. military as crimes against humanity. From the violence in Vietnam, Jean-Paul Sartre recalled the French colonial violence against the Algerian National Liberation Army.[67] By participating in the anti–Vietnam War movement, the young, left revisionist historians in Greece began to be aware of British and American colonial oppression. The United Kingdom and the United States were now understood not as the saviors who saved Greece from the tyranny of communism but as the imperialists who suppressed the radical movement that was popular with the locals from the bottom. The U.S. government's tacit support of the military coup in 1967 confirmed the Greek left's skepticism about U.S. imperialism.[68]

In East Asia, the antiwar movement in solidarity with the Vietnamese was a wake-up call for the memories of Japanese military atrocities during the "Fifteen Years' War" in the Asia-Pacific. As the Jewish community in the United States had to suppress the memory of the Holocaust to strengthen the NATO alliance at the beginning of the Cold War, the anticommunist alliance in East Asia was also suppressing the memory of the Japanese colonial atrocities. Despite the Cold War cover-up, memories of the Japanese military's wartime atrocities in its Asian neighbors could not be kept in silence forever. The lid was first lifted in Japan when Honda Katsuichi, a Vietnam war correspondent for the *Asahi Shimbun*, witnessed the U.S. military committing atrocities on site and became curious about the actions of the Japanese army on the battlefields of the Asia-Pacific War, as he had no good reason to believe the Japanese Army on Chinese front would have behaved better than the U.S. military in Vietnam. Such curiosity led him to plan a trip to China following the Japanese military attack route.[69] During the forty-day coverage in the summer of 1971, Honda collected evidence of Japanese military atrocities and documented testimonies. His travelogue transmitted a message that Japan's self-criticism of the war crimes during the Sino-Japanese War should precede the Sino-Japanese diplomatic normalization to attain a true friendship.

However, Honda's column in the *Asahi Shimbun* was met with a tremendous backlash. Japanese right-wingers claimed the Nanjing Massacre was leftist propaganda, imbued with the Comintern view of history, to defame the honor of the Japanese nation. The general readership also expressed shock in their letters to the editor. For a different reason but the same Cold War logic, Mao Zedong's communist regime also remained apathetic to the victims of the Nanjing Massacre. The main concern of the People's Republic of China was to crush the U.S. imperialists' intention to rearm Japan, and excessive interest in the Nanjing Massacre was seen as disrupting the ranks of the anti-American struggle. Until the 1960s, Nanjing was only remembered as a place of historical class struggle among the Chinese. The memory of revolutionary martyrs slaughtered by the Kuomintang's "reactionary" forces came before the Chinese, who were slaughtered by the Japanese military.[70] It was much later that the nonfiction *Rape of Nanjing* (1997), published with the subtitle *The Forgotten Holocaust of World War II*, raised public awareness of the Nanjing Massacre in communist China. Iris Chang also used the expression "the Holocaust in the Pacific" in various lectures to attract the attention of the U.S. media. In contrast to Maoist China, the percentage of affirmative responses to Honda's criticism of the Nanjing Massacre among the *Asahi Shimbun* readers in Japan amounted to 95 percent. The conscientious or critical memory in Japan was awakened by Honda's report on his journey tracing the massacre.

The Japanese self-critical memory of the Sino-Japanese War and the Nanjing Massacre surfaced in 1971. However, it was an achievement of the 1960s antiwar movement in Japan, represented by Beheiren (Citizens' Coalition for Peace in Vietnam). Born out of self-reflection on the Japanese as both victims and perpetrators of the Vietnam War, Beheiren maintained the critical self-portrait of accomplices as the Japanese economy benefited from the Vietnam War while acknowledging the pain of Japanese civilians as the Japanese archipelago became military bases for U.S. soldiers during the Vietnam War.[71] Through the antiwar movement of the 1960s, memories of the Holocaust, colonial atrocities, American slavery, and war crimes of imperial Japan became entangled in the global memory space. Indeed, the solidarity these memories formed deserves to be recognized as a global civic movement. Though May 1968 might be a failed political revolution with the old regime intact, it cannot be concluded as a failure from the perspective of the memory culture. The year 1968 was the starting point for the epic journey to disrupt the national memory culture and develop the global memory culture to empathize with the agony of national others. The historical significance of the 1968 revolution shifts from a failed political revolution to a successful mnemonic revolution in that it freed the memory culture from the nation-state and contributed to developing a global memory formation.

May 1968, as a memory revolution, was not at all spontaneous. It dates back to 1961—the year of the Eichmann trial in Jerusalem and the massacre of Algerians at an anticolonial demonstration in Paris on October 17. Maurice Papon, the prefect of Paris police who oversaw the bloody suppression that brutally murdered the Algerians and threw their bodies into the Seine in 1961, was a high-ranking official of the police under the Vichy government and a Nazi collaborator. Based on an interview with the new-left weekly magazine *Observateur*, "The Two Ghettos" (*Les deux ghettos*), an essay published by the French writer Marguerite Duras in light of the massacre, calls for mnemonic solidarity between the victims of the Holocaust and colonialism by juxtaposing the Algerian workers with the Warsaw ghetto survivors. *Les Temps Modernes* published excerpts from writings of Primo Levi and Franz Fanon in May 1961, and the Eichmann trial and the Paris Massacre in the winter issue. It was also in 1961 when Charlotte Delbo published *Les Belles Lettres*, the epistolary testimony of her experience of Auschwitz and colonial violence.

Departing from the UN Genocide Convention and a Catholic soldier's letter stating that he would refuse to participate in the mission to suppress the Algerian National Liberation Front, though he would willingly fight against the Nazis, Delbo's book raises a thesis that can be summarized in this cynical question: "Must we console ourselves by holding on to the fact that in [the Algerian internment camps]there are neither gas chambers nor crematoria?" This question adeptly implies the critical juxtaposition of the Holocaust and colonial genocide to revive and reinforce the memories of each other in France's memory culture in 1961.[72]

Also interesting is the intersection of memories of the Holocaust and colonial genocide regarding the indigenous peoples in America. The U.S. indigenous rights activist Ward Churchill once provoked controversy by comparing Christopher Columbus to Heinrich Himmler. Whether Columbus had the intention to exterminate the indigenous population when he set foot on the continent remains unproven. Still, Churchill's provocation succeeded in drawing American public attention to the massacre of indigenous peoples by the Holocaust comparison. Churchill specifically juxtaposed the Roma and Sinti victims of the Holocaust with the indigenous victims of the colonial genocide.[73] The invocation of the Holocaust was intended to make white settlers' massacre of the indigenous people recognized in American history, though that simple equalization is out of context. Instead, many suppressed memories surfaced. Seven incidents of genocide occurred in northwestern California only, from San Francisco to the Oregon border, with the victims being the peoples of Wintu, Wiyot, Tolowa, Whilkut, Pomo, Yurok, and other tribes. Though not as well-known as the Wounded Knee Massacre, genocide of the indigenous peoples was committed widely on the West Coast of the United States. The massacres followed the same process, where children, women, and elders were all murdered indiscriminately. However, the perpetrators vary: in some cases, they are the military, like the U.S. 7th Cavalry Regiment in the Wounded Knee Massacre, and in other instances, white vigilantes.[74]

The genocide of indigenous peoples of the Americas by the white vigilantes reveals an unexpected scene: the frequency and intensity of massacres are much greater under the democratic system of the settlers than under the authoritative colonial regime. Michael Mann's observation that the more democratic the decision-making structure within the settler community was, the more brutal a massacre became, insinuates much about the global memory politics surrounding colonial genocide and the Holocaust. The paradoxical union of democracy and genocide, namely, "genocidal democracies in the New World," stresses the urgent need to rescue the memory culture from not only nationalism but also Eurocentrism.[75] Once freed from Eurocentrism, the memories of genocide debunk the historical naïveté that genocide or a holocaust cannot happen in the normal West. Western democracy is not antithetical to the Holocaust but embeds the possibility of the Holocaust. Zygmunt Bauman's critique that modern civilization has the Holocaust embedded in itself echoes in American democracy.[76] The attempt to reduce the Holocaust to the particularity of German history that is "premodern" and "semifeudalistic" reeks of a political excuse. The original sin of colonial and indigenous genocide has been embedded in the liberal democracy of the United Kingdom and the United States. To quote Zeev Sternhell, fascism was not a temporary deviation but an integral part of the history of European culture.[77] If Sternhell's argument is pushed further, genocide and ethnic cleansing are a risk inherent in modern European civilization. The post-Eurocentric memory can envision the democratization of Western democracy of the twenty-first century by critically remembering the genocide of the twentieth century.

From the postcolonial perspective of global memory, the mnemonic solidarity between Germany's Muslim immigrants and the Holocaust victims is also worth noting. According to the inspiring research by Michael Rothberg and Yasemin Yildiz, Turkish immigrants have long debated, since the mass immigration in 1961, how to intervene in Germany's past, especially the memory of the Holocaust. These immigrants were enraged by the double standard of German society, which warned them against being involved in something that happened before they came, all the while criticizing them for being indifferent to the Holocaust and calling them antisemitic. For the immigrants, moving to Germany also meant moving into the memories of Germany. The Muslim immigrants in Germany did not remain passive spectators of the official commemorative rituals but started to create and express their memories as active actors. Moreover, their voices began to alter Germany's mnemoscape. The Turkish German writer Zafer Şenocak shook the national boundaries of memory in his novel *Perilous Kinship* (*Gefährliche Verwandtschaft*) by staging an encounter between the Holocaust and the Armenian genocide in the personal memory of a Turkish German. The cabaret comedian Serdar Somuncu awoke memories of the Armenian genocide by playing on stage the adaptation of the memoirs of Holocaust survivors into those of Kurdish immigrants in Germany.[78] Taner Akçam, a Turkish historian exiled to Germany, published the first-ever monograph on the Armenian genocide.

Organized by the memory activists of the Neukölln borough of Berlin, the "Neighborhood Mothers in Neukölln" project received a great deal of attention. The project started with a focus on welfare, education, and childcare and evolved to encompass political and historical problems. The participants, many of whom were impoverished immigrants, united with the volunteer groups in Germany to learn and investigate the history of the Nazis and eventually made a documentary film of their journey to Auschwitz. Most of these women, who immigrated from Turkey, Eritrea, Iraq, Sri Lanka, and Palestine, had experienced political violence, financial difficulties, racist abuse, and genocide in their home countries. The racist remarks of Polish skinheads whom they encountered on the streets of Oświęcim, where the Auschwitz concentration camp is located, were also captured in the video as an alienation effect. The racist slurs encountered at Auschwitz feel somewhat like a theatrical device that implies the potential for solidarity between the trauma of the Jews and the trauma of the Muslim minority. More important, this intervention of the immigrants bypasses the homogenizing tendency of Germany's postwar memory and provides a new impetus for reconstructing Germany as a transnational memory community. By constructing a memory culture about the past that predates their immigration, they created a fissure in the exclusive, homogeneous narrative and memory.[79]

Whether and how immigrants can be involved in the collective memory being formed here and now of the past that precedes their immigration is a new problem that faces global memory formation of the twenty-first century. The experience of participating in the memory culture of the Holocaust from the fresh perspective of the Muslim immigrants in Neukölln set a model precedent for immigrants' participation, which can be a valuable asset toward the deterritorialization of memory. For national communities to eliminate the fetters of territorialized national memory, the involvement of heterogeneous subjects who do not share the same past is necessary. Korean society's memory of the Vietnam War, for instance, will become radically deterritorialized when Vietnamese immigrants or even Cambodian immigrants join the process of memory building—at that point, the categorization as either rightist or leftist, official or grassroots, will become irrelevant. However, as we will see in the next chapter, the trajectory of global memory formation attests to the unexpectedly considerable overlap and a somewhat blurry distinction between globalization and the nationalization of memory. Even if it is evident that the globalization of memory is a movement that surpasses the nationalization of memory, it can also unpredictably accelerate and reinforce the nationalization of memory.

HISTORY TEXTBOOK CONTROVERSIES

It was not until 1978 that newspapers in South Korea began criticizing Japanese prime ministers' visits to Yasukuni Shrine.[80] The first news coverage of the Japanese prime minister's visit to the shrine was a *Dong-A Ilbo* article on August 28, 1978. The Tokyo correspondent's dispatch introduces Japanese society's debate over Prime Minister Fukuda Takeo and Chief Cabinet Secretary Abe Shintaro visiting the shrine. It foresees that "it will not be easy for Japanese society to be rid of the lure of rightward shift" due to the political pressure from the families of the war dead, postcolonial nostalgia for the imperial past, and dread of threats from the Soviet Union. Fukuda, who initially claimed that he would pay respects as a private citizen, disclosed that his intention was an official visit by signing the guestbook as prime minister while trying to avert criticism by saying the distinction between "a private citizen" and "a public figure" was blurry. The tone of the *Dong-A Ilbo* article is mildly critical, considering the circumstances. On the front page of the day's paper was a report of the Kyodo News conference where the Japanese ambassador to South Korea, Sunobe Ryojo, spoke about the need to support South Korea's economy, implying that Korea-Japan economic relations were a more crucial issue than the Yasukuni Shrine visit.[81]

Dating back to November 1977, the interview with Japanese poet Komiyama published in *Dong-A Ilbo* is also intriguing. An amicable interview with Komiyama, who tried to commemorate the war dead of colonial Korea and petition for the release of colonial Korean war criminals, also positively assesses the artist's commemoration performance of the Korean war dead at Yasukuni Shrine in September 1953 for spiritual mending of the Japan-Korea relationship.[82] Left unmentioned in the article is the problem of the commemoration of the colonial Joseon war dead at the shrine—that it appropriates the unreasonable deaths of the colonized soldiers, whether voluntary or conscripted, as sacred devotion to the Japanese empire. Compared to the vehement protests and public outrage since the mid-1980s against Japanese prime ministers' visits to Yasukuni Shrine and the inclusion of the names of colonial Korean war dead in the shrine's memorial list, this article maintains a surprising degree of congeniality.[83] On August 16, 1980, *Dong-A Ilbo* also published a photo of the Japanese prime minister, Suzuki Zenko, holding the libation at the shrine, with no significant reactions from the public. No other newspaper published even this much. There was a world of difference from August 15, 2018, when all media outlets in South Korea unanimously criticized Prime Minister Abe Shinzō's tribute at Yasukuni Shrine, a passive move on his part concerned with criticisms from neighboring countries.

In retrospect, 1982–1985 was a watershed moment: Japan's rightist turn became apparent with the Nakasone government's "total reform of postwar politics," including defense spending exceeding the upper limit of 1 percent of GDP, the Ministry of Education's instruction to mandate the national flag and anthem at all school ceremonies, and especially the prime minister's visit to Yasukuni in 1985, not to mention the textbook censorship of 1982 that attempted to dilute Japan's invasion and atrocities during the Asia-Pacific War.[84] Subsequently, in 1986, controversial issues like denials of Japan's forced annexation of Joseon and the Nanjing Massacre taunted by Minister of Education Fujio Masayuki, the historical revisionism of the political elites of the conservative Liberal Democratic Party, and the censorship of history textbooks elevated the tension between Japan and its neighboring countries over the past Japanese colonialism and the Asia-Pacific War.[85] However, the heated reactions from South Korea and other neighbors of Japan in the mid-1980s could not be reduced to the issue of Japan's radical rightward turn—the increased sensitivity toward Japan's memory culture was a good sign of East Asian memory formation. Until the 1970s, East Asian countries were not as interested in their neighbors' history textbooks or dominant memory culture. In the 1980s, however, the interest in neighboring countries' memory culture and history policy grew. While Japan's official memory remained national ego-centered, its Asian neighbors quickly extended their historical sensitivity beyond national borders.

Indeed, the nationalist turn of Japanese history textbooks in the 1980s was not new; it had already started in the mid-1950s. As the Cold War system intensified, the "red textbooks" (*akai kyokasho*) were often criticized as corrupted with dangerous historical fabrications.[86] In 1955–1956 the government censors of textbooks instructed publishers not to propel the masochist view, having estimated that the preexisting history textbooks made under the U.S. occupation instilled negative stereotypes about Japan and impeded enriching patriotism among students. Under the premise that the Asia-Pacific War was a war led by Japan to liberate Asian neighbors from Western imperialism, the textbooks transformed Japan's "invasion" into "advancement." They omitted the Nanjing Massacre—a change reminiscent of the government-approved history textbooks under the total war system.[87] However, not a single news article criticizing the issue of Japan's aggravated history textbook was printed in South Korea from 1955 to 1958. Although Japanese history textbooks subsequently went through revisions during the 1970s in light of the Ienaga trial and included the Nanjing Massacre, forced mobilization of

Koreans, and mass suicide in Okinawa, these changes did not draw the attention of Korean society either. What drew Korean society's close attention to Japan's history textbook was Japan's textbook censorship guidelines issued in 1982. These new guidelines pushed for specific alterations: Japan's "invasion" of Southeast Asia was "advancement," the March 1st Independence Movement was a "riot," and visiting the shrine was not "compelled" but "encouraged."[88] Then, concerns and criticisms flooded in from Japan's Asian neighbors.

In 1982 memory culture and history textbooks were no longer Japan's domestic issue but a shared interest of East Asia.[89] Once it heated up, the memory war again expedited the emergence of East Asian memory formation. The Nakasone administration strongly countered the criticisms of textbook censorship as an "intervention in domestic affairs," claiming that history textbooks were a matter of Japan's sovereignty. Kamei Shizuka, a member of the National Basic Issues Society, a right-wing politicians' group in Japan, warned in 1986 that a war would be possible if Korea and China did not stop interfering with Japan's domestic affairs like history textbooks and the shrine visits. Though Kamei called it "interference," the neighboring countries' criticisms of the history textbooks and demands for revision signaled the entanglement of memories of East Asian and Southeast Asian countries that reference and interpolate with each other. A new consciousness that "entangled memories" across borders need to be inclusive of the voices of people involved beyond the bounds of national sovereignty ensued. Though only in the mid-1980s did East Asian memory formation take its first step, it has since grown remarkably. Not even the sacred principle of national sovereignty that steered East Asian modernity could stop the inception of East Asian memory formation.

Published by Fushosa Publishing, the revisionist history textbook put together by the Society to Make New History Textbooks glamorizes Japan's colonialism, intending to cultivate patriots. Nevertheless, even this version of history textbook cannot entirely be unaffected by the East Asian memory formation: the inclusion of the Japanese paramilitary's mass murder of socialists and colonial Koreans during the Great Kanto earthquake; the statement that "Japanese soldiers killed lots of Chinese civilians," albeit in what it calls the Nanjing "incident" (not "massacre"); the acknowledgment of inflicting "great pain and suffering on people of many different regions in Asia including China"; and the use of verb "compel" regarding Japanese language education and shrine visits during the colonial era give an impression that even this notorious version progressed a bit from Japanese history textbooks of 1957 to the early 1970s. Of course, it continues to maintain its revisionist and denialist stance with its claims that Japan's victory in the Asia-Pacific War gave Asian peoples the hope of independence, and that the "Greater East Asia Co-Prosperity Sphere" was based on principles of each Asian country's sovereign liberalization, economic development, and abolition of racism.[90] The memory war in East Asia now results from unprecedentedly heightened attention and sensitivity toward the shared memory rather than the simple regression of Japan's memory culture. The bitter controversy over the history textbook reflects not a step back from history reconciliation but the emergence of the transnational memory space for history reconciliation in East Asia.

5

NATIONALIZATION

HIROSHIMA AND AUSCHWITZ

Dziennik Polski, a daily newspaper headquartered in Kraków, published an interesting report on January 29, 1963. Titled "The First Day of Freedom," the article reports that four Japanese antinuclear pacifism activists attended the commemoration of the eighteenth anniversary of the liberation of Auschwitz. It calls their long, crooked journey—thirty-three thousand kilometers from Hiroshima to Auschwitz, across twenty-three countries in Asia and Europe over eight months—"the Hiroshima-Oświęcim peace march." A small town in the Silesia (Śląsk) province, Oświęcim is where Auschwitz-Birkenau concentration camp was located. The report about the first encounter between the Holocaust and A-bomb memories at the commemoration ceremony of liberation in Auschwitz on January 27, 1963, was quite moving. The Japanese peace march participants brought a shard of roof tile melted in the heat of the atomic bomb, and the Auschwitz-Birkenau State Museum donated in return the ashes of Auschwitz victims in an urn. The crowd chanted "Never again Hiroshima!" (*Nigdy więcej Hiroszimy!*) and "Never again Auschwitz!" (*Nigdy więcej Oświęcimia!*) in turn. After exchanging the symbols of death from Hiroshima and Auschwitz, Stanisław Pięta, the first secretary of the Polish United Workers' Party in Kraków, delivered an opening address. Sato Gyotsu, a monk from the Nipponzan Myohoji Buddhist Temple and an Asia-Pacific War veteran, responded that he could realize the importance of denuclearization of Eastern Europe. On January 28 the contingent visited Wawel Royal Castle to see the treasures, Jagiellonian University to meet the rector, and Lenin Steelworks to meet with workers and student representatives.[1]

The thirty-six black-and-white photographs at the Museum of Modern Art in Warsaw show multifarious images of the multinational representatives in the commemoration scenes at Auschwitz. The image of the Japanese representatives holding the Buddhist funeral streamers up high and leading the march with the European participants dressed in the Polish Army uniforms and stripes of Auschwitz provides a unique mnemoscape. The highlight of this scene is the image of a stern-looking Sato chanting the Buddhist prayer in the monk's robe.[2] However, their commemoration was subject to the political instrumentalization of Cold War politics. Above the coverage of the Hiroshima-Auschwitz Peace March, a local newspaper in Łódź, *Dziennik Łódźki*, placed a small section dedicated to the news that the negotiations on denuclearization between the United States, the UK, and the Soviet Union had resumed in New York.[3] In October 1962, while Sato and others were knee-deep in the peace march, what is now known as the Cuban Missile Crisis broke out. As this crisis arose from the deployment of Soviet nuclear missiles in Cuba, the world was on the brink of nuclear war. Having realized the imminent danger of total destruction after such a close call, humanity must have found the message of the Hiroshima-Auschwitz Peace March more urgent. If I must gauge the gravity in the air of the early 1960s, the memory of Hiroshima came more desperately to people facing the threat of nuclear war than did the memory of Auschwitz.

Ran Zwigenberg, a Japanese scholar from Israel, analyzes the peace march in the Japanese context. The march was planned to seek an alternative way for Japan's peace movement after the Anpo (安保) protests against the anticommunist security treaty between the United States and Japan ended unsuccessfully in 1960. The Hiroshima peace activists aimed to revive the pacifist movement by joining the international antinuclear movement. Its jumping-off point was that the Japanese, as the only victims of atomic bombs, had a unique role in the pursuit of world peace. The four objectives proposed were: (1) to tell as many people as possible about the horrors of Hiroshima and Auschwitz; (2) to record the suffering of different people in various countries; (3) to tell people about Hiroshima and others' suffering and to hold peaceful gatherings; and (4) to make international connections based on the world religious conventions in Prague and Tokyo.[4] Not only was their intention to ask for solidarity from victims at sites of tragedy on their march route surprising, but choosing Auschwitz as the destination was also unexpected. Of course, the Hiroshima-Auschwitz march no longer seems novel compared to the cosmopolitanization of the Holocaust today, as Auschwitz has become a destination representative of "dark tourism." However, considering there was only one university class on the Holocaust available across the United States in 1962, the pioneering nature of the Japanese peace activists became evident.

According to recollections of the Japanese participants, the Hiroshima-Auschwitz Peace March was first conceived at "the meeting of activists of different faiths for peace and reconciliation" held in Kyoto in July 1961. Kuwahara Hideaki, the former chair of the Hiroshima-Auschwitz Committee, recalls that the Polish Catholic priest Jan Frankowski first proposed the march.[5] In conflict with Kuwahara's account, Polish documents profile Frankowski as a member of the PAX, a Catholic collateral organization of the Polish communist party, who worked as a legislator and religious activist representing the Catholic population. Composed of aggressive Catholic nationalists under the protection of the Polish communist party, the PAX was a somewhat unique organization. Both politically and ideologically, the PAX should not coexist with the Communist Party, but the organization fed off political compromises with relative ease. Since the Catholic nationalism of the PAX targeted West Germany and not the Soviet Union, it would not clash with the official proletarian internationalism during the Cold War. Frankowski left the PAX as it remained traditionalist Catholic after the 1956 reform and organized the Christian Social Association (Chrześcijańskie Stowarzyszenie Społeczne, ChSS) in 1957. He also served in the *Sejm* (parliament) of the Polish People's Republic from 1947 to 1972.[6]

Judging from his political footprints over twenty-five years, it seems unlikely that Frankowski's proposal for the peace march truly represented either his personal take or the Catholic Church's stance, as remembered in Japan. More a Catholic politician who unhesitatingly collaborated with the communist party than a priest, Frankowski led the "secession" from Catholic maximalism represented by Bolesław Piasecki, the leader of the PAX Association. As the leader of the minimalist movement that aspired to preserve Catholic values through negotiations with the party, Frankowski received patronage in 1956 from then general secretary of the Polish United Workers' Party Edward Ochab for his compromise.[7] Based on Frankowski's biography, his stance on the international stage can reasonably be speculated as not his personal viewpoint but a result of specific coordination with the party. The Hiroshima-Auschwitz Peace March he proposed to the Japanese antinuclear pacifists was likely part of the anti-imperial, antinuclear campaign pursued by the communist regimes of the Eastern bloc. The mention of denuclearization of Central Europe in Sato's address at the commemoration event on January 27, 1963, exhibits an aspect of the peace march embedded in the Cold War as a satisfying political message for the Polish host.

Still, it would be an unfair assessment to claim that only the communist bloc in Eastern Europe politically appropriated the Hiroshima-Auschwitz Peace March. After signing the U.S.-Japan Security Treaty, known as the Anpo joyaku (安保条約) in Japanese, Japan was not free from the Cold War restraints. Situated on the opposite end of the global Cold War from the Polish People's Republic, the Japanese government expressed reluctance to issue visas for the Hiroshima peace marchers, reasoning that it was unfair to visit only Auschwitz, the site of genocidal crime committed by the allied country West Germany, and not the Katyn Forest, where the enemy Soviet Union massacred the Polish POWs.[8] The Cold War logic that prioritized surveys of communist crimes by the evil Soviet Union over visiting the site of crimes committed by West Germany, a key member of NATO and ally of liberal democracy, was evidently at work here. Thus, the peace march in 1962, from its departure from Hiroshima to its arrival at Auschwitz, was captive to the Cold War. The good will of peace was caught between the two sides of the Cold War logic. The Cold War system could not be broken through the efforts of individual marchers. Even behind the backdrop of the peace march, the global Cold War was in operation—the emphasis was not on the peace per se but on the memory and publicity of it. The content of peace varied widely depending on whose peace it was. Thus, the Cold War logic territorialized the possibility of mnemonic solidarity in the face of the universal tragedies of humankind, namely, the atomic bombs and the Holocaust.

In June 1961, a year before the peace march began, then mayor of Dresden Hans Bonn sent a letter to the mayor of Hiroshima suggesting a sister-city relationship between the two cities. The letter was intended to convince the city of Hiroshima to participate in the peacekeeping battle against the rise of militarism across the border between East and West. Under the communist regime of East Germany, Dresden was remembered as the symbol of British and American imperial barbarity that killed twenty-five thousand "innocent" citizens and destroyed the opera house and the Frauenkirche. Judged by the cause and aspects of the sacrifice, the tragedy of Hiroshima could be better linked to Dresden than to Auschwitz. Auschwitz's symbolic power would have doubtlessly been at work for the activists to choose it as the destination for their march. Still, international politics during the Cold War would likely have been a more significant factor behind the scenes. Receiving no response from Hiroshima, the Dresden mayor wrote again in 1963 to propose a sister-city relationship, but the mayor of Hiroshima remained silent. The image of the Dresden bombing, in which the UK and U.S. air forces played the villain, could potentially evoke imperial Japan's militaristic slogan "devilish and bestial Americans and British" (鬼畜美英). The political risk of being accused of cooperating with the communist regime of East Germany would also have been a barrier. Thus, while the atomic bomb victims' empathy and sensitivity toward the victims of the Holocaust were encouraged, mnemonic solidarity with the victims of the Dresden bombing was discouraged due to the political climate of the Cold War.

The Cold War's impact on the remembrance of the Japanese atomic bomb victims has remained intact to this day in Nagasaki Peace Park, more than the thirty years since the fall of the Berlin Wall. Built near ground zero, the Peace Park is home to several monuments sent from around the world in sympathy and consolation. It is intriguing to observe these monuments standing in an area called "the peace symbol zone": the monuments and sculptures from the liberal West were sent by municipal authorities or civilians of Nagasaki's sister cities, whereas the memorials from the communist block were all sent by state authorities. The monuments sent from the liberal side in the 1980s, toward the end of the Cold War, all bear engravings such as "Porto, 1978," "Middelburg, 1983," "Pistoia, 1987," "Santos, 1988," "Ankara, 1991," or "St. Paul, 1992," indicating the mayors and citizens as their senders. The anti-communist allies were probably not eager to send monuments to the memorial park for the atomic bombing, which could be memorialized as a crime committed by U.S. imperialism. On the contrary, monuments from the communist side are marked "Czechoslovakia, 1980," "Bulgaria, 1980," "East Germany, 1981," "U.S.S.R., 1985," "People's Republic of China, 1985," "Poland, 1986," and "Cuba, 1988," denoting the states as the senders as they had no reason to avoid commemorating U.S. imperialist crimes. Though all the monuments from both sides are uniformly inscribed with "peace," "friendship," and "love," the subjects and methods of remembering the A-bombing of Nagasaki differ sharply along the Iron Curtain.

The goodwill of the Hiroshima-Auschwitz marchers fell apart from the start due to the cold-blooded political calculations of the Cold War. However, the Cold War cannot be the sole object of blame. The participants' historical consciousness was also a problem that cannot be easily dismissed. Carrying the memories of the first-ever victims of the atomic bombing, the marchers heading to Auschwitz were met with an embarrassing history in Singapore. Around the time they arrived in May 1962, hundreds of corpses of Chinese civilians massacred by the Japanese military were discovered at a construction site by a beach in Singapore. It was shocking news for the Japanese marchers who had forgotten about the Japanese war crimes committed against their Asian neighbors. Surprised by the anti-Japanese sentiment that filled the city, Sato, the leader of the peace march, led a Buddhist service in memory of the victims of the Japanese Army. The participants ended up helping in the recovery of human remains. They were perplexed by the suddenly elevated difficulty of their mission, which now included apologizing to the families of the victims of the Japanese atrocities to convince them of the march's cause—honoring Japanese atomic bomb victims. It was an unexpected encounter between the Hiroshima victims, who considered themselves the biggest victims of World War II, and the victims of Japanese imperialism.[9] The message of the peace march for solidarity between victims of Hiroshima and Auschwitz had been celebrated around the world until that point, but it began to wobble with this encounter in Singapore, which revealed that the marchers, fixated on the frame of Japan as the victim, had been oblivious of the Japanese war crimes and their victims in neighboring countries.

The experience of discovering the victims of Japanese war crimes in Asia was as significant as the experience of Auschwitz or Yad Vashem of Israel. If the march highlighted only the suffering and sacrifice of the Japanese while keeping Japanese crime in the dark, its meaning could not but fade. Unless it connected the memories of the Nanjing massacre, the Three Alls Policy that aimed for the extinction of the Chinese, forced laborers conscripted from across Asia, and the "Comfort Women," the Hiroshima-Auschwitz Peace March could, at best, reach halfway into the peace. The Second Sino-Japanese War caused ten to fifteen million deaths of Chinese people on the Chinese front alone, in addition to approximately sixty million refugees and financial damage of fifty billion dollars. In Southeast Asia, Indonesia suffered the most considerable damage: around 300,000 out of a million forced laborers died, and about three million died of famine and plague on Java alone toward the end of the war. In French Indochina under the Japanese occupation, more than a million civilians starved to death in Tonkin and Annam in 1945 due to the requisitioning of rice by the Japanese military and the naval blockade by the Allied forces. On the Korean peninsula, the death toll of colonized Koreans who were drafted into the army and forced labor was around 200,000. During the battle of Manila in 1945, up to 90,000 civilians and 30,000 soldiers died in the Philippines.[10] It is impossible to commemorate only the 300,000 Japanese civilian victims killed by the

A-bombings while turning a blind eye to the countless victims of Japanese imperial atrocities.

Japan's battle against the "white" Pacific, a racist imperial domination by the United States that likened the Japanese to monkeys and parasites and treated them as "subhuman," should not exonerate Japan's imperialist crimes against its Asian neighbors.[11] Many Asians who were initially fascinated by Japan's ostensible "Asiacentrism" soon turned their backs on Japanese imperialism because of its war crimes, imperialist arrogance, ideological self-righteousness, and racist discrimination. Japan's Orientalism vis-à-vis its neighboring Asian countries dates back to the era of the Meiji Restoration. In the popular woodblock prints that depict the First Sino-Japanese War, the Japanese soldiers are pictured as tall, fair-skinned, and almost European-looking. At the same time, the Chinese are represented as ugly stereotypes of yellow-skinned people wearing pigtails.[12] Through the First Sino-Japanese War and the Russo-Japanese War, Japan's Orientalism developed into academic disciplines such as "Oriental Studies," "Oriental History," and "Colonial Policy Studies." In Japan's historical imagination since the First Sino-Japanese War, the history of China (支那) and Korean history made up "Oriental History" peripheral to Japanese history. As attested by the slogan "Leave Asia, enter Europe" (脱亜入欧), Japan's Orientalism was a hegemonic discourse to marginalize China and Korea as the "inferior East" and establish Japan as the "superior West."[13] Underlying Japan's superiority complex over its Asian neighbors was a stubborn self-pity that reduced itself to a "subaltern empire" that was pushed out of the ring of Western imperialism.[14] It is not easy to imagine the Hiroshima-Auschwitz Peace March to have remarkably veered from the memory culture of the Japanese victimhood sustained by subaltern imperialism.

The memory of atomic bombs reinforced victimhood in Japanese society and catalyzed the nationalization of memory. When the A-bomb victims became homogenized into Japanese citizens, the noncitizen victims like the Koreans, Taiwanese, Okinawans, Chinese, Allied POWs, and other resident aliens in Japan were erased in the A-bomb memory at the expense of the nationalization of victims. An excellent example of nationalized, exclusive victimhood is the monument to the Korean victims of the atomic bombing of Hiroshima, which was built in 1970 but could not be installed in the Peace Park until 1999.[15] Indeed, nonethnic Japanese victims of the atomic bomb, who were the Japanese "nationals" under colonialism, were marginalized in postwar Japan's war memory. Insofar as the memory of Hiroshima stayed disconnected from the context of Japan's imperial past, the embarrassment felt by Sato and the marchers in Singapore was bound to recur in Japan's antinuclear pacifist movement. The idea of connecting the A-bomb victims in Hiroshima to the Holocaust victims in Auschwitz across the globe was undoubtedly a valuable asset to the deterritorialized global memory formation. However, the episode of the march shows that the connection between Hiroshima and Auschwitz could be instrumentalized in victimhood nationalism. In fact, for the nationalist right-wingers or conservatives of Japan, Auschwitz and Hiroshima were the twin evils of World War II, and the Jews and the Japanese were together the biggest victims of white racism.[16] The connection between Hiroshima and Auschwitz as absolute evils has been passed down as an indispensable pillar upholding the cultural memory of Japan's victimhood nationalism.[17]

At times in the memory culture of postwar Japan, the association between Hiroshima and Auschwitz serves to stress that the sacrifice of Hiroshima was greater than that of Auschwitz. The poems of Kurihara Sadako, a liberal poet and a peace activist from Hiroshima, uninhibitedly display such a stance. Having depicted Auschwitz and Hiroshima/Nagasaki as the two biggest holocausts in history, Kurihara also wrote with a nuance that Auschwitz was "over" but Hiroshima was not, as the survivors were still suffering from its aftereffects.[18] Interestingly, the Japanese delegation from Hiroshima and Nagasaki was the largest among the international delegates who attended the event to commemorate the fortieth anniversary of the Mỹ Lai massacre by the U.S. military during the Vietnam War on March 16, 2008. The Japanese delegates compared the atomic bombs with the impact of Agent Orange in Vietnam. Hiroshima and Nagasaki were compared with Mỹ Lai in that they were all mass murders of civilians.[19] Such a juxtaposition, which seemingly aspires to the deterritorialization of memory, winds up in the reterritorialization of memory, perhaps due to the political effect ensuing from simplified identification. By placing the memory of Japanese sacrifice in the associative network of transnational memory, the simplified identification has reinforced victimhood nationalism in the postwar Japanese mnemoscape.

WHOSE AUSCHWITZ?

Since its liberation by the Red Army on January 27, 1945, Auschwitz has been deemed a site of deterritorialized memory, symbolizing the pain of humanity across all states, nations, ideologies, and religions. Still, even the Holocaust memory was thoroughly peripheralized in the Eastern European communist bloc, especially during the Stalinist era (1948–1953). The Holocaust did not fit the official narrative that viewed World War II as the antifascist struggle of the international working class and the "great patriotic war" of the Soviet people. Even in Poland, the memory of the Holocaust was peripheralized under the communist regime, following the precedent of the Soviet Union.[20] Zionist literature of newly established Israel also depicted the Jewish Holocaust survivors as passive subjects deprived of agency.[21] The Holocaust was a topic avoided in the public sphere; when it was discussed in Israel, the discussion was limited to the memories of the heroic warriors of the Warsaw ghetto uprising. In the newborn state of Israel, the Holocaust memory was narrowed down into specific topics like "the Holocaust and ghetto uprising," "the Holocaust and heroism," and "martyrs and heroes," while the memory of victimization was suppressed. The trend of heroism was directly reflected in historiography, sublimating the warriors at Masada into the ancient Hebrew fighters for national independence. Holocaust victims were mentioned only as the backdrop to glorify these ancient and modern Hebrew heroes.[22] For different reasons, the Jewish community in the United States avoided the discussion of the Holocaust. Under the political pressure of the Cold War, Jewish Americans prioritized debunking the stereotype of "Jewish Commies." Jewish Americans had to resonate with American foreign policy that positioned

West Germany as a bulwark against Bolshevism. Their archenemy was not Nazis but "antisemitic" Bolsheviks in the Soviet Union.[23]

Nevertheless, Auschwitz as a memory site could not be forgotten. Because its universal symbolism stemmed from such a formidable scale of tragedy, Auschwitz had been a political arena where different memories of diverse victims competed. The Polish United Workers' Party set Auschwitz as the stage for the horror play that demonstrated the ultimate criminality of monopoly capitalism and had plans to turn it into an international memorial to the resistance and martyrdom of the Poles and other nations.[24] The stubborn internationalism in the Auschwitz remembrance was a screen for the ethnic nationalism of the partisan faction within the Polish communist party. The antisemitic campaign of Polish national communists led by Mieczysław Moczar in 1968 started with an attack on the editor of the *Wielka Encyklopedia Powszechna PWN* (Great universal encyclopedia PWN), published in twelve volumes in 1967; the conflict sprang from the encyclopedia's entries on "concentration camp" and "extermination camp" that defined the latter as entirely for Jews while the former was for everyone. The national communists suspected that this binary was a disingenuous attempt to emphasize the Jewish suffering and underestimate the Poles' sacrifices. The conflict was settled as the Jewish communist editor of the encyclopedia was exiled to Sweden. Still, it was only a harbinger of the nationwide anti-Zionist campaign led by the party in 1968.[25] The year 1968 reminded Jewish Poles of the experience of Auschwitz, and Holocaust survivors again had to endure ostracizing and alienation from their Polish neighbors.[26]

The layout of the Auschwitz memorial attested to the hypocrisy of proletarian internationalism proclaimed by the Polish Communist Party. By separating each building of the camp by state, the party intended to classify the Jewish victims as Greeks, Dutch, Italians, etc., according to their country of origin. Later, more exhibitions opened for victims from Czechoslovakia, Hungary, East Germany, and the Soviet Union in the 1960s; Yugoslavia, Austria, France, the Netherlands, Italy, and Poland in the 1970s–1980s; and even for Danish and Bulgarian victims who were never put in Auschwitz.[27] For a while, however, Jews were categorically nonexistent in Auschwitz, as all victims were categorized by their nationality/citizenship. According to the principle of the official commemoration in communist Poland, Jewish victims, with no state of Israel at the time of the Holocaust could be remembered only through their European citizenship. At the commemoration of the Liberation of Auschwitz in 1967, then prime minister Józef Cyrankiewicz addressed the Auschwitz victims, whose number he exaggerated to four million, without a single word about Jewish people.[28] It is difficult to imagine that Cyrankiewicz, who was imprisoned in Auschwitz as a Polish socialist resistance, was unaware of at least the rough demographics of Auschwitz.

After a series of controversies, the exhibition space for Jewish victims opened in 1968 on the last Saturday of Passover, when the antisemitic campaign in Poland was at its peak. Naturally, those who kept the Sabbath could not attend the opening.[29] Adding insult to injury, at the international commemoration event, the Polish word for Jews—Żydzi—was called at the very end of the alphabetized list of nationalities of Auschwitz victims. Under the communist regime, the official guide to Auschwitz stressed the deaths of six million "Polish citizens," the number of all victims under Nazi oppression. In memory politics, Jews were counted as Poles only when added to the number of victims to highlight the Polish sacrifices. Only a Jew who died Polish could be a great Pole. To borrow the words of Iwona Irwin-Zarecka, Jews could obtain Polish citizenship only posthumously.[30] When the "politics of numbers," which is characteristic of victimhood nationalism, attempted to maximize the number of Polish victims, the number of Jewish victims from Poland was invaluable. Thus, it is not shocking that Auschwitz, as a site of memory, became an arena for competition between Polish and Jewish victimhood under the national communist regime of Poland.

The official memory concocted by the Polish United Workers' Party was, in a nutshell, that the Nazis' target of extermination was the Poles, and that Jews were merely subject to forced migration. The memory politics of the party, such as converting the Warsaw ghetto uprising in 1943 into "a unique battle led by the Polish underground partisans," turning Auschwitz into the shrine of Polish national martyrs, and banning the screening of Claude Lanzmann's film *Shoah*, all resonated with the Polish victimhood. Jews were marginalized also in the party historiography of the Polish communist movement. The Jewish leadership who led the Social Democracy of the Kingdom of Poland (SDKP) and created the party platform, Leon Jogiches and Róża Luksemburg, was decentered in history to make way for the "pure" Polish leadership, including Cezaryna Wojnarowska.[31] A society's memory culture does not change so quickly—a poll conducted in 1992, after the fall of the communist regime and amid the swift democratization, suggests that 47 percent of Poles still remembered Auschwitz as the shrine of Polish martyrdom. Throughout the 1990s nationalist history textbooks secured a hierarchy of victims by stating that the Nazis aimed for the physical extermination of the Polish nation while Jews were simply to be banished from Europe. In this hierarchy, the Jewish victims were placed under the Polish martyrs.[32]

The debate on the Auschwitz Cross might be the most allegorical anecdote about Auschwitz as both the place of universal human tragedy and the site of Poland's national suffering, revealing the tension between deterritorialization and reterritorialization of memory. As the Catholic cross symbolized the medieval pogrom for the Jewish community, many Jews found the cross erected in Auschwitz to be a provocation from Catholics. This symbolic conflict between the Jewish and Polish peoples over the Auschwitz Cross surfaced when Pope John Paul II visited Auschwitz in 1979, where he served mass between Crematorium II and IV at Birkenau. To commemorate his mass, a Carmelite convent opened in 1984 in the building that has been used as storage for Zyklon B gas cans. The opening of the convent was not particularly upsetting, given the Polish tradition of erecting a monument where the pope visited or said mass.[33] The problem was the place—the convent built on the very site of the storage facility for the poison gas that mass murdered Jews. Many Jews felt that the Carmelite convent occupying the poison gas storage facility in Auschwitz symbolized the martyrdom and sacrifice of Polish Catholics rather than the Jewish victims of the Holocaust.

The Catholic Church of Poland introduced the Carmelite convent as the holy symbol of love, peace, and reconciliation, but rabbis had a different interpretation. Avraham Weiss, the Orthodox rabbi who led a liberal religious movement in support of the ordination of women and legalization of same-sex marriage, criticized that the convent was built as a part of the Vatican's grand scheme to de-Jewishize and Christianize the Holocaust and strongly demanded its removal.[34] The rabbis must have worried that the revival of the Jewish memories of Auschwitz that the national communists had obliterated would fall back under the name of universal love and salvation of Catholicism. In response to the unrelenting protests from the Jewish community around the world, representatives of the Roman Catholic Church and European Jewish leaders met in Geneva in 1987. They agreed to relocate the Carmelite convent by February 1989. The agreement seemed to calm the conflict, which stemmed from the fact that Auschwitz is a site of multilayered memories, at once the most prominent Jewish cemetery where over a million Jews were killed, the shrine of Catholic martyrs like Maksymilian Kolbe and Edith Stein, and the location where the Soviet POWs, socialists, the Romani people, sexual and gender minorities, and the Polish resistance perished.[35] Of course, in the age of the globalization of memory, in which people empathize with the suffering of others, antagonism and conflicts often occur in sites of multilayered memories. Sometimes, those conflictual memories can coexist to stimulate oppositional memories without being exclusive, and at other times, they obey the rule of a zero-sum game to suppress and obliterate the different memories. Unfortunately, what dominated Auschwitz was the hostile and competitive zero-sum game over memories.

Although the communist regime of Poland purged the memory of the Jewish victims after the end of World War II, the post–Cold War memory of Auschwitz progressed in the direction of "Jewishization of Auschwitz to de-Polandize Oświęcim."[36] As the pendulum swung between "Polandization/de-Jewishization" and "Jewishization/de-Polandization," Auschwitz became an arena of competition between nationalist memories that were continuously reterritorializing the cosmopolitan memory. The agreement to relocate the Carmelite convent by 1989 could not realistically be enforced. Franciszek Macharski, cardinal and archbishop of Kraków who oversaw the Oświęcim parish, disclosed that there had been difficulties in finding a new place for the convent due to the uncooperative Polish government. Complaints about the relocation burst from within the Catholic Church of Poland, not to mention from the nuns of the Carmelite convent. In July 1989 seven Jewish memory activists in stripes, including Avraham Weiss, climbed up the convent fence in protest for its immediate removal.[37] The workers at the convent poured filth on the protesters and dragged them out, under the watch of the police and the nuns. Subsequently, on July 27, a hundred members of a Jewish students organization from Western Europe staged a sit-in protest in front of the convent, chanting, "Carmelite convent must leave Auschwitz." Some residents who were watching the demonstration responded angrily to the students by yelling, "Go back to Palestine." Others tried to persuade Jewish protesters that "the nuns pray for all the victims, including the Jews."[38]

Cardinal Józef Glemp, who was the head of Roman Catholic Church in Poland, expressed relief that neither the nuns nor the convent were hurt and implored the Jews "who control the world's media" not to incite anti-Polish sentiments.[39] Because of this remark, Cardinal Glemp had to cancel his U.S. visit planned for the fall of 1989. Only after he acknowledged two years later that his remark could have reinforced negative stereotypes of the Jewish people could he visit the United States.[40] Similarly, Cardinal Macharski criticized the Jewish activists for disrespecting the human rights of the nuns and the dignity of Christians.[41] After much tumult, the Carmelite convent was relocated in 1993 by the decision of Pope John Paul II. Then, the Jewish community problematized the huge papal cross that still stood on the site—installed to commemorate the pope's mass.[42] This seven-meter-tall cross was not included in the Geneva agreement as it was yet to be erected at the time of the deal. Even after the relocation of the Carmelite convent, the Jewish community argued that they could not allow the Catholic cross at Auschwitz-Birkenau, where the Jewish deaths and pain were piled on top of each other. For the Jewish people who suffered discrimination and pogroms by Christians, the cross symbolized not love and salvation but bigotry and death. Medieval pogroms, in which the cross-holding Christian neighbors murdered Jews, were never erased from the Jewish collective memory.

In February 1998 another wave of controversy arose when Krzysztof Śliwiński, the plenipotentiary of Poland's Ministry of Foreign Affairs responsible for contacts with the Jewish diaspora, said in an interview with the French newspaper *La Croix* that the papal cross should also be removed. With Lech Wałęsa in the vanguard, devout Catholic politicians, including 130 members of the congress and 16 senators and the Catholic Church of Poland led by Cardinal Glemp, voiced that the papal cross should remain protected from the Jews. In April 1998 signs that read "Protect the cross," "Protect Jesus in Auschwitz," and "Germans killed Poles here from 1940 to 1945" were plastered on the convent's fence, which was along the route of the annual International March of the Living.[43] The newly installed crosses and slogans such as "the Jews' Holocaust of Poland, 1945–1956" attested to the gravity of the situation.[44] Such statements reflected the antisemitic and anticommunist understanding of history, in a belief that the Stalinist regime imposed on Poland was a collaborative effort between Russian Bolsheviks and Jewish communists. Thus, signs full of antisemitic bigotry, like "Jewish commies," came to decorate the convent at the Auschwitz concentration camp. Not only was the cross guarded, but more crosses, small and large, were erected. Kazimierz Świtoń, a trade union activist and a lawmaker of the ultranationalist party Confederation of Independent Poland (Konfederacja Polski Niepodległej, KPN) in the early 1990s, appointed himself as guardian of the Auschwitz Cross. Świtoń declared that he would not leave the site until there was a guarantee that the cross dedicated to the Polish victims would stand there forever.[45] He also appealed to the Polish citizens that there should be 152 more crosses erected to commemorate the 152 Polish victims who had died in Carmelite convent's front yard. His appeal brought passionate responses from Polish compatriots, resulting in 135 crosses standing there by August and 236 at the end of September 1998.

The Jewish community all over the world fiercely denounced the audacity of erecting more crosses instead of removing the controversial ones. Correspondingly, the Polish Catholic nationalists were again furious and began a campaign to erect a thousand crosses in Auschwitz.

They even threatened the Jewish protesters that they had installed booby traps under the cross to blow up if anyone tried to remove it. The Polish citizens who participated in the campaign maintained their position as if to say, "What is wrong with erecting our Catholic crosses in our country on our soil?" The memory of the communist regime that commanded the removal of crosses from public spaces added nationalist significance to the religious symbol of the crucifix, ultimately turning the Auschwitz Cross into an explosive issue. As the image of the Russians, the archenemy of the Polish nation who forced an anti-Catholic foreign ideology that was communism, overlapped with the image of the Jews who tried to break into the convent demanding that the cross be removed from Auschwitz, the Auschwitz Cross became a symbol of the affective memory that touched the emotions of the Poles. Throughout the summer of 1998, "the Valley of Crosses" laid out in the convent's courtyard became a pilgrimage site for patriotic Catholics, serving as a place of remembrance where masses, prayers, political demonstrations, and nationalist incitement met amid the web of traditional and political religions. In May 1999 the Polish Army finally cleared the Valley of the Crosses and collected 322 crosses.

However, the papal cross still stands even to this day.[46] If you stand in front of the window on the second floor of Block 11, the former prison in Auschwitz where Father Maksymilian Kolbe sacrificed himself on behalf of his fellow prisoners and Sister Edith Stein of the Carmelite convent was martyred, you can still see the papal cross standing on the other side the wall—it is impossible to miss it in this spatial setting. It is not wrong to say that the Auschwitz Cross is situated within the memory of the two Catholic martyrs, as it is located between the Auschwitz-Birkenau Memorial Museum, where virtually all the Jews were murdered, and the Auschwitz I Memorial, which includes Block 11. Therefore, Rabbi Weiss's argument that the cross as a symbol of Jewish oppression since the medieval pogroms should be removed from the most significant Jewish cemetery can be at once persuasive and dissuasive—to argue that, because the Jewish sacrifice was predominant, Auschwitz should not commemorate the victims of other faiths, including

Catholic, Jehovah's Witnesses, and the Romani people, points to religious egotism or ethnocentrism. Nevertheless, the Roman Catholic Church's worship of martyrs like Father Kolbe and Sister Stein would feel exceedingly uncomfortable from a Jewish victim's perspective. Father Kolbe is the founder of *Mały Dziennik*, a journal for most aggressively antisemitic arguments.[47] Edith Stein was a converted Jewish Catholic. Though she had been a respected symbol of interreligious communication between Judaism and Catholicism, she also reminded the Jewish people of the painful memory of coerced conversion. It was against the grain of the collective sentiment of the Jewish community that a converted "Jewish" nun dictated the Catholic memory of the Holocaust, founded on the dichotomy of the evil Nazis versus the good Catholics.[48]

The Reuters article covering the four New York rabbis, including Avraham Weiss, who attended the event for the seventy-fifth anniversary of the liberation of Auschwitz on January 27, 2020, shows the ongoing state of the memory war between the Poles and the Jews to reterritorialize Auschwitz.[49] Auschwitz had long since been selected as a World Heritage Site by UNESCO, yet the two nations were still fighting over whose heritage it was. This is not to mention that the cosmopolitanization of the Holocaust suggests that the memories of global Auschwitz victims had already spread beyond the Polish borders and Jewish community. Still, on the other side of the cosmopolitan memories the ongoing conflict that dominated the global memory formation, between the deterritorializing transnational memories and the reterritorializing national memories, has resumed. With the globalization of memory, the conflict between deterritorializing and reterritorializing memories has tended to go even deeper. As memories, which stay disconnected from each other in the past, become entangled, the competition among them intensifies. Before the globalization of memory, memory wars were limited to intranational clashes and national struggles over hegemony in domestic politics. It has expanded into a global issue, as the emerging field of international relations, "memory diplomacy," suggests.

ANNE FRANK COMES TO JAPAN

When *The Diary of a Young Girl* was first published in the Netherlands in 1947, only 1,500 copies were sold. Its German and French translations were published subsequently, but the sales stayed meager. In the United States, its theatrical adaptation, made by a Hollywood playwright for a Broadway production, drew more attention than the actual book. Later, this play was criticized for de-Jewishizing the Holocaust by foregrounding emotions that any adolescent girl might have at that age over the elements of real Jewish life at the time.[50] The first edition of the German translation published in West Germany in 1950 amounted to 4,500 books, though the market reception was lukewarm. *The Diary of a Young Girl* became known gradually. It was reprinted many times—700,000 copies were printed by 1955, and 2.5 million copies of the German translation alone were sold by the end of the twentieth century. The cover of the paperback edition in 1955 had a quote from the book ("Despite everything, I still believe that people are good at heart") that drew particular attention.[51] Sounding like forgiveness from the victim, it might have made the book more popular among German readers, who felt as if Anne Frank were forgiving them. At the same time, the quote incidentally obliterated the cruel history that murdered Anne and peripheralized the Holocaust memory. It is not entirely unreasonable that some people assume that if Anne could come back to life from the concentration camp, she would have been appalled at the absurd abuses of her diary.[52] It is surprising, however, that the country where the most copies of *The Diary of a Young Girl* have been sold is Japan: four million copies since the first publication of the Japanese translation in 1952 until the late twentieth century. Considering the copies sold of at least four different cartoon adaptations and three distinct animated films, the number of Japanese who encountered Anne Frank's diary in any form is much higher than four million.

The only Holocaust Education Center in East Asia is also in Japan. Standing in the middle of nowhere in a rice field in the small village of Fukuyama, located about eighty kilometers away from where the A-bomb landed in Hiroshima, the Holocaust Education Center had visits from more than 100,000 Japanese children on field trips since its founding in 1995.[53] Upon entering the center through the Anne Frank Rose Garden, visitors are greeted at the top of the staircase to the second floor by a plaque that reads "Never again!" in Hebrew, English, and Japanese.[54] The main exhibition space on the second floor displays a brief history of the Holocaust for laypeople, a diorama of the Auschwitz-Birkenau concentration camp, the wall made of Jerusalem stones, and the reproductions of the ghetto wall, Anne's diary, and Anne's room in the hiding place. A descendant of the chestnut tree from Anne's house in Amsterdam growing in front of the center is also impressive. Still, the 1.5 million origami cranes representing the 1.5 million Jewish children who died in the Holocaust look significant.[55] The museum explains that they are from children all over Japan who voluntarily sent their best attempts at origami. On the homepage of the center's website are messages to students from the director, Rev. Otsuka Makoto, and from Elie Wiesel. Borrowing the words of Otto Frank, Anne's father, the director writes, "Please do not just express sympathy toward Anne and the 1.5 million children but become someone who can do anything for peace." Wiesel's message suggests that students find answers to "why educated people tried to kill all the Jews; how they could look calm and kill tens of thousands of children."[56]

It is hard not to sense a specific excess in this impressive museum. This feeling of excessiveness can also be found in the locality of the center—surrounded by rice paddies in a rural town of central Japan, nine thousand kilometers away from Amsterdam—as well as in the recorded interviews of Rev. Otsuka. In his interview with the German media outlet *Deutsche Welle* in March 2015, Otsuka spoke of his incredible argument that, though historically unproven, Jews and the Japanese are of the same ancestry, and Judaism and State Shinto share many similarities. He went so far as to claim that even the Japanese language and Hebrew sounded similar.[57] Such an excess of sympathy exhibits the desire to assuage the postwar despair of the Japanese in the code of "misery loves company" and secure Japan's status as a victim within the global memory formation. Also, it was an expression of the wish to have the international community officially confirm Japan's victimhood by identifying with Anne Frank, the icon of World War II victims. More than discovering their "own" Anne Frank in Hiroshima and Nagasaki, however, the excessive identification with Jewish victims is linked to the absence of self-criticism confronting the numerous "Anne Franks" in Japan's neighboring countries whose people the Japanese military slaughtered, maimed, and deprived of human dignity. According to Otsuka Makoto, the Holocaust Education Center does not take an interest in other war crimes, as it focuses only on the Holocaust.[58] His statement makes one wonder whether the memory of the Holocaust, transplanted in Japan in connection with the memory of the atomic bombing, operates as a screen memory to cover up Japanese war crimes in the Asia-Pacific War.

Of course, the Holocaust does not continuously operate as a self-exoneration of the war crime in Japan's postwar memory culture. Here, I would like to look closely at how the Japanese translation of Viktor Frankl's *Man's Search for Meaning* (夜と霧), published in 1956, was circulated and read in Japan. According to Morita Shogo, the Japanese publisher at Misuzu Shobo, the Japanese market was the stepping stone toward becoming an international bestseller for Frankl's book, which had gone out of print in Germany after one reprint. There were critiques even in Japan of the Japanese publisher's provocative advertisement that read, "the reality of the mass murder factory that slaughtered a thousand people." Later, the Japanese editor recollected that he had hoped to make the realities of Auschwitz and the Holocaust known in Japan from a self-critical perspective and worked on the book as an "expression of everyday political determination."[59] The "letter from the publisher" included at the beginning of this edition also states that the two events, namely, the Nanjing Massacre of 1937 and the mass murder in the Nazi concentration camps, demand a profound reflection on the essence of humanity.[60] The editor's note highlights the importance of learning about the Holocaust for the Japanese to remember their war crimes. There is an important distinction to be made between realizing one's crimes reflected in the mirror image of the other and insensitive overlapping of one's tragedy onto the other's. A nuanced analogy between the Nanjing Massacre by the Japanese military and the Holocaust by the Nazis can be a helpful tool to be used in reflecting on Japan's criminal past, whereas a flat equivalence between Hiroshima and Auschwitz conflates the victims of these two different atrocities. The editor's note calling forth the Nanjing Massacre in reflection of the Holocaust differs from how the memory of the Holocaust was consumed in the 1960s and 1970s as a tool to evoke and reinforce Japan's self-exculpatory memory of war.

The Japanese right-wing nationalism that denies aggression and massacre was the opposite side of the same coin with Japan's victimhood. Hayashi Fusao, a theoretician of postwar nationalism, insisted that "Great East Asian War" helped the Asian people to break free from the oppression of Western imperialism, which was only part of Japan's "one long war spanning about a century" against the West since the opening of the port by Admiral Perry in 1853. Inspired by the Hundred Years' War of Joan of Arc, Hayashi's theory of the "Hundred Years' War in East Asia" argues that it was inevitable that the U.S. ambition to build a "white Pacific" and Japan's passionate "defense of Asia" collided over the Pacific—the Pacific was the Strait of Dover between the United States and Japan, and the Asia-Pacific War was the noble fate of Japan.[61] Japan's self-consciousness as "the victim of Western imperialism" has remained central to Japanese memory culture since 1853. The interpretation of the Meiji Restoration as an anti-imperialist struggle of Asian peoples against Western imperialism, equating the Meiji Restoration with the Sepoy Rebellion of India or the Taiping Rebellion of China, can also be understood. Japan's victory in the Russo-Japanese War of 1905 had sown hope among the marginalized resistance nationalists against Western imperialism. As Mohandas Gandhi celebrated Japan's victory in a corner of South Africa, Rabindranath Tagore led his students on a victory march. For Ottoman soldier Mustafa Kemal, schoolboy Jawaharlal Nehru at Harrow School, China's "Father of the Nation" Sun Yat-sen, Mustafa Camil in Egypt, and others, Japan's victory caused a domino effect that signaled the collapse of the imperial West. W.E.B. Du Bois also spoke of the "pride of people of color" that erupted worldwide after Japan's victory in the Russo-Japanese War.[62]

In the tradition of Japan's nationalism in resistance against the West, Hayashi Fusao's theory of the Hundred Years' War is not novel. Ishiwara Kanji, the chief of staff of the Guangdong Army who planned and executed the "Manchurian Incident" in 1931, had been convinced of the inevitability of the Asia-Pacific War since 1927. The theory of the inevitable war was, in large part, a reaction to the legal discrimination against Japanese nationals in the United States, such as the Second Alien Land Law of 1920 and the Asian Exclusion Act of 1924. In different parts of Japan, anti-U.S. protest rallies were held, and voices demanding war against the United States grew louder. Books instigating anti-American sentiment, such as *The Japan-U.S. War: Japan Will Not Lose* (1924) by Ishimaru Dota and *The Treatise of Japan-U.S. War* (1925), were published one after another. As early as 1931, Ishiwara Kanji argued that the Manchuria-Mongolia problem could not be resolved without the determination to defeat the United States and that the Asia-Pacific War was inevitable in world history. For Japanese nationalists like Ishiwara, the U.S.-Japanese War was understood not simply as "a struggle over political hegemony in the Pacific Ocean" but as "the final battle between the U.S. and Japan as the respective champions of the Western and Eastern civilizations that had advanced over thousands of years of human history." Okawa Shumei, a Japanese Asianist of the right-wing nationalist movement, similarly stressed that the clash between Japan and the United States was an inevitable historical fate to build a new world order against the Anglo-Saxon hegemony.[63]

W.E.B. Du Bois, a representative black Marxist theoretician of race in the United States, also predicted that the Japanese occupation of Manchuria would end the white domination in Asia. He expected Japan to become the leader of Asia and the people of color. After visiting Manchukuo in 1936 and speaking with Yosuke Matsuoka, president of the South Manchuria Railway Company, Du Bois concluded that Manchukuo was utterly different from Africa or the West Indies controlled by white Europe. He recognized Manchukuo under the "Five Races Under One Union" ideology as an ideal colony embodying racial equality and a multiracial community without the white capitalist mistreatment. Upon leaving Manchukuo, Du Bois was convinced that the colonial project of the colored Japanese empire was free of exploitation and subordination, unlike the colonialism of white Europe.[64] This was not just Du Bois's impression. Nationalist leaders of Africa pushed for an alliance with Japan by organizing the International League of Darker Peoples. African American writers, including John Edward Bruce, published novels about Japan's victory in the imminent war between the United States and Japan—one of which included a scene where a Japanese flag flies over the surrendered U.S. forts in the Philippines and Hawaii, much to the distress of the U.S. Intelligence Agency.[65]

If *The Diary of a Young Girl* awakened the A-bombed Japanese victimhood, most Korean readers of the book were reminded of the Korean victims of Japanese colonialism. In a book review contest for elementary school children hosted by an online bookstore, the essays submitted were overwhelmingly about how the children would have had a similar experience as Anne had they "lived as a Korean during the Japanese occupation," when "Japan invaded Korea" and "imprisoned us for no reason," comparing the Nazis with the Japanese who "brutally conducted biological experiments on Koreans whom they thought as logs."[66] An exception to this trend is a review by a fourth grader uploaded in September 2020, which expresses frustration with being confined to the house because of COVID-19 and empathizes with how frustrated and sad Anne must have felt when she had to hide as if she did not exist.[67] On the other hand, many reviews written by adults focus on the psychological topography of a sensitive adolescent girl, love, sorrow, joy, and other precious everyday emotions, insights into racism and war in general, and the organized structure of Anne's writing.[68] While the instructional frame may influence elementary school students, readers tend to become more faithful to their opinions and impressions as they grow out of the external frame.

ZIONIST HEROISM IN SOUTH KOREA

A significant difference between the memory cultures of Japan and Korea in the 1960s was that the former often referred to the Holocaust, while the latter frequently called forth the Zionist state of Israel as its model. The Japanese took a greater interest in the sacrifice of the Jewish people; Koreans were more attracted to the heroic nationalism of Israel. In contrast to the heroic nationalism under the developmental dictatorship in the 1960s and 1970s, the memory culture in today's Korea rests heavily on the "Comfort Women" and forced labor during the Asia-Pacific War. The political democratization and its mnemonic aftermath increased the empathy toward the oppressed and innocent victims. Thus, memory culture in democratized Korea pivots to victimhood nationalism even more efficiently than its Japanese counterpart. Colonial Koreans were primarily interested in the Jewish pain and suffering that ensued from losing their own country. The daily newspapers of colonial Joseon were rich in content about the Jewish Autonomous Region in Birobidzhan, the conflict between Muslims and Jewish immigrants in Palestine, lessons from the biblical people of Israel regarding the identity formation of colonial Joseon, and internationally renowned Jewish figures.[69] According to the Naver News Library, a whopping 1,622 articles are about Jews in colonial Joseon's daily newspapers from March 5, 1920, when the first daily newspaper, *Chosun Ilbo*, was published, to August 15, 1945, the day of Korea's national liberation. Such contents seem to reflect the Korean intellectuals' empathy toward the Jewish people in the diaspora, having lost their own country.

Since the founding of Israel in 1947 and of South Korea in 1948, the interests of the Korean media have shifted from empathy toward the Jewish people to admiration for Israel's state-building and national integration efforts. Between August 15, 1945 (the independence of Korea), and December 31, 1999 (the end of the twentieth century), about sixty thousand articles about Israel and Jewish people were published in South Korea. There were continued reports on the Arab-Israeli War, the Suez Crisis, the major and minor conflicts between Israel and Egypt, Syria, Jordan, and other neighboring countries, and the Six-Day War. The Jewish representation was now changed from stateless victims to the heroic nationalism that built the powerful state of Israel with unrelenting patriotism. The heroic nationalism manifested in South Korean discourse about Israel became especially apparent after Israel's legendary victory in the Six-Day War of 1967. For Korean nationalists and power elites in pursuit of a strong nation-state, Zionist Israel has been a model for the future of Korea. Intriguingly, South Korean perception of the Six-Day War as a heroic event is the opposite of French Jewry's invocation of the victimhood of the Holocaust confronting the same war.[70]

Among the news articles, what warrants special attention is the Canaan declaration by the "New Wave Student Green Cross" that divorced the student group from "childish (protest) demonstrations" and purported to help rebuild the country, the fertile Canaan land flowing with milk and honey, the Canaan Farm founded by Elder Kim Yong-ki. Park Chung-hee, who assumed the chairmanship of the supreme council after the military coup in 1961, visited the Canaan Farm in February 1962 to commend Kim Yong-ki and his family over lunch. Park looks awkward yet strangely eye-catching in the photo, where he prays as a "heretic" visiting the Canaan Farm that started the agricultural revolution and produced "Founding Tea" and "Founding Brooms," which were advertised to be better than their imported counterparts. The Canaan Farm showed Park the way to a patriotic agricultural revolution.[71] In July 1962 the South Korean government launched the "farm pioneering squad," a Korean version of the kibbutz, to which the Israeli government responded in December 1963 by donating 1,100 USD to support the publication of Korean books about the kibbutz system.[72] During the "New Village Movement" of the early 1970s, Park's love for Canaan continued, and the Canaan Farm School served as a cradle to nurture rural leaders of the movement.[73] The kibbutz, "the cradle of Israeli wealth," extended to become a model of South Korea's modernization toward the "Miracle on the Han River." Even today, for South Korea's ultra-right-wing nationalists, the "strong small state" of Israel remains the most cherished model to win the international competition for nation-building.

The opposing tendencies to remember Israel as the victim of the Holocaust and Israel as the mighty nation of Zionist heroes, taken by right-wing nationalists in Japan and Korea, reveal the complexity inherent in deterritorialization and reterritorialization of memory. It was in 1979 when the word "Holocaust" first appeared in South Korean media—thanks to the broadcasting of Korean-dubbed *Holocaust*, the American television miniseries produced by NBC in 1978. Among the 175 times the word "Holocaust" appeared from the year of national liberation (1945) to 1999, 149 appearances happened within the 1990s—a period during which the word "Jewish" was used more frequently in newspapers than was "Israel." In the 1990s the representation of Israel was shifting from a heroic warrior to an aggrieved victim. Creating new compilation guidelines to describe the Holocaust in world history textbooks in the sixth curriculum, reorganized in 1992, must have played a significant role. The new guidelines for Holocaust education were reflective of the globalization of memory. The Holocaust education to teach empathy toward victims resonated with the human rights concern. It was a sign that Korea was willing to join the victimhood competition. The nationalist struggle to recognize moral righteousness in the global memory formation had changed the nationalist discourse from heroic nationalism to victimhood nationalism. In the era of globalization of memory, victimhood nationalism, which argues for a nation's collective victimhood to gain the empathy of the global public sphere, had become the dominant narrative regulating cultural memory in many countries.

The phenomenon since the 1990s, in which a memory culture transforms from nationalist heroism to the sublimation of the Korean victims, is peculiar to "the cosmopolitanization of the Holocaust." A memory that emphasizes the veritable victimhood of one's people puts the Holocaust in a frame of reference and comparison. In Korea, the heroic nationalism modeled on Israel had shifted to victimhood nationalism, focusing on the Holocaust. Interestingly, the Holocaust reference is used frequently in Korean readers' criticisms of *So Far from the Bamboo Grove*, a story about the suffering of Japanese refugees, in the novel's Amazon review section. A reader who appears to be Korean American writes:

> This might be a "well written" book, but it is completely distorting the truth about the Japanese WW2 aggressions and atrocities. . . . If Anne Frank were a German. She was still alive to this day, and if she wrote about the mindless rapes committed by Jewish resistance fighters and Jewish American soldiers [sic] after WW2 and no mention

was made about the Holocaust during WW2. Wouldn't you think that is a DISTORTION of history?

Similar reviews appear throughout the review section. "This book is akin to an escape narrative of an SS officer's family running away from Birkenau Auschwitz [sic] concentration camp while the heroine daughter of the Nazi officer is running away from cruel and dangerous Jews freed from concentration camps and Poles. Such a narrative is morally irresponsible and disgusting material to force upon innocent children." In addition to these two reviews, negative comments prevail: "lie," "wonderful lies," "fabricated history," "horrible fiction," and "Japan's sinister scheme to make themselves look like victims by villainizing neighbor Asian nations."[74] What is interesting here is the commenters' use of the Holocaust as a rhetorical device to make American readers, who are supposedly less knowledgeable about East Asian history, understand the gravity of their concern.

The reason Korea's cultural memory changed its criterion of comparison from the discourse of Zionist heroes to the Holocaust victims is related to the emergence of victimhood nationalism centering on the memory of the Japanese military "Comfort Women." The best example would be the meeting of the Korean "Comfort Women" victims and the Holocaust survivors at the Kupferberg Holocaust Center of Queensborough Community College in New York City on December 13, 2011. Co-organized by the Korean American Civic Empowerment and the Kupferberg Holocaust Center, this meeting eloquently shows how two collective memories that emigrated to different countries are joined and interact.[75] Memories of the Korean "Comfort Women" and the Jewish survivors of the Holocaust traveled across the Pacific and Atlantic Oceans to meet in the United States. Even if the Japanese military "Comfort Women" and the Holocaust might not have been directly linked to U.S. history at the time of the tragedies, they have now become part of the memories of the United States through immigration. It is probably not a coincidence that the Korean American memory activists for "Comfort Women" often choose a Jewish cultural center as the venue of their press conference. The trajectory in which Korea's memory culture has appropriated the memory of the Holocaust since the 1990s is too evident for a coincidence. The invisible hand of victimhood nationalism lingers even over this exemplary case of globalization of memory.

The indigenization of the Holocaust in today's South Korea has more than the emergence of global memory formation as its background. Another vital setting was the democratization of 1987, which released the suppressed memories from the Cold War restrictions and facilitated the investigation into the mass killing of civilians by the state. In the process, the Holocaust as a rhetorical device was often utilized to evoke affective memories about the victims of political genocides. Lee San-ha, a left-wing nationalist poet of the 1990s, dedicated his epic poem *Hallasan* to "all revolutionaries who died heroically in battle for the national liberation and unification of our homeland." Having visited Auschwitz, he once described the Jeju uprising and other Korean political massacres as "the Korean version of Auschwitz without the gas chamber."[76] In another literary work, *Song of Sorrows* by Jeong Chan, the novel's protagonist, who is a journalist covering Chopin Conservatory of Music in Poland, falls in love with the Polish composer Henryk Górecki's *Symphony No. 3: Symphony of Sorrowful Songs* and ends up visiting the Auschwitz concentration camp.[77] In contrast to many novels about the Gwangju Uprising that express ethical resentment against state violence, Jeong Chan's story invites readers through emotions. It moves on to the question of how to cross the river of sorrow. By overlapping the Holocaust with Gwangju in the memory of victimhood, the novel transposes the rage into grief.[78]

Even for rhetorical purposes, such a metaphor that makes direct connections between Jeju, Gwangju, and Auschwitz warrants suspicion of oversimplifying history for emotional appeal—a fabulous proof that the hegemonic memory culture regulating South Korea's memory politics uses the Holocaust as a narratological benchmark. If the memory politics under the Park Chung-hee regime, which aimed for voluntary mobilization of the masses under the title of "national democracy" and "the Korean way of democracy," sought a world-historical alibi from Israel's heroic nationalism, the democracy activists who protested against the mass dictatorship in 1970s–1980s founded their criticism of the state violence on Israel's victimhood nationalism and the Holocaust. This analogy between memories would have been more convincing if it juxtaposed the anticommunist atrocities that happened in South Korea with the communist crimes by the North Korean Stalinists rather than with the Holocaust. However, the leftist intellectuals spearheading the criticism of political genocide in South Korea have often been preoccupied with the zero-sum logic of the Cold War by which they keep quiet about North Korea's political crimes, as if bringing up the state violence of North Korea would abate their critique of the ideological genocide in South Korea.

On the opposite end, North Korean democracy activists also reference the Holocaust. Organized by North Korean exiles, the photo exhibition of the "North Korean Holocaust" draws attention by making parallels between the photographs of the Nazi Holocaust and North Korea's human rights violations and of Auschwitz and political prisoners' camps in North Korea. The ad for the exhibition quotes Thomas Buergenthal, a Holocaust survivor who served as the judge for the International Court of Justice, to garner people's attention: "I believe that the conditions in the [North] Korean prison camps are as terrible, or even worse than those I saw and experienced in my youth in these Nazi camps." It also unreservedly refers to a quote by Martin Luther King Jr.: "The ultimate tragedy is not the oppression and cruelty by the bad people but the silence over that by the good people."[79] Holocaust as a rhetorical device would perhaps be the only common property shared by both leftist pro-North nationalists and anticommunist nationalist defectors from the North—that is, the political tribalism of the Cold War memory politics turned the Holocaust into an "objective" reference shared by both right and left. As attested by the case of Korea, the memory politics where victimhood nationalism is justified via simplistic juxtaposition and self-serving comparison between the Holocaust and any given nation's tragic past is problematic. It would not be much of an exaggeration to say that the most distinct problem regarding the indigenization of the Holocaust is precisely this—its oversimplified juxtaposition and comparison.

That said, such a problem does not automatically justify the Eurocentric assessment that easily generalizes non-Western societies' memories of the Holocaust as "inaccurate," "vague," and "misleading."[80] Western and Israeli memories of the Holocaust also have plenty of problems. The judgment that the Holocaust cannot have a tangible impact outside of Europe, Israel, and the United States tacitly presumes that the memories of only those who directly experienced the Holocaust are "authentic." Such a viewpoint preemptively blocks any critical intervention from the outside. It has been a long time since the Holocaust started operating as an authority for the global memory that promotes solidarity among various victims in the global memory formation. The tensions and fissures between deterritorializing and reterritorializing memories are phenomena observed not uniquely in East Asia. Such disagreements are inherent in the process of globalizing the Holocaust while emphasizing its incomparable, unique characteristics. The contradiction, which privileges Holocaust victims while vesting the memory of the Holocaust with the cosmopolitan ethics to globally protect human rights, along with the tension between the "globalized Holocaust" and the "real Holocaust," is in some ways inevitable.[81] The contradictory process in which the globalization of the Holocaust becomes the nationalization of the Holocaust also tends to make the tension between deterritorialization and reterritorialization a constant of global memory formation.

As we will see in the next chapter, the globalization and nationalization of memories and deterritorialization and reterritorialization of memories unfold in an even more complicated shape by intersecting with de- and overhistoricization.

6

DEHISTORICIZATION

MELANCHOLY OF THE DEFEATED

In October 1950 the Jewish American magazine *Commentary* published Hannah Arendt's reportage on postwar Germany suffering from the catastrophe of war. Depicting defeated Germany struggling in the ashes and ruins, Arendt's on-site report graphically delivers the agony of Germans who experienced "physical homelessness, social rootlessness, and political rightlessness."[1] "But nowhere is this nightmare of destruction and horror less felt and talked about than in Germany itself," Arendt writes. The Germans walked past the ruins everywhere in their destroyed cities without mourning for the dead or the fate of the refugees. In Arendt's eyes, the Germans could not sympathize with the pain of others. She was surprised by how deeply rooted the stubborn denial of and indifference to their past was among Germans, avoiding the painful work of self-criticism. The Germans Arendt met talked continuously about how much they suffered, and perhaps because their pain of defeat was too great, there was no sign of consideration for the Jewish victims. Arendt writes that even when they noticed she was Jewish, "no sign of sympathy, such as 'What happened to your family?'—but a deluge of stories about how Germans have suffered" followed, as if to "draw up a balance between German suffering and the suffering of others, the implication being that one side cancels the other."²

The collective mindset of victimhood nationalism, which believes that emphasizing the damage our nation had suffered would somehow reduce the damage done to others by us, was already present in postwar Germany. Arendt also had a hard time understanding the Germans' denials and excuses, which blamed all their suffering on the occupying forces. A widely held belief at the time among Germans was that the occupying troops were imposing unreasonable hardships on Germans for their problems—the British because they were afraid of competing with Germany in the future, the French due to their helpless nationalism, and the U.S. military because of its lack of understanding of the European mindset. German newspapers unreservedly used the word "*Schadenfreude*" to accuse the Allied forces of finding perverted pleasure in German misfortunes. Most Germans felt spiteful about the "victors." With the *Schadenfreude* discourses, Germans buried the accountability for Nazism, the Holocaust, and World War II under the pains inflicted by the occupying forces' malice and ignorance. The poster that pointed the finger at Germans, saying, "You are a sinner," with the backdrop of the Buchenwald concentration camp, could never awaken the German conscience and was considered as the Allies' wicked anti-German propaganda. "An otherwise quite normally intelligent woman" whom Arendt met in southern Germany even surprised her by telling her "the Russians had begun the war with an attack on Danzig."³ Despite the facts and realities of the war that had been revealed over the five years since its end, many Germans, like that woman, did not believe Nazism was the cause of World War II.

The Germans wanted to establish their self-image as noble sacrifices and cleanse the sins of humanity by replacing the concrete facts about World War II with vague, abstract questions like "Why must humans wage war?" They equated their pain of defeat to the punishment given to Adam and Eve for eating the forbidden fruit; the pain seemed worth it if it was the price of redemption for the sins of all humankind.⁴ The Germany Arendt witnessed in 1950 was completely different from

Germany today, the leading figure of critical memory to apologize and compensate for its crimes. The Germans' self-exculpatory memory that Arendt encountered in the early 1950s is also demonstrated by the polls conducted at the time: in a survey conducted in U.S.-occupied Germany in November 1946, 37 percent of German respondents expressed that they believed "the extermination of Jews, Poles, and other 'non-Aryans' was necessary for the safety of Germans." In the same survey, one out of three responded, "Jews cannot have the same rights as people of the Aryan race." Another poll done in 1952 showed a similar result: approximately 37 percent of the respondents answered that it was better for Germany to be rid of Jews. Even long after the war, many Germans held on to the belief that "Nazism was a good idea wrongly applied."[5] The minutes of the Bundestag of West Germany show how Germans firmly maintained their position as victims, first of Hitler and later of the Allies. In their collective memory, the German victims were abundant, yet the victims of German perpetration were nowhere to be found.[6] For a decade after the end of the war, students in West Germany spent more time reading Homer's *Iliad* in Greek than discussing World War II and the Holocaust, and history lectures stopped abruptly during the Weimar era.[7] No class time was allotted to learning about German crime during World War II.[8]

Denazification of postwar Germany was a myth. While high-ranking Nazis resisted denazification by avoiding punishment with fake identifications bought from the black market, the average Germans resisted by booing and neglecting the enforced de-Nazifying efforts. In the U.S.-led POW camp where seventeen-year-old boy soldier Günter Grass was imprisoned, the German POWs were always in firm denial of the appalling photographs of Buchenwald and Bergen-Belsen concentration camps presented to them by the American educators in starched and ironed shirts. Thinking the photos were U.S. propaganda, the German POWs would ask questions about how "negros" were treated in the United States to distract the American educators trying to lecture about the horror of racism.[9] At a youth meeting of the Christian Democratic Union in U.S.-occupied Hessen, a speaker warned the audience that denazification would bring about the Bolshevization of Germany. There also emerged a conspiracy theory that the German Jews who left Germany and came back with the Allied forces were the masterminds behind all German hardships.[10] The opposite was true in East Germany—the Jewish communists who returned to East Germany after the war were celebrated as the symbols of the antifascist struggle that strengthened the political authenticity of East Germany. There existed, however, a particular hierarchy between victims, even in East Germany. Communist sacrifices often overshadowed the Jewish sufferings there. The sacrifices made by Jews were only belatedly highlighted after the reunification with West Germany. Even those highlights were not for the sake of Jewish victims. The Jewish victims were often brought up when Daniela Dahn, Christa Wolf, and others expressed their nostalgia for East Germany as the antifascist hometown.[11]

Whether capitalist West or socialist East, postwar Germany maintained a passive attitude toward apology and compensation for Israel. Even aside from rebuttals concerning the positivistic law, such as "Why should we pay state-level compensation for the Holocaust to Israel, a country that did not even exist at the time?," then chancellor of West Germany Konrad Adenauer faced political rejections from both ends of the ideological spectrum for his compensation plan. Adenauer's Christian Democratic Union (CDU), the ruling conservative party, worried the compensation would instigate antisemitism among those who opposed special treatment of the Jewish population. The Communist Party of Germany (KPD) was also against the compensation plan for the reason that it would benefit only the capitalists and financiers of Israel. The diplomatic corps voiced their concerns that the Germany-Israel reconciliation would alienate the potential allies of Germany in the Arab League. Popular opinion was no different—according to a 1951 poll, over one-fifth of respondents rejected any compensation, while about 10 percent of respondents supported compensation for Jewish victims of Nazis.[12] The compensation plan passed by the Bundestag of West Germany in 1953 received 239 votes in favor of the program out of 360 members. The social democrats unanimously voted yes, whereas most Conservatives, including the Christian Social Party and CDU members, abstained to show their disapproval. Interestingly, all thirteen members of the KPD voted no; the resistance from the Communist Party was more stubborn than that of the Conservatives.[13]

Communist East Germany was also lukewarm in coming to terms with the Nazi past, albeit for different reasons. The antifascist history of the East German leadership came to symbolize the new identity of East Germany, yet the very symbolism exonerated East Germans in general from the Nazi crimes. The ruling Socialist Unity Party (Die Sozialistische Einheitspartei Deutschlands, SED) considered Nazism as the crime of monopoly capitalism of the West and set it aside as the past that only West Germany had to deal with. Some argued that the Nazis and capitalists in West Germany were traitors to the nation, and only the communists who led the battle against fascism were the true representatives of the German nation. The communists sacrificed in the antifascist struggles were the heroic martyrs who dedicated themselves to the socialist future. Anyone who denied the historical legitimacy of East Germany was considered a fascist.[14] Separately from the socialist martyrs of antifascist struggles, those who perished unreasonably without knowing why also settled in the memory of East Germany—they were the innocent civilian casualties during the Allies' bombardment that sabotaged the building of socialism in East Germany. The reductionist memory of the Holocaust to the monopoly capitalism was paired with the official memory that remembered the Dresden bombing as evidence of the destructive impulse of Western imperialism. As such, anti-Western political instrumentalism of the Cold War was at the helm of East German memory.[15]

Walter Ulbricht, then first secretary of the Communist Party in East Germany, even declared Germany's anticolonial war against U.S. imperialism, the core of cosmopolitanism. He lamented that the United States colonized West Germany.[16] Ulbricht, the first secretary of the Socialist Unity Party, valued East German communism for its resistance against American imperialism. In the opinion of the East German leaders, the imminent danger for Germany was losing its independence to the Marshall Plan and the formation of NATO and becoming relegated to a colony of Western imperialism. Therefore, the battle against Western imperialism was the most pressing political undertaking, and asking whether someone was a Nazi in the past was discouraged as an undermining act against the National Front; what was important was not the Nazi crimes of the past but the anti-imperialist struggle of the present.[17] Those who kept problematizing the past Nazism were deemed anachronistic communists or perpetual cosmopolitans—that is, Jewish communists who were unable to acclimate themselves to the change of the era. The popular argument was that Germany would naturally overcome its Nazi past once it defeated imperialism and capitalism. This way, hundreds of perpetrators and collaborators of Nazi crimes and the Holocaust became off the hook in "anti-Nazi" East Germany; now, the ordinary people of East Germany were no longer Nazi collaborators but the victims of U.S. imperialism.[18]

East Germany's schematic historical materialism, by which mass murders and the Holocaust were reduced to the capitalist system, was indeed problematic. In this view, what should be punished was not perpetrators but the impersonal structure. However, it was a human who pulled the trigger at a Jew kneeling next to a pit in the Eastern forest and pushed the button to release the gas in the Auschwitz gas chamber. What kills a person is not a structure but another person. As the Nazi collaborators in East Germany blamed the capitalist system for their crimes, the communists who fought in the antifascist battle were actively praised as liberators of the Jewish people.[19] In the communist way of coming to terms with the Nazi past, ordinary East Germans became victims first of Western imperialism and capitalism and then of Stalinism after the Fall, to be ultimately turned into the triple victims of Nazism, U.S. imperialism, and Russian Stalinism.[20] There were only victims and no perpetrators in East Germany.

The mindset of postwar Japan's memory culture was similar to the anti-imperialist political code of East Germany. The pillar that upheld the cultural memory of Japan was the "national victimology," which defined the fifteen years of the military's takeover from 1931 to 1945 as "a moment of historical aberration along the path of an otherwise successful modernization process" and purported that all Japanese, including the emperor, were victims of the military misdeeds.[21] Under the rule of the Supreme Commander of the Allied Powers after the war, the Japanese thought they were placed in a postcolonial situation[22]—the memory of the vast empire that spanned north to Inner Mongolia and Manchuria and south to New Guinea, east to the Aleutian Islands and west to Burma, was reconstructed in the postcolonial grammar to justify victimhood nationalism of postwar Japan. More radical sects like the Society to Make New History Textbooks devised an image of Japan as a victim not only of the Western imperialism of the United States and the United Kingdom but also of the nationalism of neighboring countries like China and Korea. From their perspective, Japan, at war against U.S. imperialism and its goal of the "white Pacific," was subject to "Japan bullying" led by the aggressive Korean and Chinese nationalists.[23] The postcolonial memory in the postimperial state of Japan has disrupted the postwar reconciliation in East Asia. The question of to whom and for what postcolonial Japan should apologize remained an obstacle to dialogue about the shared past.

To conservative voters in Japan, the impression of Japanese modern history was deeply ingrained as the history of rightful self-defense against both the "red terror" and "white terror" inflicted, respectively, by Russian communism and American imperialism.[24] A young monk at Yasukuni Shrine once told Ian Buruma that the Asia-Pacific War was not a war to invade other countries. It was a matter of sustenance for the Japanese nation and liberation for all Asian nations, and the said nations had rightly been grateful for Japan's intervention.[25] Exhibitions at Yushukan, the museum at Yasukuni Shrine renovated in 2002, center on the conspiracy theory–like interpretation of history that then U.S. president Franklin Roosevelt dragged Japan, a country without many natural resources, into war to reinvigorate the American economy hit hard by the Great Depression. Founded on March 27, 1999, in Chiyoda, Tokyo, the National Showa Memorial Museum (Shōwakan) focuses on exhibiting the Japanese experience as victims, ranging from the blockade imposed by Western countries and the incendiary bombing of Tokyo to the atomic bombings.[26] The argument for Japan's right to commemorate the Asia-Pacific War, countering the fact that the U.S. perpetrators built the Vietnam War memorial in Washington, D.C., also could not be easily overlooked.[27] Postwar Japan's memory culture, which represents itself as a postcolony and not a postempire, was constructed around victimhood.

The myth of national victimology was deeply rooted not only in the minds of rightwing ideologues or conservative voters but also among supporters of the Peace Constitution. Japan's violent oppression of its neighboring Asian countries had to be erased or marginalized behind the façade of the Peace Constitution. The antiwar narrative of the peace movement tended to endorse the myth of Japan as an innocent victim of the war. The mismatching three, namely, the Supreme Command of Allied Powers as the main force of the occupation, the rightwing political constellation joined by many war criminals, and the leftwing political groups and social activists who led the peace movement, maintained their strange cohabitation in postwar Japan's memory culture living on victimhood. The occupational force acquiesced in Japan's victimhood to sever average citizens from the military leadership and militarist national elites, while the right wing that embraced war criminals fled from their accountability through the identification of Japan as a victim. The left wing, on the other hand, strove to build the image of Japan as a victim of the war to criticize the anticommunist military alliance between the United States and conservative Japan and prompt antiwar sentiments.[28] To some extent, it is a continuity of prewar critical intellectuals who welcomed the victorious attack on Pearl Harbor.

The self-pity of Japan as a victim knew no end. The vehement memory of the Asia-Pacific War, whose early victory signaled Japan's liberation from its inferiority complex vis-à-vis the "whites" in the United States and the United Kingdom, stayed alive and well even after Japan's defeat in the war. What served to fade Japan's self-reflection on its accountabilities for the war and colonialism was the regret that the military, bureaucrats, and institutions suffocated the people's autonomy and creativity, resulting in the country's defeat in the war.[29] Japan's postwar adaptation to democracy was one of the answers to how not to lose again. The gap between the United States as the victor and Japan as the loser was likened to the difference between an atomic bomb and a bamboo spear; the regret that Japan had lost the battle of science and technology had brought forth policies focusing on science and technology.[30] The "real" problem, it seemed, was that they had lost the "morally just" war against racism. Oyadomari Josei, an Okinawan captain who committed suicide immediately after the battle on September 2, 1945, wrote that the Asia-Pacific War ended in Japan's moral victory. In his view, Japan started the war with "the moral spirit of contributing to the world peace and happiness for all humankind," but the United States "used the brutal atomic bombs unprecedented in human history."[31] The critical memory of the war was more about the defeat rather than the responsibilities for how the war started and the war atrocities committed by the Japanese military. It was based on regret of defeat rather than repentance of guilt. The Japanese war crimes against the Asian neighbors could not be settled within this memory culture. The melancholy of defeat overshadowed the critical engagement with the colonialist past.[32]

Fujio Masayuki, Japanese minister of education during the mid-1980s, disclosed to Buruma that the Tokyo Tribunal was "a racist retaliation to weaken Japan's power."[33] Upon Japan's withdrawal from the League of Nations in 1933 in protest against the Lytton Report that denounced Japan's colonization of Manchuria, Ambassador Plenipotentiary Matsuoka Yosuke gave an austere speech about Japan's determination as the crucified nation. He compared Japan with Jesus Christ on the cross to emphasize the Japanese victimhood by Western imperialism since Perry's invasion in 1853.[34] At the 1964 Tokyo Olympics, when runner Tsuburaya Kokichi, a soldier in the Japan Self-Defense Force who entered the stadium in second, was overtaken by Basil Heatley of the United Kingdom just 150 meters away from the finish line and missed the silver in the men's marathon, the Japanese in the audience let out a long sigh.[35] Abebe Bikila, the Ethiopian runner who came in first, was not Tsuburaya's competition to begin with. Still, the fact that a Japanese runner was overtaken right before the finish line by a British runner revived the sorrow of defeat among the Japanese spectators. When Tsuburaya took his own life before the Mexico City Olympics in 1968 for the burden of upholding the nation's honor, Japan's most renowned writers across the political spectrum—Mishima Yukio, Kawabata Yasunari, and Oe Kenzaburo, among others—expressed their condolences.[36] Another bitter aspect of Japan's victimhood nationalism was the meteoric fame

Rikidōzan enjoyed as the symbol of national pride who had avenged the defeat by knocking down giant American wrestlers with his karate chop.[37]

After the war, the historical status of the collective victim was preempted by Axis powers like Germany and Japan, which started the war and invaded neighboring countries. In the memory culture of the Axis countries, World War II came to be remembered as a sudden, indiscriminate natural disaster in which there were only victims and no perpetrators.[38] With the naturalization of human disaster, any search for the historical responsibility of the human-made tragedy must have taken place in the realm of god, fate, or nature. Once the war became dehistoricized, perpetrators usurped the position of victims to promote their victimhood nationalism. Victimhood nationalisms of postwar Germany and Japan have each established a collective identity that revolves around the memories of the Allies' air raids and atomic bombings, refugees *Vertriebene* and *Hikiagesha*, and forced labor at the Soviet POW camps. In the postwar global memory formation, German and Japanese memory cultures have procured ontological security by sharing the memories of victims. For many members of these societies, the victimhood memories held an ontological meaning beyond mere remembrance. Therefore, the critique of victimhood nationalism is often interpreted as the negation of their national existence and emotionally evokes vehement reactions.

BOMBED INNOCENT

The most salient symbol of victimhood in East Germany was the British-American aerial bombing of Dresden. Formerly called "Florence of the Elbe," Dresden was more appealing than other industrial cities bombed by the Allies to be made the symbol of innocent victimhood. Immediately following the war's end, only the "fascist criminals" were held accountable for destroying Dresden, while the British and American air forces faced no criticism. Along with the establishment of East Germany in 1949, the antifascist rhetoric was converted into anti-Western, anti-imperial chants. The official memory of East Germany viewed the Allies as sharing a common interest in imperialism with Hitler's Nazi Germany, and the reckless bombing and destruction of Dresden were declared crimes against humanity committed by British and American imperialism. Innocent Germans fell prey to Western imperialism.[39] The government of East Germany advised the textbook authors to indicate "the terrorist attacks by the UK. and U.S." and explain that the "real" reason for bombing Dresden was to impede Soviet governance and intimidate the socialist enemies by boasting the Allies' destructive power. While comparing the Allies' bombing of Dresden to the bombings of Guernica, Warsaw, and Rotterdam by the Nazis, Minister-President of Saxony Max Seydewitz simultaneously illustrated the antisemitic oppression during *Kristallnacht* to induce a decontextualized association between the Holocaust and the Dresden attack.[40] Dresden, along with Auschwitz, became a symbol of the cruelty of war in East Germany's remembrance. Auschwitz and Dresden were both marked as the crime scene of the secret collusion between fascism and monopoly capitalism.[41]

Also, the official memory of East Germany drew a connection between the tragedy of Dresden and the threat of nuclear war. There emerged a claim that Hiroshima accidentally became the first victim of the atomic bomb. The bomb was initially planned to be dropped on Dresden, but the Soviet Army advanced too quickly. Walter Weidauer's *Inferno Dresden* of 1965 was where this claim first appeared.[42] The attempts to juxtapose Hiroshima and Dresden within the memory of World War II were also present in West Germany. A *Die Zeit* review of the book *The Destruction of Dresden* (1963) by David Irving, who would later become known as a Holocaust denier, reads: "The world's greatest mass murder in the history of mankind that took place during one single day, probably was not suffered by the population of Hiroshima, as one was inclined to presume earlier, but by the inhabitants of Dresden."[43] When Irving was writing about Dresden in the early 1960s, he firmly believed that Stalin requested the bombing. Unable to find evidence to support his claim, Irving resorted to a theory that the bombing of Dresden was consequentially helpful for Soviet advancement and that the USSR certainly welcomed the air raid. Irving's assessment was in agreement with the political interpretation of the U.S. State Department that the massive air raid on Dresden was due to Stalin's continuous request to alleviate the Nazi strain on the Soviet Army on the Eastern Front.[44]

Irving stated that the Dresden air raid caused 202,040 casualties, which was about eight times more than the official statistics of 25,000 and closer to the estimation made by historians of West Germany. The official report by East Germany also maintained approximately 25,000 deaths, adding collateral damage to the 18,375 deaths reported by the Dresden Police Department. As the documents from the Police Departments of Dresden and Berlin were uncovered one after another, Irving could not but admit that he exaggerated the death toll. The official party historians of East Germany argued that there must be a reason the anticommunist and imperialist historians of West Germany insisted on the hyperbolic 250,000 deaths—the reason, East German historians thought, was to demonstrate there was not much difference in the destructive effect between the atomic bomb and a conventional air raid, which justifies NATO's preparation for nuclear war. This argument did not have much credibility, despite its possible political impact.[45] West Germany's estimation of 250,000 deaths also includes exaggeration and omitted details. Under the surface of West Germany's 250,000 deaths hypothesis, a direct adaptation of the statistics immensely hyperbolized by the Nazi propaganda about the Allies' brutality, was the logic of the Cold War that emphasized the sacrifices of German refugees who fled to Dresden to escape the advancing Red Army. If innocent refugees who escaped from the advancing Soviet military were massacred by the relentless aerial bombings requested by Stalin, the main perpetrators must have been Stalin and his coteries.

In the end, the divided memory of the Dresden bombing pointed the finger at the UK-U.S. alliance in East Germany and at Stalin and the Soviet Union in West Germany. The memory of the bombing also played a significant role in making German civilians, in both East and West, victims. The bombing that came like a "natural disaster to our beautiful city of Dresden" generated a dehistoricized memory that is oblivious to the chronology of the war and focuses only on the pain and tragedy of the aerial bombing.[46] Winfried G. Sebald et al. argued that speaking of the relentless British-American aerial attacks was taboo in West Germany. They condemned the German writers who kept quiet about the vicious bombings that destroyed German cities. As Sebald admitted in the postscript to his lecture in Zürich, the real issue was the literary form through which the memory was depicted. What ultimately embarrassed Sebald was that the memory of the bombing was instrumentalized for postwar national reconstruction rather than testifying to the people's suffering. Also impressive is Sebald's critical sensibility, which found surprising that the depictions of Berlin Zoo with the charred corpse of a lion in a cage, dead lizards with their bodies coiled in pain, an extinct elephant whose huge body needed to be cut apart to be transported out of the cage, were more detailed than the description of human suffering. Nevertheless, it cannot be overlooked that realistic depictions of the victims' suffering often entail the dehistoricization of the perpetrator's crimes. Without the experience of the SS that incinerated the massive pile of Jewish corpses at Treblinka, cremating the 6,865 victims of the bombing in the old Dresden square would have caused many more logistic difficulties.[47]

Jörg Friedrich argued that Nazi Germany's air raid on London was concentrated on military targets like the airfield, airplane factory, shipyards, and harbor facilities, in contrast to the Allies' indiscriminate bombings of residential areas to damage the Germans' morale.[48] This is adjacent to facts yet omits other historical facts not to Friedrich's taste. On the first day when Nazi Germany invaded Poland, the squadron leader who led the air strike on Wieluń, a small town in Poland, commanded that the center of a crowded market be hit. The attack killed 1,200 Polish civilians and destroyed 70 percent of the village.[49] At the beginning of the war, the Polish civilian death toll due to Nazi airstrikes rose to 20,000. The supreme commander of the bombing of Wieluń was General Field Marshal of Luftwaffe Wolfram Freiherr von Richthofen, who also commanded the Condor Legion that bombed Guernica during the Spanish Civil War. This contemptuous high official of the Nazi air force later wrote that the incendiaries were very effective from the outset of the bombing of Stalingrad.⁵⁰ Friedrich's book suggests that the Allies' bombings of Germany had a higher death toll than that of an atomic bomb by presenting the death statistics of an airstrike on a small German city where one in three was killed compared to one in seven in Nagasaki.⁵¹ However, the author kept silent about the Nazi airstrikes on Guernica and Wieluń. Friedrich's description even compares the suffering of the German civilians to the suffering of European Jews through linguistic association—by referring to Bomber Command 5 as *Einsatzgruppe* (killing commandos), cellars and bomb shelters as "crematoria," and the bombing victims as "exterminated." Though many Germans involved in the Nazi war crimes were undeniably "victimized," it was not "guiltless" deaths.⁵²

In Japan, the memory of the atomic bombing has overridden the memory of air raids, as evidenced by the analysis of the many television specials scheduled in 1995 for the fiftieth anniversary of the defeat. Japan's uniqueness as the "only victim of the A-bomb in the world" situated the country in a convenient position to convert its history of perpetration into a memory of suffering. The fact that Japan had been the only victim of the atomic bombing in human history functioned as a "screen memory" that conceals Japan's war crimes against its Asian neighbors. Paired with Auschwitz, the atomic bombing of Hiroshima has been, at least for the Japanese anti-Western nationalists, the most representative war crime of white supremacy.⁵³ Considered en masse as the victims of "absolute evil," the victims of Hiroshima and Auschwitz have been treated as equals in Japan's memory culture. In the lectures of "Memory Keepers," the semi-official designation for the atomic bomb survivors who traveled around the world to speak on their past suffering and a future without nuclear weapons, Hiroshima was often juxtaposed with the Holocaust.⁵⁴ The May 1995 issue of *Shokun!* (諸君), a nationalist monthly magazine, institutionalized such a trend by calling the Allies' aerial attacks, including the atomic bombings, "genocide."⁵⁵

The ruling Liberal Democratic Party of Japan and conservative voters have viewed the Asia-Pacific War as a battle against "red peril" (of Russian Bolshevism) and "white peril" (the threat of the UK and U.S.

imperialism), fought simultaneously by Japan as the leading figure of Asia. Such has been the postwar reference to the "holy war." The logic of the Japanese nationalists' defense is that the crimes committed by Japan's colonialism caused less than one-tenth of the damage inflicted by Western imperialism.[56] Justice Radhabinod Pal of the Tokyo Tribunal also claimed that the use of atomic bombs by the United States was an atrocious act comparable to the Nazi war crimes.[57] Dehistoricized memories about Hiroshima are used even more frequently by leftwing peace activists, among whom the idea that the atomic bomb was an evil, racist military experiment that was dropped to intimidate the Soviet Union is a widely held view. Under the surface of this view is the premise of leftist pacifism that Japanese militarism was punished by the judgment of history with the atomic bombing. The Japanese, therefore, have the right and responsibility to intervene should the United States pose even a slight threat of nuclear war against the antinuclear peace spirit of Hiroshima.[58] This is, in effect, the leftwing peace activists in Hiroshima employing the same rhetoric used in East Germany's official discourse of the Dresden bombing with emphasis on the Anglo-American imperialist threat to the Red Army.

The narrative strategy of the Hiroshima Peace Memorial Museum epitomizes the dehistoricized memory. At the beginning of its permanent exhibition, the museum delivers a message to the international audience:

> A single atomic bomb indiscriminately killed tens of thousands of people, profoundly disrupting and altering the lives of the survivors. Through belongings left by the victims, A-bombed artifacts, testimonies of A-bomb survivors, and related materials, the Hiroshima Peace Memorial Museum conveys to the world the horrors and the inhumane nature of nuclear weapons. It spreads the message of "No More Hiroshimas."[59]

The exhibition entitled *Hiroshima on August 6* unreservedly displays the gruesome aftermath of the bombing—including photos of burnt clothes of student volunteers who were helping repair buildings, of a man burnt to death, of a woman whose back is burnt, and of a child whose face and both hands are severely burnt, and a drawing of a victim holding an eyeball in their hand. Following these images, the gallery opens its way to the victims' testimonies, the history of the museum, and the explanation of the effect of nuclear weapons. The history of Hiroshima as a military base since the Sino-Japanese War is briefly touched on at the end of the exhibition, though it is insufficient to win back the audience's historical impartiality after all the sensational, dreadful images of postbombing Hiroshima.[60] The message of peace unequivocally occupies the centerpiece of the exhibition's narrative. What is paradoxical is that the more robust the message of peace is, the vaguer the historical context and political accountability for the bombing and the war gets. It is not surprising that the films, cartoons, novels, and paintings made during the 1950s that visualize the memories of Hiroshima often depict the experience out of its historical context as if it were a natural disaster. Indeed, many Japanese considered the war itself as a kind of natural disaster, just as many Germans did.[61] The pain and wounds stayed in their memory, but the history was erased.

ABSOLUTIST PACIFISM

Absolutist pacifism, which defines all wars as the "absolute evil," tends to overlook the historical context. During the invasion of Yugoslavia by NATO in 1998, the Japanese media, from conservative magazines like *Bungeishunjū* and *Seiron* to liberal leftists like *Sekai*, unanimously stood against NATO's bombing. Their emphasis on unconditional peace was an extension of the absolutist pacifist principles and the opposite of that of Germany, where the bombing received almost unanimous support from the Social Democratic Party, Christian Democratic Union, and even the Green Party. Absolutist pacifism is unperturbed by historical context. Considering that no war should be contextually rationalized, a comprehensive assessment of the war's heterogeneous context is still indispensable to debunk self-exonerative memories of war. The footage of NATO's air strike on Belgrade was often overlaid in the Japanese media with the image of A-bombed Hiroshima or Tokyo destroyed by the B-29 carpet bombing.[62] The thorny question of how to hold Serbia accountable for its killing of Muslim Albanians in Kosovo and set its relation to the NATO bombing was absent in Japan's critical gaze on the bombing of Belgrade. The issue of accountability for starting the war is similarly missing in Japan's antiwar peace movement.[63] There is no accountability as there is no subject, and the problem is constantly reduced to "the absolute evil" of war. Dehistoricized and decontextualized, absolutist pacifism unfalteringly problematizes war and atomic bombs but rarely demands Japan's accountability for the war or the U.S. guilt for dropping those nuclear bombs.

In preparation for the fiftieth anniversary of the end of the war in 1995, a controversy arose surrounding the exhibition of *Enola Gay*, a bomber that dropped the atomic bomb on Hiroshima, curated by the Smithsonian Museum. The exhibition proposal, which included the Manhattan Project, the U.S. decision-making process to drop the nuclear bombs, the preparation of *Enola Gay*, the frightful aftermath of the bombings, and the legacy of nuclear power, met with fierce opposition from World War II veterans. The U.S. Senate condemned the exhibition as historical revisionism. At the request of the museum, wary of potential cuts in government funding, the exhibition's focus was readjusted to the physical aircraft displayed at the Air and Space Museum. The American veterans' principal stance was that the Asia-Pacific War was a "just" war against the Japanese attack. They argued that the use of the A-bomb expedited the end of the war and thus saved numerous lives of both Americans and Japanese. American veterans not only justified the atomic bombing but also rekindled the issue of accountability, which was the inception of the atomic bomb.[64] Backlash erupted in Japan against the lack of acknowledgment and commemoration of the Japanese victims in the United States. Many Japanese felt it was hypocrisy that the United States erected monuments to the Confederate soldiers who died in support of slavery and built the Vietnam War memorial that insinuated the U.S. victimhood.[65] The exhibition in the Yushukan Museum within Yasukuni Shrine also consists of a narrative that Japan was dragged into the war by Franklin Roosevelt's plot, and the U.S.-led Tokyo trial was the trial of the vengeful winner.

Detached from historical contexts, absolutist pacifism is naive. When the Senate passed a resolution to cancel the exhibition in 1994, Kurihara Sadako wrote: "If the atomic bombing was mercy/ so was the imperial army's massacre of 20 thousand in Nanjing/ so was the Nazis' gas chamber that massacred 6 million/ mercy."[66] Considering Kurihara's career as an antiwar peace activist, the reader can easily assume that the poet's intention was not to condone the Holocaust and the Nanjing Massacre. That said, the poem unexpectedly stimulates associations that pardoning the atomic bombing equals canceling out Japan's atrocity in Nanjing. Intriguingly, the person born on the day the atomic bomb blasted Hiroshima was chosen as the final torch bearer for the Tokyo Olympics in 1964. A baby born as Hiroshima *hibakusha*, representing the Olympic spirit of peace, symbolizes absolutist pacifism in postwar Japan. Above all other things, the history of the Hiroshima Peace Memorial Museum is quite disturbing. Tange Kenzo, then assistant professor at Tokyo University, won the Peace Memorial Park and Museum design competition in 1949. The complex was built according to his design and opened in August 1955.[67] Ironically, Tange's design originated from the Greater East Asia Co-Prosperity Sphere Commemorative Building Project in 1942, which was to be built at the base of Mt. Fuji to celebrate the Japanese imperial achievement. It projected a grandiose, State Shintoesque architecture incorporating the prewar nationalist aesthetics of "overcoming modernity." This plan was scrapped as Japan's defeat in the Asia-Pacific War became evident, but its spirit remained to be realized later in the Peace Memorial Park.[68]

Dehistoricized absolutist pacifism can be no less problematic than outright imperialist nostalgia or historical revisionism. Similarly, it was Japanese imperial nationalists who insisted on special relief measures for the Korean victims of the atomic bomb, attesting to the logic of the Greater East Asia Co-Prosperity. Their sympathy for the Korean A-bomb victims was born out of the imperialist reasoning, not consideration for universal human rights deprived of the victims. To them, the Korean victims were imperial subjects who helped fight Japan's battle against

Western imperialism.[69] To a certain degree, absolutist pacifism and antinuclear fundamentalism can be attributed to the strict censorship by the U.S. occupying forces, whose suppression of the A-bomb memory backfired in the reinforcement of Japan's ahistorical victimhood. As the Allies' indiscriminate bombing obliterated the memory of perpetration against Guernica and Wieluń, the Japanese Air Force's reckless bombing of China was efficiently overwritten with the memories of Hiroshima and Nagasaki. As the memories of the civilian victims of the atomic bombing were highlighted, the facts that Kure, a satellite city of Hiroshima, was the home port for Japan's Central Pacific Fleet and that Mitsubishi Heavy Industries in Nagasaki built the warships were buried. Effectively decontextualized, the dark history of the victims who participated in the war crimes could be put aside.

In general, the bombers could absolve themselves of a guilty conscience because the perpetrators floating in the air were detached from the results of the "unilaterally mechanized world of slaughter" of air raids.[70] This point is also raised by Bauman's insightful writing about "moral invisibility," which made mechanized mass violence easier.[71] The memory of air raids is also distorted by the rage of Japanese society against the Western media that compared the al-Qaeda attacks on the World Trade Center to Kamikaze. The outrage is justified by the logic that purports that Kamikaze, which focused only on military targets, was qualitatively different from the al-Qaeda attacks that targeted civilian buildings and that it was more suitable to compare 9/11 with the bombing of Hiroshima, as both were indiscriminate attacks on civilians.[72] On a wall of the temporary 9/11 memorial was hung a garland made of Sadako's paper cranes, a symbol of peace and friendship sent by the mayor of Hiroshima.[73] The paper crane garland has the impact of negating the comparison between the al-Qaeda attacks and Kamikaze and superimposing the memories of 9/11 victims in New York on the A-bomb victims in Hiroshima. The memories of air strikes on civilian targets are also ethnocentric.

Also telling in this regard is Okunoshima (Okuno island) in the Seto Inland Sea, a short forty-minute ride by ferry from Hiroshima. Upon arrival on this pastoral island, dubbed "bunny island," visitors are welcomed by rabbits descended from the rabbits used for experiments in the chemical weapons facility. The Okunoshima Poison Gas Museum is in a small concrete building by the island's pier. On this island, where the gigantic poison gas factory of the Japanese empire used to be, more than 5,000 laborers, including women and children, worked, and 1,600 of them died of the aftereffects of the poison gas. According to a Chinese source, approximately 80,000 Chinese people were killed by the chemical weapons produced here. That is not a negligible number, considering that it is only slightly less than the total number of civilian victims of the Allied bombing in sixty-three cities across Japan, excluding Tokyo. However, the Japanese government, which kept the existence of the chemical weapons facility confidential, continuously feigned ignorance. It was only in 1988 that the one-room museum could open on the ruins of the facility, thanks to the ceaseless demands and efforts of the survivors of the aftereffects of the poison gas. Now a well-known stop for dark tourism, as many Korean tourist bloggers write, the Okunoshima Poison Gas Museum is often neglected as an addendum to Hiroshima.[74]

VICTIMIZED PERPETRATORS

In postwar Germany and Japan, the experiences of expellees and Soviet POWs were also crucial in converting the perpetrator's history into the victim's memory. In the last phase of the war, approximately twelve million Germans were expelled from their homes in Eastern Europe. What these Germans suffered during the expulsion included bombardment and air raids by the Red Army, sexual violence on an unprecedented scale, revenge murders and violence by Poles and Czechs, inclement cold weather, and famine. The civilian deaths among the expellees are estimated to be around at least 500,000 and at most two million. As the historical position of victims was reestablished in the anticommunist frame during the Cold War era, the expellees' memory of the "barbaric" communist revenge took over the silenced history of the Holocaust and

Nazi genocides, especially in West Germany.[75] The Nazis' war on the Eastern front was one of the worst racist wars of the twentieth century. The sacrifices inflicted on the German expellees and the Slavic neighbors were incomparably disproportionate. The total sum of fear felt by the German victims was different from that of the Polish or Russian victims.[76] The Nazis' overwhelming violence, which systematically dehumanized the victims, was decidedly different from the primitive brutality of the Slavic neighbors. If the Nazis' systematic violence aimed primarily at physical extermination, the Red Army's violence was more sporadic in inflicting lifelong psychological damage on living victims.[77]

Indeed, the sacrifices made by the Poles under Nazi occupation and the suffering of German expellees may seem asymmetrical both qualitatively and quantitatively. For the Poles, one of the biggest victims of Nazi Germany, the readjustment of the borders meant a recurrence of their sacrifice. At the Potsdam Conference, which shaped the political map of postwar Europe, Poland handed its eastern area, including Vilnius/Wilno, Lviv/Lwów, and Grodno, over to the Soviet republics like Lithuania, Ukraine, and Belarus. The area amounted to one-third of the entire prewar Polish territory. In exchange, Poland received from Germany the Pomorze/Pommern region of East Prussia, Gdańsk/Danzig as a free city-state before the war, Silesian cities including Wrocław, and the western territory with steel and coal mines. A mass of refugees from the eastern territories was forced to migrate to the reclaimed West, emptied by the evacuation of German inhabitants. It was only natural that the Poles, with their vivid memories of the three partitions by Prussia and the horror of Nazi occupation, were anxious for Germany's official recognition and promise of security for its "regained territory" (*ziemia odzyskana*). Although Poland secured the Oder-Neisse line by signing the Treaty of Zgorzelec/Görlitz with East Germany on July 6, 1950, there remained a possibility of border disputes with West Germany and no diplomatic relations. Unlike the case for Germany-France relations, the historical reconciliation between Poland and Germany still seemed far off.[78]

Until the early 1960s, the cultural memory of West Germany was far from today's image of Germany as the model country for critical memory and self-reflection. In the memory of average Germans, the Nazi atrocities and the Holocaust were the crimes committed by Hitler and his aides, for whom justice had been served through the Nuremberg Trials. On the other hand, ordinary Germans could not be rid of the feeling that they, as "the first and last victims of Hitler," were the victims of unjust memories. The pain they experienced was genuinely enormous: mass killings of civilians, including women and children, by the indiscriminate bombings by the Allies, pillage and rape by the advancing Soviet Army, and expulsion from East Prussia and Silesia, to name a few of the long list of hardships the Germans had to suffer.[79] The civilian expellees had especially been tormented by their conditions on the road. In the end, many settled in West Germany and formed a powerful voting bloc that no political group in West Germany could ignore. Their memories of victimhood were intense and provocative.

Most horrifying memories came from the German expellees of the detention camps in Poland and Czechoslovakia. Detention camps were often run by vicious professional criminals and operated in a manner that was a replica of Nazi concentration camps. Filling up the empty concentration camps built by the Nazis for Jews and Slavs, the German expellees were retaliated against for most of the Nazi brutalities against Jews. As all the Jews under the Nazi regime had to wear the letter "J" on their chest, the Germans had to wear the letter "N" for Niemiec, the Polish word for German. Especially notorious was the Lamsdorf/Łambinowice camp in Poland, where its eighteen-year-old warden Cesaro Gimborski abused and murdered more than six thousand German expellees, including eight hundred children. One German professor in the Lamsdorf camp who wore glasses was beaten to death for looking like an intellectual. The process through which the Polish teenage correctional officers ruthlessly tortured and murdered the German intellectuals, entrepreneurs, and bourgeois is almost reminiscent of the Khmer Rouge of Cambodia.[80] The situation was not much different in Czechoslovakia, where President Edvard Beneš cursed that "the Germans be damned!" despite his vision of a harmonious and multiethnic country. He overtly instigated people to wipe out Germans. The Czech Revolutionary Guards fired machine guns at more than ten thousand German civilians gathered at the Strahov stadium, "just for fun." Thousands of Germans were dead for their entertainment. On July 31, 1945, the Revolutionary Guards threw a German whom they met on a bridge into the river and shot about fifty people in a small city of Ústí in Sudetenland.[81] What the German Czechoslovaks had to experience through their urgent move from Sudetenland to Germany was not different from the indescribable pain suffered by the East Prussian refugees.

Memories of the German expellees are often more vivid and, in a way, more painful than memories of the Allied bombings: the Soviet soldier rapists or the Eastern European perpetrators had faces, while bombs had no face. If East Germans' memory of the bombings by the imperialist Allies was about the faceless victimizers, the West Germans' memory of being retaliated against by East Europeans was a concrete memory in which the faces of victimizers remained unobscured. Anticommunism and the red complex in West Germany also contributed to emphasizing the brutal violence committed by communists. The victims of German expulsion founded the Federation of the Expellees (Bund der Vertriebenen, BdV) and demanded apologies from the Soviet Union, Poland, Czechoslovakia, and other Eastern European countries that expelled them. As it was taboo in East Germany to remember the comrade communist state as a perpetrator, West Germany was the sole keeper of the memory of expulsion. It was not an accident that about 7.5 million out of 12 million expellees had settled in West Germany. The number is about 70 percent of the total survivors among expellees. Most of these survivors had a close relationship with the German Catholic Church. Many of them had voted for the Nazi Party in the past and, after the war, became the main supporter base for the Christian Democratic Party (CDU) and the Christian Socialist Party (CSU). Though the Federation of the Expellees became peripheralized after May 1968 by the postmemory generation with a critical memory culture, they maintained significant political influence until the late 1960s.

Immediately following the end of the war, the Church of West Germany criticized the German expulsion from Eastern Europe and supported the Charter of German Expellees (Charta der Deutschen

Heimatvertriebenen) of 1950. Expellees were the crucial supporters of the traditional church. Hans-Christoph Seebohm, minister of transport during the Konrad Adenauer administration, took one step forward and attempted to decontextualize the history by equating the suffering of German expellees with that of the Jewish victims of the Holocaust. When, in reality, twenty out of thirty leading figures who signed the charter were either former high-ranking Nazi SS officers or members of the Nazi Party and a third of the two-hundred-person staff of the Federation of the Expellees were former Nazis, equating them with the Holocaust victims meant trivializing and vulgarizing the Holocaust to erase the history of Nazi atrocities. West Germany's foreign policy also acknowledged displaced East Prussians' "right to the homeland" (Recht auf die Heimat).[82] However, convincing the Poles of the German expellees' right to return home was nearly impossible. The Poles viewed these former Nazis-turned-expellees as perpetrators before victims, and the armed people of Poland and Czechoslovakia who attacked the retreating Germans deemed themselves as victims before perpetrators.

The "collective guilt" closes our eyes to the suffering of the innocent members of the perpetrating nations. In contrast, "collective innocence" ignores crimes committed by the individual perpetrators of the victimized nations. From the ontological viewpoint of the individual victims, every sacrifice comes as painfully and insufferably as any other loss in the world. In principle, all victims are equal. Yet the historical grain of the sacrifice appears differently once an individual victim's suffering converts into a social memory. What matters in the social memory is the historical contextualization of individual victims and perpetrators. Detached from the historical context, hierarchizing victims is an abuse of memory, and homogenizing all victims into abstract suffering is a misuse of memory. We must empathize with the victims' pain without loosening the guard over hierarchization and homogenization of suffering in global memory formation. Understanding that complexity should not endorse "an age-old strategy of self-exculpation, one guilt set against the other and thereby reduced to zero."[83] Guilt and suffering are not either/or choices. The contradiction of guilt and suffering in the German memory culture can be perceived insofar as the agony of German expellees and POWs does not acquit the perpetrators among themselves. In short, those Germans were also victims of the unprecedentedly macabre violence initiated by Nazi Germany and often themselves.

Though on a smaller scale than their German counterparts, the Japanese expellees had also gone through considerable suffering. A report by the Ministry of Health of Japan estimates the number of returnees to Japan in 1945–1963 at 6.29 million, among which civilian expellees are estimated at around 3.2 million.[84] The number of 3.2 million civilian expellees is about a quarter of the 12 million German expellees. Although the repatriation of the Japanese living in Korea, Taiwan, and China began in October 1945, the death toll of *hikiagesha* in Manchuria and the Korean peninsula amounts to 110,000 and 18,000, respectively.[85] The Japanese death toll is much lower than German civilian deaths during expulsion, estimated at 500,000 to 2 million. Despite the statistics that show notable quantitative differences, the experiences were strikingly similar. Most of them were deprived of all their property and suffered retaliation from the locals while roaming about asking for food in inclement weather. Sexual violence was a constant threat to the female *hikiagesha* on the road. Many Japanese women who married Korean men were kicked out of their homes, often by their husbands. Even after they returned to Japan, the *hikiagesha* encountered prejudice and discrimination from the mainland Japanese. Those who used to be POWs in the Soviet Union and China were suspected of being brainwashed by the communists. It was difficult for them to find jobs or return to their prewar workplaces. The Red Purge of 1949–1950 even took away the jobs those returnees had secured with much trouble.[86]

Both *So Far from the Bamboo Grove* by Yoko Kawashima Watkins and *Crabwalk* by Günter Grass depict the suffering of Japanese and German expellees who had to return immediately to their homeland toward the end of World War II. However, there is a world of difference between the political topologies of memory illustrated in these two novels. This difference is not because of a considerable discrepancy between the metadiscourses or ideologies toward which the two writers are inclined; it also is not because one distorts history and the other seeks historical truths. There is but a subtle difference in perspective that is almost invisible. Once through the hypersensitized circuit of memory, this subtle difference becomes the cause of an insurmountable discrepancy. What distinguishes these two novels is historical contextualization—the stark contrast between Günter Grass and Yoko Watkins lies not only in their literary style of artistic merit as writers but, more importantly, in their historical imagination to contextualize and problematize their personal memories. The point becomes even more apparent when we comb through the narrative details of the two novels. As explained in chapter 2, *So Far from the Bamboo Grove* tends to unilaterally highlight the pain and suffering of the Japanese expellees without taking into account Japan's imperial past from the Asian perspective. The novel fails to critically reflect on the historical injustice inflicted on Asian neighbors by Japanese colonialism, not to mention the war crimes committed by the Japanese military. The author could have maintained a more balanced view by trying to historicize her suffering within the historical context of Japanese colonialism.

Crabwalk, by German Nobel Laureate Günter Grass, deals with the sinking of the *Wilhelm Gustloff*.[87] On January 30, 1945, the *Wilhelm Gustloff*, with about ten thousand German expellees on board, was departing the port of Gotenhafen in East Prussia (now Gdynia of Poland) when it was struck by Soviet torpedoes and sank. This tragic event, in which most of the civilian passengers, including four thousand children, were buried under the cold water of the Baltic Sea, was made into a movie in West Germany in 1959. At that time, the *Gustloff* tragedy was considered one of the evident testimonies of the suffering of German expellees in the face of retaliation by the Soviet Red Army. However, as the self-critical reflection on Nazi Germany became a dominant theme of West Germany's memory culture in the late 1960s, this monumental incident that positioned German expellees as victims faded from the memory of West Germans. Prime Minister Willy Brandt's Eastern policy that sought historical reconciliation with Eastern Europe also, in some ways, encouraged such oblivion. Also, in East Germany, the sinking of the *Gustloff* remained taboo as it implied the brutality of the Soviet communist brothers. Suppressed under the Western memory of the Holocaust and the Eastern banner of proletarian internationalism, the *Gustloff* incident resurfaced in the public sphere with the radical political change caused by the collapse of the Soviet Union and the reunification of Germany in 1990.

In the post–Cold War era, the memory of World War II began to be reconfigured with a new set of codes. Especially as the Eastern European countries were joining the European Union and NATO, Europe's mnemoscape was restructured accordingly to incorporate the East European memories. In the process, the problem of remembering the victims of Stalinist terror fueled the restructuring of the expanded European memory formation, including Eastern Europe. The tragedy of the *Gustloff* came under the spotlight again, with a push from the victims and political conservatives. The neo-Nazis who emerged from regions of former East Germany also welcomed this change. Confronting such complicated memory politics, Günter Grass argued that the pains of the German victims should not be overlooked despite the huge sin they committed. He criticized especially the leftists, now overwhelmed by the guilt of the Holocaust, who left the historical task of rightly remembering the suffering of ordinary Germans to the political conservatives. According to Grass, the balanced memory would be possible only after the leftists' acknowledgment of the German expellees' suffering was added to the scale. The writer might have wished to critically remember the tragedy within the historical context instead of completely erasing its memory by the leftists or absolutizing its ethnocentric memories by the rightists.

Published in 2002, Grass's novel had indeed invigorated international discussions about Germans as victims. Grass's presence as a writer representing the German intellectual conscience must have provided significant impetus for the debate. Stunned that such an argument came from not neo-Nazis but Grass, some leftist critics claimed that *Crabwalk* might consequentially justify Nazism. Nevertheless, it would be a mistake to conclude that the novel supports and justifies Nazism just because it focuses on the unreasonable deaths of around eight thousand passengers on the ship *Gustloff*. Grass, a writer with a relentless gaze on history, fostered a memory complex where perpetrators and victims intersect even within one individual. Throughout the novel, he placed historical facts, such as that the ship was named after Wilhelm Gustloff, the Gauleiter of the Swiss Nazi Party; that it was a propaganda tool for the "Strength Through Joy" program that cajoled the labor class; that it was also stained with blood as it carried the infamous Condor Legion that bombed Guernica back home after the Spanish Civil War; and that the approval rate for the Nazi Party was exceedingly high among the German expellees from the East, primary victims of the sinking. The author's stance on the suffering of the German expellees is evident: albeit stressed in the novel, it was the victimhood put in the parentheses of Nazi Germany's crimes against humanity.

The difference between Günter Grass's *Crabwalk* and Yoko Kawashima Watkins's *So Far from the Bamboo Grove* becomes apparent at this juncture. Grass's unique perspective on the German expellees from the East originates from his skepticism about the dichotomous boundary between a victim and a perpetrator. In an unpredictably tumultuous history, a perpetrator often becomes a victim, and a victim frequently finds oneself in a perpetrator position. Still, deconstructing the dichotomous boundary should not mean the reversal of positions between the perpetrator and the victim or indiscriminately lumping the memories of both together through the logic of "ultimately, everyone is a victim." Grass's historical gaze, which critically contextualizes and disturbs the boundary between the victim and the perpetrator instead of essentializing the boundary, may have upgraded the version of critical memory. His dogged investigation that does not loosen the grip of contextual details would not allow the dehistoricization or decontextualization of *So Far from the Bamboo Grove*. The problem with the memory culture of postwar Japan and Germany was not mere fabrication or distortion of history but more dehistoricization and decontextualization. The disproportionate memories, with the history of perpetration erased and victimhood emphasized, were problematic not because they were false but because they dehistoricized the memory of the victimhood.

The memories of German POWs detained in Soviet prison camps were also dehistoricized to reinforce the history of oppression and persecution under the Asiatic Slavic communists. What waited for POWs returning from Soviet prison camps to West Germany in the 1950s were trials. The returned POWs who informed Stalin's secret police of their colleagues with Nazi pasts were labeled "comrade abusers" (*Kameradenschinder*) and punished even more harshly than the Nazi criminals. At the court of West Germany, where the Nazi criminals were generously deemed to have no agency and "merely followed the order," "comrade abusers" of Soviet prison camps were tried and punished for their agency. The West German Court was eager to avenge the POWs, whom it criticized for "having lost the virtue of being a man and camaraderie."[88] The masculine virtue and camaraderie the West German Court stressed in the 1950s were the main reasons that the members of Reserve Police Battalion 101 participated in the massacre of Jews in Józefów, Poland, in 1942. The members who refused or hesitated to join in the killings were called "assholes" and "cowards" by their comrades; to them, what ultimately mattered was their reputation among their peers rather than a human connection with the Jewish victims.[89] In East Germany, the informants in the Soviet prison camps were highly regarded as the champions of antifascist struggle and ideal citizens; in West Germany, they were blamed for the defeat and met with disdain and cold stares.

The predicament of the Japanese POWs, who suffered from various diseases, famine, and severe weather in Soviet Central Asia or Siberia, is also conceivable. Such painful experiences often bring about dehistoricizing memories. The memoir of Yonehara Mari, the simultaneous interpreter between Russian and Japanese at the first official meeting between the Japanese POWs and the Soviet representatives, tells about an exciting episode. In 1990, when the Soviet system was on the verge of collapse, the Soviet government sent a delegation to host a symposium in Tokyo to come to terms with the past of Japanese POWs in Siberia. The seminar was filled with indignation, insults, and heckling. It was the first official meeting of the Japanese POWs who were detained in the Soviet Union, now old, and the Soviet delegates. An uproar began when a historian in the Soviet delegation said the Soviet troops "entered" Manchuria. "How can you say they simply 'entered' when they invaded, violating the Neutrality Pact?" Amid the pandemonium, the Soviet historian resumed speaking: "Shut your mouth, where were you then? Are you saying Manchuria was your territory?" The room went silent at once.⁹⁰ Also interesting is the dialogue that Noda Masaaki, a Japanese psychiatrist, had with a painter: the painter gave a passionate speech about his bleak experience as a detainee in Siberia—dead comrades' faces, severe cold, starvation, hard labor, and the decrepit condition of the camp. When Noda asked about his experience in Northeast China, that is, Manchuria, the eloquent painter was suddenly at a loss for words.⁹¹ The dehistoricization of memory is an easy path to bury the contextual imbalance among victims and stress the egocentric victimhood.

The returned POWs in Japan and West Germany shouldered, on top of the responsibility for the defeat, the blame for ever-increasing physical violence and price gouging. It was common in the postwar cultural imagination to associate the POWs and the war leaders who pushed for total war with the delinquency of the bootleg market in ruins.⁹² The Japanese POWs at the Chinese front could finally return home after writing emotive apologies and repenting self-criticism. Although it was an obligatory part of the political reeducation program of the People's Republic of China, general suspicion hung in the sky that the communist propaganda brainwashed them to betray Japan and the Japanese nation. Around the port cities, where the returnees first set foot in Japan, rumors spread that a POW from the Soviet prison camp whom the communist ideology had brainwashed had sworn to join the Japanese Communist Party on a mission to Sovietize Japan.⁹³At the same time, the suffering of POWs was used as a card to cancel out the crimes of their home countries. In Nazi Germany, 3.3 million out of 5.7 million Soviet POWs died of abuse and famine, whereas 8,348—4 percent of the total of 232,000 —Allied POWs lost their lives. The Nazis' racist war on the Eastern Front is evident in the death toll of POWs at Nazi camps.⁹⁴ The German and Japanese POWs who were detained at the Soviet prison camps until 1956, when the last POW was sent home, were often called forth to counterbalance the agony of Allied POWs. The death toll of Japanese detainees in Siberia reached 61,855, slightly exceeding 10 percent of the total number of detainees—609,448. In comparison to one million deaths out of three million German POWs, the Japanese death toll was considerably smaller.

However, the voices of the Japanese POWs were much louder than their German counterparts. In contrast to German soldiers, the Japanese did not have a chance to commit crimes against the Soviet Union, which joined late in the Asia-Pacific war. Japanese civilians and soldiers in Manchuria were helplessly victimized as the Red Army advanced. They had no reason to feel guilty toward the Soviet Union. From the viewpoint of punitive justice, the Japanese POWs in China are more comparable to German POWs in Russia for their war crimes. Similarly, the memory of the Japanese civilians abducted by North Korean agents could be so energetically consumed without any guilty feeling. While some atomic bomb victims, *hikiagesha*, and POWs were implicated in the Japanese imperial project, the Japanese civilian abductees were innocent victims who were not involved in wartime or colonialist perpetration. A "tiny" number of Japanese abductees, between thirteen (North Korean confirmation) and seventeen (Japanese estimation), is a drop in the ocean of the Asia-Pacific War victims. It is the rarest case of the Japanese pure victims without being implicated so that the Japanese ethnocentric victimhood could be expressed without filtering, however tiny. Recently, many Koreans could witness Japanese prime minister Kishida wearing a blue ribbon badge on his jacket during his official visit to Korea, a symbol of the Japanese victims abducted by North Korea.[95]

HISTORICAL INDULGENCE

Immediately after the war, the soldiers and citizens of the Axis powers began to claim they were genuine victims, regardless of how deeply they were implicated in war crimes. These victims of the Axis countries directed their anger toward the fanatic Nazis, Fascists, and militarist leadership, which brought about a predicament of defeat. Italians believed they were victims of the "alien" Fascism. As Benedetto Croce, a representative intellectual of postwar Italy, defined Fascism as "a parenthesis in history," Fascism for many Italians was not the mainstream of Italian history but a foreign political ideology enforced from outside.[96] The neorealist cinema dominant in postwar Italy strove for the representation of antifascist morality, with the core message that the decadent bourgeoisie and foreign influence were to be blamed for Fascism; the German soldiers, drug addicts, gays, and sadist criminals were responsible for the moral and physical atrocities committed under the name of Italian Fascism.[97] The binary between "pure, real Italy" and "Fascist, fake Italy" was the basic grammar governing postwar Italy's memory culture. Fascism, in short, was deemed "not Italian"; Italian history and Mussolini's Fascism were two separate entities. As "good Italian" and "bad Fascist" must have been differentiated, holding the "good," average Italians accountable for the Fascist atrocities was not possible. The Nuremberg Trials were thus not even a possibility in postwar Italy, where Fascism readily faded into the black hole of the past.[98] It shows how postwar Italy's self-hypnotizing image as the nation of victims came into existence. How the memory of Italians as the victims of Fascism correlates with the increasing popularity of the Mussolini calendar, composed of photos of bare-chested Il Duce giving a speech, remains a mystery.[99]

In Central Europe, Austrians competed against Germans over the position of the Nazis' first victim. The Moscow Conference of 1943 declared null Nazi Germany's forced annexation of Austria on March 12, 1938, and stipulated that Austria was "the first free country to fall victim to Hitlerite aggression." Before this, Winston Churchill promised in a speech in 1942 to liberate Austria from the "Prussian yoke." Since the enemies of the Allies were a few feudalistic Prussian Junkers and the Nazis, a lot of Austrians who passionately supported the annexation and desired to be incorporated into the Third Reich could hide behind the cloak of the "evil" Nazi-Prussian villains. As the ruling Socialist Party denounced the Nazi war criminals and accomplices as Austrian national traitors, most ordinary Austrians who collaborated with the Nazis could remain victims of betrayal.[100] However, the reality of these Austrian victims was a bit more complicated. Out of the entire population of seven million, those who joined the Nazi Party amounted to 693,007—second only to Germany. What is more, 127,000 of them were dedicated Nazis who joined the Nazi Party despite the watch and persecution from the Engelbert Dollfuss government before the annexation. Austrians occupied only 8 percent of the population of the Third Reich, yet 14 percent of the SS. The percentage of Austrians who participated in mass murder in any form, from the "euthanasia" program to Auschwitz, was a whopping 40 percent.[101] Of 110 members of the Berlin Philharmonic, 8 were Nazi Party members—compared to 45 Nazis among the 117 members of the Vienna Philharmonic, minus the 13 members kicked out for being against the annexation or Jewish.[102]

Vienna's Jewish population steeply dropped from 200,000 to 6,500 through the war. Only 200 Jews could hide in the houses of Austrian Viennese. The Austrian neighbors who took over Jewish homes during the war greeted the returned Jewish survivors with an unwelcoming question: "You still alive?"[103] Much can be inferred about the Austrian memory culture from the survey conducted by *Der Standard*, a Viennese daily newspaper, for the seventy-fifth anniversary of the Nazi annexation of Austria in March 2013. More than half of respondents—54 percent to be precise—said that the Nazi Party would win the next election if it were a legal political party now. Also, 42 percent responded that life under Nazism was not at all that bad. What is more surprising is that 39 percent of respondents believed that antisemitic oppression could resume in Austria—together with 17 percent saying that it was highly likely, a total of 56 percent acknowledged the possibility of antisemitic oppression. Still, 61 percent felt the country's effort to liquidate its Nazi past was enough as it was. While 53 percent responded that Austria freely agreed to be annexed by Nazi Germany, 46 percent maintained that Austria fell prey to the Nazis by the 1938 annexation. The German weekly *Stern* wrote that this survey was shocking, though the Austrian readers were not so surprised.[104]

Victimhood, which dominated both East and West Germany during the late 1940s, returned to the center of Germany's memory culture with the collapse of the Berlin Wall. A survey conducted by *Spiegel* in 1995 shows the opinion that the German expulsion was a Holocaust-like crime against humanity was not the minority. This tendency was stronger among the elders who directly experienced the expulsion, as about 40 percent of respondents age sixty-five or older agreed.[105] Some even argued that the suffering of Germans was more painful than that of Jews.

In the mid-1990s, almost as much as in the late 1940s, perpetration against Germans was emphasized over German perpetration against others. In the post–Cold War era, the image of Germans extended beyond the collective perpetrators to the complex victims. Once the ideological chains of the Cold War were unlocked, the politically repressed memories were emancipated. To break the normative equation between Germans and perpetrators, the tendency to highlight the memory of Germans as "absolute victims" emerged down the road.[106] Prime Minister Helmut Kohl's cultural politics, designating German victimhood as the new national identity for Reunified Germany, also contributed to the revival of victimhood memory. In response, British prime minister Tony Blair expressed concerns over Reunified Germany's promotion of national victimhood. Especially in the dichotomy of "a few Nazi criminals" and "most innocent Germans," ordinary Germans became Hitler's first and last victims. To "most Germans," Nazism was a "foreign phenomenon" that originated from outside of the national history of Germany.[107] Even the accountability for the Holocaust should have been directed to the few Nazi villains who were extraneous to Germany's national tradition.

The average Japanese also believed that the military leadership deceived them. The Japanese victimhood, which erased the people's complicity with the total war efforts under the name of the Imperial Rule Assistance (翼賛体制), was in epistemological collusion with the Orientalism of the Supreme Commander for the Allied Powers (SCAP). To emphasize that the ordinary Japanese were victims of the totalitarian military government, SCAP applied the Orientalist logic of "the feudalistic Japanese who slavishly obey the authority." Even though the people of Japan loyally sent their wholehearted support to the emperor, all their efforts were in vain due to the betrayal by the military leadership.[108] SCAP's stance absolved many Japanese who proactively collaborated with the total war state from the guilt and accountability for war. The Tokyo Trials also indulged the average Japanese by eliciting a sense of betrayal by the military leadership. Thus, the perpetration was solely attributed to abstract entities like leadership, militarism, and system, while the ordinary Japanese were rendered innocent victims of the war and militarism. Then created was the image of Japanese and other Asian peoples as the communal victims of the Japanese military.[109] In 1946 an extremely rare opinion was Maruyama Masao's reflective view that the perpetrators of the inhuman atrocities committed by the Japanese military during the Asia-Pacific War were the rank-and-file soldiers, and even a "lowly" private in the barracks could assume an infinitely superior position as a member of the Imperial Army in the occupied territories.[110]

A personal memory stems from each individual's direct experience, but a collective memory is deeply integrated into the discursive frame of public history. A cultural memory that encourages communal thinking and engagement in the past, present, and future is inseparably related to society's dominant historical consciousness and discourse. The postwar historiography of both Germany and Japan shared the paradigm of *Sonderweg,* which stresses the historical peculiarity of the capitalist development, the unyielding remnants of colonialism and feudalism, the feudalization of the bourgeoisie, and industrialization led by feudal aristocrats, a failed bourgeois-democratic revolution; weak parliamentary democracy, oppressive politics of developmental dictatorship, the working class deprived of the basic labor and social rights and stuck in the "class in itself" (*Klasse an sich*), the state existing as a powerful patron; immaturity of the modern individual subject, and the unliberal, antipluralistic political culture.[111] According to this interpretation, shared by Marxist historiography that values the unilinear development modeled on the United Kingdom and the Whig-bourgeois historiography and considers the British and American liberal democracy as the universal way toward modernity, German Nazism or Japanese militarism was an inevitable outcome of the abnormal development of capitalism. In other words, Germany and Japan walked the fascistic, top-down road to a revolution where the collusion among the feudal ruling class, military, and big capitalists was possible due to the remnants of premodernity and deviatory development of capitalism.

The *Sonderweg* thesis sits with a premise that most ordinary people of Germany and Japan, including the liberal bourgeoisie, office workers, mid- to low-level bureaucrats, the working class, and peasants, were the real victims of top-down fascism and forced modernization. Claiming that a few Nazis and militarists forced innocent people into the war, the *Sonderweg* thesis held the abstract social system and structure responsible. Nevertheless, the structure does not kill. Only individuals can kill. It was the "small" actors living and moving on site who cornered the victims and killed them. The *Sonderweg* thesis was a historical discourse that functioned as an acquittal for the small actors who perpetrated atrocities on site. The ordinary Germans and Japanese were already the first victims of the evil Nazis and military leaders even before the war; by the end of the war, they became the last victims. In 1940, two years into the war, the dead and missing German soldiers amounted to 62,700 and 64,500, respectively—the numbers soared through 1944 to 458,800 and 1,527,600, which were respectively seven times and twenty-five times more.[112] While the statistics can be proof that the German soldiers who believed sacrifice for the national community to be the greatest virtue were, in fact, the worst victim, they also suggest the soldiers' loyalty toward the Nazi state that operated the machines for destruction and slaughter to the best of its ability even when defeat was unavoidable. Among the 3.1 million Japanese casualties since the Asia-Pacific War broke out in December 1941, 2.3 million were soldiers and military civilians, and 800,000 were civilians. The statistics that show that 91 percent of them, accounting for more than two million soldiers and most civilian victims, died after January 1, 1944, are interestingly similar to the death trend of Nazi German soldiers.[113] The soldiers who expired in a flash during the "hopeless resistance" were indeed victims of the top-down fascist system, but the meaning of their deaths was far more complex.

7

OVERHISTORICIZATION

HOMO JEDVABNECUS

So often, perpetrators in history transform into victims in memories: historical perpetrators disown their historical agency and hide behind the structure of history. In the whirlwind of history, individual actors cannot but become helpless in the face of overwhelming circumstantial forces. However, a unilateral emphasis on the structural power of history is problematic. Relinquishing historical agency to the historical structure is a convenient way for individual perpetrators to disown their personal responsibility for their actions. The Laudański brothers—Kazimierz, Zygmunt, and Jerzy—two of whom (Zygmunt and Jerzy) were sentenced to fifteen and twelve years, respectively, in prison by the court of postwar communist Poland for the murder of their Jewish neighbors in Jedwabne, are an excellent example. A letter that the eldest brother, Kazimierz, sent to the Polish daily *Gazeta Wyborcza* on December 5, 2000, was not only an excuse but also a full-fledged provocation. In his letter, Kazimierz claimed that the genuine culprits of the Jedwabne pogrom were not Poles like himself but the Nazi German troops. He also blamed the "Jewish commies" who collaborated with Stalin's secret police to make the long list of Poles to be exiled to Siberia. He strongly warned against demonizing his brothers, who adhered to the patriotic family tradition. Culminating in a clichéd message that the Laudański brothers "have always been ready to contribute to the country for the public good, and still are," the letter strained the patience of Adam Michnik, then editor-in-chief of *Gazeta Wyborcza*, and the editorial team started seriously delving into the story.[1]

On December 16, 2000, Anna Bikont, a journalist from *Gazeta Wyborcza*, interviewed the brothers in Pisz, a Polish town 100 kilometers from Jedwabne. Kazimierz had become a successful beekeeper with regular clients, some of them even from Germany. In his house, where he served tea and homemade gingerbread, Bikont interviewed the brothers for over three hours. Well prepared for the interview, the brothers answered all Biknot's questions in a calm, orchestrated manner. After the interview, Bikont canceled her hotel reservation and drove back to Warsaw through the night on the icy road. She could not sleep, haunted by the brothers' pushing for their innocence while "the scenes of 1941 replaying under their eyelids." Jerzy, the youngest, who was identified in Jedwabne by survivor Szmuel Wasersztajn's testimony as one of the Poles who had been at the burning where Jewish victims had been locked inside, explained his circumstantial innocence by the fact that he had stayed as far away from the barn as 30 meters. Saying that other Polish neighbors had been standing much closer to the barn, he smirked at Bikont, who later recalled that she wanted to drive as quickly and as far away as possible from the brothers' plea: "Do you even know what Jews did under the postwar Communist regime? Should that make Poles and Jews point fingers at each other now?" When she was about to leave after wrapping up the interview, Kazimierz Laudański warned her not to reopen the past wounds, as they had no issues with Jews.[2]

The phrase the Laudański brothers blurted out just before Bikont left, *Żydokomuna* [Jewish commies], revealed their subconscious bias. The label "Jewish commies" justifies the inverted memory in which Poles were not antisemitic perpetrators but the victims of Jewish communists even to this day. According to this memory, the Poles under the Soviet occupation from 1939 to 1941 upon the Molotov-Ribbentrop Pact were victimized by Jewish communists, who allegedly denounced the Polish anticommunist partisans to the Soviet secret police and expelled them to Central Asia or Siberia. Accused also of looting food from Polish peasants during World War II, the Jews were viewed as the most radically disloyal ethnic group to the Polish Underground State and ethnic Poles.[3] In this version of history, the victims were Poles, not Jews. Polish Jews were merely traitors who sold their fellow citizens to the Soviet Union. The denialists hence redefined the Soviet occupation as the "Soviet-Jewish occupation" to highlight the Jewish betrayal for the oppression of ethnic Poles. As an example of the antisemitic language of the interwar period, the stereotype of Jewish commies was typical of anticommunism combined with antisemitism. The practice of labeling the opposition as Jewish commies still pervades political discourse, and Poland's memory politics in the twenty-first century is not immune to it.

Kazimierz Laudański's plea that the brothers were the real victims of communism, a foreign ideology imposed by the Soviet Union, seems indefensible in the face of a letter sent to the Polish Secret Police by Zygmunt Laudański about seventy years earlier. Zygmunt was in prison for murder when he wrote the letter to appeal for leniency to the Secret Police of the Polish Communist Party in 1949. In it, he asks for consideration of his record as a loyal communist who risked his life to serve the NKVD until the Nazis reoccupied Poland in 1941. He rejoined the party and the agricultural collective when the Soviet military stationed again after the Nazis' defeat. He spent six months hiding in the woods after the Red Army had invaded in 1939 and Jedwabne had become incorporated into the Byelorussian Soviet Socialist Republic. Something must have been off with him. He came out of the woods and joined the NKVD only after he had felt sure of his safety. He then worked as an NKVD informer when the Soviet military occupied the region (1939), as a Nazi collaborator in killing Jews under the Nazi occupation (1941), and again as a communist zealot once the communist regime came to power in Poland (1945). His track record reminds me of, and in a way seems more dramatic than, Chon Kwangyong's novel *Kapitan Lee*, in which the Korean protagonist turns from a pro-Japanese collaborator of the colony to a pro-Soviet collaborator in North Korea and later to a pro-American anticommunist in South Korea.[4]

Another quixotic opportunist is Karol Bardoń, who had been sentenced to death for his participation in the Jedwabne pogrom but died of a stroke in prison. Formerly a watchmaker, Bardoń had been promoted to the manager of a tractor repair factory while helping Stalin's secret police and other administrative bureaus after the Soviet occupation in 1939. When the Nazis occupied the village in 1941, he actively participated in the massacre of Jews.[5] As attested to by the life of Bolesław Piasecki, the "perfect opportunist" who had an impressive career as a fascist leader during the interwar period and a Catholic politician friendly with the communist regime after the war, blending fascism, antisemitism, communism, Catholicism, and nationalism was not a problem for such opportunists.[6] Thus, it is not particularly surprising that these opportunists, wrapped in a pragmatism so flexible that it would make the literary imagination blush, remember themselves as "the victims of 'Jewish commies'" in twenty-first-century anticommunist Poland. Audacious trespassers of the fine web of ideology and system, the opportunists dubbed "small fish" flaunt excuses that should not be dismissed simply as distortions of memory on the individual level. For an in-depth analysis, it is necessary to question the historical grammar of Poland's postwar memory culture and the narrative model that restructures the criminal past of the Laudański brothers into the memory of victims.

Hannah Arendt's conceptual pair of "collective guilt" and "collective innocence" would be the most compelling reference point for understanding this inversion of perpetrators and victims. Collective guilt promotes categorical thinking by which one feels guilty about, or deems oneself guilty for, things done in the name of the nation even though one was not involved in the actions.[7] "Collective innocence" stands opposite to "collective guilt," although the two embody the same logic to categorically decide one's guilt or innocence based on one's national belongingness. In memory politics, the two play by the same rules from opposite ends of the table. Arendt claims that both "collective guilt" that enshrouds an entire nation with the guilt of the previous, or even ancient, generation and "collective innocence" that covers individuals' perpetration under the name of the victimized nation foster a situation where everyone in a collective is either guilty or innocent.[8] Invoking "collective innocence," the Laudański brothers could justify themselves as victims for having been part of the Polish nation even though they murdered their Jewish neighbors. By identifying themselves with the Polish nation that suffered from both Nazism and Stalinism and, as of late, from Western capitalism, they buried history and memories of their perpetration beneath multicolored victimhood nationalism. Victimhood nationalism provided perpetrators with a screen memory to cover up their crimes, be they leftists or rightists. It occurs globally that the absolutization of collective positionality highlights the nation's victimhood and thus pardons individual perpetrators in the name of the victimized nation.

It is often the case that perpetrators preach victimhood nationalism while the real victims suppress their traumatic memories in silence. It is more so because genuine victims tend to feel survivors' guilt for outliving their fellow victims. Such is the paradox of victimhood nationalism. For perpetrators, victimhood nationalism is a priceless mnemonic asset that conceals their guilt and justifies their unfounded rage.[9] The Polish nationalists' denial of the Kielce pogrom on July 4, 1946, which was prompted by an eight-year-old's lie about himself being kidnapped by a Jew and almost sacrificed at a religious ritual, reflects the psychology of "collective innocence." This pogrom, which started absurdly with the little boy who lied to avoid a scolding after staying a night outside picking cherries with a friend who lived twenty-six kilometers away, resulted in at least forty Jewish deaths, two Polish deaths, and tens of people injured. Of the forty Jews murdered, thirty were stoned to death by the angry mob. The communist authorities promptly criticized the massacre as a ploy by the underground anticommunist group linked to the government in exile in London. They sent twelve suspects to the military tribunal, where nine of them were executed by firing squad. Happening in communist Poland after its liberation from Nazi occupation, the Kielce pogrom came as an immense shock for Jewish survivors who were still living with the trauma of the Holocaust.

However, the Kielce pogrom was hardly a one-time occurrence. From Poland's liberation by the Red Army in November 1944 to

December 1945, 351 Jews were murdered. The total number of deaths by Judeocide between 1944 and 1947 in liberated Poland is estimated to be over a thousand.[10] Between June and December 1945, about thirty assaults against Jewish survivors, of which eleven were robberies and five were conflicts over the ownership of prewar Jewish properties, were reported from liberated Kielce, Kraków, and other Polish cities.[11] The pinnacle of antisemitic assaults in Poland since its liberation from the Nazis, the Kielce pogrom prompted the Jewish migration during which sixty thousand Jews left their homes in Poland between July and September 1946. The new normal was for the Jewish Holocaust survivors to leave their dear homes in Poland to settle in the "refugee camps" in Germany, where the remnants of the Nazis still prevailed.[12] What was even more depressing about the Kielce pogrom was that the perpetrators were not limited to ultranationalists or despicable mobsters. According to the newspapers of the time, the main actors of the massacre were ordinary Poles, among whom were members of the local branch of the Polish Socialist Party (PPS) and about a thousand workers from the factories of Ludwików Steelworks. Analogous to the Japanese neighbors who murdered *josen-jin* (racist term for colonial Koreans in Japanese) and communists during the Great Kanto Earthquake, the Polish perpetrators in Kielce also had a strong sense of self-consciousness as justice-serving vigilantes.[13] If it was the feeling of fulfilling civic duties, as in Rembrandt's painting *The Night Watch*, that galvanized the people, genocide is the potential danger immanent in modern statecraft.

The reaction was not much different from that of ordinary workers who did not partake in the massacre. The working class, in general, was reluctant to criticize the Kielce pogrom, with some even complaining that the Polish Workers' Party (PPR) was too philo-semitic. As the massacre unfolded, Józef Kalinowski, then secretary of the Kielce PPR, refused to follow the order from the Central Bureau to appease the angry crowd. Even after the massacre, the "moral terrorism" against Jews continued among the lower-ranking members of the PPS and PPR.[14] On the nationalist side, antisemitism was more overt. At the Peasant Party (Stronnictwo Chłopskie) convention held at the Paradise (Raj) theatre in Kraków on August 19, 1945, a delegate delivered a resolution to expel the Jews with a speech that they "should thank Hitler for exterminating Jews," which was met with applause from over a thousand delegates.[15] The party, police, military, and public security agency were all impotent in the face of the deep wave of grassroots antisemitism. The nascent communist power was reluctant to go against the public sentiment to fight antisemitism. What dominated the party's official discussions at that time were nationalist slogans such as "national unification" and "the will of the nation." Before the Kielce pogrom, the party's public security department was already inundated with furious memoranda from the local Jewish committee that there needed to be more disciplinary measures to prevent assaults and looting of Jewish residents by the locals.[16]

Again, the Kielce pogrom was the pinnacle of the development of grassroots antisemitism rather than a historical anomaly. Although Poland was liberated, the Nazis' inhumane rule and war brutality had normalized moral decadence, which justified shameless selfishness by the logic of survival.[17] The legacy of the Nazis, especially in Eastern Europe, compelled the surrender of all moral codes in exchange for survival, and "the society as a whole became beastlike or demonic."[18] The Nazis could no longer be held accountable for the pogroms after the war. *Kuźnica*, a weekly magazine that dates back to the era of the "moderate revolution" and the Enlightenment constitution of the late eighteenth century, wrote sarcastically, "Today Kielce is *Judenrein*. Hitler's plan has been executed in Kielce to perfection."[19] Kazimierz Wyka's poignant essay in *Rebirth* (*Odrodzenie*) analyzes the postwar pogrom in the Kraków ghetto on August 11, 1945, as an indicator of the Polish paradox. The essay states that the tragedy in Poland was paradoxically derived from the absence of a collaborative political organization with the Nazis, such as the Quisling regime of Norway. The legacy of antisemitism in the well-organized Polish resistance movement made the country's battle against antisemitism more difficult.[20] This paradox of Polish nationalism delineated by Wyka was later adopted and developed by Adam Michnik in the Jedwabne debate. Unlike the ultranationalists of the Quisling regime, Vichy France, Hungary, Slovakia, Ukraine, and the Baltic states who collaborated with the Nazis, Polish ultranationalists refused to cooperate and thus maintained their historical legitimacy.

Polish antisemites even tried to rescue Jews to save the honor of the Polish nation. As a result, antisemitism remained the symbol of Polish patriotism, not of pro-Nazi collaboration.[21]

RESCUING NEIGHBORS, RESCUING NATION

It is not that difficult to rediscover those at the intersection of contradictory labels, such as indigenous fascists, heroes of anti-Nazi resistance, and antisemites who saved Jewish lives among the impassioned Poles who lived under the Nazi occupation. Zofia Kossak-Szczucka, the symbol of female resistance fighters, was one such figure. Also known by her code name "Weronika," Kossak-Szczucka cofounded the Front for the Rebirth of Poland (Front Odrodzenia Polski), a Catholic nationalist resistant group, and the Polish Council to Aid Jews (Rada Pomocy Żydom, also known by its codename Żegota).[22] In August 1942 Kossak-Szczucka disseminated five thousand copies of a leaflet entitled "Protest," a call to help Jews at the crossroads of extermination. A nationalist prose writer whose high repute predated the war, Kossak-Szczucka reported on the heinous atrocity at the Warsaw ghetto, where tens of thousands of Jews were helplessly waiting to be killed behind the ghetto wall. She condemned the Polish and worldwide silence facing the massacre of millions of unarmed civilians: "Those who remain silent in the face of murder are accomplices of the crime." In other words, not denouncing murder is akin to accepting the murder. For her, the protest against the Holocaust was by God's command against murder and, therefore, the duty of "us Polish Catholics." The Christian code of ethics, which allegorized neglecting the Holocaust as the actions of Pontius Pilatus, who crucified Jesus and washed the blood off his hands, inspired the Polish Catholics to rescue the Jews. Kossak-Szczucka, while stressing the duty of "us Polish Catholics" to save the Jewish lives, maintained that her belief that the Jews were the "political, economic, ideological enemy of Poland" would remain unchanged.[23]

Interestingly, in Kossak-Szczucka's record, there coexists the activism through Żegota, risking her own life to save the Jews, and the antisemitic belief that antagonized Jews. The paradox of "an antisemite saving Jewish lives" was possible due to Kossak-Szczucka's unyielding nationalism. For the honor of the Polish nation, even antisemites threw themselves into the rescue effort of the Jews. It was the duty and pride of Polish nationalism, in the depths of which lay the desire to save the abstract honor of the nation by saving the lives of Jews who were facing extermination on Polish soil. In September 1943 Kossak-Szczucka was stopped, questioned, and arrested by the Nazis. She was sent to Auschwitz-Birkenau concentration camp, escaped, and participated in the Warsaw Uprising in August 1944. After the war, she was blacklisted by the Communist Party due to her right-wing nationalism. Still, she could flee to Western Europe with the help of Jakub Berman, who initially supervised the Ministry of Public Safety and owed Kossak-Szczucka for the life of his Zionist brother, Adolf Berman. A hardcore nationalist with exceptional love for her country, Kossak-Szczucka returned to Poland in 1957 after the de-Stalinization. For Żegota's Jewish rescue efforts, Kossak-Szczucka was posthumously named one of the Righteous Among the Nations in 1985 by Yad Vashem. In 2009 the National Bank of Poland issued coins commemorating her. In 2018 she was awarded the Order of the White Eagle, the highest Polish order. The legend of Jewish rescue was a peculiar code of memory that reaffirmed the "collective innocence"—had the nationalist patriots of Poland, the most significant collective victim of the Nazis, voluntarily sacrificed themselves to save their Jewish neighbors, the "collective innocence" of the Polish nation could once again be validated.

Not only nationalist elites but also ordinary peasants sacrificed their lives to rescue Jews. On the night of March 24, 1944, a Nazi police detachment raided the farmhouse of Józef Ulma in a small town called Markowa and killed eight Jews who were hiding in the attic. The Nazis then dragged Józef Ulma, his wife Wiktoria Ulma, who was seven months pregnant, and their six children to the town square and executed them while the villagers were forced to watch. It is presumed that the overnight massacre ensued from information provided by their Polish neighbor, who was after the wealth of Szall and Goldman, the Jewish families hiding at the Ulmas' farmhouse. The Nazis' show of force was enough to intimidate the Polish peasants. The following day, a total of twenty-four Jewish corpses were abandoned in nearby fields. Polish peasants, worried about their own safety, murdered the Jews they had been sheltering and discarded the bodies in the fields.²⁴ Józef and Wiktoria Ulma were named the Righteous Among the Nations on September 13, 1995, at Yad Vashem. Even so, they were remembered by only a few Holocaust experts in Poland. In March 2018 the Sejm passed a decree declaring March 24 as "the National Day of Remembrance of Poles who saved Jews under German occupation." The decree, initiated by the ruling Law and Justice Party (PiS), states that the national holiday is in tribute to the "heroes who fulfilled the ethos of the sovereign Republic of Poland and epitomized the highest ethical values and Christian philanthropy through their heroic actions, invincible bravery, solidarity and compassion for fellow human beings."²⁵

Prior to this designation, the Polish Catholic Church named Józef and Wiktoria Ulma as "servants of God" and began the process of their beatification. In 2006 an elementary school in Markova changed its name to "School of Servants of God Ulma Family." In March 2016 the Ulma Family Museum of Poles Saving Jews in World War II opened in Markowa. In attendance were high-profile figures, including then president Andrzej Duda. In October 2016 the presidents of the four countries in the Visegrád Group visited the museum to lay flowers and lit candles in front of the granite wall with names of Poles who saved Jews. In 2018 Mateusz Morawiecki, prime minister of Poland, held a press conference for foreign journalists on the Amendment to the Act on the Institute of National Remembrance in the Ulma Family Museum.²⁶ The amendment included an article that read: "Whoever claims, publicly and contrary to the facts, that the Polish Nation or the Republic of Poland is responsible or coresponsible for Nazi crimes committed by the Third Reich . . . shall be liable to a fine or imprisonment for up to 3 years."²⁷ Academic activities made punishable by this law ranged from the use of vague terminology such as "Polish concentration camp" to the claims that Poles collaborated with the Nazis or in the Holocaust. If followed strictly, the law could also punish Jan Gross for writing about the Jedwabne pogrom, where the Poles murdered their Jewish neighbors. By this point, Gross had already been subjected to threats of prosecution by the Polish Public Prosecutor's Office. The Ulma Family Museum, as the site of memory symbolizing Poland's collective innocence, was an opportune example to countervail the national image as collaborators in the Holocaust.

The use of memories of Jewish rescue as a means to justify nationalism is also found in Japan. Intriguing is the Japanese quiet enthusiasm for Sugihara Chiune (杉原千畝), the "Japanese Schindler" who saved the lives of up to 6,000 Jewish refugees from mass murder by issuing 2,193 transit visas as the acting consul at the Japanese Consulate in Kaunas, Lithuania. Nicknamed the Baltic Casablanca, Kaunas was full of diverse refugees, conspirators, secret agents, brokers and crooks and was an ideal place for the adventurous heroes. In various Japanese history textbooks on Japanese literature, world history, and ethics, the image of Sugihara as the "Japanese Schindler" is emphasized. For instance, one ethics textbook for middle school remarks about Sugihara's "transit visa for life" under the rubric of "world peace and love for humanity." Tsuruga, where the Jewish refugees landed, is described as a "port of humanism."[28] A few national language textbooks, even in primary school, introduce the story of Sugihara with phrases like "social justice," "gratitude," and "joy of survival."[29] The visitor's books at Sugihara museums in Kaunas and Tsuruga have been filled with notes from young Japanese students expressing their pride in being a Japanese thanks to Sugihara Chiune, a rescuer of Jews who risked his career. The Jews in Kaunas were fleeing the Russian Bolsheviks, the new occupier of Kaunas and Lithuania after the Molotov-Ribbentrop agreement. There is no mention that Sugihara, as a professional diplomat, operated an intelligence ring against the Soviet Union and oversaw the diplomatic affairs of Manchukuo or even in Kaunas.

The memory politics of the Xi regime in China regarding "China's Schindlers," namely, Ho Feng-Shan (何鳳山) and Qian Xiuling (錢秀玲), likewise calls for a more detailed assessment, as the spotlight under which the Chinese government placed the Chinese people who saved Jewish lives is suspected to have been a "screen memory" to hide its violation of human rights at the Uighur internment camps in Xinjiang.[30] The "rescuer's turn" in Holocaust memory politics is witnessed in East

Asia and is no longer peculiar to the European mnemoscape.³¹ Sometimes it tends to overhistoricize the role of rescuers. It is not comfortable to see that the Chinese leader Xi Jinping praises John Rabe, a member of the Nazi Party and Siemens representative in Nanjing, as "a great humanitarian" for rescuing the Chinese from the Japanese Army's Nanjing Massacre. Instrumentalizing memories of rescuing Jews as a means to justify nationalism is also found in North Africa. For reasons similar to their Polish counterpart, the memory of Sultan Mohammed V of Morocco, who saved the lives of 240,000 Jewish citizens of Morocco despite the antisemitic measures enforced by Vichy France during World War II, is now an ineluctable part of the national narrative of postwar Morocco. Yet in the Moroccan memory of Jewish rescue stands the forced labor camp established by the Vichy regime in North Africa. Mohammed V, whose courage and benevolence saved Moroccan Jews, is curiously absent in this memory of the labor camp. It was for a similar reason that the German artist Oliver Bienkowski's Holocaust monument near Marrakesh was deinstalled: the monument was not to commemorate the king but installed in memory of the LGBT victims of the Holocaust, whose identities were still punishable by Moroccan law.³²

The story of the Ulma family has secured its place in the official wartime narrative of the Museum of the Second World War in Gdańsk. The museum, subjected to attacks from right-wing nationalists throughout its opening process for being "not Polish enough," "divisive for the Polish nation," "cosmopolitan," and "pseudo-universalist," could display the story of the Ulmas only after its director resigned for unfathomable political reasons.³³ The way out of the maze of memory politics for them is simple—the exit is at the end of the road following the message that Poles, who were at once the biggest victims of Nazism and Stalinism and the good neighbors who risked their lives to save Jewish lives, could never victimize others. It is where the memory of the Ulma family meets that of the Laudański brothers: once the frame of collective innocence structures the collective memory of Polish society, denialism of not only the Jedwabne killing but also the Kielce pogrom pokes its head through the cracks. They are framing the collective memory of contemporary Poles that the pogroms were a conspiracy by Stalin's Secret Police or communist Polish intelligence to taint the reputation of Polish nationalism, and the Polish perpetrators were innocent victims of such a conspiracy. Under the slogan that it was not the Kielce pogrom (*pogrom kielecki*) but the security service pogrom (*pogrom ubecki*) resonating through the megaphones of skinheads in front of 7 Planty Street in Kielce, where Jews were massacred, the overhistoricized concept of "collective innocence" becomes the tool of memory terrorism.[34]

In February 2021 another turmoil erupted in Polish society upon the Institute of National Remembrance's appointment of Tomasz Greniuch, who had been a leading member of the far-right nationalist organization Obóz Narodowo-Radykalny (ONR), as the head of its Wrocław office. The ruling PiS braced itself against the protests of the mayor of Wrocław and historians to process this appointment. When the photo of himself doing a Nazi salute was revealed and stirred controversy, Greniuch dismissed the criticism by explaining that it was a traditional Roman salute, to much outrage from his critics.[35] Greniuch's political stride, modeled on the Catholic fascism of the Falange of Spain, was possible through the cultural memory of Poland, which had collective innocence as its backdrop. More important, the official memory of the Polish state formulated collective innocence through the series of "memory laws" and memory-related trials. On February 9, around the same time as the appointment of Greniuch, the Warsaw court ruled that the historians Jan Grabowski and Barbara Engelking must issue a written apology for defaming the plaintiff's grandfather, who was a Holocaust survivor.[36] The legal logic that employed "apology" as a means of penalty was strange, but the wrath of Polish nationalists was directed at Grabowski and Engelking's denial of the collective innocence of the Polish nation. The transposed memory of the eldest Laudański brother, Kazimierz, as manifested in his statement, "As all other Poles, we suffered under the rules of the Soviet Union, Germany, and Polish People's Republic," exhibits the modus operandi of collective innocence as the matrix of cultural memory.[37]

Forsaking the morally comfortable position of the victims was undoubtedly difficult to endure for ordinary Poles. A sociologist's argument that the Jedwabne debates brought forth a "moral revolution" engaging the whole of civil society helps us understand the gravity of the question in Poland.³⁸ Upon the collapse of the communist regime, the dominant historical discourse in 1990s Poland was that the international community did not adequately acknowledge the suffering of the Polish nation.³⁹ Since reflecting on the communist crime was central to coming to terms with the past, accountability for the Holocaust under the Nazis was marginalized in the Polish memory culture.⁴⁰ The Polish professional criminals (*szmalcownicy*) who blackmailed the Jews or sold them to the Nazis were omitted entirely from World War II history, and the Polish indifference to the Jewish population was reductively attributed to insuperable external reasons such as the Nazis' reign of terror. As a result, the deep-rooted grassroots antisemitism within Poland was deliberately overlooked. Poland's experience portends the great danger of a memory culture based on the collective innocence of an entire nation. The moralism of victimhood nationalism stays immoral as long as it complies with the overhistoricized self-righteousness upheld by collective innocence rather than consciously demanding responsibility from each individual.

COLONIAL GUILT AND COLLECTIVE INNOCENCE

From the newly liberated Republic of Korea, Ahn Dongwon went on an around-the-world trip in 1948 and published his trip record in 1949. His travelogue recounts a mishap Ahn faced in the soccer stadium in London: Ahn said yes when asked, "You, Korean?" by a British man, who in return blurted out "*bakayaro, bakayaro*" and tried to hit Ahn. Though Ahn protested by explaining he was not a "Jap" but a Korean, the British man, who then said Koreans were even worse, was unstoppable. This reckless stranger claimed revenge for the beatings and insults he had received from Koreans. Later, Ahn learned that the British man had been detained for three years at the Japanese POW camp in Singapore. His memory of the POW camp was filled with starvation, abuse, and inhumane treatment, and his hostility was directed toward the colonial

Korean POW camp guards. Those whom he had faced every day on site had been lower-ranking Korean jailers rather than Japanese Army officials. That explains why Koreans were the target of his revenge for all the abuses he had endured. Ahn felt "spiteful of those who evoked such hostility toward Koreans" in this man by being overly subservient to imperial Japan.[41] The painful and resentful memories of abuse by the Korean guards in Japanese POW camps in Southeast Asia were more intense than Ahn imagined. In 1951 the British government, with the backing of former POWs whose resentment against Koreans was too strong to be ignored, opposed the Korean government's joining the Treaty of San Francisco.[42]

Koh Hwang Kyung, the chief of the Women's Bureau installed by the U.S. military government in South Korea and founder of Seoul Women's University, had a similar experience when she attended the Asian Relations Conference held in New Delhi in 1947. Sitting in the hotel lobby, Koh was approached by one of the Malaysian delegates, who complained to her about his family being tortured by Korean soldiers. Koh, to not further upset the delegate who had openly expressed his hatred and disdain, explained the unfortunate situation of the colonial Korean soldiers desperate to prove their loyalty to the Japanese empire. To Koh's attempts to justify the Korean soldiers' cruelty by ultimately ascribing it to Japanese colonialism, the Malaysian delegate coldly responded by pointing out that the Koreans were still accountable, even considering the historical circumstances. In *Travel to India*, Koh recounts feeling an "electric shock" about the notoriety of Koreans as vicious aggressors against their Asian neighbors.[43] The official memory of the newly independent Republic of Korea as the victim of Japanese colonialism was laid bare in the face of the grassroots memories of its Asian neighbors that testified to the brutality of colonial Koreans in service of the Japanese Imperial Army. The Asian Relations Conference in 1947 was held to elucidate the ideological fallacy of the Greater East Asian Co-Prosperity Sphere and promote new unity in postwar Asia. For Koh Hwang Kyung, however, the conference was a moment of revelation about Koreans as, at once, the victims of Japanese colonialism and perpetrators of violence against their Asian neighbors.

Colonial Korean guards were also present in constructing the Thailand-Burma Railway, which became widely known via the movie *The Bridge on the River Kwai*. The project's record speed, built at an average of 840 meters per day through dense forest, over small and large river streams, and across ravines, took the lives of numerous workers. Of 125,000 mobilized for the construction of this bridge, including 55,000 Allied POWs and 70,000 local workers, 44,000 died. A quarter of the Allied POWs perished due to the ferocious work environment involving malnourishment, disease, and daily physical abuse.[44] At the war crimes trials to hold those who inflicted forced labor on POWs accountable for the breach of the Geneva Convention, 111 were convicted out of 120 indicted for their crimes related to the Thailand-Burma Railway. Of those indicted, 35 were Korean guards and 33 were found guilty. Koreans made up one-third of the war criminals, second only to the Japanese. The punishments were also relatively harsher for the Koreans—of 32 sentenced to death, 13 were Koreans. Of the 13, 4 received a sentence reduction and 9 were executed. Of the 111 class BC Korean war criminals who were found guilty, 32 were sentenced to death, 16 to life in prison, and 64 to imprisonment. Severe sentences amount to about 50 percent of the 33 convicted Korean war criminals, among whom 9 were sentenced to death, 7 to life in prison, and 17 to imprisonment.[45] In the trials of class BC war crimes in the Asia-Pacific War held in forty-nine regions in Asia, including Japan, a total of 5,700 were prosecuted. Among them, 4,403 were convicted, and 948 were sentenced to death. Among those convicted, 148 were Koreans, 23 of whom were sentenced to death. Of the 148 Korean convicts, 129 were jailers in the POW camps.

Since December 1941 many Koreans have been selected through the four-step selection process and trained in the Noguchi detachment in Busan. After two months of training, they were assigned to POW camps in Southeast Asia, Seoul, and Incheon: a total of 3,223 Korean military workers were dispatched through this process, and 3,016 of them were relocated to Southeast Asia. In a 4.27 out of 100 ratio, 129 became war criminals.[46] The 4.27 percent is just a little higher than the percentage of war criminals in the notorious Japanese military police—4.25 percent, for 1,534 convicted out of 36,073. Such a high conviction rate of Korean military workers was related to the high death rate of Allied POWs in Japanese prison camps. Of the 132,134 Allied POWs captured by the Japanese military, 35,756 died, setting the death rate at a whopping 27 percent. This is about seven times higher than the 4 percent death rate of the Allied POWs captured by the Nazi German and Italian military (9,648 died out of 235,473). Such a high number of deaths was enough to readily convince the court of the existence of particular criminal violence against the POWs. The death rate of 27 percent was even much higher than the death rate of the Japanese POWs detained in Siberia, which supported the victimhood of postwar Japan. The death rate of the Japanese POWs in Siberia was 10.1 percent (61,855 deaths out of 609,448), roughly one-third of the death rate of the Allied POWs in Japanese prison camps.[47] The high death rate of the Allied POWs was also linked to the ideology of imperial Japan—*Daily News* (每日申報), the publication of the government-general of colonial Korea, wrote that supervising the insolent white POWs was a task that "enriched one's deference to the Japanese Empire" and took delightful revenge for the hundred years of arrogant British and American exploitation.[48] Even in the prison camps in colonial Joseon, the persistent tendency to abuse POWs for ideological propaganda showed off to colonial Koreans the power of the Japanese empire by putting the "white" British and American prisoners on display and "extinguishing the remaining admiration for the United Kingdom and United States in the minds of Koreans."[49]

Though international law indicted the Korean military workers in Japanese POW camps as war criminals, they are still remembered as victims by the postcolonial public memory in South Korea. The permanent exhibition *Those Who Became War Criminals* at the National Museum of Japanese Forced Mobilization in Busan explains: "The Korean jailers became the easiest target for the Allied forces after the war. Japan passed its accountability for brutality on to the Korean jailers. The Allied POWs who could not distinguish Koreans from the Japanese accused the Koreans of war crimes." Another explanation is that "the POWs' resentment was directed at the Korean jailers in front of them, and from there, the concept of 'abusive Koreans' was conceived," meaning that the POWs supposedly misunderstood and falsely accused the Korean jailers of war crimes. According to the museum's official exhibition statement, the Korean war criminals were essentially victims. Dedicated to those sacrificed in the railway construction, the museum's special exhibition in 2020, *The Thai-Burma Death Railway*, touched on the "tragic lives of the Korean jailers who in reality were victims of forced mobilization under the Japanese occupation but were accused of and executed for the crimes against the Allied POWs."[50]

"전범이 된 조선청년들" (The young Joseon men who became war criminals), a documentary film produced by KBS, the national broadcaster of South Korea, has a similar plot line. In the sequence that explains that the reason the Japanese military pushed through such a laborious construction plan was that "the Allied POWs and Korean jailers were there," the film alludes to the fact that the POWs and Koreans shared a common fate as victims. To the viewers, the oppositional relationship between the Japanese perpetrators and the POWs–Korean jailers as victims would seem evident.[51] The film stretches even further to narrate how the fate of those young Korean men was even harsher than that of the Allied POWs. In the documentary, as in the exhibition, the memories of the local workers, whose casualties outnumbered those of the Korean jailers or the Allied POWs, are omitted; they appear in glimpses only as witnesses who indirectly suggest the victimhood of the Korean war criminals. Prosecuted as war criminals, ostracized in the Republic of Korea as Japanese collaborators, and exempted from the support law in Japan, these Koreans indeed walked a heartbreaking journey. Amid the somber, sorrowful melody of *Les Larmes de Jacqueline*, the film continues its depiction of "unfortunate Joseon youths" who were incarcerated as war criminals in a foreign prison far from home.

Such a tragedy of these young Korean men whose history started with being mobilized against their will by Japanese imperialism and ended with execution in an alien country would make anyone watching emotional. Lee Hak-Rae, a former jailer who was initially sentenced to death and later had his sentence reduced to life imprisonment, testifies in the film that he "could not but give absolute obedience to the commands of the Japanese military, and had to supervise the prisoners to accomplish the mission." Jang Soo-eob, another former jailer sentenced to death at the war crime trials, also defends himself by saying that he was "in a tough situation where he had to obey the orders as a colonial Korean under Japanese rule." The bottom line of the Korean war criminals' arguments was that, according to the military order, they brutalized the prisoners who broke the rules. Jo Moon-sang, who was sentenced to death by hanging for war crimes against the British and executed in 1947, testified that he was taught that "physical violence was the only way to confront a prisoner bigger in size than you" since the days of jailer training at the Noguchi detachment in Busan.[52] The "small perpetrators" on site evaded their accountability by saying that they, as civil servants, were merely obeying orders. At the same time, the people in charge, "desk murderers," claimed they had never committed violence with their own hands.

The pleas of the Korean war criminals and the collective memory in postcolonial Korea are composed of the logic of collective innocence and "mediation of action" that absolve the Korean jailers. The famous question, "If the 'armband' of perpetrators was 'enforced' on the Korean jailers, could they be punished for simple acts of violence?," epitomizes collective innocence.[53] After all, the number of applicants for the jailer position exceeded the available spots by ten times despite the selective requirements, including Japanese language proficiency, a high level of education, and physical fitness. The sophistry of collective innocence that has exonerated colonial Koreans en masse takes the logical leap from the victimhood of Koreans as a colonized nation to the argument that every Korean was a victim under the colonial rule. The overhistoricizing national victimhood buries the history of individual perpetrators into the memory of collective innocence. "Mediation of action" is also a logical tool frequently used by perpetrators to appeal their innocence.[54] According to this logic, everyone who had been involved in the massacre would be innocent: the commanders, for they had not directly murdered anyone, and the rank and file, as they could not but follow the commands forced on them. Still, Lee Hak-rae's testimony that he could not avoid the order to abuse the POWs also means his admission of guilt, however "unavoidable" the crime might have been. Lee later visited Australia to apologize for the violence in the prison camps. Moon Tae-bok, former chair of Dongjinhoe, the association of ex-jailer war criminals and their families founded in 1955 to demand reparations from the Japanese government, also expressed his wish to apologize to the British POWs.[55]

Their apologies and regrets aside, personal and official memories of the Korean jailers have been markedly self-defensive, as attested by a series of government reports in postcolonial Korea. Published by the Committee for Investigation of Damage Inflicted by Forced Mobilization During the Period of Resistance Against Japan and Aid for Victims of Forced International Migration, the reports "defined the registered 86 out of the 129 ex-jailer war criminals as victims of forced mobilization as of April 2011." In the reports, the Korean jailers were "conscripted for Japan's war of aggression under the colonial rule and blamed as the convicts by the Allied forces for the war crimes." The report also claims that Korean camp guards "were mobilized against their will for Japan's war of aggression," rendering them as the "genuine" victims who were faced with the double misfortunes. "The Koreans victimized by the forced mobilization became the abusers of the Allies" because "the Koreans were deliberately and continuously pushed to the sites of perpetration by the Japanese." In short, the guilty here were not the Korean jailers but the Japanese imperialists. The Korean war criminals were "double victims" of both Japanese imperialism and the Allied powers' war tribunal: the Japanese empire was their first victimizer, and the Allies who did not take the historical context into account were the second victimizer.[56] Even though the former jailers themselves either issued an apology or expressed their willingness to apologize to the Allied POWs they victimized, the Korean government's report describes them as "double victims." The document does mention their apologies at the end of the report, but its overall tenor emphasizes the Koreans' victimhood.

The Korean government's report employs a logic that is surprisingly similar to that of the Laudański brothers' self-exoneration of their crimes in the Jebwabne pogrom. Although they participated in the Jedwabne pogrom of 1941, the brothers claimed they were the real victims because they were Poles who were "doubly victimized" by the Nazis and the Soviet Union. This is not unique to the Laudański brothers. Many perpetrators and accomplices in the Holocaust in Ukraine, the Baltic states, Hungary, and the Balkan peninsula often stress their double victimhood under Nazism and Stalinist terror. The reversal of memory, by which individual perpetrators hide their agency behind the curtain of national victimhood and even reposition themselves as victims, is a dangerous subterfuge. The way of thinking that an individual's act of violence is absolvable for one's membership of the victimized nation is categorically antisemitic in that it determines whether someone is guilty or innocent based not on their actions but on their ethnicity or nationality. The memory code of distinguishing victims and perpetrators based on race, ethnicity, or nationality is as pernicious as the mindset of the genocide, which categorically incriminates the entire ethnic or national group. Distancing from the logic that turns the Korean jailer-perpetrators into victims of Japanese colonialism, a critical question to ask at this juncture would be how to hold the Japanese government accountable for withholding from those colonial Korean jailers the rehabilitation support it provided for the Japanese war criminals.

Even more intricate problems arise regarding subjectivity or historical agency. For instance, Kim Chul-soo, a Korean camp guard in Indonesia, could send about eighty yen every month to his family back home in South Chungcheong Province. This amount at the peak of his career far exceeded the salary for the town chief, who was paid fifty yen monthly at that time. On average, Korean jailers were paid wages seven times higher than rank-and-file Japanese Imperial Army soldiers. For the youths of impoverished Joseon, deciding to enlist for the military-civilian position of two-year terms and better salaries rather than being conscripted into forced labor or the military was more than reasonable.[57] The decision was not morally desirable, but it would be unfair to label the destitute colonial Korean youths who tried to appropriate the colonial conditions as immoral "Japanese collaborators." The lives of historical actors who wound their ways in the world so hostile to them cannot be measured by abstract ideologies. Their crooked life trajectories are good evidence of their everyday struggles to ride out the colonial hardship at the grassroots level. For this reason, grassroots memories of the subalterns who survived not inside the hegemonic memory but on the margins of deterritorialized memory are precious.

Life on the margins of memory is well-illustrated by the story of Yang Chil-seong, a former Korean jailer who joined the Indonesian National Armed Forces to fight for the liberation of Indonesia and was later executed by a Dutch military firing squad. His furrowed life path was not something that could be contained within a frame of one specific territorialized memory: he was at once a colonial Korean, Japanese imperial subject, Japanese military civilian, war criminal, Indonesian national liberation fighter, and third-country victim of Dutch colonialism. Now buried in the national heroes' cemetery in the small Javanese town of Garut, Yang Chil-seong lived through the margins across the postwar memory spaces of the Koreas, Japan, the Netherlands, and Indonesia. Yang and the Korean military civilians were not the only ones on the historical threshold of memory: the Taiwanese military civilians who turned their backs on the empire, the defeated Japanese soldiers who once believed in the grand cause of the Greater East Asia Coprosperity Sphere, and the Gurkhas who advanced to Indonesia as part of the British Colonial Army also joined Indonesia's independence movement led by Achmed Sukarno.[58] In the official memory of the twenty-first-century Korean government that distinctly describes the Korean jailers as victims, there is minimal room to include people like Yang, who stayed on the threshold of memory.

Since the code of collective innocence dominates the memory culture, the space for memories of (post)colonial Koreans as potential or actual perpetrators gets even more limited. A quintessential example would be Korean society's memory of the Wanpaoshan (萬寶山) incident. In April 1931 a conflict arose between Korean and Chinese peasants over constructing a waterway in marshlands near Wanpaoshan in Changchun, Manchuria. The Korean peasants tried to resolve the dispute by relying on the military forces of the Japanese empire, causing the Japanese authorities on the side of the Korean peasants to intervene on July 1. However, the conflict spread to the Korean peninsula as the Manchurian branch of *Joseon Ilbo* misreported the incident as physical attacks on the Koreans by the Chinese. As a result, ethnic Chinese residents in more than thirty regions on the Korean peninsula, including Iri, Seoul, Kaesong, Pyongyang, Wonsan, Sariwon, and Incheon, were brutalized and murdered from July 3 to July 30, 1931. According to the Lytton Report of the League of Nations, the Wanpaoshan incident left 127 dead and 393 injured in the Chinese population in Korea.[59] However, the actual casualties might have been higher than the numbers reported. Just in Pyongyang on July 7, 59 were reported as missing, 819 were injured, and 479 homes were destroyed. Up until July 13 the number of Koreans arrested for their involvement in the massacre was 1,840: 490 from Gyeonggi Province, 750 from Pyongan Province, and 600 from other regions. By the conclusion of the trials in September 1931, nearly a thousand Koreans were sentenced to a fine or prison.[60]

Oh Ki-young remembers that the tragedy was the first of its kind in the long history of Pyongyang, where "bodies of infants and women beaten to death were everywhere." His recollection depicts the sight of horror, though in a snippet.[61] Considering the number of victims or punishment imposed on the perpetrators, the massacre of the Chinese in Korea was more significant in scale than the Kielce pogrom of 1946. In this book, I suggest an alternative name for the Wanpaoshan incident: "the Joseon Chinese pogrom." Used frequently in the official memories and the current academy in Korea, the "Wanpaoshan incident" may be enough to explain the conflict between the Korean and Chinese peasants in Changchun, Manchuria. Still, it may also obscure the massacre and plunder that ensued in the Korean peninsula. The linguistic practicality of the "Wanpaoshan incident" is analogous to "the Nanjing incident." The wording "incident" tends to underestimate the scale of tragedy by covering the violent massacre. The news articles on Wanpaoshan that filled *Dong-A Ilbo* and *Chosun Ilbo* for the entire month of July 1931 are a testament to the press's obsession. What is interesting is that the articles make an apparent distinction between the Wanpaoshan incident and the Joseon Chinese pogrom: the conflict between the Korean and Chinese peasants in Manchuria is called "the Wanpaoshan incident," while the sequential attacks on and murders of the Chinese in Joseon were entitled "attack on Chinese," "Manbosan [Wanpaoshan] and Pyongyang incidents," "conflict in Incheon," "Joseon incident," and the like. It is difficult not to feel that the memory culture of contemporary Korean society that consolidates the conflict in Wanpaoshan and the massacre of the Chinese in Joseon into the abstract "Wanpaoshan incident" has regressed from that of the journalists of colonial Joseon in 1931.[62]

Compared to the scale of the shock the Chinese pogrom caused in colonial Joseon society, the memory of it in postliberation Korea is vague at best. Under the blanket term "the Wanpaoshan incident," the massacre of the Chinese in Joseon was eclipsed by the conflict in Manchuria. In postcolonial Korea, the collective memory was heavily influenced by the conspiracy theory that the pogrom was a ruse planted by the Japanese to justify its invasion of Manchuria by pitting Koreans against the Chinese. According to this conspiracy theory, detectives of the governor-general of Joseon bribed Korean A-frame porters to attack the Chinese people and businesses so the porters could commit arson, looting, and vandalism at the nod of the Japanese police. What is more, the author of *Land*, one of the most popular Korean epic novels set mainly in the colonial era, hypothesized that there were Japanese people disguised in *hanbok* hiding themselves in the crowd.[63] Such a hypothesis is reminiscent of the Stalinist conspiracy theories that the Kielce pogrom was a ruse of the Polish Communist Party or that it was led by a high-ranking NKVD officer who happened to work later for the Soviet Embassy in Tel Aviv in the 1960s.[64] Pushed to the extreme of its logic, the conspiracy theory can transform the Korean perpetrators into the victims of the Japanese scheme. In its moderate version, the main villain is the Japanese imperialism that pitted the peoples of Joseon and China against each other, while the Korean perpetrators are sympathizers or accomplices at worst. Postcolonial Korean memory of the Chinese pogrom does not veer far from this theory of the Japanese conspiracy, which reconfirms the collective innocence of colonial Koreans.

Nevertheless, all conspiracy theories are conducive to becoming a matter of political belief rather than undergoing scientific verification.

Because they mainly stem from unverifiable hypotheses, conspiracy theories tend to override verifiability. What is left, then, depends on "believe it or not"—the unjust binary of us versus them, "believing" versus "unbelieving," naturally becomes dominant. Collective innocence as the a priori premise of the Korean nation meets the logic of conspiracy theory at this juncture. Not believing in the theory that the Chinese pogrom in Joseon was Japan's imperial conspiracy can quickly turn one into an antinational villain who refutes the existential premise of the Korean nation. In 2003, almost sixty years after the liberation, the history of "the Wanpaoshan incident" could finally enter the realm of Korea's official memory as the government-approved high school history textbook included it. Also, the term "Anti-Chinese Riots" used in these studies may be one step forward from the "Wanpaoshan incident." However, I still believe that it would be more reasonable to refer to the 1931 massacre of the Chinese people in Joseon as a "pogrom," which implies a combination of ethnic prejudice, jealousy, and competition. Still, the textbook follows the logic of the conspiracy theory and fails to formulate a critical memory of the Chinese pogrom.[65] The memory culture reflected in the contemporary school textbook is far more irresponsible and immature than the article published in *Chosun Ilbo* nearly a century before, in July 1931, that separated the Wanpaoshan incident of Manchuria from the massacre of the Chinese and stressed the Koreans' accountability for the massacre.

The memory of Manchukuo posed a serious threat to the national victimhood and collective innocence of the colonial Koreans. Japan's imperialism in Manchuria was marked by the policy of "osmotic expansion through Koreans as proxy immigrants."[66] To Korean immigrants, Manchuria was the El Dorado of the Japanese empire; to indigenous Manchurians, the colonial Koreans seemed like the proxies for Japanese colonialism. The number of colonial Koreans who emigrated to Manchuria reached about two million, including a million agricultural workers, thirteen thousand mid- to lower-ranking bureaucrats, and two thousand medical workers, along with drug smugglers, pimps, and other adventurers looking for easy money. Although the historical legacy of Manchukuo, such as a planned economy and nationalist mobilization, continued in the developmental dictatorship of South Korea and the Kim Il Sung dictatorship in North Korea, the memory of Manchuria was utterly obliterated.[67] Also forgotten were the memories of "the Wanpaoshan incident" and the Chinese pogrom. The reality that lacks even rudimentary research on the colonial Korean perpetrators of the Chinese pogrom is perhaps only a natural consequence. Since the perspective of collective innocence views a colonial Korean perpetrator as a nonexistent actor, researching a subject that had never actually existed in history would be an impossible task.

The affirmation of Koreans' collective innocence is often paired with vehement condemnation of its Japanese counterpart. An editorial published in *Joongang Ilbo* on May 20, 2013, wrote that the atomic bombing of Japan was "the god's punishment and revenge for Asians," with much controversy. The language of the article was riddled with nationalistic hostility and spite. The column, which included expressions like "as if the screams of the victims of Unit 731 reached the heavens, the heat flash of the atomic bombs struck Hiroshima and Nagasaki" and "it would be up to the god's will to decide whether . . . there needed to be more firestorms to punish the Japanese," caused an uproar. Suga Yoshihide, then chief cabinet secretary of Japan, denounced it as "a perspective that the only A-bomb victims in the world can be never tolerated." *Joongang Ilbo* issued a statement that the editorial was based on the editor's personal opinion and did not reflect the official viewpoint of the newspaper.[68] Korean *hibakusha* spearheaded the public rebuke of the article in Korea. Their scathing criticism pointed out that the bombing of Hiroshima and Nagasaki took numerous lives of not only Japanese civilians but also foreign nationals, including some seventy thousand colonial Koreans, Chinese, Taiwanese, international students from South Asia, Allied POWs, and missionaries, and that the Republic of Korea has, in fact, the second largest number of victims of the atomic bombs.[69] The colonial Korean victims' fierce protest against the expression "the god's punishment" suggests the potential of grassroots memories as critical ammunition against the nationally framed memories. The scandal over the *Joongang Ilbo* article explicitly revealed problems of standardized narrative and memory culture operating in binary opposition between collective innocence and guilt, dehistoricization, and overhistoricization of memory.

HEREDITARY VICTIMHOOD AND ISRAEL

In a survey about Israeli identity in 1992, around 80 percent of students at a teachers' college responded that they were all "survivors of the Holocaust."[70] The college students in 1992 would have mostly belonged to the generation born from the mid-1960s to early 1970s. Born twenty or so years after the end of World War II, this generation could not have directly experienced the Holocaust, and it was existentially impossible for them to have been either a victim or a survivor of the Holocaust. It was through the transcendental power of cultural memory that the Jewish sons and daughters who had not yet been born during the Holocaust could become hereditary victims. Emblematizing the Holocaust as its symbol, the memory culture of Israel passed down the status of Holocaust victims to the postwar generation, the so-called children of the Holocaust.[71] While "postmemory" is the memory acquired primarily through an individual's developmental stages from the traumatic memories of their parents or relatives,[72] cultural memory that promotes hereditary victimhood requires no family trauma as its premise. In Israel's memory culture, the status of "the children of the Holocaust" as hereditary victims is accessible to every Jewish person regardless of whether their parents or grandparents were victims of the Holocaust. What is also meant by this self-identifying as a hereditary victim of the Holocaust, regardless of one's family history, is obtaining Israeli memory citizenship.

Hereditary victimhood has not always been the dominant code in Israel's cultural memory. On the contrary, heroism prevailed initially in the memory culture of the newly founded state of Israel. A Bergen-Belsen concentration camp survivor, Werner Weinberg, writes in his memoir that Israelis treated a Holocaust survivor like "a museum piece, a fossil, a freak, a ghost."[73] David Shaltiel, Israel's founding father and first prime minister David Ben Gurion's special envoy to Western Europe, curtly commented after visiting the refugee camps in Germany: "Those who survived did so because they were egotistical and cared primarily about themselves."[74] The language of Zionist literature is even more harsh and violent when describing Jewish diasporic victims. The famed Zionist poet Haim Nahman Bialik wrote that the Jewish victims "fled like mice, scurried like roaches, and died like dogs" in Europe, in lines that reveal the Zionist's disdainful hostility toward the Jewish diaspora who, ignoring the Zionist desire to help build Zion "here" in Palestine, stayed "there."[75] Israel's official memory could not veer much from the dichotomy between "masculine, active Zionist heroism" and "weak, feminine, and passive diaspora Jewish victims." In it, the Holocaust was even symbolized by the image of a female prostitute bearing a tattoo that said "for officers only."[76] In brief, it was "a sexist reconstruction of history" that feminized and peripheralized the Holocaust survivors.[77]

Zionist activists considered diaspora Jewish victims as an unnecessary burden, thus objectifying and instrumentalizing them with labels like "human resource."[78] In the Zionist official memory in Israel, Holocaust survivors were turned into passive objects deprived of agency. The Zionists' hostile gaze on the Jewish diaspora is also palpable in the attitudes of Zionist newspapers' reporting on the Holocaust during wartime. For example, the *Palestine Post* on November 25, 1942, only briefly touches on the report issued by the Polish government-in-exile regarding the Final Solution devised by Heinrich Himmler. In the same issue, information on the Soviet victory in Stalingrad and the Allies' advance on Tunisia was given far more weight in both priority and length. The report on Himmler's Final Solution was handled with even less importance than a story about the Asia-Pacific War. To the Jewish papers in Palestine at the time, political issues of the local party were much more urgent and vital than the fate of the diasporic Jews.[79] Zionists saw Hitler's coming to power as the failure of Jewish assimilationists. Ben-Gurion expected the Nazi reign to catalyze Jewish migration to Palestine, ultimately fostering an environment conducive to Zionism. The agreement between Nazi Germany and Ha'avara, which represented the Jewish population in Palestine, paved the way for German

Jews migrating to Palestine to exchange their assets for German goods instead of cash. While the Jewish community in the United States boycotted German products, an abundant supply of them flowed into Palestine.[80]

After the end of the war, American Jewry was also drawn not to the Holocaust victims but to masculine war heroes. The American Jews who crossed the Atlantic to the New World had to be a nation of victors, not victims. The self-image of American Jews was of victorious heroes embodying healthy American traits, whereas Holocaust victims were the Jews they left behind in the Old World. As the end of World War II approached, John Slawson, executive vice president of the American Jewish Committee (AJC), said a proper Jewish representation should "avoid representing the Jew as weak, victimized, and suffering. . . . There needs to be an elimination or at least a reduction of horror stories of victimized Jewry. . . . War hero stories are excellent."[81] The cultural code prevalent among American Jews was their inclusion on the side of victors rather than of victims. There is a world of difference between the AJC's heroic memories and today's Holocaust-centered memories stressing the victimhood of exclusive singularity. Also interesting is the Anti-Defamation League's critique of *The Anatomy of Nazism*, a documentary film that the ADL leadership reckoned to be "too narrowly focused on Jewish suffering." Max Horkheimer, a central figure of the Frankfurt School, also expressed concern about emphasizing Jewish sacrifice, as it could provoke a negative influence. Stereotyping of Jews as victims was what they all feared.[82]

The global Cold War also played a significant role in the suppression of Holocaust memories within American Jewry. On top of the fact that 50–60 percent of the Communist Party USA were Jews, the Rosenbergs' espionage case, in which Jewish American couple Julius and Ethel Rosenberg delivered confidential information about nuclear weapons production to the Soviet Union, further cornered Jewish Americans. As the Cold War intensified, the most urgent matter for the Jewish population in America was to be rid of the label "Jewish commies." Under the circumstances where Washington politics considered West Germany as the bulwark in Europe against Bolshevism, evoking the memories of the Holocaust could be interpreted as a political challenge posed by Jewish communists to vilify West Germany. The charge of aiding communism by disrupting the anticommunist front line of NATO was something that should not only be worrying but also actually frightening. Therefore, discussions of the Nazi Holocaust gave way to those of Stalin's antisemitism and Eastern Europe's purge of Jewish communists, as if antisemitism was a communist problem and not a Nazi problem. Prompted by the trial of Rudolf Slánský staged by Czechoslovakian Stalinists, American Jewry began to stress the antisemitism of the Communist Bloc. Though Stalinist antisemitism pushed Holocaust memories aside, the Jewish community in the United States could, in exchange, be rid of the stereotype of Jews as communists.[83] The plan to build a memorial museum in New York for survivors of the Warsaw ghetto uprising and the Holocaust between 1946 and 1948 also was not supported by the Jewish community. The Warsaw ghetto fighters, including Mordechai Anielewicz, were connected to the Bund, a Jewish communist movement, which made American Jews reluctant to support the plan.[84] It is not surprising that Brandeis University was the only school in the United States in 1962 that offered a course about the Holocaust.

If in the United States, the Cold War logic was what suppressed Holocaust memories, in Israel it was the Zionist historical discourse that hindered productive discussions about the Holocaust. The catastrophe dawned on the Jews who refused to relocate to Palestine and stayed in Europe, which seemed to attest to the Zionist outlook that rebuilding an independent state on Israeli soil—old Palestine—was the only viable option.[85] Most victims of the Holocaust were the assimilationists who refused to leave Europe. The defeat of assimilationism, which left the issue of the nation to the civic choice, reinforced the Zionists' ethnic nationalism in Israel.[86] There must not have been enough room for the Holocaust in such historical discourse. In the nascent state of Israel, the memory of the Holocaust was focused on the Warsaw ghetto uprising and the fighters. In 1951 Knesset, Israel's parliament, passed a resolution to designate the twenty-seventh day of the Hebrew month of Nissan (a week after Passover—May 3, 1951, by the Gregorian calendar) as Yom HaShoah, the Holocaust Remembrance Day, to commemorate the Warsaw ghetto uprising that happened on the eve of Passover in 1943. Prior to this, in December 1943, a kibbutz was named Yad Mordechai after the ghetto fighter Mordechai Anielewicz. In 1951 a memorial to Anielewicz was erected in the kibbutz in light of the designation of Yom HaShoah.[87] In 1959 the Martyrs' and Heroes Remembrance (Yad Vashem) Law was passed to regulate the commemorative rituals, including a two-minute silence and flags flying at half-staff.

The memory culture that commemorated the heroic ghetto fighters and their martyrdom more readily than Holocaust victims was in harmony with the mythologized memory of Masada created by a Zionist in the nineteenth century. The Hebrew warriors of Masada, who put up a three-year resistance to the overwhelming Roman Army and, in the end, chose to commit group suicide rather than surrender, were the symbol of the struggle for national liberation of ancient Israel. Despite the Judaic doctrine that forbade suicide, the group suicide of the Masada warriors was glorified as holy "martyrdom." In contrast to the passive death of assimilated Jews during the Holocaust, the Masada warriors were considered the alternative model for the struggle for national liberation. The Masada myth appealed especially to the younger generation who were born in Palestine and educated in Hebrew by a Zionist curriculum.[88] The culture that sublimates and worships individual deaths to bring forth the nation's revival is typical of civil religion. To borrow the words of Zeev Sternhell, the state of Israel, centered on the concept of nation, was "a classical product of modern nationalism as it materialized in Eastern Europe and the Third World."[89] In the memory culture dominated by the warlords of Masada who threw themselves to save the Jewish nation, the victims of the Holocaust could not help but be marginalized. In 1950s Israel, the memory of the Holocaust was focused on the ghetto uprising fighters. Calling the Holocaust victims "Jews" while the ghetto fighters were "Zionists" and "Hebrew Youths," the politics of naming revealed Israel's Zionism-tinted memory culture, which, in essence, began by denying diaspora.[90]

Nevertheless, the Holocaust continued to exist in the shade of heroism as a cultural memory to persuade the raison d'etat of Israel. This point is most successfully attested to in the official memory articulated by the Israeli Declaration of Independence. The document denotes that "the massacre of millions of Jews in Europe was [a] clear demonstration of the urgency of solving the problem . . . by re-establishing in Eretz-Israel the Jewish State." According to it, "the State of Israel will be open for Jewish immigration and for the Ingathering of the Exiles; it will foster the country's development for the benefit of all its inhabitants."[91] Yet, at the grassroots memory level, the Holocaust victims came to the notice of Israelis through the Eichmann trial. Begun on April 11, 1961, and lasting until December 15 of the same year, the trial was held in a kind of court of public opinion broadcast not only to the people of Israel but also throughout the world, from Mossad's capture of Eichmann in Argentina to his death sentence. Through the Eichmann trial, the prosecutor with "six million accusers," Gideon Hausner, hoped to build a national saga that would resonate across generations of Israeli people.[92] The protagonists of the heart-rending saga were the Holocaust survivors on the stand to testify. As the Holocaust was recounted in stark detail through the voices of witnesses, empathy for the victims' suffering proliferated among the people of Israel and worldwide. Holocaust survivor Yehiel De-Nur collapsed while giving testimony and was transferred to the hospital, adding a dramatic effect to the trial.

Watching the trial, Israelis, old and young, started to empathize and eventually identify with the suffering of the Holocaust victims, affirming once again the legitimacy of the state of Israel. Young Israelis now criticized the world for letting Jews perish in the concentration camps instead of denouncing the Holocaust victims. Hausner later recalled that "it was enough to let the archive speak; a fraction of them would have sufficed to get Eichmann sentenced ten times over," yet he "needed a living record of a gigantic human and national disaster."[93] What required testimonies was not the trial but the public sentiment, in that the witnesses were first selected based on their published memoirs and finalized through interviews.[94] Of 121 trial sessions, 62 were survivor testimonies—the focus was on effectively delivering the victims' suffering to move people watching the trial rather than on verifying facts.[95] The Eichmann trial was a massive success in terms of Israel's national unity. The trial linked the suffering and death of diaspora Jews to the raison d'etat of Israel and rationalized Ben-Gurion's teleological view of history that turned the diaspora and the Holocaust into a process toward the establishment of the Jewish state.[96] In correspondence between the official memory and grassroots memories, the Holocaust was given a hegemonic status in Israel's memory culture. Likewise, victimhood nationalism became fixed as the canonical historical narrative that frames the past, defines the present, and designs the future.

Though Mossad's meticulous operation to abduct Eichmann drew both admiration and criticism from the international community, the original function of the agency was not tracking down war criminals but rather for the national security of Israel, with missions of searching for spies and building an intelligence network in the Middle East. The riots of Sephardic Jews in Wadi Salib, an impoverished neighborhood of Haifa, in 1959 shocked both the government and the people of Israel. Mostly immigrants from Middle Eastern countries, Sephardic Jews were subject to Ashkenazi Jews from Europe in terms of their political power, social status, financial status, and level of education. They were subalterns in Israel. To the Zionist founders of Israel, Sephardic Jews were mere objects of anthropological interest. However, when European Jews were murdered en masse due to the Holocaust, the 750,000 Jews in the Middle East suddenly emerged after the war as the alternative target demographic for immigration to Israel, a newly founded state in dire need of people to populate its land. Sephardi Jews emigrated to Israel due to their Middle Eastern neighbors' hostility following the Arab-Israeli War, only to be stuck on the bottom rung of Israel's social ladder. In consequence, the conflict between Ashkenazi and Sephardic Jews intensified, more so than the conflict between Zionists and Holocaust survivors, as their social gap grew more significant after the reparation money from Germany flowed into Israeli society.[97]

The riots started by Sephardic Jews were deemed a threat to the hegemony of Ashkenazi Jews, who were central to Zionism. As a new state surrounded by enemy states with an incomparably more extensive scale, Israel was desperate for a patriotic catharsis to resolve the conflict between the two major Jewish ethnic subgroups and unite the nation as a whole. To achieve such national unity, Ben-Gurion tried to formulate a cultural memory of the Holocaust by explaining to those who "lived in Asia and Africa and had no idea what Hitler was doing."[98] Circumstantial factors like these were primarily why the Eichmann trial became the court of public opinion that appealed to Israel's national sentiment. The Six-Day War of 1967 further reinforced the oneness among the people of Israel, and Israel heightened the anxiety of the nation, who fretted about the possibility of genocide. The CIA accurately predicted that Israel would repel its enemies in a week to ten days. However, the ontological anxiety was more overwhelming than the realist calculation. About the thoughts he had during the Six-Day War, a young soldier recalled: "People believed we would be exterminated if we lost the war. We got this idea—or inherited it—from the concentration camps. It is a concrete idea for anyone who has grown up in Israel, even if he did not experience Hitler's persecution."[99] Here, it is evident that hereditary Holocaust victimhood is contiguous emotionally to the existential insecurity among Israelis. As suggested by Raymond Aron's concept of "state-cide,"[100] the Middle Eastern Arab enemy's threat against Israel was interpreted as the matter of the ontological insecurity rather than international politics.

A phenomenon characteristic of post–Six-Day War Israel was that the state as an actor began to actively hanker after the status of the victim. Calling the new border after the 1967 war "Auschwitz Lines," Israel's hereditary victimhood became at once the people's modus vivendi and the state's modus operandi.[101] Whereas the leaders of both North and South Korea after the liberation stressed the necessity to build a more robust nation-state in order not to relive the agony of the past, in Israel, historical discourse on the Holocaust and Masada prevailed in the public sphere—the lesson that served to reason the great power Israel's hegemony in the Middle East. The tendency to engage hereditary Holocaust victimhood in the existential imperative of the state of Israel became more prominent during the incumbency of Prime Minister Menachem Begin. Founder of the Likud, Begin compared Yasser Arafat, then leader of the Palestinian Liberation Front, to Hitler and the Palestinian Declaration of Independence to *Mein Kampf*. He also explained that the bombing of Iraq's nuclear reactor in 1981 was a necessary measure to "protect our nation, a million and a half of whose children were murdered by the Nazis in the gas chambers." He also spoke at a cabinet meeting preliminary to the Israeli invasion of Lebanon in 1982: "You know what I did and what we all did to prevent war and bereavement, but it is our fate that in Eretz Israel there is no escape from fighting with dedication. Believe me, the alternative is Treblinka, and we have decided there will be no more Treblinka."[102]

As the criticism from the international community heightened after the invasion of Lebanon, Begin claimed that the international community had lost the right to demand a response from Israel for its actions after the Holocaust. He also bawled in the Israeli parliament that "no nation on Earth can preach morality to our nation."[103] In the *Encyclopedia of the Holocaust* published in Israel, the entry for the mufti Amin al-Husseini, the nationalist leader of Palestine during World War II, is about double in length compared to the entry on Joseph Goebbels or Hermann Göring and longer than those on Heinrich Himmler and Reinhard Heydrich combined. Among all the entries on people, only the one on Hitler is longer than that of al-Husseini. At the World Zionist Congress held in Jerusalem in October 2015, the hawkish Israeli prime minister Benjamin Netanyahu left the participants aghast by accusing the mufti of planting the idea of the Holocaust in Hitler, whose initial plan was to expel Jews from Europe.[104] As attested to by such examples, the cultural memory of the Holocaust was often permeated by political calculations to justify the state-cide of Palestine. The official memory of Israel, which prides itself on being the most morally righteous country in the world due to the sacrifice of the Holocaust, also reveals the darker side of victimhood nationalism.

Often, at the grassroots level, the Holocaust memory functioned as the antithesis of aggressive Zionism. When the Israeli soldiers murdered fifty civilians who were returning home after work in the small town of Kfar Kassem in the Sinai peninsula in October 1956 amid the Suez Canal crisis, voices of self-reflection burst from Israeli society decrying that it was shame and dishonor of the entire Israeli nation and that the Israelis were no different from the Nazis or the antisemitic perpetrators in Eastern European pogroms. Here, the Holocaust was also used within Israeli society as the ground of moral imperative for universal human rights.[105] As victimhood nationalism encroached on Holocaust memories, however, the potential to bring about mnemonic solidarity through the Holocaust could not wake up. The Israeli military's total ban on visiting the Ghetto Fighters' Museum after the Palestinian Intifada eloquently indicates the case. The commanders were afraid that the Israeli soldiers could be reminded of their treatment of Palestinian youths by looking at the history of the Nazis' brutal suppression of the Warsaw ghetto uprising.[106] Such concern had become a grotesques reality—expressions of racist hostility against Arabs were rampant, the Israeli soldiers who conspired to murder Arabs called themselves the "Mengele squad," and other nicknames like "the Auschwitz platoon" and "the Demjanjuk squad" were also present within the military.[107] As victimhood nationalism developed in Israel's memory politics, the memory of the Holocaust stopped being the weapon of the victims.

The premise of victimhood nationalism, with its dichotomy between victims and perpetrators, disallows fundamental critiques of the likes of colonialism, genocide, and the Holocaust. Instead of changing the rules that caused the tragedies of world history, victimhood nationalism tends to induce a desire to preempt the position of the victor over that of the loser, of the victimizer over that of the victim, by using the same set of rules. Emotionally, it is full of regret and denunciation of the nation's history of being victimized. It can, on the other hand, readily accept the rules of colonialism and the Holocaust insofar as the positions are invertible. The historical introspection, which allows people to free themselves from "hereditary victimhood" and become aware of their capability to victimize others, should be the narrative framework for cultural memories of the twenty-first century. Inscribed deeply in the collective memory of a nation, victimhood nationalism fundamentally blocks criticisms of the latent or already palpable danger of colonialism. The sinister lesson of the Holocaust is not that it can happen to victimize us again but that we can also perpetrate such an atrocity ourselves.[108] The real danger of victimhood nationalism lies not only in that it turns perpetrators into victims but also in its hindering of victims' critical awareness of being potential victimizers under different historical settings. Nothing is more dangerous than moral self-righteousness without reflection.

8

JUXTAPOSITION

RADICAL JUXTAPOSITION

Juxtaposition is the modus operandi of global memory formation. If comparison is the starting point of historical imagination, juxtaposition is the starting point of cultural memory. As all national histories, intentionally or unintentionally, peep into other nations' histories in comparative history, a nation's cultural memory juxtaposes one's collective memory with that of others. Thus, national history and memory contribute to constructing one's national collective. The juxtaposition of memory is often a product of meticulous political calculation when memory politics is globally at work to insidiously highlight specific memories while suppressing and erasing others. It may seem novel, but juxtaposition is a time-honored and widespread practice. It garners less attention from academia for its stealthy operation. Unlike the concept of "entangled memories" that seems evident to even the thoughtless, the juxtaposition of distant memories constructs cultural memory covertly and impalpably. Like the cofiguration of particular "national history" and universal "world history," victimhood nationalism juxtaposes the suffering of one's own nation and that of other countries in the same memory narrative.[1] In the global memory formation, the competition of victimhood nationalism over who suffered more and whose suffering carries a universal significance is predicated on the juxtaposition of memory. The juxtaposition of memory essentializes and justifies the nation's victimhood nationalism with relative ease without creating a new framework for elaborate theorization or emotional appeal. It warrants a critical assessment of juxtaposition as a comparison tool to uphold victimhood nationalism.

Juxtaposition is not always used to justify victimhood nationalism. For instance, "radical juxtaposition" reveals unexpected commonalities through a montage of different memories while disrupting the linear order of memory and rejecting hierarchy.[2] Though not often, it challenges the complacency of the national memories to stimulate critical memories globally. This chapter is built on the method of radical juxtaposition to critically examine the political operation of juxtaposed memories in global memory formation. Viewed through the lens of radical juxtaposition, unrelated and distant societal memories are often unexpectedly intimately connected. The memories of the Vietnam War, for instance, may seem unrelated to the Holocaust memory as the former is increasingly faded and peripheralized while the latter occupies more and more space in the U.S. public sphere. However, a critical juxtaposition can help discover a deep connection between these two memories: whereas the Holocaust memory draws the portrait of the United States as the mighty and righteous country that rescued European Jews from Nazism, the Vietnam War memory reminds the United States of the defeat, guilt, shame associated with the civilian massacre, and ecocide by Agent Orange. The memory boom of the Holocaust and the disremembrance of the Vietnam War in U.S. memory culture are two faces of one and the same memory politics to strengthen the status quo.[3] The Vietnam War is also absent in most American history textbooks. Most textbooks in the United States do not mention the likes of the Mỹ Lai massacre, indiscriminate area bombings, and the environmental calamity of Agent Orange. College textbooks are more critical, but it is still difficult to make out that the Vietnam War was a U.S. war crime.

Descriptions of the Vietnam War in American history textbooks are far more self-apologetic than even the government-censored Japanese textbooks are on the issue of the Asia-Pacific War, let alone German school books on making critical memories.[4] The oblivion of the Vietnam War as a recent past in the 1960s–1970s is in sharp contrast with the memory of the Japanese internment camp during World War II. The latter is remembered as a tragic, shameful, dishonorable, and grave criminal act. U.S. history textbooks also included photos of Japanese-American women and children standing in line to enter the camp as a mnemonic device to overlap with European Jews arriving at the death camps.[5] The exhibition dedicated to the Japanese American internment camp in the Japanese-American National Museum in the Little Tokyo area of Los Angeles, California, in 2023 was titled *Don't Fence Me In*. Among the many notable artifacts on display was a Heart Mountain barracks, an original structure saved and preserved from the "concentration camp" in Wyoming.[6] How the three distinct memories—of the Holocaust, the Vietnam War, and the Japanese internment camp—are juxtaposed in U.S. memory culture alludes to an interesting point: juxtaposition allows a genealogical analysis of cultural memory by bringing together memories that are absent and present beyond a surface-level comparison of memories of the immediate past. The question of why specific memories are highlighted while others are obliterated becomes the starting point of the genealogical analysis of memory politics.

The case of Serbia seems much more extreme. The Jasenovac Committee of the Holy Assembly of Bishops of the Serbian Orthodox Church represents Serbian nationalist memory activism. The Jasenovac concentration camp (1941–1945) was run not by Nazi Germans but by Ustasha, a Croatian fascist organization. The committee calls Jasenovac the "Kosovo of Serbia," disclosing its intention to turn the site into a symbol of Serbian suffering. At this juncture, the Holocaust is evoked to at once emphasize the national suffering of Serbia and publicize the nation's moral rectitude in the international community.[7] The Holocaust is summoned to the memory politics of Serbian nationalists who stress mnemonic solidarity between Jews and Serbs over their shared suffering. The problem is that the Jasenovac extermination camp functions as more than a tool to justify Serbia's victimhood nationalism, but as a screen memory that covers up the war crimes committed by Serbia during the civil wars in former Yugoslavia. What is more, the Jasenovac

Committee's memory politics camouflages Serbian Chetniks' war crimes against Muslims and Croats and against communist-led Yugoslav Partisans through its leveraging of the Holocaust to revive the fight against Ustasha.[8] The memory of the Holocaust, which the committee loudly revitalized by even dragging in a rock band, is an apparatus to erase the memory of ethnic cleansing perpetrated by Serbian nationalists during the Yugoslav Wars. Holocaust memory has been appropriated as such by Serbian nationalism. The declaration of restoring the memory of the shared suffering of Yugoslav peoples and their battle against Fascism remained only in the realm of words.

The reality of the rehabilitated memory in the name of socialist brotherhood was the reterritorialized memory in service of Serbian nationalism. An awareness of themselves as victims of the Holocaust, just like or even more so than the Jews, spread among Serbs. The anti-Serbian sentiment across Europe after the Yugoslav War was interpreted as equivalent to antisemitism. Thus, it is not surprising that the Museum of Genocide Victims in Serbia depicts the nation's pain and suffering inflicted by Croatian fascists through the lens of the Holocaust.[9] Serbia's memory politics is interesting because it is the complete opposite of its Croatian counterpart, which severs the Holocaust memory from the Ustasha massacre of Serbs. In Croatia, the local fascists and German residents actively partook in the Holocaust, with only three thousand Jews surviving as a result. Upon entering the postcommunist era of the 1990s, Croatia's memory culture progressed toward the obliteration of the memories of communist partisans and Serbian victims. It even pushed for the idea of entombing the Ustasha militia killed by communist partisans and Croatian soldiers who died in the Yugoslav War with the remains of the Holocaust victims from the Jasenovac camp, in an attempt at the historical reinstatement of Ustasha.[10] The instrumentalization of the Holocaust to historically reinstate antisemitic nationalist fascists is not unique to the former Yugoslavia. In general, postcommunist Eastern Europe has incorporated Holocaust images in the process of emphasizing each nation's sacrifice enforced by communism as an alien ideology. Such an inclination to juxtapose the Holocaust with Stalinist crimes under the slogan of "there is no hierarchy among victims" could be observed in the former Communist Bloc countries, including East Germany. From the existential perspective of individual victims, it is difficult to assert that the pain of any individual Holocaust victim was more significant than that of an individual victim of Stalinist terror. All victims carry their own pain.

The narcissistic analogization of themselves to the Jewish Holocaust victims in postcommunist Eastern Europe reflects a certain ambivalence. Holocaust memory in the European East has been at once an adamant expression of their will to share the cosmopolitan narrative promoted by the European Union and a tactical remembering device to hijack the Holocaust for their respective nationalist aims. The postcommunist narrative in which two totalitarianisms, namely, Nazism and Stalinism, tyrannized the people is also shared by the Baltic states. The Molotov-Ribbentrop Pact of 1939 has often been cited as the unsubtle evidence of the joint conspiracy between Nazism and Stalinism. Nazism and Stalinism are delineated as an "equally evil" political parallel at this juncture.[11] Yet, in Eastern Europe, the Stalinist crime has often garnered more scrutiny for its persistence and tenacity in this evil parallel. For example, Estonia's National Day of Mourning perceived the Gulag to be a worse evil than Auschwitz. The national suffering under Soviet occupation often peripheralizes the Holocaust.[12] More aggressive critics would repeat Ernst Nolte's stance during the *Historikerstreit* that Nazism was brought on as a repercussion of Stalinist terror. Scarcely any reason can challenge the legitimacy of communism better than that it caused Nazism and the Holocaust. Appropriating the Holocaust memory to reproach communist crimes, such memory politics intends to erase East European memories of their connivance and collaboration with Nazism during the Holocaust. The result we see now is the emergence of the far-right nationalist memory regime in Eastern Europe.[13]

What is disturbing about such a reversal of memory in Eastern Europe is that it is not contained within the far-right nationalist sector but popularized among grassroots memories. A worrying example is Ukraine's Maidan Revolution in 2013–2014, during which the participants called themselves the "Banderites" (Banderivtsi) and reinstated the Ukrainian ultranationalist Stepan Bandera as the symbol of resistance against the corrupt, pro-Russian government.[14] Meanwhile, in western Ukraine, a movement to revive Ukrainian nationalism that shares an ideological affinity with Nazism gained traction—the members would call the day the Nazis conquered Lviv the "independence day" from Poland's oppressive rule and confront Poland about the memory of Volhynia massacre. Apparently, Putin and Russian ultranationalists abused this Ukrainian nationalist memory politics as an excuse to invade Ukraine. In postcommunist Eastern Europe, the indigenizing process of the Holocaust memory erased the communist-led antifascist efforts in exchange for the mythologization of antisemitic, racist ultranationalism.[15] While different from the Holocaust denialism of the United States or Western Europe, it may be an even more deceptive form of denialism in that it appropriates the Holocaust to reinstate the historical antisemitism of far-right nationalism. It is worth noting that the Holocaust memory has also been appropriated in the global memory formation as a means to justify state violence, such as a preemptive strike, through political catastrophization to invoke an apocalyptic premonition of genocide.[16]

SAINTS OF AUSCHWITZ AND NAGASAKI

In East Asia, the juxtaposition between the Holocaust and the atomic bombing in Japan is notable as both a narrative technique and a hegemonic device to structuralize the memory of the Asia-Pacific War. Especially eminent is the connection between Maksymilian Kolbe, the Polish priest revered as the "Saint of Auschwitz," and Nagai Takashi, dubbed the "Saint of Nagasaki." In Nagasaki, nicknamed "Rome of East Asia," these two Catholic "martyrs" bridged the gap between secular death and religious sanctity. Kolbe, who had worked as a missionary in Nagasaki from 1930 to 1936, returned to Poland and was imprisoned in Auschwitz after the Nazis had invaded Poland. Kolbe sacrificed his life on August 14, 1941, to save a fellow prisoner, Franciszek Gajowniczek, in a punishment cell of Block 11 at the Auschwitz concentration camp. A devout Catholic and physician in Nagasaki, Nagai lost his wife to the atomic bomb that also severely injured him. Though all his children were safe, the loss of his wife, who was burnt almost entirely in the heat and identified only by the slight trace of the rosary on her bone, left an insurmountable pain in the family.[17] The essays Nagai wrote as he was dying of leukemia contain peculiar accounts of the tragedy of the atomic bombing. In Japan's postwar memory culture, Auschwitz and Nagasaki, the Holocaust and the atomic bomb, became entangled through these two figures.

Nagai was working at Nagasaki University Hospital when the atomic bomb was dropped on August 9, 1945. The shattered glass left numerous cuts on the right side of his upper body. One of the shards ruptured an artery in his head, resulting in a severe injury. By mid-September his condition had deteriorated so much that he was in the throes of death. Realizing that his time had come, Nagai made a general confession to a priest and received the Sacrament of the Anointing of the Sick. While slowly drifting into unconsciousness, Nagai suddenly felt a cold sensation in his mouth and heard his mother whispering, "This is Lourdes water." In his eyes, "the Lourdes Grotto with roses in full bloom and the pure image of the Holy Mother seemed so clear," he heard a voice telling him to pray to Father Maksymilian Kolbe for intercession.[18] The miracle of Lourdes water reoccurred as he drank the water that stopped the bleeding and healed the wound. However, the water that treated Nagai was brought not from Lourdes in France but from the Hongouchi Seminary in the Militia of the Seibo no Kishi [Immaculate] Monastery, where Kolbe had built a replica of the spring of Lourdes.[19] What made this miracle on Nagai's deathbed remarkable was the appearance of Father Kolbe. The part of this story where Nagai prays to Father Kolbe for intercession is especially striking.[20] Nagai recalls in his memoir that he paid a medical visit to Kolbe at the Hongouchi Seminary in 1935. Kolbe had tuberculosis in both lungs. From the physician's perspective, it was incredible that someone who had lost about 80 percent of both of his lungs' functionality could still passionately immerse himself in the publication of the *Seibo no Kishi* (聖母の騎士, Immaculate). When Nagai asked how Kolbe could continue, the Polish priest held up his rosaries and said, "This. This is how."[21]

Catholicism has been the matrix of cultural memory in Nagasaki, the so-called Holy Land of the East. Incidentally, the date of the Japanese attack on Pearl Harbor in 1941 was December 8, the Feast of the Immaculate Conception. Nagai recalled that upon hearing about the attack on Pearl Harbor, a premonition that Urakami might be turned entirely into ashes sent a shiver down his spine.[22] When the atomic bomb exploded in Nagasaki on August 9, 1945, confessions were being held at Urakami Cathedral. All the priests, subpriests, and lay followers who were gathered for the mass died on the spot. The official name of Urakami Cathedral, the Immaculate Conception Cathedral, originated in the Militia Immaculatae (Rycerstwo Niepokalanej), which Saint Maksymilian Kolbe founded. Aside from the personal connection between Father Kolbe and Dr. Nagai, the memory of the Nagasaki bombing was intricately woven together with that of Christian persecution. Not only was Urakami Cathedral at the hypocenter of the blast, but the apocalyptic image of the atomic bombing served as an ideal motif that could be combined with the cultural memory of Christian persecution. The persecution of Christians in Nagasaki had been widely known outside Japan even before the war. Raphael Lemkin, who coined the term and concept of "genocide," included the Christian persecution in Nagasaki in his world history of genocide, along with the colonial genocides in Namibia and the Congo, and the massacre of Roma, American Indians, Aztecs, Incas, Armenians, and European Jews.[23] The atomic bombing amplified the grimness of genocide by casting an apocalyptic shade over the region's Christian persecution. Within this context, Maksymilian Kolbe bears great significance in Nagasaki's memory culture.

Nagai came to fame even before Father Kolbe was canonized in 1982. After the war, Nagai wrote meditative essays in his sickbed in Nyokodo (如己堂), a small teahouse named after Mark 12:31, "Thou shalt love thy neighbor as thyself." These consoling writings bestowed religious meanings on the unreasonable deaths of the atomic bomb victims there. A compilation of these essays was published titled *The Bells of Nagasaki* in 1949, selling 110,000 copies in six months. The publication was approved with the premise that it would include as an appendix the report of Japanese military atrocities in Manila because the American censors required a balanced account of the Japanese between the atomic bomb victims and the war criminals. Nagai's book offered an interpretation of the bombing in Nagasaki as God's will to cleanse the original sin of the Japanese. It moved many who were unable to find meaning in the carnage of war and innocent deaths. The year 1949 also marked the four-hundredth anniversary of Saint Francisco Xavier's missionary work in Japan. A contingent from the Vatican served a special mass in the ruins of Urakami Cathedral and the Twenty-Six Martyrs Museum, where tens of thousands of Japanese Catholics gathered.[24] Subsequently, Nyokodo was visited by Helen Keller, the Japanese emperor, and even the papal envoy to meet Nagai. By then, Nagai was deemed the symbol of peace and healing and called the "saint of Urakami" despite having never been officially canonized. When Nagai died in 1951, the city government organized his funeral with twenty thousand attendees. The bells of all churches and shrines in Nagasaki pealed to mourn his death.

The motto of Nyokodo, to treat others as yourself, corresponds to the verse that represents Kolbe's martyrdom, John 15:13: "Greater love hath no man than this, that a man lay down his life for his friends." The personal encounter between the "saint of Urakami," Nagai Takashi, and the "saint of Auschwitz," Maksymilian Kolbe, has functioned as a link that places the memory of the atomic bomb and of Auschwitz next to each other. Through this peculiar juxtaposition, Nagasaki's nuclear bomb victims could avoid being regionally isolated and secure the universality of its tragedy. They could communicate with the global memory of the Holocaust. Through its entanglement with the memory of Auschwitz, represented by Kolbe, the memory of Nagasaki became the first step toward peace as a universal memory reflective of the pain of war and genocide. Still, such an attempt to deterritorialize the memory of Nagasaki had to continuously negotiate with the challenges posed by the force to reterritorialize the memory. Nagasaki's memory culture, with its emphasis on solidarity, has maintained instead a tendency to overlook the historical context of the Asia-Pacific War that caused the tragedy of the atomic bombing. The dehistoricized memory of Nagasaki has been used at times to justify Japan's victimhood nationalism. The complex tension between universalism, particularism, internationalism, and nationalism in the postwar global memory space is also unmistakably present in Nagasaki's memory culture.

At this juncture, one can see how Japan's obsession with comparing the Holocaust with the atomic bombing played the screen memory as in former Yugoslavia. As the aggressive wing of victimhood nationalists professes that the Japanese and Jews are both the most representative victims of white racism, such an obsession provokes Japan's victimhood nationalism more emotionally through a crude juxtaposition. Also interesting to note is the opening of the Anne Frank and Holocaust exhibition in Hiroshima and Nagasaki in August 1995, as a countermemory to the Holocaust denial scandal in Bungei Shunju's *Marco Polo* in February 1995.[25] How the memories of Maksymilian Kolbe at Auschwitz and atomic bomb victims in Nagasaki are juxtaposed in Japan's memory culture draws attention in this sense. Being juxtaposed does not necessarily mean that two distinct memories are organically intertwined within the global memory space. At times, the memories are regionally fragmented or deliberately selected to be placed next to each other. Just as the controversy surrounding Kolbe's antisemitism that heated Europe and the United States did not cause the Japanese concern, Nagai Takashi's use of the term *hansai* (燔祭), the literal translation of "holocaust," in his address to commemorate the atomic bomb victims at Urakami Cathedral on November 23, 1945, did not have an impact in the European and U.S. memory space. The mere juxtaposition, not to mention the close entanglement, of these two memories was enough to construct a complex meaning. As attested to by the consolidation between the memories of Auschwitz and of Nagasaki through Father Kolbe, transnational memory can indeed operate to consolidate and justify nationalist memories across borders.

Nagai Takashi's contribution to global memory formation is that he originated the "Urakami *hansai*" theory. At the memorial mass held at Urakami Cathedral for the atomic bomb victims on November 23, 1945, Nagai gave a eulogy quoting the word *hansai*, a Japanese translation of the term "Holocaust," meaning burnt offering. The word appears in chapter 22 of Genesis, when God said to Abraham, "Sacrifice him [Isaac] there as a burnt offering on a mountain I will show you." Thus began the Urakami Holocaust theory. Soon after the atomic bombing, a rumor spread among the non-Christians in central Nagasaki that the victims of Urakami Cathedral were punished for worshipping not the Japanese gods but the Western God, as attested to by the decimation of some eight thousand Catholics, eighty of whom were praying during the mass at the cathedral at the time of the bombing. This rumor shows how deeply rooted religious and social prejudice against the Christian *burakumin* (the lowest social caste in Japan) of Urakami had been. In a challenging way, the Christians of Nagasaki referred to the horrors of the atomic bombing as the fifth persecution. They viewed the bombing as a continuation of historical Christian persecution, which started during the Toyotomi Hideyoshi era and continued through the Tokugawa Shōgunate to the fourth persecution from the 1860s until 1873 after the opening of Japan. Urakami Cathedral was the largest cathedral in East Asia and had been built on a site where persecuted Japanese Catholics had previously had to step on a *fumi-e*, or sacred image, and demonstrate to the state their apostasy. The cathedral symbolized the revival and ultimate victory of Japanese Catholicism; the fifth persecution, namely, the atomic bombing, caused consternation among Catholics in Nagasaki.[26]

The atomic bombing of Nagasaki that centered on Urakami Cathedral cast an apocalyptic shade on the tragedy. The apocalyptic image of the bombing provided the Nagasaki victims with a religious sublime aura. The A-bomb victims were turned into the subjects of an unavoidable fate, whether divine intervention or societal persecution, against which no human agency could stand. The Catholic victims believed that the deaths testified to their actual innocence and faith in themselves, who repented and were punished on behalf of humanity. To them, Nagai's 2,502-character eulogy was an attempt to recover their lost agency. Nagai read the eulogy, entitled "Funeral Address for the Victims of the Atomic Bomb," at the requiem mass, where the attendants held eight thousand candles to symbolize eight thousand Catholic victims of the bombing.[27] In his speech, Nagai emphasized that the fact that the Urakami Cathedral was at the hypocenter of the nuclear bomb blast was divine providence. Furthermore, he asserted that it was not a coincidence that the date of August 15, when "the whole world welcomed a day of peace" following "the Imperial Rescript which put an end to the fighting," also happened to be the Feast of the Assumption of Mary.

To Nagai, the formation of the hypocenter of bombing over the cathedral did not feel like a chance event. The atomic bomb had initially been planned to be dropped in the city center of Nagasaki but was dropped in the northern town of Urakami due to dense clouds that obstructed sight at the time. Of all places, the bomb hit the cathedral, where eighty or so priests and believers were gathered for the mass to prepare the ceremony of the Assumption of Mary. Their deaths in the very cathedral dedicated to the Holy Mother added to the fatalistic tone of the tragedy. According to Nagai, "Urakami church was chosen not as a victim but as a pure lamb, to be slaughtered and burned on the altar of sacrifice to expiate the sins committed by humanity in the Second World War."[28] If Nagai's logic is to be taken to the extreme, the sacrifice of the Catholics of Urakami had brought a swift end to the war, saving billions of human lives that otherwise would have been ravaged. Furthermore, if the Catholics of Urakami, who had overcome persecution for four hundred years and maintained their orthodox faith, had been chosen as a sacred offering on the altar of the Lord, they would have been graced and blessed by God. Nagai's eulogy assigned a resolute humanitarian meaning to the unreasonable deaths of the Catholics of Urakami Cathedral: "How noble, how splendid was that holocaust of August 9th, when flames soared up from the cathedral, dispelling the darkness of war and bringing the light of peace! In the depth of our grief, we reverently saw here something beautiful, pure, and good."[29]

Praising the victims of the bombing for sacrificing themselves as burnt offerings to God, Nagai's eloquent speech sublimated the regrettable deaths into the sacred sacrifice for peace. "Holocaust," as it appears in the Bible, means the ritual where a pure, unsullied animal is burned alive to be offered to God.[30] Therefore the theory of the "Urakami Holocaust" was to remember the victims of the Nagasaki bombing on the same level as the Jewish victims of the Nazi Holocaust. As pure and unsullied lambs, they became the holy sacrifice of the great Holocaust, chosen to be offered on the altar of God and burned by the atomic bomb. They were also martyrs of peace, who died not only for the absolution of others from their sins committed during the war but also so that the war could be brought to an end, preventing any more innocent victims. As per René Girard's interpretation, the Catholics' theory of persecution was the basis of their belief in themselves as altruistic sacrifices that were punished on behalf of "sinners." It is a sin to kill a sacrifice for the holy ritual, but the sacrifice cannot be made holy unless it is destroyed.[31]

Claiming that "God finally accepted the sacrifice when Urakami went in flames and listened to the human suffering to reveal to the Emperor to make the holy decision of ending the war," Nagai's eulogy is surprisingly similar in tone to the Japanese emperor's "Jewel Voice Broadcast," which emphasized the emperor's determination to "pave the way for a grand peace for all the generations to come" reflected in his "noble act" to surrender to save the Japanese nation and humanity from the increasingly cruel enemy and their weapons. Based on this logic, the war itself becomes the biggest perpetrator, while the Japanese are holy victims who sacrificed themselves for the peace of humanity.[32] Such rhetoric to sublimate the victims' premises that the "conventional" wartime atrocities perpetrated by the Japanese military were nothing compared to the sacrifices caused by the atomic bomb. This is not so different from the collective sentiment of Japan's antinuclear movement, which focused on designing the future of Japan as a peaceful nation rather than reflecting on its past as invaders. Victimhood was also the crux of Japan's postwar leftist peace activism.[33]

Even if it spoke for the Catholic victims' emotional devastation, Nagai's "Urakami Holocaust" theory was subject to endless criticism. From the perspective of memory politics, it was a discourse of "double exemption" that simultaneously erased the Japanese emperor's war responsibility and the United States for the atomic bombing. Poet and Nagasaki bombing survivor Yamada Kan denounced the theory as misleading pro-U.S. propaganda that tried to appease the "grudge of the people" with the phrase "divine providence." Writer Inoue Hisashi also argued that the notion of "divine providence" obfuscated the question of who should be held accountable for the use of atomic bombing.[34] These critiques make a valid point regarding the political effect created by the eulogy, which sublimated the deaths caused by the bombing of Nagasaki into a holy sacrifice for world peace through "divine providence."

Dehistoricizing, as well as religiously essentializing, the historically unprecedented tragedy of the atomic bombing was to erase the political responsibility for the victims' innocent deaths. Once dehistoricized, the victimhood of Nagasaki could again catalyze Japan's absolutist pacifism. Nagai's Catholic existentialism stands opposite the memory politics of Hiroshima, which is politically instrumentalizing the victims. It is expected of the survivors to seek existential meanings beyond the level of politics from the requiem for the dead. Assigning the meaning of holy sacrifice to the unreasonable, innocent deaths was also to grant an ontological value to the deceased beyond the political judgment. Though the Urakami Holocaust theory deserves the political criticism that it induced the exoneration of political responsibility for the war and atomic bombing, the criticism is counterbalanced by its restoration of the survivors' capacity to affirm their existential value and meaning of the victims' deaths through the notion of religious sublimation.

Among the Catholic mourners in Nagasaki, survivor's guilt was quite common. In Nagai's words, "In large-scale destructions such as an atomic bomb explosion, humans . . . die if they follow their conscience. To avoid dying, one must turn away from one's conscience." The extreme circumstances of the atomic bombing demanded a choice to be made between morality or rationality, between "saving a friend groaning in pain before your eyes and to be engulfed in flames, or fleeing the scene and leaving your friend there to die." "In the face of waging atomic war, any country would say, 'Do not be concerned about others, just save yourself. Do not even think about your duty. Your own life must be saved.'" In such a desperate situation, it is challenging to follow the teaching that "you must love others; negate yourself and give love; fulfill your duty."[35] Affected by the powerlessness survivors had to feel facing the deaths of family, friends, and neighbors, survivor's guilt is a matter of faith and morality before it is political. As attested to by Primo Levi's painful account, survivor's guilt is connected with "self-accusation, or the accusation of having failed in terms of human solidarity."[36] It is not surprising that a guilty conscience similar to that of the Holocaust survivors can be identified in Nagai and other atomic bomb survivors. Nagai asks himself, "Haven't the survivors merely held up the hundreds of thousands of victims burned by the atomic bomb as examples, using them as the driving force to keep the peace movement going? Although the citizens affected by the atomic bombing (*hibakusha*) of Hiroshima and Nagasaki have been praying for peace, what sacrifices have those survivors made for their prayers?"[37]

This guilt is distinct, by virtue of its self-reflexive existentialist tone, from Hiroshima's political victimhood. Memory in Hiroshima is more politicized due to the atomic bombing of Hiroshima being defined as a product of American racism and a symbol of absolute evil that ranks alongside the horrors of Auschwitz. Indeed, there is some truth in the assertion that, in the case of Nagasaki, the survivor's guilt at leaving dying friends behind gave rise to feelings of atonement or even newfound respect for cases of martyrdom or self-sacrifice that contradicted the egoistic instinct to save oneself. Survivor's guilt is also apparent in the affectionate esteem Japanese Catholics felt toward the "Saint of Auschwitz," Maksymilian Kolbe, who had given up his life to save a fellow prisoner. Similarly, Brother Ozaki Tōmei writes about his own survivor's guilt in a book called *Father Kolbe of Nagasaki*. At the "vigorous age of 17 years," Ozaki was exposed to radiation from the atomic bomb while he was working at an arms factory in Urakami. He would later recall that, "Seeing the chaos of the wounded lying around, I fled the scene in shock. Two months later, I entered the monastery."[38] Here, it is implied that he had felt a sense of guilt about having "fled the scene" and abandoned those who were dying from the aftereffects of the atomic bomb was the reason behind his decision to knock on the door of the Seibo no Kishi Monastery.[39] That Ozaki was drawn to the "martyr of charity, Father Kolbe, who gave his life in place of another during the war" would have owed much to the pangs of guilt he was experiencing.

ANTI-WESTERNISM AND ANTISEMITISM

Japanese author Endō Shūsaku, who introduced Kolbe to many Japanese readers through his novel *A Woman's Life, Part Two: The Case of Sachiko*, which was first serialized in *Asahi Shimbun*, writes in the novel's epilogue about the subtle guilty consciousness one has as a survivor: "Rather than these difficult words, it may just be the honest feeling that 'we really all contrived to survive.' We all contrived to survive. However, hidden behind this feeling are more complex emotions. They are the sadness and pain of knowing that even though I may have survived, the ones that I longed for, loved, and was close friends with were lost during or after the war."[40] As a devout Catholic, Endō portrays Kolbe in his novel as frequently quoting the Bible verse, "There is no greater love than to lay down one's life for one's friends," thereby constantly evoking the guilt of those who had survived. Kolbe, who sacrificed his life by taking the place of a fellow prisoner, was thus a martyr who had made substitutionary atonement for the guilt of survivors.

The common theme running through *A Woman's Life, Part One* and *A Woman's Life, Part Two* is the self-sacrifice of devoting a pure and earnest love to another, to the extent of giving up one's life. Kiku, who appears in *Part One*, gives up her life for her beloved, Seikichi. Vomiting blood, she dies in front of the statue of the Mother Mary of Oura Cathedral. Kiku had given up everything, even defiling her own body, for her beloved Mother Mary, who comforts Kiku by saying, "You have lived this world for love, just as my son [Jesus Christ] has," thereby creating an overlap between Kiku's love for Seikichi and her love of Christ.[41] The Mother Mary of Oura Cathedral statue is the one before which the "Saint of Auschwitz," Father Kolbe, used to kneel in prayer daily while teaching at Oura Seminary. In *Part Two*, Sachiko, Kiku's grandniece, is seen praying in front of the same statue of Mother Mary. Interestingly, the three protagonists in *Part Two* are Sachiko, Kiku's grandniece; Shuhei, the object of Sachiko's pure and ardent love, who dies in war as a kamikaze pilot; and Father Kolbe.

Part Two was written using a "parallel plot" structure, in which the tragic love story between Sachiko and Shuhei intersects with the story of the priest, Maksymilian Kolbe. In the novel, Father Kolbe gives Sachiko a sacred printed image of Maria containing the Bible verse from John 15:13: "There is no greater love than to lay down one's life for one's friends."[42] Endō also writes that the minds of the romantic lovers sacrificing themselves for their beloved are "very similar to the mentality of a saint giving his life over to God, forsaking everything else."[43] The sacrificial love of Kiku, who gave her own life for her beloved, and the martyr's love of Father Kolbe, who gave his life in place of a fellow prisoner, allow survivors to realize their guilt and achieve a religious catharsis through substitutionary atonement. Endō's understanding of Christianity, according to which indifference toward others' pain and misfortune is a sin, and one becomes salvageable only when one feels guilty for such indifference, was a vital link that connected Kolbe and Nagasaki in his novel.[44] The martyrdom at Auschwitz of Father Kolbe, with his secure connection to Nagasaki, was an excellent motif for the process of introspection provoked by the guilt experienced by the Catholic survivors of the Urakami holocaust.

In the photographs taken during his stay in Nagasaki, Kolbe wears his trademark long, dark beard. However, the photos taken after his return to Poland show him clean shaven. According to Ozaki Tōmei interpretation, Kolbe had grown a long beard to soften his interactions with the Japanese by emulating the traditional image of a wise man of the East.[45] Upon arriving at Nagasaki, Kolbe and his party came under suspicion by the Japanese police of being Russian spies. The conflict between Japan and the Western imperialist countries, including United States, had escalated after the Japanese invasion of Manchuria. As the Asia-Pacific War was thought to be imminent, the pressure exerted on the Catholic Church by the Japanese military and the Special Higher Police intensified.[46] Catholicism was not favorably perceived in Japanese society, and the image of the Catholic Church was connected to Western colonialism. Even Endō, who was a devout Catholic, could not but be conscious of the disapproving eyes being leveled at Catholicism for its involvement with colonialism. It is symbolic that Endō's work began by coming to terms with the distance between the West and Japan, and Christianity and Japan's pantheistic aesthetics.[47]

In *A Woman's Life, Part One*, Endō takes up the church's complicity with Western colonialism through the words of Hondo Shuntaro of the Nagasaki Magistrate's Office. Hondo, after rejecting the French and U.S. ministers' request to release Christians as interference in internal affairs, rebukes: "Why has the so-called Pope of Christians kept mum about the rampant stealing, invading, and killing in the Eastern lands being committed by the Christian countries?" Following this pointed question is Endō's apt depiction of the embarrassment of Father Petitjean, the French priest who is made to admit the Christian hypocrisy, without any excuse to justify the invasion and colonization of Asia and Africa by Western Christian countries. Upon hearing Hondo's more or less personal attack—"Father Petitjean, while you have stirred up trouble in Japan and the village of Urakami and the Christians of Urakami are locked in prison, you are comfortably rested in this room"—the French priest is at a loss for words.[48] Here, the contrast between Father Kolbe from the East and Father Petitjean from the West is most pronounced. Indeed, Poland, as a (semi)peripheral state of Europe, could be regarded as "the East within the West" and free from the guilt of colonialism, having been a nation oppressed by the three partitioning states of Russia, Prussia, and Austria for 120 years. Since Poland had maintained a close relationship with Japan by sharing the common enemy of Russia since the Russo-Japanese War, Kolbe from the underprivileged Poland within Europe was at an advantage in Japan's memory culture.[49]

According to the recollections of his fellow friars, Kolbe was met with hostility from Bishop Hayasaka and Father Urakawa of Oura Cathedral, who were skeptical of his simple and humble approach to missionary work. It was rare for missionaries from the West to experience such inhospitality in Japan. All Kolbe's eccentricities as a priest—from his childlike habit of calling the Holy Mother *Mamusia* ("Mommy" in Polish) and insistence on living in honest poverty to the extent that he suffered from malnutrition to his simple missionary approach that relied solely on *Seibo no Kishi*—made him distinctly different from other missionaries from the West.[50] Endō's portrayal of the arrival of Kolbe and his party at Nagasaki is intriguing: unlike typical Westerners, who tended to travel by first class, Kolbe and five other Polish friars took third-class seats in a ship named *Nagasakimaru*. Tamaki, a Nagasaki police commissioner, was puzzled at seeing them in the third-class cabin, carrying only a few pieces of clothing and a couple of books. Tamaki felt both pity and frustration toward these poor "Westerners" who spoke hardly a word of Japanese and very little English. After their arrival, the Polish men, carrying their suitcases and not knowing where to go, stood confused in the middle of the street rather than taking a rickshaw, until they received help from Detective Kaneda, who walked them to Oura Cathedral.[51] The mixture of curiosity, pity, and irritation Kaneda felt toward the Polish clergy would have been quite different from the fear of Western colonialism that captured Hondo when he was meeting Father Petitjean in the Nagasaki Magistrate's Office.

Kolbe's stance, which supported the Japanese empire against the "Western" colonialism of the United States, Britain, France, and the Netherlands in the Pacific and Southeast Asia, was not something generally expected from a Western missionary. Father Sergius, who aided Kolbe, recalled in vivid detail an anecdote Kolbe had shared after his trip to India in 1932: "Japan is preparing to go to war with Russia. Japan is afraid of nothing. It is not afraid even of the United States. The Holy Mother is giving them good guidance. Japan may seize all of Asia in its hand. Even Europe, if the time is ripe. This is very good for the Militia of the Immaculate Mary. Let us go out there with the Japanese and distribute *Seibo no Kishi*."[52] It is hard to establish how well-known Kolbe's stance vis-à-vis the Japanese empire had been in Japan. What can be inferred, though, is that Kolbe's Polish origin and its marginalized position in world history and international politics, namely, East in the West, allowed him to be relatively free from the charge of being a Catholic agent of "Western" colonialism. Compared to other missionaries from the West, Kolbe, coming from Poland, could enjoy the privilege of being underprivileged. He was one of the few Europeans who could be readily accepted by Japan's postwar memory culture. Another crucial factor was the historical camaraderie that the Japanese empire and Polish nationalists had formed through their international solidarity against the common enemy, Russia; it was to the extent that in fall 1931, the Soviet intelligence agency reported that Poland and Japan had signed an agreement to attack the USSR at the same time.[53] Though this report turned out to be a false alarm, the suspicion was a testament to the tight relationship between the two countries at the time.

Sono Ayako's exceptional love for Maksymilian Kolbe is also noteworthy. Author of *Kiseki* (Miracle), documenting the priest's life in a biographical novel, Sono arrived in Poland on September 21, 1971, on the way to attend Kolbe's beatification at the Vatican on October 17. With the guidance of Tadeusz K. Oblak, a Polish Jesuit, the Japanese writer searched for traces of Kolbe in Poland for more than three weeks. It was a long journey, starting at Zduńska Wola, which was Kolbe's hometown, then moving on to Niepokalanów Monastery and Zakopane, where Kolbe stayed at a sanatorium to recover from his illness, and ending at the Auschwitz concentration camp in Oświęcim. Sono also visited Franciszek Gajowniczek, whose life was saved by Kolbe's sacrifice, and talked with him about Kolbe. While in Poland, Sono was astonished at how little was known about the story of Gajowniczek and Kolbe. She tacitly accused the Polish media of indifference by claiming that if this had been Japan, the media attention would have taken over Gajowniczek's everyday life.[54] Sono published her travel notes as a series of articles, which ran for a year in the Catholic journal *Catholic Club*, beginning in January 1972. Having gathered her travelogue, based on the French version of Maria Winowska's biography of Kolbe, with the materials collected during her travels in Poland and her artistic creativity, Sono penned *Kiseki*.

In Sono's understanding, Kolbe was a Catholic patriot. According to her, he had wanted to punish the foreign enemies that had occupied Poland. Still, he realized that real revenge lay in winning over people worldwide by spreading God's word rather than resorting to violence. She was also told an anecdote by Father Anselmo in Kraków, according to which Kolbe's father had fought in the Brigade of the Polish Legions under Józef Piłsudski during the First World War. During a battle, Kolbe's father was captured by Soviet troops and executed.[55] Piłsudski was the leader of the Polish Socialist Party who secured the Polish-Japanese front against Russia during his visit to Japan in July 1904 at the request of the General Staff Office of Japan.[56] The patriotism of Kolbe, whose father had devoted himself to the national movement, resonated with the historical cliché of Polish Catholicism acting as the representative of the crucified nation.[57] It is an anecdote but not confirmed history. Perhaps mindful of the controversy surrounding Kolbe's recognition as a Christian martyr at his beatification, Sono wrote that the golden rule of Christianity is love, and to lay down one's life for one's friends, as Father Kolbe of Auschwitz did for Gajowniczek is the greatest love. In other words, when devotion to Jesus is taken to its furthest point, it is accompanied by death. Had he ignored Gajowniczek's cries for mercy and his pleas to be allowed to see his family again, Kolbe may have been alive physically, but as a priest and spiritually, he would have been as good as dead.[58]

Sono reconfirms Kolbe's martyrdom, and Endō elaborates on this in his novel by ensuring that Sachiko of Nagasaki and Kolbe of Auschwitz cross paths. In his famous essay "Father Kolbe," which has been included in a certified Japanese high school textbook, Endō defines the meaning of a miracle as follows: "I do not think that a miracle is curing an incurable disease or turning a stone into gold. A miracle is doing what we cannot do. In the appalling purgatory of a Nazi concentration camp, Father Kolbe gave a love that we cannot give. This is what I call a miracle."[59] The short essay communicated Father Kolbe's love to Japanese high school students through the Japanese National Language textbook. Once published in a high school textbook, it made Father Kolbe's existence known to ordinary Japanese people who were neither Catholics nor literary enthusiasts.

While Sono Ayako was at a Paris airport waiting to board a plane headed to Warsaw on September 21, 1971, a heated debate erupted in Poland over Father Kolbe's eligibility for his forthcoming beatification. *Tygodnik Powszechny*, a liberal Catholic weekly magazine published in Kraków with widespread support from critical intellectuals, published on September 19 a reader's letter suspecting Kolbe of antisemitism. The writer of the letter was the critical left-wing intellectual and renowned publicist Jan Józef Lipski. Lipski began his letter with the premise that Kolbe's beatification was an issue that, by and large, belonged to the Catholic Church. Yet, he still expressed concern from the perspective of a secular member of the Polish nation. According to his letter, *Mały Dziennik*, of which Kolbe was the founder and editor-in-chief, was pandering to extreme antisemitism and inciting hatred and contempt. The letter exposed that *Mały Dziennik* had close connections with antisemitic members of the ultranationalistic National Radical Camp (Obóz Narodowo-Radykalny, ONR).[60] Lipski also rejected the widespread notion that Kolbe had admitted his wrongdoings and repented of his sins by sacrificing his life by stating that it was simply wishful thinking on the part of the Polish Catholic.[61]

After consulting with Dr. Joachim Bar of the Catholic Theology Academy of Warsaw, who was to oversee Kolbe's beatification, the editors of *Tygodnik Powszechny* published an editor's note based on Bar's response along with Lipski's critical letter on the same page. The editor's note stated, to refute Lipski's claim, that Father Kolbe was not directly involved in the editing of the first issue of *Mały Dziennik*, published in May 1935, as he had been in Nagasaki. The note also included a letter from Kolbe in Nagasaki to the acting editor-in-chief of the Polish devotional magazine *Rycerz Niepokalanej* on July 12, 1935. In that letter, Kolbe advised the editor of *Mały Dziennik* "to refrain from unnecessary hostility toward other people, parties, or nations . . . speaking of the Jews. I would devote great attention not to stir up accidentally nor to intensify to a greater degree the hatred of our readers against them." The editors of *Tygodnik Powszechny* added that Kolbe had returned to Poland in 1936 and then immersed himself in work at the Niepokalanów monastery, while the editors in Warsaw were responsible for publishing *Mały Dziennik* without his supervision.[62] This controversy quickly sank into obscurity once *Tygodnik Powszechny* had run an article on the front page for October 17, the day of Kolbe's beatification, about Cardinal Karol Wojtyła raising Father Kolbe to the honors of the altar.[63]

Although the controversy surrounding Kolbe's antisemitism made headlines just before Sono Ayako arrived in Warsaw, not a single word about it could be heard from the writer. Sono might be unaware of this controversy due to the language barrier. However, given that Father Oblak accompanied them as a guide and translator for the entirety of the trip, and considering the influence *Tygodnik Powszechny* had among Polish intellectuals, it would have been somewhat awkward for her to have no clue at all. Furthermore, the controversy emerged just a month before Kolbe's beatification, and Sono was interacting with Catholic intellectuals in Poland precisely at that time. Only Sono herself would know if she had any prior knowledge of Kolbe's alleged antisemitism. Nevertheless, she left a hint that allows some speculation by revealing that Kolbe often used aggressive expressions when he founded the Militia Immaculatae (Rycerstwo Niepokalanej), prompted by the celebration of Freemasonry's two-hundredth anniversary in Rome in 1917. Citing Maria Winowska's biography of Kolbe, Sono explains that when Father Kolbe saw "a black flag showing the Archangel St. Michael beneath the feet of Lucifer . . . beneath the windows of the Vatican. . . . Right then, [Father Kolbe] conceived the idea of organizing an active society to counteract Freemasonry and other slaves of Lucifer."[64]

As Sono's citation shows, Kolbe was a steadfast opponent of the Freemasons.[65] In his writings, they were often portrayed as part of an axis of evil that also recruited socialists and Jews. *The Protocols of the Elders of Zion*, an antisemitic text fabricated to spread the Jewish conspiracy theory, was sometimes quoted as supporting evidence for this claim.[66] Kolbe's recollection of the Freemason demonstrations in Rome often arises whenever controversy about his antisemitism surfaces. It is intriguing that Sono paid attention to this passage at the critical time of his imminent beatification, especially given that she had likely been aware of the controversy. Considering the paths Sono went on in later years, it was not so out of character for her to intentionally keep quiet about Kolbe's antisemitism. In 2015 she became the talk of the press worldwide for a column she contributed to *Sankei Shimbun*, which suggested that the Abe Shinzō administration should consider South African Apartheid and racial segregation as a potential model for Japan's immigration policy. She came under fire again in 2016 for unreservedly making discriminatory comments about people with disabilities.[67] Sono has mostly played the role of ideologue for the Abe regime, and it makes sense that from her ideological point of view, Kolbe's alleged antisemitism was never a particular problem. Sono's indifference to the allegations surrounding Kolbe's antisemitism went hand in hand with her enthusiastic support for Catholic nationalism.

Her positive views of nationalism and patriotism were consistent with her criticism of Oe Kenzaburo's book-length essay *Okinawa Notes*. In "The Story Behind the Myth: Group Suicides on Okinawa and Tokashiki Islands," Sono took issue with Oe's critique of the former commander of the Kerama Islands, who ordered about 430 residents to commit mass suicide. She accused Oe of standing in the "viewpoint of God" and judging the commander who ordered the suicides as sinful. How Sono felt about this matter is apparent in the following passage: "Why should those who made the beautiful sacrifice of giving up their lives for their country be made into something less clean, their deaths defiled by someone saying after the war that they were forced to kill themselves by military order?"[68] In Sono's transnational memory, the residents of the Kerama Islands who died in an act of forced mass suicide are aligned with Father Kolbe, who died a martyr's death at Auschwitz, because all of them "made the beautiful sacrifice of giving up their lives." In response, Oe remarked, "Those who claim [the likes of Sono's argument] are defiling humanity." Sono's affection toward those who died for their "beautiful, patriotic souls" aptly represents the collective sentiment of postwar Japan's nationalism sublimating into civil religion.[69]

Around the time of Kolbe's canonization in 1982, the controversy about his antisemitism reemerged, this time beyond the Polish national borders and covered by major international media outlets, including the *New York Times* and the *Washington Post*.[70] Any international Catholic intellectual, regardless of their ability to speak Polish, would have struggled to feign ignorance. The issue appeared again in an obituary for Gajowniczek published in the March 15, 1995, issue of the *New York Times*.[71] The question of Kolbe's antisemitism was brought up again in John Gross's review of Patricia Treece's biography of Kolbe, "A Man for Others: Maximilian Kolbe, Saint of Auschwitz, in the Words of Those Who Knew Him," published in the *New York Review of Books* on February 17, 1983. Gross's claim was refuted by some readers in their letters to the editor, eliciting a reply from Gross.[72] It is undeniable that Kolbe believed in the authenticity of *The Protocols of the Elders of Zion*, as well as that he claimed that the Masonic Mafia was instigating atheistic communism. He believed that international Zionism was the driving force behind this. However, Kolbe was not a typical antisemitic extremist in that he advocated the conversion of Jews and did not reject those who had converted. It is attested to again by the anecdote where he sheltered about 1,500 Jews who were fleeing Nazi persecution and sought refuge in the monastery of Niepokalanów. According to testimony by Rosalia Kobla, who lived near the monastery, Father Kolbe advised that she should also give Jews bread to eat "because all men are our brothers."[73] As Kolbe's advocates have argued, of the more than 10,000 letters and 369 editorials and columns he wrote, only 31 mentioned the Jewish question, and even in these, his main concern was the conversion of Jews to Catholicism.[74]

Considering that hardline antisemites do not allow the conversion of Jews into Christians, Kolbe was not a hardliner. Whether Kolbe was a hardline antisemite is not my primary concern. I am more interested in puzzling out Japanese Catholic intellectuals' silence over the controversy regarding Father Kolbe's antisemitism. It is not surprising that Sono Ayako, who commended the Apartheid system of South Africa as a model for migration policy in Japan, would not be concerned about Father Kolbe's antisemitism. It might not be a serious question to her. However, it is perplexing to see Endō Shūsaku, deemed a comparatively liberal Catholic intellectual, also keeping silent. Reconciling his silence on Kolbe's antisemitism with his postcolonial engagement with Franz Fanon in Lyon in the 1950s remains a challenge. Still, it is possible that Endō was unaware of the controversies surrounding Kolbe's antisemitism. Considering that he was a devout subscriber of the leftist Catholic magazine *Esprit* when he was studying in France and that he tried to apply the problematics of Japan to Franz Fanon's discussions of race, colonialism, and liberation that we read in the magazine, Endō's silence regarding Kolbe's antisemitism was odd, indeed.[75] To imagine that Endō from East Asia could have been connected with Fanon from Martinique-Algeria on the intellectual horizon beyond the regional confines is exciting; it would be even better if we could find more explicit evidence of their conceptual encounter. It could have been another stimulating example of how the hitherto separately regarded memories of decolonization, namely, of Africa's anticolonialism and decolonization and of postwar East Asia under the Cold War system, are entangled in the global memory formation. However, the charge of antisemitism against Kolbe, who was deeply involved in the memory of the bombing of Nagasaki, drove a wedge in the mnemonic solidarity between Nagasaki and Auschwitz.

MARTYRDOM IN GRASSROOTS MEMORY

It was not until after Father Kolbe's canonization on October 10, 1982, that his martyrdom at Auschwitz became widely known in the global memory space. Earlier, however, on June 7, 1979, Pope John Paul II had delivered a sermon during his first visit to Poland since his election, in which he said that Father Kolbe and Sister Edith Stein of the Carmelite convent signified the triumph of the Catholic faith in a dire situation such as Auschwitz.[76] In February 1981 the pope visited Nagasaki and paid his respects before Kolbe's statue at the Seibo no Kishi Monastery in Hongouchi. In April 1982 Mother Teresa visited Nagasaki. In Japan around the same time, between November 1980 and February 1982, Endō Shūsaku wrote *A Woman's Life* in serialized form for *Asahi Shimbun*. In 1981 he started to gather data on Father Kolbe and launched a campaign to raise funds to build a Kolbe memorial in Nagasaki. Also in 1981, the Modern Film Association and the Women's Society of Saint Paul of Japan produced a low-budget film, *The Life of Father Kolbe: The Miracle of Love in Auschwitz* (コルベ神父の生涯: アウシュビッツ 愛の奇跡), which won the best movie prize at the third Japanese Red Cross Film Festival. Kolbe was remembered just as fervently, if not more, in Japan as in Poland, considering that the first Polish biographical film of Kolbe, *Life for Life* (Życie za życie), was not made until 1991 when the communist regime collapsed. As the influence of Catholicism in Japanese society is minuscule compared to that in Poland, the scope of the Kolbe memory cult in Nagasaki and Japan implies something more significant than the Catholic Church.

Kolbe returned to public attention in Poland when a TV documentary about him aired in 2007. In 2010 the Polish Senate declared 2011, the seventieth anniversary of Kolbe's martyrdom, to be the year of Saint Maksymilian Kolbe. Kolbe had already been made patron saint of his hometown, Zduńska Wola, in 1998, which was still later than when the cult of Kolbe spread in Japan. He had become an essential part of Poland's national memory. The first parish church dedicated to Kolbe was one in Kałków-Godów, dubbed "the Golgotha of the Polish nation." It was built to commemorate the 136 Polish peasants murdered on May 24 and November 11, 1943, when the Nazis violently evacuated the residents to retaliate against the Polish partisans. Begun as a small chapel in 1981, the parish church raised funds to build a proper church as a protest against the communist regime's martial law that prohibited free labor unions on December 13, 1981, and was able to complete its ground floor in 1983. Its first mass, on November 11, 1984, was dedicated to the "motherland"; in 1986 the church was named "the Golgotha of the Polish nation." As implied by the name "Golgotha," it has become a memory site where the Polish victims of Nazism and communism were remembered as martyrs.[77]

Since his beatification in 1971, Father Kolbe had come to be regarded as a symbol of martyrdom against atheistic communism. From the perspective of the Polish Catholic Church, the significance of Kolbe's antifreemasonry and antisemitism lay in the sense that they formed the ideological root of anticommunism. However, the attention to Kolbe's martyrdom quickly moved on to another priest, Jerzy Popiełuszko, who was kidnapped and brutally murdered by the Communist Secret Police on October 19, 1984.[78] The anticommunist vernacular memory culture in Poland bestowed the status of representative martyr upon Popiełuszko (who had been killed by atheist communists) rather than Kolbe. The political significance of the murder of Popiełuszko, who had fallen victim to a communist crime, outweighed that of the death of Kolbe, whom the Nazis had killed. While persecution by Nazis had become a faint memory, the memory of communist persecution was still fresh and vivid. Even into the 1990s, the iconic twentieth-century Polish Catholic martyr was Father Popiełuszko.[79] This story may explain why Kolbe was initially more popular as the object of worship in Japan than in Poland. Kolbe's popularity in Japan comes from his status as a moral referent for the sanctification and remembrance of the Nagasaki Catholic victims. A comparison could quickly be drawn between the Catholic atomic bomb victims in Nagasaki, who had given up their lives on the altar of world peace as a "burnt offering," and Father Kolbe, who sacrificed his own life to save another in Auschwitz. This idea was shared not only by Catholic intellectuals like Nagai Takashi or Endō Shūsaku but also among quite a few ordinary Japanese people.

Despite their fragmentary nature, guest books from the Oura Saint Kolbe Memorial Museum and the Kolbe Museum of Seibo no Kishi offer a glimpse into how the Japanese think about Father Kolbe. Based on the number of visitor book entries, Japanese visitors are most numerous, followed by Koreans. The number of Polish visitors is also continually increasing. The guest books show that Japanese visitors are from various backgrounds, while Koreans and Poles are mostly Catholic pilgrims. While Polish visitors often express their pleasant surprise at finding a trace of another Polish compatriot, Father Kolbe, in Nagasaki, Korean Catholic pilgrims' comments focus more on their wish for national unification and peace and the happiness and well-being of their families and church communities. They are mostly out of context. Compared to the comments made by Koreans and Poles in the guest books, those by Japanese predominantly include their memory of visiting Auschwitz and a prayer for peace. While most of the entries by Japanese name one of Endō's essays or novels as their first encounter with the story of Father Kolbe, a few mention that they first learned of him through their visit to the Auschwitz concentration camp. Interestingly, no Polish visitors mention Auschwitz in their note.

Another conspicuous commonality among the comments made by Japanese is the mention of the Great East Japan Earthquake. There is an interestingly long comment left on March 17, 2014, by a second-generation atomic bomb survivor who said he was the same age as when Father Kolbe died as a martyr. He wrote about his mother's sudden death and the radiation leak from the Fukushima nuclear power plant and urged that everyone under a capitalist system that relies on nuclear energy must follow Father Kolbe's noble footsteps. An entry made on June 24, 2018, says that a book by Brother Zeno, who worked as a missionary in Japan alongside Father Kolbe, brought immense consolation to the victims of the Great East Japan Earthquake in 2011. Father Kolbe has become a symbol that not only binds together three memories—of the Christian persecution in Tokugawa in Japan, of the Holocaust at Auschwitz, and of the atomic bombing of Nagasaki—but is also connecting them to the memory of a more recent event, the earthquake of 2011. Combining these four memories is possible because the visitors can psychologically restructure and reorganize the timeline of competing memories surrounding Kolbe.[80] Japan's grassroots memories summon the memory of Kolbe at Auschwitz as a point of reference that facilitates a better understanding of today's nuclear tragedies.

The visitors, then, are not merely passive receivers of the curated discourse in the museum but active participants who interact with and intervene in the exhibition through their own interpretations. Japan's grassroots memories, which temporally reconstruct Kolbe's memory to align it with their historical path that ultimately includes the Great East Japan Earthquake, create an intriguing mnemonic process for the memories of Auschwitz and Nagasaki. The significance of the guest books also lies in the Japanese visitors' active participation and contribution to making an interactive memory culture. It can be said that the experience of the earthquake has extended into the rehistoricization of the bombing of Nagasaki. On the other hand, this mnemonic "retiming" strategy cannot eliminate the charge of dehistoricization and decontextualization of Kolbe's martyrdom. The Japanese grassroots memories have forgotten about the controversy surrounding Kolbe's antisemitism yet remain complacent with the story of a saint who practiced the miracle of love in Auschwitz. The dehistoricized memory of Kolbe shares the logical structure of decontextualization with postwar Japan's victimhood nationalism that ignores imperial Japan's invasion and oppression of its neighboring countries in Asia and emphasizes its status as the world's first and only atomic bomb victim. For the sacrifices of Auschwitz and Nagasaki to continue to hold their true significance, breaking away from the practice of justifying and rationalizing such sacrifices would be the first step.

During his visit to Japan, Pope Francis spoke at the Hiroshima Peace Park on November 24, 2019. In contrast to John Paul II, his speech suggested a direction to deterritorialize the remembrance of the atomic bombings of Hiroshima and Nagasaki in the global memory formation. He noted that the victims of the atomic bombing in Hiroshima "came from many different places, each had their own name, some of them spoke different languages," and that he "remembers all victims associated with this place." He also showed compassion for non-Japanese atomic bomb victims by shaking hands and having a conversation with Park Namjoo, a Korean-Japanese Catholic victim of the bombing, at a pray-for-peace event held at the Peace Memorial Park in Hiroshima.[81] Pope Francis's visit to Japan in commemoration of all victims of the atomic bombing, regardless of their nationality or place of origin, is very different from the message of Pope John Paul II from Poland, who expressed great interest specifically in Father Kolbe's memory. What is left for us is to ponder the paradox that the only way a sacrifice can have meaning is by "sacrificing the sacrifice," as articulated by Zizek.[82]

9

DENIAL

DENIALIST INTERNATIONAL

In December 2006 an incident that alarmed global memory formation occurred in Tehran, Iran: an international conference with the title "Review of the Holocaust: Global Vision." This event, officially sponsored by the Department of Foreign Affairs of Iran, boasted a list of sixty-seven participants from thirty countries that included then Iranian president Mahmoud Ahmadinejad, other high-profile government officials, far-right racists like a member of the Ku Klux Klan (KKK), Holocaust deniers, Islamic extremists, and the ultra-orthodox rabbis of Neturei Karta, who believed that the secular Zionist state of Israel was against the Judaic principle. A sort of Denialist International was formed through this conference. Following the opening address by Ahmadinejad, who vowed to one day "wipe Israel off the face of the Earth," was a keynote speech by former KKK leader David Duke. He spoke to incite antisemitism among Muslims by decrying the West's public sentiment that criminalized even mere questioning of the Holocaust. In the twenty-first century, Duke and white supremacists began to expand the scope of their activities into the Middle East to bypass the legal system of the West where Holocaust denialism is a punishable offense. Duke also asserted that he had persuaded the Iranian government to sponsor the international gathering.[1] Historically, antisemitism had been a unique phenomenon of the West—the Islamic world had been much more welcoming of Jews than the medieval Christian world. It was not until the bloody war of 1948 between Jews and Arabs over the founding of Israel that antisemitism began to spread in the Islamic world. Holocaust denialism was also disseminated as a discourse to denigrate the legitimacy of Israel's founding.

This historical background had inspired Duke to take an interest in the Islamic world. Affiliation with the Islamic world helped dilute the racist tone of Holocaust denialism. White supremacists such as Duke are also responsible for the recent spread of the phrase "white separatism," which appropriates the rhetoric of national self-determination. At the conference in Tehran, Duke was accompanied by Robert Faurisson and other notorious deniers from various countries, including Sweden, Malaysia, Switzerland, Austria, Hungary, and Australia.[2] It would not be an exaggeration to state that Iran had risen as the new leader of the "Holocaust Deniers International" through this event. Ayatollah Khomeini, who had led the Iranian Revolution in 1979, was an antisemitic Islamic theologian, and antisemitism had officially been incorporated into Iran's government policies after the revolution as the result of the Iranian government's continual appeal to Holocaust deniers. The *Tehran Times* published unfiltered claims of deniers like David Irving and Robert Faurisson, and Iranian radio stations aired interviews with Ernst Zündel and Mark Weber. Iran also granted political asylum for Jürgen Graf, a Holocaust denier from Switzerland.[3] The claims the participants brought to the conference in Tehran were nothing new: all were typical, already worn-out denialist "facts" such as that the actual number of victims at Auschwitz was only about two thousand, that a mere five thousand had died at Treblinka due to illness, and that there had been no gas chamber.

However, the conference was only the tip of the denialist iceberg. Regrettably, the list of denialist claims is endlessly long. They come in numerous different and diverse forms: the personal denials of murderers claiming their innocence, the state-level denials that negate accountabilities for genocide, the opportunistic denials to hog media attention, defense of denialism posing as freedom of press and scholarship, the denials of evidence manipulation, the denialist "definitionalism" that splits hairs between mass murder and genocide, the contextualist denials through historical relativization, the ethnocentric denials that singularize one's nation as the only victim of genocide, the denials that vulgarize genocide, and many more.[4] The metalanguage of denialism contains messages to instigate genocide, and it is a hazardous form of verbal violence whose severity warrants being called "the last stage of genocide."[5] When denialism does not stop within the official memory of the perpetrator nation but functions as the narrative template that regulates a society's memory culture, it can potentially lay the theoretical foundation for future genocide. The crux of denialism lies in expunging memories. Victims die again with the death of memories. By denying memories as the moral determination to acknowledge victims who died stripped of human dignity, deniers obscure responsibility and dismiss the "justice of others." Disremembering extermination is yet another extermination. Hence the genocide of memory is the last stage of genocide.

During World War II the Nazi murderers had already launched the foundation for denialism. The architect of the Gestapo, Reinhard "the Butcher" Heydrich, placed a strict ban on taking photographs of massacre sites. The "No Photos" signs surrounding the concentration camps testify to the Nazis' deliberate attempt to obliterate memories. The Nazis understood that the optimal condition for the success extermination of Jews was if no one outside believed what had happened inside the camps.[6] Heinrich Himmler, Reichsführer-SS, was a pioneer of Holocaust denialism—with his utmost focus on destroying evidence of the Holocaust, Himmler shredded documents and blew up the sites that could be traced back to the Nazi atrocities, such as the crematorium.[7] The SS under Himmler declared that not even one witness would walk out of the camp alive. Indeed, no one walked out of the gas chamber alive. Nobody could survive the poison gas. The Nazis' grotesque obsession, which surpassed mass murder and aimed at the destruction of forensic evidence like the victims' corpses, attests to how eager they were to erase memories. When most physical evidence has been destroyed, we must resort to imagination to remember against the obliteration of memory. Imagination is requisite to reconstruct the past from mere traces, which do not allow us the minute linguistic, visual, and acoustic details by reading between the lines of trauma-laden testimonies that are sparse and fragmented.

This chapter will reach beyond the superficial critique of denialism to cover cultural memory as a faculty of imagination that re-creates the past with destroyed, or only faint, evidence. Auschwitz was not an imagination but a reality. The "Comfort Women" system of the Japanese military existed as a reality before it was discovered through reenactment of the past. The Bosnian genocide in Srebrenica was a tragedy that happened before it was labeled "ethnic cleansing." Auschwitz, Japanese military "Comfort Women," and Yugoslav "ethnic cleansing" were all realities before they were discourse. However, historical realities cannot be recognized outside discourse and thus cannot exist outside discourse. Our history is not history as the "thing-in-itself" (*Ding an sich*) that exists beyond human consciousness, but rather the history that we recognize. What matters is not the past itself but memory that acknowledges the past; then, memory culture as a set of rules or discourse that directs, regulates, and constitutes memory is concerned. In this chapter I will first examine how different forms of denialism imitate and reference one another within global memory formation. Then I will knock on the possibility of solidarity across borders by investigating how victims' memories unite against the Denialist International. The Denialist International refers to the discursive umbrella of denialist episteme, logic, ideas, and statements rather than an organizational network among deniers as persons. Under the rubric of "Denialist International," the chapter scrutinizes the elevation of Holocaust denial into generic negationism by finding out the methodological and rhetorical common threads that unite deniers worldwide.

TOPOGRAPHY OF DENIALISM

In the topography of denialism that constitutes global memory formation, the most outstanding is simple denialism. Dating back to Himmler during the Holocaust, denialism of this kind is violent yet discernible to the eyes of any sensible person for its overtness and lack of depth. Simple denial emerges primarily in the early stage of denialism. It kills memories that challenge the official or dominant history. Armed with the most simplistic and unfounded logic, denialists often use words of the immediate impact, like "lie," "despicable manipulation," "distortion of truth," "factually fabricated," "invented history," "cheap fiction," "footnoted fiction," and "hundreds of lies." This category of denialism includes the extreme Holocaust denialists gathered at the International Conference in Tehran, the ultra-right-wing pundits of Japanese deniers, and genocide denialism at sites of ongoing memory wars. Holocaust denialism, which claims that the Holocaust was a lie invented by the Allies' Jewish propaganda machine, that the *Kristallnacht* of 1938 was staged not by the Stormtroopers but by Jewish demagogues, that there was no gas chamber at Auschwitz and only 50,000 Jews were victimized in the camp, and that the total number of Holocaust victims did not exceed 200,000; denialism of Japanese military atrocities committed during the Asia-Pacific War, including the Nanjing Massacre and the Japanese military "Comfort Women" system; and the "Stolen Generations" denialism that denies the white Australian government's abduction of aboriginal children all fall under this category.[8] If Holocaust memory is now an industry, Holocaust denialism too has become an industry.[9] It would not be a stretch to say that genocide denialism as a whole has become industrialized.

Genocide denialism hardly stops at denying facts—instead, it continues to suppress memories and actively insult victim-witnesses mustering the courage to recount traumatic memories.[10] However, simple denials are often observed not only among the perpetrators but also within the victim group. The more a nation has affirmed the moral rectitude of its victimhood nationalism, the less likely its people would accept that they had been perpetrators. The dichotomy between collective guilt and collective innocence further solidifies their belief. For instance, the immediate rhetoric of simple denials is often utilized by Polish nationalists, who call Jan Gross a liar for disclosing that the murderers of the Jedwabne pogrom were Polish neighbors, and nationalists of Korea and Eastern Europe, with their denials of the life-threatening experience of Japanese civilian *hikiagesha* and German civilian expellees through hunger and rape as historical distortion. As touched on in chapter 7, nationalists in Poland and Korea argue that the book by Gross or Watkins is disguised as historical or autobiographical fiction to disseminate a conspiracy theory among the naïve Western readership and international media unfamiliar with other histories. According to the nationalists' argument, the book is the enemy's defamatory plot against the Polish or Korean nation. Regrettably, this is not so different from Japan's ultraright "Comfort Women" denialists, who have maintained that the Japanese military's sexual slavery is the Korean nationalists' fabrication to defame the Japanese nation. On the psychological basis of this denialism lies the discomfort about being reminded by the "Comfort Women" of the complicity of many hundreds of ordinary men of the Japanese military in systemized sexual assault.[11]

Even more obscene than straightforward denialism is suspicion-based denialism. What is incredibly offensive about accusatory denialism comes from the performative nature of language. Once accused, whether the suspicion is factual or how close it is to the truth matters no longer. Through linguistic performativity, accusatory denialism transforms the issue of historical facts into that of moral feelings at the moment of its utterance. In most cases, the accusation is based on suspicious rumors, but it is still effective in achieving its goal: to provoke angry emotions among the audience against the suspect. Its effectiveness is not reduced even if the accusation is later proven false; when it is debunked, the initial emotions it provoked already dominate the collective memory. The accusation itself is thus already half a success if it spreads. Once spread, the factuality of the claim is immaterial. Deniers often instrumentalize accusations in propaganda campaigns to discredit victims and stir negative emotions. Deniers do not need to verify their accusations—it would be even better if they turn out to be true, but veracity is secondary to propagation. Linguistic performativity ensures that publicizing is enough to sow doubt, mistrust, skepticism, and anger about the accused. Deniers have nothing to lose, even if their actions entail lawsuits or are punishable by memory laws, as long as they can advertise their own cause.

When litigated, deniers often politically galvanize their supporters by identifying themselves as victims of the media and the court that suppresses freedom of speech.[12] As a result, deniers win even when they lose—this is why accusation is the most useful tool for them to scar the historical authenticity of critical memory and tamper with its credibility.

Amid the debate surrounding the Jedwabne pogrom, deniers and critics with a nationalist streak targeted Szmul Wasersztajn, the survivor whose testimony Jan Gross cited as the primary source in his book *Neighbors*. They claimed that Wasersztajn was not even present at the site of the massacre during the Jedwabne pogrom and that he served as a member of the Soviet Secret Police and middle-ranking officer of the Security Service of communist Poland. There also arose a hypothesis that the Soviet Union or Polish Stalinists scripted Wasersztajn's testimony, which made his emigration to the United States possible—even the minutes of the 1949 trial or interrogation records cited by Gross were false confessions that the Polish defendants and their families were coerced into making through torture and blackmailing from the communist secret police. Therefore, the very foundation of Gross's argument was bogus. Under the surface of this argument was the premise that the claim that the Poles murdered their Jewish neighbors in Jedwabne was a lie contrived by anti-Polish Stalinists and pro-Russian Jewish communists in Poland. Not a few have opined that *Neighbors* was written to defame Poland by redirecting the blame onto Poles instead of Germans, who were the real perpetrators. Such a claim, spread through social media, including the book's customer review page on Amazon.com, was a charge shrewdly chosen to discredit Gross's book.[13]

The conspiracy theory surrounding the Kielce pogrom is similar in its premise and logic. On July 4, 1946, an angry mob ambushed a Jewish refugee shelter at 7/9 Planty Street and murdered forty-two Jews who had survived the Holocaust. The massacre was triggered by a rumor that the Jews tried to kidnap and sacrifice a Polish boy to use the blood of a Catholic for their secretive ritual. Apropos of the massacre, the right-wing pundits in exile began spreading word that the person who directed the attack in uniform turned out to be a major of the Polish Secret Police.

Then he was considered a member of the Soviet Secret Police. Some even argued that the person in question was spotted at the Soviet Embassy in Israel in the 1960s. What all these rumors meant was that the Kielce pogrom was a tragedy plotted by the Soviet or Polish Communist Secret Police. The real culprit, the rumors suggested, was not the Poles but the Soviet Secret Police.[14] Such a charge that sprouted in the corners of academia spread exponentially through social media. Another book by Jan Gross, *Fear*, which covers the Kielce pogrom, was deemed a collective effort to slander Poland to push the responsibility for Stalinist crimes onto the Poles. At the same time, it was supposedly a challenge to the Polish nation and the Roman Catholic Church, as well as a libel on Cardinal Adam Stefan Sapieha. Accusatory denialism also came into play as some appealed to grassroots anticommunism by implying collusion between Gross and communists, arguing that the reason Gross kept lying was that Poles ruined his dream of a communist utopia.[15]

Nowhere in the sourcebook on the Kielce pogrom compiled by the Institute of National Remembrance can be found evidence suggesting Soviet or Polish Secret Police intervention. However, there is ample evidence that the masses voluntarily committed violence on the street.[16] But suspicion is enough for an accusation to function. The anticommunist accusation against the Kielce pogrom tends to spread into the international space of social media. The review sections of online bookstores like Amazon.com have been a crucial space for Polish nationalist memory activists as they could campaign for the legitimacy of Poland's victimhood nationalism to international readers unfamiliar with Poland's domestic affairs, be it political, linguistic, or cultural. Unsurprisingly, the heated online debate over *So Far from the Bamboo Grove* in East Asia was reenacted in the book's review page on Amazon in the United States. The internet space, including the online review platforms of English, as lingua franca, anglophone-based social media, and especially the "dark web" that exists outside legal restrictions, is the new cradle of denialism. Just as in Asia and Europe, the Japanese military "Comfort Women" denialism, denials of sexual violence brought to light by the #MeToo movement, American alt-right slavery denialism, Holocaust denialism of the Neo-Nazis, and nationalist denialisms of Poland and Korea are interestingly alike; it is thus urgent to conduct a thorough study on denialist memory culture being generated in the "dark web" and other blind spots of the internet.

The "North Korean intervention hypothesis" about the May 18 Gwangju Democratic Uprising of 1980 in South Korea bears similarities to the Stalinist conspiracy theory about the Kielce pogrom. In July 2015 Jee Man-won, who first raised the North Korean intervention hypothesis, published on his website "System Club" and in the online newspaper *Newstown* an article claiming North Korean military intervention in Gwangju along with a comparison between photos of a citizen who participated in the uprising and of a high-ranking official of North Korean military. He also distributed 300,000 copies of the *Newstown* issue that contained his article, not only in cities like Seoul and Daegu but also in front of Gwangju City Hall and the South Jeolla Provincial Office, where the massacre occurred. Jee took down from his website his serial column entitled the "Gwangsoo Series," which alleged the citizens of Gwangju to be the agents of North Korean special forces, soon after the Supreme Court of Korea found him guilty of libel and ordered him to compensate for damages he caused on September 26, 2019.[17]

According to Jee, the North Korean government live-streamed Gwangju in May 1980 as they would do a soccer match—the North Koreans even mentioned the name of their spy: "When the citizen militia stole the truck and rushed across Gwangju, they said 'oh, that is good, that is good' and then 'he is Gwangsoo, see, that is Gwangsoo.'" Jee argues that the name "Gwangsoo" in the title of his column was first taken from the moment in this footage where the North Korean soldier says, "There is 'Gwangsoo' we know." He also says that the photos that support the North Korean intervention hypothesis were sent from an anonymous donor with the username "homeless blanket," who allegedly found the 632 pictures of the North Korean special forces present in the protest masses of Gwangju. Although Jee asserts that this anonymous donor is an image analytics expert who manages a team of eight and used to work for a U.S. intelligence agency, he has never once seen this person's face or spoken to them over the phone.[18] Presumably, Jee deliberately misinterpreted the confidential images from the Defense Security Command's database as the photos of the North Korean agents.[19]

Former South Korean president responsible for the atrocities in Gwangju Chun Doo-Hwan, who initially stated that he had never heard about North Korea's intervention in his June 2016 interview with *New Dong-A*, changed his story by writing in his 2017 memoir that "the Gwangju incident was the North Korean special forces' guerrilla attack on the city."[20] However, what holds more gravity than Chun's memoir is that many still believe in Jee's conspiracy theory. Even after Jee removed the "Gwangsoo" series from his website, his accusatory denialism lingered in the public sphere. A comment on a news article about the removal of columns from Jee's website attests to the tenacious impact of accusatory denialism: "Dr. Jee, please stay patient and strong. I think many of your claims, if not all, are true. The truth will be discovered when the nation is reunited, and secret documents from North Korea are disclosed. I do not know about 'Gwangsoo,' but other than that, many circumstantial details, such as those so-called militias, seem unreasonable if done by ordinary citizens. The truth shall come out. It shall."

Accusatory denialism never retreats just because the accusation proves false. Until new evidence is discovered to validate it, a charge remains forever as an accusation. That is why an allegation without proof exerts more power than a fact. For its believers, accusatory denialism works like an onion—when an old charge is lifted, a new charge appears. The accusation continues no matter how many layers are lifted. Another believer in the North Korean intervention hypothesis in the comment section asserts that it has been verified as fact and that "the North Korean textbooks state that North Korea was behind the Gwangju incident, and there is a monument to special force veterans who died in 1980."[21] Admittedly, I have not checked the North Korean textbooks. Still, the hypothesis is not necessarily disadvantageous for the North Korean government, which identifies itself as the democratic base for revolution in South Korea. It can be used, paradoxically, also by the North Korean government as proof that the North Korean Worker's Party and its "great leader" have assumed a leading role in performing the South Korean revolution.

The charge against Yoko Kawashima-Watkins's father for serving in notorious Unit 731 is also enjoyable. Raised during the *So Far from the Bamboo Grove* controversy of 2007, this accusation bears no proof that the author's father was an officer of Unit 731, despite the high probability that he might have been involved in Japan's colonial enterprise or military invasion based on circumstantial evidence. Nevertheless, factuality holds little weight. The charge of being the daughter of a heinous war criminal was itself an implication of Kawashima-Watkins's upbringing, which would naturally have influenced her "distorted" recollection of the past. The logic was that although the author portrayed herself and her family as victims if her father was the vile Japanese officer of Unit 731 who regularly committed medical experiments, the family could never be considered victims. "Cyber Diplomatic Delegation Group" VANK, a nationalist nongovernmental organization, published a cartoon book that takes another step forward. The book says that the Japanese were never treated harshly or out of hostility by Koreans, but they instead refused to receive help from Koreans who tried to hand water to them for fear that the Koreans might have poisoned the water. That was because "the Unit 731 officers on the run with their families, who used to murder people with contaminated chemicals, did not trust the Koreans' favor because they were afraid the Koreans would retaliate against them in the same way." What has been proven up until now is that in *So Far from the Bamboo Grove*, Kawashima-Watkins's father refused water handed out by a Korean. This anecdote is allegedly the most crucial evidence that he served in Unit 731.

According to VANK's "accurate" history, the Japanese were never attacked or harassed by Koreans, and the narrative where the angry mobs in a vengeful spirit raped women seems more "applicable" to the testimonies of Korean girls who were kidnapped by the Japanese soldiers to be made into sexual slaves. Appearing next in the book are photographs, one of the "comfort woman" Park Young-Shim and others with a caption that reads "Japanese soldiers threatening 'Comfort Women' with guns and swords."[22] Deep down in their "accurate" history is the simplistic view that the photo of young, pregnant Park Young-Shim is somehow more accurate evidence than the testimony of women's rights activist Lee Yong-Soo, another "comfort woman" survivor who is now old and weary. Such a simplistic understanding can readily dismiss the context in which these "accurate" images are juxtaposed. However difficult it is to grasp why the Japanese soldiers threatened the "Comfort Women" not with scrip but with weapons at their own "comfort station," rather unreasonably in a weedy field, according to the explanations of the photos presented by VANK, whose "accurate" history prioritizes highlighting the image of the Japanese military as perpetrators. While it is factual that Kawashima-Watkins's father was detained at the Soviet POW camp in Siberia, no evidence has confirmed he was an official of Unit 731. Nevertheless, this does not matter, either. The evil of accusatory denialism is precisely in that just by raising it, the integrity of testimony is already undermined, and the victim-witness has to get hurt again in the process.

The mastermind behind accusatory denialism is positivistic denialism, which goes far back in history as "science" armed with positivist epistemology. The biggest paradox of this "scientific" denialism is that those who destroyed historical evidence suddenly designate themselves as strict positivists. Often, those deniers shout "evidence!" in unison because they are confident there is no evidence. For positivistic deniers, positivism is merely an ideology frequently called forth to discredit victims' memories as inaccurate. Positivism as an ideology refuses to be checked empirically. It was first used as a weapon of denialism by Holocaust deniers, who claimed the history of the Holocaust and the gas chamber was made up based on a few testimonies rather than scientific proof. The tenor of such a claim is that witnesses' memories are too subjective and emotionally charged to be trusted. It gnaws at the inaccurate nature of testimonies, in which, for example, all Nazi doctors are described as Josef Mengele in the memories of Auschwitz survivors. Another critical aspect of positivistic denialism is the intimidating demand for unequivocally textualized documents, as testimonies that only exist in victims' voices are not credible. Deniers know that the victims only have their experiences and voices, whereas the perpetrators control the archives and historical narratives.

The obsession with "accurate documentary sources" over "inaccurate testimonies" justifies positivistic denialism—e.g., Hitler cannot be held accountable because no document signed by Hitler to implement the Holocaust has been discovered. Unless a letter signed by Hitler falls from the sky one day, Hitler's responsibility for Holocaust is denied as what victims fabricated in their testimonies. Promising a thousand dollars for anyone who brought him written documentation of Hitler's order for the massacre, David Irving's bluff was to insult the survivors under the name of positivism.[23] As Christopher Browning testified in the court, Hitler repeatedly spoke about his expectations to his aides, who—the likes of Heinrich Himmler—could sufficiently understand the Führer's will. In the testimony, Browning called the absence of official documents regarding Hitler's orders the "Richard Nixon complex," in comparison with Nixon's conspiracy to destroy the evidence of his involvement in the Watergate scandal.[24] The Holocaust deniers' logic on Hitler's role is surprisingly similar to that of May 18 Gwangju deniers, who claim that then president Chun cannot be held accountable for the massacre of civilians because there is no written proof that he ordered the shooting—so much so that it can also be called the "Chun Doo-hwan complex."

In his memoir in 2017, Chun states that his hand was not in the suppression of the democracy movement in Gwangju and that he was crucified as a sacrifice for a "cleansing ritual." No one, including himself, deliberately ordered the shooting, and "such an order did not even exist," writes Chun in denial of his responsibility for the mass murder. The psychological state at which Chun arrives that he was the real victim of memory politics to heal the wounds of the Gwangju tragedy chillingly overlaps with Irving's positivistic denialism. The Supreme Court of Korea acknowledged the comprehensive responsibility for the shooting order as it convicted Chun of "murder for the purpose of rebellion" on April 17, 1997. However, the Court did not specify Chun as the one who gave the order because by then, the crucial evidence, including *The Data File of Command from Chief of Staff* (May 3–June 29, 1980), *Regular Military Brief '80* (April 24–June 22, 1980), and *New Military Administration Plans for Current Affairs* had vanished.[25] As expected, to a certain extent, the "Investigative Committee for Past Events" within the Ministry of National Defense could not find the written proof of Chun's shooting order after a long, arduous search. Today, the evidence closest to proving Chun's responsibility is the record of his attendance at a meeting of chief commanders during which "His Excellency Chun" stressed the "invocation of the martial law army's self-defense power." From a strict positivist viewpoint, this is only circumstantial evidence, not direct evidence; there is no "smoking gun." It is unrealistic to expect a written order signed by Chun himself to appear suddenly out of a void one day. A societal memory that keeps its dogged watch on Chun Doo-hwan and his military administration is required rather than being caught up in the positivist debate.

The logic of those who deny the existence of the Japanese military "Comfort Women" system during the Asia-Pacific War is also similar. They frame all testimonies by the victims as perjury, for there does not remain any textual documentation of the perpetrators' crime. One of the "Comfort Women" deniers, Fujioka Nobukatsu, argues that the victims' testimonies are fabricated as there are no official documents from the military that enforced the mobilization of the victims. By this, he abruptly limited the historical discussion over the Japanese military "Comfort Women" to the issue of forced mobilization. According to Fujioka, the testimonies are not "facts" because the survivors cannot recall the specific times of their mobilizations and locations of the Comfort Women station, and there is no documentary source to confirm their claims. Adding insult to injury, he also questions whether "there is anything to prove those grandmas were Comfort Women."[26] The hidden agenda under this remark is that those grandmas were prostitutes. In his denialism, positivism operates as a deflecting scheme to veer from the essence of the "Comfort Women" issue, which is systemic sexual violence by the Japanese military. The human rights violation in his purportedly "scientific" or "positivist" framing of victims as liars is even more problematic. Latent behind the deniers' reckless infringement of human rights is the political malice to intimidate the victims, who mustered the courage to testify despite their traumas and drown their voices back in silence. Denialism is the genocide of memories and, thus, the final stage of genocide.

The same positivist logic is applied to denials of the Nanjing Massacre—by emphasizing erroneous parts, it negates the foundation of the entire claim. The deniers' empirical evidence is that the total number of victims of the Nanjing Massacre is forty-seven, or that John G. Magee, the witness who testified at the war criminal trial, directly witnessed only three incidents of murder. There are undeniable factual errors in the documents presented as evidence of the Nanjing Massacre at the trial. It seems unlikely that the photo of a Japanese soldier slaying a Chinese, exhibit A of the Nanjing trial, was taken during the massacre in December, as the soldier is in his summer uniform. The deniers also argue that the report, sent by fourteen Americans to the U.S. Embassy to petition for the Chinese, also does not mention that the Japanese military shot the Chinese people. Thus, a systemic massacre orchestrated by the Japanese Army had not taken place—what is not mentioned in the official records of the Japanese military is considered manipulated by anti-Japanese zealots. In short, deniers assert that anything that was not recorded did not happen.[27]

There are also deniers of the Great Vietnamese Famine of 1945. The Vietnamese government's official stance explains that two million people, a monumental number that amounts to 15 percent of the entire population of Vietnam at the time, starved to death. The dispute comes from the fact that there is scarcely any documentary source to support the official statistics about the Great Famine. Also, the memory of the Great Famine had long been repressed, even in Vietnam. At the same time, the country focused on the heroic memory of the national liberation struggle—analogous to how the Chinese Communist Party's official stance against the United States repressed the memory of Nanjing, and Korea's male-centric heroic nationalism suppressed the memory of "Comfort Women." Perhaps unintentionally, the official memories of Korea, the People's Republic of China, and Vietnam during the Cold War partially overlapped with the denialism of Japanese right-wing nationalism. If the Japanese nationalists' positivistic denialism is the violence of facts against memories, the heroist official memories of China, Korea, and Vietnam that suppressed the victims' memories were the violence of the present against the past, male chauvinism against women, national collective rights against individual human rights, and official memory against the personal and vernacular memories.

There are unlimited examples in which positivism refuses to be examined or verified. Even the so-called Ienaga Saburo trial of 1997 at the Supreme Court of Japan, which confirmed that the Nanjing Massacre, the Japanese military "Comfort Women" system, and Unit 731 were undeniable historical truths, could not change the opinions of Japanese positivistic deniers.[28] The deniers' positivism is a unique strain that can readily deny empirical, "positive" facts whenever necessary. At eight trials among the ten lawsuits filed by the "Comfort Women" victims in Korea, the Philippines, Taiwan, and the Netherlands against the Japanese government, the Japanese judges concluded that even though the compensation demanded is invalidated under the positive law, the plaintiff's claims about the abduction and physical and psychological abuses were "undeniable historical evidence" and truths. The conclusion explained in the preface and supplement to the judgment is also reconfirmed in the Japanese legal circle's review of the "Comfort Women" trials.[29] The steadfast denialism of positivistic deniers is a testament to how unimportant the existence of evidence/documentation is to them, for whom positivism is merely a pretext. What is important to them is not the evidence itself but the politics of evidence. As exemplified by Irving's attitude during the *Irving v. Lipstadt* trial, positivistic deniers do not hesitate to deflect into postmodern relativism or agnosticism as soon as there emerges proof that is inconvenient for their argument.[30] No one can perfectly represent the past. Deniers use positivism not to establish their argument but to invalidate the opposition, to delve not into the documents but into the vulnerable points of the opposition's testimony to discredit its integrity. Deniers do not prioritize proof or science. They use positivism only when it is instrumental as an ideology to justify their denials.

It is for this reason that conspiracy theories abound. Allegedly, the testimonies of the "Comfort Women" victims are lucrative lies backed by the "anti-Japanese groups in and out of the country" aiming to dishonor the Japanese nation. Still, conspiracy theorists are not particularly eager to verify their theories because their "positivistic" aim is to discredit the testimonies rather than to determine facts. Likewise, the celebrities accused of committing sexual violence in light of the recent #MeToo movement often feign bravado by demanding definitive evidence, reducing the victims' testimonies as a plot against their fame and reputation. The anemic impact of the #MeToo movement in Japan is paired with the ascendancy of "Comfort Women" denialism, which is not limited to right-wing politicians or leading deniers. On the rise are the likes of a Japanese airport banning its staff from wearing tote bags made by Marymond, a fashion brand that sponsors the "Comfort Women" survivor-victims; major TV broadcasters labeling as anti-Japanese the companies that support the "Comfort Women" memory activism; and demands that the government funding for research on the "Comfort Women" be withdrawn. The chain that links the "Comfort Women" denialism with the misogynous reactions to the #MeToo movement is patriarchy that oppresses the voices of women.[31] The patriarchal perpetrators are hiding under the blanket defense that a testimony, unless verified by documents, cannot be evidence.

Also favored by deniers is the tactic that invalidates the victim's memory by questioning the testimony's historical authenticity for minor discrepancies. As mentioned earlier, the Nanjing Massacre denialism uses this tactic. However, a more widely known example would be the cancellation of the exhibition about the atrocities committed by the German military, *War of Annihilation: Crimes of the Wehrmacht 1941 to 1944*. Scheduled to be held in New York after five years of traveling across Germany since 1995, the exhibition was suddenly canceled just a couple of weeks before the opening because the photos of people victimized by Hungarian and Finnish troops incorporated in the German military were described as "victims of the German military." Among the 1,443 photographs of the exhibition, less than 20 were subject to this error, which was unlikely to negate the historical authenticity of numerous other photos that attested to the crimes committed by the German military but still enough to cause the scandal that ultimately canceled the exhibition. The photos of German atrocities bear witness to different perpetrator groups other than the regular German soldiers, including the Waffen-SS, Einsatzgruppen of the Security Police, local paramilitaries, and Reserve Police Battalion, all of whom were part of "the German military" through incorporation or collaboration. Also, the corpses in the photos in which a Jew recovers abandoned bodies near the Galician city of Borysław and Złoczów seem to belong, unequivocally, to the victims of the Soviet Secret Police, not the German military—yet the Jew in the photo was murdered by German soldiers immediately after he recovered the corpses.[32]

An interesting point about this episode is that Bogdan Musiał and Krisztián Ungváry, who publicly raised the issues regarding the factuality of photos, were both historians from Poland and Hungary. Especially unrelenting was the critique from Musiał, who had also criticized Jan Gross in the Jedwabne debate from the standpoint that defended the Polish nation. Musiał argued that the Holocaust had been politicized, commercialized, instrumentalized, and sacralized as a secular religion in the American context. Gross's research was a mere reiteration of the Holocaust thesis that had been dogmatized in the United States. Musiał also unreservedly denounced Gross by claiming he neglected professional criticality as a historian when directly quoting the Jedwabne pogrom survivor Szmuel Wasersztajn. Musiał equated Gross's *Neighbors*, which "subjugated facts to ideological pressure," with the exhibition that "fundamentally manipulated the source rather than precisely analyzing the photos and documents" in his critique.[33] However, Musiał's positivism was also for his own sake rather than something everyone could agree on. Upon reviewing Musiał's argument and the sources he used, Omer Bartov discovered that Musiał was also not innocent of the desire to instrumentalize his sources politically: to support the argument that the corpses in the Borysław massacre photos belonged to the victims of the Soviet Secret Police, Musiał quoted Irene Horowitz's memoir, in which the author states, immediately following the quoted part, that the German soldiers mobilized local Ukrainians to orchestrate the massacre of Jews.[34] While it is unclear whether Musiał deliberately omitted the German military's plan for the massacre, his positivist analysis of the text was insufficient. His research trend that emphasizes Polish victimhood under the Russian red totalitarianism might have influenced such an oversight.[35]

Nevertheless, determining the validity of Musiał's positivist criticism is not my focus here. I am interested in how this Polish historian's research is consumed, disseminated, and reproduced in Germany. If a German historian publicly contradicted the German military's involvement in the Holocaust, they would face accusations of defending the Nazi past. This is because a German historian, no matter how logically critical of the collective guilt, cannot be emotionally free from the original sin of the Holocaust. The same argument could be received because it was spoken by a historian from Poland, a country that Nazi Germany victimized. When Poland's anticommunist victimhood nationalism that emphasizes Stalinist victimization crosses the border to Germany's memory culture, a relative discount on Nazi crimes takes place in its historical assessment. This is a precious example of the covert mechanism of denials reproduced across borders. Korean scholars' research that dilutes the impact of coercion on the colonial Joseon victims, like "Comfort Women," is appropriated by the Japanese deniers. Amplified in the "pro-Japanese" sentiment via Japan's memory culture, the Japanese version of the Korean research is once again translated by pro-Japanese/anti-Chinese nationalists of Taiwan to defend Taiwanese nationalism against PRC nationalism.[36] Across borders, mnemonic solidarity occurs not only in the realm of deterritorialized critical memory but also in reterritorializing, defensive memories, and denialism. The emergence of transnational denialism is also a peculiarity in the globalization of memory.

FACT, TRUTH, AUTHENTICITY

The scandal over the *War of Annihilation* exhibition allows us to ponder the positivity of photographs provided as historical evidence. The gray zone between fact and fiction, past and representation, and real and fake expands ad infinitum. It is also in this gray zone where the crude dichotomy between "real" and "fake" images and naïve realism that believes "photographs are the objective, mechanical documentation free of human intervention" fall flat. The photos taken by Yamahata Yosuke, who served as a military journalist for the Japanese Imperial Army during the Asia-Pacific War, are a typical example. Depicting a child holding a rice ball at the site of the Nagasaki bombing, the childlike Japanese soldiers playing with Chinese children at the Chinese front, and Emperor Hirohito portrayed as a family man after the war, these photos are not "contrived" or "fake" per se, as they captured the scenes as they were.[37] Still, the boundary between truth and lie is blurry, considering the historical interpretations and meanings these photos attempt to convey. Photographs cannot be objective to begin with. Even if it candidly captures a scene, the end product is inevitably affected by the photographer's selection and omission, which manipulate and adjust, rather than catch mechanically, the reality. In Yamahata's photos, Hirohito is not a war criminal but a peace-loving family man, and the Japanese soldiers who led the horrendous massacre in the Sino-Japanese War are turned into warm-hearted young men hanging out with Chinese children. The innocent eyes of the child standing at the site of the Nagasaki bombing create the image of the innocent Japanese victims, leaving aside the historical background of World War II.[38] The gaze of Yamahata, who was not only the military journalist for the Imperial Army but also the court photographer for the Hirohito family, overlaps with the memory culture in postwar Japan.

The gray zone of visual representation between fact and fiction is also present in the works of amateur photographers. A German film and video company, Polar Film, released in 2004 a DVD compilation of 16mm documentary films shot by Nazi German soldiers. Entitled *The Third Reich Private: Life and Survival* (*Das Dritte Reich privat: Leben und Überleben*), this compilation has soundtracks accompanying the originally silent films.[39] In a scene where the Nazi soldiers pick blueberries in an occupied forest, the sound of birds chirping is added on top of the actor Matthias Ponnier's sonorous voice-over narration, rendering the Nazis into wide-eyed boys fit for the peaceful, quiet landscape. At the expense of the violence of Nazism and invasion, the horror of war and Nazi crimes were substituted with an idle peace in between missions. The effect of a soundtrack is also prominent in the sequence where a topless Romani girl in occupied Russia is dancing in front of the German soldiers. Despite being tantamount to the exoticizing photos taken by Western colonizers traveling Africa/Asia, this film of a dancing Romani girl and the cheering German soldiers who surround her does not provide the viewers with concrete details about the situation—it might have been recorded as evidence that the Nazis could force people into doing whatever they wanted, as it seems unlikely the young Romani girl would have voluntarily stripped herself to dance in front of physically overwhelming strangers.

However, the "gypsy-style" music added to this sequence completely changes its mood, as if the girl is dancing for her own pleasure and is infatuated with the tune.[40] The sequence reminds one that sound effects play as important a role as visual effects in media representations. Although the added soundtracks do not directly distort or fabricate the images, accepting the reality presented in the films still feels awkward. By adding sound effects, Polar Film designed a particular interpretation of the films in *The Third Reich Private*. The description on the back of the DVD cover covertly reveals the editor's intention: "free spaces in nooks and crannies of everyday lives in various forms."[41] Thus, this digitization project of old 16mm films reflects more than an application of new technology to better restore the images; through the editing process in which sounds were added to originally silent visual sources, the everyday violence of war is represented as peaceful and idyllic times. It would be an exaggeration to interpret this DVD compilation of Nazi German soldiers' daily lives in occupied territories as containing a message of denialism. However, it would be overly naïve to interpret the documentary film with added soundtracks as an honest display of reality in the occupied territories. The study of positivistic denialism teaches us an unequivocal lesson: it is not easy to prove positivism positively.

In a book of interviews published in 2018, Jan Gross recounts his first encounter with Wasersztajn's testimony, which graphically describes the tragic massacre in Jedwabne:

> Wasersztajn's testimony was so shocking when I first read it that I was left stupefied for a while without knowing how to write about this

person. I thought he went mad after surviving something overwhelmingly shocking. As a reader, I thought the one who was giving the testimony must have experienced something truly awful, but what he described was too horrible to have actually happened.... Murdering every one of your Jewish neighbors in your own small, ordinary town, let alone burning them alive in a barn.[42]

In short, the first reaction the author of *Neighbors* had to the testimony was wondering whether Wasersztajn suffered from hallucination after witnessing something too harrowing. Irena, Gross's spouse, also did not react much differently to the testimony at first, when she said, "Isn't he mad?" Gross initially hesitated even about using Wasersztajn's testimony as a primary sources in his book. Gross somewhat vaguely indicates the transition of his interest as a historian from documentary sources to testimonies along the gradual evolution of his thoughts into realizing what happened in Jedwabne "had a logic of its own, a certain rhythm that he could not ultimately understand."[43] Gross's retrospection offers a valuable insight into the relationships between a historian and witness, fact and representation, and history and memory.

As shocking as Gross's retrospection is Raul Hilberg's inquiry, "Is it not equally barbaric to write footnotes after Auschwitz?" Asked by Hilberg, a representative of practicing positivistic research on the Holocaust boasting eight kilometers of bookshelves full of documentary sources he inspected, this question is without doubt a parody of Theodor Adorno's famous quote, "To write poetry after Auschwitz is barbaric." What is more interesting is the essay title in which Hilberg asks this question. Though simple on the surface, the title "I Was Not There" reflects a chillingly fraught implication.[44] To me, the essence is that a prominent positivist historian who studied the Holocaust in the archives realized the limitation of history represented by documentary sources. From the perspective of historical epistemology, it seems that Hilberg's essay offers a fundamental question on the delicate tension between "fact" and "authenticity" in representing the past. When the "accurate" official documents about a past event and "inaccurate" memories of the witnesses who directly experienced it compete, fact and authenticity can be mutually exclusive.

It was Hilberg's way of describing the historian's dilemma, amid the conflict between fact and authenticity, of choosing either work ethics as a historian or humanitarian ethics to empathize with the victim.[45] Although Marc Bloch's warning that "there is no good eyewitness" about the inaccurate nature of testimonies reminds historians of the solemn work ethics regarding facts, an obsession with facts has assigned historians the role of prosecutor and depreciated empathy with the victim-witness. Even so, Gross's assertion that "a historian deals not with the issue of explanation but with the issue of ethics" feels pretty far-fetched.[46] At its deepest level, memory studies have ultimately to confront the issue of ethics, but that does not mean a historian can forsake the duty to pass through the intricate maze of historical explanation. Fact and authenticity are anything but the objects of competition or either-or selections. The truth may lie somewhere in the contest between fact and authenticity. However, it is difficult to deny that our understanding of the past is broadened from history to memory and fact to authenticity, along with the emergence of global memory formation.

The dramatic scenes of the Eichmann trial, aired worldwide, catalyzed such a shift. Especially when Holocaust survivor Yehiel Dinur fainted during his testimony on a live broadcast, the international audience could empathize even more with the protagonist of this tragedy. The trial became an episode of a televised drama, and its cast reshaped the global sentiment toward the tribunal. The criticism that Mossad's abduction of Eichmann was a breach of international law and Argentina's sovereignty also vanished. Critical voices of Karl Jaspers or Martin Buber that the Nazi crimes against humanity should be tried at the international court rather than the Israeli court were also subdued by the moving scenes of victims' testimonies.[47] Though there were enough documentary sources to prove Eichmann guilty, Israeli prosecutor Gideon Hausner brought him to court and carefully selected witnesses to appeal to the emotions of the audience watching the trial on TV. After initially selecting candidates by studying published testimonies and memoirs, Hausner interviewed them and finalized his witnesses who were to be in front of the court camera.[48] As the witnesses began to appear in the courtroom, Eichmann was no longer the star of the trial.

The witnesses, who survived their traumas and began to recount their deeply buried memories, were the new focus of the audience's attention. Respect and awe were directed toward the Holocaust survivors as they began to unravel their memories as the trial progressed. At last, the fact that they were the victims or survivors of the Holocaust was not something to hide or feel ashamed of.

From the perspective of memory, the importance of the Eichmann trial lies in that it liberated the Holocaust survivors from the fear of testifying. The fear that no one would believe or pay attention to their stories hindered the survivors from accessing their memories.[49] A community of empathetic listeners had to form first for the witness's private memories to be societally communicated and converted into cultural memories. The goal of the victim's testimony was not to verify the facts of the Holocaust but to draw the audience's empathy by expressing their intimate emotions.[50] What the Eichmann trial occasioned in Israel was a listener community for the Holocaust victims, which would expand into the world concomitantly with the globalization of the Holocaust. A reassessment of the trial's approach and focal shift from fact-checking to listening and empathizing also ensued when Dinur fell momentarily unconscious as he was too disheartened and enraged by the judges who pried into the uncertain details of his memory.[51] It would not be an exaggeration to say that memory studies emerged from the critique of historical positivist methodologies in the process of analyzing Holocaust survivors' testimonies.[52] Under the foundation of its emergence was a concern for protecting witnesses against the violence of positivism, which purported that documents were the only verifiable proof. It was for this concern that Lipstadt's lawyers decided not to call Holocaust survivors as witnesses during the *Irving v. Lipstadt* trial. Under the circumstances where it was expected that Irving would insult the survivors and negate the meaning of testimony, they would instead protect the rights and dignity of the survivors rather than take the easy road to winning the case.[53]

The victim-centered perspective ultimately brought about the democratization of historical episteme. The emphasis on human rights generated empathy for victims, and from the empathy stemmed the recognition of the testimony as important a source as a document—the raw voices of victims began to create fissures within the stronghold of researchers armed with emotional distance and textual positivism. No one is without a name, as Nathan Beyrak states in the Slovak Jewish Memory Restoration project, an extension of Yale University's Holocaust oral history project Fortunoff Archive. Testimony collection of oral history was significant in restoring personal history by discovering individual victims' names and faces from anonymous statistics.[54] When the victims recovered their names, history split into multiple individual stories—the pursuit of personal history transformed the political categories of history into psychological ones.[55] The advent of oral history meant that undocumented oral sources could assume a more significant role than merely a complementary one that supports official documents. Focusing on the victims' voices streaming against the official narrative and textual archives dominated by the establishment became a crucial political engagement with the past. From the standpoint of "history politics," recovering plural voices of the grassroots that have been suppressed and erased by the official narrative means democratization of the past. It also affirmed the existential meaning of subalterns in "here/now" by revaluing their agency and historical impacts that had been overlooked.

Popularized in the 1970s, testimonies and life histories of ordinary people enabled the recovery of the voices of marginalized people and rewriting history in their own words. Through the public recounting and empathetic listening of their own stories, the victims could empower themselves and depart from the status of "passive victims." For democratizing historical actors, testimony was a revolution in historical episteme beyond a self-empowerment. The emergence of testimony signaled a challenge to the institutional power-knowledge and the power network that monopolized the images of the past in the name of scientific history and academic truth by dominating archives, public education, and media. It came to public consciousness that compared to the institutional authority wielded by the perpetrators, what the victims had were mainly their own experiences and voices.[56] Just as the victims' voices surfaced on the front page of the cultural memory, the center of gravity in recognition of the past also shifted from documentation to testimony. The subaltern positionality often attached to the victims of tragic history highlighted the importance of testimony and memory again. A catalyst for the democratization of historical episteme and representation was the inception of memory studies that put as much weight on testimonies as documentary sources. Aside from Israel's internal political calculations, the significance of the Eichmann trial lies in the elevated moral empathy toward Holocaust victim-witnesses and democratization of the past through their personal memories as one of the epistemological pillars of representation.

Pioneer of the genre of "voice novel," Svetlana Alexievich once called herself "a historian who cares for people's souls."[57] From the positivistic tradition of history as an academic discipline, a good historian had not been "a historian of the soul." The task of a historian had been to take careful steps toward dry historical facts and truths free of emotional influence from within and correct minute details of private memories heavily affected by trauma, sorrow, rage, loneliness, grief, pride, or joy. "A historian who cares for people's souls," in turn, sounded like an oxymoron. Since the emergence of memory studies, attending to the soul became a virtue of historians, not a vice. As the center of representation shifted from documents to testimony and the purview of recognition of the past broadened, the authority of written evidence and historical narrative began to be dismantled. In a memory war against the perpetrators who dominate documentation and official narratives, the victims only have their own experiences and voices. Facing the perpetrators' weapon of positivism, called forth when it was necessary to paint the victims' memories as exaggerated, inaccurate, politically motivated, and even fabricated, grassroots memories from the bottom often rely on testimony. Therefore, they must consider the relative upper hand speech has over written text. Only an unskilled historian would believe that the historical truth reveals itself when the traumatized witness is scrupulously cross-examined against documentary sources. The issue of embracing the ethical sensitivity of memory studies is perhaps one of the biggest challenges history faces in the twenty-first century.

A Jewish American psychiatrist originally from Romania, Dori Laub, had long been in charge of Yale University's Holocaust Survivors Film Archive Project, for which he conducted interviews and psychoanalyzed the survivors. To question the relationship between testimony and historical truth, Laub uses as an example a witness in her late sixties who had sorted the belongings of those sent to the gas chambers at the "Canada camp." To the audience's surprise, this tiny woman who was testifying in almost a whisper suddenly raised her voice when she recounted the Auschwitz uprising, as if she could still hear the loud bang, gunfire, and screams from the battle on the other side of the barbed wire fence. Her voice amplified in a flash as the vivid memory of the past came back. Then, she returned to her usual monotonous murmur as she accounted the suppression of the uprising. Laub played a recording of this testimony at an academic conference on Holocaust education, where the attending historians uniformly pointed out the testimony's inaccuracy: she testified that four chimneys had been destroyed during the uprising, although only one had been. The historians unanimously agreed that this woman's testimony was at odds with the historical facts and, therefore, cannot be trusted.[58]

Against the distrust from the professional historians, Laub argued that the crux of the historical truth was not the number of chimneys destroyed but the armed uprising of the camp inmates—the witness was testifying to the very truth of history that the enforced stricture of Auschwitz, where an armed uprising shouldn't have, and couldn't have, occurred, had been broken. What she witnessed was the reality of an unimaginable occurrence. In this surreal reality, "she testified to the breakage of the framework. That was historical truth."[59] Charlotte Delbo's comparison between "intellectual memory" (about ordinary facts) and "deep memory" (of traumas) provides excellent insight into the truth and fact. If applied to Delbo's dichotomy, the fact that one chimney had been destroyed is in the realm of "intellectual memory," whereas the contradicting destruction of four chimneys belongs to the realm of "deep memory."[60] An innovative take on the witness's testimony is possible through this framework: it is not that the testimony is untrustworthy because it does not match the historical facts, but it is more authentic because it is recalled from the deep memory inconsistent with the fact. According to Laub, witnesses of an event that is too incredulous tend to remember it in exaggeration. Donald Spence's distinction between "factual truth" and "narrative truth" is also suggestive—while a factual truth bases itself on a close observation of a past event, a narrative truth is derived from the concurrent act of remembering as the event unfolds.[61]

History and memory are at once complementary and contradictory. Coined by Giorgio Agamben, "The Aporia of Auschwitz" accounts for "a reality that necessarily exceeds its factual elements" brought to light by the experience of Auschwitz.[62] The paradox of representation where fact and truth, proof and understanding remain distinct from each other offers sharp insight into the complex relationships among facts, authenticity, and truth beyond the dichotomy of testimony and documentation. As attested by Binjamin Wilkomirski's fake memoir *Fragments: Memories of a Wartime Childhood* (*Bruchstücke: Aus einer Kindheit 1939–1948*), the irony that fake survivor memoirs "more perfectly" restore the facts is also interesting at this juncture.[63] This is because counterfeit memoirs are usually written with meticulous research on historical evidence. Ironically, survivors' testimonies that focus on delivering their pain can be free from the obsession with facts. In contrast, fake memoirs that rely on published testimonies or documentary sources must stick to the details of factual truth. The dilemma that factually inaccurate deep memory has more authenticity than strictly factual intellectual memory will remain as the aporia of Auschwitz that demands our continued rumination on the historical reality.

Even authenticity can be fabricated sometimes. As "excess" became the norm of popular culture with the spectacular development of the mass media, the Holocaust survivors began to be consumed as cultural icons that testified to the excess of tragedy. For their suffering of unimaginable horror and tragedy, the survivors were expected to satisfy the masses' "melancholic pleasure" by recounting their stories. Unlike the voices of perpetrators enshrouded in historical narratives, the "raw" voices of victims had more potential to be rendered into melodramatic aesthetics.[64] Captured by TV cameras, the dramatic scene of Dinur fainting during testimony at the Eichmann trial began with a tragedy. However, the culture of confession in the 1960s mass media evolved through TV shows, films, and talk shows on the Holocaust, elevating the "democracy of pain" to the highest value.[65] For this, the mass media have also attempted to fix the role of victim-witnesses on dramatic testimony of "disbelief," relegating them to the objects to satisfy society's "melancholic pleasure" consuming victims' memories. Victims must look enough like victims, and the sacrificed must have sacrificed sufficiently; they are not accepted as ordinary persons with different desires. The violence of collective memory is inflicted on individual victims in the sublimation process of their personal memories into the official narrative of victimhood nationalism.

The victim-survivors of overwhelming violence, such as the Holocaust, reaffirm the truth by proving the cruelty of perpetrators. This process inevitably renders the victims pathetic and abject to no end. Korean society's consumption of the "Comfort Women" testimonies is not much different. The desire to hear about the incredulous atrocities inflicted on the Japanese military "Comfort Women" victims is quite different from the desire to learn about the proud struggles of the long-term political prisoners. The audience listens to the latter's accounts of their historical actions with the underlying glory and grandeur. From the former "Comfort Women," however, the society forcefully extracts memories of the heinous crimes of Japan to further objectify them as helpless victims. The staged contrast between proud male fighters and pitiful female victims had been a familiar scene in political rallies. When Lee Yong-soo said that she was not a "victim of the Japanese military 'Comfort Women' system" but a women's rights activist, it was her vehement refusal of the Korean memory culture that had continuously pigeonholed the former "Comfort Women" as witnesses who were obligated to constantly testify against the Japanese imperial atrocities and sexual violence.[66] To this day, Korean society has yet to answer Lee's piercing question: "Why must I be called a comfort woman and a sexual slave?"

SILENCE VERSUS VERISIMILITUDE

In contrast to the Holocaust victims on the witness stand to speak of the "disbelief dramatically," the countless ellipses in Alexievich's voice novel testify in silence. The ellipses inserted at each articulation of memory by women witnesses show us that the gap between our intellectual words and the deep stories of our hearts cannot be quickly closed. A Korean feminist anthropologist's retrospection about the Jeju *halmangs* (meaning an older woman in the Jeju dialect), the victims of the Jeju April 3 Massacre of 1948 that resulted in a significant number of civilians murdered, tells a similar story. The *halmangs* initially refused to tell the "ugly" story. Both the Russian women witnesses "sorry" in Alexievich's novel and the Jeju *halmangs*' "ugly story" indicate the "deep memories" long buried in the speakers' minds.[67] They are memories the speakers cannot tell, reenact, retrieve, or deliver to someone who does not share the experience. As traumas are, memories buried deep inside oneself are unexcavatable and inexplicable. The ellipses used often in Alexievich's novel are a creative device to speak on the unspeakable by omitting the words. As the author says, an ellipsis is an effective literary mechanism that allows readers to access "when the most important stories are written in silence" and encounter the dormant silences under the speaker's deep consciousness. It can also provide a passage to empathy by letting the readers into what is unspoken by the speaker. An expressive method for unspeakable memory that is more extreme than the ellipsis of the living is summoning the dead to properly commemorate their tragic deaths, as demonstrated in the research by Kwon Heon-Ik that restored the voices of the Vietnamese through their ghosts and by Kim Seongnae in which the Jeju shamans summoned the dead to rekindle the memories of the April 3 massacre.[68]

Photography also represents silence, but it stands opposite of an ellipsis. While an ellipsis indicates a deeply buried memory, a photograph sometimes discloses a memory like a speech. If an ellipsis speaks on the unspeakable by omission, a shot visually representing the past edits the memory in a much more diverse and meticulous way. The photo of the Auschwitz-Birkenau concentration camp, in which the two railroad tracks toward the camp merge before the main gate, is a representative example. Anyone looking at this photo would assume it was taken from outside the camp, facing the main entrance. It was taken from inside the camp facing out. The single railroad continues inside the camp until it passes the gate, where it diverges—supposedly to arrange new arrivals of Jews promptly. Interestingly, nowhere in the description of the photo is explained the direction of the railroad that heads out from inside the camp, perhaps as the image of multiple tracks converging in front of the camp would be more fitting to the fact that the Jews were transferred into Auschwitz from different places in Europe.[69] It is unfair to say this photo was "manipulated," but viewers may be confused when they learn where the railroad tracks were headed. This photo delicately reveals the distance between reality and vividness. The photography acquires the verisimilitude of literary realism.

During the critical debate started by activist Lee Yong-soo on the oppressive memory politics of the Korean Council for Justice and Remembrance for the Issues of Military Sexual Slavery by Japan, Korean Broadcasting System (KBS) published footage initially filmed by the U.S. Army Signal Corps. The film footage is real, but the context is questionable. Broadcast on May 28, 2020, this clip shows a frontal close-up of a pregnant woman presumed to be the "comfort woman" Park Young-shim, establishing a curious contrast between Park, who died in 2006 in North Korea, and Lee, a living survivor. It must not have been an accident that the film was aired when the public sentiment began to condemn Lee.[70] By proclaiming that she was an activist, Lee protested the official memory of the victimhood nationalism, which had homogenized the "Comfort Women" into a single entity of passive victims and negated individual agency as a historical actor. As Kim Han-sang's poignant words point out, the footage was aired on public television to insinuate that "the black-and-white, silent film footage recording Park's victimization was deemed more credible than living Lee Yong-soo."[71] Publicizing the clip was aimed at the positivistic illusion that utilized photographic evidence to invalidate Lee's testimony as a survivor whose language embodied multifaceted aspects of the subject. Underneath it lay the positivistic belief that anything captured by the photographic media is technological proof of the past as fact and that the suffering of the "Comfort Women" victims was more scientifically, hence effectively, conveyed when visualized in photographs. Such a paranoiac obsession with photographic evidence of victimization is also palpable in the photos of the victims where their dark wounds in the original black-and-white image are digitally painted in bright red to accentuate blood.[72] Again, we must remind ourselves that the signifier-signified relation in photographic images is rather dependent on the interpretive discourse and practice than objective or scientific visuals.

The film *Schindler's List* is more direct with its editing and manipulation of the images. Faced with opposition from the Jewish community, the film was shot in a set built outside of the Auschwitz-Birkenau concentration camp. In the set, the barracks, the platform that received newly arrivals, and the crematorium could all be captured from one angle. Thanks to this set, the audience could see the entire camp at a glance, which would not have been possible in the actual camp. It is too large, and its facilities are too spread out to be captured in one shot. The set provided a stage that effected a more realistic scene than the actual site. Authenticity is a "cultural composition" for it relies on how meaning or interpretation is made, invention and application of the means of representation, and discourse that appropriates and juxtaposes images, symbols, and metaphors that constitute representation of reality.[73] Steven Spielberg deliberately shot scenes like the military mission to shut down the ghetto with a handheld camera, which would inevitably make subtle trembles. According to Janusz Kamiński, the cinematographer of *Schindler's List*, 40 percent of the entire film was shot with a handheld camera. As a result, the storytelling, scenario, and shooting technique that gives the audience the illusion of journalistic footage rendered the film more realistic. The narratological method that allows the audience to grasp the scope of reality, expressed with the maximized visual effects to justify its fictitiousness, also notably contributed to the film's huge success. In remembering and representing the past, reality and plausibility often conflict. More often than not, verisimilitude wins over reality when it comes to appealing to the audience.

10

FORGIVENESS

VIOLENCE OF FORGIVENESS

Forgiveness and reconciliation are the salient ethics and desirable goals of memory politics, but they may be the most difficult virtues to practice. As difficult as it is for the perpetrator to properly apologize and ask for forgiveness, it is not easy for the victim to forgive the perpetrator. Regarding apology and forgiveness that went out of sync, Rabbi Abraham Joshua Heschel shares a story of a rabbi known as a scholar and a noble soul in the Eastern borderland. On a return trip from Warsaw, the rabbi was invited by merchants sitting next to him on the train to join their card game. Having never played cards before, the rabbi politely turned down the invitation. One of the merchants, who did not like that the rabbi refused to play with them, then grabbed him by the collar and dragged him out of the compartment, so the rabbi had to stand in the vestibule until his destination. When the train stopped at the destination, the merchants were surprised to see a crowd recognizing the rabbi on the platform and running to him to ask for a handshake. Only then did the merchant realize that the passenger he kicked out was a respected rabbi of Brest-Litovsk and ask for his forgiveness. The rabbi did not forgive him.

Feeling uncomfortable, the merchant went to the rabbi's house that evening and offered three hundred rubles as a recompense. The rabbi briefly responded that he could not accept that. His stubbornness perplexed everyone. How could such a noble soul be so petty about forgiving something that small? In a subsequent conversation, when the rabbi spoke of the commandment that one must forgive someone when asked more than three times, his son reminded him of the merchant who had been begging for his forgiveness. The rabbi responded, "I cannot forgive him no matter how much I want to—as he did not know who I was on the train, he wronged that nameless person, not me. He should ask for that person's forgiveness, not mine." This anecdote pertains to the Judaic teaching that no one can forgive on behalf of someone else. Even from the standpoint of ontological common sense, it is questionable whether a "third party" can forgive the perpetrator on behalf of the victim.[1] The "rabbi on the train" story was Heschel's allegorical response to a challenging question posed by Simon Wiesenthal.

In his small book *The Sunflower* (*Die Sonnenblume*), published in 1969, Wiesenthal recalls an anecdote buried deep inside him and asks for opinions from spiritual leaders and conscientious intellectuals of the world. Considered one of the most poignant moral questions raised by the experience of World War II, his story dates back to the summer of 1942, when he was incarcerated in the Janowska concentration camp in L'viv, in Western Galicia. As if mocking the devastation of war, sunflowers bloomed everywhere without a care in the world that summer—their beauty, in sharp contrast to the wretched life at the camp, was a testament to the world's irrationality. With the surreal sunflowers as a backdrop, Wiesenthal had to commute outside the camp to work in forced labor. Now in stripes, starved and exhausted, he walked the familiar streets where he used to waste his youth wandering around before the war. One day, he was assigned to fatigue duty at his alma mater, L'viv Polytechnic, which had been turned into a temporary hospital by the Nazis. His job was to clear out medical waste, reeking of disinfectants and discharges from wounds. In the middle of his work, a nurse approached him and asked whether he was a Jew. When he said he was, she took him inside the building. Reminiscing about his school days, Wiesenthal followed the nurse until they reached a ward where a man shrouded in white bandages lay immobile on the only cot in the room. This dying man, named Karl, was said to have enlisted in the SS and been sent to the Eastern Front, where he was fatally wounded.

Upon hearing that Jews from concentration camps were working at the hospital, Karl requested on his deathbed that he meet any one of them so he could apologize for the horrible crimes he perpetrated on Jews before he closed his eyes for good. To Wiesenthal, who now stood awkwardly by the cot, the dying Karl confessed the brutalities his unit committed on the Eastern Front, saying that he could not find peace waiting for death, as the faces of dead Jews kept appearing before his eyes. From his childhood as a happy altar boy at the church and adolescence as a Hitler Youth whose fanaticism for the Nazis had drawn him away from his social democrat father, to adulthood as a member of the SS perpetrating war crimes on the Eastern Front, he confessed everything in repentance. The memory of herding Jews into a shed, which was then set on fire, and machine-gunning anyone running out of the shed haunted him. The Jewish man who jumped from the second floor, covering his child's eyes with his clothes on fire, was another image he could not shake from his mind. The child's face, with black hair and brown eyes, was too sharp and clear for Karl to die in peace. Thus, he thought he should confess everything and apologize to any Jewish person he could before his death. That was when Wiesenthal came across him. To Karl, begging desperately for forgiveness so he could die peacefully, Wiesenthal said nothing and quietly walked out of the room. He did not forgive. Or rather, he could not forgive.

This encounter continuously disturbed Wiesenthal. Whether refusing to forgive the "little lamb" in the face of death was heartless, whether it was okay to turn down the last will of a dying person, he could not be sure. His campmate Josek consoled him after hearing the story: he, too, would not have forgiven, but he would have verbally expressed his rejection instead of walking out in silence. It was not within their rights to forgive what that young Nazi SS member did to other Jews.[2] Wiesenthal had brooded on this episode for more than two decades before he asked his readers, "What would you have done?" In light of this question, many philosophers, theologians, and intellectuals worldwide pondered how intricate and complicated forgiving was. As in Rabbi Heschel's allegory, neither Wiesenthal, Josek, nor anyone else could forgive the Nazi on behalf of his victims. Whether to forgive the perpetrator was solely up to the victim. It would be ludicrous for someone to forgive a murderer as a proxy for the victim. From a Judaic perspective, Wiesenthal's not forgiving the "dying lamb" was not something to feel guilty about. Forgiving the perpetrator when you are not the victim is not only impossible but immoral, let alone forgiving someone who did not ask to be forgiven. From the perspective of Catholicism, which stresses the importance of forgiveness, it is also possible to find fault in disallowing an opportunity to repent for someone who sincerely regrets an action and asks for forgiveness.

From a secular perspective, it is difficult to deny that Karl, a Nazi SS member who had been an active participant in the genocide of Jews with a firm belief, was ultimately incapable of reflecting critically on racist politics. His wish to be forgiven by "any" Jew was still under the influence of Nazi ideology that demonized all Jews as a monolith. Even on his deathbed, this Nazi pushed his burden of making a moral decision onto the shoulders of Wiesenthal, a stranger and a Jew, who was suddenly asked to grant him final forgiveness. For his peace of mind in the face of death, the Nazi criminal apologized to *any* Jew rather than *the* Jews he murdered, and he forced an absurd ultimatum onto the randomly selected Jewish stranger who was then made to feel self-critical for being unable to forgive him. According to Primo Levi's piercing charge, the Nazis once again used a Jew in exchange for a peaceful death. Karl merely wanted to unload his guilt and anguish on someone else in the selfish and shameless act. Considering that he was precisely the kind of person who would repent only when his death or Germany's defeat was imminent, it is doubtful if he would have genuinely regretted his actions and begged for forgiveness if the Third Reich had been on a winning streak and he could have indulged in the privileges of the victor.[3]

The act of forgiving is often violent. Especially from Rabbi Heschel's standpoint, forgiving a murderer on behalf of the dead victim is analogous to denying the victims their exclusive right to forgive. Therefore, it can be another form of violence. Even if the victim's parents forgive the murderer, the forgiveness they grant would be for taking their most loved one from them, not for the murder, which only the murdered can forgive. Forgiving on behalf of a lover or friend is just as problematic: what "I" can forgive is only the infliction of grief on "me." No one can claim the life of another in the name of love. If one does, it is a mere illusion. Aside from logic, the risk of forgiving is that it enables forgetting. Once forgiveness is granted, people consider the tug-of-war over reconciliation finished and return to their daily lives as if nothing happened. Yet, what is essential in memory politics is not hastened closure—instead, it is to painfully admit that even such a heinous action is still part of humanity and seek a better way to remember lest the abhorrent aspect of humanity ever resurfaces. For this reason, we should approach with more caution toward the Catholic ideal of forgiveness, which may seem more generous than the austere stances of Levi and Heschel.

As attested by *The Confessions of St. Augustine*, the Catholic ideal of forgiveness draws a clear distinction between a subject who did wrong and a subject to be punished—this is to restrict the object of forgiveness to one who did wrong to distinguish between forgiving a person and absolution of sin.[4] Where forgiving a person who wronged you falls in the realm of humans, absolution of punishable sin is in the realm of God. From a Christian perspective, forgiving frees both the forgiver and the forgiven from the burden of the past and helps heal the damaged relationship. Though humans must repent for God to forgive them, in human relationships, forgiveness sometimes precedes repentance—to wait for repentance from the forgiven after forgiveness is granted.[5] Forgiveness is also a crucial virtue of human society as it is a highly ethical determination to prevent another evil not by negating the evils done in the past but by liberating the victim from vengeful desires.[6] Still, the political discourse that demands forgiveness from the perpetrator's side is sometimes used to condemn the victim for not forgiving, weakening the victim's ethical-political stance. Those who want to expunge their uncomfortable past compel the victim to forgive. Victims, on the other hand, can also exploit the act of forgiving to maintain their morally privileged status and subjugate the perpetrator—this is the instrumentalization of forgiveness to affirm one's moral superiority.[7] The understanding of violence inherent in forgiveness also serves as a critical weapon against the "theological antisemitism" that pits "vengeful, unforgiving" Judaism against "loving, benevolent" Christianity.[8]

If we shift our focal point from the existential realm of each individual to the political realm, forgiveness is not an absolute virtue. In global memory politics, forgiveness is a double-edged sword that can either deconstruct or reinforce victimhood nationalism. In this chapter I will investigate the issue of forgiveness and victimhood nationalism that revolves around the pastoral letter that Polish Catholic bishops sent to German bishops on November 18, 1965, on the occasion of the twentieth anniversary of the end of World War II. This letter became an "event" as soon as it was made public.[9] At first glance, the letter was just one of the fifty-six letters the Polish bishops sent to episcopates around the world near the end of the Vatican Council. What made this one stand out was its content: signed by thirty-five bishops and an archbishop with Cardinal Stefan Wyszyński at the head, the letter was written mainly to initiate reconciliation between the Polish Catholic Church and its German counterpart. The Catholic Church of Poland, as the biggest victim of Nazi Germany, sending a message to forgive the German brothers and sisters was indeed surprising, but what was even more shocking was the ending of the letter, where the Polish victims asked for forgiveness from the German perpetrators. This pastoral letter from the Polish bishops subverted the secular common sense that the perpetrator must seek forgiveness from the victim first. Known for its vital part, "we forgive and ask for forgiveness," this letter written in subversive imagination inevitably garnered public attention since it instantaneously relocated the Catholic meaning of "forgiveness" from the personal to the political realm.[10]

DRAFTING RECONCILIATION

It seems that not only Archbishop Bolesław Kominek, who wrote the letter's first draft, but also the other signatories thoroughly anticipated the impact of the letter. According to an intelligence report sent by the Polish Ministry of Interior and Administration to the party central on November 13, five days before the letter was published, Archbishop Kominek told people around him that the letter would be a "real bomb."[11] The archbishop and all the other Polish bishops who signed the letter braced themselves for a harsh backlash from the authorities and society. That worry soon became a reality—the German episcopate published a lukewarm, vague statement in reply, and the Polish Communist Party and media did not hesitate to denounce the Catholic Church. The party's propaganda machines came up with the slogan "We neither forgive nor ask to be forgiven," in a mocking parody of the Polish bishops' letter. The party's official newspaper and national media went even further and called the bishops "national traitors" and the letter a "surrender document to German retaliation" and an "anticitizen act." Some even chanted, "Expel the (national traitor) cardinal from Poland!"[12] The main argument of such condemnation was that the bishops were traitors who sold Poland's national interest to the imperialists of West Germany.[13] At a time of the ongoing Cold War between communist Poland and West Germany, when historical reconciliation regarding the Nazi genocide still had far to come, the outcry could damage the church's reputation.

In terms of population, Poland suffered the most deaths in World War II. Excluding the 150,000 in the Soviet-occupied regions, the final Polish death toll is estimated at 5.4–5.6 million in the Nazi-occupied area, including approximately 3 million Jews. That is about 20 percent of the entire population at the time. Poland's loss was also significant beyond numbers: more than half of its lawyers, 40 percent of doctors, and one-third of university professors and high school teachers perished. Catholic priests were not an exception to the Nazis' mass murder of Polish intellectuals. Two thousand pastors and five bishops were executed or killed in the concentration camp and elsewhere, which amounted to 25 percent of the country's entire pastoral population.[14] Nevertheless, Poland did not receive an official apology from either Germany for two decades after the end of the war. According to East Germany's official stance, the evils of Nazism were the responsibility of West German capitalists who had betrayed the national interest of the

German people by supporting imperialism and militarism. On the other hand, West Germany, which officially had no diplomatic relations with Poland, had neither the means nor the willingness to apologize. Poland secured the Oder-Neisse line by signing the Zgorzelec Treaty with East Germany on July 6, 1950, but the risk of a border dispute with West Germany remained present. Consisting mainly of expellees from East Prussia, Silesia, Sudetenland, and other Eastern European regions, the Catholic Church of West Germany was not ready to concede the new border. Its stance was based on the critique of Eastern Europe's expulsion of German civilians and advocacy for the Charter of German Expellees.

The bishops' letter was initially written with the intent of breaking the deadlock and initiating reconciliation between the two countries by inviting the Catholic brothers of West Germany to the millenary anniversary of the acceptance of Christianity in 1966. The anniversary event was a precious opportunity for the Polish Catholic Church to reaffirm the importance of Christianity as an intangible national asset to compete with the communist ideology. It signaled the return from the communist atheism of the Eastern Bloc to the Christian traditions of the West. Making peace with West Germany would be a first step toward the Western turn. Despite the intention, the letter put the Polish Catholic Church in a difficult position. Having competed with the church for sociocultural hegemony since the communist regime came to power, the ruling communist party (PZPR) attacked the national legitimacy of Catholicism through the propaganda war against the bishops' pastoral letter. The party's antichurch propaganda that painted the church as traitorous worked exceptionally well when the public learned that the German bishops' reply did not transparently acknowledge the Oder-Neisse line. The church suffered a great turmoil not only from the outside but also from within: more than half of Polish priests who answered the survey conducted by the Polish government said they disagreed with the bishops' pastoral letter, and Cardinal Wyszyński was not content with this backlash from the younger generation of priests.[15]

That said, the letter's imagination that subverted the preconceived notion of forgiveness, which needs to be asked for by the perpetrator and granted by the victim's side, was a masterful political tactic to induce an apology from postwar Germany.[16] Having received the letter asking for forgiveness from victims, the German bishops would have felt uncomfortable without apologizing themselves. The letter was a great success at the international level as it broke the ice between Poland and West Germany. Its historical significance became more palpable through the series of amicable settlements between the two countries that ensued in the post–Cold War era: the exchange of peace signs between West German chancellor Helmut Kohl and Polish prime minister Tadeusz Mazowiecki in 1989, the international reaffirmation of the Oder-Neisse line, the reunification of Germany, and Poland's joining of the European Union. The letter expanded the meaning of forgiveness that had hitherto remained private in Catholic culture into the arena of international politics. In Catholicism, forgiveness is an ethical and emotional device to liberate the victim from vindictive desires. As the historical reconciliation between Poland and Germany progressed, the bishops' letter belatedly received praise, such as "the avant-garde of reconciliation" (Robert Żurek), "the greatest foresight in Polish history since World War II" (Jan Józef Lipski), "a touching documentation of reconciliation" (Helmut Kohl), "the letter that inspired the Polish-German dialogue" (Tadeusz Mazowiecki), and "a document that tore down the psychological wall" (Adam Michnik).[17]

With the dawn of the twenty-first century, the letter broadened the contours of historical reconciliation beyond Poland-Germany relations. At the bishops' conference held in Warsaw in June 2005, the sixtieth anniversary of the war's end, the Polish bishops read a letter modeled on the 1965 letter to endorse mutual reconciliation between Poland and Ukraine. This new letter was also read at the Orthodox churches in the town of Zarvanytsia in Ternopil and in L'viv, which used to be a multicultural city populated with Poles, Jews, and Ukrainians.[18] Ternopil is a city in the Volhynia (Волинь/Wołyń) region adjoining the Polish-Ukrainian border and the site of tragedy in which the Polish nationalist resistance force and Ukrainian nationalists in alliance with the Nazis massacred more than a hundred thousand Polish and Ukrainian peasants in retaliation against each other. The memory of the wartime ethnic cleansings in Volhynia, suppressed in the name of the socialist brotherhood during the Cold War era, has been a thorny issue that had obstructed the historical reconciliation between Poland and Ukraine since the 1990s. In 2013 the Polish Catholic Church and the Orthodox Church of Ukraine cooperated to declare a joint statement for mutual forgiveness and reconciliation.[19] Though liberal politicians and critical intellectuals in both countries had continuously reiterated the necessity of historical reconciliation since the mid-1990s, the two churches drafted the historical document for reconciliation. Also, the Bolesław Kominek Youth European Forum was launched in 2019 with the support of the EU to remember Archbishop Kominek and is held every summer to facilitate the exchange of ideas and experiences among youths across Europe about historical reconciliation.

"WE FORGIVE AND ASK FOR YOUR FORGIVENESS"

Breaking the deadlock of the historical reconciliation between Poland and West Germany required a new set of meta-ethics that surpassed the conventional calculation to determine who was the more tragic victim and who had to apologize first. The Catholic Church of both countries volunteered to play the role of the transnational agent of remembrance. Upon his arrival in Rome to attend an ecumenical council in February 1962, Cardinal Wyszyński invited the German cardinal Julius Döpfner to dinner. As the secretaries for the Vatican Council, the two cardinals maintained a close relationship with each other. Cardinal Döpfner was a representative of the liberal tradition of the German Catholic Church that historicized the suffering of expellees within the historical context of Nazi crimes. At the dinner, Cardinal Döpfner tipped Cardinal Wyszyński off on internal information from West German authorities that Chancellor Adenauer hoped to affirm the Oder-Neisse line but was reluctant to publicly declare it considering the political stance of the expellees. Döpfner leaked the information that the Adenauer administration of West Germany was serious about stabilizing its relationship with People's Poland.[20]

Aside from the two cardinals' close friendship, the German bishops also suggested to the Polish Catholic Church a coproposal to the Vatican for the canonization of the Polish priest Maximilian Kolbe, who had sacrificed himself on behalf of another inmate in Auschwitz. In 1964 members of the German Catholic peace organization Pax Christi-Bewegung visited Poland on a reconciliatory mission. Karol Wojtyła, then archbishop of Kraków and later Pope John Paul II, welcomed the visitors at the front gate of Auschwitz. Also, during a sermon at the twentieth anniversary of the end of World War II held in Wrocław in 1965, Archbishop Kominek blessed not only the Polish residents but also the Germans who were expelled from Wrocław. Ultimately, he called for mutual understanding and peace between Poles and Germans. By implying the possibility of a "shared cultural legacy," the sermon by the archbishop of Wrocław, an Upper Silesian native familiar with German-Polish cultural hybridity, presented an alternative perspective from the Polish nationalist historiography that Silesia "originally belonged to Poland."[21] In contrast to the dominant paradigm of national history at the time, Archbishop Kominek's idea of "shared cultural legacy" pioneered the "transnational history," "overlapping history," or "border history" that garnered the support of East European historians only half a century later.[22] One can easily bridge between shared cultural legacy and border history of hybrid cultures or overlapping history. In the 1960s the mood was ripe for communication.

On October 14, 1965, the Evangelical Church in Germany (EKD) published a memorandum known as the *Ostdenkschrift* (East memorandum) for the twentieth anniversary of the end of the war. This memorandum was a step toward reconciliation by affirming the Oder-Neisse line and Poland's ownership of the ceded German territories. The *Ostdenkschrift* opened the gate of mutual understanding between the Polish victims and German perpetrators by contextualizing the historical relationship between the Nazis and German expellees without failing to acknowledge the latter's pain and suffering. The memorandum's affirmation of Poland's sovereignty over its "reclaimed" western territories, against the general resentment among the East Prussian expellees to whom the land signified their home, set a true milestone in a new way toward historical reconciliation. It broke the taboo of West German society.[23] When the memorandum was published, Znak, an association of liberal Catholic intellectuals in Poland who were relatively free from communist control, was the first to pay attention to it, believing that the time had come for the conversation. It was anticipated that the *Ostdenkschrift* would counteract the Polish Communist Party's nationalistic anti-German propaganda about West German "revanchists" attempting to reseize the "reclaimed" western territories.[24]

The more significant meaning of the memorandum was that it thawed the ice of distrust between the two countries. Interestingly, the reports of the Polish military inspectorate in West Berlin and the Polish Trade Representative in Cologne favored the *Ostdenkschrift*. The Polish military inspectorate reported on the press conference held by the EKD about the issues regarding German expellees and Germany–East Europe relations. Neither enthusiastic nor apathetic, it explained the mood in a bureaucratic tone without a critical edge.[25] The Polish trade representative reported on the contact with the editor-in-chief of the SPD Party newspaper. According to the report, Dr. Gustav Heinemann expressed his hope to visit Poland. A member of the EKD leadership, Heinemann hoped to see firsthand reactions to the memorandum from the Polish government and the public. The report painted a positive picture of Poland's invitation by informing about Heinemann's background: he Heinemann was initially a member of the CDU but left the party in protest of West Germany's rearmament, joining the SPD.[26] A few days later, the Polish trade representative invited Eugen Gerstenmaier to a luncheon at the Foreign Press Club in Bonn, where Gerstenmaier had a long conversation with a Polish official. One of the reports states that Gerstenmaier expressed the need for reconciliation between Poland and West Germany and his hope to visit Poland as a private citizen to learn about Poland's reaction to the *Ostdenkschrift*. The report carefully suggests that the Polish Institute of International Affairs in Warsaw be the host institution for his visit to Poland.[27]

The *Ostdenkschrift* caused a great sensation not only among the Polish authorities but also within the Catholic Church. The first among the bishops to notice the meaning of the memorandum was Bolesław

Kominek, archbishop of Wrocław. A German territory ceded to Poland due to the postwar border adjustments, and typical of what the Poles called "reclaimed land," Wrocław was where the cultures of Germany and Poland intermingled. Born and raised in Wrocław and familiar with the German language and culture, Archbishop Kominek later confessed that the EKD's *Ostdenkschrift* had inspired him to draft the pastoral letter with other bishops.[28] The tremendous significance of the *Ostdenkschrift* is that it recognizes the Germany-Polish border marked by the Oder-Neisse line and acknowledges Poland's sovereignty over the "reclaimed land." In effect, the memorandum could become a watershed in Poland-Germany relations, as Władysław Gomułka, first secretary of the party, considered normalization of Poland-West Germany relationship and reconciliation possible if West Germany affirmed the Oder-Neisse line. For Gomułka, a national communist who chose a route independent of the Soviet Union, reconciliation between Poland and West Germany was desperately needed as a preventive measure against intervention from the Soviet Union, which had voluntarily taken the role of intermediary in Central Europe.[29] Indeed, he might have also expected economic aid through reparations and compensation as a result of the normalization.

The progressive members of the EKD had already demanded through the Memorandum of Tübingen that the West German government recognize the Oder-Neisse line as the official national border between postwar Germany and Poland and abolish its plan for nuclear armament. Signed by eight renowned Protestant theologians on November 6, 1961, and sent to several members of the parliament, the memorandum was made public in February 1962, giving rise to heated controversy in West German society. The expellees living in West Germany vehemently criticized the memorandum, their main argument being that it ignored the political sovereignty of people in East Germany and Eastern Europe and colluded with communism, which worshipped corruption and violence. The expellees' voice emerged through the controversy, which had a considerable impact in West German society. It revealed that the West German public was not ready to affirm the new border along the Oder-Neisse line. Neither was the SPD prepared to implement the decision. Although the SPD would later adopt the demands of the memorandum as party policy, it hesitated at that time, wary of being labeled as "fatherlandless fellas" (*Vaterlandslose Gesellen*). Even Willy Brandt, the initiator of the *Ostpolitik*, thought the party's official stance should not be based on the memorandum as its radical stance could upset West German voters.[30]

It is hard to say that the general sentiment in West Germany in the autumn of 1965, after the publication of the *Ostdenkschrift* and the Polish bishops' letter, was notably different from that of 1962. The bishops' letter carried a message of enormous impact that could at once break the stalemate between Poland and Germany. Still, vernacular memories in both West Germany and Poland were not ready to decipher the futuristic message of the letter. The Polish bishops' pastoral letter differed remarkably from the Polish Communist Party's nationalist-communist view of history even at the level of vocabulary: it refrained from using Polono-centric expressions such as "originally Polish" (*Ur-polnisch*) and "reclaimed land" (*ziemia odzyskana*) to describe the ceded territory from Germany. In drafting the letter, Archbishop Kominek used instead more neutral expressions like "Potsdam Western territories" (*Potsdamer Westgebiete*) and terms that were widely used in West German memory culture, such as "refugees" (*Flüchtlinge*) and "expellees" (*Vertriebene*), to convey empathy with the pain of Germans expelled from the East.[31] Such West German terms were taboo in Poland in the 1960s as they had different political implications from the official East German term *Umsiedler* or the Polish *przesiedlony*, meaning "resettlers." Whereas the West German terminology reflected the pain and suffering of the expellees, the East German and Polish counterparts bore a meaning that was emotionally neutralized. Though seemingly minuscule, this semantic difference was later used by the Polish Communist Party as the critical reason for its condemnation of the bishops' letter.

Beginning with an invitation for the German bishops to the celebration of the millennium anniversary of the baptism of Poland to be held in Jasna Góra in May 1966, the letter expresses gratitude to Otto the Great for Poland's acceptance of Roman Catholicism, not Greek Orthodox Christianity. It also acknowledges with modesty that German merchants, architects, artists, and settlers have historically been a cultural bridge between Poland and the West since the Middle Ages. Candidly stating that Magdeburg's rights introduced by Germans liberated the urban air of Poland, it also describes the German influence in Poland's national culture and artistic exchange between the two countries.[32] Between the lines of the statement that explains how Polish and German cultures share the common foundation in Roman Catholicism lies the historical implication that Polish culture is more akin to Western Europe than to Eastern Europe of the Greek Orthodox belief. It also vaguely hints at the implicit message that Soviet-enforced communism is a foreign "Eastern" ideology.[33] The letter was exceedingly progressive for its time also because of its historical paradigm. It does, on the surface, unfalteringly acknowledge the German influence on Polish culture, yet it does not approve of Germany's colonialist view on history. According to the letter, Germany's historical role as a cultural bridge between Poland and Western Europe differed from colonialism in the late era. Its view of history is also far from the autochthonism of the nationalists who deny any trace of foreign cultural import within Poland's historical domain.[34] At a time when the national history paradigm was dominant and transnational histories, such as border history, global history, entangled history, and overlapping history, had a long way to go, this 1965 letter's take on history was remarkably ahead of its time.[35]

The letter emphasizes that "Catholic saints who, instead of taking what the brother nation has, handed out their own cherished culture according to God's will." It draws a clear distinction between the evangelical vocation of Christianity and aggressive colonialism. Taking as a model Paweł Włodkowic, rector of the Kraków Academy (now Jagiellonian University), who stressed the human rights of non-Christians and supported propagation through religious mercy at the Council of Constance in 1414, the letter poignantly criticizes the Teutonic knights who tried to convert heathens with fire and swords and as a result are remembered as a terrible burden for European Christianity and an insulting nightmare for Poles. In this way, the letter maintains a critical tone toward the Teutonic Order—it traces the lineage of Frederick the Great of Prussia, Bismarck, and Hitler back to the order's belligerent desire for colonialism that engulfed the peaceful mission of Christianity that ultimately turned Poland into the land of death where smoke fumed day and night from the crematoria at the Nazis' concentration camps. The Nazi regime's targeted killing of the Polish Catholic priests, including five bishops among the two thousand priests killed, was a testament to the brutal colonial rule that had long replaced the Christian tradition of peaceful propagation. For example, 278 priests, or 47 percent of the priesthood, were executed in the diocese of Chełmno alone in the early stage of the war. There are numerous such examples. The Nazis' apocalyptic destruction during World War II left Poles only the ruins and rubble, poverty and disease, tears and deaths.[36]

Archbishop Komineck expected his German brothers to understand the reason for the Poles' distrust of their nearest neighbor and strong demand for the recognition of the Oder-Neisse line and border security. The letter clarifies that the reconciliation's premise was acknowledging the Oder-Neisse line as the Polish-German border. Having ceded the eastern borderlands to the Soviet Union, Poland, in the aftermath of the Nazis' intentional destruction, deserved to be recompensated with the western territories, including Silesia and Pomerania. For Poles, it was a cry for survival. The main point of the letter was that such a demand by Poland was entirely different from the Nazis' colonial conquest of Eastern Europe and their demand for a more expansive "living space" (*Lebensraum*) for the Aryan race. The letter also calls forth the tradition of nineteenth-century Poland's national liberation movement, which dreamed of liberating not only the nation but also neighboring nations, to imply that Poland's safety and peace would entail Germany's safety and peace, and that Poland's freedom and Germany's freedom are tightly entangled. The letter stood in the spirit of "for our and your freedom" (*Za wolność naszą i waszą*), a slogan of the Polish irredentist movement in 1831 that appeared in crucial historical turning points of the twentieth century in 1956, 1968, 1980, and 1989. Most recently, in 2022, Lithuanian president Gitanas Nausėda quoted this slogan in his tweet: "It remains relevant now when Ukraine is withstanding Russian war."[37]

It was also in the context of the nineteenth-century tradition that the letter deeply empathized with the suffering of German expellees from

East Prussia and the "pain of conscience" Germans had had to endure under the Nazis. It paid tribute to the "White Rose" and other German anti-Nazi resistant movements that had attempted the assassination of Hitler and shed light on the considerable number of Germans who had met the same fate as their Polish peers in the concentration camp. The letter had no room for the simplistic national binary of collective guile and collective innocence. The Polish bishops in the letter ultimately offer a hand of reconciliation to the German bishops sitting opposite of them at the council and invite them to the celebration of the millennium anniversary of Poland's Christianity, ending the letter with the famous line "We forgive, and ask for forgiveness" (*wir . . . gewähren Vergebung und bitten um Vergebung*).[38] As a parody of the ancient Roman poet Horace's aphorism "*Veniam damus petimusque vicissim*," this line was also quoted by Pope Paul VI on October 17, 1963, in his request to stop the continuous disputes for the reunification of churches worldwide. Resolving conflicts and initiating reconciliation through written correspondence between priests have been Christian traditions since the Roman Empire in the third to fourth centuries.[39] Thus, neither the form nor the function of the bishops' letter was unprecedented or particularly scandalous in the history of Catholicism.

Still, this letter in 1965 was so far ahead of its time that even its complimentary nickname, "the avant-garde of reconciliation," falls short of describing its progressiveness. The letter was written with the belief that pain was pain regardless of "whose pain," and sharing pain and sorrow was a just action, even if each bore a different political significance.[40] Its message carries the highly developed ethics of reconciliation, forgiveness, and a restrained sense of victimhood. In this regard, it is distinct from the rhetoric of the Federation of Expellees (BdV) more than fifty years later, which overlaps the suffering of German expellees with the Holocaust by appropriating expressions like "extermination camps," "forced labor," and "crematoria."[41] The offer of empathy and reconciliation from the victims of more significant pain to the other victims who had previously victimized them was a resolute moral decision to reject a hierarchy among victims. As *Die Welt* writes, many Germans were touched by the Polish bishops' letter because they resonated with its message, which acknowledges the pain of German expellees for the first time and aims to bring justice to them from Poland. Rather than invalidating the Germans' suffering by comparing the magnitude of each nation's suffering, the letter delivered warm empathy to the German readers and overcame the dichotomy between collective guilt and collective innocence in the national frame of German perpetrators versus Polish victims.

The overcoming of the conventional perpetrator-victim relations without losing historical contexts was also an essential achievement of the letter by the Polish bishops, who initially thought initiating reconciliation was the responsibility of the German Church. Acknowledging the pain of German expellees had long been a taboo in postwar Poland's memory culture and therefore required tremendous courage. It could also have been a gamble, as many German expellees at the time misconstrued the Poles' crime against them to be worse than what Germany had done to Poland. The avant-garde leadership reflected in the letter is even more unique, considering that the Catholic Church of West Germany was taking a relatively passive stance toward reconciliation as the expellees from East Prussia had significant influence over the church.[42] The Polish bishops' letter overthrew the "zero-sum game" of victimhood that uses quantitative inequality of suffering as the logical base to highlight one's own "greater" suffering by denying or countering the "smaller" sufferings of others.[43] The letter's reconciliatory effort sets an example amid memory cultures of victimhood that belittle or negate others' pain and misery to glorify the suffering of one's nation. By demonstrating the ethics of forgiveness, the letter left a legacy of historical reconciliation between Poland and Germany.

GERMAN BISHOPS ON VERTICAL RECONCILIATION

Traditionally in theology, God's top-down forgiveness of humans was the predominant form of forgiveness. The discourse on reconciliation likewise centered on the vertical reconciliation between God and humans. The World Council of Churches (WCC) theologians first led horizontal reconciliation between humans. Considering the WCC theology's tendency to seek harmony among all creations of God, its pursuit of horizontal reconciliation between humans was only natural.[44] The passion for horizontal reconciliation diminished as evangelical churches joined and conservatized the WCC, but it is still alive and a topic of discussion. Separately from the WCC, horizontal reconciliation also gained traction within the Lausanne movement. The Christian community could not but to heed the elevated conflicts between races, nations, and ethnicities since the mid-1990s, such as the September 11 attacks, the Israeli-Palestinian conflict, the Yugoslav Wars, the ethnic cleansing in the Balkans, and the Rwandan genocide, to name a few. The Lausanne movement listed racism, American slavery, the Holocaust, ethnic cleansing, and colonial genocide as real-life examples of ethnic conflict and demanded that Christians constructively engage in reconciliatory efforts. Composed of daily rituals for reconciliation, such as "forgive the perpetrator and challenge injustice for others," "welcome neighbors from the enemy side and pursue reconciliation," and "accept pain and death rather than destruction and revenge," the movement emphasized "the lifestyle of reconciliation" as a way of Christian practice.[45] However, this "lifestyle" remained somewhat more rhetorical than practical.

Standing face-to-face with the reality of the twenty-first century, where the road toward horizontal reconciliation is still rough, the letter by Polish bishops in 1965 in which the victim asks forgiveness of the perpetrator seems ever more innovative. Such bold ethics of reconciliation that subverted the secular convention were made possible by differentiating offense from the offender. Once the distinction was made, punishing the offense while forgiving the offender became possible. To borrow Paul Ricoeur's logic, the fate of the punishable subject was left up to God's mercy, but the victim could forgive the perpetrator. Through this act of forgiving, the Poles averted the risk of committing another evil by letting go of their vengeful desire against Germany.[46] Albeit in a germinal form, a postcolonial problem, beyond colonial problems, can be sensed at this juncture. The letter was an expression of the Polish bishops' determination to rescue the memory of World War II from the victimhood nationalism of Poland and Germany and go into historical reconciliation and Christian forgiveness. Unlike vertical reconciliation, where the sinner asks for God's forgiveness with the premise of repentance and God forgives the repentant sinner, horizontal reconciliation between humans has more room to be flexible; a reverse reconciliation, where forgiveness precedes repentance, is possible between humans.[47]

At the foundation of the Polish bishops' upfront forgiveness was the novel arrangement to morally pressure Germans into repentance and apology to Poles. For such a contrarian move to be effective, however, the reaction from the addressee, the German episcopate, was crucial. If the perpetrator group, the target of forgiveness, did not express enough willingness to repent to be accepted by the victims, the meaning of forgiveness offered by the victim group would be reduced in half. This was a time when Germans still held on to solid racial/national biases against Poles. If the Polish bishops had not only forgiven but also asked for forgiveness from the perpetrators who had yet to repent, ordinary, secular Poles would have felt that the bishops were overusing forgiveness. In contrast, Germany found it easier to reconcile with France, which was considered of equal or superior cultural standing, than with Poland.[48] Unfortunately, the German bishops' reply was disappointingly weak, enough to make Poles think the Polish bishops indeed wasted forgiveness. The reply acknowledges at the beginning the German nation's violent attacks on the Polish nation but spends much more space unfolding the suffering of German expellees and thanking the Polish bishops for mentioning them. The central argument is that the right to home should have been respected for the German expellees who did not intend to invade but were invited by the Slavic rulers of the region at the time to live a quiet, honest life. According to a report from the Polish Intelligence Agency, the German episcopate privately requested their Polish counterpart to alter the parts of the letter where the Teutonic Order and Bismarck are negatively described.[49]

Historical interpretation may be crucial, but it was only secondary to the letter's central issue: whether to acknowledge the new national border adjusted after World War II along the Oder-Neisse line. The German bishops' reply that stressed the expellees' rights to return home was, in short, a rejection of the Oder-Neisse line as the national border. While the Polish bishops' letter focuses on the horizontal reconciliation between humans, the German bishops' reply emphasizes the vertical reconciliation between God and humans. Based on their logic, all human wrongdoings were first and foremost a sin against God, and therefore the sinners must ask for God's mercy before they do fellow humans; only after God's forgiveness was granted could the sinners ask for forgiveness from people around them.[50] Such a viewpoint, namely, that of "vertical reconciliation," dehistoricizes memories of victimhood from different historical backgrounds by stressing the equal footing of all sinners. In other words, the German bishops took a passive stance on historical reconciliation by responding to the Polish bishops' request for horizontal reconciliation with vertical reconciliation—a move that was frustratingly conservative from the perspective of the WCC. When the German bishops' reply was revealed, Cardinal Wyszyński could not hide his discomfort. In his letter to Cardinal Döpfner, Wyszyński shows his disappointment that the German bishops' reply was far more rigid than the Protestant *Ostdenkschrift*, that it was "too restrained and reserved."[51]

About the reply being so listless compared to the groundbreaking letter from the Polish bishops, Cardinal Döpfner later regretted that they could have "responded more warmly," even though they had to consider the expellees who constituted the majority of the German Catholic Church. While most West Germans were not desperate to reconcile with Poland, many of them were also steeped in victimhood nationalism and believed that Poland committed more significant crimes than Germany did. They thought the last line of the Polish bishops' letter, where they asked for forgiveness, was a sign that the Poles finally admitted their guilt. The stiff victimhood nationalism among German expellees also contributed to the church's political anxiety that if it affirmed Poland's stance on the Oder-Neisse line, it would lose support from the over seven million expellees and jeopardize its relationship with the CDU and CSU.[52] In 1968 the Bensberger Kreis also criticized the reply as insufficient and claimed that it could have made sure of its affirmation of the Oder-Neisse line as the national border to mitigate the Poles' fear and anxiety, as did the *Ostdenkschrift*.[53] Though the Bensberger Memorandum was positively received by Polish Catholic intellectuals like Bartoszewski and Mazowiecki, the German bishops' reply had already raised the ire of the Polish public.

The Internal Security Agency of Poland promptly translated the reply and sent it to the party leadership, and the party's propaganda outlets started a full-fledged anti-Catholic campaign. They often quoted the German media to support their claim that the anti-Polish groups in West Germany were the most pleased by the Polish bishops' letter, along with their own biased takes that the conservative media in Germany complained about the letter's interpretation of the history and that the Polish bishops did not accept the Oder-Neisse border. As the lead story in *Die Welt* reads, "The right to home continues," and the German media's German-centric reporting helped the party's anti-Catholic campaign, which alleged that while the German bishops advocated for their country, the Polish bishops went against their own.[54] The Polish bishops were met with harsh reproaches that they were national traitors who sold their national interest to West German imperialists. The party's organ *Trybuna Ludu* reported in fury that the bishops of Poland and West Germany compared the German expellees with the Holocaust victims and equated the suffering of the former to that of six million Poles whom the Nazis barbarically slaughtered. The self-praise of Wenzel Jaksch, president of the Federation of Expellees, who turned the bishops' letter into his achievement, was a testament to how dangerous it is to compromise with West German imperialism.[55] The party's propaganda outlets did not miss this chance to also rebuke the Catholic Church for choosing to cooperate with imperialist West Germany over East Germany, which was free of the complication regarding expellees and divorced from the Nazis' chauvinist tradition.

The party's propaganda machine also problematized the use of West German conservatives' terminology "expellees" (*Vertriebene/wygnancy*) instead of "resettlers" (*Umsiedler/przesiedleńcy*). The East German term *Umsiedler* was a depoliticized, neutral term, whereas its West German counterpart, *Vertriebene*, contained the historical meaning of innocent refugees driven out of their hometown. The party's official organs raised concern about the phrase "Potsdam Western territories" (*Potsdamer Westgebiete*) as it was considered an expression already corrupted by West German imperialists and history revisionists. Instead of "reclaimed land" (*ziemia odzyskana*) to connote that Silesia and Pomerania were originally Polish territories, the use of "Potsdam Western territories" attracted much criticism.[56] Aside from the rebuke from official party authorities, Cardinal Wyszyński received letters of complaint from individuals. Mostly from residents of the "reclaimed land," the letters called the cardinal "traitor of Poland" and "deplorable servant of capitalism" and challenged him with questions like, "How come the perpetrator Germany does not ask for forgiveness yet our bishops do," and "Are you really Polish?" Chants like "kick the cardinal out of Poland" were heard often. Still, the cardinal did not falter—he maintained his belief that the Polish bishops' letter was "the shining evidence of our Christian spirit and symbol of maturity of the history of Catholicism that exceeds a thousand years."[57]

Most political denunciations from the party stemmed from deliberate misinterpretation. As attested to by the official letter from the state secretary of the Polish People's Republic, the backlash was intense among party elites who saw the church as a spiritual power interfering with the state's diplomatic affairs.[58] That the Polish bishops wrote the letter only in German and did not translate it into Polish was also a huge oversight, as it enabled the party's propaganda machines to (mis)translate it to support their argument. For the church, therefore, the question of whether the Catholic Church had the right to forgive the perpetrator on behalf of individual victims was the most biting criticism. Albeit politically motivated, the party's criticism that nobody granted the Catholic bishops the right to represent the Polish nation also had its point. The Catholic Church did not represent non-Catholic Poles, and even within the Catholic community, declaring to forgive Germans in the name of the church on behalf of individual Polish victims who were not ready to forgive was problematic. Victims' consent to the ethics of forgiveness and confirmation of the German perpetrators' will to repent were left out in the process. Such an oversight became a reason that the Polish bishops' letter, despite its foundation of transnational reconciliation between Germany and Poland, cannot be free of criticism that it overused forgiveness.[59]

CATHOLIC DIALOGUE IN EAST ASIA

Transplanted into the memory space of East Asia, where not only official memories but also personal and vernacular memories between Korea, Japan, and China are in bitter conflict over Japan's imperial past and the Asia-Pacific War, the Polish bishops' pastoral letter ceases being the past and unexpectedly becomes the future of East Asia. This does not mean another political instrumentalization of the 1965 letter by arbitrarily erasing its historical context. Instead, it aims at a critical inquiry about how to revive the spirit of the 1965 letter in the context of twenty-first-century East Asia. Reflecting on the bishops' letter and its history in the memory space of East Asia now is also a search for new possibilities to solve the dilemma of the East Asian history disputes through an extension of political performativity and ethical implications demonstrated by the Polish Catholic Church as a transnational agent for historical reconciliation. Under East Asia's current circumstances, where both governments and civil societies are bound by the rules of international politics and unable to find a breakthrough, the precedent set by the Catholic Church for open communication beyond borders has a special meaning. A cross-historical reflection on the Polish bishops' letter of 1965 will hint at how to establish reconciliation and forgiveness as the rule of the game that steers East Asia's memory politics beyond politics. Considering that the Catholic Church belongs to the minority in South Korea and the extreme minority in Japan, its initiative for history reconciliation may remain a symbolic one. However, that transnational symbolic initiative, with which many East Asians can sympathize, is urgently needed.

Thirty or so years after the Polish bishops' letter, the Japanese bishops published an episcopal statement, "Determination Toward Truth," commemorating the fiftieth anniversary of the end of World War II on

February 25, 1995. The statement acknowledges and apologizes that "the Japanese military destroyed the lives of people in Joseon, China, the Philippines, and other regions, ... violated dignities of other humans, and massacred countless civilians including unarmed women and children in their brutal acts of destruction." It also stresses that the Japanese perpetrators are responsible for healing the "wounds inflicted on Asians," a responsibility the postwar generations of Japanese should keep.[60] To many Korean Catholics, that statement in 1995 showed the Japanese bishops' sincere repentance and confession that became an important first step for the church to start the journey toward forgiveness and reconciliation with its relationship with Korea. The statement occasioned regular meetings of Korean and Japanese bishops, the first of which, in 1996, discussed the issue of history textbooks. As the meetings thenceforth covered controversial topics such as "the lesson from the massacre of Koreans during the Great Kanto Earthquake (2003)" and "East Asia's denuclearization/nuclear power phase-out (2012)," the role of the Catholic Church in peace and historical reconciliation between Korea and Japan became increasingly crucial.

Another important document in the journey toward historical reconciliation is the Japan Catholic Council for Justice and Peace statement delivered on Assumption Day, August 15, 2019. Signed by Bishop Katsuya Taiji, this statement refers to the "emotional gap between the Japanese government's stance that takes no responsibility for the history of colonization and Koreans as the victim nation who are enraged by such a stance" as the obstacle that hinders Korea-Japan reconciliation. The statement reaffirms the validity of the individual victims' rights to claim reparations for personal damages after signing the 1965 Treaty on Basic Relations Between Japan and the Republic of Korea and once again demands that the Japanese government acknowledge its accountability for damages inflicted due to colonization. It denotes that the Council for Justice and Peace stands officially for individual reparations to Korean forced laborers, as is the case for Chinese forced laborers for whom the Japanese companies acknowledged and compensated for their exploitation of labor, highlighting the historical and moral legitimacy of reparations for individual victims of the Japanese empire's inhumane acts. The statement also references the cancellation of the Statue of Peace exhibition planned in Japan due to the public museum director's hate speech in its stern request for Japan's accountability for the elevated state of the Korea-Japan conflict.[61]

As if to respond to the statement, Bishop Constantine Bae Ki Hyun, head of the Justice and Peace Committee of the Catholic Bishops' Conference of Korea, expressed his will to "correspond in solidarity with the invitation of the Japanese Catholic Council for Justice and Peace" while still making clear that "Japan's economic sanctions against the Korean nation who had their language, country, and even customs taken away by Japan was a new kind of oppression, and a treatment to avoid genuine regret and reflection." He also proposed "repentance and purification" as the premise for peace between Korea and Japan.[62] Before this, the Korean Bishops' Conference published the "Statement in Commemoration of the Hundredth Anniversary of the March 1st Movement" in March 2019 to reflect and repent of the wrongs of the Catholic Church during the colonial era, including neglecting the Koreans' pain and suffering and instead advising them to participate in Japan's war of invasion and pay tribute to the shrine.[63] In response, the Japanese Council issued another statement acknowledging the Japanese Catholic Church's undue intervention in the Korean church during the colonial era and encouragement of its members to participate in the war, and that Japan's policy of invasion was also responsible for the Korean War and the partition of the peninsula.[64] Under the current circumstances where the historical reconciliation between Korea and Japan has once again reached a deadlock, these corresponding statements commemorating the centennial of the March 1st Movement are precious documentation of how the church's self-criticism and critical understanding of history worked in harmony as a system.

At this moment, when the communication channels at all levels of political circles and civil society organizations are mostly inoperative, the role of the Catholic Church as a transnational actor for peace and reconciliation has become ever more crucial. Thus, the statements leave much to be desired, as neither could reach beyond Japan's unilateral apology and reflection on the colonial past. While repentance and reflection on the part of Japan as the perpetrator are obvious requisites for reconciliation, they do not fully account for the necessary and sufficient conditions: the Catholic Church as a transnational institution of memory is capable of maintaining its postcolonial criticism of the victimhood nationalism of Korean society while demanding reflection and repentance from Japanese society. Latent in the victim's act of forgiving the perpetrator is an opportunity for the former to be finally rid of the desire for revenge and remorse for the fact that they had to be the victim, not the perpetrator; the colonized, not the colonizer. Unless the chain of oppression and injustice between colonizer and colonized, perpetrator and victim, and oppressor and oppressed is broken rather than simply reversing positions, the injustice of colonialism will continue to be reproduced. With this concern in mind, it seems the reality of the Korean Catholic Church is that the anticolonial rage overpowers decolonial reflection. For it to unfold its subversive imagination to induce apology and repentance from the perpetrator by forgiving first, as did the Polish Catholic Church, the Korean Catholic Church must free itself from the political and emotional confines of victimhood nationalism.

Established over a long period that exceeds two thousand years, the Catholic Church is a representative example of transnational actors in world history. For this reason, it is expected to take a transnational leadership role in East Asia's historical reconciliation. Amid the current situation in East Asia, where nationalist antagonism and conflicts over history become increasingly aggravated, a novel, convention-defying idea such as the Polish bishops' letter in 1965 is needed more urgently than ever. What would be immensely useful at this juncture is a transnational memory initiative that can introduce a way out of the current communication model of East Asia where "each nation is confined within its nationalist narrative, developing a plot of reconciliation that is neither heard nor understood by each other."[65] When it walks away from the "enforced dichotomy" between heartless perpetrator and guiltless victim, the discourse on reconciliation and forgiveness will be able to pay due attention to the "universality of sorrow."[66]

What would be the "East Asian way" toward transnational reconciliation and forgiveness surpassing binary oppositions between guilt and suffering, perpetration and victimization, and apology and reconciliation? Can the revolutionary imagination in the Polish bishops' letter also fuel the "avant-garde of reconciliation" in twenty-first-century East Asia? What roles can the Catholic Church in East Asia assume for historical reconciliation and forgiveness? What did the Japanese Catholic Church have to consider to understand and empathize with the suffering on the Korean peninsula, and how would the Korean Catholic Church accept and understand the pain felt by the Japanese during the Asia-Pacific War? How do Christianity's universal ethics regarding reconciliation, forgiveness, and memory politics that are historically contextualized coalesce and collide? These questions for East Asia's transnational reconciliation remain open to multiple, contradictory answers.

CODA

Beyond Mnemonic Eurocentrism

Globalization has dramatically reconfigured the mnemoscape in the third millennium. The global mnemoscape showed an exceedingly dynamic picture—the Holocaust became a reminder of the transatlantic slave trade and colonial genocide. In turn, the memory of colonial atrocities, including sexual violence, reciprocally evoked the memory of the Holocaust, the Soviet Gulag, and other genocides. The globalization of memory propelled memory studies beyond the mnemonic Eurocentrism. With its critical memory of Western colonialism, the postcolonial memory regime raised doubts about the Eurocentric self-reflection of the Holocaust as the point of continuous return for Western civilization to reconfirm its humanistic values. If I may borrow Zygmunt Bauman's words, Western civilization or the West-led global modernity is not antithetical to the Holocaust but embeds the possibility of the Holocaust. Thus, the postcolonial memory culture disquieted "the moral comfort of self-exculpation" of the West. If the Holocaust and colonial genocide are a risk inherent in global modernity, the Holocaust becomes a global question beyond the specific ethnic and national boundaries. The post-Eurocentric memory can problematize the history of global modernity through the critical gaze at the West as the implicated agency of the colonial genocide and Holocaust. The widespread belief that only the "imported antisemitism" in Muslim milieus is problematical indicates the moral complacency of the West's self-exculpation. The escalation of tension between the mnemonic Eurocentrism and postcolonial memories has been palpable in global memory formation.

Memory war in today's Germany is telling in this regard. On March 23, 2020, Lorenz Deutsch, a Free Democratic Party (FDP) politician in Nordrhein-Westfalen, issued an open letter to denounce Achille Mbembe, accusing the prominent postcolonial theorist from Cameroon of an "antisemitic critique of Israel, Holocaust relativization, and extremist disinformation."[1] In the letter, Deutsch suspects Mbembe's essay "The Society of Enmity" of Holocaust relativization because of a comparison between Apartheid in South Africa and the Israeli occupation of Palestinian territories. What Mbembe makes in the essay is by no means a simple equation. He lays out South African Apartheid and the destruction of Jews in Europe as "two emblematic manifestations of [the] fantasy of separation," with a careful proviso about the Holocaust's extremity.[2] Mbembe had made clear that he stood against all racism and colonialism, and reasonable criticisms of colonialism and racism bore no connection to the relativization of the Holocaust.[3] Mbembe's comparison was neither deviant nor unwarranted. Memory activists in the non-West tend increasingly to employ the Holocaust as a metonym to help ignorant European readers/listeners understand and visualize the colonial crime in the global memory formation.

The juxtaposition of the Holocaust and the Apartheid regime in South Africa can be traced back to the Apartheid era. Anti-Apartheid activists in South Africa drew the analogy to Nazi Germany to mobilize international support for the anti-Apartheid movement as the most critical moral battle in the postcolonial world. As mentioned in the "Black Atlantic and the Holocaust" section of chapter 4, many prominent anti-Apartheid activists, including Nelson Mandela, made the connection between Apartheid and the Holocaust. The successive exhibition *Nazisme in Zuid-Afrika* at the Anne Frank House in Amsterdam in the early 1970s shed light on this juxtaposition.[4] No one accused organizers of "antisemitism" or "Holocaust relativization" at that time. In stark comparison to the 1970s, the memory war in today's Germany, loud with buzz words of "antisemitic critique of Israel, Holocaust relativization, and extremist disinformation," attests to an unfortunate setback from the global to the national.[5] In 2019 the Bundestag declared the anti-Israel Boycott, Divestment, and Sanctions (BDS) movement to be antisemitic, further accelerating the judicialization of memories. The declaration reflects Germany's anxiety about the danger of downplaying Nazi crimes and German responsibility. However, that anxiety shrinks the historical meaning of the Holocaust from a "crime against humanity" to "crime against Jews." Here, what we are witnessing is a divide between deterritorialization and reterritorialization. In Natan Sznaider's words, there is tension between the UN's Universal Declaration of Human Rights (1984) and Israel's Declaration of Independence (1948), a divide between human rights and national rights.[6] More fundamentally, a tension between mnemonic Eurocentrism and the postcolonial memory regime underlies all these polemics on the Mbembe debate.[7]

Allegations of the Holocaust relativization have been rendered effective at an epistemological level, which precludes comparison at all. After the *Historikerstreit* in 1980s, "relativization" belonged to the *Index Expurgatorius* of German history and memory. Ernst Nolte's mechanical juxtaposition of the crimes of Nazism and Stalinism, with an implication of Nazism as a defensive response to Stalinism, represented a revisionist perspective to shift Nazi Germany's responsibilities for the Holocaust on to Bolshevik Russia and, at best, relativize the Nazi crime in comparison with the Stalinist crime. Since then, the scarlet letter "R" has been attached to any effort to compare the Holocaust with other kinds of genocide, namely, colonial ethnocide and Stalinist political genocide.[8] The Mbembe debate of 2020 can be deemed an aftershock of the *Historikerstreit* in 1986–1987. To elevate the present discussion into "*Historikerstreit* 2.0," as Michael Rothberg suggests, we need to find a way to critical relativization replacing the "German Catechism" or "new McCarthyism."[9] Considering the universality or incomparable uniqueness of the Holocaust underlies most attacks on Mbembe as an antisemite, how to articulate the critical relativization would be crucial. Ussama Makdisi's question, "How can a nation meaningfully repent for its past if it makes another nation pay the price for this repentance?," remains unanswered by German critics of the postcolonial comparison.[10]

As a coda to this book, I will call forth critical relativization and radical juxtaposition as the conceptual tools to criticize both the relativist dismissal of German accountability and the reductionist negation of the Holocaust's comparability. Its underlying questions are how to overcome the mnemonic Eurocentrism, how to highlight the multidirectional mnemonic interactivities of colonialism, the Holocaust, and Stalinism, and how to draw a nonhierarchal montage of entangled memories through critical relativization and radical juxtaposition in the global memory formation.[11] Dirk Moses's sarcastic remark about the influence of postcolonial studies being "tantamount to the barbarian conquest of Rome" for the aging 1968 generation insinuates the difficulty of this task in the German context.[12] More than a generational conflict, the task entails a paradigm shift from the national memory of the *Historikerstreit* to the global memory of the *Historikerstreit* 2.0 in the post–Cold War era.[13] The Mbembe debate indicates that the German national conscience of the Holocaust guilt can impede the building of the transnational conscience of the colonial guilt and even the Holocaust itself. Breaking the taboo on the Holocaust comparability is closely entwined with deprovincializing Germany's national memory. Focusing on the Global Easts, mainly Eastern Europe and East Asia, I intend to revisit the question of critical relativization and radical juxtaposition in the German and global memory space.[14]

In the heat of the Mbembe debate, Jan Grabowski raised grave concerns about the German conscience and its failure. Grabowski criticized Germany's politically palatable claim of exclusive responsibility for the crimes against humanity, the Holocaust.[15] In a joint communique to *Spiegel* on May 7, 2020, then German foreign minister Heiko Maas and contemporary historian Andreas Wirsching in Munich stressed the exclusive German responsibility for the Holocaust.[16] As a Polish Holocaust historian, Grabowski expressed the discomfort he felt from the German scholars' "goodwill" and "political correctness" to carry the burden of the Holocaust among themselves. Grabowski's point was that the German historians' conscientious stance vis-à-vis Holocaust memory had unwittingly hindered a debate like the *Historikerstreit* in Eastern Europe. From the Polish perspective, Maas and Wirsching's argument that anyone who disagrees with Germany's sole guilt "does injustice to victims and makes history instrumental" is problematic. Simply, it overlooks the complicity among East Europeans under Nazi occupation, which helps East European local collaborators to gloss over their perpetration. It is uncomfortable to find the mnemonic complicity between Germany's conscientious stance on its "sole responsibility" for the Holocaust and Eastern European nationalists' Holocaust denialism—"the Holocaust happened on our soil, but our hands are clean." Germany's goodwill may sound ethical at the national level, but it can be morally flawed in the transnational mnemonic nexus because it consequentially exonerates the wartime Nazi collaborators in Eastern Europe.[17] As a historian of the Global Easts, I cannot agree with Maas and Wirsching's conscientious stance for its mnemonic Eurocentrism.

Coming to terms with the Holocaust in Central-Eastern Europe cannot be reduced to Germany-Israel's binational memory diplomacy. In the global memory nexus, provincializing the mnemonic Eurocentrism and deprovincializing the German national memory are the head and tail of the same coin.[18] The debate among Polish historians on the Eastern European antipathy toward Islamic refugees in 2015 is also intriguing. Jan Gross sparked the discussion by publishing an article titled "East Europeans Have No Shame" in *Die Welt* on September 13, 2015. He argued that "East Europeans have revealed themselves to be intolerant, illiberal, xenophobic, and incapable of remembering the spirit of solidarity that carried them to freedom a quarter-century ago" in light of the influx of Islamic refugees.[19] Gross attributed the root cause of Islamophobia in Eastern Europe to "World War II and its aftermath"—that the failure of the Holocaust memory left East Europeans unabashedly hostile to the refugees, which indicates the unethical memory practice.[20] Gross juxtaposed today's antirefugee sentiment and the suppressed shame regarding their Holocaust complicity in postcommunist Poland.

Polish historians, including Marcin Zaremba and Aleksander Smolar, immediately refuted Gross. They tried to invalidate Gross's radical juxtaposition by stressing the absence of aggressive colonialism in Eastern Europe, including Poland. In contrast to the West, Poland has never kept colonialism to rule over indigenous peoples of different cultures. So, East European countries were not experienced in dealing with indigenous people of different colors and cultures.[21] Zaremba and Smolar pushed for a surprisingly anticolonial charge against Western European colonialism: "You are guilty of colonialism, but we are innocent. So, the refugee problem is your problem." Inadvertently, however, such anticolonial rhetoric bespeaks the ambivalence of Polish Orientalism: being Orientalized by the West while Orientalizing the imagined Others within Poland. An in-depth investigation of the trajectories of irredentist nationalism in partitioned Poland confirms the Polish ambivalence. Poles were colonizers of their Lithuanian and Ukrainian neighbors in the *kresy* (Eastern borderland) while German settlers colonized Western and Baltic Poland. Treated as a hinterland, the first model of underdevelopment, and "a neglected suburb of Europe," Poles have never been free from the West's "intellectual project of demi-Orientalization."[22] In the reverse but same way, Poles have developed their version of Orientalism toward their "more Eastern" and "less Western" Slavic neighbors.[23]

This version of Orientalism reflects Poland's status of in-between, subaltern vis-à-vis Germany and the "West," yet as a subaltern empire fully incorporated in the global hierarchy of domination as the repressive local agent of the great powers.[24] Also, internal colonialism structured interwar Poland as a multiethnic state under the *Sanacja* regime, which responded to the demands of ethnic minorities by setting up the internment camp at Bereza Kartuska in 1934. Internal colonialism, demi-Orientalism against the *kresy* and the more Eastern Slavic neighbors, and the fusion of antisemitism and anti-Bolshevism in official discourse colluded rhetorically with the Nazi's anti-Slavic and antisemitic propaganda. The radical juxtaposition of Islamic refugees and the Holocaust in the Polish mnemoscape revealed the ambivalent desire and resentment of Polish subaltern colonialism. From the postcolonial perspective, the colonial experience was not absent in Poland. It is also true that Poland accepted 100,000 Chechen refugees or exiles after the Russian invasion of Chechenia, which refutes the proposition that Islamophobia is a fixed memory template in postcommunist Poland. However, the recent refugee crisis has seen a dramatic shift from empathy to apathy in the Polish attitude toward Chechens.[25]

Gross's criticism that the Polish hostility to Islamic refugees represents its failure to come to terms with the past of the Holocaust echoes Mbembe's juxtaposition of Apartheid and the Holocaust to some extent. The Polish debate on Islamophobia and the Holocaust, provoked again by Gross, bespoke the lack of postcolonial self-criticism in the Polish memory culture. The combination of tropes counts, however. The post-dependent memory of *colonial* occupation under Nazism and Stalinism operates as a screen memory to suppress the past of Poland's internal colonialism and colonialist complicity. Regrettably, the mnemonic shift of the Polish positionality from innocent victim to "Homo Jedvabnecus" after 2000 was not connected to postcolonial criticism. The radical juxtaposition of Islamic refugees and the Holocaust provides a gaze at the postcolonial lens's critical relativization of Polish victimhood. The discursive connection between antisemitism and Islamophobia is no secret in contemporary Poland—it is well manifested in this widespread political "joke": "We are ready to accept refugees because we have always had concentration camps."[26]

In the Polish memory culture, one can see emotional resistance to situating the Nazi occupation within the context of global colonialism. An implicit Eurocentrism insists that "the Holocaust stands out from other genocides because it was committed in the heart of civilized Europe rather than in (supposedly) primitive or barbaric societies."[27] As early as 1950, Aimé Césaire pinpointed the dilemma: "[The European bourgeois] has a Hitler inside him ... and ... what he cannot forgive Hitler for is not the *crime* in itself, the *crime against man*, it is not *the humiliation of man as such*, it is the crime against the white man, and the fact that he applied to Europe colonialist procedures which had until then been reserved exclusively for the Arabs of Algeria, the 'coolies' of India, and the 'niggers' of Africa."[28] Remarkably, communist Poland published a translation of Césaire's earliest version of *Discours sur le colonialisme* in 1950—an example of how Poland's communist postcolonialism drew an analogy between the Slavic East of the "Third Europe" and the postcolonial states of the "Third World." The Polish translation of Aimé Césaire was meant to simultaneously criticize the Nazi occupation of Poland and Western imperialism in Asia and Africa.[29] However, the mnemonic nexus of the Holocaust and postcolonial criticism has been regrettably neglected among historians in postcommunist Poland.

The Holocaust memory, when dissociated from the postcolonial discourse, often serves as the mnemonic leverage for reterritorialization or renationalization of the collective memory. Polish nationalist historians have used "forgotten Holocaust" and "Poland's Holocaust" to stress Polish victimhood around World War II and claimed that that Poles were the first nation to experience the Holocaust.[30] Allegedly, "Poles were even more exposed than Jews to arrest, deportation, and death," especially during 1939–1941.[31] Paradoxically, the Holocaust rhetoric is employed to make a case for Polish victimhood nationalism and instead marginalize the Holocaust. The nationalist appropriation of the Holocaust is not particular to Poland but a widespread phenomenon in Eastern Europe. The appropriation of the Holocaust as an analogy to the Slavic suffering by local memory activists inevitably banalizes the historical specificities in attempts to make the comparison plausible. The cosmopolitanization of the Holocaust could occur weirdly through anachronistic and superficial comparisons. When the distance between cosmopolitanization and vulgarization of the Holocaust memory turns out to be much closer than expected, critical relativization bears the utmost significance.

New memory activism in Eastern Europe nationalized Holocaust remembrance in the name of multiculturalism—East European memory activists often invoked the Holocaust to stress the national victimhood by the "foreign" Stalinist oppression. One of the most prominent cases is the recent development in Serbia, where Serbian nationalists have activated the Holocaust as a screen memory covering the Serbian war crimes and atrocities in the Yugoslavian civil war of the 1990s. The Holocaust memory has become a device of affection to provoke emotions in association with Serbia's victimhood nationalism. Postcommunist politics, especially in Serbia, the Baltic States, Hungary, and Ukraine, has appropriated the memory, symbols, and imagery of the Holocaust to stress one's own national victimhood under the Stalinist terror. Both the Holocaust memory and the memory of Stalinist oppression must be subject to critical relativization; it is not acceptable or imaginable that the spirit of the Prague Declaration on "the equal treatment and non-discrimination of victims of all the totalitarian regimes" leaves out the Islamic refugees. In this sense, critical relativization of the absolute promotes the "multidirectional memories" between the West and East.

In the age of globalization of memories, diverse local memories interact with the Holocaust, and the Holocaust is used as a metonym for plural crimes against humanity and the mnemonic touchstone of evil. This globalized version of the Holocaust covertly undermines the uniqueness of the Holocaust.[32] Once the Holocaust becomes an ethical template to think about genocide and other crimes in the global memory formation, it ceases to be an exclusively Jewish experience. To make the Holocaust comparable to other crimes can engender de-/overcontextualization, or worse, ahistoricization prone to political instrumentalization. However, the non-European indigenization of the Holocaust does not necessarily confirm mnemonic Eurocentrism, which regards global memories of the Holocaust as "imprecise," "inaccurate," and "misleading" because the Holocaust supposedly has "no real resonance" outside of Europe, Israel, and the United States.[33] In Israel, Benjamin Netanyahu exploits the Holocaust to brutalize the Palestinians by stripping them of fundamental human rights in the name of the survivors of the Holocaust.[34] The anticommunist liberal democracy of the United States and multiculturalism of the UK have never hesitated to conjure up the Holocaust to justify their political regimes.[35] Anti-abortionists called the legalization of abortion the "American Holocaust," American gay rights activists suffering from the AIDS crisis appealed to the public by using the term "AIDS holocaust," and animal rights activists coined the slogan "Buchenwald for animals." Even the National Rifle Association made a blatant remark that the Warsaw ghetto uprising could erupt with only ten pistols.[36] Holocaust memories have become banal and vulgar in the West, too.

It is difficult to justify the mnemonic Eurocentrism to encapsulate the Holocaust memory within the dichotomy between East and West. This dichotomy presupposes that the West has matured the unique historical conditions necessary for democracy and human rights, whereas democracy remains underdeveloped in the East. In this regard, mnemonic Eurocentrism is complicit with the German *Sonderweg* in seeing antisemitism as a distinctly German prejudice. Both are profoundly misleading to make believe that fascism and the Holocaust can be reduced to manifestations of the premodern peculiarities of the East. The peculiarity argument plays into the historical alibi for the colonialist genocide of the modern West, which is thus exempted from association with the "premodern barbarity." In reality, however, Western colonialism was what provided an important historical precedent for the Nazis' genocidal thinking. The Nazi utopia of a racially "pure" German empire cannot be separated from the Nazis' mimetic aspiration for Western colonialism, for "turning imperialism on its head and treating Europeans as Africans."[37] The colonial genocide and the Holocaust were both "categorial murders" in line with the essentialist obsession to categorize others based on race, ethnicity, class, and so on.[38]

The mnemonic Eurocentrism is enforced and more often internalized in the East. As shown in chapter 5 on nationalization and chapter 8 on juxtaposition, memory activists in Global Easts frequently mobilized mnemonic Eurocentrism of the Holocaust as an absolute memory template to win the global recognition of their own national suffering. One finds an excellent example of the self-exonerating process in the juxtaposition of Saint Maksymilian Kolbe at Auschwitz and the A-bomb Catholic victims in Nagasaki. In this juxtaposition, a critical gaze at Father Kolbe's antisemitism and the colonial atrocities of the Japanese empire is absent. Arguably, the most conspicuous result of this juxtaposition is the dissociation of Nagasaki and Auschwitz from the critical memory of postcolonial politics. Its callous political effect can be found in the remarks of Sono Ayako, a Catholic protagonist of the Maksymilian Kolbe cult in Japan and the late premier Abe Shinzō's political advisor, that South African Apartheid and racial segregation is a potential model for Japan's migration policy. No less problematic is the Korean ultranationalist way of appropriating the Israelis' Zionist memory to justify the developmental dictatorship at the cost of human rights. What matters in the juxtaposition of distant memories is not whether but how.

The critical relativization resonates with the criticism against Ernst Nolte's relativist dismissal of German responsibility during the *Historikerstreit* in the 1980s. Nolte's mechanical juxtaposition of the crimes of Nazism and Stalinism had the problem of relativizing and exonerating the Holocaust. Comparison and relativization remain too euphemistic to characterize Nolte's thesis of "European Civil War," which propelled the reductionist thinking that Nazism was a necessary evil to defend the Christian West from the Bolsheviks' aggression. The hysterical condemnation of Achille Mbembe may stand in continuity with the grave concern about the shameless relativization of the Holocaust. On the other hand, in the *Historikerstreit* 2.0 triggered by the Mbembe controversy, the political constellation is almost opposite to the *Historikerstreit* in the 1980s. It is now primarily conservatives who stand for the uniqueness of the Holocaust, whereas leftists argue for the postcolonial nexus of the Holocaust.[39] What matters in these debates is no longer relativization per se, but the kinds of relativization. All historical events, including the Holocaust, are singular. The historical singularity of the Holocaust does not mean it is incomparable. To delve even deeper into semantics, incomparability itself presupposes a previous comparison. Only after having tried a comparison can one judge if they are incomparable. Therefore, that the Holocaust is often deemed "incomparable" does not categorically negate its comparability. Mnemonic Eurocentrism has rendered the colonial genocide into a secondary crime against humanity by comparing it with the Holocaust. History of comparison in the disguise of incomparability proves the urgency and gravity of critical relativization and radical juxtaposition.

The racial and ethnic conflicts in the United States often overlap with the tension between mnemonic Eurocentrism and postcolonialism. In mid-May 2021, Ali Velshi said on *MSNBC Live*, "One look at a current map of Israel, Gaza, and the occupied territories conjures up only one other example: Apartheid-era South Africa and the 'Bantustans' or 'homelands' into which Black Africans were forced."[40] Congresswoman Rashida Tlaib from Michigan went even further, saying, "What they are doing to the Palestinian people is what they continue to do to our black brothers and sisters here; . . . it is all interconnected."[41] On the hundredth anniversary of the Tulsa massacre, in 2021, one Holocaust researcher at the University of Charleston argued that the Tulsa Race Massacre should be called "pogrom" rather than a racial uprising.[42] On the other hand, juxtaposing the centrality of the Holocaust against the oblivion of the Vietnam War shed light on the peculiarity of the mnemonic Eurocentrism in U.S. memory culture.[43] Through the Holocaust memory, the United States has perpetuated its self-image as the righteous savior of Jews under Nazi oppression. The profound influence of the Holocaust memory is in stark contrast to the absence of the Vietnam War memory in U.S. history textbooks. American cultural memory has simultaneously suppressed the memories of defeat, guilt, and shame from the Vietnam War and promoted the memories of rescuing Jews from Nazi concentration camps. Images of U.S. soldiers saving Jews from Nazi villains screened images of U.S. soldiers killing civilians in Mỹ Lai, Vietnam.

After the Israel-Hamas War broke out, the Israeli diplomats wore the yellow Star of David patch in the UN Security Council meeting on October 30, 2023, to condemn the Hamas terrorist attack. On October 23, on the other side of the Pacific, the Palestinian diplomatic representation in Tokyo tweeted on its X account in Tokyo a comparison of the Israeli bombardment of Gaza with the "Little Boy," the atomic bomb dropped on Hiroshima. When three Palestinian teenagers laid a wreath at the altar of atomic bomb victims at the Hiroshima Peace Memorial, the University of Cologne announced it would disinvite the Jewish American philosopher Nancy Fraser as Albert Magnus Professor for 2024 on the grounds that she had signed the "Philosophy for Palestine." The host considered the statement Fraser signed to be relativizing the October 7 attack by Hamas "in a way to justify it." When Masha Gessen was almost not awarded the Hannah Arendt Prize in December 2023, the *Guardian* sarcastically wrote that "Hannah Arendt would not qualify for the

Hannah Arendt prize. She would be canceled in Germany today for her political position on Israel and opinions about contemporary Zionism, which she remained critical of from 1942 until she died in 1975."[44] On Black Sunday, many Hamas sympathizers quoted Frantz Fanon to claim that "the massacre conducted by Hamas was a direct and inevitable reaction to Israel's 'colonial' oppression." Adam Schatz, the most comprehensive biographer of Franz Fanon, infers that Fanon would have been skeptical of the Hamas's October 7 attack.[45] Nothing implicitly shows the paradox of today's global memory formation more than that Arendt and Fanon would not qualify for intellectual and political leadership in their territories.

Memory is not linear. The critical relativization and radical juxtaposition are potential tools for deconstructing the hegemonic hierarchization of memories in global memory formation. Mnemonic solidarity among conflictual memories is never achieved by flattening different memories into one linear composition. Mnemonic solidarity is sustained by maintaining the critical tension among the cacophony of discrete memories confronting and intertwining within global memory formation.[46] When the memory of victimization escapes from the "zero-sum" game of victims, from reterritorialization that prioritizes one's own nation's sacrifice and ranks others' suffering under one's own, and finally from victimhood nationalism, diverse, even if conflicting, memories will finally be able to conjoin to form the flood of mnemonic solidarity. This book concludes that mnemonic solidarity in global memory formation is inconceivable without sacrificing victimhood nationalism.

NOTES

1. MNEMOHISTORY

1. Ulrich Beck, "The Cosmopolitan Perspective: Sociology of the Second Age of Modernity," *British Journal of Sociology* 51, no. 1 (2000): 79–105; Andreas Wimmer and Nina Glick Schiller, "Methodological Nationalism and Beyond: Nation-State Building, Migration and Sociology," *Global Networks* 2, no. 4 (2002): 301–34.
2. Marc Bloch observed that all history is tainted with the comparative history and hinted at the transnationality of nationalist imagination in historiography. For the cofiguration and comparison, see Naoki Sakai, *Translation and Subjectivity: On "Japan" and Cultural Nationalism* (Minneapolis: University of Minnesota Press, 1997), 40–71.
3. Timothy Mitchell, "The Stage of Modernity," *Questions of Modernity*, ed. T. Mitchell (Minneapolis: University of Minnesota Press, 2000), 4.
4. Benedict Anderson, *Imagined Communities: Reflections on the Origin and Spread of Nationalism*, rev. ed. (London: Verso, 1991), 47–65; C.L.R. James, *The Black Jacobins: Toussaint L'Ouverture and the San Domingo Revolution*, 2d ed., rev. (New York: Vintage Books, 1989); Susan Buck-Morss, *Hegel, Haiti and Universal History* (Pittsburgh, Pa.: University of Pittsburgh Press, 2009); Eric J. Hobsbawm, *Nations and Nationalism Since 1780* (Cambridge: Cambridge University Press, 1990), 46–79; Paul Gilroy, *Postcolonial Melancholia* (New York: Columbia University Press, 2005); Sakai Naoki, *The End of Pax Americana: The Loss of Empire and Hikikomori Nationalism* (Durham, N.C.: Duke University Press, 2022).
5. My idea of victimhood nationalism was inspired by Zygmunt Bauman's concept of "hereditary victimhood." Zygmunt Bauman, *Modernity and the Holocaust* (Ithaca, N.Y.: Cornell University Press, 2000), 238. For the lineage of victimhood nationalism, see my previous works, 임지현, "희생자의식 민족주의" [Victimhood nationalism],

『역사비평』 15 (2007); "犧牲者意識の民族主義 [Victimhood nationalism] (特集 シンポジウム グローバル化時代の植民地主義とナショナリズム)—(問題提起)," 『立命館言語文化研究』 95 (2009): 57–62; Jie-Hyun Lim, "Victimhood Nationalism in Contested Memories—National Mourning and Global Accountability," in *Memory in a Global Age: Discourses, Practices and Trajectories*, ed. Aleida Assmann and Sebastian Conrad (Basingstoke, UK: Palgrave Macmillan, 2010), 138–62; Lim, "Narody-ofiary i ich megalomania," trans. Marek Darewski, *Więź*, no. 616–17 (2010): 22–34; Lim, "Victimhood Nationalism and History Reconciliation in East Asia," *History Compass* 8, no. 1 (2010): 1–10; Lim, "Victimhood Nationalism in the Memory of Mass Dictatorship," in *Mass Dictatorship and Memory as an Ever-Present Past*, ed. Jie-Hyun Lim, Barbara Walker, and Peter Lambert (Basingstoke, UK: Palgrave Macmillan, 2014), 36–61.

6. Dan Diner, "Negative Symbiose. Deutsche und Juden nach Auschwitz," *Babylon* 1 (1986): 9; Sebastian Wogenstein, "Negative Symbiosis? Israel, Germany, and Austria in Contemporary Germanophone Literature," *Prooftexts: A Journal of Jewish Literary History* 33, no. 1 (2013): 106–10; Tom Segev, *The Seventh Million: The Israelis and the Holocaust*, trans. Haim Watzman (New York: Owl Book, 2000), 15–20, 29–31.

7. Dan Diner, "Cumulative Contingency: Historicizing Legitimacy in Israeli Discourse," *History and Memory: Studies in Representation of the Past* 7, no. 1, Special Issue: *Israel Historiography Revisited*, ed. Gulie Ne'eman Arad (1995): 153–55, 160–63; Anita Shapira, "Politics and Collective Memory: The Debate Over the 'New Historians' in Israel," *Israel Historiography Revisited*, 9–11; Ilan Pappe, "Critique and Agenda: The Post-Zionist Scholars in Israel," *Israel Historiography Revisited*, 69–73.

8. Ashis Nandy, *The Intimate Enemy*, 2d ed. (Oxford: Oxford University Press, 2009).

9. Larry Wolff, *Inventing Eastern Europe: The Map of Civilization on the Mind of the Enlightenment* (Stanford, Calif.: Stanford University Press, 1994); Jan Kieniewicz, "The Eastern Frontiers and the Civilisational Dimension of Europe," *Acta Poloniae Historica*, no. 107 (2013); Jerzy Jedlicki, *A Suburb of Europe: Nineteenth-Century Polish Approaches to Western Civilization* (Budapest: Central European University Press, 1999); Lucy Mayblin, Aneta Piekut, and Gill Valentine, "'Other' Posts in 'Other' Places: Poland Through a Postcolonial Lens?," *Sociology* 50, no. 1 (2016): 60–76; Jie-Hyun Lim, "A Postcolonial Reading of the Sonderweg: Marxist Historicism Revisited," *Journal of Modern European History* 12, no. 2 (2014): 280–94.

10. Jie-Hyun Lim, *Global Easts: Remembering, Imagining, Mobilizing* (New York: Columbia University Press, 2022), part 2, 129–248.

11. Martin Krygier, "Letter from Australia: Neighbors: Poles, Jews and the Aboriginal Question," *East Central Europe* 29, no. 1/2 (2002): 297–309; Dan Stone, "The Historiography of Genocide: Beyond 'Uniqueness' and Ethnic Competition," *Rethinking History* 8, no. 1 (2004): 127–38; Carol Gluck, "Operations of Memory: 'Comfort Women' and the World," in *Ruptured Histories: War, Memory and the Post-Cold War in Asia*, ed. Shelia Miyoshi Jager and Rana Mitter (Cambridge, Mass: Harvard University Press, 2007); Michael Rothberg and Yasemin Yildiz, "Memory Citizenship: Migrant Archives of Holocaust Remembrance in Contemporary Germany," *Parallax* 17, no. 4 (2011): 32–48; Shirli Gilbert, "Anne Frank in South Africa. Remembering the

Holocaust During and After Apartheid," *Holocaust and Genocide Studies* 26, no. 3 (2012): 366–93; A. Dirk Moses, "The Holocaust and World History," in *The Holocaust and Historical Methodology*, ed. Dan Stone (New York: Berghahn Books, 2012); Roberta Pergher et al., "Scholarly Forum on the Holocaust and Genocide," *Dapim: Studies on the Holocaust* 27, no. 1 (2013): 40–73.

12. "Transnational history," "world history," and "global history" are used indiscriminately and interchangeably to denote the alternative to the dominant paradigm of "national history." These terms are distinguishable only by their slight tonal variation rather than conceptual differences from each other. However, this book preferentially uses the term "global history" because investigating victimhood nationalism requires a *global* approach that reaches beyond binational relations. For the history of the global usage of these terms, see Sven Beckert and Dominic Sachsenmaier, eds., *Global History Globally* (London: Bloomsbury, 2018); Douglas Northrop, ed., *A Companion to World History* (Chichester, UK: Wiley-Blackwell, 2012).
13. Aleida Assmann and Sebastian Conrad, "Introduction," in *Memory in a Global Age*, 1.
14. Astrid Erll, "Travelling Memory," *Parallax* 17, no. 4 (2011).
15. In this book, I will only use the term "global memory formation," although I have used "transnational memory formation" elsewhere prior to this book. See Jie-Hyun Lim, "Transnational Memory Formation: Memory-History-Culture," in *The Routledge Companion to World Literature and World History*, ed. May Hawas (London: Routledge, 2018), 266–76.
16. To learn more about memory studies and the history of emotion, see Aleida Assmann, "Impact and Resonance: Towards a Theory of Emotions in Cultural Memory," *Söndertörn Lectures*, no. 6 (2011); Tea Sindbæk and Barbara Törnquist-Plewa, eds., *Disputed Memory: Emotions and Memory Politics in Central, Eastern and South-Eastern Europe* (Berlin: Walter de Gruyter, 2016).
17. Matthias Böckmann et al., eds., *Jenseits von Mbembe: Erinnerung, Politik, Solidarität* (Berlin: Metropol Verlag, 2022); Jie-Hyun Lim, "Triple Victimhood: On the Mnemonic Confluence of the Holocaust, Stalinist Crime, and Colonial Genocide," *Journal of Genocide Research* (April 2020).
18. Paul Ricoeur, *Memory, History, Forgetting*, trans. Kathleen Blamey and David Pellauer (Chicago: University of Chicago Press, 2004), 1–2.
19. Chiara De Cesari and Ann Rigney, "Introduction," in *Transnational Memory: Circulation, Articulation, Scales*, ed. Chiara De Cesari and Ann Rigney (Berlin: Walter de Gruyter, 2014), 3.
20. Jie-Hyun Lim, "Second World War in Global Memory Space," in *Cambridge History of Second World War*, ed. Michael Geyer and Adam Tooze (Cambridge: Cambridge University Press, 2015), 3:698–724.
21. Ever-resonant in my concern over the moral implication of global memory formation are Zygmunt Bauman's caution that the historical lesson of the Holocaust is "not the likelihood that 'this' could be done to us, but the idea that we could do it," and Christopher Browning's insight that saw a portrait of not an ordinary "German" but

an ordinary "man" in the faces of Nazis. Bauman, *Modernity and the Holocaust*, 152; Christopher R. Browning, *Ordinary Men: Reserve Police Battalion 101 and the Final Solution in Poland* (New York: Harper Perennial, 1993), 189, 222–23; Michael Mann, *The Dark Side of Democracy: Explaining Ethnic Cleansing* (Cambridge: Cambridge University Press, 2005), 9.

22. Jean-Marc Dreyfus and Marcel Stoetzler, "Holocaust Memory in the Twenty-first Century: Between National Reshaping and Globalization," *European Review of History* 18, no. 1 (2011): 75.

23. Giorgio Agamben, *Remnants of Auschwitz: The Witness and the Archive*, trans. Daniel Heller-Roezen (New York: Zone Books, 1999), 12; Marianne Hirsch and Leo Spitzer, "The Witness in the Archive: Holocaust Studies/Memory Studies," *Memory Studies* 2, no. 2 (2009): 156, 159, 161.

24. For the interaction of multidimensional memories, see Gluck, "Operations of Memory," 52–58.

25. Brent J. Steele elaborates on the importance of collective memory and national identity in international relations, citing "ontological security," in his *Ontological Security in International Relations: Self-Identity and the IR State* (London: Routledge, 2008).

26. Renan's argument that suffering in common unifies more than joy does, and griefs are of more value than triumphs where national memories are concerned, seems to have prognosticated the advent of "affective memory" characteristic of victimhood nationalism. Methodologically, "affective memory" is also where memory studies meet the history of emotions. Ernest Renan, "What Is a Nation?," trans. Martin Thom, in *Nation & Narration*, ed. Homi K. Bhabha (London: Routledge, 1990), 19.

27. Ronald Smelser and Edward J. Davies II, *The Myth of the Eastern Front: The Nazi-Soviet War in American Popular Culture* (Cambridge: Cambridge University Press, 2007), 39–63.

28. Kata Bohus, Peter Hallama, and Stephan Stach, eds., *Growing in the Shadow of Antifascism: Remembering the Holocaust in Communist Eastern Europe* (Budapest: Central European University Press, 2021); Michal Brumlik and Karol Sauerland, eds., *Umdeuten, verschweigen, erinnern: die spaete Aufarbeitung des Holocaust in Osteuropa* (Frankfurt am Main: Campus Verlag, 2010), 7–22.

29. Assmann and Conrad, eds., *Memory in a Global Age*; Lim, "Triple Victimhood"; A. Dirk Moses, "Conceptual Blockages and Definitional Dilemmas in the 'Racial Century': Genocides of Indigenous Peoples and the Holocaust," *Patterns of Prejudice* 36, no. 4 (2020): 7–36; Jie-Hyun Lim and Eve Rosenhaft, eds., *Mnemonic Solidarity: Global Interventions* (London: Palgrave Macmillan, 2021).

30. "美정부 1호 위안부기림비 뉴저지서 제막식" [First comfort women monument in the U.S. to unveil in New Jersey], 『조선일보』, March 9, 2013.

31. Entangled memory is a parallel to entangled history (*historie croisée*). For entangled history, see Michael Werner and Bénédicte Zimmermann, "Beyond Comparison: Histoire Croisée and the Challenge of Reflexivity," *History and Theory* 45, no. 1 (2006): 30–50. For entangled memories, see Lim, "Second World War In Global Memory

1. MNEMOHISTORY 321

Space," 3:699; Marius Henderson and Julia Lange, "Introduction," in *Entangled Memories: Remembering the Holocaust in a Global Age*, ed. Marius Henderson and Julia Lange (Heidelberg: Universitätsverlag, 2017), 3–16.

32. Daniel Levy and Natan Sznaider, "Memory Unbound: The Holocaust and the Formation of Cosmopolitan Memory," *European Journal of Social Theory* 5, no. 1 (2002): 87. Unlike Levy and Sznaider, I do not confine the term "internal globalization" to the Holocaust as a universal memory.

33. Lynn Hunt, *Inventing Human Rights: A History* (New York: Norton, 2008), 17–18, 29–31; Lea David, "Moral Remembrance and New Inequalities," *Global Perspectives* 1, no. 1 (2020).

34. United Nations, "Report of the Special Rapporteur in the Field of Cultural Rights, Farida Shaheed: Memorialization Processes" (2014), 5–6, https://digitallibrary.un.org/record/766862.

35. Antony Polonsky and Joanna Michlic, "Introduction," in *The Neighbors Responded: The Controversy Over the Jedwabne Massacre in Poland*, ed. Antony Polonsky and Joanna Michlic (Princeton, N.J.: Princeton University Press, 2004), 9. A recently disclosed document from the Israeli Ministry of Foreign Affairs reveals how the Israeli government colluded with consulates and embassies to reduce the impact of the First International Conference on the Holocaust and Genocide. As a result, Yad Vashem, Tel Aviv University, and Elie Wiesel, who organized the event, withdrew from the conference, which by then had become significantly reduced in scale. The Ministry of Foreign Affairs maintains that its interference with the conference was due to potential threats from the Turkish government to the Jews crossing the Turkish border to migrate to Israel. However, Israel Charny, the Armenian Genocide scholar and one of the organizers, claims that the ministry's reasoning is unfounded. Ofer Aderet, "How Israel Quashed Efforts to Recognize the Armenian Genocide—to Please Turkey," *Haaretz*, May 2, 2021.

36. Lea David, "Human Rights, Micro-solidarity, and Moral Action: Face-to-Face Encounters in the Israeli/Palestinian Context," *Thesis Eleven* 154, no. 1 (2019): 66–79.

37. Samuel Moyn, *The Last Utopia: Human Rights in History* (Cambridge, Mass.: Harvard University Press, 2010); Samuel Moyn, *Christian Human Rights* (Philadelphia: University of Pennsylvania Press, 2015); Lea David, "Human Rights as an Ideology? Obstacles and Benefits," *Critical Sociology* 46, no. 1 (2020).

38. Similar examples can be found in the silence of Korean leftwing nationalists who hide behind the "internal approach" theory and shove North Korea's human rights issues under the rug, and the Chinese government's rebuke of the Japanese government's denunciation of human rights abuses against Uighurs, backed by the reason that Japan also committed terrible atrocities, such as the Nanjing Massacre and the Japanese Military "Comfort Women" system. See also "유엔북한인권사무소 설치의 문제점" [The problem with the installation of the UN Human Rights Office in North Korea], 『자주시보』, August 15, 2015; "대북전단금지법 두고 내정간섭하는 미국 규탄" [Condemning the U.S. intervention in domestic affairs regarding the ban on the balloon propaganda campaigns], 『자주시보』, December 23, 2020; "난징 학살 자행 일본, 신장 인권 말할

자격 있나" [Can Japan speak on human rights in Xinjiang without confronting its own history of the Nanjing Massacre], *YTN*, March 26, 2021.
39. Kay Schaffer and Sidonie Smith, "Venues of Storytelling: The Circulation of Testimony in Human Rights Campaigns," *Life Writing* 1, no. 2 (2004): 3.
40. Lewis A. Coser ed., *Maurice Halwachs on Collective Memory* (Chicago: University of Chicago Press, 1992); Jan Assmann, *Moses the Egyptian: The Memory of Egypt in Western Monotheism* (Cambridge, Mass.: Harvard University Press, 1997), 15; Jan Assmann and John Czaplicka, "Collective Memory and Cultural Identity," *New German Critique*, no. 65 (1995): 125–33; Jan Assmann, *Erinnerungsräume: Formen und Wandlungen des kulturellen Gedächtnisses* (Munich: Beck, 2003), 133–34; Jan Assmann, *Das kulturelle Gedächtnis: Schrift, Erinnerung und politische Identität in frühen Hochkulturen* (Munich: Beck, 1999). See also Jeffrey K. Olick, *The Politics of Regret: On Collective Memory and Historical Responsibility* (New York: Routledge, 2007), 10; Ann Rigney, "Plenitude, Scarcity and the Circulation of Cultural Memory," *Journal of European Studies* 35, no. 1 (2005): 11–28; Marek Tamm, "History as Cultural Memory: Mnemohistory and the Construction of the Estonian Nation," *Journal of Baltic Studies* 39, no. 4 (2008); Tamm, ed., *Afterlife of Events: Perspectives on Mnemohistory* (Basingstoke, UK: Palgrave Macmillan, 2015).
41. Assmann and Czaplicka, "Collective Memory and Cultural Identity," 128–29.
42. Gluck, "Operations of Memory," 52–58.
43. Nathan Wachtel, "Introduction," in *Between Memory and History*, ed. Marie-Noëlle Bourguet, Mucette Valensi, and Nathan Wachtel (London: Harwood Academic Publishers, 1990), 4–5. Henry Russo, who was an active participant in the foundation of Institut d'Histoire du Temps Présent, has clarified that the reason for naming the institute "Temps Présent" was not to signal "contemporary history" but in consideration of the history of memories being made here and now. Henry Russo, personal conversation with the author, May 9, 2011.
44. For the distinction between memory politics as practices and memory culture as structural hegemony, see Berthold Molden, "Resistant Pasts Versus Mnemonic Hegemony: On the Power Relations of Collective Memory," *Memory Studies* 9, no. 2 (2016): 125–42. In this book, I will interchange Assmann's "cultural memory" and Molden's "memory culture," depending on contextual details. Sometimes Holwachs's "collective memory" is also invoked.
45. Michael Rothberg, *Multidirectional Memory: Remembering the Holocaust in the Age of Decolonization* (Stanford, Calif.: Stanford University Press, 2009). Compared to Rothberg's original idea, the global history of victimhood nationalism shows the seamy side of multidirectional memories.
46. Jie-Hyun Lim and Eve Rosenhaft, eds., *Mnemonic Solidarity: Global Interventions* (London: Palgrave Macmillan, 2021); Jie-Hyun Lim, *Opfernationalismus: Erinnerung und Herrschat in der postkolonialen Welt* (Berlin: Verlag Klaus Wagenbach, 2024).
47. Amos Goldberg, "Forum: On Saul Friedlander's *The Years of Extermination 2*. The Victim's Voice and Melodramatic Aesthetics in History," *History and Theory* 48, no. 3 (2009): 234.

48. David Blackburn and Geoff Eley, *The Peculiarities of German History* (Oxford: Oxford University Press, 1984), 7, 164, and passim; Jürgen Kocka, "Asymmetrical Historical Comparison: The Case of the German *Sonderweg*," *History and Theory* 38, no. 1 (1999): 41; Jie-Hyun Lim, "A Postcolonial Reading of the *Sonderweg*: Marxist Historicism Revisited," *Global Easts*, 280–94.
49. Bauman, *Modernity and the Holocaust*; Enzo Traverso, *The Origins of Nazi Violence*, trans. Janet Lloyd (New York: The New Press, 2003); Jürgen Zimmerer, "Die Geburt des Ostlandes aus dem Geiste des Kolonialismus: Die nationalsozialistische Eroberungs- und Beherrschungspolitik in (post-)kolonialer Perspektive," *Sozial Geschichte* 19, no. 1 (2004): 10–43; Benjamin Madley, "From Africa to Auschwitz: How German South West Africa Incubated Ideas and Methods Adopted and Developed by the Nazis in Eastern Europe," *European History Quarterly* 35, no. 3 (2005): 429–64; Robert Gerwarth and Stephan Malinowski, "Der Holocaust als kolonialer Genozid? Europäische Kolonialgewalt und nationalsozialistischer Vernichtungskrieg," *Geschichte und Gesellschaf* 33, no. 3 (2007): 439–66; A. Dirk Moses, "Empire, Colony, Genocide: Keywords and the Philosophy," in *Empire, Colony, Genocide: Conquest, Occupation, and Subaltern Resistance in World History*, ed. A. Dirk Moses (New York: Berghahn Books, 2008).
50. Lucy Mayblin et al., "'Other' Posts in 'Other' Places: Poland Through a Postcolonial Lens?," *Sociology* 50, no. 1 (2016): 66; Larry Wolff, *Inventing Eastern Europe: The Map of Civilization on the Mind of the Enlightenment* (Stanford, Calif.: Stanford University Press, 1994), 9; Jedlicki, *A Suburb of Europe*, xiii; David Furber, "Near as Far in the Colonies: The Nazi Occupation of Poland," *International History Review* 26, no. 3 (2004): 559; Kristin Kopp, *Germany's Wild East: Constructing Poland as Colonial Space* (Ann Arbor: University of Michigan Press, 2012).
51. Reto Hoffmann and Max Ward, eds., *Transwar Asia: Ideology, Practices, and Institutions, 1920–1960* (London: Bloomsbury Academic, 2022).

2. GENEALOGY

1. The article was reprinted as a booklet in 1996: Jan Błoński, *Biedni Polacy patrzą na getto* (Kraków: Wydawnictwo Literackie, 1996).
2. Jerzy Turowicz, "Ethical Problems of the Holocaust: Discussion Held at International Conference on the History and Culture of Polish Jewry in Jerusalem on Monday, 1 February 1988," in *My Brother's Keeper? Recent Polish Debates on the Holocaust*, ed. Antony Polonsky (London: Routledge, 1990), 215.
3. "The Poor Poles Look at the Ghetto," https://www.tygodnikpowszechny.pl/the-poor-poles-look-at-the-ghetto-144232, last accessed July 23, 2024.
4. In everyday use of Polish, *grzech* (sin) and *grzeszny* (sinful) often denote actions that incur not necessarily religious but moral guilty conscience, such as infidelity.
5. Richard Bernstein, "An Epic Film About the Greatest Evil of Modern Times," *New York Times*, October 20, 1985; Roger Ebert, "Shoah," RogerEbert.com, November 24, 1985, https://rogerebert.com/reviews/shoah-1985.

6. Interestingly, such reaction from the PZPR and the communist regime in 1985 was quite parallel to the argument of the Catholic right-wing nationalists and PiS, the ruling party of Poland as of 2020, which attempted to legislate a memory law to penalize defamation of the Polish nation.
7. Lawrence Baron, "Kino w krzyżowym ogniu polemiki żydowsko-polskiej," in *Polacy i Żydzi: kwestia otwarta*, ed. Robert Cherry and Annamaria Orla-Bukowska (Warsaw: Więź, 2008), 60.
8. Claude Lanzmann, *Shoah: The Complete Text of the Acclaimed Holocaust Film* (New York: De Capo Press, 1995), 77–79.
9. Lanzmann, 24.
10. Lanzmann, 120–21.
11. For the official historiography and memory of the Red Court, see Elizabeth Kridl Valkenier, "The Rise and Decline of Official Marxist Historiography in Poland, 1945–1983," *Slavic Review* 44, no. 4 (1985): 663–80; Joanna Wawrzyniak, *Veterans, Victims, and Memory: The Politics of the Second World War in Communist Poland*, trans. Simon Lewis (Frankfurt am Main: Peter Lang, 2015); Jie-Hyun Lim, "'The Good Old Cause' in the New Polish Left Historiography," *Science & Society* 61, no. 4 (1997/98): 541–49; Jie-Hyun Lim, "The Nationalist Message in Socialist Code: On Court Historiography in People's Poland and North Korea," *Making Sense of Global History: The 19th International Congress of Historical Sciences*, ed. Solvi Sogner (Oslo: Universitetsforlaget, 2001); Jie-Hyun Lim, "역사의 금기와 기억의 진정성-21세기 폴란드 역사학과 '희생자의식'" [Historical taboos and authentic memories—victimhood in Polish historiography in the twenty-first century], 『서양사론』 111 (2011): 147–74.
12. A. Kemp-Welch, *Poland Under Communism: A Cold War History* (Cambridge: Cambridge University Press, 2008), 158–59; Dariusz Stola, "Fighting Against the Shadows: The 'Anti-Zionist' Campaign of 1968," in *Anti-Semitism and Its Opponents in Modern Poland*, ed. Robert Blobaum (Ithaca, N.Y.: Cornell University Press, 2005), 285, 292; Stola, *Kampania antysyjonistyczna w Polsce 1967–1968* (Warsaw: ISP PAN, 2000).
13. Andrzej Walicki, *Trzy patriotyzmy* (Warsaw: Res Publica, 1991), 35–36.
14. Adam Michnik, "Nationalism," *Social Research* 58 (Winter 1991): 759.
15. Timothy Snyder, *Bloodlands: Europe Between Hitler and Stalin* (New York: Basic Books, 2010), 406.
16. Jakub Berman's younger brother Adolf Berman founded CENTOS, an aid organization for Jewish children in the Warsaw Ghetto during the Nazi occupation. He was a politician, writer, and active member of the leftist Zionist party Poalej Syjon. For more about Adolf Berman, see Natalia Aleksiun, "Adolf Berman. W głównym nurcie historii. Żydowski Instytut Historyczny im. Emanuela Ringelbluma," October 17, 2013, https://web.archive.org/web/20161005115834/http://www.jhi.pl/blog/2013-10-17-adolf-berman-w-glownym-nurcie-historii.
17. Mateusz Gniazdowski, "Losses Inflicted on Poland by Germany During World War II. Assessments and Estimates—an Outline," *Polish Quarterly of International Affairs* 16, no. 1 (2007): 107–8, 116.

2. GENEALOGY   325

18. Wojciech Materski and Tomasz Szarota eds., *Polska 1939–1945: Straty osobowe i ofiary represji pod dwiema okupacjami*, 2009, Institute of National Remembrance (IPN), https://web.archive.org/web/20120323161233/http://niniwa2.cba.pl/polska_1939_1945.htm.

19. The Belarusian and Ukrainian death tolls continue to increase in the twenty-first century. If the victims of the Holodomor enforced by Stalinist collectivization were to be taken into account, the proportion of victims in the Ukrainian population of the time surpasses that of the Polish. Nevertheless, the current upsurge in death tolls reflects the politics of counting at work, and the exact estimation will take longer to come. For example, the nationalist historiography of Ukraine sometimes overestimates the number of the Holodomor victims to be 6.3 million, which seems to be a rhetorical strategy to emphasize its bigger scale than the 6 million Jewish victims of the Holocaust.

20. As I wrote this chapter, on November 1, 2020, the German parliament reached a bipartisan agreement on erecting a monument to the Polish victims of World War II in Askan Square in central Berlin. That this monument would be the first Nazi victims' memorial dedicated to a single nation other than Jews and Romani signified the scale of Polish suffering under the Nazis. Stuart Dowell, "German Parliament Says 'Ja' to the Polish War Memorial," *First News*, November 2, 2020, https://www.thefirstnews.com/article/german-parliament-says-ja-to-polish-war-memorial-17224.

21. About the statistics of victims in each Asian country during the Asia-Pacific War, see United Nations, Economic and Social Council, 2nd Year, 4th Session, *Report of the Working Group for Asia and the Far East*, Supplement no. 10, 1947; John W. Dower, *War Without Mercy: Race and Power in the Pacific War*, 7th ed. (New York: Pantheon Books, 1993), 295–99; "異域에서不歸客된七萬英靈에慰靈祭" [Commemorating seventy thousand deceased in alien lands], 『東亞日報』, January 16, 1946. Japanese scholar Yoshida Yutaka estimates the total of colonial Korean deaths, of both soldiers and civilians, during the Asia-Pacific War at 200,000. This estimate is bigger than the Taiwanese death toll of 30,000 and the Malay/Singaporean death toll of 100,000, but considerably smaller than the death tolls of Indonesia, Vietnam, and the Philippines, each of which amounts to over a million. 吉田裕『日本軍兵士』[Japanese soldiers] (東京:中央公論新社, 2017), 24. It is very hard to uncover the number of Korean deaths, partly because Korea was not invited to participate in the War Crimes Trial. All numbers are speculated more than calculated. Still, the death toll of Koreans is surprisingly low. See also R. J. Rummel, *Statistics of Democide* (Honolulu: University of Hawaii Press, 1997), chap. 3, https://www.hawaii.edu/powerkills/SOD.CHAP3.HTM.

22. For Asian cases, see Dower, *War Without Mercy*, 296–97.

23. Gniazdowski, "Losses Inflicted on Poland," 103–4. The Polish parliamentary committee to calculate German reparations estimates the Polish deaths at 5.1 million, including the 3 million Jewish deaths, and the material damage around US$54 billion. Considering the impracticability of obtaining exact statistics, approximately over 5 million deaths and US$50 billion of material damage seem to be the generally

accepted numbers. "Poland Totals WWII Occupation's Cost Amid Germany Claim Talk," *AP News*, September 1, 2018.
24. Jan T. Gross, *Fear: Anti-Semitism in Poland After Auschwitz* (New York: Random House, 2006), 98, 121–22.
25. The trope of Crucified Jesus was a recurring theme used in glorifying a nation as the sublime martyr for all humanity. A year before Japan's withdrawal from the League of Nations, Matsuoka Yosuke, the chief Japanese delegate to the League of Nations, likened Japan to Jesus crucified by the international media, to much of the world's surprise. Ian Buruma, 『근대 일본』 [Modern Japan], trans. 최은봉 (서울: 을유문화사, 2004), 98.
26. Joanna Szczęsna, "25 lat sporów o 'Shoah,'" *Gazeta Wyborcza*, March 24, 2010, http://wyborcza.pl/1,76842,7694169,25_lat_sporow_o__Shoah_.html.
27. Feliks Tych, "민족문제와 폴란드 공산주의 체제의 전술-유대인 정책" [The nationalist tactics of the Communist regime in Poland: The policy toward the Jews], 임지현·김용우 엮음, 『대중독재 II: 정치종교와 헤게모니』 [Mass dictatorship II] (서울: 책세상, 2005), 306. Also noteworthy is Harry Hartoonian's recently published memoir, which talks about the Armenian Genocide in the context of "dispossession." Harry Hartoonian, *The Unspoken as Heritage: The Armenian Genocide and Its Unaccounted Lives* (Durham, N.C.: Duke University Press, 2019), 98–113.
28. Gross, *Fear*, 47, 98, 120, and passim.
29. According to Dariusz Stola in a private conversation with me, Andrzej Paczkowski remarked that Błoński's change of wording in Miłosz's poem from "poor Christians" to "poor Poles" provoked a furious reaction as it alluded to the collective guilt of the Polish nation rather than a long conflict between Christians and Jews. Unfortunately, there is no way to know whether this modification was done with Miłosz's tacit consent. Anthony Polonsky recalls the meeting between Miłosz and Błoński at Somerville College, Oxford, in June 1984, but no clue about this. Antony Polonsky, "You Need to Speak Polish: Interviewed by Konrad Matyjaszek," *Studia Litteraria et Historica* 6, no. 2017 (September 7, 2016): 25–26, https://doi.org/10.11649/slh.1401.
30. Błoński, *Biedni Polacy*, 26–27.
31. Błoński, 18. For an English translation of this essay, I referred to Polonsky, *My Brother's Keeper*, 42.
32. Benjamin Meed, "Benjamin (Ben) Meed Describes the Burning of the Warsaw Ghetto During the 1943 Ghetto Uprising," interview by Michael Berenbaum, March 1, 1990, United States Holocaust Memorial Museum Collection, videocassettes, 3:18, https://encyclopedia.ushmm.org/content/en/oral-history/benjamin-ben-meed-describes-the-burning-of-the-warsaw-ghetto-during-the-1943-ghetto-uprising?parent=en%2F3636.
33. Czesław Miłosz, "Campo dei Fiori," trans. David Brooks and Louis Iribarne, Poetry Foundation, https://www.poetryfoundation.org/poems/49751/campo-dei-fiori.
34. Perhaps it is a coincidence that the underground tunnel was under Bonifraterska Street. Still, one cannot but feel the irony of the street name of "good brothers," which divided the Jewish ghetto from the Aryan side in Warsaw under the Nazi occupation.
35. Lanzmann, *Shoah*, 184.

36. Ewa Berberyusz, "Guilt by Neglect," in *My Brother's Keeper*, 70–71.
37. Błonski, *Biedni Polacy*, 12.
38. Błonski, 13–14.
39. Stanisław Salmonowicz, "The Deep Roots and Long Life of Stereotypes," in *My Brother's Keeper*, 55–56, 58.
40. Władysław Siła-Nowicki, "A Reply to Jan Błonski," in *My Brother's Keeper*, 61–62, 67.
41. Berberyusz, "Guilt by Neglect," in *My Brother's Keeper*, 70.
42. Teresa Prekerowa, "The Just and the Passive," in *My Brother's Keeper*, 75.
43. Jerzy Turowicz, "Polish Reasons and Jewish Reasons," in *My Brother's Keeper*, 141.
44. One can remember Ian Kershaw's famous dictum that "the road to Auschwitz was built by hate, but paved with indifference." See Kershaw, *Popular Opinion and Political Dissent in the Third Reich: Bavaria 1933–45* (Oxford: Clarendon Press, 2002), 277.
45. Jerzy Jastrzębowski, "Differing Ethical Standpoints," in *My Brother's Keeper*, 119–20.
46. Jastrzębowski, 120.
47. Zygmunt Bauman, "On Immoral Reason and Illogical Morality," *Polin: A Journal of Polish-Jewish Studies* 3 (1990): 296.
48. Bauman, 298.
49. Jan Gross, *Sąsiedzi: Historia zagłady żydowskiego miasteczka* (Sejny: Pogranicze, 2000). Also available in English as Jan Gross, *Neighbors: The Destruction of the Jewish Community in Jedwabne* (Princeton, N.J.: Princeton University Press, 2001). Contrary to Gross's estimate, the Institute of National Remembrance suggests the number of victims to be around 340, based on the exhumation of the massacre site in 2001. See Radoław J. Ignatiew, "On final findings of investigation S 1/00/Zn into the killing of Polish citizens of Jewish origin in the town of Jedwabne, on 10 July 1941, i.e. pursuant to Article 1 point 1 of the Decree of 31 August 1944," http://ipn.gov.pl/eng_konf_jedwabne_press.html. The disparity in numbers does not change the nature of the Jedwabne pogrom.
50. The documentary's original title was *Sąsiedzi*, like Gross's book title. Later the title was changed to "*Gdzie Mój Starszy Syn Kain*." See Tadeusz Sobolewski, "'Sąsiedzi' Agnieszki Arnold: Każdy ma swoje Jedwabne," *Gazeta Wyborcza*, April 2, 2001, https://wyborcza.pl/1,75410,207852.html.
51. Paweł Machcewicz, "In the Shadow of Jedwabne," in *Thou Shalt Not Kill: Poles on Jedwabne* (Warsaw: Więź, 2001), 141.
52. Anna Bikont, *The Crime and the Silence: Confronting the Massacre of Jews in Wartime Jedwabne*, trans. Alissa Valles (New York: Farrar, Straus and Giroux, 2015), 9.
53. "Idzie po nas Ida czyli film zrobiony z nienawiści. Przypominamy poruszający felieton prof. Aleksandra Nalaskowskiego z tygodnika 'w Sieci," *wPolityce.pl*, December 26, 2014, https://wpolityce.pl/kultura/227316-idzie-po-nas-ida-czyli-film-zrobiony-z-nienawisci-przypominamy-poruszajacy-felieton-prof-aleksandra-nalaskowskiego-z-tygodnika-w-sieci.
54. Joanna Kurczewska, "From the Editor," *Polish Sociological Review* 137, no. 1 (2002): 4.
55. "Jej dokument ujawnił prawdę o Jedwabnem," TOK FM, July 7, 2017, https://www.tokfm.pl/Tokfm/7,103454,22035601,jej-dokument-ujawnil-prawde-o-jedwabnem-mam-poczucie-porazki.html.

56. Ireneusz Krzemiński, "Polish-Jewish Relations, Anti-Semitism and National Identity," *Polish Sociological Review* 137, no. 1 (2002): 45.
57. Marek Ziółkowski, "Memory and Forgetting After Communism," *Polish Sociological Review* 137, no. 1 (2002): 19, 22.
58. See Marek Jan Chodakiewicz, *The Massacre in Jedwabne July 10, 1941: Before, During, and After* (Boulder, Colo.: East European Monographs, 2005), 12; Paweł Machcewicz, "Wokół Jedwabnego," in *Wokół Jedwabnego: Studia* Tom. 1 (Warsaw: IPN, 2002), 55–59.
59. Those extreme interpretations are supported by the contributions to the Jedwabne controversies by Antoni Macierewicz, Jan Nowak-Jeziorski, and others. See A. Polonsky and J. A. Michlic, eds., *The Neighbors Respond* (Princeton, N.J.: Princeton University Press, 2004).
60. Poland's ruling Law and Justice Party (PiS) maintains a stance that is not far from this: Germany is entirely accountable for the massacre, and any interpretation that refutes the sole German accountability or raises the question of Polish involvement would be deemed an attack on the national identity of Poland and the Polish values and customs, and a scheme to disgrace the Polish nation. About the right-wing stance and interpretations of the Jedwabne pogrom, see Joanna Beata Michlik, "'At the Crossroads': Jedwabne and Polish Historiography of the Holocaust," *Dapim: Studies on the Holocaust* 31, no. 3 (2017): 296–306; Jörg Hackmann, "Defending the 'Good Name' of the Polish Nation: Politics of History as a Battlefield in Poland, 2015–18," *Journal of Genocide Research* 20, no. 4 (2018): 587–606. The phrase *pedagogika wstydu* (the pedagogy of shame), frequently used by right-wing nationalists to attack critical history, bears remarkable similarity to the Japanese ultraright's rhetorical trope 自虐史観 (masochistic view of history). Korean New Right revisionist historians use the same jargon of masochistic history in blaming the leftist historiography critical of the South Korean dictatorship.
61. Zygmunt Bauman, "Afterword to the 2000 Edition," *Modernity and the Holocaust* (Ithaca, N.Y.: Cornell University Press, 2000), 236.
62. 임지현, "지그문트 바우만 인터뷰: 악의 평범성에서 악의 합리성으로" [Interview with Zygmunt Bauman: From the banality of evil to the rationality of evil)],『당대비평』21 (2003): 12–32.
63. 林志弦, "世襲的犠牲者意識と脱植民地主義の歴史学" [Hereditary victimhood and postcolonial historiography], 三谷博他 偏『東アジア歴史対話—国境と世代を超えて』 (東京: 東京大学出版会, 2007), 167–86.
64. I referred to the online versions of *Chosun Ilbo, Dong-A Ilbo, Joongang Ilbo, Hankyoreh*, and Yonhap News Agency. According to an article published in the *Boston Globe*, the Consulate General of the Republic of Korea in Boston sent a letter to the Massachusetts Department of Education on January 16, condemning *So Far from the Bamboo Grove* for its distorted view of history depicting Koreans as evil perpetrators. Considering the fourteen-hour difference between Korea and the East Coast of the United States, the Korean consulate sent the letter at approximately the same time as the Korean news outlets reported in unison about *So Far from the Bamboo Grove*. The fact that the Korean consul in Boston was a former news reporter at the time might

have contributed to this simultaneous action. Interestingly, the "reclusive North Korean government" joined the criticism later on February 3. See Lisa Kocian, "Korean Officials Join Fray on Book," *Boston Globe*, February 14, 2007.
65. 김성현, "열두살 일본 소녀가 겪은 전쟁" [The war through the lens of a twelve-year-old girl], 『조선일보』, May 6, 2005, https://www.chosun.com/site/data/html_dir/2005/05/06/2005050670221.html.
66. 厚生省社会・援護局援護50年史編集委員会, 『援護50年史』 [A history of the fifty years of relief policies], ぎょうせい (1997), 11, 17, 28, 32.
67. 厚生省援護局, 『引揚げと援護三十年の歩み』 [*Hikiage* and social relief—a sketch of last thirty years], ぎょうせい (1978): 690.
68. 山田陽子, 『図説満州：日本人の足跡をたどる』 [Illustrated Manchu—in search of the trajectory of the Japanese] (大阪：梅田出版, 2011), 80–98.
69. James Orr, *The Victim as Hero: Ideologies of Peace and National Identity in Postwar Japan* (Honolulu: University of Hawaii Press, 2001), 161.
70. 洪郁如、田原開起,「朝鮮引揚者のライフ・ヒストリー：成原明の植民地・引揚げ・戦後」『人文・自然研究』10 (2016): 160–75.
71. 이광수, 『일본 역사왜곡 1편: 요코 이야기의 진실을 찾아라』 개정판 [Japan's historical revisionism, vol. 1: Searching for the truth of *So Far from the Bamboo Grove*—rev. ed.] (서울: 키네마인, 2010), 52–57.
72. For the relationship between collective memory, mnemonic identity, and ontological security, see Maria Mälksoo, "'Memory Must Be Defended': Beyond the Politics of Mnemonical Security," *Security Dialogue* 46, no. 3 (2015).
73. 이광수, 『일본 역사왜곡 1편』, 173–86.
74. ヨーコ・カワシマ・ワトキンズ,『竹林はるか遠く――日本人少女ヨーコの戦争体験記』[So far from the bamboo grove], 都竹恵子訳 (東京: ハート出版, 2013).
75. "So Far from the Bamboo Grove," Amazon Japan, accessed January 2, 2022, https://www.amazon.co.jp/Bamboo-Grove-Yoko-Kawashima-Watkins/dp/0688131158; 빙문신, "눈재인 정부의 아이러니 ... '일본 진보가 고립되고 있다'" [The irony of the Moon Jae-In administration: Japanese progressives are alienated], *SBS News* Online, last modified March 12, 2021, https://news.sbs.co.kr//news/endPage.do?newsId=N1006237883#lv-container.
76. Jie-Hyun Lim, "Victimhood Nationalism: Compelling or Competing?," *Korea Herald*, April 29, 2007.
77. Joshua Simon, *The Ideology of Creole Revolution: Imperialism and Independence in American and Latin American Political Thought* (Cambridge: Cambridge University Press, 2019), 1–2.

3. SUBLIMATION

1. In my paper published in the Polish liberal Catholic journal *Więź*, after consulting a translator, victimhood nationalism was translated as "Nations: Victims and Their Megalomania" because of the semantic difference between English and Polish.

Although the ambivalence of the term *ofiara* was also problematic, the negative undertone of nationalism in Polish was the most significant factor in our decision to translate it. Jie-Hyun Lim, "Narody-ofiary i ich megalomania," Polish translation by Marek Darewski, *Więź*, no. 616/7 (2010): 22–34.

2. In postwar Germany, especially in West Germany, the nuance of *Opfer* leaned toward the meaning of passive victim rather than active sacrifice to emphasize the German suffering after the war. Robert G. Moeller, "Responses to Alon Confino," *Cultural Analysis* 4 (2005): 67.

3. Zuzanna Bogumił and Małgorzata Głowacka-Grajper, *Milieux de Mémoire in Late Modernity*, trans. Philip Palmer, Geschichte-Erinnerung-Politik no. 24 (Berlin: Peter Lang, 2019), 33. The Christian martyr who obtains power by killing themself comes in contact with Émile Durkheim's idea of "altruistic suicide," which displays a determination to sacrifice oneself for the community. About Durkheim's altruistic suicide, see Steven Stack, "Émile Durkheim and Altruistic Suicide," *Archives of Suicide Research* 8, no. 1 (2004): 9–22; Lung-chang Young, "Altruistic Suicide: A Subjective Analysis," *Sociological Bulletin* 21 (1972): 103–21.

4. Ami Pedahzur, Arie Perliger, and Leonard Weinberg, "Altruism and Fatalism: The Characteristics of Palestinian Suicide Terrorists," *Deviant Behavior* 24, no. 4 (2003): 405–23; Lori Allen, "There Are Many Reasons Why: Suicide Bombers and Martyrs in Palestine," *Middle East Report*, no. 223 (2002): 36.

5. Søren Kierkegaard, *The Journals of Kierkegaard*, trans. Alexander Dru (New York: Harper Torchbooks, 1959), 151.

6. George L. Mosse, *Fallen Soldiers: Reshaping the Memory of the World Wars* (Oxford: Oxford University Press, 1990), 25.

7. Mosse, 29–32.

8. Oasis Music Choir, "현충일 노래" [South Korean Ceremony Song—'Song of Memorial Day'] (Seoul: Oasis Record Music Company, 1984), https://www.youtube.com/watch?v=ID5fLCpCmd4&ab_channel=Rhee.

9. Oasis Music Choir, "제헌절 노래" [South Korean Ceremony Song—'Song of Constitutional Day'] (Seoul: Oasis Record Music Company, 1984), https://www.youtube.com/watch?v=owq5B_wSdw4.

10. Benedict Anderson, *Imagined Communities*, rev. ed. (London: Verso, 1991), 145.

11. Jie-Hyun Lim, "Transnational Memory Activism and the Performative Nationalism," in *Handbook of Memory Activism*, ed. Yifat Gutman and Jenny Wüstenberg (Oxford: Oxford University Press, 2022), 93–102.

12. Ernest Renan, "What Is a Nation?," trans. Martin Thom, in *Nation & Narration*, ed. Homi K. Bhabha (London: Routledge, 1990), 19.

13. For political religions, civil religions, and secular religions, see Emilio Gentile, "The Sacralisation of Politics: Definitions, Interpretations and Reflections on the Question of Secular Religion and Totalitarianism," *Totalitarian Movements and Political Religions* 1, no. 1 (Summer 2000): 18–55; Gentile, *The Sacralization of Politics in Fascist Italy*, trans. Keith Botsford (Cambridge, Mass.: Harvard University Press, 1996). Despite my continued reservations about his binary categorization between political

religion in the dictatorship and civil religion in the democracy, I still find Gentile's theoretical elaboration very helpful in understanding victimhood nationalism as a political religion.

14. For the "soul-consoling" aspect of premodern East Asian funeral rites for the war dead, see 강인철, 『전쟁과 희생: 한국의 전사자 숭배』 [War and sacrifice: The cult of war dead in Korea] (서울: 역사비평사, 2019), 76–80; 이욱, "조선 전기 유교국가의 성립과 국가제사의 변화" [The formation of the Confucian state and the state rituals in the early Joseon], 『한국사연구』 118 (September 2002): 161–93.

15. Pericles's eulogy in Ancient Athens seems different among the premodern mourning rituals. Celebrating the war dead who chose "to die resisting, rather than to live to submit," the eulogy seems closer to modern states' sublimation of the war dead than the traditional rituals of East Asia to pacify vengeful spirits. The armed soldiers of Athens were closer to the civilian militia of the modern era than medieval mercenaries in that they exchanged civil rights for military duties. As a text, Pericles's eulogy was perfect for the modern nationalist sublimation of the war dead that sought the ideological culprit from ancient republicanism. See Thucydides, *History of the Peloponnesian War*, 2.42, Perseus Digital Library Project, http://www.perseus.tufts.edu/hopper/text?doc=Thuc.+2.42&fromdoc=Perseus%3Atext%3A1999.01.0200, excerpted from Thucydides, *The Peloponnesian War* (London: Dent; New York: Dutton, 1910).

16. Goerge L. Mosse, *The Nationalization of the Masses* (New York: Howard Fertig, 1975); Mosse, *Fallen Soldiers: Reshaping the Memory of the World Wars* (Oxford: Oxford University Press, 1990).

17. Anthony D. Smith, "Neo-Classicist and Romantic Elements in the Emergence of Nationalist Conception," in *Nationalist Movements*, ed. Anthony D. Smith (London: Macmillan, 1976), 77–79.

18. K. R. Minogue, "Nationalism and the Patriotism of City-States," in Smith, ed., *Nationalist Movements*, 64. The Enlightenment interpretation, which appropriated ancient Greco-Roman Mediterranean civilization as the Western tradition, coincided with the emergence of the nation-state system and national commemoration of dead soldiers.

19. Martin Bernal, *Black Athena: The Afroasiatic Roots of Classical Civilization* (New Brunswick, N.J.: Rutgers University Press, 1987), especially chaps. 4, 5, 6.

20. George L. Mosse, *The Fascist Revolution* (New York: Howard Fertig, 1999), 71, 83–86.

21. Chris K. Huebner, "Between Victory and Victimhood: Reflections on Culture and Martyrdom," *Direction: A Mennonite Brethren Forum* 34, no. 2 (2005): 228–40, http://www.directionjournal.org/article/?1402.

22. Remarkably, the democratization of death has been prevalent among war veterans. They were more likely to think all the deaths of fellow soldiers were equal. For instance, Lazare Ponticelli, one of the last World War II veterans in France, refused Jacques Chirac's proposal to bury him in the Pantheon, in solidarity with his fellow fallen soldiers buried in other cemetaries. See Margaret MacMillan, *Dangerous Games: The Uses and Abuses of History* (New York: Modern Library, 2008), 18.

23. Oded Wolkstein and Dror Mishani, "Interview with Slavoj Žižek: The World Is a Disaster Area," *Haaretz*, June 10, 2006, https://www.haaretz.com/1.4872454.
24. Yael Zerubavel, "The Death of Memory and the Memory of Death: Masada and the Holocaust as Historical Metaphors," *Representations*, no. 45 (Winter 1994): 87.
25. Amos Goldberg, "Forum: On Saul Friedlaender's *The Years of Extermination* 2. The Victim's Voice and Melodramatic Aesthetics in History," *History and Theory* 48, no. 3 (2009): 225–26, 232–34.
26. Laura Jeffery and Matei Candea, "Introduction: The Politics of Victimhood," *History and Anthropology* 17, no. 4 (2006): 289, 292.
27. Lea David, *The Past Can't Heal Us: The Dangers of Mandating Memory in the Name of Human Rights* (Cambridge: Cambridge University Press, 2020); William Miles, "Third World Views of the Holocaust," *Journal of Genocide Research* 6, no. 3 (2004): 371–93, https://doi.org/10.1080/1462352042000265855.
28. Jie-Hyun Lim, "Victimhood Nationalism in Contested Memories—National Mourning and Global Accountability" in *Memory in a Global Age: Discourses, Practices and Trajectories*, ed. Aleida Assmann and Sebastian Conrad (Basingstoke, UK: Palgrave Macmillan, 2010); Jie-Hyun Lim, "Victimhood Nationalism and History Reconciliation in East Asia," *History Compass* 8, no. 1 (November 2010).
29. Lim, "Victimhood Nationalism and History Reconciliation," 74–76.
30. Gentile, *The Sacralization of Politics*, 18.
31. For Rousseau's advice to Poles to establish a civil religion, see Jerzy Robert Nowak, *Myśli o Polsce i Polakach* (Warsaw: wydawnictwo Unia, 1993), 81.
32. Mosse, *The Fascist Revolution*, 70.
33. Mosse, *Fallen Soldiers*, 18–19.
34. The debate between Cardinal Mercier of Belgium and Cardinal Villot of France on whether to admit those who died for the country as Christian martyrs is an exemplary moment of intellectual tension at a turning point where religious martyrdom becomes patriotic martyrdom. Ernst H. Kantorowicz, "Pro Patria Mori in Medieval Political Thought," *American Historical Review* 56, no. 3 (1951): 472–73.
35. Mosse, *Fallen Soldiers*, 78.
36. Anderson, *Imagined Communities*, 8.
37. Tzvetan Todorov, "Totalitarianism: Between Religion and Science," *Totalitarian Movements and Political Religions* 2, no. 1 (2001): 41.
38. Anderson, *Imagined Communities*, 10–12.
39. Anderson, 251–52.
40. Robert Mallet, "Foreword," *Totalitarian Movements and Political Religions* 1, no. 1 (2000): ix.
41. Jay Winter, *Sites of Memory, Sites of Mourning: The Greatest War in European Cultural History*, Canto ed. (Cambridge: Cambridge University Press, 1998), 15–17.
42. Winter, 23–24.
43. Elias Canetti, *Masse und Macht* (군중과 권력), Korean trans. by 강두식, 박병덕 (서울: 바다출판사, 2002), 191–95, 351.

44. Michał Łuczewski, *Kapitał moralny. Polityki historyczne w późnej nowoczesności* (Kraków: Ośrodek Myśli Politycznej, 2017), 97. Even though Łuczewski highlights the "moral asset" as a characteristic of late modernity, it is not necessary to narrow it down specifically as a late modern phenomenon. As Max Weber argued, re-enchantment and disenchantment are the two sides of modernity. The origin of political religion can be traced back to the Jacobin era, marked by its attempt at the establishment of Deism.
45. Gentile, *The Sacralization of Politics*; Michael Burleigh, "National Socialism as a Political Religion," *Totalitarian Movements and Political Religions* 1, no. 2 (2000): 3–11.
46. Gentile, *The Sacralization of Politics*, ix, x, 1, 4–18, 34–38.
47. Michael Burleigh, "Political Religion and Social Evil," *Totalitarian Movements and Political Religions* 3, no. 2 (2002): 2.
48. Gentile, *The Sacralization of Politics*, 22.
49. 高橋哲哉, 『国家と犠牲』 [State and sacrifice] (東京: 日本放送出版協会, 2005), 174–75, 190–91.
50. 高橋哲哉, 『靖国問題』 [Yasukuni question] (東京: 筑摩書房, 2005), 59.
51. Gentile, *Sacralization of Politics*, 14.
52. 高橋哲哉, 『国家と犠牲』, 174–75.
53. Franz Stangl, a former SS commander and commandant of the Sobibor and Treblinka exterminations camps, testified in his interview with Gitta Sereny that he had to sign an agreement that he would cut all ties with the church when he joined the Nazi Party. This testimony provides a meaningful insight into the Nazis' competition as a secular religion against the Roman Catholic Church. Gitta Sereny, *The German Trauma: Experiences and Reflections, 1938–2001* (London: Penguin Books, 2001), 102.
54. 강인철, 『전쟁과 희생』, 113–14.
55. Akiko Takenaka, *Yasukuni Shrine: History, Memory, and Japan's Unending Postwar* (Honolulu: University of Hawai'i Press, 2015), 46–48.
56. Takenaka, 11–13, 57–71, 132–35.
57. Although his descendants failed in building the Olympia stadium, Kuroita's proposal was at least partially materialized by the Chidorigafuchi National Cemetery, Nippon Budokan, National Showa Memorial Museum, Science Museum, and National Museum of Modern Art, all surrounding the shrine and the Imperial Palace.
58. 李成市, "植民地文化政策の価値について見た歴史認識" [Historical consciousness represented by colonial cultural policies], paper presented to the Kyoto Forum of Public Philosophy, March 13, 2004.
59. Akiko Takenaka, "Mobilizing Death: Bodies and Spirits of the Modern Japanese Military Dead," in *The Palgrave Handbook of Mass Dictatorship*, ed. Paul Corner and Jie-Hyun Lim (London: Palgrave Macmillan, 2016), 353–55.
60. 高橋哲哉, 『国家と犠牲』, 85–87.
61. 이영진, 『죽음과 내셔널리즘: 전후 일본의 특공위령과 애도의 정치학』 [Death and ationalism: The emorial for the special units in postwar Japan and the politics of mourning] (서울: 서울대학교출판문화원, 2018), 10–11.

62. Emiko Ohnuki-Tierney, *Kamikaze, Cherry Blossoms, and Nationalisms: The Militarization of Aesthetics in Japanese History* (Chicago: University of Chicago Press, 2002), chap. 6.
63. 강인철, 『전쟁과 희생』, 171–73.
64. 강인철, 184–85, 200, 202.
65. 강인철, 200.
66. 강인철, 129–33.
67. "추도순례" [Memorial pilgrimage], 일제강제동원피해자지원재단 [Foundation for Victims of Forced Mobilization by Imperial Japan], https://fomo.or.kr/eng/contents/92.
68. "十勇士의壯烈한戰鬪經過 肉彈으로陣地粉碎" [Ten heroic sacrifices that destroyed the enemy fortress], 『동아일보』, May 21, 1949; "祖國守護의精華 李總理 肉彈十勇士讚揚" [Ten heroes sacrificed for the national defense], 『경향신문』, May 21, 1949; "壯하다!不滅의靈魂 十勇士·戰沒將兵葬儀式嚴修" [Eternal lives of the ten heroes], 『경향신문』, May 29, 1949; "十勇士에慰問金遝至" [Donation to ten heroes], 『조선일보』, May 24, 1949.
69. Takenaka, *Yasukuni Shrine*, 127.
70. 小熊英二, 『民主と愛国：戦後日本のナショナリズムと公共性』 [Democracy and patriotism: Nationalism and publicness in postwar Japan] (東京: 新曜社, 2002), 34.
71. Fritz Wüllner, *Die NS-Militärjustiz und das Elend der Geschichtsschreibung: ein grundlegender Forschungsbericht*, 2d ed. (Baden-Baden: Nomos, 1997), 168.
72. Ariel Merari et al., "Making Palestinian Martyrdom Operations/ Suicide Attacks Interview with Would-Be Perpetrators and Organizers," *Terrorism and Political Violence* 22, no.1 (2009): 102–19.
73. Bethany Bell, "Austria Unveils World War Two Deserters' Memorial," *BBC News*, October 24, 2014, http://www.bbc.com/news/world-europe-29754386#story_continues_1.
74. Around thirty thousand conscientious objectors and deserters from the German Wehrmacht were sentenced to death by the Nazi military courts from 1939 to 1945. Approximately twenty thousand of them were executed, including fifteen hundred Austrian nationals. "Austrian Memorial for WW II Deserters," *Deutsche Welle*, October 24, 2014, https://www.dw.com/en/austria-inaugurates-memorial-to-wehrmacht-deserters-killed-by-the-nazis/a-18019168.
75. "Denkmal für die Verfolgten der NS-Militärjustiz in Wien," https://deserteursdenkmal.at/wordpress/home/.
76. 「ギュンター・グラス」 [Günter Grass] 『朝日新聞』, May 17, 1995; 「大江健三郎」 [Oegenzabro] 『朝日新聞』, May 18, 1995.
77. Michael Hardt and Antonio Negri, *Empire* (Cambridge, Mass: Harvard University Press, 2000), 205.
78. Ingar Solty, "The Man Who Tried to Whistle Against an Ocean: Kurt Tucholsky (1890–1935)," *Socialism and Democracy* (2020), https://doi.org/10.1080/08854300.2020.1821337.
79. Steven R. Welch, "Commemorating 'Heroes of a Special Kind': Deserter Monuments in Germany," *Journal of Contemporary History* 47, no. 2 (April 2012): 370–76.

80. Peter Taylor-Whiffen, "Shot at Dawn: Cowards, Traitors or Victims?" *BBC*, March 3, 2011, http://www.bbc.co.uk/history/british/britain_wwone/shot_at_dawn_01.shtml.
81. 찰스 암스트롱, "가족주의, 사회주의, 북한의 정치종교" [Familism, socialism, and the political religion in North Korea], in 임지현·김용우 엮음 『대중독재 II: 정치종교과 헤게모니』 [Mass dictatorship II: Political religion and hegemony] (서울: 책세상, 2005), 168–89.
82. Mosse, *Nationalization of the Masses*, 215–16.
83. Goldberg, "Forum: On Saul Friedlaender's *The Years of Extermination 2*," 225–26.
84. Tzvetan Todorov, *Facing the Extreme: Moral Life in the Concentration Camps*, trans. A. Denner and A. Pollack (London: Weidenfeld & Nicolson, 1999), 11, 15, 20.

4. GLOBALIZATION

1. Ian Buruma, *Year Zero: A History of 1945* (New York: Penguin Press, 2013).
2. "Declaration of the Stockholm International Forum on the Holocaust," International Holocaust Remembrance Alliance, accessed December 13, 2022, https://www.holocaustremembrance.com/sites/default/files/stockholm_4csilver.pdf.
3. "Declaration of the Stockholm International Forum on the Holocaust."
4. Benoît Challand, "1989, Contested Memories and the Shifting Cognitive Maps of Europe," *European Journal of Social Theory* 12, no. 3 (2009): 399.
5. Jan Surmann, "Zwischen Restitution und Erinnerung. Die US-Restitutionspolitik am Ende des 20. Jahrhunderts und die Auflösung der Tripartite Gold Commission," in *Universalisierung des Holocaust? Erinnerungskultur und Geschichtspolitik in internationaler Perspektive*, ed. Moisel Eckel, Beitrage zur Geschichte des Nationalsozialismus, vol. 14 (Göttingen: Wallstein, 2008), 135–55; Stuart Eizenstat, *Imperfect Justice: Looted Assets, Slave Labor and the Unfinished Business of World War II* (New York: Public Affairs, 2003).
6. "Declarations of the Task Force for International Cooperation on Holocaust Education, Remembrance, and Research," in *A Teacher's Guide to the Holocaust*, produced by the Florida Center for Instructional Technology, College Education, University of South Florida, December 3, 1998, https://fcit.usf.edu/holocaust/resource/assets/decl.htm.
7. Jean-Marc Dreyfus and Marcel Stoetzler, "Holocaust Memory in the Twenty-first Century: Between National Reshaping and Globalisation," *European Review of History* 18, no. 1 (2011): 70.
8. Larissa Allwork, "Holocaust Remembrance as 'Civil Religion': The Case of the Stockholm Declaration (2000)," in *Revisiting Holocaust Representation in the Post-Witness Era*, ed. Diana I. Popescu and Tanja Schult (Basingstoke, UK: Palgrave Macmillan, 2015), 288.
9. Dan Diner, "Memory and Restitution: World War II as a Foundational Event in a Uniting Europe," in *Restitution and Memory: Material Restitution in Europe*, ed. Dan Diner and Gotthart Wunberg (New York: Berghahn Books, 2007), 9; Alon Confino,

Foundational Past: The Holocaust as Historical Understanding (Cambridge: Cambridge University Press, 2012), 5–6.

10. Leszek Kołakowski, "Amidst Moving Ruins," *Daedalus* 121, no. 2 (1992): 56.
11. This number is from the foundation's official report. See Michael Jansen and Günter Saathoff, *A Mutual Responsibility and a Moral Obligation: The Final Report on Germany's Compensation Programs for Forced Labor and Other Personal Injuries* (Basingstoke, UK: Palgrave Macmillan, 2009), 25, 27. The number has since increased to about twenty million, including forced laborers in the occupied territories.
12. U.S. Department of the Treasury, "Treasury Deputy Secretary Stuart E. Eizenstat International Conference on the Impact of the Holocaust on Contemporary Society Brandies University," March 26, 2000, https://home.treasury.gov/news/press-releases/ls501.
13. Author's dialogue with Michael Jansen and Günter Saathoff, Berlin, August 16, 2016.
14. According to the National Memorial Museum of Forced Mobilization Under Japanese Occupation, 7,554,764 colonial Koreans were mobilized for industrial and agrarian labor, 63,312 for civilian military service, and 209,279 for military service. Of the total 7,827,355, about 6.5 million were mobilized to work in the Korean peninsula. The statistics need to be investigated thoroughly, but the official memory of the Japanese colonial past in Korea perceives this as a solid fact.
15. "獨 '나치 노역자 150만명 배상'...1인당 최고 8백만원" [German reparations for one and a half million forced laborers—eight million KRW per person], 『동아일보』, July 12, 2000, https://www.donga.com/news/article/all/20000713/7558376/1; "獨 '나치배상'참회 세계가 격찬" [Global community in praise of the German repenting compensation for Nazi crimes], 『문화일보』, July 18, 2000, http://www.munhwa.com/news/view.html?no=200007189000401; "독일재계, 나치노역 피해보상 근거마련 환영" [German CEOs welcoming the reparations for the forced labor under Nazi rule], 『중앙일보』, May 23, 2001, https://news.joins.com/article/4080761; https://www.mk.co.kr/news/home/view/2000/07/88039/; "나치 강제노역 국제보상협정 7개국 서명" [Seven countries signing the International Treaty of Recompensation], 『매일경제』, July 17, 2000, https://www.mk.co.kr/news/home/view/2000/07/88039/.
16. "'나치 과거사' 보상 마무리 日과 대조적" [Germany in contrast with Japan in compensating the Nazi past], 『경향신문』, June 12, 2007, http://news.khan.co.kr/kh_news/khan_art_view.html?art_id=200706121835171.
17. 정현백·송충기, "통일 독일의 과거 청산-강제징용된 외국인 노동자에 대한 배상" [United Germany's coming to terms with its past—restitution to the foreign victims of forced mobilization], Friedrich Ebert Stiftung Korean Cooperation Office, *FES-Information-Series 2000–06*, 12.
18. Judges of the Women's International War Crimes Tribunal on Japan's Military Sexual Slavery, "Transcript of Oral Judgment," articles 16–26, 27–28, 30–31, Women's Caucus for Gender Justice, December 4, 2001, http://iccwomen.org/wigjdraft1/Archives/oldWCGJ/tokyo/summary.html.
19. Judges of the Women's International War Crimes Tribunal, "Transcript of Oral Judgment," article 153.

20. Danielle Paquette, "Turning Pain Into Hope: Rwanda's Children of Rape Are Coming of Age—Against the Odds," *Washington Post*, June 11, 2017, https://www.washingtonpost.com/sf/world/2017/06/11/rwandas-children-of-rape-are-coming-of-age-against-the-odds/.
21. Maki Kimura, *Unfolding the "Comfort Women" Debates: Modernity, Violence, Women's Voices* (Basingstoke, UK: Palgrave Macmillan, 2016), 6–8; Rumi Sakamoto, "The Women's International War Crimes Tribunal on Japan's Military Sexual Slavery: A Legal and Feminist Approach to the 'Comfort Women' Issue," *New Zealand Journal of Asian Studies* 3 (2001): 49–50.
22. Carol Gluck, "Operations of Memory: 'Comfort Women' and the World," in *Ruptured Histories: War, Memory and the Post-Cold War in Asia*, ed. Shelia Miyoshi Jager and Rana Mitter (Cambridge, Mass.: Harvard University Press, 2007), 69, 74.
23. Carol Gluck, "What the World Owes the Comfort Women," in *Mnemonic Solidarity-Global Interventions*, ed. Jie-Hyun Lim and Eve Rosenhaft (London: Palgrave Macmillan, 2020), Entangled Memories in the Global South Series, vol. 1, 92ff.
24. R. Charli Carpenter, "Surfacing Children: Limitations of Genocidal Rape Discourse," *Human Rights Quarterly* 22 (2000): 428–77; Alison Desforges, *Leave None to Tell the Story: Genocide in Rwanda* (New York: Human Rights Watch, 1999), 163.
25. Though the Dutch-hosted Batavia War Crimes Trials prosecuted and punished the perpetrators who forced the Dutch women in the Japanese detention camp to serve as military "Comfort Women," the indictment was more about the perpetration of the racial taboo where an Asian man sexually assaulted a white woman rather than the men's sexual exploitation and violence against women in general. See Gluck, "Operations of Memory," 67.
26. International Criminal Court, Situation in the Democratic Republic of Congo in the Case of the *Prosecutor v. Germain Katanga*, July 2, 2007, https://www.icc-cpi.int/CourtRecords/CR2007_04166.PDF; Melanie O'Brien, "'Don't Kill Them, Let's Choose Them as Wives': The Development of the Crimes of Forced Marriage, Sexual Slavery and Enforced Prostitution in International Criminal Law," *International Journal of Human Rights* 20, no. 3 (2016): 386–87, 393–95.
27. Dustin Lewis, "Unrecognized Victims: Sexual Violence against Men in Conflict Settings Under International Law," *Wisconsin International Law Journal* 27, no. 1 (2009): 1–49; Sandesh Sivakumaran, "Sexual Violence Against Men in Armed Conflict," *European Journal of International Law* 18, no. 2 (2007): 253–76; Sandesh Sivakumaran, "Lost in Translation: UN Responses to Sexual Violence Against Men and Boys in Situations of Armed Conflict," *International Review of the Red Cross* 92, no. 877 (2010): 259–77.
28. Gluck, "Operations of Memory," 72.
29. J. K. Yamamoto and Mikey Hirano Culross, "Comfort Women Monument Unveiled In Glendale," *Rafu Shimpo: Los Angeles Japanese Daily News*, August 2, 2013, http://www.rafu.com/2013/08/comfort-women-monument-unveiled-in-glendale/.
30. White House petition to remove the "Comfort Woman" monument by Japanese Americans accusing Koreans of harassing the Japanese by false claims about the

"Comfort Women" system, https://petitions.whitehouse.gov/petition/remove-monument-and-not-support-any-international-harassment-related-issue-against-people-japan/FPfs7p0Q. Last accessed January 20, 2019 (petition platform dissolved on January 20, 2021).

31. Nikkei for Civil Rights and Redress, "About NCRR," accessed March 8, 2020, http://www.ncrr-la.org/about.html.
32. 신기영, "일본군 위안부 문제: 보수의 결집과 탈냉전 세계정치의 사이에서" [The Japanese military "comfort women" issue: Between the conservative rally and post–Cold War international politics], 조판자 엮음, 『탈 전후 일본의 사상과 감성』 (서울: 박문사, 2017), 237.
33. Yamamoto and Culross, "Comfort Women Monument Unveiled in Glendale."
34. ReflectSpace, "(dis)Comfort Women: Sex Slaves of the Japanese Imperial Army," https://www.reflectspace.org/post/dis-comfort-women-sex-slaves-of-the-japanese-imperial-army.
35. ReflectSpace at the Glendale Central Library, "ReflectSpace / City of Glendale," last accessed March 8, 2020 (link no longer active), http://www.glendaleca.gov/government/departments/library-arts-culture/central-library-grand-re-opening-may-1-2017/reflectspace.
36. 무타 카즈에, "『'위안부'문제는 '#미투다!'』 동영상 공격으로 보는 일본" [The "Comfort Women" issue is a #MeToo issue: Japan's video attacks], 허윤, 무타 가즈에, 도미야마 이치로, 권김현영 지음, 『전쟁, 여성, 폭력: 일본군 '위안부'를 트랜스내셔널하게 기억하기』 CGSI e-Pub, 41, http://cgsi.ac/bbs/board.php?bo_table=eng_e_Pub&wr_id=3.
37. C. Sarah Soh, *The Comfort Women: Sexual Violence and Postcolonial Memory in Korea and Japan* (Chicago: University of Chicago Press, 2008), 32.
38. 무타, " 『'위안부'문제는 '#미투다!'』 ," 45–46.
39. Gluck, "What the World Owes," 117.
40. On December 28, 2015, the South Korean and Japanese governments announced an agreement to resolve the "Comfort Women" issue at the diplomatic table. In light of the contemporary interest and concerns regarding the Japanese military "Comfort Women" issue, *Bloomberg News* published an article urging society to act for the women abducted as sex slaves by the Islamic State and Boko Haram. Noah Feldman, "Apology Isn't Justice for Korea's 'Comfort Women,'" *Bloomberg News*, December 29, 2015, http://www.bloombergview.com/articles/2015-12-28/how-korea-s-deal-with-japan-fails-comfort-women-.
41. Christa Paul, *Zwangsprostitution. Staatlich errichtete Bordelle im Nationalsozialismus* (Berlin: Edition Hentrich, 1994).
42. 정용숙, "나치 국가의 매춘소와 강제성매매-그 실제와 전후 시대의 기억" [State-run brothels and forced sexual labor under the Nazis—the realities and the postwar memories], 『여성과 역사』 29 (2018): 385–87.
43. "Louis Harap's Letter to W.E.B. Dubois. Feb. 13, 1952," W.E.B. Du Bois Papers (MS 312), Special Collections and University Archives, University of Massachusetts Amherst Libraries.

44. W.E.B. Dubois, "The Negro and the Warsaw Ghetto," in *The Oxford W.E.B. Dubois Reader*, ed. Eric. J. Sundquist (Oxford: Oxford University Press, 1996), 470.
45. Ela Kwiecinska, "An 'India of Europe': Stanisław Szczepanowski (1846–1900) and Galician-Indian Pararells in 'The Misery of Galicia,'" *Artha Journal of Social Sciences* 20, no. 2 (2021): 57–73.
46. Dubois, "The Negro and the Warsaw Ghetto," 470–72.
47. Paul Gilroy, *The Black Atlantic: Modernity and Double Consciousness* (London: Verso, 1993), 207–8.
48. Rebecca Wolpe, "From Slavery to Freedom: Abolitionist ExpressionsiIn Maskilic Sea Adventures," *AJS Review* 36, no. 1 (2012): 61–62.
49. Toni Morrison,『보이지 않는 잉크』[Invisible ink] 이다희 옮김 (서울: 바다출판사, 2021), 160.
50. Ann Curthoys and John Docker, "Defining Genocide," in *The Historiography of Genocide*, ed. Dan Stone (Basingstoke, UK: Palgrave Macmillan, 2010), 16–21. Regarding the political abuse and misuse of Lemkin's theoretical heritage by left and right wings in Europe, America, Eastern Europe, Israel, and the Arab states, see James Loeffler, "Becoming Cleopatra: The Forgotten Zionism of Raphael Lemkin," *Journal of Genocide Research* 19, no. 3 (2017): 34–60.
51. Dan Goldberg, "An Aboriginal Protest Against the Nazis, Finally Delivered," *Haaretz*, October 10, 2012, http://www.haaretz.com/jewish-world/jewish-world-features/an-aboriginal-protest-against-the-nazis-finally-delivered.premium-1.483806.
52. "Australian Foreign Minister to Visit Yad Vashem Sunday and Participate in Event Marking Establishment of Chair for the Study of Resistance During the Holocaust, in Tribute to William Cooper," Yadvashem.org, December 9, 2010, https://www.yadvashem.org/press-release//09-december-2010-13-00.html.
53. Shirli Gilbert, "Anne Frank in South Africa: Remembering the Holocaust During and After Apartheid," *Holocaust and Genocide Studies* 26, no. 3 (2012): 366, 374.
54. Gilbert, 374–76.
55. Bernice L. McFadden, *The Book of Harlan* (New York: Akashic Books, 2016). The reviews on goodreads.com praise it as a moving story (Brina K, Lauren Cecile, lark benobi, J. Beckett, Jamise, and others) yet rate it poorly for its historical representations (Lisa, Chrissie, Missy J, and others). "The Book of Harlan," goodreads.com, https://www.goodreads.com/book/show/22642465-the-book-of-harlan.
56. "Rhineland Mongrels" was an epithet for the multiracial children born to the colonial African soldiers and German women during the French and Belgian occupation of the Ruhr (1923–25). Eve Rosenhaft, "히틀러의 흑인 희생자를 상상하기: 다방향기억과 최근의 홀로코스트 소설" [Imagining a Black victim of Hitler: Multidirectional memory and Holocaust fictions], 문수현 역,『독일연구』42호 (2019): 118.
57. Karol Radziszewski, "August Agbola O'Brown (1895–1976), zolnierz powstania warszawskiego; z cyklu 'Ali,'" 2015, Akryl na plotnie, Muzeum Warszawy.
58. René Aguigah, "The Conviction and Conscience of Achille Mbembe: Interview with Achille Mbembe," *New Frame*, April 23, 2020, https://www.newframe.com/the

-conviction-and-conscience-of-achille-mbembe/; "Call to Replace Felix Klein as the Federal Government Commissioner for the Fight Against Antisemitism," April 30, 2020, https://www.scribd.com/document/459345514/Call-on-German-Minister-Seehofer.

59. Michael Rothberg, "On the Mbembe Affair: The Specters of Comparison," Goethe Institut, *Latitude: Rethinking Power Relations—for a Decolonised and Non-racial World*, https://www.goethe.de/prj/lat/en/dis/21864662.html.
60. Natan Sznaider, "The Summer of Discontent: Achille Mbembe in Germany," *Journal of Genocide Research* (December 2020): 2, https://doi.org/10.1080/14623528.2020.1847862
61. Rothberg, "On the Mbembe Affair."
62. Geoff Eley, "Nazism, Politics and the Image of the Past: Thoughts on the West German Historikerstreit 1986–1987," *Past & Present*, no. 121 (1988); Charles Maier, *The Unmasterable Past: History, Holocaust and German National Identity*, 2d ed. (Cambridge, Mass.: Harvard University Press, 1997); Siobahn Kattago, *Ambiguous Memory: The Nazi Past and German National Identity* (Westport, Conn.: Praeger, 2001), 56–62.
63. Michael Rothberg, *Multidirectional Memory*. For critical relativization, see Jie-Hyun Lim, *Global Easts: Remembering-Imagining-Mobilizing* (New York: Columbia University Press, 2022), part 1.
64. Jan Józef Lipski, "Europa, ale jaka?," in *Pisma Polityczne: Wybór* (Warsaw: Wydawnictwo Krytyki Politycznej, 2011), 81.
65. Regarding the colonialist oblivion in postwar German memory culture, see Reinhart Kössler, *Namibia and Germany: Negotiating the Past* (Windhoek: University of Namibia Press, 2015), 49–50, 59–63, About the colonialist project of Nazi Germany in Eastern Europe, see Kristin Kopp, *Germany's Wild East: Constructing Poland as Colonial Space* (Ann Arbor: University of Michigan Press, 2012); Edward B. Westermann, *Hitler's Ostkrieg and the Indian War: Comparing Genocide and Conquest* (Norman: University of Oklahoma Press, 2016); Carroll P. Kakel, III, *The American West and the Nazi East: A Comparative and Interpretive Perspective* (Basingstoke, UK: Palgrave, 2013); James Q. Whitman, *Hitler's American Model* (Princeton, N.J.: Princeton University Press, 2017); Thaddeus Sunseri, "Exploiting the 'Urwald': German Post-colonial Forestry in Poland and Central Africa," *Past & Present*, no. 214 (2012).
66. Telford Taylor, *Nuremberg and Vietnam: An American Tragedy* (Chicago: Quadrangle Books, 1970).
67. Berthold Molden, "Vietnam, the New Left, and the Holocaust: How the Cold War Changed Discourse on Genocide," in *Memory in a Global Age: Discourses, Practices and Trajectories*, ed. Aleida Assmann and Sebastian Conrad (Basingstoke, UK: Palgrave Macmillan, 2010), 79–96.
68. Mark Mazower, "The Cold War and the Appropriation of Memory: Greece After Liberation," in *The Politics of Retribution in Europe: World War II and Its Aftermath*, ed. István Deák, Jan T. Gross, and Tony Judt (Princeton, N.J.: Princeton University Press, 2000), 224–25.

69. Honda Katsuichi, "Author's Preface to the U.S. Edition," in *The Nanjing Massacre: A Japanese Journalist Confronts Japan's National Shame*, trans. Karen Sandness (London: Routledge, 1998), xxvi.
70. Daqing Yang, "The Malleable and the Contested: The Nanjing Massacre in Postwar China and Japan," in *Perilous Memories: the Asia-Pacific War(s)*, ed. T. Fujitani, Geoffrey M. White, and Lisa Yoneyama (Durham, N.C.: Duke University Press, 2001), 50–86.
71. 針生一郎, "日本の68年" [1968 in Japan], 『環：歴史・環境・文明』33 (2008): 196–205.
72. Michael Rothberg, "Between Auschwitz and Algeria: Multidirectional Memory and the Counterpublic Witness," *Critical Inquiry* 33, no. 1 (2006): 158–60, 169, 170; Rothberg, "From Gaza to Warsaw: Mapping Multidirectional Memory," *Criticism* 53, no. 4 (2011): 528.
73. Ward Churchill, "American Holocaust: Structure of Denial," *Socialism and Democracy* 17, no. 1 (2003): 26, 30, 61. In a similar vein, local Catholic missionaries during the Nigerian Civil War compared the Biafra victims to the Jewish Holocaust victims. Pol Pot's massacre was also often referred to as the "Cambodian Holocaust," and Killingfield the "Auschwitz of Asia." The Holocaust was the most frequently summoned metaphor when emphasizing the tragedy of victims in global memory formation. Even the antisemitic Polish nationalists also used the term "forgotten Holocaust" to shed light on the Nazi massacre of non-Jews and Poles. The Middle East was no exception in using the term "Holocaust" to underscore the sacrifice of the weak. In the 1980s, the Mujahideen in Afghanistan accused the Soviet invasion of being more vicious than the Nazi Holocaust, and Saddam Hussein became a worse villain than Hitler during the First Iraq War in 1991. The Simon Wiesenthal Center revealed that German companies built the "gas chambers" for the dictator of Iraq. When Serbian forces and militias slaughtered Bosnian Muslims in 1992, a Muslim college student moaned that he was like a Jew under Nazi rule. Paul Preston, an English historian of the Spanish Civil War, titled his new book *The Spanish Holocaust*. Although some Jewish intellectuals complained about making the Holocaust too trivial, the term "Holocaust" was used everywhere. For conservative Christians in the United States, the legalization of abortion was the "American Holocaust," and animal rights activists raised their voices on the "animal Holocaust" taking place on fur farms. Gay rights activists warned that the "AIDS Holocaust" was taking place amid social apathy. Anti-gun control groups boasted of the homemade guns used in the ghetto uprising to make a statement that the Holocaust could have been prevented if guns were allowed in Nazi Germany. Smokers appealed that the strict antismoking policy was the "smoker Holocaust." It is indeed challenging to shake off the impression that the Holocaust is being trivialized and ridiculed in the process of globalizing memory.
74. Northwestern California Genocide Project, https://nwgenocide.omeka.net/.
75. Michael Mann, *The Dark Side of Democracy: Explaining Ethnic Cleansing* (Cambridge: Cambridge University Press, 2005), 4.
76. Zygmunt Bauman, *Modernity and Holocaust* (Ithaca, N.Y.: Cornell University Press, 2000), 243.

77. Zeev Sternhell, *The Birth of Fascist Ideology*, trans. David Maisel (Princeton, N.J.: Princeton University Press, 1995), 3.
78. Michael Rothberg and Yasemin Yildiz, "Memory Citizenship: Migrant Archives of Holocaust Remembrance in Contemporary Germany," *Parallax* 17, no. 4 (2011): 35, 37–38.
79. Rothberg and Yildiz, 39–43.
80. 이채주, "日本 右傾化의 季節—安保意識변화와 太平洋戰爭 재평가" [Japan's rightist turn—reevaluating the Pacific War], 『동아일보』, August 28, 1978.
81. "日本大使가 對韓經濟支援必要" [Japanese ambassador stresses the need of economic support for Korea], 『동아일보』, August 28, 1978.
82. 유경현, "日「韓國文化協」회장 小見山씨 韓·日「정신적和解」에 노력" [Komiyama's efforts for the Korean-Japanese spiritual reconciliation], 『동아일보』, November 10, 1977.
83. "日首相의 神社참배 15일 公式단행할 듯" [Japanese prime minister will pay an official visit to Yasukuni], 『동아일보』 August 10, 1985; "中曾根首相의 千일" [Thousand days of Prime Minister Nakasone], 『동아일보』, August 21, 1985; "國旗게양·國歌제창 義務化 日本 文部省 初中高행사에 지시" [Hinomaru and Kimigayo will be obligatory in official ceremony], 『동아일보』, September 6, 1985.
84. The textbook controversy in 1982 was triggered by a report on changing the term "invasion" to "advancement" in the certification process. However, the replacement of terms had already taken place in the late 1950s. In the 1982 revision, Japan's invasion of Southeast Asia was rewritten as "advancement," and the March 1 Movement in colonial Joseon was called a "riot." While it is true that the Liberal Democratic Party launched a campaign to criticize textbooks when many of them started to include the Nanjing Massacre and forced mobilization of Koreans as historical facts, the replacement of the term "invasion" with "advancement" regarding China was not the result of the 1982 revision. 福岡良明, 『「戦争体験」の戦後史』 [Postwar history of war experience] (東京: 中公新書, 2009), 231–32.
85. "日문부상"韓-日합방 侵略아니다" [Annexation of Korea was not an invasion)], 『조선일보』 September 7, 1986; "「外交고비」넘겨도 皇國史觀이 문제" [Emperor-centered history matters], 『동아일보』, September 6, 1986; "日本史의 왜곡기술" [Fabrication of history in Japan], 『동아일보』, June 7, 1986.
86. Takashi Yoshida, "A Battle Over History: The Nanjing Massacre in Japan," in *The Nanjing Massacre in History and Historiography*, ed. Joshua Fogel (Berkeley: University of California Press, 2000), 76.
87. Yoshiko Nozaki, *War Memory, Nationalism and Education in Postwar Japan, 1945–2007: The Japanese History Textbook Controversy and Ienaga Saburo's Court Challenge* (London: Routledge, 2008), 20–25.
88. "侵略歷史왜곡에 底意있다: 日敎科書 날조의 背後" [What is behind the fabrication of history in Japanese textbook], 『경향신문』, July 26, 1982; "日本 歷史교과서 歪曲 부분 史實은 이렇다" [Facts against the distortion in Japanese history textbook], 『동아일보』, July 29, 1982.
89. The diplomatic pressure from neighboring Asian countries led the Japanese government to establish the "neighboring countries clause" [近隣諸國條項] to respect and

cooperate with the international understanding of history and then chief cabinet secretary Gotoda Masaharu to state in 1986 that the government would refrain from visiting Yasukuni Shrine. In August 1993 a statement from the chief cabinet secretary, Kono Yohei, and a press conference by Prime Minister Miyazawa Kiichi solidified a reformative stance by acknowledging the military involvement in the installation and operation of the "comfort stations," forced mobilization, and Japan's war of aggression. This was followed by Prime Minister Murayama Tomiichi's statement on August 15, 1995, which expressed remorse and apology for the history of colonial rule and invasion. 吉田裕,「せめぎあう歴史認識」[Alternative history], 成田龍一・吉田裕 編,『記憶と認識の中のアジア・太平洋戦争：岩波講座アジア・太平洋戦争戦後編』(東京：岩波書店, 2015), 56–57.

90. 아시아평화와 역사교육연대,『후쇼샤 일본중학교 역사교과서: 2005년 검정합격본·검토용』(Fushosha Middle School history textbook) (서울, 2005) 비매품, 189–207.

5. NATIONALIZATION

1. "Pierwszy dzień wolności . . .," *Dziennik Polski*, no. 24 (5908), 29 stycznia, 1963.
2. "Fotoreportaże/Wybrane Fotoreportaże/Marsz Pokoju Hiroszima-Oświęcim, 1963," nr. ilustracji: 8611, 8612, 7631, 4994, Archiwum Eustachego Kossakowskiego, Museum of Contemporary Art, Warsaw.
3. "Uczestnicy Marszu pokoju zwiedzają polski," *Dziennik Łódzki*, no. 26 (5027), 30 stycznia, 1963.
4. English translation in Ran Zwigenberg, "The Hiroshima-Auschwitz Peace March and the Globalization of the Moral Witness," *Dapim—Studies on the Holocaust*, December 2, 2013.
5. "Interview with Kuwahara Hideki," *Hiroshima*, July 2, 2010, quoted in Ran Zwigenberg, *Hiroshima: The Origins of Global Memory Culture* (Cambridge: Cambridge University Press, 2014), 179. The "Kuwahara Hideki" appearing in Zwigenberg's book is actually 桑原英昭, whose name is transcribed as "Hideaki." Sawada Katsumi, who translated the book into Japanese, corrected this. See 林志弦,『犠牲者意識ナショナリズム——国境を超える「記憶」の戦争』[Victimhood nationalism] 澤田克己 (翻訳) (東京:東洋經濟新聞社, 2022), 411.
6. "Jan Frankowski," in *Słownik biograficzny katolicyzmu społecznego w Polsce* T. 1, A–J (Lublin: Towarzystwo Naukowe Katolickiego Uniwersytetu Lubelskiego, 1994).
7. Ariel Orzełek, "U genezy Chrześcijańskiego Stowarzyszenia Społecznego. Powstanie i rozpad pierwszego zespołu redakcyjnego tygodnika 'Za i Przeciw,'" *Kwartalnik Historyczny* 126, no. 4 (2019): 723, 727–28, 730.
8. Zwigenberg, *Hiroshima*, 180–81. Fifty-seven years after the massacre, the Osaka Peace Museum held a photo and data exhibition titled "Katyn Forest Incident—the Whereabouts of 22,000 Polish Officers" from March 1 to May 12, 2019. Sponsored by the Polish Embassy in Japan, the special exhibition featured images of Nazi German excavations and artifacts from the site of the massacre at the Katyn Forest provided by

the Western Institute (Instytut Zachodni) in Poznań, and Polish-language articles published in Kraków during the Nazi occupation. The exhibition was structured to make the audience walk through the memorial garden dedicated to the 12,620 deaths and 2,173 missing persons in the aftermath of the U.S. air raids on Osaka to enter the exhibition gallery, seamlessly overlapping the memories of the civilian victims of the Osaka air raids and Polish military officers killed in the Katyn Forest by the Soviet secret police. I happened to see this exhibition while visiting Osaka for a lecture on April 19, 2019. To me, the time, place, and materials on view felt disorganized and without historical context. I'm still looking for the answer to the questions I had at the exhibition: Why at that exact time? Why at that exact place? One possible, broad answer may be that Japan and Poland have been emotionally friendly beyond international diplomacy thanks to their common enemy, Russia, since the Russo-Japanese War.

9. Zwigenberg, *Hiroshima*, 189–94.
10. John W. Dower, *War Without Mercy: Race and Power in the Pacific War* (New York: Pantheon Books, 1986), 296–97.
11. On the U.S. military's white supremacist propaganda and military strategy on the Pacific front, see Dower, 9, 14, 7, 38, 65, and passim.
12. Buruma, 『근대일본』 [Modern Japan], 54–55.
13. Stefan Tanaka, *Japan's Orient: Rendering Pasts Into History* (Berkeley: University of California Press, 1993), 4–60.
14. Jordan Sand, "Subaltern Imperialists: The New Historiography of the Japanese Empire," *Past and Present*, no. 225 (2014): 275.
15. Lisa Yoneyama, *Hiroshima Traces: Time, Space, and the Dialectics of Memory* (Berkeley: University of California Press, 1999), 152–66.
16. Ian Buruma, *The Wages of Guilt: Memories of War in Germany and Japan* (New York: NRB, 2015), 92.
17. Takahashi Tetsuya, "The Emperor Showa Standing at Ground Zero: On the (Re-) configuration of a National 'Memory' of the Japanese People," *Japan Forum* 15, no. 1 (2003): 6.
18. Sadako Kurihara, "The Literature of Auschwitz and Hiroshima," *Holocaust and Genocide Studies* 7, no. 1 (1993): 86–87.
19. Fujimoto Hiroshi, "Towards Reconciliation, Harmonious Coexistence and Peace: The Madison Quakers, Inc. Projects and the Hibakusha's Visit to My Lai in March 2008," *Nanzan Review of American Studies* 37 (2015): 14, 15, 20; "My Lai Survivors Gather to Pray for Victims, Peace 40 Years After Massacre," AP, March 16, 2008, http://www.foxnews.com/story/2008/03/16/my-lai-survivors-gather-to-pray-for-victims-peace-40-years-after-massacre.html; MQI Vietnam, *Winds of Peace*, nos. 1–12 (December 1999–October 2005), http://www.mqivietnam.org/archives.
20. Michael C. Steinlauf, *Bondage to the Dead: Poland and the Memory of the Holocaust* (Syracuse, N.Y.: Syracuse University Press, 1997), 63–74.
21. Idith Zertal, *From Catastrophe to Power: Holocaust Survivors and the Emergence of Israel* (Berkeley: University of California Press, 1998), 217, 221.

22. Dan Diner, "Cumulative Contingency: Historicizing Legitimacy in Israeli Discourse," *History and Memory*, Special Issue: *Israel Historiography Revisited*, 7, no. 1 (1995): 153, 155, 157.
23. Peter Novick, *The Holocaust and Collective Memory* (London: Bloomsbury, 2001), 91, 98, 116, 121, and passim.
24. Michael C. Steinlauf, "Teaching About the Holocaust in Poland," in *Contested Memories: Poles and Jews During the Holocaust and Its Aftermath*, ed. Joshua D. Zimmerman (New Brunswick, N.J.: Rutgers University Press, 2003), 264.
25. Steinlauf, 265.
26. Barbara Engelking, *Holocaust and Memory* (London: Leicester University Press, 2001), 282–83. When I visited Auschwitz for the first time in January 1991, I was bewildered to spot antisemitic graffiti in the neighborhood in Oświęcim, a vivid memory that still haunts me.
27. Lawrence Weinbaum, *The Struggle for Memory in Poland: Auschwitz, Jedwabne and Beyond* (Jerusalem: Institute of the World Jewish Congress, 2011), 15.
28. Weinbaum, 17. The official stance of the Polish authorities was that two million of the four million victims of Auschwitz were Jewish, and one million were Polish. After the fall of the communist regime, the statistics of the dead changed to 1.1 million, 90 percent of whom were recognized as Jews.
29. In Poland's Second Republic during the interwar period, Jewish citizens' civil rights were recognized, but the Sabbath tradition still made it difficult for them to get jobs in the government or large corporations. To be faithful to the Jewish tradition, they had no choice but to work at smaller factories for Jewish employers or as self-employed workers.
30. Iwona Irwin-Zarecka, "Poland After the Holocaust," in *Remembering for the Future: Working Papers and Addenda*, ed. Yehuda Bauer et al. (New York: Pergamon Press, 1989), 147.
31. Jie-Hyun Lim, "The Nationalist Message in Socialist Code: On Court Historiography in People's Poland and North Korea," in *Making Sense of Global History: The 19th International Congress of Historical Sciences Commemorative Volume*, ed. S. Sogner (Oslo: Universitetsforlaget, 2001), 373–80.
32. Steinlauf, "Teaching About the Holocaust in Poland," 266.
33. Geneviève Zubrzycki, *The Crosses of Auschwitz: Nationalism and Religion in Post-Communist Poland* (Chicago: University of Chicago Press, 2006), 4–5.
34. Peter Steinfels, "Move by Vatican Applauded in U.S.," *New York Times*, September 20, 1989.
35. Zubrzycki, *Crosses of Auschwitz*, 5.
36. Zubrzycki, 112.
37. "Auschwitz-Birkenau: Auschwitz Convent," *Jewish Virtual Library*, https://www.jewishvirtuallibrary.org/auschwitz-convent; "A Polish Paper Accuses Jews from Bronx in Nuns' Attack," Reuters, July 16, 1989.

38. John Tagliabue, "Strife Returns to a Convent at Auschwitz," *New York Times*, July 27, 1989.
39. John Tagliabue, "Cardinal in the Auschwitz Whirlwind," *New York Times*, September 5, 1989.
40. Peter Steinfels, "Polish Cardinal Acknowledges Distress He Caused in 1989 Homily," *New York Times*, September 21, 1991.
41. John Tagliabue, "Polish Prelate Assails Protests by Jews at Auschwitz Convent," *New York Times*, August 11, 1989.
42. The cross was already standing in front of the convent when Rabbi Abraham Weiss and others staged a protest at the convent in summer 1989. Shortly after the incident, Rabbi Weiss argued in the *New York Times* that the cross should be removed along with the convent. Avraham Weiss, Opinion: "We Did Not Go to Auschwitz to Be Beaten," *New York Times*, September 12, 1989.
43. The march along the three-kilometer path from Auschwitz to Birkenau was designated as an annual educational program for participants from around the world "to study the history of the Holocaust and to examine the roots of prejudice, intolerance and hatred." International March of the Living, https://www.motl.org/about/, accessed December 12, 2021.
44. Zubrzycki, *Crosses of Auschwitz*, 8–9.
45. Roger Cohen, "Poles and Jews Feud About Crosses at Auschwitz," *New York Times*, December 20, 1998; "Świtoń Kazimierz. Konflikt na żwirowisku," *Gazeta Wyborcza*, July 28, 1998, https://wyborcza.pl/7,75248,139041.html.
46. Zubrzycki, *Crosses of Auschwitz*, 9–10.
47. Chapter 8 of this book discusses Maksymillian Kolbe in more detail.
48. Janine P. Holc, "The Remembered One: Memory Activism and the Construction of Edith Stein's Jewishness in Post-Communist Wrocław," *Shofar: An Interdisciplinary Journal of Jewish Studies* 29, no. 4 (2011): 78, 91.
49. "Rabbis Call for Removal of Church at Auschwitz," Reuters, January 26, 2020, https://www.haaretz.com/world-news/wires/1.8446689å.
50. Novick, *Holocaust and Collective Memory*, 117.
51. Daniel Levy and Natan Sznaider, *The Holocaust and Memory in the Global Age* (Philadelphia: Temple University Press, 2006), 60–63.
52. Alvin H. Rosenfeld, "Popularization and Memory: The Case of Anne Frank," in *Lessons and Legacies: The Meaning of the Holocaust in a Changing World*, ed. Peter Hayes (Evanston, Ill: Northwestern University Press, 1991), 265; Lawrence L. Langer, "The Uses—and Misuses—of a Young Girl's Diary: 'If Anne Frank Could Return from Among the Murdered, She Would Be Appalled,'" in *Anne Frank: Reflection on Her Life and Legacy*, ed. Hyman Aaron Enzer and Sandra Solotaroff-Enzer (Urbana: University of Illinois Press, 2000).
53. My interview with Akio Yoshida, deputy director of the Fukuyama Holocaust Education Center, August 7, 2012. According to him, the founder, Otsuka Makoto, opened the memorial hall after meeting Otto Frank by chance during a pilgrimage to the Holy Land in Jerusalem and through Frank's donations of relics and various materials. It

is difficult to understand from the perspective of Western Christianity and Judaism that a Christian Protestant pastor would find and run a memorial hall for Jews.
54. "Never Again" is translated as "Do Not Forget" in Japanese.
55. Sadako Sasaki, an atomic bomb victim in Hiroshima, folded a thousand paper cranes in her bed before dying of leukemia in 1955 at the age of eleven. The paper cranes later became a symbol of antiwar peace in honor of innocent child victims. Since then, Anne Frank and Sasaki Sadako have often appeared next to each other in Japan's transnational memory discourse on children's war victims. Eric Margolis, "Anne Frank and Sadako Sasaki: Two Girls That Symbolize the Horrors of War," *Japan Times*, December 28, 2020, https://www.japantimes.co.jp/community/2020/12/28/issues/2020-in-review-world-war-ii-75th-anniversary-anne-frank-sadako-sasaki/.
56. 「ホロコースト記念館」 [Holocaust memorial], http://www.hecjpn.org/index.html.
57. Julian Ryall, "Japanese Retain a Fascination with Anne Frank," *Deutsche Welle*, March 2, 2015, https://www.dw.com/en/japanese-retain-fascination-with-anne-frank/a-18284457.
58. "Why Are the Japanese So Fascinated with Anne Frank?" *Haaretz*, January 22, 2014, https://www.haaretz.com/jewish/anne-frank-the-japanese-anime-1.5314070. A submission in response to this article, by a Japanese reader named Kurokawa, claims that Israelis might be oblivious to the fact that the Japanese Army saved twenty thousand Jews (presumably in Shanghai) during World War II. In contrast, Korean visitors' general response is nonhistorical. According to Deputy Director Yoshida Akio, most of the Korean group visitors to the center were college students studying architecture, and their attention was primarily focused on the architecture of the building rather than the contents of the exhibition.
59. 金井元貴, "永遠のロングセラーはどう生まれたか。みすず書房と『夜と霧』の60年" [Sixty years of *Man's Search for Meaning*], 新刊 JP, December 30, 2017, https://www.sinkan.jp/news/8255?page=1.
60. V. E. フランクル著,『夜と霧――ドイツ強制収容所の体験記録』 [*Man's Search for Meaning*] (霜山德爾訳東京: みすず書房, 1956), 1.
61. 林房雄,『大東亞戰爭肯定論』 [Affirming the Great East Asian War] (東京: 中央公論新社, 2014), 7, 19, 149, 228.
62. Pankaj Mishra,『제국의 폐허에서: 저항과 재건의 아시아 근대사』 [In the ruins of the empire: The modern history of Asia in resistance and restoration], 이재만 옮김, (서울: 책과 함께, 2013), 11–20.
63. 山室信一『キメラ―満州国の肖像』 [Chimera—a portrait of Manchukuo] (東京:中公新書, 2004), 47–51.
64. 하영준, "일본제국과 범아프리카주의의 '트랜스-퍼시픽 커넥션': W. E. B. 듀보이스와 C. L. R. 제임스의 동아시아 담론을 중심으로" [The transpacific connection between the Japanese empire and pan-Africanism], *Homo Migrans* 18 (2018): 166–69.
65. Yuichiro Onishi, "The New Negro of the Pacific: How African Americans Forged Cross-Racial Solidarity with Japan, 1917–1922," *Journal of African American History* 92, no. 2 (2007): 199–200.

66. "『안네의 일기』 어린이 독후감 대회 참여작" (The participating essays in the children's *The Diary of a Young Girl* review contest), http://www.yes24.com/Product/Goods/1418754. The part about the biological experiment on "Koreans as logs" seems to indicate that the writer mistakenly remembered the word "Maruta" of Unit 731 as a "log." A mistake like this is frequently possible considering that an elementary school student wrote it. The point is that almost all book reports equate Japanese colonial rule with Anne Frank's Holocaust experience.

67. "안네의 일기" [*The Diary of a Young Girl*], http://www.yes24.com/campaign/KidsImpression/viewkids.aspx?qChild_Mem_Id=outself&qChild_Mem_Nm=%bd%c5%bc%d2%c1%f8&qReport_seq_no=385790.

68. "안네의 일기 줄거리 독후감" [A review of *The Diary of a Young Girl*], https://m.blog.naver.com/PostView.nhn?blogId=sbbamtol&logNo=220064081996&proxyReferer=https:%2F%2Fwww.google.com%2F; "안네의 일기" [*The Diary of a Young Girl*], https://bookbugs.tistory.com/entry/%EC%95%88%EB%84%A4%EC%9D%98-%EC%9D%BC%EA%B8%B0-%EC%95%88%EB%84%A4-%ED%94%84%EB%9E%91%ED%81%AC-%EC%A0%80; "안네의 일기" [*The Diary of a Young Girl*], http://joungul.co.kr/after/after1/%EB%8F%85%ED%9B%84%EA%B0%90_52984.asp.

69. "猶太共和國" [The republic of Jews], 『朝鮮日報』, October 22, 1928; "回回教徒와 猶太教徒의 軋轢" [The conflict between Islam and Judaism], 『東亞日報』, April 24, 1936; "팔레스타인에서 民族的鬪爭激化" [The international struggle elevates in Palestine], 『朝鮮日報』, April 24, 1936; "世界史에 나타난 猶太係의 偉人" [The great Jews in world history], 『東亞日報』, July 9, 1934.

70. For French Jews' response to the Six-Day War, see Joan B. Wolf, "Anne Frank Is Dead, Long Live Anne Frank: The Six-Day War and the Holocaust in French Public Discourse," *History and Memory* 11, no. 1 (1999): 106.

71. "朴議長, 晴耕雨讀을 남기고 . . ." [Chairman Park's diligence and studiousness], 『京鄕新聞』, February 10, 1962; "萬坪開墾한 農事革命" [The agricultural revolution reclaims ten acres], 『京鄕新聞』, February 10, 1962; "朴正熙 議長 눈감고 祈禱" [Chairman Park Chung-hee prays with his eyes closed], 『東亞日報』, February 10, 1962; "農村을 위한 朴議長의 지시를 보고 . . ." [Upon reading Chairman Park's instructions for the farmlands], 『京鄕新聞』, February 11, 1962.

72. "이스라엘에서 千餘佛 再建運動위해 寄贈" [Israel donates over a thousand USD to the land reclamation project], 『京鄕新聞』, December 2, 1963.

73. "朴大統領 가나안 農軍修了式에 農畜舍建立費 등 보내" [President Park endows the Canaan Farmhand School with the funds to be used toward the construction of sheds and other facilities], 『東亞日報』, November 17, 1973.

74. "Customer reviews" for *So Far From the Bamboo Grove*, filtered by "all critical reviews," Amazon.com, accessed January 2, 2023, https://www.amazon.com/Bamboo-Grove-Yoko-Kawashima-Watkins/product-reviews/0688131158/ref=cm_cr_arp_d_viewpnt_rgt?ie=UTF8&reviewerType=all_reviews&filterByStar=critical&pageNumber=1.

75. KACE, "Compilation of Korean News Articles on Comfort Women Survivors and Holocaust Survivors' Meetings," December 21, 2011, http://kace.org/2011/12/21

/compilation-of-news-articles-on-comfort-women-survivors-and-holocaust-survivors%27-meeting/.

76. 권미강, "4.3항쟁 담은 이산하 시인 시집 <한라산> 복간" [*Hallasan*, a poetry collection about the Jeju Uprising by Yi Sanha, is republished], *Ohmynews*, April 2, 2018, http://www.ohmynews.com/NWS_Web/View/at_pg.aspx?CNTN_CD=A0002419620.
77. It is also suggestive that Jung Chan inserted patriotic songs from the nineteenth-century Polish national movement in his novel and seemed to prefer Górecki, with a strong "national music" flavor, over Schoenberg's "A Survivor from Warsaw," a modern musical take on the Holocaust.
78. 정찬, 『슬픔의 노래』 [The Song of Sorrow] (서울: 조선일보사, 1995).
79. "감옥의 문은 밖에서 열어야 . . . 북한-홀로코스트 사진전 개최" [The prison gate opens from the outside—an exhibition of photographs from North Korea and the Holocaust], *World News*, April 13, 2021, https://www.thewordnews.co.kr/mobile/article.html?no=24365; 정상윤, "北인권 실상 담은 '북한-홀로코스트 사진전시회' 개막" [The North Korea-Holocaust photo exhibition opens to disclose the current state of human rights in North Korea], *NewDaily*, last modified April 13, 2021, https://www.newdaily.co.kr/site/data/html/2021/04/13/2021041300237.html.
80. Alon Confino, "The Holocaust as a Symbolic Manual," in *Marking Evil: Holocaust Memory in the Global Age*, ed. Amos Goldberg and Haim Hazan (New York: Berghahn Books, 2015), 56.
81. Amos Goldberg, "Ethics, Identity, and Anfifundamental Fundamentalism," in *Marking Evil*, 21; Haim Hazan, "Globalization Versus Holocaust," in *Marking Evil*, 31.

6. DEHISTORICIZATION

1. Hannah Arendt, "The Aftermath of Nazi Rule," *Commentary* (October 1950): 342. Because Arendt speaks only of the U.S., UK, and French occupation and not the Soviet-occupied regions, "Germany" in this report seems to refer to West Germany.
2. Arendt, 342–43.
3. Arendt, 345, 347–349, 344.
4. Arendt, 343–44. The concept of "redemptive suffering" was also adopted by the atomic bombing victims in Hiroshima and Nagasaki as a moral/religious apparatus to assuage their suffering. I will explain this in detail in chapter 8.
5. Tony Judt, *Postwar: A History of Europe Since 1945* (New York: Penguin Press, 2005), 58–59.
6. Maja Zehfuss, *Wounds of Memory: The Politics of War in Germany* (Cambridge: Cambridge University Press, 2007), 92–93.
7. Peter Schneider, "Sins of Grandfathers," *New York Times*, December 3, 1995.
8. It is intriguing that Germans began to celebrate the *Volkstrauertag*, the People's Mourning Day, remembering the war dead and victims of violent oppression in 1950. It has its origin in commemorating the war dead after the World War II. In 1934 Nazis replaced the *Volkstrauertag* with *Heldengedenktag* (Heroes Remembrance Day),

which was replaced again by *Volkstrauertag* in 1950. Its commemoration day was changed to the second Sunday before the Advent, to distinguish it from the Nazis' celebration.
9. Ian Buruma, *Year Zero: A History of 1945* (New York: Penguin Press, 2013), 280.
10. Buruma, 289.
11. Katharina von Ankum, "Victims, Memory, History: Antifascism, and the Question of National Identity in East German Narratives After 1990," *History and Memory* 7, no. 2 (1995): 42, 45.
12. Robert G. Moeller, *War Stories: The Search for a Usable Past in the Federal Republic of Germany* (Berkeley: University of California Press, 2001), 26–27. When Chancellor Adenauer, while the negotiation on compensation was still going on, leaked to Jewish newspapers that Germany was considering two million in state compensation for Israel, Ben-Gurion was so furious that he proposed declaring war on West Germany at a ministerial meeting. Despite that in the international Cold War system Israel had no option but to side with the Western bloc, and that it needed strong ties not only with the United States and the United Kingdom but also with Germany and France to be accepted by the Western bloc, Ben-Gurion's proposal to declare war on West Germany attested to how furious and discouraged he was. Tom Segev, *The Seventh Million: The Israelis and the Holocaust*, trans. Haim Watzman (New York: An Owl Book, 2000), 191, 200–201.
13. Moeller, *War Stories*, 27. One may recall from the West German Communist Party's insistence against reparations for Israel and Jews the rigidity of the "social fascism" theory of the 1930s that equated social democracy with fascism.
14. Jeffrey Herf, *Divided Memory: The Nazi Past in the Two Germanys* (Cambridge, Mass.: Harvard University Press, 1997), 33–36.
15. Bill Niven, "Introduction: German Victimhood at the Turn of the Millenium," in *Germans as Victims*, ed. Bill Niven (Basingstoke, UK: Palgrave/Macmillan, 2006), 2.
16. Herf, *Divided Memory*, 109–13.
17. Walter Ulbricht, "Warum Nationale Front des demokratischen Deutschlands?," in *Zur Geschichte des Deutschen Arbeiterbewegung: Aus Reden und Aufsätzen*, vol. 3 (Berlin: Dietz Verlag, 1954), 491. Cited in Herf, *Divided Memory*, 110.
18. Herf, *Divided Memory*, 109–12.
19. A monument in Meissen depicting communist political prisoners supporting a Jewish prisoner on the verge of collapsing in a concentration camp represents the image of the East German communist as a savior of Jews.
20. Sarah Farmer, "Symbols That Face Two Ways: Commemorating the Victims of Nazism and Stalinism at Buchenwald and Sachsenhausen," *Representations*, no. 49, Special Issue: *Identifying Histories: Eastern Europe Before and After 1989* (Winter 1995): 113.
21. Takashi Fujitani, Geoffrey M. White, and Lisa Yoneyama, "Introduction," in *Perilous Memories: The Asia-Pacific War(s)*, ed. T. Fujitani et al. (Durham, N.C.: Duke University Press, 2001), 7.

22. Carol Gluck, "Operations of Memory: Comfort Women and the World," in *Ruptured Histories: War, Memory and the Post-Cold War in Asia*, ed. Shelia Miyoshi Jager and Rana Mitter (Cambridge: Harvard University Press, 2007), 51.
23. 林房雄,『大東亞戰爭肯定論』, 7, 19, 149; Tessa Morris-Suzuki,『일본의 아이덴티티를 묻는다』[Asking Japan's identity] 박광현 옮김 (서울: 산처럼, 2002), 55–56.
24. John W. Dower, "'An Aptitude for Being Unloved': War and Memory in Japan," in *Crimes of War: Guilt and Denial in the Twentieth Century*, ed. Omer Bartov, Atina Grossmann, and Mary Nolan (New York: New Press, 2002), 219.
25. Ian Buruma, *The Wages of Guilt: Memories of War in Germany and Japan* (New York: New York Review of Books, 2015), 224.
26. Roger B. Jeans, "Victims or Victimizers? Museums, Textbooks, and the War Debate in Contemporary Japan," *Journal of Military History* 69, no. 1 (2005): 157–59.
27. Dower, "'An Aptitude for Being Unloved,'" 230.
28. James J. Orr, *The Victim as Hero: Ideologies of Peace and National Identity in Postwar Japan* (Honolulu: University of Hawaii Press, 2001), 2–3, 7.
29. 小熊英二,『民主と愛国』, 43–50, 67–70.
30. John Dower, "The Bombed: Hiroshima and Nagasaki in Japanese Memory," *Diplomatic History* 19, no. 2 (1995): 278–79.
31. 親泊朝省,「草芥の文 [Writing by a grassroot], cited in 『民主と愛国』, 155.
32. 大沼保昭,『東京裁判から戦後責任の思想へ』(From the Tokyo trial to the idea of postwar responsibility] (東京: 有信堂, 1985), 86; 櫻井均,『テレビは戦争をどう描いてきたか: 映像と記憶のアーカイブス』[How television has described the war: The archive of images and memories] (東京: 岩波書店, 2005).
33. Buruma, *The Wages of Guilt*, 199. In an interview conducted in October 1986, Fujio compared the Nanjing Massacre with the atomic bombings of Hiroshima/Nagasaki and argued that it was evident which of the two was on a larger scale and more intentional. He was later dismissed for this interview.
34. David John Lu and Howard John Waitzkin, *Agony of Choice: Matsuoka Yōsuke and the Rise and Fall of the Japanese Empire, 1880–1946* (Lanham, Md.: Lexington Books, 2002), 85. For the entire speech, see「國際聯盟總會に於ける松岡代表の演説」データベース『世界と日本』[World and Japan] 政策研究大学院大学・東京大学東洋文化研究所, https://worldjpn.grips.ac.jp/documents/.
35. Roy Tomizawa, "The Triumphant Tragedy of Marathoner Kokichi Tsuburaya, Part 1: The Marathon Sprint That Broke the Hearts of the Japanese," *The Olympians*, May 3, 2017, https://theolympians.co/2017/05/03/the-triumphant-tragedy-of-marathoner-kokichi-tsuburaya-part-1-the-marathon-sprint-that-broke-the-hearts-of-the-japanese/.
36. Roy Tomizawa, "The Triumphant Tragedy of Marathoner Kokichi Tsuburaya, Part 4: A Suicide Note That Captures an Essence of the Japanese, and Endures as Literature," *The Olympians*, May 10, 2017, https://theolympians.co/2017/05/10/11080/.
37. 이타가키 류타, "동아시아 기억의 장소로서의 역도산" [Rikidōzan as an East Asian memory space],『역사비평』 95호 (2011): 127–60.

38. The post-3/11 discourse, which overlays the aftermath of the Great East Japan Earthquake, tsunami, and Fukushima nuclear accident on March 11, 2011, with the postwar conditions after August 15, 1945, can be understood similarly. 심정명, "3·11과 전후의 끝: 무의미한 죽음과 애도의 문제" "March 11 and the end of the postwar: The problem of mourning and meaningless death," 조관자 엮음, 『탈전후 일본의 사상과 감성』 [The post-postwar Japanese thought and sensibilities] (서울: 박문사, 2017), 64–65.
39. Dorothee Wierling. "Krieg im Nachkrieg: Zur oeffentlichen und privaten Präsenz des Krieges in der SBZ und frühen DDR," in *Der Zweite Weltkrieg in Europa. Erfahrung und Erinnerung*, ed. Jörg Echternkamp and Stefan Martens (Paderborn, Ger.: Schöningh, 2007), 237–51.
40. Max Seydewitz, *Die unbesiegbare Stadt. Zerstung und Wiederaufbau von Dresden* (Berlin: Kongress Verlag, 1956), 41, 183, 214–15, cited in Bas von Benda-Beckmann, *A German Catastrophe? German Historians and the Allied Bombings, 1945–2010* (Amsterdam: Amsterdam University Press, 2010), 124–25.
41. von Benda-Beckmann, 159–60.
42. von Benda-Beckmann, 132. von Benda-Beckmann's argument is based on Walter Weidauer's book *Inferno Dresden* (1965). However, as mentioned in chapter 5, then Dresden mayor Hans Bonn sent a letter in June 1961 to the mayor of Hiroshima to propose a sisterhood between Dresden and Hiroshima and join the "fight to protect peace against militarism emerging across East-West boundaries." In East Germany's official memory culture, attempts to juxtapose Dresden and Hiroshima had already begun by the early 1960s, and it seems the threat of nuclear war through the Cuban missile crisis and other incidents had only intensified the bond.
43. Hofmann, "Als Dresden in Trümmer sank," cited in von Benda-Beckmann, *A German Catastrophe?*, 142.
44. von Benda-Beckmann, 146.
45. von Benda-Beckmann, 144–51.
46. W. G. Sebald, 『공중전과 문학』 [On the natural history of destruction] 이경진 옮김 (서울: 문학동네, 2013), 41.
47. Sebald, 112, 126–27, 134.
48. Jörg Friedrich, *The Fire: The Bombing of Germany 1940–1945* (New York: Columbia University Press, 2006), 59.
49. Tadeusz Olejnek, *Wieluń. Polska Guernika* (Wieluń: BWTN, 2004).
50. Anthony Beevor, *The Second World War* (New York: Little, Brown, 2012), 337.
51. Friedrich, *The Fire*, 91.
52. Zehfuss, *Wounds of Memory*, 94.
53. Buruma, *The Wages of Guilt*, 92–98.
54. Sakiko Masuda, "'Memory Keeper' Yumie Hirano to Visit Poland in May, Convey Survivors' Experiences of Atomic Bombing," *Chugoku Shimbun*, April 18, 2016, http://www.hiroshimapeacemedia.jp/?p=59331.
55. Philip A. Seaton, *Japan's Contested War Memories: The Memory Rifts in Historical Consciousness of World War II* (London: Routledge, 2007), 135.
56. Seaton, 82.

57. Dower, "'An Aptitude for Being Unloved,'" 219, 226.
58. Buruma, *The Wages of Guilt*, 98.
59. Hiroshima Peace Memorial Museum, "Message from the Hiroshima Peace Memorial Museum," https://hpmmuseum.jp/modules/exhibition/index.php?action=CornerView&corner_id=20&lang=eng.
60. Hiroshima Peace Memorial Museum, "Permanent Exhibitions," https://hpmmuseum.jp/modules/exhibition/index.php?action=FacilityView&facility_id=4&lang=eng.
61. Noma Field, "War and Apology: Japan, Asia, the Fiftieth, and After," *Positions* 5, no. 1 (1997).
62. 藤原帰一,『戦争を記憶する：広島・ホロコーストと現在』[Remembering war: Hiroshima, Holocaust, and the present] (東京：講談社現代新書、2001), 105–7.
63. 藤原帰一, 124.
64. John W. Dower, "Triumphal and Tragic Narratives of the War in Asia," *Journal of American History* 82, no. 3 (1995): 1125. Harold Agnew, who flew as a scientific observer on the Hiroshima bombing mission on August 6, 1945, disappointed the Japanese victims on the sixtieth anniversary of the war by flatly refusing to apologize and insisting that he, too, had lost many friends in the war that began with the Japanese attack on Pearl Harbor. "I do not apologize. Those [the Japanese leadership] are the people who should apologize," he said to the Japanese victims who demanded an apology from him. More interesting, however, are the 13,220 comments left by Korean readers under the news article covering Agnew's refusal to apologize. Most of them condemn Japan's posing as a victim and agree that the United States was right to refuse to apologize for the use of the atomic bombs. "히로시마 원폭피해자들에게 돌직구 날리는 원폭 개발자" [The physicist who helped develop the A-bomb slams the Hiroshima victims with facts],『생생일본뉴스』, August 6, 2020, https://youtu.be/ufZym-LkkBw.
65. Dower, "'An Aptitude for Being Unloved,'" 230.
66. 「原爆展の米上院決議に憤り込め60行の詩 詩人・栗原貞子さん／広島」[A poet angry at U.S. Senate's resolution against the *Enola Gay* exhibition],『朝日新聞』, November 19, 1994.
67. Hiroshima Peace Memorial Museum, "Construction of Peace Memorial Park," https://hpmmuseum.jp/modules/exhibition/index.php?action=ItemView&item_id=131&lang=eng.
68. Lisa Yoneyama, *Hiroshima Traces: Time, Space, and the Dialectics of Memory* (Berkeley: University of California Press, 1999), 1–3.
69. Yoneyama, 25. See also 유경헌, "日「韓國文化協」회장 小見山씨 韓・日「정신적화해」에 노력" [Komiyama's efforts for the Korean-Japanese spiritual reconciliation],『동아일보』, November 10, 1977.
70. 吉田敏浩,『反空爆思想』[Anti-air bombing thought] (東京：日本放送出版協会、2006), 151, 164, 165.
71. Zygmunt Bauman, *Modernity and the Holocaust* (Ithaca, N.Y.: Cornell University Press, 2000), 24.
72. Seaton, *Japan's Contested War Memories*, 83.
73. 「サダコの折り鶴寄贈／ＮＹ、テロ追悼施設に」[Sadako's paper cranes to the memorial hall of the 9.11 terror], 共同通信, September 13, 2007.

74. For records of such "dark tourism," see these blog entries (in Korean): 재하, "바다와 함께한 서일본 일주 (3일차)—독가스섬 오쿠노시마에 남겨진 전흔 [West Japan trip along the sea: The scars of war in Okunoshima, the 'Poison Gas Island'"], last modified June 10, 2019, https://blog.naver.com/jcjw1234/221558239896; 열씨미, "히로시마 여행-오쿠노시마 (토끼섬, 독가스섬)" [Hiroshima trip—Okunoshima], last modified May 21, 2019, https://blog.naver.com/jbm993/221543384914. On the other hand, many travelogues write only about the beautiful sunset and cute bunnies on Okunoshima, attesting to the Poison Gas Museum's lack of presence and impact. 기기, "[일본] 히로시마 토끼섬 오쿠노시마 (大久野島)" [Japan's Bunny Island in Hiroshima], last modified August 25, 2019, https://blog.naver.com/xjvmgksrldnj/221627795080
75. Niven, "Introduction: German Victimhood," 15.
76. On collective memory in postwar Poland, see Karolina Wigura, *Wina Narodów: Przebaczenie jako strategia prowadzenia polityki* (Gdansk: Scholar, 2011); Joanna Wawrzyniak, *Veterans, Victims and Memory* (Frankfurt am Main: Peter Lang, 2015); Małgorzata Pakier and Joanna Wawrzyniak, eds., *Memory and Change in Europe: Eastern Perspectives* (New York: Berghahn, 2016), part 4; Janine Holc, *The Politics of Trauma and Memory Activism: Polish-Jewish Relations Today* (London: Palgrave Macmillan, 2018); Zusanna Bogumił and Małgorzata Głowacka-Grajper, *Milieux de mémoire in Late Modernity* (Frankfurt am Main: Peter Lang, 2019).
77. The woeful scale and depth of violence may explain why it is so difficult nowadays to find Eastern European victims' memoirs like *A Woman in Berlin* (*Eine Frau in Berlin*), 익명의 여인, 『베를린의 한 여인』, 염정용 옮김 (서울: 해토, 2004).
78. German historicism is also largely responsible for this. Its traditional view of history recognized France as an equal of Germany since the nineteenth century yet maintained the orientalist attitude toward Poland. See also Jan M. Piskorski, ed., *Historiographical Approaches to Medieval Colonization of East Central Europe* (New York: Columbia University Press, 2002).
79. Bill Niven ed., *Germans as Victims* (Basingstoke, UK: Palgrave Macmillan, 2006); Moeller, *War Stories*; and Herf, *Divided Memory*.
80. Buruma, *Year Zero*, 94–95, 157. The history of this camp is much more complicated. A German POW camp from 1870, it was used to imprison Soviet and Polish soldiers, especially the resistance fighters of the Warsaw ghetto uprising in 1943, during World War II and then turned into a German internment camp from summer 1945 to fall 1946. The camp became the center of controversy in the 1990s when the ethnic Germans living in Śląsk, Poland, cited it as a symbol of Polish crime against Germans. Maren Roeger, "News Media and Historical Remembrance: Reporting on the Expulsion of Germans in Polish and German Magazines," in *Mediation, Remediation, and the Dynamics of Cultural Memory*, ed. Astrid Erll and Ann Rigney (Berlin: Walter de Gruyter, 2009), 194–96.
81. Niven, "Introduction: German Victimhood," 18.
82. Moeller, *War Stories*, 32–35; Norbert F. Pötzl, "Versöhnen oder Verhöhnen: Dauerstreit um die Stiftung 'Flucht, Vertreibung, Versöhnung,'" in *Die Deutschen im Osten*

Europas: Eroberer, Siedler, Vertriebene, ed. Annette Grossbongardt et al. (Munich: Deutsche Verlags-Anstalt, 2011), 240–24.

83. Aleida Assmann, "On the (IN)Compatability and Suffering in German Memory," *German Life and Letters* 59, no. 2 (2006): 194.
84. 若槻泰雄,『戦後引揚げの記録』[Records of the postwar *hikiage*] (東京: 時事通信社, 1991), 252–53.
85. 山田陽子,『図説満州:日本人の足跡をたどる』[Illustrated trajectories of the Japanese in Manchuria] (東京: 梅田出版, 2011), 80–98.
86. Lori Watt, *When Empire Comes Home: Repatriation and Reintegration in Postwar Japan* (Cambridge, Mass: Harvard University Press, 2009), 133.
87. Günter Grass,『게걸음으로』[Crabwalk] 장희창 역 (서울: 민음사, 2015).
88. Frank Biess, "Between Amnesty and Anti-communism: The West German Kameradenschinder Trials, 1948–1960," in *Crimes of War: Guilt and Denial in the Twentieth Century*, ed. Omer Bartov, Atina Grossmann, and Mary Nolan (New York: New Press, 2002), 141–46, 149–52; Frank Biess, *Homecomings: Returning POWs and the Legacies of Defeat in Postwar Germany* (Princeton, N.J.: Princeton University Press, 2006), 154–66.
89. Christopher Browning,『아주 평범한 사람들: 101예비경찰대대와 유대인 학살』[Ordinary men: Reserve Police Battalion 101 and the final solution in Poland], 이진모 옮김 (서울: 책과 함께, 2010), 107, 116.
90. 米原万里,『魔女の1ダース—正義と常識に冷や水を浴びせる13章』[A dozen pencils at witch] (東京: 新潮文庫, 2000), 106–9.
91. 米原万里,『打ちのめされるようなすごい本』[A great book beating you] (東京: 文藝春秋, 2006), 120.
92. Buruma, *Year Zero*, 140; 逆井聡人,『〈焼跡〉戦後空間論』[Postwar space after the ashes] (東京: 青弓社, 2018), 25, 32, 54–55.
93. Watt, *When Empire Comes Home*, 128–29, 136–37.
94. Michael Burleigh, *The Third Reich: A New History* (New York: Hill and Wang, 2001), 512; "Prisoners of War of the Japanese 1939–1945," https://www.forces-war-records.co.uk/prisoners-of-war-of-the-japanese-1939-1945.
95. "한국은 기시다 '푸른리본' 배지...'" [Blue ribbon on Kishida...],『한겨레신문』, May 8, 2023.
96. Mirco Dondi, "The Fascist Mentality After Fascism," in *Italian Fascism: History, Memory and Representation*, ed. R.J.B. Bosworth and Patrizia Dogliani (New York: St. Martin's Press, 1999), 141.
97. Ruth Ben-Ghiat, "Liberation: Italian Cinema and the Fascist Past, 1945–50," in *Italian Fascism*, 84.
98. Paul Corner, ed., *Popular Opinion in Totalitarian Regimes: Fascism, Nazism, Communism* (Oxford: Oxford University Press, 2009), 122–23.
99. Angela Giuffrida, "Gifts for Fascist Friends: Mussolini's Calendar Comeback," *Guardian*, December 27, 2018, https://www.theguardian.com/world/2018/dec/27/gifts-for-fascist-friends-mussolinis-calendar-comeback. New editions of Mussolini calendars continue to be sold on Amazon.

100. Matti Bunzl, "On the Politics and Semantics of Austrian Memory: Vienna's Monument Against War and Fascism," *History and Memory* 2, no. 2 (1996): 11–13.
101. Evan Burr Bukey, *Hitler's Austria: Popular Sentiments in the Nazi Era, 1938–1945* (Chapel Hill: University of North Carolina Press, 2000), 43–44.
102. Norman Lebrecht, "Beautiful Music Does Not Drown Out Shameful History of the Past," *Jewish Chronicle*, March 15, 2013, https://www.thejc.com/comment/opinion/beautiful-music-does-not-drown-out-shameful-history-of-the-past-1.42994.
103. Bunzl, "On the Politics," 11–12, 24. Polish neighbors' attitudes toward Holocaust survivors who returned to their homes were not very different either. The returnees who managed to survive were often killed in property disputes with Polish neighbors occupying their homes. Bozena Szaynok, "The Impact of the Holocaust on Jewish Attitudes in Postwar Poland," in *Contested Memories: Poles and Jews During the Holocaust and Its Aftermath*, ed. Joshua D. Zimmerman (New Brunswick, N.J.: Rutgers University Press, 2003), 240.
104. Conrad Seidl, "Umfrage: 42 Prozent sagen 'Unter Hitler war nicht alles schlecht,'" March 8, 2013, https://www.derstandard.at/story/1362107918471/umfrage-42-prozent-sagen-unter-hitler-war-nicht-alles-schlecht; "UMFRAGE ZUR NS-VERGANGENHEIT: Österreicher schocken mit Umfrage zur Nazi-Zeit," March 10, 2013, https://www.stern.de/panorama/gesellschaft/umfrage-zur-ns-vergangenheit-oesterreicher-schocken-mit-umfrage-zur-nazi-zeit-3107244.html.
105. Robert Moeller, "War Stories: The Search for a Usable Past in the Federal Republic of Germany," *AHR* 101, no. 4 (1996): 1009–10.
106. Niven, "Introduction: German Victimhood," 19; Moeller, "War Stories," 1010–13.
107. Konrad H. Jarausch and Michael Geyer, *Shattered Past: Reconstructing German Histories* (Princeton, N.J.: Princeton University Press, 2003), 37–45.
108. Orr, *The Victim as Hero*, 7, 14, 15, 16.
109. Orr, 3, 9–13.
110. 丸山眞男, 『超国家主義の論理と心理』 [The logic and psyche of ultranationalism] (東京: 岩波文庫, 2015), 3.
111. Sebastian Conrad, *The Quest for the Lost Nation: Writing History in Germany and Japan in the American Century* (Berkeley: University of California Press, 2010); Jie-Hyun Lim, *Global Easts: Remembering-Imagining-Mobilizing* (New York: Columbia University Press, 2022), 129–50.
112. Michael Geyer, "There Is a Land Where Everything Is Pure: Its Name Is Land of Death," in *Sacrifice and National Belonging in Twentieth-Century Germany*, ed. Greg Eghigian and Matthew Paul Berg (Arlington: Texas A&M University Press, 2002), 122–23.
113. 吉田裕, 『日本軍兵士』 [Japanese soldiers], 23–26.

7. OVERHISTORICIZATION

1. Anna Bikont, *The Crime and the Silence: Confronting the Massacre of Jews in Wartime Jedwabne*, trans. Alissa Valles (New York: Farrar, Straus and Giroux, 2015), 10.

7. OVERHISTORICIZATION   357

2. Bikont, 16–17.
3. M. J. Chodakiewicz, *Po Zagładzie. Stosunki polsko-żydowskie 1944–1947* (Warsaw: Instytut Pamięci Narodowej, 2008), 58.
4. Jan T. Gross, *Neighbors: The Destruction of the Jewish Community in Jedwabne* (Princeton, N.J.: Princeton University Press, 2001), 73–75; 전광용, 『꺼삐딴 리, 전광용 단편선 [Captain Lee and other short stories by Jeon Kwangyong]』 (서울: 문학과 지성사, 2009).
5. Gross, 72–73.
6. Mikołaj Stanisław Kunicki, *Between the Brown and the Red: Nationalism, Catholicism, and Communism in 20th Century Poland—the Politics of Bolesław Piasecki* (Athens: Ohio University Press, 2012).
7. Hannah Arendt, *Eichmann in Jerusalem: A Report on the Banality of Evil*, rev. and enl. ed. (New York: Penguin Books, 1994), 278.
8. Arendt, 297–98.
9. In the communist era, Poles were taught that the Holocaust was a conspiracy led by German Jewish capitalists against the Polish nation. The most popular history textbook in Poland taught this even after Poland transitioned from communism. Michael C. Steinlauf, "Teaching About the Holocaust in Poland," in *Contested Memories: Poles and Jews During the Holocaust and Its Aftermath*, ed. Joshua D. Zimmerman (New Brunswick, N.J.: Rutgers University Press, 2003), 264–66.
10. Anna Cichopek, "The Cracow Pogrom of August 1945," in Zimmerman, *Contested Memories*, 221.
11. Bożena Szaynok, "The Jewish Pogrom in Kielce, July 1946—New Evidence," *Intermarium* 1, no. 3, March 4, 2016, https://ece.columbia.edu/files/ece/images/kielce.html.
12. After the Kielce Pogrom, the party moved about 100,000 surviving Jews to the "reclaimed land" (*ziemia odzyskana*), a desperate measure to protect them from the Polish neighbors' antisemitism because western Poland and the "reclaimed land" were not as antisemitic as eastern Poland. See Frank Golczewski, "Die Ansiedlung von Juden in den ehemaligen deutschen Ostgebieten Polens 1945–1951," in *Umdeuten, verschweigen, erinnern: die späte Aufarbeitung des Holocaust in Osteuropa*, ed. Micha Brumlik and Karol Sauerland (Frankfurt am Main: Campus Verlag, 2010), 93–104.
13. Jan T. Gross, *Fear: Anti-Semitism in Poland After Auschwitz* (New York: Random House, 2006), 118.
14. These two parties merged in 1948 to form the Polish United Worker's Party (PZPR), the ruling party of the communist regime.
15. Gross, *Fear*, 225. That Poland's then deputy prime minister Andrzej Lepper positively assessed Hitler in an interview with the German weekly magazine in 2006 can be understood similarly. Jan. M. Piskorski, "Lepper nie powinien wychwalac Hitlera," *Gazeta Wyborcza*, May 12, 2006, https://classic.wyborcza.pl/archiwumGW/4629833/Lepper-nie-powinien-wychwalac-Hitlera; "Andrzej Lepper kontra prof. Jan M. Piskorski," *Gazeta Wyborcza*, May 17, 2006, https://wyborcza.pl/7,76842,3352331.html.
16. Gross, *Fear*, 120–21, 126.

17. Antisemitism after the war was not unique to Poland. On April 19, 1945, about four hundred Parisians demonstrated under the slogan "France for the French." It was an antisemitic protest provoked by an incident where a Holocaust survivor asked a French man who had occupied his house without permission to leave. Netty Rosenfeld, a Jewish Dutch Holocaust survivor, said her job application to the Dutch Resistance radio station was rejected because her last name was "unsuitable for public broadcasting." Jews were also excluded from Belgium's national compensation policy for World War II victims because they were killed not due to their political resistance but for being Jewish. Pieter Lagrou, "Victims of Genocide and National Memory: Belgium, France and the Netherlands 1945–65," *Past & Present* 154 (1997):182, 193, 198–99; Ian Buruma, *Year Zero: A History of 1945* (New York: Penguin Press, 2013), 134–35.
18. Szewach Weiss, "To co pisze Gross, to nie są bzdury," http://wiadomosci.gazeta.pl/wiadomosci/1,114873,8988721,Szewach_Weiss__to_co_pisze_Gross__to_nie_sa_bzdury.html.
19. Quoted in Gross, *Fear*, 129.
20. Gross, 130.
21. Adam Michnik, "Poles and Jews: How Deep the Guilt?," in *The Neighbors Responded: The Controversy Over the Jedwabne Massacre in Poland*, ed. Antony Polonsky and Joanna Michlic (Princeton, N.J.: Princeton University Press, 2004), 435.
22. Żegota was the only state-sponsored organization in occupied Europe that was set up with the aim of saving Jews. Polin Museum of the History of Polish Jews, https://sprawiedliwi.org.pl/en/o-sprawiedliwych/the-council-to-aid-jews.
23. "Odezwa 'Protest!' konspiracyjnego Frontu Odrodzenia Polski pióra Zofii Kossak-Szczuckiej, sierpień 1942 r." ["Protest!" appeal of the clandestine Front for the Rebirth of Poland written by Zofia Kossak-Szczucka, August 1942], http://www.zydziwpolsce.edu.pl/biblioteka/zrodla/r3_5d.html.
24. "Paying the Ultimate Price: Józef and Wiktoria Ulma," in *I Am My Brother's Keeper: A Tribute to the Righteous Among the Nations*, Yad Vashem, https://www.yadvashem.org/yv/en/exhibitions/righteous/ulma.asp.
25. "Ustawa. Z dnia 6 marca 2018 r. o ustawieniu Narodowego Dnia Pamięci Polaków ratujących Żydów pod okupacją niemiecką," http://orka.sejm.gov.pl/opinie8.nsf/nazwa/1947_u/$file/1947_u.pdf.
26. Zuzanna Bogumił and Małgorzata Głowacka-Grajper, *Milieux de Mémoire in Late Modernity: Local Communities, Religion and Historical Politics* (Frankfurt am Main: Peter Lang, 2019), 188–89ff.
27. "Dziennik Ustaw Rzeczypospolitej Polskiej," Warsaw, dnia 14 lutego 2018 r. Poz. 369, https://dziennikustaw.gov.pl/D2018000036901.pdf. Regarding the international criticism with which it was met at the time, see Marc Santora, "Poland's 'Death Camp' Law Tears at Shared Bonds of Suffering with Jews," *New York Times*, February 6, 2018.
28. 『中學道德』 [Textbook of moral education in middle school] (岐阜: 日本文教出版株式會社, 2021), 44–47, 55.

29. Elementary School Moral Textbook, https://www.doutoku.info/plan1/view/504. 「杉原千畝―大勢の人の命を救った外交官」[Sugiharatsiune—a diplomat to save Jewish lives] (日本文教出版6年, p. 98「社会正義の実現」);「五十五年目の恩返し」[Gratitude after 55 years] (光村図書6年, p. 138「感謝」);「六千人の命を救った決断―杉原千畝」[A decision to save 6,000 people—Sugiharatsiune] (光文書院6年, p. 114「社会正義」);「六千人の命のビザ―杉原千畝―」[Visa to save 6,000 people—Sugiharatsiune] (教育出版6年, p. 72「よりよく生きる喜び」).
30. 김정안, "유대인 4000명 구한 '중국판 쉰들러' 있었다" [The "Chinese Schindler" who saved the lives of 4,000 Jews],『동아일보』, July 21, 2015; 예영준, "'중국의 쉰들러' 실화소설 선물 . . . 시진핑, 벨기에 국왕 마음 얻다" [Xi Jinping wins the heart of the Belgian king with a novel based on the "Chinese Schindler"],『중앙일보』, June 26, 2015.
31. For the rescuer's turn, see Natalia Aleksiun, Zofia Wóycicka, and Raphael Utz, eds., *The Rescue Turn and the Politics of Holocaust Memory* (Detroit, Mich.: Wayne State University Press, forthcoming).
32. Aomar Boum and Daniel Schroeter, "Why Did Morocco Just Demolish a Holocaust Memorial?" *Haaretz*, September 22, 2019.
33. "Rootless cosmopolitanism" was one of the key terms of the Polish Communist Party's antisemitic campaign. Regarding the controversy surrounding the Museum of the Second World War in Gdańsk, see the work of Paweł Machcewicz, who served as the head of the preparatory committee and the museum's first director. Paweł Machcewicz, *The War That Never Ends: The Museum of the Second World War in Gdańsk* (Berlin: De Gruyter, 2019).
34. The documentary film *Bogdan's Journey* by Two Points Film shows the skinheads in the protest. The simple yet strange rhyme that rings when they sing the slogan "pogrom ubecki" instead of "pogrom kielecki" indeed leaves an eerie aftertaste.
35. Tomasz Pajączek, "Związki szefa wrocławskiego IPN z ONR. Nowe fakty," ONET, February 19, 2021, https://wiadomosci.onet.pl/wroclaw/zwiazki-tomasza-greniucha-z-onr-nowe-fakty/zhsn7w2.
36. Jie-Hyun Lim, Zoom conversation with Aleksandra Gliszczyńska-Grabias, Jan Grabowski's lawyer in Warsaw, February 4, 2021; Andrew Higgins, "A Massacre in a Forest Becomes a Test of Poland's Pushback on Wartime Blame," *New York Times*, February 8, 2021, https://www.nytimes.com/2021/02/08/world/europe/poland-massacre-jews-nazis-blame.html.
37. Bikont, *The Crime and the Silence*, 119. The innocence defense of the Laudanski brothers is similar to the defense of the Ukrainian Nazi camp guard John Demjanjuk. On March 17, 2012, when Demjanjuk, a former Ukrainian guard at the Sobibor Extermination Camp, died, his son claimed his father was "a victim of barbaric Soviet Union and Germany since childhood" and that "Germany made the innocent Ukrainian POWs a scapegoat to push blame for what Nazi Germany did." Ofer Aderet, "John Demjanjuk Dies at 91, Taking His Secret to the Grave," *Haaretz*, March 18, 2012, https://www.haaretz.com/1.5206052. Demjanjuk, also known as "Ivan the Terrible," was the subject of one of the last Nazi war crimes trials. For a detailed account of this

trial, see Lawrence Douglas, *The Right Wrong Man: John Demjanjuk and the Last Great Nazi War Crimes Trial* (Princeton, N.J.: Princeton University Press, 2016).

38. Joanna Kurczewska, "From the Editor," *Polish Sociological Review* 137, no. 1 (2002): 4.
39. Ireneusz Krzemiński, "Polish-Jewish Relations, Anti-Semitism and National Identity," *Polish Sociological Review* 137, no. 1 (2002): 45.
40. Marek Ziółkowski, "Memory and Forgetting After Communism," *Polish Sociological Review* 137, no. 1 (2002): 19, 22.
41. 안동원, 『세계일주기』 [Traveling around the world] (서울: 태극서관, 1949), 71–73. Regarding the predicament faced by intellectuals in postliberation Korea as the accomplices of the Japanese empire, see 장세진, 『슬픈아시아: 한국지식인들의 아시아 기행, 1945–1966』 [Sad Asia: Korean intellectuals' travelogues to Asia] (서울: 푸른역사, 2012).
42. Alexis Dudden, *Troubled Apologies: Among Japan, Korea, and the United States* (New York: Columbia University Press, 2008), 74.
43. 고황경, 『인도기행』 [Traveling India] (서울: 을유문화사, 1949), 167.
44. The 25 percent death rate for POWs was very high, but the death rate for local workers was even higher. However, local war crimes trials only accounted for the abused Allied prisoners and the Japanese/Korean war criminals who abused them.
45. 内海愛子, 村井吉敬, 『赤道下の朝鮮人叛乱』 [Chosenjin's rebellion at the equator] (東京: 勁草書房, 1980), 87–88.
46. 内海愛子, 『朝鮮人B・C級戦犯の記録』 [Records of B·C war criminal Chosenjins] (東京: 岩波現代文庫, 2015), iv–v.
47. Nevertheless, no numbers regarding the abuse of prisoners can be compared to the three million Soviet prisoners who died in Nazi concentration camps. Such a horrendous scale of mass murder was partially due to the Nazis' racist ideology that deemed the Slavs "lower humans."
48. 「半島人 青年의 光榮. 米英人 捕虜監視員에 大量採用」 [Massive employment of Korean youth as POW camp guards], 『每日申報』, May 23, 1942; 「快消息에 感激爆發. 半島青年의 榮譽인 米英人 俘虜의 監視指導」 [Cheers for the good news: Glory to the Korean youth], 『每日申報』, May 23, 1942.
49. 内海愛子, 『朝鮮人B・C級戦犯の記録』, 108.
50. "기획전시, 죽음의 태국-버마 철도" [Special exhibition, The Thailand-Burma Death Railway], 국립일제강제동원역사관 [National Memorial Museum of Forced Mobilization Under Japanese Occupation], May 12–August 30, 2020, https://www.fomo.or.kr/museum/kor/CMS/Board/Board.do?mCode=MN0065&&mode=view&board_seq=2592.
51. KBS 파노라마 플러스, "전범이 된 조선청년들" [The young Joseon men who became war criminals], KBS, August 1, 2014, https://vod.kbs.co.kr/index.html?source=episode&sname=vod&stype=vod&program_code=T2013-0132&program_id=PS-2014073429-01-000&broadcast_complete_yn=Y&local_station_code=00&section_code=05&section_sub_code=05.
52. 조건(조사1과) 책임 조사 작성, "조선인 BC급 전범에 대한 진상조사-포로감시원 동원과 전범 처벌 실태를 중심으로" [An investigation of the Joseon BC class war criminals with a

focus on the mobilization of the jailors and the punishment of the war criminals], 『대일항쟁기강제동원피해조사 및 국외강제동원희생자등지원위원회보고서』 (서울: 일제하강제동원피해자지원재단, 2011), 발간등록번호 11-1655026-000007-01. 41, 44, 55.

53. 조건(조사1과) 책임 조사 작성, 47.
54. Zygmunt Bauman, *Modernity and the Holocaust* (Ithaca, N.Y.: Cornell University Press, 2000), 24–25. A representative use of it was by Adolf Eichmann, who insisted on his innocence by arguing that he had never been an antisemite and had never so much as even once slapped a Jew, but merely followed the orders as a civil servant.
55. 内海愛子, 『朝鮮人B・C級戰犯の記錄』, 312.
56. 조건(조사1과) 책임 조사 작성, "조선인 BC급 전범에 대한 진상조사," ii, 5.
57. 内海愛子·村井吉敬, 『赤道下の朝鮮人叛亂』, 45–47, 49–50, 123.
58. 内海愛子·村井吉敬, 4, 17–18, 21–23, 32–35.
59. 박영석 역, 『리턴보고서』 [Lytton Report] (서울: 탐구당, 1986), 138.
60. 윤상원, "한국 역사학계의 만보산사건 연구동향과 과제" [The research trend in Korean academia regarding the Wanpaoshan incident and its challenges], 『한국역사연구』 51집 (2016), 15.
61. 오기영, "평양폭동사건 회고" [Remembering the Pyongyang riots], 『東光』, September 1931: 10–12.
62. "朝鮮과万宝山, 両事件은無関係" [Joseon and Wanpaoshan], 『東亞日報』, July 29, 1931; "衝突事件의政府方針決定" [Regarding government policy on the conflict], 『朝鮮日報』, July 9, 1931; "中人襲擊事件第一次公判" [First trial of the Chinese attackers], 『朝鮮日報』, August 13, 1931. A Holocaust researcher at the University of Charleston argued that the Tulsa Race Massacre should be called a "pogrom" rather than a racial uprising in 2021, the hundredth-anniversary year. This drew my interest as it was similar to my argument that the "Wanpaoshan incident" should be called the "Joseon Chinese Pogrom." Joshua Shanes, "The Tulsa Massacre Wasn't a 'Race Riot'—It Was a Pogrom," *Forward*, May 31, 2021.
63. 윤해동, "만보산 사건과 동아시아 기억의 터-한국인들의 기억을 중심으로-" [The Wanpaoshan incident and the site of East Asian memory with a focus on the Korean memory], 『사이間 SAI』 14 (2013): 495–96.
64. Gross, *Fear*, 133.
65. Studies by Kang Jin-A, Son Seung-hoe, and other researchers discuss the competition between colonial Joseon and Chinese workers, the proxy colonialism of Manchukuo Koreans, and the general oppression of ethnic Chinese in colonial Joseon from the perspective of global history, but these studies have not yet been the main current. See also Jin-A Kang, "The Enforcement of Immigration Control in Colonial Korea and the Rise of Nationalism in the Chinese Media," *Translocal Chinese: East Asian Perspectives* 9, no. 1 (2015): 142–69; 강진아, "滿洲事變 前後 朝鮮華僑 問題의 樣相- 朝鮮総督府 外事課와 在韓中国領事館 간 往復 文書를 중심으로-" [On the Chinese diaspora in Joseon around the Manchurian Incident], 『東洋史學研究』 120 (2012): 262–305; 손승회, "1931년 植民地朝鮮의 排華暴動과 華僑" [Anti-Chinese riots and Chinese diaspora in colonial Joseon], 『중국근현대사연구』, 제41집 (2009): 141–65.

66. Suk-Jung Han, "The Suppression and Recall of Colonial Memory: Manchukuo and the Cold War in the Two Koreas," in *Mass Dictatorship and Memory as Ever Present Past*, ed. Jie-Hyun Lim et al. (Basingstoke, UK: Palgrave Macmillan, 2014), 168.
67. Suk-Jung Han, 172–74.
68. 박은하, "원폭은 신의 징벌 중앙일보 칼럼에 일 술렁" [The *Joongang Ilbo* article that calls the atomic bomb a divine punishment causes an uproar in Japan], 『경향신문』, May 25, 2013, http://m.khan.co.kr/amp/view.html?art_id=201305241933191.
69. 김치관, "원폭피해단체들, '김진 칼럼'에 "한국은 두 번째 원폭 피해국" [The atomic bomb victims respond to the *Joongang Ilbo* article: "Korea is the second biggest victim of the atomic bomb"], 『통일뉴스』, May 26, 2013, http://www.tongilnews.com/news/articleView.html?idxno=102692.
70. Yahir Oron, *Jewish-Israeli Identity* (Tel Aviv: Sifriat Poalim, 1992), 58. Quoted in Tom Segev, *The Seventh Million: The Israelis and the Holocaust*, trans. Haim Watzman (New York: Owl Book, 2000), 516.
71. Bauman, *Modernity and the Holocaust*, 238.
72. For the concept of postmemory, see Marianne Hirsch, *The Generation of Postmemory: Writing and Visual Culture After the Holocaust* (New York: Columbia University Press, 2012). Regarding the postmemory of U.S. Japanese internment camps, see Marita Sturken, "Absent Images of Memory: Remembering and Reenacting the Japanese Internment," in *Perilous Memories: The Asia-Pacific War(s)*, ed. Takeshi Fujitani, Geoffrey M. White, and Lisa Yoneyama (Durham, N.C.: Duke University Press, 2001), 34–47.
73. Werner Weinberg, *Self-Portrait of a Holocaust Survivor* (Jefferson, N.C.: Mcfarland, 1985), 152.
74. Idith Zertal, *From Catastrophe to Power: Holocaust Survivors and the Emergence of Israel* (Berkeley: University of California Press, 1998), 217.
75. Segev, *The Seventh Million*, 110.
76. Segev, 179–80.
77. Ilan Pappe, "Critique and Agenda: the Post-Zionist Scholars in Israel," *History and Memory*, Special Issue: *Israel Historiography Revisited*, 7, no. 1 (1995): 72.
78. Zertal, *From Catastrophe to Power*, 221.
79. Peter Novick, *The Holocaust and Collective Memory* (London: Bloomsbury, 2001), 35–36.
80. Segev, *The Seventh Million*, 18; Arendt, *Eichmann in Jerusalem*, 58–60.
81. Novick, *The Holocaust and Collective Memory*, 121.
82. Novick, 116, 122, 123.
83. Novick, 91, 98, 116, 121, 123.
84. Annette Wieviorka, *The Era of the Witness*, trans. Jared Stark (Ithaca, N.Y.: Cornell University Press, 2006), 48–49.
85. Dan Diner, "Cumulative Contingency: Historicizing Legitimacy in Israeli Discourse," *History and Memory*, Special Issue: *Israel Historiography Revisited*, 7, no. 1 (1995): 153–55.
86. Uri Ram, "Zionist Historiography and the Invention of Modern Jewish Nationhood: The Case of Ben Zion Dinur," *History and Memory*, Special Issue: *Israel Historiography Revisited*, 7, no. 1 (1995): 110, 117.

87. Elon Gilad, "The History of Holocaust Remembrance Day," *Haaretz*, April 27, 2014, https://www.haaretz.com/the-history-of-holocaust-remembrance-day-1.5246317.
88. Yael Zerubavel, "The Death of Memory and the Memory of Death: Masada and the Holocaust as Historical Metaphors" *Representations*, no. 45 (1994): 75–89.
89. Zeev Sternhell, *The Founding Myths of Israel*, trans. David Maisel (Princeton, N.J.: Princeton University Press, 1998), xii.
90. Born as a rabbi's child in France and moving to Israel in the mid-1960s, Michel Warschawski writes about the shock he felt when he first learned that "savonette," a slur against Holocaust survivors, was also used to refer to a weak person. Weakness was considered a character flaw in Israel until the mid-1960s. Michel Warschawski, *On the Border*, trans. Levi Laub (Cambridge, Mass.: South End Press, 2005), 153–54.
91. "The Declaration of the Establishment of the State of Israel," May 14, 1948, https://main.knesset.gov.il/en/about/pages/declaration.aspx.
92. Segev, *The Seventh Million*, 333.
93. Gideon Hausner, *Justice in Jerusalem* (New York: Holocaust Library, 1977), 291.
94. Wieviorka, *The Era of the Witness*, 71. Leo Hurwitz's camera work also played a crucial role. A legendary cinematographer of Hollywood, Hurwitz was blacklisted in the industry due to the vicious McCarthyism of the 1950s and 1960s for his political beliefs until he directed the television coverage of the Eichmann trial.
95. Marianne Hirsch and Leo Spitzer, "The Witness in the Archive: Holocaust Studies/Memory Studies," *Memory Studies* 2, no. 2 (2009): 152, 155.
96. Idith Zertal, *Israel's Holocaust and the Politics of Nationhood*, trans. Chaya Galai (Cambridge: Cambridge University Press, 2005), 111.
97. Segev, *The Seventh Million*, 121, 185, 186, 249, and passim.
98. Segev, 328.
99. Quoted in Segev, 389.
100. Wieviorka, *The Era of the Witness*, 105.
101. Tadek Markiewicz and Keren Sharvit, "When Victimhood Goes to War? Israel and Victim Claims," *Political Psychology* (September 2020): 3–5, https://doi.org/10.1111/pops.12690.
102. Quoted in Segev, *The Seventh Million*, 399.
103. Segev, 399.
104. Interesting to note is the distance between Netanyahu's speech and the Israeli government's demand for an apology from Christiane Amanpour, the CNN anchor who compared Donald Trump to the Nazis. "Netanyahu: Hitler Didn't Want to Exterminate the Jews," *Haaretz*, October 21, 2015, https://www.haaretz.com/israel-news/netanyahu-absolves-hitler-of-guilt-1.5411578; Raphael Ahren, "Israel Calls on CNN's Amanpour to Apologize for Comparing Trump to Nazis," *Times of Israel*, November 2020, https://www.timesofisrael.com/israel-calls-on-cnns-amanpour-to-apologize-for-comparing-trump-to-nazis/.
105. Segev, *The Seventh Million*, 299–301.
106. Segev, 408.

107. Shiri Tsur, "The Mengele Squad," *Haaretz*, October 1, 2010, https://www.haaretz.com/2010-10-01/ty-article/the-mengele-squad/0000017f-f84f-d887-a7ff-f8ef5b4a0000.
108. Bauman, *Modernity and the Holocaust*, 152.

8. JUXTAPOSITION

1. For cofiguration of the national and global, East and West, see Naoki Sakai, *Translation and Subjectivity: On "Japan" and Cultural Nationalism* (Minneapolis: University of Minnesota Press, 1997), 40–71; Jie-Hyun Lim, *Global Easts: Remembering, Imagining, Mobilizing* (New York: Columbia University Press, 2022), 151–78.
2. Susan Stanford Friedman, "Planetarity: Musing Modernist Studies," *Modernism/modernity* 17, no. 3 (2010): 493.
3. Yến Lê Espiritu and Diane Wolf, "The Appropriation of American War Memories: A Critical Juxtaposition of the Holocaust and the Vietnam War," *Social Identities: Journal for the Study of Race, Nation, and Culture* 19, no. 2 (2013): 188–203.
4. James W. Loewen, "The Vietnam War in High School American History," in *Censoring History: Citizenship and Memory in Japan, Germany, and the United States*, ed. Laura Hein and Mark Selden (Armonk, N.Y.: Sharpe, 2000), 150–72; David Hunt, "War Crimes and the Vietnamese People: American Representations and Silences," in *Censoring History*, 173–200.
5. Laura Hein and Mark Selden, "The Lessons of War, Global Power, and Social Change," in *Censoring History*, 36–37.
6. See *Don't Fence Me In*, a special exhibition at the Japanese American National Museum, https://www.janm.org/exhibits/dont-fence-me-in; and the permanent exhibition at the JANM, *Common Ground: The Heart of Humanity*, https://www.janm.org/exhibits/commonground.
7. Lea David, "Holocaust Discourse as a Screen Memory: The Serbian Case," in *History and Politics in the Western Balkans: Changes at the Turn of the Millenium*, ed. Srdan M. Jovanović and Veran Stancetic (Belgrade: Center for Good Governance Studies, 2013), 66.
8. David, 65, 67, 69, 71, 79.
9. Jelena Subotić, *Yellow Star, Red Star: Holocaust Remembrance After Communism* (Ithaca, N.Y.: Cornell University Press, 2019), 65–66.
10. Subotić, 123–35.
11. Martin Evans, "Memories, Monuments, Histories: The Re-thinking of the Second World War Since 1989," *National Identities* 8, no. 4 (December 2006): 318–21; "Gespräch zwischen Micha Brumlik und Karol Sauerland," in *Umdeuten, verschweigen, erinnern: die spaete Aufarbeitung des Holocaust in Osteuropa*, ed. Michal Brumlik and Karol Sauerland (Frankfurt am Main: Campus Verlag, 2010), 7–15.
12. Siobhan Kattago, "Agreeing to Disagree on the Legacies of Recent History: Memory, Pluralism and Europe After 1989," *European Journal of Social Theory* 12, no. 3 (2009): 382.
13. Subotić, *Yellow Star, Red Star*, 6, 8, 9, 11.

14. Grzegorz Rossoliński-Liebe, "Debating, Obfuscating and Disciplining the Holocaust: Post-Soviet Historical Discourses on the OUN–UPA and Other Nationalist Movements," *East European Jewish Affairs* 42, no. 3 (2012): 199–241; William J. Risch, "What the Far Right Does Not Tell Us About the Maidan," *Kritika: Explorations in Russian and Eurasian History* 16, no. 1 (2015): 137–44.
15. On the nationalist appropriation of Holocaust memories in other Eastern European countries, see Brumlik and Sauerland, eds., *Umdeuten, verschweigen, erinnern*; Aro Velmet, "Occupied Identities: National Narratives in Baltic Museums of Occupations," *Journal of Baltic Studies* 42, no. 2 (2011).
16. A. Dirk Moses, "Genocide and the Terror of History," *Parallax* 17, no. 4 (2011): 91.
17. 永井隆, "死床日記:ロザリオの鎖" [Diary at the deathbed: Rosary], 『永井隆全集』(東京: サンパウロ, 2003), 第三巻, 162.
18. 永井隆, "ルルドの奇跡:如己堂随筆" [Miracle of Lourdes], 『永井隆全集』, 第二巻, 103–5.
19. This miraculous "Lourdes water" from Hongouchi Seminary is still being sold at the St. Kolbe Museum at the entrance of the hill to the Oura Church in Nagasaki.
20. Nagai met Father Kolbe while in a coma before the news of Kolbe's martyrdom was reported. Kolbe's martyrdom in Auschwitz was not even known to the Polish friars in Hongouchi at the time. Those Polish friars who believed in the "religion of the enemy nation" were transferred to the Tochinoki Hot Springs in Aso Mountain on the night of August 2, 1945, and were kept under house arrest until they returned to Nagasaki after the end of the war. Only then did they learn of Father Kolbe's martyrdom, through *Seibo no Kishi*, which arrived from Poland on September 21, 1946. Immaculate Conception Province Conventual Franciscans of Japan, 『聖コルベ來日75周年記念誌』[Memorial book to celebrate St. Kolbe's visit to Japan] (長崎: 聖母の騎士社, 2005), 88. Nagai also donated one hundred yen from his cousin to Polish friars after they returned to Hongouchi. 永井隆, "死床日記:ロザリオの鎖" [Diary at the deathbed], 『永井隆全集』, 第三巻, 170.
21. 永井隆, "微笑の秘訣" [Secret of the smile], 『聖母の騎士』(May 1980): 15. Nagai also reported the news from the front in *Seibo no Kishi* while serving on the Chinese Front as a medic in the service of the Fifth Division Medical Corps from summer 1937 to February 1940, after Father Kolbe left Japan.
22. 永井隆, "亡びぬものを" [Foreverness], 『永井隆全集』, 第三巻, 462–63.
23. A. Dirk Moses, "The Holocaust and World History," *The Holocaust and Historical Methodology*, ed. Dan Stone (New York: Berghahn Books, 2012), 276.
24. Susan Southhard, *Nagasaki: Life After Nuclear War* (New York: Penguin Books, 2016), 169–70.
25. Rotem Kowner, "Tokyo Recognizes Auschwitz: The Rise and Fall of Holocaust Denial in Japan, 1989–1991," *Journal of Genocide Research* 3, no. 2 (2001), 261.
26. Gwyn Maclelland, "Guilt, Persecution, and Resurrection in Nagasaki: Atomic Memories and the Urakami Catholic Community," *Social Science Japan Journal* 18, no. 2 (2015): 239.
27. The text quoted in this chapter is excerpted from Nagai's handwritten script in consideration of Professor Shinji Takahashi's criticism that the funeral address

rewritten and published in *Bells of Nagasaki* (1949) was very different from the original. The facsimile of the handwritten script is in Konishi Tetsuro, "The Original Manuscript of Takashi Nagai's Funeral Address at a Mass for the Victims of the Nagasaki Atomic Bomb," *Journal of Nagasaki University of Foreign Studies*, no. 18 (2014): 55–68.

28. Nagai in Tetsuro, 61.
29. Nagai in Tetsuro, 62.
30. According to the late Feliks Tych, who served as director of the Jewish Historical Institute in Warsaw, Yad Vashem and the Jewish Historical Institute had argued over who first used the term "Holocaust." Regardless of which one first used it, it remained an unfamiliar term in the West until the end of the 1950s. It is remarkable that Nagai already used the term "Holocaust" (*hansai*), albeit in Japanese translation, in 1945.
31. René Girard, 『폭력과 성스러움』 [Violence and the sacred], 김진식·박무호 옮김, (서울: 민음사, 1997), 9–10, 14.
32. John Dower, 『패배를 껴안고』 [Embracing the defeat], 최은석 옮김, 민음사, 2009, 33–34, 248.
33. John Dower, "The Bombed: Hiroshima and Nagasaki in Japanese Memory," *Diplomatic History* 19, no. 2 (1995): 290–91.
34. 권혁태, "'나가사키의 종'은 어떻게 울렸나?" [How did the "Bell of Nagasaki" toll?], 『한겨레21』, December 18, 2014; 전은옥, "'원폭은 천벌'... 그것은 정말 '신의 뜻'이었나?" [The atomic bomb as a divine intervention—was it really the "god's will?"], 『오마이뉴스』, April 23, 2013. However, it was Dr. Akizuki Tatsuichiro (秋月辰一郎), a disciple of Nagai, who first raised such criticism. Southard, *Nagasaki*, 172–76.
35. 永井隆, "原子野の声：如己堂随筆" [Voice from the field of A-bomb], 『永井隆全集』, 第二巻, 119. There perhaps was this kind of guilty conscience beyond the Bible's lessons in the psychological background of Nagai's naming of his late residence Nyokodo [如己堂].
36. Primo Levi, *The Drowned and the Saved*, trans. Raymond Rosenthal (New York: Simon & Schuster, 1988), 64.
37. 永井隆, "原子野の声," 153.
38. 小崎登明, 『長崎のコルベ神父』[Father Kolbe in Nagasaki] (長崎: 聖母の騎士社, 2010), 363–64.
39. Father Ozaki Tōmei died of pancreatic cancer on April 15, 2021, and his obituary in *Nagasaki Shimbun* writes that he was in charge of rescuing the injured and burial of the dead, a description that is inconsistent with Tōmei's own account. This discrepancy warrants further investigation. "小崎登明さん死去　被爆修道士　コルベ神父語り部" [Ozaki Tōmei dead, hibakusha brother and a biographer of Father Kolbe], 『長崎新聞』, April 16, 2021. Professor Watanabe Naoki of Musashi University kindly sent me this information.
40. 遠藤周作, 『女の一生：二部・サチ子の場合』[A life of a woman: Part 2—Sachiko] (東京: 新潮文庫, 1986), 569.
41. 遠藤周作, 『女の一生：一部・キクの場合』[A life of a woman: Part 1—Kiku] (東京: 新潮文庫, 1986), 563–64.

42. 遠藤周作,『女の一生：二部・サチ子の場合』, 27–28.
43. 遠藤周作,『心の夜想曲』[Nocturnes of heart] (東京: 文春文庫, 1989), 72–73.
44. 金承哲,「遠藤周作の『イエスの生涯』について-神学と文学の間で」[About Endō Shusaku's "Life of Jesus"—between theology and literature],『キリスト教文藝』28 (2012): 125.
45. 小崎登明,『長崎のコルベ神父』, 351.
46. 小崎登明, 268–70; 永井隆,「亡びぬものを」, 488.
47. 金承哲, "遠藤周作の『イエスの生涯』について-神学と文学の間で," 126.
48. 遠藤周作,『女の一生：一部・キクの場合』, 302–4.
49. For more about the "Asianness" of Eastern Europe, including Poland, see Larry Wolff, *Inventing Eastern Europe* (Stanford, Calif.: Stanford University Press, 1994); Kristin Kopp, *Germany's Wild East: Constructing Poland as Colonial Space* (Ann Arbor: University of Michigan Press, 2012); Jan Kieniewicz, "The Eastern Frontiers and the Civilisational Dimension of Europe," *Acta Poloniae Historica*, no. 107 (2013); Jie-Hyun Lim, *Global Easts*. About the friendly relationship between the Japanese empire and the Polish national movement during the Russo-Japanese War, see 阪東宏, "ポーランド人と日露戦争" [Poles and the Russo-Japanese War] (東京: 青木書店, 1995), 215–56.
50. 小崎登明,『長崎のコルベ神父』, 169–70, 208, 239–40.
51. 遠藤周作,『女の一生：二部・サチ子の場合』, 6–13.
52. 小崎登明, 『長崎のコルベ神父』, 182.
53. Timothy Snyder, *Bloodlands: Europe Between Hitler and Stalin* (New York: Basic Books, 2010), 37.
54. 曽野綾子,『奇蹟』[Miracle] (東京: 毎日新聞社, 1973), 112–15.
55. 曽野綾子, 72, 77.
56. 阪東宏,『ポーランド人と日露戦爭』, 123, 129–37; Wacław Jędrzejewicz, "Sprawa 'Wieczuru' Józef Piłsudski a wojna japońsko-rosyjska, 1904–1905," *Zeszty Historyczne*, no. 27 (1974), 60–65.
57. Sono deliberately uses the term "patriotism" when referring to the nationalism of the Kolbe family. This may have been influenced by the Polish dichotomy of "bad nationalism" and "good patriotism."
58. 曽野綾子,『奇蹟』, 122–27.
59. 遠藤周作, "コルベ神父 [Father Kolbe],"『新編國語總合』改訂版 (東京: 代修館書店, 2018), 186ff. This essay is a reprint of an article originally published in the *Asahi Shimbun* column "Kaleidoscope" on April 5, 1992.
60. On November 11, 2018, the centennial anniversary of Poland's national liberation, the National Radical Camp (ONR) demonstrated its historical affiliation to the interwar period antisemitism by organizing massive anti-immigrant/anti-Islam protests with the European far-right in large Polish cities such as Warsaw. Tomasz Greniuch, who was appointed amid controversy as the head of the Wrocław office of the Institute of National Remembrance in February 2021, also served as a longtime member in the leadership of the ONR.
61. Jan Józef Lipski, "Ojciec Kolbe i, Mały Dziennik,'" *Tygodnik Powszechny*, no. 38 (1182), September 19, 1971.

62. *Tygodnik Powszechny*, no. 38 (1182), September 19, 1971.
63. Kardynał Karol Wojtyła, "Znak Naszej Epoki," *Tygodnik Powszechny*, no. 42 (1186), October 17, 1971. Cardinal Karol Wojtyła, who later became Pope John Paul II, was a big fan of Kolbe and orchestrated his canonization ceremony as a pope. He even visited the monastery of Immaculate, founded by Kolbe in Nagasaki. Kolbe's criticism of antisemitism was received as a criticism of Pope John Paul II and the entire church. Stanisław Karjski, "Przedmowa," *Św. Maksymilian Maria Kolbe o Masonerii i Żydach: pisma wybrane* (Krzeszowice, Pol.: Dom Wydawniczy Ostoja, 2010), 3.
64. 曽野綾子,『奇跡』, 72–74.
65. Kolbe considered Freemasons to be the biggest and most potent enemy of the Catholic Church. Karjski, *Św. Maksymilian Maria Kolbe*, 7.
66. Karjski, 42.
67. Elaine Lies and Takashi Umekawa, "Japan PM Ex-adviser Praises Apartheid in Embarrassment for Abe," Reuters, February 13, 2015; David McNeill, "Japanese Prime Minister Urged to Embrace Apartheid for Foreign Workers," *Independent*, February 13, 2015;"安倍首相の盟友·曽野綾子も野田聖子議員に障がい者ヘイト!'子どもの治療に税金を使っているのを申し訳なく思え,'" *Litera*, August 1, 2016, https://lite-ra.com/2016/08/post-2463.html.
68. 曽野綾子,『ある神話の背景――沖縄・渡嘉敷島の集団自決』[Background of a myth—collective suicide in Okinawa and Kerama Islands] (東京: 文藝春秋, 1973), 167, 259;大江健三郎,『定義集』[Book of definitions] (東京: 朝日新聞出版, 2016), 88–91.
69. For more about Japan's civil religion, see chapter 3.
70. Richard Cohen, "Sainthood," *Washington Post*, December 14, 1928; Henry Kamm, "The Saint of Auschwitz Is Canonized by Pope," *New York Times*, October 11, 1982; Daniel Schlafy and Warren Green, reply by John Gross, "Kolbe & Anti-Semitism," *New York Review of Books*, April 14, 1983.
71. David Binder, "Franciszek Gajowniczek Dead; Priest Died for Him at Auschwitz," *New York Times*, March 15, 1995.
72. John Gross, "Life Saving," *New York Review of Books*, February 17, 1983; "Kolbe & Anti-Semitism," *New York Review of Books*, April 14, 1983.
73. Becky Ready, "Was St. Maximilian Kolbe an Anti-Semite?," Eternal World Television Network, accessed December 22, 2022, https://www.ewtn.com/catholicism/library/was-st-maximilian-kolbe-an-anti-Semite-1068, taken from Becky Ready, *Immaculata Magazine* (May/June 1996).
74. Ronald Modras, "John Paul, St. Maximilian, and Anti-Semitism," in *Martyrs of Charity*, part 2 (Washington, D.C.: St. Maximilian Kolbe Foundation, 1989), 373.
75. Regarding the intellectual connection between Endō and Fanon, see Christopher Hill, "Crossed Geographies: Endō and Fanon in Lyon," *Representations* 128, no. 1 (2014): 96–105.
76. John Paul II, "Apostolic Pilgrimage to Poland, Holy Mass at the Concentration Camp, Homily of His Holiness John Paul II," Auschwitz-Bierkenau, June 7, 1979, https://w2.vatican.va/content/john-paul-ii/en/homilies/1979/documents/hf_jp-ii_hom_19790607_polonia-brzezinka.html.

77. Zuzanna Bogumił and Małgorzata Głowacka-Grajper, *Milieux de mémoire in Late Modernity: Local Communities, Religion and Historical Politics* (Frankfurt am Main: Peter Lang, 2019), 53–55, 72–73.
78. Michael T. Kaufman, "Poles Vow to Continue Slain Priest's Masses," *New York Times*, November 26, 1984.
79. Father Popiełuszko has already been recognized as a martyr within the Roman Catholic Church and is now in the process of canonization after his beatification on June 6, 2010.
80. This resembles the discursive strategy of "retiming." See also Chaim Noy, "Memory, Media, and Museum Audience's Discourse of Remembering," *Critical Discourse Studies* 15, no. 1 (2018): 31–32.
81. 이세원, "히로시마 방문한 교황, 재일한국인 피폭자 박남주 씨 만나" [The pope visits Hiroshima and meets Park Namjoo, a Zainichi-Korean A-bomb victim],『연합뉴스』, November 25, 2019, https://www.yna.co.kr/view/AKR20191125037200073.
82. Slavoj Žižek,『시차적 관점』[The parallex view], 김서영 옮김 (서울: 마티, 2009), 175–77.

9. DENIAL

1. George Michael, "Mahmoud Ahmadinejad's Sponsorship of Holocaust Denial," *Totalitarian Movements and Political Religions* 8, no. 3/4 (2007): 667–68.
2. Michael, 669.
3. William F. S. Miles, "Indigenization of the Holocaust and the Tehran Holocaust Conference: Iranian Aberration or Third World Trend?," *Human Rights Review* 10, no. 4 (2009): 506–7.
4. For a detailed classification of denialism, see Israel W. Charny, "A Classification of Denials of the Holocaust and Other Genocides," *Journal of Genocide Research* 5, no. 1 (2003): 11–34, https://doi.org/10.1080/14623520305645.
5. Israel W. Charny and Daphna Fromer, "Denying the Armenian Genocide: Patterns of Thinking as Defence-Mechanisms," *Patterns of Prejudice* 32, no. 1 (1998): 48, https://doi.org/10.1080/0031322X.1998.9970246.
6. Georges Didi-Huberman,『모든 것을 무릅쓴 이미지들-아우슈비츠에서 온 네 장의 사진』[Images in spite of all: Four photographs from Auschwitz]), 오윤성 옮김 (서울: 레베카, 2017), 36.
7. Lucy Dawidowicz, *The War Against Jews* (London: Penguin Books, 1975), 191–92.
8. Pierre Vidal-Naquet, *Assassins of Memory: Essays on the Denial of the Holocaust*, trans. Jeffrey Mehlman (New York: Columbia University Press, 1992), 1–211; Berel Lang, "Six Questions on (or About) Holocaust Denial," *History and Theory* 49, no. 2 (2010): 157–68; James Najarian, "Gnawing at History: The Rhetoric of Holocaust Denial," *Midwest Quarterly* 39, no. 1 (1997): 74–78; Daqing Yang, "The Challenges of the Nanjing Massacre: Reflections on Historical Inquiry," in *The Nanjing Massacre in History and Historiography*, ed. Joshua Fogel (Berkeley: University of California

Press, 2000), 146–47; Robert Manne, "In Denial: The Stolen Generations and the Right," *Australian Quarterly Essay* 1 (2001); Bai Attwood, "The Stolen Generations and Genocide: Robert Manne's 'In Denial: The Stolen Generations and the Right,'" *Aboriginal History* 25 (2001): 163–72.

9. Paul Behrens, "Introduction," in *Holocaust and Genocide Denial: A Contextual Perspective*, ed. Paul Behrens, Nicholas Terry, and Olaf Jensen (New York: Routledge, 2017), 2.

10. Michael Salter, "Countering Holocaust Denial in Relation to the Nuremberg Trials," in *Holocaust and Genocide Denial*, 21.

11. Laura E. Hein and Mark Selden, "The Lessons of War, Global Power, and Social Change," in *Censoring History: Citizenship and Memory in Japan, Germany, and the United States* (Armonk, N.Y.: Sharpe, 2000), 29.

12. 이소영, "역사부정 규제를 둘러싼 기억의 정치: 5·18왜곡처벌법안 관련 논의를 중심으로" [The memory politics around the censorship of historical denialism: A discussion regarding the Special Act on the Punishment of Historically Distorting the May 18 Movement], 『법과 사회』 61호 (2019): 176–79.

13. For instance, Chris Janiewicz, Stefan Komar, and Janusz Paciorek argue in such a way. These are just people on the internet (names may very well be fake); their reviews can be deleted anytime, so citing specific reviewers may not be effective for a long-term argument. I did not disclose the names of reviewers for Kawashima-Watkins's book in chapter 5. I would rather keep them anonymous and cite the whole review page instead, because deniers will likely continue even if these three reviewers happen to delete theirs. "Customer Reviews" for *Neighbors: The Destruction of the Jewish Community in Jedwabne, Poland*, filtered by "all critical reviews," Amazon, accessed December 30, 2022, https://www.amazon.com/Neighbors-Destruction-Jewish-Community-Jedwabne/product-reviews/0142002402/ref=cm_cr_arp_d_viewpnt_rgt?ie=UTF8&showViewpoints=0&filterBy=addOneStar&filterByStar=critical&pageNumber=1.

14. Carla Tonini, "The Jews in Poland After the Second World War: Most Recent Contributions of Polish Historiography," *Quest. Issues in Contemporary Jewish History. Journal of Fondazione CDEC*, no. 1 (2010): 61–62.

15. "Customer Reviews" for *Fear: Anti-Semitism in Poland After Auschwitz*, filtered by "all critical reviews," Amazon, https://www.amazon.com/-/ko/product-reviews/0812967461/ref=acr_dp_hist_1?ie=UTF8&filterByStar=one_star&reviewerType=all_reviews#reviews-filter-bar.

16. Łukasz Kamiński and Jan Żaryn, eds., *Wokół Pogromu Kieleckiego* (Warsaw: IPN, 2006).

17. 김용희, "5·18 단체 강력한 대응 . . . 지만원 '광수 시리즈' 내렸다" [Ji Man-Won took down the "Gwangsu" series after a strong backlash from the May 18 Memorial organizations], 『한겨레신문』, May 6, 2020, https://www.hani.co.kr/arti/area/honam/943738.html.

18. "지만원이 북한군이라던 '김 군.' . .직접 찾아봤더니" [We found "the boy named Kim" whom Ji Man-Won claimed to be a North Korean soldier], *MBC* 뉴스데스크, May 13, 2019, https://www.youtube.com/watch?v=dDAPiGOvBBc.

19. "'5·18이 북한군의 소행'? 37년 만에 공개된 기무사 사진첩 . . . 드러나는 그날의 진실" [The truth uncovered regarding the accusation that May 18 was a North Korean military ploy, as photographs from the Defense Ministry's Intelligence Agency become public after 37 years], *SBS 더저널리스트*, January 11, 2018, https://www.youtube.com/watch?v=jy_sstg6dLw&t=121s.
20. 전두환,『전두환회고록 1권: 혼돈의 시대』 [The memoir of Chun Doo-Hwan 1: The era in chaos] (서울: 자작나무 숲, 2017), 534–35.
21. 김용희, "5·18 단체 강력한 대응 . . . 지만원 '광수 시리즈' 내렸다" [The May 18 Memorial organizations push back—Ji Man-Won takes down the "Gwangsu" series],『한겨레신문』, May 6, 2020, https://www.hani.co.kr/arti/area/honam/943738.html.
22. 이광수,『반크 역사바로찾기 3: 요코 이야기의 진실을 찾아라!』 (VANK's history corrections vol. 3: Seeking the truth of *So Far from the Bamboo Grove*!] (서울: 키네마인, 2009), 124–32.
23. D. D. Guttenplan, *The Holocaust on Trial: History, Justice and the David Irving Libel Case* (London: Granta Books, 2002), 46.
24. Also, interesting to note is the dispute in the course of Irving's denial trial over whether Irving was racist. Irving presented to the court pictures of a man of color who worked in his home and claimed they were excellent evidence that he was not a racist. Richard Evans, an expert witness for the defense, retorted, "Do you have any direct documentary proof to prove that you are not a racist?" and left Irving speechless. Guttenplan, 211, 221.
25. "[팩트체크] 전두환 '발포명령 없었다?' . . . 검증해보니" [Fact check: Chun's claim that there was no "open fire" order], *JTBC 뉴스*, April 3, 2017, https://news.jtbc.joins.com/article/article.aspx?news_id=NB11448607.
26. 藤岡信勝, "【教科書が歪めた歴史1 [Distorted history in history textbook 1]】『従軍慰安婦』 [Comfort Women] 虚偽の記述が独り歩き,"『産経新聞』, September 27, 1996; "中学教科書の『従軍慰安婦』記述　東大で討論会" [Descriptions of "Comfort Women" in the middle school history textbooks—discussion at Todai],"『産経新聞』, November 27, 1997.
27. Daqing Yang, "The Challenges of the Nanjing Massacre," 145–46; Takashi Yoshida, "A Battle Over History: The Nanjing Massacre in Japan," in *The Nanjing Massacre in History and Historiography*, 107–8.
28. Yoshida, "A Battle Over History," 104.
29. Carol Gluck, "What the World Owes the Comfort Women," 80. On the ruling and the case analysis of the Shimonoseki-Busan trial on April 27, 1998, see 坪川宏子・大森典子,『司法が認定した日本軍「慰安婦」-被害・加害事実は消せない!』 [The court recognizes the comfort women: The facts of victimization cannot be erased] (京都: かもがわ出版, 2011), 2, 4–5, 12, 63–64; "社說: 国の怠慢が厳しく裁かれた" [The leniency of the state was harshly tried],『西日本新聞』, April 28, 1998; "關釜裁判, 判決文" [The Shimonoski-Busan trial, ruling, April 28, 1998], http://kanpusaiban.bit.ph/saiban/shimonoseki_hanketsu.pdf.
30. Evans's point about postmodern historical interpretation's responsibility for denialism in the Irving trial is understandable in this regard, but it cannot be applied

generally. Denialists use anything for their argument, whether it is epistemological positivism or relativism, despite obvious contradictions. Guttenplan, *The Holocaust on Trial*, 229-30.

31. 카즈에 무타, "위안부 문제는 미투다" [The "Comfort Women" issue is a #MeToo issue]. 牟田和恵, "「慰安婦」問題は#MeTooだ！" 서강대학교 트랜스내셔널인문학 연구소, 『전쟁, 여성, 폭력: 일본군 '위안부'를 트랜스내셔널하게 기억하기』e-pub., http://cgsi.ac/bbs/board.php?bo_table=eng_e_Pub&wr_id=3.

32. Omer Bartov, "The Wehrmacht Exhibition Controversy: Politics of Evidence," in *Crimes of War: Guilt and Denial in the Twentieth Century*, ed. Omer Bartov, Atina Grossmann, and Mary Nolan (New York: New Press, 2002), 41-42, 51-52.

33. Bogdan Musiał, "Historiografia mityczna," *Rzeczpospolita*, 24 lutego, 2001; Piotr Forecki, *Od Shoah do Strachu: spory o polsko-żydowską przeszłość i pamięć w debatach publicznych* (Poznań, Pol.: wydawnictwo poznańskie, 2010), 306-9.

34. Irene and Carl Horowitz, *Of Human Agony* (New York: Shengold, 1992), 82. Quoted in Bartov, "The Wehrmacht Exhibition Controversy," 52.

35. In his next book, *Stalins Beutezug* [Stalin's plundering raid], Musiał also argues that the production tools and industrial infrastructure Stalin's plundering units looted from Poland and East Germany greatly contributed to the Soviet Union's postwar rise to power. Bogdan Musiał, *Stalins Beutezug: die Plünderung Deutschlands und der Aufstieg der Sowjetunion zur Wehrmacht* (Berlin: List, 2011).

36. 朴裕河, 『帝国的慰安婦：殖民統治與記憶政治』[Comfort Women of the empire: Colonial rule and memory politics] (劉夏如訳, 台北, 2017).

37. Tessa Morris-Suzuki, 『우리 안의 과거』 [The past within us] 김경원 역 (서울: 휴머니스트, 2006), 127-33.

38. Morris-Suzuki, 131-32.

39. *Das Dritte Reich privat: Leben und Überleben*, directed by Karl Höffkes (Essen, Ger.: Polar Film, 2004), DVD.

40. Matt Jönsson, "Innocence by Association? Everyday Nazism on DVD," in *Imagining Mass Dictatorships: The Individual and the Masses in Literature and Cinema*, ed. Karin Sarsenov and Michael Schoenhals (Basingstoke, UK: Palgrave Macmillan, 2013), 162-82.

41. *Das Dritte Reich privat: Leben und Überleben*.

42. Jan Tomasz Gross and Aleksandrą Pawlicką, . . . *bardzo dawno temu, mniej więcej w zeszły piątek* (Warsaw: Wydawnictwo WAB, 2018), 137-38.

43. Gross and Pawlicką, 140-141, 143.

44. Raul Hilberg, "I Was Not There," in *Writing and the Holocaust*, ed. Berel Lang (New York: Holmes & Meier, 1988), 17, 20, 25.

45. Ever since his was a doctoral student, Hilberg had been a historian who was moved more by facts than by the authenticity of testimony or empathy for witnesses. A well-known anecdote is that Franz Neumann, Hilberg's advisor and a Jewish intellectual who defected from Germany, advised him to remove the criticism of the Jewish Council's cooperation with the Nazis. Götz Aly, "Geschichte reicht in die Gegenwart: Ein Gespräch mit dem Historiker Raul Hilberg," *Neue Züricher Zeitung*, December 10, 2002.

46. Jan Gross, "Poduszka pani Marx," *Tygodnik Powszechny*, March 4, 2001.
47. Hannah Arendt, *Eichmann in Jerusalem: A Report on the Banality of Evil* (New York: Penguin Books, 1994), 251–52.
48. Annette Wieviorka, *The Era of the Witness*, trans. Jared Stark (Ithaca, N.Y.: Cornell University Press, 2006), 67–72.
49. Wieviorka, 72.
50. Wieviorka, 24.
51. This also occasioned a paradigm shift called the "emotional turn" in future historical research.
52. However, memory studies would introduce emotion later than history did. Peter Stearns's research in the mid-1980s is usually cited as the start of emotional history, whereas in memory studies the importance of emotion was first emphasized by Aleida Assmann in 2011. See Peter N. Stearns and Carol Z. Stearns, "Emotionology: Clarifying the History of Emotions and Emotional Standards," *American Historical Review* 90, no. 4 (1985): 813–36; Aleida Assmann, "Impact and Resonance: Towards a Theory of Emotions in Cultural Memory," *Söndertörn Lectures*, no. 6 (2011).
53. Guttenplan, *The Holocaust on Trial*, 306.
54. The slogan of Slovakia's Bardejov Jewish Preservation Committee (BJPC), in which Beirak was involved, is also remarkable: *ǩdí človek má svoje meno* (everyone has a name). Finding a name means a lot. https://www.facebook.com/mestobardejovofficial/photos/pcb.4688961001154123/4688957987821091.
55. Wieviorka, *The Era of the Witness*, 141–43.
56. Goldberg, "Forum: On Saul Friedlaender's *The Years of Extermination 2*. The Victim's Voice and Melodramatic Aesthetics in History," 222.
57. Svetlana Alexievich, 『전쟁은 여자의 얼굴을 하지 않았다』 [The unwomanly face of war: An oral history of women in World War II], 박은정 옮김 (서울: 문학동네, 2015); 위지현, "정말 중요한 이야기는 침묵으로 기록된다: 스베틀라나 알렉시예비치 강연회" [The most important stories are written in silence: On Svetlana Alexievich], 『문학과 사회』 119 (2017).
58. Dori Laub, "Bearing Witness, or the Vicissitudes of Listening," in *Testimony: Crises of Witnessing in Literature, Psychoanalysis, and History*, ed. Shoshana Felman and Dori Laub (New York: Routledge, 1992), 59–60.
59. Laub, 60.
60. Charlotte Delbo, *Days and Memory*, trans. Rosette Lamont (Marlboro, Ver.: Marlboro Press, 1990); Delbo, *Auschwitz and After*, trans. Rosette Lamont (New Haven, Conn.: Yale University Press, 1995). Quoted in Marianne Hirsch and Leo Spitzer, "The Witness in the Archive: Holocaust Studies/Memory Studies," *Memory Studies* 2, no. 2 (2009): 156.
61. Hirsch and Spitzer, "The Witness in the Archive," 161–62.
62. Giorgio Agamben, *Remnants of Auschwitz: The Witness and the Archive*, trans. Daniel Heller-Roazen (New York: Zone Books, 1999), 12.
63. Stefan Maechler, *The Wilkomirski Affair: A Study in Biographical Truth*, trans. John E. Woods (New York: Schocken Books, 2009); Daniel Ganzfried, *. . . alias Wilkomirski*.

Die Holocaust-Travestie, ed. Sebatian Hefti (Berlin: Jüdische Verlagsanstalt, 2002); *W.-What Remains of the Lie*, directed by Rolando Colla (2020), https://www.myfilm.ch/asset/wwasvonderluegebleibt-ID2846_59EA01c.

64. Amos Goldberg, "Forum: On Saul Friedlaender's *The Years of Extermination* 2, the Victim's Voice and Melodramatic Aesthetics in History," *History and Theory* 48, no. 3 (2009): 220–22.
65. Goldberg, 233–34.
66. "위안부 피해자 이용수 할머니 기자회견 현장 [원본]" [Live from the former comfort woman Lee Yong-soo's press conference], 『TV조선』, May 25, 2020, https://www.youtube.com/watch?v=sfXEoFzpyig.
67. 김은실의 발언. "스베틀라나 알렉시예비치 초청 강연토론회" [A conversation with Svetlana Alexievich], 서강대학교 트랜스내셔널인문학연구소, May 24, 2017, http://cgsi.ac/bbs/board.php?bo_table=kor_seminar&wr_id=30.
68. Heon-Ik Kwon, *Ghosts of War in Vietnam* (Edinburgh: University of Edinburgh Press, 2013); Seongnae Kim, "The Work of Memory: Ritual Laments of the Dead and Korea's Cheju Massacre," in *A Companion to the Anthropology of Religion*, ed. Janice Boddy and Michael Lambeck (Oxford: Wiley Blackwell, 2013), 223–38; Monica Black, "Ghosts of War," in *The Cambridge History of Second World War*, vol. 3, ed. Michael Geyer and Adam Tooze (Cambridge: Cambridge University Press, 2015), 654–74.
69. Dorothee Brantz, "Landscapes of Destruction: Capturing Images and Creating Memory Through Photography," in Geyer and Tooze, *The Cambridge History of the Second World War*, vol. 3, 737–40.
70. "KBS 발굴 '만삭의 위안부' 구출 당시 영상 최초 공개" [The first broadcast of the footage of the "parturient comfort woman" being rescued—KBS found footage], *KBS 뉴스*, https://www.youtube.com/watch?v=xDACtH6u8JU.
71. 김한상, "발견된 푸티지 속의 박영심은 무엇을 말하는가(혹은 말하지 못하는가)?: 사진적 생존자의 영화적 현전과 포스트/식민 아카이브의 냉전 지식체제" [What Park Young-shim in the found footage can and can't speak of: The cinematic presence of a photographic survivor and the Cold War system of knowledge in the postcolonial archives], 『문학과영상』 21, no. 3 (2020): 683.
72. 김한상, 688–89.
73. Christoph Classen and Kirsten Wächter, "Balanced Truth: Steven Spielberg's *Schindler's List* Among History, Memory, and Popular Culture," *History and Theory* 47, no. 2 (2009): 88–89.

10. FORGIVENESS

1. Abraham Joshua Heschel, "Symposium," in *The Sunflower: On the Possibilities and Limits of Forgiveness*, by Simon Wiesenthal (New York: Schocken Books, 1997), 170–71.
2. Wiesenthal, "The Sunflower," in Wiesenthal, *Sunflower*, 3–96.
3. Primo Levi, "Symposium," in Wiesenthal, *Sunflower*, 191–92.

4. Piotr H. Kosicki, "*Caritas* Across the Iron Curtain? Polish-German Reconciliation and the Bishops' Letter of 1965," *East European Politics and Societies* 23, no. 2 (2009): 218–19.
5. Urszula Pękała, "The Abuse of Forgiveness in Dealing with Legacies of Violence," in *Forgiveness: Philosophy, Psychology, and the Arts*, ed. Tim McKenry and Charlotte Bruun Thingholm (Oxfordshire, UK: Inter-Disciplinary Press, 2013), 78.
6. Józef Tischner, *Pomoc w rachunku sumienia* (Kraków: Znak, 2002), 23; Karolina Wigura, "Alternative Historical Narrative: Polish Bishops' Appeal to Their German Colleagues of 18 November 1965," *East European Politics and Societies and Cultures* 27, no. 3 (2013): 404.
7. Pękała, "The Abuse of Forgiveness," 79–80.
8. Adam Sacks, "The Coercive Christian Takeover of the Holocaust," *Haaretz*, April 20, 2020, https://www.haaretz.com/jewish/holocaust-remembrance-day/.premium-the-holocaust-s-christian-makeover-8783146.
9. Although the letter referred to them as "German bishops," what the Polish bishops meant was "West German bishops." The term "Germany" used in this chapter regarding the Catholic Church of West Germany often means "West Germany." I mostly retain the term "Germany" to respect the original text but resort to "West Germany" whenever necessary in context. The German original texts for the Polish bishops' letter and the German bishops' reply, the crude Polish translation by the Polish government, and the English translation used at the Atlantic Forum referenced in this chapter are as follows: "Hirtenbrief der polnischen Bischöfe an ihre deutschen Amtsbrüder vom 18. November 1965"; "Die Antwort der deutschen Bischöfe vom 5. Dezember 1965," http://cdim.pl/1965-11-18-botschaft-der-polnischen-an-die-deutschen-bisch-fe, 2942; Ministerstwo Spraw Zagranicznych, 498/Rap/65, https://msz.gov.pl/resource/8fd59e91-0bb9-4fd7-bce3-fd81dfc421dd:JCR; *German Polish Dialogue: Letters of the Polish and German Bishops and International Statements* (Bonn: Edition Atlantic Forum, 1966).
10. Wigura, "Alternative Historical Narrative," 402–4.
11. Wojciech Kucharski, "Prawdziwa bomba. Jak powstawało Orędzie biskupów polskich do biskupów niemieckich," *Więź*, no. 615 (2010): 123.
12. Ewa Czaczkowska, "Rola Kardynała Stefana Wyszyńskiego W Powstaniu Orędzia Biskupów Polskich Do Niemieckich Nieznane Dokumenty W Archiwum Prymasa Polski," *Przegląd Zachodni*, no. 3 (2016): 199.
13. Andrzej Gajewski, "Confrontation and Cooperation: 1000 Years of Polish–German–Russian Relations," *Journal of Kolegium Jagiellońskie: Toruńska Szkoła Wyzsza* 2 (2015): 9–10.
14. Karolina Wigura, *Wina Narodó . . . Przebaczenie jako strategia prowadzenia polityki* (Gdańsk: Scholar, 2011); Joanna Wawrzyniak, *Veterans, Victims and Memory* (Frankfurt am Main: Peter Lang, 2015); Małgorzata Pakier and Joanna Wawrzyniak, eds., *Memory and Change in Europe: Eastern Perspectives* (New York: Berghahn Books, 2016), part 4; Janine Holc, *The Politics of Trauma and Memory Activism: Polish-Jewish Relations Today* (London: Palgrave Macmillan, 2018); Zusanna Bogumił and

Małgorzata Głowacka-Grajper, *Milieux de mémoire in Late Modernity* (Frankfurt am Main: Peter Lang, 2019). See also chapter 2 of this book.
15. Kosicki, *"Caritas* Across the Iron Curtain?," 225.
16. Piotr Madajczyk, "S. Gawlitta, 'Aus dem Geist des Konzils! Aus der Sorge der Nachbarn!' Der Briefwechsel der polnischen and deutschen Bischöfe von 1965 und seine Kontexte," *Kwartalnik Historyczny* 125, no. 2 (2018): 187.
17. Robert Żurek, "Avantgarde der Versöhnung: Über den Briefwechsel der Bischöfe und die Ostdenkschrift des EKD von 1965," https://www.dialogmagazin.eu/files/gestaltung/illustration/Ausschnitt%20Ausgabe%20DIALOG%20Bischoefe.png; Wigura, "Alternative Historical Narrative," 402–8.
18. Letter of Bishops of Poland and Ukraine on Reconciliation, "We Have to Rise Above the Legacy of History, Forgive One Another," *Zenit*, August 29, 2005, https://zenit.org/articles/letter-of-bishops-of-poland-and-ukraine-on-reconciliation/.
19. "Polish and Ukrainian Bishops Sign Reconciliation: Polish and Ukrainian Church Leaders Signed an Appeal for Reconciliation in Warsaw on Friday, Marking the 70th Anniversary of WWII Massacres," Radio Poland, June 28, 2013, http://archiwum.thenews.pl/1/10/Artykul/139811,Polish-and-Ukrainian-bishops-sign-reconciliation.
20. Kosicki, *"Caritas* Across the Iron Curtain?," 222; Czaczkowska, "Rola Kardynała Stefana Wyszyńskiego," 194–95.
21. Basil Kerski and Robert Zurek, "Einführung," in *Wir Vergeben und Bitten Um Vergebung: Der Briefwechsel der polnischen und deutschen Bischöfe von 1965 und seine Wirkung*, ed. Kerski, Kycia, and Zurek (Osnabruck, Ger.: Fibre, 2006), 17–22.
22. Matthias Middell and Lluis Roura, eds., *Transnational Challenges to National History Writing* (Basingstoke, UK: Palgrave Macmillan, 2013).
23. Rainer Clos, "Ein Tabubruch: Die Ostdenkschrift der EKD von 1965," September 17, 2015, https://www.evangelisch.de/inhalte/124873/17-09-2015/ekd-ostdenkschrift-1965-verstaendigung-mit-polen-kirche-und-politik.
24. Kosicki, *"Caritas* Across the Iron Curtain?," 229–30.
25. "5 listopada 1965, szyfrogram szefa Polskiej Misji Wojskowej w Berlinie Zachodnim o konferencji prasowej w sprawie Memorandum Wschodniego," https://msz.gov.pl/resource/6d3747e9-f26a-4328-88a1-7641b59f2365:JCR.
26. "12 listopada 1965, szyfrogram szefa Przedstawicielstwa Handlowego w Kolonii w sprawie Memorandum Wschodniego," https://msz.gov.pl/resource/fd5e75f7-f61e-4765-b6c2-a002caba7fec:JCR.
27. "16 listopada 1965, szyfrogram szefa Przedstawicielstwa Handlowego w Kolonii o sytuacji po ogłoszeniu 'Memorandum Wschodniego,'" https://msz.gov.pl/resource/a7ca81dd-ab4c-40c6-a0e5-3daf730df49f:JCR. The Gerstenmeier in the text seems to indicate Eugen Gerstenmaier, then president of the Bundestag and a member of the Christian Democratic Union.
28. Gerhard Besier (Dresden) und Katarzyna Stokłosa (Sønderborg), "Kirchliches Versöhnungshandeln im Interesse des deutsch-polnischen Verhältnisses (1962–1990)," *KZG/CCH* 24 (2011): 303.

29. "Gespräch mit Mieczsław Rakowski," in *Wir Vergeben und Bitten Um Vergebung*, 143, 145.
30. Besier und Stokłosa, "Kirchliches Versöhnungshandeln," 297.
31. "Hirtenbrief der polnischen Bischöfe"; *German Polish Dialogue*, 15–16.
32. *German Polish Dialogue*, 7, 9, 10–11.
33. Wigura, "Alternative Historical Narrative," 407.
34. For the nationalist historiography of Central and Eastern Europe and its alternatives, see Jan M. Piskorski, ed., *Historiographical Approaches to Medieval Colonization of East Central Europe* (New York: Columbia University Press, 2002); and Frank Hadler and Mathias Mesenhoeller, eds., *Vergangene Grösse und Ohnmacht in Ostmitteleuropa: Repräsentationen imperialer Erfahrung in der Historiographie seit 1918* (Leipzig: Akademische Verlagsanstalt, 2007).
35. Considering that it was only in 2000 that art historians of Poland and Germany worked together on the exhibition *Common Heritage* in Warsaw, Berlin, and Dresden, the progressiveness of the letter cannot be stressed enough. For the exhibition, see Klaus Ziemer, "Introduction," in *Memory and Politics of Cultural Heritage in Poland and Germany*, ed. Ziemer (Warsaw: Cardinal Stefan Wyszyński University in Warsaw, 2015), 8.
36. "Hirtenbrief der polnischen Bischöfe," 13–15.
37. "Prezydent Litwy o Konstytucji 3 maja: obchodzimy to święto razem z Polską," Deon.pl, https://deon.pl/swiat/prezydent-litwy-o-konstytucji-3-maja-obchodzimy-to-swieto-razem-z-polska,2031668.
38. "Hirtenbrief der polnischen Bischöfe," 16, 18.
39. Gajewski, "Confrontation and Cooperation," 10.
40. "Die polnische Gesellschaft war auf einen solchen Schritt nicht vorarbeitet: Gespräch mit Tadeusz Mazowiecki," in Kerski, Kycia, and Zurek, *Wir Vergeben und Bitten Um Vergebung*, 101.
41. See Stefan Berger, "On Taboos, Traumas, and Other Myths: Why the Debate About German Victims of the Second World War Is Not a Historians' Controversy," in *Germans as Victims*, ed. Bill Niven (Basingstoke, UK: Palgrave Macmillan, 2006), 214, 220; and chapter 6 of this book.
42. Basil Kerski and Robert Zurek, "Der Briefwechsel zwischen den polnischen und deutschen Bischöfen von 1965: Entstehungsgeschichte, historischer Kontext und unmittelbare Wirkung," in Kerski, Kycia, and Zurek, *Wir Vergeben und Bitten Um Ergebung*, 26, 37.
43. Michael Rothberg, *Multidirectional Memory: Remembering the Holocaust in the Age of Decolonization* (Stanford, Calif.: Stanford University Press, 2009), 3, 9, 11, and passim.
44. 김은수, "선교과제로서의 화해와 치유" [Reconciliation and healing as missionary work], 『선교신학』 21 (2009); 안승오, "에큐메니칼 화해 개념 이해 [Understanding the ecumenical concept of reconciliation]," 『신학과 목회』 , 45 (2016).
45. 박보경, "로잔운동에 나타나는 화해로서의 선교" [Missionary work as reconciliation in the Lausanne movement], 『선교신학』 38 (2015).

46. Kosicki, "Caritas Across the Iron Curtain?," 219; Wigura, "Alternative Historical Narrative," 404.
47. Pękała, "The Abuse of Forgiveness," 78.
48. Urszula Pękała, "Asymetrie pojednania. Pojednanie niemiecko-polskie i niemiecko-francuskie po II wojnie światowej," in *Perspektywy dialogu: Studia na temat niemiecko-polskich procesów transferowych w przestrzeni religijnej*, ed. Aleksandra Chylewska-Tölle (Słubice, Pol.: Collegium Polonicum, 2016), 98–100.
49. Gajewski, "Confrontation and Cooperation," 11.
50. "Die Antwort der deutschen Bischöfe an die polnischen Bischöfe vom 5. Dezember 1965," http://cdim.pl/1965-11-18-botschaft-der-polnischen-an-die-deutschen-bisch-fe,2942.
51. Kosicki, "Caritas Across the Iron Curtain?," 223; Wigura, "Alternative Historical Narrative," 406.
52. Kerski and Jurek, ""Einführung," 34–41.
53. The memorandum signed by 160 Catholic intellectuals, including Joseph Ratzinger, then a young theology professor, was released in 1968 when the New Eastern Policy (Ostpolitik) was discussed at the Social Democratic Party (SPD) convention in Nuremberg.
54. "The Polish Bishops," *Die Welt*, December 4, 1965; "The Answer," *Hessische Allgemeine*, December 7, 1965, in *German Polish Dialogue*, 118, 121.
55. "Regarding the Message of the Bishops," *Trybuna Ludu*, December 12, 1965, in *German Polish Dialogue*, 47–48.
56. "Declaration of the PAX Federation," *Słowo Powszechna*, December 29, 1965; "Letter from the President of the Council of Ministers of the Peoples Republic of Poland to the Bishops of the Roman Catholic Church," March 5, 1966, in *German Polish Dialogue*, 55, 71, 73.
57. Czaczkowska, "Rola Kardynała Stefana Wyszyńskiego," 198–99.
58. "Questions of the Authors of the 'Message,'" *Życie Warszawy*, January 14, 1966; "Letter from the President of the Council," in *German Polish Dialogue*, 61–62, 72–73.
59. Pękała, "The Abuse of Forgiveness," 80.
60. 日本カトリック司教団教書、[平和への決意　戦後五十年にあたって] [Decision toward peace confronting 50 years after the end of war], February 25, 1995, https://www.cbcj.catholic.jp/wp-content/uploads/2016/10/heiwa_ketsui-1.pdf.
61. 日本カトリック正義と平和協議会、"日韓政府関係の和解に向けての会長談話" [Chairperson's statement on the reconciliation between Japan and Korea], August 14, 2019, https://www.cbcj.catholic.jp/2019/08/14/19330.
62. 주교회의 정평위원장 배기현 주교, "한일관계 새로운 질서 찾자" [In search of new order in the Korean-Japanese relationship], https://www.cpbc.co.kr/CMS/news/view_body.php?cid=760302&path=201908, accessed March 31, 2020.
63. 한국 천주교 주교회의, "3·1 운동 100주년 기념 담화" [Statement on the centennial of March 1st Movement]," http://www.cbck.or.kr/Notice/13013764, accessed March 31, 2020.

64. 日本カトリック正義と平和協議会会長談話, "3・1独立運動100周年を迎えて" [Commemorating the centennial of the March 1st Movement], https://www.cbcj.catholic.jp/2019/03/05/18627/, accessed March 31, 2020.
65. 양권석, "기억의 치유: 이야기와 실천의 새로운 길을 찾아서" [The healing of memory: Toward the new road to storytelling and practice], 『동아시아 기억의 연대와 평화: 한일 가톨릭 교회의 역할』 학술대회(2019/10/31) 종합토론 기조 발제문.
66. Aleida Assmann, "On the (In)Compatability and Suffering in German Memory," *German Life and Letters* 59, no. 2 (April 2006): 194.

CODA

1. Lorenz Deutsch, "Offener Brief an Intendantin Der Ruhrtriennale," https://www.lorenz-deutsch.de/antisemitismus-keine-buehne-bieten/2234/.
2. Achille Mbembe, "The Society of Enmity," *Radical Philosophy* 200 (November/December 2016): 24–25. See also Michael Rothberg, "On the Mbembe Affair: The Specters of Comparison," *Latitude*, May 2020, https://www.goethe.de/prj/zei/en/pos/21864662.html; Rothberg, "Comparing Comparisons: From the 'Historikerstreit to the Mbembe Affair,'" *Geschichte der Gegenwart*, September 23, 2020, https://geschichtedergegenwart.ch/comparing-comparisons-from-the-historikerstreit-to-the-mbembe-affair/.
3. René Aguigah, "The Conviction and Conscience of Achille Mbembe: Interview with Achille Mbembe," *New Frame*, April 23, 2020.
4. Shirli Gilbert, "Anne Frank in South Africa: Remembering the Holocaust During and After Apartheid," *Holocaust and Genocide Studies* 26, no. 3 (2012): 366, 374–75.
5. Itay Mashiach, "In Germany, a Witch Hunt Is Raging Against Critics of Israel. Cultural Leaders Have Had Enough," *Haaretz*, December 10, 2020, https://www.haaretz.com/israel-news/2020-12-10/ty-article-magazine/.highlight/in-germany-a-witch-hunt-rages-against-israel-critics-many-have-had-enough/0000017f-db0d-df0f-a17f-df4fa21b0000.
6. Natan Sznaider, "The Summer of Discontent: Achille Mbembe in Germany," *Journal of Genocide Research*, December 4, 2020, https://doi.org/10.1080/14623528.2020.1847862. However, Sznaider seems to have become more inclined toward the raison d'etat of the Israeli state, as attested to by his most recent book. See Natan Sznaider, *Fluchtpunkte der Erinnerung: Über die Gegenwart von Holocaust und Kolonialismus* (Munich: Carl Hanser Verlag, 2022).
7. For the most updated version of my criticism, see Jie-Hyun Lim, *Opfernationalismus: Erinnerung und Herrschaft in der postkolonialen Welt* (Berlin: Verlag Klaus Wagenbach, 2024): 57–94.
8. In the current debates on "Causa Mbembe," the conservatives stand for the uniqueness of the Holocaust and against the postcolonial view of the Holocaust in the

context of global colonialism. See Jürgen Zimmerer und Michael Rothberg, "Erinnerungskultur: Enttabuisiert den Vergleich!," *Die Zeit*, no. 14, March 31, 2021, https://www.zeit.de/2021/14/erinnerungskultur-gedenken-pluralisieren-holocaust-vergleich-globalisierung-geschichte/.

9. A. Dirk Moses, "Der Katechismus der Deutschen," *Geschichte der Gegenwart*, May 23, 2021, https://geschichtedergegenwart.ch/der-katechismus-der-deutschen/; Bascha Mika, "Interview with Micha Brumlik:Israel-Kritik: Wer bestimmt eigentlich, was antisemitisch ist?," *Frankfurter Rundschau*, March 8, 2020, https://www.fr.de/kultur/gesellschaft/micha-brumlik-ich-bezeichne-das-als-eine-neue-form-des-mc-carthyismus-90017108.html.

10. Ussama Maksidi, "Atonement at the Expense of Another," *The New Fascism Syllabus*, June 12, 2021, http://newfascismsyllabus.com/opinions/atonement-at-the-expense-of-another/.

11. While critical relativization is my term, I borrowed the term "radical juxtaposition" from Susan Sontag and Allan Kaprow, "An Art of Radical Juxtaposition," *The Second Coming Magazine* (January 1965), 2026; Susan Stanford Friedman, *Planetary Modernisms* (New York: Columbia University Press, 2015); and Yến Lê Espiritu and Diane Wolf, "The Appropriation of American War Memories: A Critical Juxtaposition of the Holocaust and the Vietnam War," *Social Identities: Journal for the Study of Race, Nation, and Culture* 19, no. 2 (2013), 188–203. See also Jie-Hyun Lim, "Postcolonial Reflections on the Mnemonic Confluence of the Holocaust, Stalinist Crimes, and Colonialism," in *Mnemonic Solidarity-Global* Interventions, ed. Jie-Hyun Lim and Eve Rosenhaft (Basingstoke, UK: Palgrave/Macmillan, 2021), 15–44.

12. Moses, "Der Katechismus der Deutschen."

13. Peter Leo im Gespräch mit Kolja Unger, "Historikerstreit 2.0 über Shoah: Historiker Peter Leo fordert globale Perspektive auf NS-Verbrechen," *Deutschlandfunk*, July 11, 2021, https://www.deutschlandfunk.de/historikerstreit-2-0-ueber-shoah-historiker-per-leo-fordert-100.html.

14. The "East" in the Global Easts is not a geographically fixed entity but a liquid position where events, questions, and actors are discursively located in global interactions.

15. Jan Grabowksi, "Germany Is Fueling a False History of the Holocaust Across Europe," *Haaretz*, June 22, 2020, https://www.haaretz.com/world-news/2020-06-22/ty-article-opinion/.premium/germany-is-fueling-a-false-history-of-the-holocaust-across-europe/0000017f-f497-d887-a7ff-fcf75b480000. According to Grabowski, he first sent this essay to German newspapers such as the *FAZ* and *Spiegel*, which in unison refused to publish it; he ultimately had to translate it into English and publish it in *Haaretz*. Grabowski email message to the author, June 7, 2021.

16. Heiko Maas and Andreas Wirsching, "75 Jahre Kriegsende: Keine Politik ohne Geschichte," *Spiegel*, May 7, 2020, https://www.spiegel.de/politik/deutschland/keine-politik-ohne-geschichte-a-d74deffe-c0f3-4ff7-a6af-dc713e74c6f3.

17. To my surprise, German historians' good intentions are very similar to the Japanese "conscientious (良心的) intellectuals" who unconditionally advocate nationalism in

both Koreas and China. See "日本の讀者へ" [Introduction to Japanese readers], 『犠牲者意識ナショナリズム―国境を超える「記憶」の戦争』 [Victimhood Nationalism] 澤田克己 (翻訳) (東京:東洋經濟新聞社, 2022): iv–v.

18. I prefer "deprovincializing German national memory" to "globalization of German responsibility" because the latter suggests diluting German responsibility. For "globalization of German responsibility," see Claudius Seidl, "War der Holocaust eine koloniale Tat?," *FAZ*, March 1, 2021, https://www.faz.net/aktuell/feuilleton/streit-um-gedenkkultur-war-der-holocaust-eine-koloniale-tat-17217645.html.

19. Jan Gross, "Die Osteuropäer haben kein Schamgefühl," *Die Welt*, September 13, 2015, https://www.welt.de/debatte/kommentare/article146355392/Die-Osteuropaeer-haben-kein-Schamgefuehl.html.

20. Especially in Poland and Baltic countries, the Holocaust has been deemed peripheral to the national suffering under the Stalinist oppression. See Siobhan Kattago, "Agreeing to Disagree on the Legacies of Recent History: Memory, Pluralism and Europe After 1989," *European Journal of Social Theory* 12, no. 3 (2009): 382; Martin Evans, "Memories, Monuments, Histories: The Re-thinking of the Second World War Since 1989," *National Identities* 8, no. 4 (2006): 320.

21. Bartosz T. Wieliński, "'Polska nie chce uchodźców, bo nie rozliczyła się ze zbrodni na Żydach.' Oburzenie po tekście Grossa," *Gazeta Wyborcza*, September 15, 2015, https://wyborcza.pl/7,75968,18817369,polska-nie-chce-uchodzcow-bo-nie-rozliczyla-sie-ze-zbrodni.html; Aleksander Smolar, "Smolar: Gross szokuje," *Gazeta Wyborcza*, September 16, 2015, https://wyborcza.pl/7,75968,18824173,smolar-gross-szokuje.html.

22. Lucy Mayblin et al., "'Other' Posts in 'Other' Places: Poland Through a Postcolonial Lens?," *Sociology* 50, no. 1 (2016): 66; Larry Wolff, *Inventing Eastern Europe: The Map of Civilization on the Mind of the Enlightenment* (Stanford, Calif.: Stanford University Press, 1994), 9; Jerzy Jedlicki, *A Suburb of Europe: Nineteenth-Century Polish Approaches to Western Civilization* (Budapest: Central European University Press, 1999), xiii.

23. For instance, see Clare Cavanagh, "Postcolonial Poland," *Common Knowledge* 10, no. 1 (2004): 82–92; Maxim K. Waldstein, "Observing *Imperium*: A Postcolonial Reading of Ryszard Kapuscinski's Account of Soviet and Post-Soviet Russia," *Social Identities* 8, no. 3 (2002): 481–99.

24. For subaltern empires, see Viatcheslav Morozov, "Subaltern Empire? Toward a Postcolonial Approach to Russian Foreign Policy," *Problems of Post-Communism* 60, no. 6 (2013): 16–28; Jordan Sand, "Subaltern Imperialists: The New Historiography of the Japanese Empire," *Past and Present*, no. 225 (November 2014): 273–88. For its in-between position, Poland has been called a "little imperialism."

25. See the interview with Malika Abdoulvakhabova, a Chechen refugee living in Poland, in Marek Rymsza, "Dyskusja: czy to nasza sprawa?" *Więź*, no. 662 (2015): 36, 38, 39.

26. Rymsza, 42.

27. Dan Stone, "The Historiography of Genocide: Beyond 'Uniqueness' and Ethnic Competition," *Rethinking History* 8, no. 1 (2004): 133.

28. Aimé Césaire, *Discourse on Colonialism*, trans. J. Pinkham (New York: Monthly Review, 2000), 36.
29. Adam F. Kola, *Socjalistyczny Postkolonializm: Rekonsolidacja pamięci* (Toruń, Pol.: NCU Press, 2018), 2–3.
30. See Richard C. Lukas, *Forgotten Holocaust: The Poles Under German Occupation*, rev. ed. (New York: Hippocrene Books, 2005); Tadeusz Piotrowski, *Poland's Holocaust: Ethnic Strife, Collaboration with Occupying Forces and Genocide in the Second Republic, 1918–1947* (Jefferson, N.C.: McFarland, 1998).
31. Lukas, *Forgotten Holocaust*, 34–35.
32. Amos Goldberg, "Ethics, Identity, and Anti-fundamental Fundamentalism: Holocaust Memory in the Global Age," and Haim Hazan, "Globalization Versus Holocaust," in *Marking Evil: Holocaust Memory in the Global Age*, ed. Amos Goldberg and Haim Hazan (New York: Berghahn Books, 2015), 20–21, 31.
33. Alon Confino, "The Holocaust as a Symbolic Manual," in Goldberg and Hazan, *Making Evil*, 56.
34. Hagai El-Ad, "Netanyahu Exploits the Holocaust to Brutalize the Palestinians," *Haaretz*, January 23, 2020, https://www.haaretz.com/israel-news/2020-01-23/ty-article-opinion/.premium/netanyahu-exploits-the-holocaust-to-brutalize-the-palestinians/0000017f-e0b3-d804-ad7f-f1fb6fc40000.
35. Jean-Marc Dreyfus and Marcel Stoetzler, "Holocaust Memory in the Twenty-first Century: Between National Reshaping and Globalization," *European Review of History* 18, no. 1 (February 2011): 74–75.
36. Peter Novick, *The Holocaust and the Collective Memory* (London: Bloomsbury, 2001), 241.
37. Mark Mazower, *Dark Continent: Europe's Twentieth Century* (New York: Vintage Books, 1998), xiii.
38. Zygmunt Bauman, *Modernity and the Holocaust*, rev. ed. (Ithaca, N.Y.: Cornell University Press, 2000), 227–28.
39. Jürgen Zimmerer und Michael Rothberg, "Erinnerungskultur: Enttabuisiert den Vergleich!," *Die Zeit*, no. 14, March 31, 2021, https://www.zeit.de/2021/14/erinnerungskultur-gedenken-pluralisieren-holocaust-vergleich-globalisierung-geschichte/.
40. Ali Velshi, "Israel's Bombing of Gaza Ignores Palestinians' Right to Exist," *MSNBC Live*, last modified May 20, 2021, https://www.msnbc.com/opinion/israel-s-bombing-gaza-ignores-palestinians-right-exist-n1267585.
41. Alan Macleod, "Why the Overton Window Has Suddenly Shifted on Israel-Palestine," *Mintpressnews*, May 24, 2021, https://www.mintpressnews.com/why-overton-window-suddenly-shifted-israel-palestine/277338/.
42. Joshua Shanes, "The Tulsa Massacre Wasn't a 'Race Riot'—It Was a Pogrom," *Forward*, May 31, 2021.
43. Espiritu and Wolf, "The Appropriation of American War Memories."
44. Samantha Hill, "Hannah Arendt Would Not Qualify for the Hannah Arendt Prize in Germany Today," *Guardian*, December 18, 2023, https://www.theguardian.com/commentisfree/2023/dec/18/hannah-arendt-prize-masha-gessen-israel-gaza-essay.

45. Etan Nechin, "Would Frantz Fanon Have Supported the Oct. 7 Massacre? His Biographer Isn't So Sure," *Haaretz*, February 2, 2024, https://www.haaretz.com/life/books/2024-02-02/ty-article-magazine/.premium/would-frantz-fanon-have-supported-the-oct-7-massacre-his-biographer-isnt-so-sure/0000018d-63eb-d480-adbd-ebfbaa3a0000.
46. For an alternative approach to mnemonic solidarity, see Anna Cento Bull and Hans Lauge Hansen, "On Agonistic Memory," *Memory Studies* 9, no. 4 (2015): 390–404.

BIBLIOGRAPHY

OFFICIAL DOCUMENTS, COMMUNIQUÉS AND GOVERNMENT REPORTS

『조선인 BC 급 전범에 대한 진상조사—포로감시원 동원과 전범 처벌 실태를 중심으로』 [An investigation of the Joseon BC class war criminals with a focus on the mobilization of the jailors and the punishment of the war criminals]. 대일항쟁기강제동원피해조사및국외강제동원희생자등지원위원회 보고서. 2011. 발간등록번호: 11-1655026-000007-01.

"한국 천주교 주교회의, 3·1 운동 100 주년 기념 담화" [Statement on the centennial of March 1st Movement] 한국천주교주교회의 담화문. March 2, 2019. http://www.cbck.or.kr/Notice/13013764?page=3&gb=K1300.

"한일관계 새로운 질서 찾자" [In search of new order in the Korean-Japanese relationship]. 주교회의 정평위원장 배기현 주교. https://www.cpbc.co.kr/CMS/news/view_body.php?cid=760302&path=201908 Accessed March 31, 2020.

"平和への決意 戦後五十年にあたって" [Decision toward peace confronting 50 years after the end of war]. 日本カトリック司教団教書. February 25, 1995. https://www.cbcj.catholic.jp/wp-content/uploads/2016/10/heiwa_ketsui-1.pdf.

"3・1独立運動１００周年を迎えて" [Commemorating the centennial of the March 1st Independence Movement]. 日本カトリック正義と平和協議会. March 5, 2019. https://www.cbcj.catholic.jp/2019/03/05/18627/.

"日韓政府関係の和解に向けての会長談話" [Chairperson's statement on the reconciliation between Japan and Korea]. 日本カトリック正義と平和協議会. August 14, 2019. https://www.cbcj.catholic.jp/2019/08/14/19330/.

厚生省援護局『引揚げと援護三十年の歩み』 [*Hikiage* and social relief—a sketch of last thirty years]. ぎょうせい、1978年.

厚生省社会・援護局援護50年史編集委員会『援護50年史』 [A history of social relief in last fifity years]. ぎょうせい、1997年.

"Call to Replace Felix Klein as the Federal Government Commissioner for the Fight Against Antisemitism, 30 April 2020." Statement to German Minister Seehofer by Jewish Scholars and Artists. https://www.scribd.com/document/459345514/Call-on-German-Minister-Seehofer.

"Dziennik Ustaw Rzeczypospolitej Polskiej. Warszawa, dnia 14 lutego 2018 r. Poz. 369." *Dokument podpisany przez Marek Guluch Data.* https://dziennikustaw.gov.pl/D20180000 36901.pdf.

Instytut Pamięci Narodowej. "On Final Findings of Investigation S 1/00/Zn Into the Killing of Polish Citizens of Jewish Origin in the Town of Jedwabne, on 10 July 1941, i.e., Pursuant to Article 1 Point 1 of the Decree of 31 August 1944." http://ipn.gov.pl/eng konf _jedwabne_press.html.

International Holocaust Remembrance Alliance. "Declaration of the Stockholm International Forum on the Holocaust." https://www.holocaustremembrance.com/sites/default /files/ stockholm_4csilver.pdf.

Israel Ministry of Foreign Affairs. "Declaration of Establishment of State of Israel, May 14, 1948." https://mfa.gov.il/mfa/foreignpolicy/peace/guide/pages/declaration%20 of%20est ablishment%20of%20state%20of%20israel.aspx.

"Louis Harap's Letter to W.E.B. Dubois. Feb. 13, 1952." W.E.B. Du Bois Papers (MS 312). Special Collections and University Archives, University of Massachusetts Amherst Libraries.

Maas, Heiko, and Andreas Wirsching. "75 Jahre Kriegsende: Keine Politik ohne Geschichte," *Spiegel.* Online ed., May 7, 2020.

Museum of Contemporary Art in Warsaw. "'Marsz Pokoju Hiroszima-Oświęcim, 1963' nr. ilustracji: 8611, 8612, 7631, 4994." *Archiwum Eustachego Kossakowskiego.*

Odezwa "Protest!" konspiracyjnego Frontu Odrodzenia Polski pióra Zofii Kossak- Szczuckiej, sierpień 1942 r. http://www.zydziwpolsce.edu.pl/biblioteka/zrodla/r3_5d.html.

"Prague Declaration on European Conscience and Communism," June 3, 2008.

"Prezydent Litwy o Konstytucji 3 maja: obchodzimy to święto razem z Polską." Deon.pl. https://deon.pl/swiat/prezydent-litwy-o-konstytucji-3-maja-obchodzimy-to-swieto -razem-z-polska,2031668.

Sejm Rzeczypospolitej Polskiej. "USTAWA z dnia 6 marca 2018 r. o ustanowieniu Narodowego Dnia Pamięci Polaków ratując ych Żydów pod okupacją niemiecką." http:// orka.sejm.gov.pl/opinie8.nsf/nazwa/1947_u/$file/1947_u.pdf.

Serwis Rzeczypospolitej Polskiej. "5 listopada 1965, szyfrogram szefa Polskiej Misji Wojskowej w Berlinie Zachodnim o konferencji prasowej w sprawie Memorandum Wschodniego." https://msz.gov.pl/resource/6d3747e9-f26a-4328-88a1-7641b59f2365:JCR.

———. "Ministerstwo Spraw Zagranicznych. 498/Rap/65." https://m sz.gov.pl/resource /8fd59e91-0bb9-4fd7-bce3-fd81dfc421dd:JCR.

———. "12 listopada 1965, szyfrogram szefa Przedstawicielstwa Handlowego w Kolonii w sprawie Memorandum Wschodniego." https://msz.gov.pl/reso urce/fd5e75f7-f61e-4765 -b6c2-a002caba7fec:JCR.

———. "16 listopada 1965, szyfrogram szefa Przedstawicielstwa Handlowego w Kolonii o sytuacji poogłoszeniu Memorandum Wschodniego." https://ms z.gov.pl/resource/a7ca81dd -ab4c-40c6-a0e5-3daf730df49f:JCR.

"Transcript of Oral Judgment, delivered in The Hague, The Netherlands, 4 December 2001." Statement by Judges of the Women's International War Crimes Tribunal on Japan's Military Sexual Slavery. http://iccwomen.org/wigjdraft1/Archives/oldWCGJ/tokyo/summ ary.html.

United Nations Digital Library. "Report of the Special Rapporteur in the Field of Cultural Rights, Farida Shaheed: Memorialization Processes." https://digitallibrary.un.org/record/766862

"United Nations, Economic and Social Council, 2nd Year, 4th Session." *Report of the Working Group for Asia and the Far East.* Supplement no. 10 (1947).

"Ustawa. Z dnia 6 marca 2018 r. o ustawieniu Narodowego Dnia Pamięci Polaków ratujących Żydów pod okupacją niemiecką." http://orka.sejm.gov.pl/opinie8.nsf/nazwa/1947_u/$file/1947_u.pdf.

Washington Conference on Holocaust-Era Assets. "Declarations of the Task Force for International Cooperation on Holocaust Education, Remembrance, and Research. December 3, 1998." https://fcit.usf.edu/holocaust/resource/assets/decl.htm.

DAILY NEWSPAPERS, WEEKLIES, AND PERIODICALS

경향신문 [Kyunghyang Shinmun]
産經新聞 [Sankei Shinbun]
長崎新聞 [Nagasaki Shinbun]
동광 [Tong'kwang]
동아일보 [Dong-A Ilbo]
매일경제 [Maeil Business Newspaper]
매일신보 [Maeil Sinbo]
머니투데이 [Money Today]
문화일보 [Munhwa Daily]
朝日新聞 [Asahi Shinbun]

新刊 JP [Shinkan JP]
오마이뉴스 [Ohmy News]
자주시보 [Jajusibo]
연합뉴스 [Yonhap News Agency]
조선일보 [Chosun Daily]
통일뉴스 [Tongil News]
한겨레 [Hankyoreh]
한겨레21 [Hankyoreh21]
cpbcNews
Litera

AP News
BBC
Bloomberg
Chugoku Shimbun
Daily Telegraph
Der Standard
Deutsche Welle
Die Welt
Dziennik Łódzki
Dziennik Polski
Evangelisch.de
First News
Forward

Korea Herald
Neue Züricher Zeitung
New Frame
New York Review
New York Times
Olympians
Onet
Polityka
Radio Poland
Rafu Shimpo
Reuters
Rzeczpospolita
Słowo Powszechna

388 BIBLIOGRAPHY

Fox News
Frankfurter Allgemeinezeitung
Frankfurter Rundschau
Gazeta Wyborcza
Guardian
Haaretz
Hessische Allgemeine
Independent
Japan Times
JTA

Spiegel
Stern
Times of Israel
TOK FM
Trybuna Ludu
Tygodnik Powszechny
Washington Post
Zenit
Życie Warszawy

FILMS, DOCUMENTARIES, AND OTHER AUDIO/VISUAL SOURCES

다큐멘터리 <KBS 파노라마 플러스—전범이 된 조선청년들> [The young Joseon men who became war criminals]. KBS, September 2, 2014. https://www.youtub e.com/watch?v =yk1IQv7F6Ec&t=86s.

뉴스 <KBS 발굴 '만삭의 위안부' 구출 당시 영상 최초 공개> [The first broadcast of footage of the "parturient comfort woman" being rescued—KBS found footage]. KBS, May 28, 2020. https://www.youtube.com/watch?v=xDACtH6u8JU.

뉴스 <지만원이 북한군이라던 '김 군.'. .직접 찾아봤더니> [We found "the Boy Named Kim" whom Ji Man-Won claimed to be a North Korean soldier]. MBC, May 13, 2019. https://www.youtube.c om/watch?v=dDAPiGOvBBc.

뉴스 <'5.18 이 북한군의 소행?' 37 년 만에 공개된 기무사 사진첩..드러나는 그날의 진실> [The truth uncovered regarding the accusation that May 18 was a North Korean military ploy, as the photographs from the Defense Ministry's intelligence agency become public after 37 Years]. SBS 뉴스, January 11, 2018. https://www.youtube.com/watch?v=jy_sstg6dLw &t=121s.

뉴스 <[팩트체크] 전두환 "발포명령 없었다"? . . . 검증해보니> [Fact check: Chun's claim that there was no "open fire" order]. JTBC, April 3, 2017. https://news.jtbc.join s.com/article /article.aspx?news_id=NB11448607.

뉴스 <난징학살 자행 일본, 신장 인권 말할 자격 있나> [Can Japan speak on human rights in Xinjiang without confronting its own history of the Nanjing Massacre]. YTN, March 26, 2021. https://news.naver.com/ main/read.nhn?mode=LSD&mid=tvh&oid=052&aid=00 01567703&sid1=289#.

뉴스 <문재인 정부의 아이러니..." 일본 진보가 고립되고 있다> [The irony of the Moon Jae-In administration: The Japanese progressives are alienated]. SBS, March 11, 2021. https://news.sbs.co. kr/news/endPage.do?newsId=N1006237883#lv-container.

<위안부 피해자 이용수 할머니 기자회견 현장 [원본]> [Live from the former "Comfort Woman" Lee Yong-soo's press conference]. TV 조선, May 25, 2020. https://w ww.youtube.com /watch?v=sfXE0Fzpyig.

<히로시마 원폭피해자들에게 돌직구 날리는 원폭 개발자> [The physicist who helped develop the A-bomb slams the Hiroshima victims with facts]. 생생일본뉴스. August 6, 2020. https://youtu.be/ufZym-LkkBw.

Arnold, Agnieszka. 1999. *Gdzie mój starszy syn Kain*. Telewizja Polska - I Program https://www.youtube.com/watch?v=fbf1acGB0j8.

Białek, Bogdan. 2016. *Bogdan's Journey*. Two Points Film.

Höffkes, Karl. 2004. *Das Dritte Reich* privat: *Leben und Überleben*. DVD. Polar Film.

"Jej dokument ujawnił prawdę o Jedwabnem." TOK FM, July 7, 2017. https://www.tokfm.pl/Tokfm/7,103454,22035601,jej-dokument-ujawnil-prawde-o-jedwabnem-mam-poczucie-porazki.html.

Lanzmann, Claude. 1985. *Shoah*. New Yorker Films.

BOOKS, MONOGRAPHS, AND ARTICLES

IN KOREAN

강인철.『전쟁과 희생: 한국의 전사자 숭배』[War and sacrifice: The cult of war dead in Korea]. 역사비평사, 2019.

고황경.『인도기행』[Traveling India]. 을유문화사, 1949.

다카하시 데쓰야(高橋哲哉).『(결코 피할 수 없는) 야스쿠니 문제』[Yasukuni question]. 현대송 옮김. 역사비평사, 2005.

―――.『국가와 희생―개인의 희생 없는 국가와 사회는 존재하는가?』[State and sacrifice—can there be a state and society without the sacrifice of individuals?]. 이목 옮김. 책과함께, 2008.

사카사이 아키토(逆井 聡人).『'잿더미' 전후 공간론』[Charred ruins—a discussion of postwar spaces]. 박광현 옮김. 이숲, 2020.

아시아평화와 역사교육연대.『후쇼샤 일본 중학교 역사교과서―2005년 검정합격본·검토용』(비매품). [Fushosha middel school history textbook]. 2005.

안동원.『세계일주기』[Traveling around the world]. 태극서관, 1949.

이광수.『일본 역사왜곡 1편: 요코 이야기의 진실을 찾아라』개정판 [Japan's historical revisionism, vol. 1: Searching for the truth of *So Far from the Bamboo Grove*--revised edition]. 키네마인, 2010.

이다.『반크 역사바로찾기 3: 요코 이야기의 진실을 찾아라!』[VANK's history corrections, vol. 3: Seeking the truth of *So Far from the Bamboo Grove*!]. 키네마인, 2009.

이영진.『죽음과 내셔널리즘―전후 일본의 특공위령과 애도의 정치학』[Death and nationalism—the memorial for the special units in postwar Japan and the politics of mourning]. 서울대학교출판문화원, 2018.

임지현.『희생자의식 민족주의』[Victimhood nationalism—a global history]. 휴머니스트, 2021.

―――.『그대들의 자유, 우리들의 자유―폴란드 민족해방운동사』[For our freedom and yours—a history of the Irredentist movement in Poland]. 아카넷, 2000.

―――.『적대적 공범자들』[Antagonistic complicity]. 소나무, 2005.

임지현·김용우 엮음.『대중독재 I—강제와 동의의 사이에서』 [Mass dictatorship I: Between coorsion and consent]. 책세상, 2004.

———.『대중독재 II: 정치종교와 헤게모니』 [Mass dictatorship II: Political religion and hegemony]. 책세상, 2005.

———.『대중독재 III—일상의 욕망과 미망』 [Mass dictatorship III: Between collusion and evasion]. 책세상, 2007.

임지현·이성시 엮음.『국사의 신화를 넘어서』. [Beyond the myth of national history]. 휴머니스트, 2004.

장세진.『슬픈아시아: 한국지식인들의 아시아 기행(1945-1966)』 [Sad Asia: Korean intellectuals' travelogues to Asia (1945-1966)]. 푸른역사, 2012.

전광용.『꺼삐딴 리—全光鏞創作集』 [Captain Lee]. 을유문화사. 1992.

전두환.『전두환 회고록』 [The memoir of Chun Doo-Hwan]. 민정기 엮음. 자작나무숲, 2017.

정찬.『슬픔의 노래』 [The song of sorrow]. 조선일보사, 1995.

김은수.「선교과제로서의 화해와 치유—2005 아테네 CWME 를 중심으로」 [Reconciliation and healing as missionary work].『선교신학』 21 (2009): 1-29.

김준현.「한국의 문학/지식 장에서 '만보산 사건'이 기억되어 온 몇 가지 방식」 [Several ways to commemorate Wanpaoshan incident in the literary and knowledge field in Korea (1931~1987)].『한국문학연구』 51 (2016): 39-74.

김철.「몰락하는 신생(新生): '만주'의 꿈과 『농군』의 오독(誤讀)」 [Collapsing rebirth: Dream of Manchuria and misreading of "Nong-Gun"].『상허학보』 9 (2002): 123-59.

김한상.「발견된 푸티지 속의 박영심은 무엇을 말하는가(혹은 말하지 못하는가)?—사진적 생존자의 영. 화적 현전과 포스트/식민 아카이브의 냉전 지식체제」 [What Park Young-shim in the found footage can and can't speak of: The cinematic presence of a photographic survivor and the Cold War system of knowledge in the postcolonial archives].『문학과영상』 21, no. 3 (2020): 679-709.

니시무라 아키라(西村明).「위령(慰靈)과 폭력: 전쟁사망자에 대한 태도 이해를 위해」 [Soul consoling and violence]. 이세영 옮김.『종교문화비평』 2 (2002): 251-53.

무타 카즈에(牟田和惠),「'"위안부"문제는 '#미투다'!」 동영상 공격으로 보는 일본」 [The "Comfort Women" issue is a #MeToo issue]. 허윤·무타 카즈에·도미야마 이치로·권김현영.『전쟁, 여성, 폭력: 일본군 '위안부'를 트랜스내셔널하게 기억하기』 (2019): http://cgsi.ac/bbs/board.php?bo_table=eng_e_Pub&wr_id=3.

박보경.「로잔운동에 나타나는 화해로서의 선교—2004 년 파타야 포럼과 케이프타운 서약문을 중심으로」 [Missionary work as reconciliation in the Lausanne movement].『선교신학』 38 (2015): 141-70.

배묘정.「노래 부르기의 정치학—<임을 위한 행진곡>의 제창·합창 논란에 대한 수행적 관점의 분석」 [The politics of singing: A performative analysis of the controversy over compulsory singing and the voluntary singing of "Marching for Our Beloved"].『서강인문논총』 59 (2020): 205-42.

손승회.「1931 년 植民地朝鮮의 排華暴動과 華僑」 [Anti-Chinese riots and Chinese diaspora in colonial Joseon].『중국근현대사연구』 41 (2009): 141-65.

———.「근대 한중관계사의 새로운 시각 모색: 萬寶山事件 연구에 대한 적용가능성을 중심으로」 [Searching for new perspective on modern Korea-China relations: Focusing on the applicability to the research on Wanpaoshan incident].『역사학보』 202 (2009): 381-408.

신기영.「글로벌 시각에서 본 일본군 '위안부' 문제—한일관계의 양자적 틀을 넘어서」 [Rethinking Japanese wartime "Comfort Women" from a global perspective: Beyond Korea-Japan bilateral relations].『일본비평』 8, no.2 (2016): 282-309.

———.「일본군 위안부 문제: 보수의 결집과 탈냉전 세계정치의 사이에서」 [The Japanese military "Comfort Women" issue: Between the conservative rally and the post-Cold War international politics]. 조관자 엮음.『탈 전후 일본 의사상과 감성』. 박문사, 2017.

심정명.「3.11 과 전후의 끝: 무의미한 죽음과 애도의 문제」 [March 11 and the end of the postwar: The problem of mourning and meaningless death]. 조관자 엮음.『탈 전후 일본의 사상과 감성』. 박문사, 2017.

안승오,「에큐메니칼 화해 개념 이해」 [Understanding the concept of ecumenical reconciliation].『신학과 목회』 45 (2016): 151-72.

양권석.「기억의 치유—이야기와 실천의 새로운 길을 찾아서」 [The healing of memory: Toward the new road to storytelling and practice].『동아시아 기억의 연대와 평화: 한일 가톨릭 교회의 역할』 학술대회 종합토론 기조 발제문. 2019.

윤상원.「한국 역사학계의 만보산사건 연구동향과 과제」 [The research trend in Korean academia regarding the Wanpaoshan incident and its challenges].『한국문학연구』 51 (2016): 7-38.

윤상인.「수난담의 유혹: '요코이야기'와 민족주의」 [The alluring narrative of the tragedy: Yoko monogatari and nationalism].『비평』 15 (2007): 177-202.

윤상인.「근대문명과 신체정치」 [Modern civilization and body politics].『관정일본리뷰』 26 (2021): 1-4.

윤해동.「만보산 사건과 동아시아 기억의 터—한국인들의 기억을 중심으로」 [The Wanpaoshan incident and the site of East Asian memory with a focus on the Korean memory].『사이間 SAI』 14 (2013): 479-514.

이브 로제네프트 [Eve Rosenhaft].「히틀러의 흑인 희생자를 상상하기—다방향기억과 최근의 홀로코스트 소설」 [Imagining Hitler's Black victims: Multidirectional memory and recent holocaust fictions]. 문수현 옮김.『독일연구』 42 (2019): 107-40.

이소영.「역사부정 규제를 둘러싼 기억의 정치—5 18 왜곡처벌법인 관련 논의를 중심으로」 [The memory politics around the censorship of historical denialism: A discussion regarding the special act on the punishment of historically distorting the May 18 movement].『법과 사회』 61 (2019): 157-84.

이욱.「조선 전기 유교국가의 성립과 국가제사의 변화」 [The formation of the Confucian state and the state rituals in the early Joseon].『한국사연구』 118 (2002): 161-93.

이타가키 류타(板垣竜太).「동아시아 기억의 장소로서 力道山」 [Rikidōzan as East Asian memory space].『역사비평』 95 (2011): 127-60.

임지현 · 미하우 실리바.「폴란드 사회주의 운동사 연구의 반성과 전망」 [Reflections and prospects for history of Polish socialist movements].『역사비평』 32 (1996): 230-51.

임지현.「희생자의식 민족주의」 [Victimhood nationalism].『비평』 15 (2007).

———.「역사의 금기와 기억의 진정성—21 세기 폴란드 역사학과 '희생자의식'」 [A taboo-breaking memory of Jedwabne: Victims and perpetrators in the Polish historiography in the 21st century].『서양사론』 111 (2011): 147-74.

———.「독재는 민주주의의 반의어인가? 대중독재의 모순어법과 민주주의의 민주화」 [Mass dictatorship as a conceptual oxymoron: How are dictatorships interwoven with democracies?].『서양사론』 116 (2013): 39-63.

———.「동아시아 역사포럼—선사시대에서 역사시대로의 이행」[East Asian History Forum for criticism and solidarity]. 宮嶋博史·李成市·尹海東·林志弦 엮음. 『植民地近代の視座 (朝鮮と日本)』. 東京: 岩波書店, 2004.

———.「전지구적 기억공간과 회생자의식—홀로코스트, 식민주의 제노사이드, 스탈린주의 테러의 기억은 어떻게 만나는가?」[Entangled memories of the Holocaust, colonial genocide and Stalinist terror]. 『대구사학』 125 (2016): 110–34.

———.「정말 중요한 이야기는 침묵으로 기록된다—스베틀라나 알렉시예비치 초청 강연회」.[The most important stories are written in silence: A lecture by Svetlana Alexievich]. 『문학과 사회』 119 (2017): 338–48.

———.「지그문트 바우만 인터뷰—악의 평범성에서 악의 합리성으로」[Interview with Zygmunt Bauman—from banality of evil to rationality of evil]. 『당대비평』 21 (2003): 12–32.

정용숙.「나치 국가의 매춘소와 강제성매매—그 실제와 전후 시대의 기억」[State-run brothels and forced sexual labor under the Nazis--the realities and the postwar memories]. 『여성과 역사』 29 (2018): 375–420.

정현백·송충기.「통일 독일의 과거 청산—강제징용된 외국인 노동자에 대한 배상」[United Germany's coming to terms with its past--restitution to the foreign victims of forced mobilization]. 『FES-Information-Series』 (2000): 1–12.

찰스 암스트롱 [Charles K. Armstrong].「가족주의, 사회주의, 북한의 정치종교」[Familism, socialism, and the political religion in North Korea]. 임지현·김용우 엮음. 『대중독재 II—정치종교과 헤게모니』, 책세상, 2005.

펠릭스 티호 [Feliks Tych].「민족문제와 폴란드 공산주의 체제의 전술—유대인 정책」[The nationalist tactics of the communist regime in Poland: The policy toward the Jews]. 임지현·김용우 엮음.『대중독재 II: 정치종교과 헤게모니』. 책세상, 2005.

하영준.「일본제국과 범아프리카주의의 '트랜스-퍼시픽 커넥션'—W.E.B. 듀보이스와 C.L.R. 제임스의 동아시아 담론을 중심으로」[The transpacific connection between the Japanese empire and pan-Africanism: A study on the East Asian discourse of W.E.B. Du Bois and C.L.R. James]. 『Homo Migrans』 18 (2018): 159–203.

IN JAPANESE

内海愛子. 『朝鮮人B・C級戰犯の記錄』[Records of B·C war criminal Chosenjins]. 岩波現代文庫, 2015.

内海愛子、村井吉敬.『赤道下の朝鮮人叛亂』[Chosenjin's rebellion at the equator]. 勁草書房, 1980.

遠藤周作. 『女の一生：一部　キクの場合』[A life of woman: Part 1—Kiku]. 新潮文庫, 1986.

———.『女の一生：二部・サチ子の場合』 [A life of a woman: Part 2—Sachiko]. 新潮文庫, 1986.

———.『心の夜想曲』[Nocturnes of heart]. 文春文庫, 1989.

———.『人生の踏繪』[Life's Fumie]. 新潮社, 2017.

大江健三郎.『定義集』 [Book of definitions] 朝日新聞出版, 2016年.

林志弦. 『犧牲者意識ナショナリズム――国境を超える「記憶」の戰爭』 [Victimhood nationalism]. https://澤田克己 (翻訳). 東京：東洋經濟新聞社, 2022.

金承哲.「遠藤周作の『イエスの生涯』について―神学と文学の間で」[About Endo Shusaku's "Life of Jesus"—between theology and literature] 『キリスト教文芸』 28 号, 2012, 128–48.

洪郁如・田原開起.「朝鮮引揚者のライフ・ヒストリー: 成原明の植民地・引揚げ・戦後」["Life history" of Chosen repatriates: Narihara Akira's colonialism, repatriation, and postwar].『人文・自然研究』10号、2016, 160–75.

小熊英二.『民主と愛国: 戦後日本のナショナリズムと公共性』[Democracy and patriotism: Nationalism and publicness in postwar Japan] 新曜社、2002.

小崎登明.『長崎のコルベ神父』[Father Kolbe in Nagasaki]. 聖母の騎士社、2010.

厚生省援護局.『引揚げと援護三十年の歩み』[*Hikiage* and social relief—a sketch of last thirty years] ぎょうせい、1978.

厚生省社会・援護局援護50年史編集委員会.『援護50年史』[A history of the fifty years of relief policies] ぎょうせい、1997.

坂井久能.『名誉の戦死—陸軍上等兵黒川梅吉の戦死資料』. [Death in honor: Documents on the death in battle of army private Umekichi Kurokawa]. 岩田書院、2006.

逆井聡人.『〈焼跡〉の戦後空間論』[Postwar space after the ashes]. 青弓社、2018.

曾野綾子.『ある神話の背景—沖縄・渡嘉敷島の集団自決』[Background of a myth—collective suicide in Okinawa and Kerama Islands]. 文藝春秋、1973.

———.『奇蹟』[Miracle]. 毎日新聞社、1973.

高橋哲哉.『国家と犠牲』[State and sacrifice]. 日本放送出版協会、2005.

———.『靖国問題』[Yasukuni question]. ちくま新書、2005.

俵義文.『戦後教科書運動史』[History of revision movements on postwar school textbooks]. 平凡社新書、2020.

坪川宏子・大森典子.『司法が認定した日本軍「慰安婦」—被害・加害事実は消せない!』[The court recognizes the Comfort Women: The facts of victimization cannot be erased]. かもがわ出版、2011.

テッサ・モーリス=スズキ.『批判的想像力のために: グローバル化時代の日本』[For the critical imagination: Japan in the age of globalization]. 平凡社、2013.

中野敏男.『大塚久雄と丸山真男—動員、主体、戦争責任』[Otsuka Hisao and Maruyama Masao. Mobilization, subject, and war responsibility]. 青土社、2001.

永井隆.『永井隆全集 (第二巻)』[The complete works of Nagai Takashi, vol. 2] サンパウロ、2003.

———.『永井隆全集 (第三巻)』[The complete works of Nagai Takashi, vol. 3] サンパウロ、2003.

———.「微笑の秘訣」[Secret of the smile].『聖母の騎士』. 5月号、1980, 15.

成田龍一、吉田裕編.『記憶と認識の中のアジア・太平洋戦争: 岩波講座アジア・太平洋戦争戦後編』[Memory and perception of the Asia-Pacific War: Iwanami lectures on post–Asia-Pacific War]. 岩波書店、2015.

西川長夫.『国民国家論の射程——あるいは"国民"という怪物について』[The range of the nation-state theory: or, the monster called the "Nation"]. 柏書房、2012.

針生一郎.「日本の68年—「全共闘」・「美共闘」の可能性と問題点」[1968 in Japan: Possibilities and problems of "Zenkyoto" and "Bikyoto"].『環: 歴史・環境・文明』33、2008, 178–95.

林房雄.『大東亜戦争肯定論』[Affirming discourses on the Greater East Asian War]. 中公文庫、2014.

阪東宏.『ポーランド人と日露戦争 (明治大学人文科学研究所叢書)』[Polish in the Russo-Japanese War]. 青木書店、1995.

藤原帰一.『戦争を記憶する: 広島・ホロコーストと現在』[Remembering war: Hiroshima, Holocaust, and the present]. 講談社現代新書、2001.

山室信一.『キメラ―満州国の肖像』[Chimera: A portrait of Manchukuo]. 中公新書、2004.
吉田敏浩.『反空爆の思想』[Anti-air bombing thoughts]. 日本放送出版協会、2006.
吉田裕.『日本軍兵士―アジア・太平洋戦争の現実』[Japanese soldiers: The realities of the Asian-Pacific War] 中公新書、2017.
ヨーコ・カワシマ・ワトキンズ.『竹林はるか遠く―日本人少女ヨーコの戦争体験記』[So far away from the Bamboo Grove]. 都竹恵子訳、ハート出版、2013.
山田陽子.『図説 満洲―日本人の足跡をたどる』[Illustrating Manchuria: In the footsteps of the Japanese]. 梅田出版、2011.
米原万里.『打ちのめされるようなすごい本』[A great book beating you]. 文藝春秋、2006.
―.『魔女の1ダース―正義と常識に冷や水を浴びせる13章』[A dozen pencils at witch]. 新潮文庫、2000.
遠藤周作.「コルベ神父」[Father Kolbe].『新編国語総合』. 大修館書店、2017/
李成市.「植民地文化政策の評価を通してみた歴史認識」[Historical consciousness represented by colonial cultural policies]. 三谷博・金泰昌編、『東アジア歴史対話―国境と世代を越えて』東京大学出版会、2007, 187-206.
林志弦. ""世襲的犠牲者" 意識と脱植民地主義の歴史学」[Hereditary victimhood and postcolonial historiography] 三谷博、金泰昌編、『東アジア歴史対話――国境と世代を超えて』東京大学出版会、2007.
―.「犠牲者意識の民族主義 (特集 国際シンポジウム グローバル化時代の植民地主義とナショナリズム) ―(問題提起)」[Victimhood nationalism]『立命館言語文化研究』20巻3号、2009, 57-62.
―.「グローバルな記憶空間と犠牲者意識」[Global memory space and victimhood nationalism].『思想』no. 1116, 2017, 55-73.
―.「東アジア歴史フォーラム――先史時代から歴史時代への移行」[East Asian History Forum for criticism and solidarity: A transition from prehistory to history]. 河かおる訳、宮嶋博史、李成市、尹海東、林志弦編、『植民地近代の視座』. 岩波書店、2004.
若槻泰雄.『戦後引揚げの記録』[Records of the postwar hikiage]. 時事通信社、1991.
Immaculate Conception Province Conventual Franciscans of Japan.『聖コルベ来日75周年記念誌』[Memorial book to celebrate St. Kolbe's visit to Japan]. 聖母の騎士社、2005.
V. E.フランクル、『夜と霧―ドイツ強制収容所の体験記録』[Man's search for meaning]. 霜山徳爾訳、みすず書房、1956.

IN ENGLISH, GERMAN, OR POLISH

Aleksiun, Natalia. "Adolf Berman. W głównym nurcie historii. Żydowski Instytut Historyczny im. Emanuela Ringelbluma." October 17, 2013, https://web.archive.org/web/20161005115834/http://www.jhi.pl/blog/2013-10-17-adolf-berman-w-glownym-nurcie-historii.

Allen, Lori. "There Are Many Reasons Why: Suicide Bombers and Martyrs in Palestine." *Middle East Report* 223 (2002): 34-37.

Aly, Götz. "Geschichte reicht in die Gegenwart: Ein Gespräch mit dem Historiker Raul Hilberg." *Neue Züricher Zeitung*, December 10, 2002.

Anderson, Benedict. *Imagined Communities: Reflections on the Origin and Spread of Nationalism*. London: Verso, 1991.

Anonyma. *Eine Frau in Berlin: Tagebuchaufzeichnungen vom 20. April bis 22. Juni 1945.* Frankfurt am Main: Eichborn, 2003.
Arendt, Hannah. "The Aftermath of Nazi Rule." *Commentary* 10 (1950): 342–53.
——. *Eichmann in Jerusalem: A Report on the Banality of Evil.* New York: Penguin Books, 1994.
Assmann, Aleida. "Impact and Resonance: Towards a Theory of Emotions in Cultural Memory." *Söndertörn Lectures* 6 (2011): 41–70.
——. "On the (In)Compatability and Suffering in German Memory." *German Life and Letters* 59, no. 2 (2006): 187–200.
Assmann, Aleida, and Sebastian Conrad, eds. *Memory in a Global Age: Discourses, Practices and Trajectories.* Basingstoke, UK: Palgrave Macmillan, 2010.
Assmann, Jan. *Moses the Egyptian: The Memory of Egypt in Western Monotheism.* Cambridge, Mass.: Harvard University Press, 1997.
Assmann, Jan, and John Czaplicka. "Collective Memory and Cultural Identity." *New German Critique* 65 (1995): 125–33.
Ayako, Sono. *Miracles: A Novel*, trans. Kevin Doak. Portland, Me.: Merwin Asia, 2016.
Bartov, Omer. "The Wehrmacht Exhibition Controversy: Politics of Evidence." In *Crimes of War: Guilt and Denial in the Twentieth Century*, ed. Omer Bartov, Atina Grossmann, and Mary Nolan. New York: New Press, 2002.
Bartov, Omer, Atina Grossmann, and Mary Nolan. *Crimes of War: Guilt and Denial in the Twentieth Century.* New York: New Press, 2002.
Bauer, Yehuda, Franklin H. Littell, and Alice L. Eckardt, eds. *Remembering for the Future: Working Papers and Addenda.* New York: Pergamon Press, 1989.
Bauman, Zygmunt. *Modernity and the Holocaust.* Ithaca, N.Y.: Cornell University Press, 2000.
——. "On Immoral Reason and Illogical Morality." *Polin* 3 (1988): 294–330.
Beck, Ulrich. "The Cosmopolitan Perspective: Sociology of the Second Age of Modernity." *British Journal of Sociology* 51, no. 1 (2000): 79–105.
Beckert, Sven, and Dominic Sachsenmaier, eds. *Global History, Globally.* London: Bloomsbury, 2018.
Beevor, Anthony. *The Second World War.* New York: Little, Brown, 2012.
Behrens, Paul, Nicholas Terry, and Olaf Jensen, eds. *Holocaust and Genocide Denial: A Contextual Perspective.* New York: Routledge, 2017.
Ben-Ghiat, Ruth. "Liberation: Italian Cinema and the Fascist Past, 1945–50." In *Italian Fascism: History, Memory and Representation*, ed. Richard J. B. Bosworth and Patrizia Dogliani. London: Palgrave Macmillan, 1999.
Bender, Ryszard. *Słownik biograficzny katolicyzmu społecznego w Polsce: A-J.* Lublin, Pol.: Towarzystwo Naukowe Katolickiego Uniwersytetu Lubelskiego, 1994.
Berger, Stefan. "On Taboos, Traumas and Other Myths: Why the Debate About German Victims of the Second World War Is Not a Historians' Controversy." In *Germans as Victims*, ed. Bill Niven. Basingstoke, UK: Palgrave Macmillan, 2006.
Bernal, Martin. *Black Athena: The Afroasiatic Roots of Classical Civilization.* New Brunswick, N.J.: Rutgers University Press, 1987.

Besier, Gerhard, and Katarzyna Stoklosa. "Einleitung: Kirchliches Versöhnungshandeln im Inter esse des deutsch-polnischen Verhältnisses (1962–1990)." *Kirchliche Zeitgeschichte* 24, no. 2 (2011): 295–306.

Bessel, Richard. *Life in the Third Reich*. Oxford: Oxford University Press, 1987.

Biess, Frank. "Between Amnesty and Anti-communism: The West German Kameradenschinder Trials, 1948–1960." *Crimes of War: Guilt and Denial in the Twentieth Century*, ed. Omer Bartov, Atina Grossmann, and Mary Nolan. New York: New Press, 2002.

———. *Homecomings: Returning POWs and the Legacies of Defeat in Postwar Germany*. Princeton, N.J.: Princeton University Press, 2006.

Bikont, Anna. *The Crime and the Silence: Confronting the Massacre of Jews in Wartime Jedwabne*, trans. Alissa Valles. New York: Farrar, Straus and Giroux, 2015.

Black, Monica. "Ghosts of War." In *The Cambridge History of the Second World War*, vol. 3, ed. Michael Geyer and Adam Tooze. Cambridge: Cambridge University Press, 2015.

Blackburn, David, and Geoff Eley. *The Peculiarities of German History*. Oxford: Oxford University Press, 1984.

Blobaum, Robert, ed. *Anti-Semitism and Its Opponents in Modern Poland*. Ithaca, N.Y.: Cornell University Press, 2005.

Błoński, Jan. *Biedni Polacy patrzą na getto*. Kraków: Wydawnictwo Literackie, 1996.

Bogumił, Zuzanna, and Małgorzata Głowacka-Grajper. *Milieux de Mémoire in Late Modernity: Local Communities, Religion and Historical Politics*. Frankfurt am Main: Peter Lang, 2019.

Bohus, Kata, Peter Hallama, and Stephan Stach, eds. *Growing in the Shadow of Antifascism: Remembering the Holocaust in Communist Eastern Europe*. Budapest: Central European University Press, 2021.

Bourguet, Marie-Noëlle, Mucette Valensi, and Nathan Wachtel, eds. *Between Memory and History*. London: Harwood Academic Publishers, 1990.

Brantz, Dorothee. "Landscapes of Destruction: Capturing Images and Creating Memory Through Photography." In *The Cambridge History of the Second World War*, vol. 3, ed. Michael Geyer and Adam Tooze. Cambridge: Cambridge University Press, 2015.

Browning, Christopher R. *Ordinary Men: Reserve Police Battalion 101 and the Final Solution in Poland*. New York: HarperPerennial, 1993.

Brumlik, Micha, and Karol Sauerland, eds. *Umdeuten, verschweigen, erinnern: die späte Aufarbeitung des Holocaust in Osteuropa*. Frankfurt am Main: Campus Verlag, 2010.

Buck-Morss, Susan. *Hegel, Haiti, and Universal History*. Pittsburgh, Pa.: University of Pittsburgh Press, 2009.

Bukey, Evan Burr. *Hitler's Austria: Popular Sentiments in the Nazi Era 1938–1945*. Chapel Hill: University of North Carolina Press, 2000.

Bull, Anna Cento, and Hans Lauge Hansen. "On Agonistic Memory." *Memory Studies* 9, no. 4 (2015): 390–404.

Bunzl, Matti. "On the Politics and Semantics of Austrian Memory: Vienna's Monument Against War and Fascism." *History and Memory* 7, no. 2 (1995): 7–40.

Burleigh, Michael. "The Cardinal Basil Hume Memorial Lectures-Political Religion and Social Evil." *Totalitarian Movements and Political Religions* 3, no. 2 (2002): 1–60.

———. "National Socialism as a Political Religion." *Totalitarian Movements and Political Religions* 1, no. 2 (2000): 1–26.

———. *The Third Reich: A New History*. New York: Hill and Wang, 2001.

Buruma, Ian. *Inventing Japan, 1853–1964*. New York: Modern Library, 2004.

———. *The Wages of Guilt: Memories of War in Germany and Japan*. New York: New York Review of Books, 1994.

———. *Year Zero: A History of 1945*. New York: Penguin Press, 2013.

Canetti, Elias. *Masse Und Macht*. Hamburg, Ger.: Claassen, 1960.

Carpenter, R. Charli. "Surfacing Children: Limitations of Genocidal Rape Discourse." *Human Rights Quarterly* 22 (2000): 428–77.

Cavanagh, Clare "Postcolonial Poland." *Common Knowledge* 10, no. 1 (2004): 82–92.

Césaire, Aimé. *Discourse on Colonialism*, trans. J. Pinkham. New York: Monthly Review, 2000.

Challand, Benoît. "1989, Contested Memories and the Shifting Cognitive Maps of Europe." *European Journal of Social Theory* 12, no. 3 (2009): 397–408.

Chang, Iris. *The Rape of Nanking: The Forgotten Holocaust of World War II*. New York: Basic Books, 1997.

Charny, Israel W. "A Classification of Denials of the Holocaust and Other Genocides." *Journal of Genocide Research* 5, no. 1 (2003): 11–34.

Charny, Israel W., and Daphna Fromer. "Denying the Armenian Genocide: Patterns of Thinking as Defence-Mechanisms." *Patterns of Prejudice* 32, no. 1 (1998): 39–49.

Cherry, Robert, and Annamaria Orla-Bukowska, eds. *Polacy i Żydzi: kwestia otwarta*. Warsaw: Więź, 2008.

Chodakiewicz, M. Jan. *The Massacre in Jedwabne July 10, 1941: Before, During, and After*. Boulder, Colo.: East European Monographs, 2005.

———. *Po Zagładzie. Stosunki polsko-żydowskie 1944–1947*. Warsaw: Instytut Pamięci Narodowej, 2008.

Chow, Rey. "Sacrifice, Mimesis, and the Theorizing of Victimhood (A Speculative Essay)." *Representations* 94, no. 1 (2006): 131–49.

Churchill, Ward. "An American Holocaust? The Structure of Denial." *Socialism and Democracy* 17, no. 1 (2003): 25–75.

Cichopek, Anna. "The Cracow Pogrom of August 1945." In *Contested Memories: Poles and Jews During the Holocaust and Its Aftermath*, ed. Joshua D. Zimmerman. New Brunswick, N.J.: Rutgers University Press, 2003.

Classen, Christoph, and Kirsten Wächter. "Balanced Truth: Steven Spielberg's *Schindler's List* Among History, Memory, and Popular Culture." *History and Theory* 48, no. 2 (2009): 77–102.

Confino, Alon. *Foundational Past: The Holocaust as Historical Understanding*. Cambridge: Cambridge University Press, 2012.

———. "The Holocaust as a Symbolic Manual." In *Marking Evil: Holocaust Memory in the Global Age*, ed. Amos Goldberg Haim Hazan. New York: Berghahn Books, 2015.

Conrad, Sebastian. *The Quest for the Lost Nation: Writing History in Germany and Japan in the American Century*. Berkeley: University of California Press, 2010.

Corner, Paul, and Jie-Hyun Lim, eds. *The Palgrave Handbook of Mass Dictatorship*. London: Palgrave Macmillan, 2016.

Corner, Paul, ed. *Popular Opinion in Totalitarian Regimes: Fascism, Nazism, Communism*. Oxford: Oxford University Press, 2009.

Coser, Lewis A., ed. *Maurice Halwachs on Collective Memory*. Chicago: University of Chicago Press, 1992.

Curthoys, Ann, and John Docker. "Defining Genocide." In *The Historiography of Genocide*, ed. Dan Stone. Basingstoke, UK: Palgrave Macmillan, 2010.

Czaczkowska, Ewa K. "Rola kardynała Stefana Wyszyńskiego w powstaniu Orędzia biskupów polskich do niemieckich. Nieznane dokumenty w archiwum prymasa Polski." *Przegląd Zachodni* 360, no. 3 (2016): 193–203.

David, Lea. "Holocaust Discourse as a Screen Memory: The Serbian Case." In *History and Politics in the Western Balkans: Changes at the Turn of the Millenium*, ed. Srdan M. Jovanović and Veran Stancetic. Belgrade: Center for Good Governance Studies, 2013.

———. "Human Rights as an Ideology? Obstacles and Benefits." *Critical Sociology* 46, no. 1 (2020): 37–50.

———. "Human Rights, Micro-solidarity and Moral Action: Face-to-Face Encounters in the Israeli/Palestinian Context." *Thesis Eleven* 154, no. 1 (2019): 66–79.

———. "Moral Remembrance and New Inequalities." *Global Perspectives* 1, no. 1 (2020). https://do i.org/10.1525/001c.11782.

———. *The Past Can't Heal Us: The Dangers of Mandating Memory in the Name of Human Rights*. Cambridge: Cambridge University Press, 2020.

Dawidowicz, Lucy. *The War Against Jews*. London: Penguin Books, 1975.

De Cesari, Chiara, and Ann Rigney, eds. *Transnational Memory: Circulation, Articulation, Scales*. Berlin: Walter de Gruyter, 2014.

Delbo, Charlotte. *Auschwitz and After*, trans. Rosette Lamont. New Haven, Conn.: Yale University Press, 1995.

———. *Days and Memory*, trans. Rosette Lamont. Marlboro: Marlboro Press, 1990.

Desforges, Alison. *Leave None to Tell the Story: Genocide in Rwanda*. New York: Human Rights Watch, 1999.

Didi-Huberman, Georges. *Images Malgré Tout*. Paris: Les Éditions de Minuit, 2003.

Diner, Dan. "Memory and Restitution: World War II as a Foundational Event in a Uniting Europe." In *Restitution and Memory: Material Restitution in Europe*, ed. Dan Diner and Gotthard Wunberg. New York: Berghahn Books, 2007.

———. "Negative Symbiose. Deutsche und Juden nach Auschwitz." *Babylon* 1, no. 1 (1986): 9–20.

Diner, Dan, and William Templer. "Cumulative Contingency: Historicizing Legitimacy in Israeli Discourse." *History and Memory* 7, no. 1 (1995): 147–70.

Diner, Dan, and Gotthart Wunberg, eds. *Restitution and Memory: Material Restitution in Europe*. New York: Berghahn Books, 2007.

Dondi, Mirco. "The Fascist Mentality After Fascism." In *Italian Fascism: History, Memory and Representation*, ed. Richard J. B. Bosworth and Patrizia Dogliani. New York: St. Martin's Press, 1999.

Douglas, Lawrence. *The Right Wrong Man: John Demjanjuk and the Last Great Nazi War Crimes Trial*. Princeton, N.J.: Princeton University Press, 2016.

Dower, John W. "An Aptitude for Being Unloved: War and Memory in Japan." In *Crimes of War: Guilt and Denial in the Twentieth Century*, ed. Omer Bartov, Atina Grossmann, and Mary Nolan. New York: New Press, 2002.

———. "The Bombed: Hiroshimas and Nagasakis in Japanese Memory." *Diplomatic History* 19, no. 2 (1995): 275-95.

———. *Embracing Defeat: Japan in the Wake of World War II*. New York: Norton, 1999.

———. "Triumphal and Tragic Narratives of the War in Asia." *Journal of American History* 82, no. 3 (1995): 1124-35.

———. *War Without Mercy: Race and Power in the Pacific War*. 7th ed. New York: Pantheon Books, 1993.

Dreyfus, Jean-Marc, and Marcel Stoetzler. "Holocaust Memory in the Twenty-first Century: Between Bational Reshaping and Globalisation." *European Review of History* 18, no. 1 (2011): 69-78.

Dubois, W.E.B. "The Negro and the Warsaw Ghetto." In *The Oxford W.E.B. Dubois Reader*, ed. Eric. J. Sundquist. Oxford: Oxford University Press, 1996.

Duden, Alexis. *Troubled Apologies: Among Japan, Korea, and the United States*. New York: Columbia University Press, 2008.

Echternkamp, Jörg, and Stefan Martens, eds. *Der Zweite Weltkrieg in Europa. Erfahrung und Erinnerung*. Paderborn, Ger.: Schöningh, 2007.

Eckel, Moisel, ed. *Universalisierung des Holocaust? Erinnerungskultur und Geschichtspolitik in internationaler Perspektive, Beitrage zur Geschichte des Nationalsozialismus*, vol. 21. Göttingen, Ger.: Wallstein, 2008.

Eizenstat, Stuart. *Imperfect Justice: Looted Assets, Slave Labor and the Unfinished Business of World War II*. New York: Public Affairs, 2003.

Eley, Geoff. "Nazism, Politics and the Image of the Past: Thoughts on the West German Historikerstreit 1986-1987." *Past & Present* 121 (1988): 171-208.

Engelking, Barbara. *Holocaust and Memory*. London: Leicester University Press, 2001.

Enzer, Hyman A., and Sandra Solotaroff-Enzer, eds. *Anne Frank: Reflection on Her Life and Legacy*. Urbana: University of Illinois Press, 2000.

Espiritu, Yến Lê, and Diane Wolf. "The Appropriation of American War Memories: A Critical Juxtaposition of the Holocaust and the Vietnam War." *Social Identities* 19, no. 2 (2013): 188-203.

Evans, Martin. "Memories, Monuments, Histories: The Re-thinking of the Second World War Since 1989." *National Identities* 8, no. 4 (2006): 317-348.

Farmer, Sarah. "Symbols That Face Two Ways: Commemorating the Victims of Nazism and Stalinism at Buchenwald and Sachsenhausen." *Representations* no. 49 (1995): 97-119.

Felman, Shoshana, and Dori Laub, eds. *Testimony: Crises of Witnessing in Literature, Psychoanalysis, and History*. New York: Routledge, 1992.
Field, Norma. "War and Apology: Japan, Asia, the Fiftieth, and After." *Positions: East Asia Cultures Critique* 5, no. 1 (1997): 1–51.
Fogel, Joshua, ed. *The Nanjing Massacre in History and Historiography*. Berkeley: University of California Press, 2000.
Forecki, Piotr. *Od Shoah do Strachu: spory o polsko-żydowską przeszłość i pamięć w debata ch publicznych*. Poznań, Pol.: wydawnictwo poznańskie, 2010.
Friedman, Susan Stanford. "Planetarity: Musing Modernist Studies." *Modernism/modernity* 17, no. 3 (2010): 471–99.
Friedrich, Jörg. *The Fire: The Bombing of Germany, 1940–1945*. New York: Columbia University Press, 2008.
Fujitani, Takashi, Geoffrey M. White, and Lisa Yoneyama, eds. *Perilous Memories: The Asia-Pacific War(s)*. Durham, N.C.: Duke University Press, 2001.
Furber, David. "Near as Far in the Colonies: The Nazi Occupation of Poland." *International History Review* 26, no. 3 (2004): 541–79.
Gentile, Emilio. *The Sacralization of Politics in Fascist Italy*, trans. Keith Botsford. Cambridge, Mass.: Harvard University Press, 1996.
Gentile, Emilio, and Robert Mallett. "The Sacralization of Politics: Definitions, Interpretations, and Reflections on the Question of Secular Religion and Totalitarianism." *Totalitarian Movements and Political Religions* 1, no. 1 (2000): 18–55.
German Polish Dialogue: Letters of the Polish and German Bishops and International Statements. Bonn: Edition Atlantic Forum, 1966.
Gerwarth, Robert, and Stephan Malinowski. "Der Holocaust als kolonialer Genozid? Europaeisch e Kolonialgewalt und nationalsozialistischer Vernichtungskrieg." *Geschichte und Gesellschaft* 33, no. 3 (2007): 439–66.
"Gesprach zwischen Micha Brumlik und Karol Sauerland." In *Umdeuten, verschweigen, erinnern: die spaete Aufarbeitung des Holocaust in Osteuropa*, ed. Michal Brumlik and Karol Sauerland. Frankfurt am Main: Campus Verlag, 2010.
Geyer, Michael. "There Is a Land Where Everything Is Pure: Its Name Is Land of Death." In *Sacrifice and National Belonging in Twentieth-Century Germany*, ed. Greg Eghigian and Matthew P. Berg. Arlington: Texas A&M University Press, 2002.
Geyer, Michael, and Adam Tooze, eds. *The Cambridge History of the Second World War*, vol. 3. Cambridge: Cambridge University Press, 2015.
Gilbert, Shirli. "Anne Frank in South Africa: Remembering the Holocaust During and After Apartheid." *Holocaust and Genocide Studies* 26, no. 3 (2012): 366–93.
Gilroy, Paul. *The Black Atlantic: Modernity and Double Consciousness*. London: Verso, 1993.
——. *Postcolonial Melancholia*. New York: Columbia University Press, 2005.
Girard, René. *La Violence et le Sacré*. Paris: Éditions Bernard Grasset, 1972.
Gluck, Carol. "Operations of Memory: Comfort Women and the World." In *Ruptured Histories: War, Memory and the Post-Cold War in Asia*, ed. Shelia Miyoshi Jager and Rana Mitter. Cambridge, Mass.: Harvard University Press, 2007.

——. "What the World Owes the Comfort Women." In *Mnemonic Solidarity-Global Interventions*, ed. Jie-Hyun Lim and Eve Rosenhaft. London: Palgrave Macmillan, 2020.

Gniazdowski, Mateusz. "Losses Inflicted on Poland by Germany During World War II. Assessments and Estimates—an Outline." *Polish Quarterly of International Affairs* 16, no. 1 (2007): 94–126.

Golczewski, Frank. "Die Ansiedlung von Juden in den ehemaligen deutschen Ostgebieten Polens 1945–1951." In *Umdeuten, verschweigen, erinnern: die spaete Aufarbeitung des Holocaust in Osteuropa*, ed. Michal Brumlik and Karol Sauerland. Frankfurt am Main: Campus Verlag, 2010.

Goldberg, Amos. "Forum: On Saul Friedländer's The Years of Extermination 2. The Victim's Voice and Melodramatic Aesthetics in History." *History and Theory* 48, no. 3 (2009): 220–37.

Goldberg, Amos, and Haim Hazan, eds. *Marking Evil: Holocaust Memory in the Global Age*. New York: Berghahn Books, 2015.

Grabowski, Jan. "Germany Is Fueling a False History of the Holocaust Across Europe" *Haaretz*. June 22, 2020.

——. *Hunt for the Jews: Betrayal and Murder in German-Occupied Poland*. Bloomington: Indiana University Press, 2013.

Grajewski, Andrzej. "Over the Wall. The Letter of the Polish Bishops in the Context of the Eastern Policy of Vatican." *Journal of Kolegium Jagiellonskie: Toruńska Szkoła Wyzsza* 2, no. 1 (2015): 4–15.

Grass, Günter. *Im Krebsgang. Eine Novelle*. Göttingen, Ger.: Steidl, 2002.

Gross, Jan T. "Die Osteuropäer haben kein Schamgefühl." *Die Welt*. Online ed. September 13, 2015.

——. *Fear: Anti-Semitism in Poland After Auschwitz*. New York: Random House, 2006.

——. *Neighbors: The Destruction of the Jewish Community in Jedwabne*. Princeton, N.J.: Princeton University Press, 2001.

——. *Sąsiedzi: Historia zagłady żydowskiego miasteczka*. Sejny, Pol.: Pogranicze, 2000.

Gross, Jan T., and, Aleksandrą Pawlicką. . . . *bardzo dawno temu, mniej więcej w zeszły piątek*. Warsaw: Wydawnictwo WAB, 2018.

Guttenplan, D. D. *The Holocaust on Trial: History, Justice and the David Irving Libel Case*. London: Granta Books, 2002.

Hackmann, Jörg. "Defending the "Good Name" of the Polish Nation: Politics of History as a Battlefield in Poland, 2015–18." *Journal of Genocide Research* 20, no. 4 (2018): 587–606.

Hadler, Frank, and Mathias Mesenhoeller, eds. *Vergangene Grösse und Ohnmacht in Ostmitteleuropa: Repräsentationen imperialer Erfahrung in der Historiographie seit 1918*. Leipzig, Ger.: Akademische Verlagsanstalt, 2007.

Han, Suk-Jung. "The Suppression and Recall of Colonial Memory: Manchukuo and the Cold War in the Two Koreas." In *Mass Dictatorship and Memory as Ever Present Past*, ed. Jie-Hyun Lim et al. Basingstoke, UK: Palgrave Macmillan, 2014.

Hardt, Michael, and Antonio Negri. *Empire*. Cambridge, Mass.: Harvard University Press, 2000.

Hartoonian, Harry. *The Unspoken as Heritage: The Armenian Genocide and Its Unaccounted Lives*. Durham, N.C.: Duke University Press, 2019.

Hausner, Gideon. *Justice in Jerusalem*. New York: Holocaust Library, 1977.

Hayes, Peter, ed. *Lessons and Legacies. The Meaning of the Holocaust in a Changing World*. Evanston, Ill.: Northwestern University Press, 1991.

Hein, Laura E., and Mark Selden, eds. *Censoring History: Citizenship and Memory in Japan, Germany, and the United States*. Armonk, N.Y.: Sharpe, 2000.

Henderson, Marius, and Julia Lange, eds. *Entangled Memories: Remembering the Holocaust in a Global Age*. Heidelberg, Ger.: Universitätsverlag Winter, 2017.

Herf, Jeffrey. *Divided Memory: The Nazi Past in the Two Germanys*. Cambridge, Mass.: Harvard University Press, 1997.

Hilberg, Raul. "I Was Not There." In *Writing and the Holocaust*, ed. Berel Lang. New York: Holmes & Meier, 1988.

Hill, Christopher. "Crossed Geographies: Endō and Fanon in Lyon." *Representations* 128, no. 1 (2014): 93–123.

Hiroshi, Fujimoto. "Towards Reconciliation, Harmonious Coexistence and Peace: The Madison Quakers, Inc. Projects and the Hibakusha's Visit to My Lai in March 2008." *Nanzan Review of American Studies* 37 (2015): 3–23.

Hirsch, Marianne. *The Generation of Postmemory: Writing and Visual Culture After the Holocaust*. New York: Columbia University Press, 2012.

Hirsch, Marianne, and Leo Spitzer. "The Witness in the Archive: Holocaust Studies/Memory Studies." *Memory Studies* 2, no. 2 (2009): 151–70.

Hobsbawm, Eric J. *Nations and Nationalism Since 1780*. Cambridge: Cambridge University Press, 1990.

Holc, Janine P. *The Politics of Trauma and Memory Activism: Polish-Jewish Relations Today*. London: Palgrave Macmillan, 2018.

———. "The Remembered One: Memory Activism and the Construction of Edith Stein's Jewishness in Post-Communist Wrocław." *Shofar: An Interdisciplinary Journal of Jewish Studies* 29, no. 4 (2011): 67–97.

Horowitz, Irene, and Carl Horowitz. *Of Human Agony*. New York: Shengold, 1992.

Huebner, Chris K. "Between Victory and Victimhood: Reflections on Culture and Martyrdom." *Direction: A Mennonite Brethren Forum* 34, no. 2 (2005): 228–40. http://www.directionjournal.org/article/?1402.

Hunt, David. "War Crimes and the Vietnamese People: American Representations and Silences." *Bulletin of Concerned Asian Scholars* 30, no. 2 (1998): 72–82.

Hunt, Lynn. *Inventing Human Rights*. New York: Norton, 2007.

Irwin-Zarecka, Iwona. "Poland After the Holocaust." In *Remembering for the Future: Working Papers and Addenda*, ed. Yehuda Bauer, Franklin H. Littell, and Alice L. Eckardt. New York: Pergamon Press, 1989.

Jager, Sheila Miyoshi, and Rana Mitter, eds. *Ruptured Histories: War, Memory and the Post-Cold War in Asia*. Cambridge, Mass.: Harvard University Press, 2007.

James, C.L.R. *The Black Jacobins: Toussaint L'Ouverture and the San Domingo Revolution*. London: Secker & Warburg, 1938.

Jansen, Michael, and Günter Saathoff. *A Mutual Responsibility and a Moral Obligation: The Final Report on Germany's Compensation Programs for Forced Labor and Other Personal Injuries*. Basingstoke, UK: Palgrave Macmillan, 2009.

Jarausch, Konrad H., and Michael Geyer. *Shattered Past: Reconstructing German Histories*. Princeton, N.J.: Princeton University Press, 2003.

Jeans, Roger B. "Victims or Victimizers? Museums, Textbooks, and the War Debate in Contemporary Japan." *Journal of Military History* 69, no. 1 (2005): 149–95.

Jedlicki, Jerzy. *A Suburb of Europe: Nineteenth-Century Polish Approaches to Western Civilization*. Budapest: Central European University Press, 1999.

Jędrzejewicz, Wacław. "Sprawa 'Wieczoru': Józef Piłsudski a wojna japońsko-rosyjska 1904–1905." *Zeszyty Historyczne (Paryż)* 27 (1974): 3–103.

Jeffery, Laura, and Matei Candea."Introduction: The Politics of Victimhood." *History and Anthropology* 17, no. 4 (2006): 287–96.

Jönsson, Matt. "Innocence by Association? Everyday Nazism on DVD." In *Imagining Mass Dictatorships: The Individual and the Masses in Literature and Cinema*, ed. Karin Sarsenov and Michael Schoenhals. Basingstoke, UK: Palgrave Macmillan, 2013.

Jovanovic, Srdan M., and Veran Stancetic, eds. *History and Politics in the Western Balkans: Changes at the Turn of the Millenium*. Belgrade: Center for Good Governance Studies, 2013.

Judt, Tony. *Postwar: A History of Europe Since 1945*. New York: Penguin Press, 2005.

Kamiński, Łukasz, and Jan Żaryn, eds. *Wokół pogromu kieleckiego*. Warsaw: Instytut Pamięci Narodowej, 2006.

Kantorowicz, Ernst H. "Pro Patria Mori in Medieval Political Thought." *American Historical Review* 56, no. 3 (1951): 472–92.

Karjski, Stanisław. *Św. Maksymilian Maria Kolbe o masonerii i Żydach: pisma wybrane*. Krzeszowice, Pol.: Dom Wydawniczy Ostoja, 2010.

Katsuichi, Honda. *The Nanjing Massacre: A Japanese Journalist Confronts Japan's National Shame*, trans. Karen Sandness. London: Routledge, 1998.

Kattago, Siobahn. "Agreeing to Disagree on the Legacies of Recent History: Memory, Pluralism and Europe After 1989." *European Journal of Social Theory* 12, no. 3 (2009): 375–95.

———. *Ambiguous Memory: The Nazi Past and German National Identity*. Westport, Conn.: Praeger, 2001.

Kemp-Welch, Anthony. *Poland Under Communism: A Cold War History*. Cambridge: Cambridge University Press, 2008.

Kerski, Basil, Thomas Kycia, and Robert Zurek, eds. *Wir Vergeben und Bitten um Vergebung: Der Briefwechsel der polnischen und deutschen Bischöfe von 1965 und seine Wirkung*. Osnabruck, Ger.: Fibre, 2006.

Kieniewicz, Jan. "The Eastern Frontiers and the Civilisational Dimension of Europe." *Acta Poloniae Historica* 107 (2013): 165–75.

Kierkegaard, Søren. *The Journals of Kierkegaard*, trans. Alexander Dru. New York: Harper Torchbooks, 1959.

Kim, Seongnae. "The Work of Memory: Ritual Laments of the Dead and Korea's Cheju Massacre." In *A Companion to the Anthropology of Religion*, ed. Janice Boddy and Michael Lambeck. Oxford: Wiley Blackwell, 2013.

Kimura, Maki. *Unfolding the "Comfort Women" Debates: Modernity, Violence, Women's Voices.* Basingstoke, UK: Palgrave Macmillan, 2016.

Kocka, Juergen. "Asymmetrical Historical Comparison: The Case of the German *Sonderweg.*" *History and Theory* 38, no. 1 (1999): 40–50.

Kola, Adam F. *Socjalistyczny Postkolonializm: Rekonsolidacja pamięci.* Toruń, Pol.: NCU Press, 2018.

Kołakowski, Leszek. "Amidst Moving Ruins." *Daedalus* 12, no. 2 (1992): 43–56.

Kopp, Kristin. *Germany's Wild East: Constructing Poland as Colonial Space.* Ann Arbor: University of Michigan Press, 2012.

Kosicki, Piotr H. "Caritas Across the Iron Curtain? Polish-German Reconciliation and the Bishops' Letter of 1965." *East European Politics and Societies* 23, no. 2 (2009): 213–43.

Kössler, Reinhart. *Namibia and Germany: Negotiating the Past.* Windhoek: University of Namibia Press, 2015.

Kowner, Rotem. "Tokyo Recognizes Auschwitz: The Rise and Fall of Holocaust Denial in Japan, 1989–1999." *Journal of Genocide Research* 3, no. 2 (2001): 257–72.

Krygier, Martin. "Letter from Australia: Neighbors: Poles, Jews and the Aboriginal Question." *East Central Europe* 29, no. 1–2 (2002): 297–309.

Krzemiński, Ireneusz. "Polish-Jewish Relations, Anti-Semitism and National Identity." *Polish Sociological Review* 137, no. 1 (2002): 25–51.

Kucharski, Wojciech. "Prawdziwa bomba. Jak powstawało Orędzie biskupów polskich do biskupów niemieckich." *Więź* 53, no. 615 (2010): 123–32.

Kunicki, Mikołaj S. *Between the Brown and the Red: Nationalism, Catholicism, and Communism in 20th Century Poland—the Politics of Bolesław Piasecki.* Athens: Ohio University Press, 2012.

Kurczewska, Joanna. "From the Editor." *Polish Sociological Review* 137, no. 1 (2002).

Kwon, Heonik. *After the Massacre: Commemoration and Consolation in Ha My and My Lai.* Berkeley: University of California Press, 2006.

——. *Ghosts of War in Vietnam.* Cambridge: Cambridge University Press, 2008.

Lagrou, Pieter. "Victims of Genocide and National Memory: Belgium, France and the Netherlands 1945–1965." *Past & Present* 154 (1997): 181–222.

Lang, Berel. "Six Questions on (or About) Holocaust Denial." *History and Theory* 49, no. 2 (2010): 157–68.

Langer, Lawrence L. "The Uses—and Misuses—of a Young Girl's Diary: 'If Anne Frank Could Return from Among the Murdered, She Would Be Appalled.'" In *Anne Frank: Reflection on Her Life and Legacy*, ed. Hyman A. Enzer and Sandra Solotaroff-Enzer. Urbana: University of Illinois Press, 2000.

Lanzmann, Claude. *Shoah: The Complete Text of the Acclaimed Holocaust Film.* New York: De Capo Press, 1995.

Laub, Dori. "Bearing Witness or the Vicissitudes of Listening." In *Testimony: Crises of Witnessing in Literature, Psychoanalysis, and History*, ed. Shoshana Felman and Dori Laub. New York: Routledge, 1992.

League of Nations. *Commission of Enquiry Into the Sino-Japanese Dispute Contributor, and Edward Robert Bulwer-Lytton Lytton. Situation in Manchuria: Report of the Lytton Commission of Inquiry.* Geneva: League of Nations, 1932.

Lee, Sung-si. "Shokuminchi bunka seisaku no kachi wo tsuujite mita rekishi ninsiki [Historical consciousness represented by colonial cultural policies]." Paper presented to Kyoto Forum of Public Philosophy, March 13, 2004.

Leo, Peter. "Gespräch mit Kolja Unger: Historikerstreit 2.0 über Shoah: Historiker Peter Leo fordert globale Perspektive auf NS-Verbrechen." *Deutschlandfunk*, July 11, 2021.

Levi, Primo. *The Drowned and the Saved*, trans. Raymond Rosenthal. New York: Simon & Schuster, 1988.

Levine, Hillel. *In Search of Sugihara*. New York: Free Press, 1996.

Levy, Daniel, and Natan Sznaider. *The Holocaust and Memory in the Global Age*. Philadelphia: Temple University Press, 2006.

———. "Memory Unbound: The Holocaust and the Formation of Cosmopolitan Memory." *European Journal of Social Theory* 5, no. 1 (2002): 87–106.

Lewis, Dustin. "Unrecognized Victims: Sexual Violence Against Men in Conflict Settings Under International Law." *Wisconsin International Law Journal* 27, no. 1 (2009): 1–49.

Lim, Jie-Hyun. "Displacing East and West: Towards a Postcolonial Reading of 'Ostforschung' and 'Myśl Zachodnia (2010).'" http://www.transeuropeennes.eu/en/articles/354/Displacing_East_an d_West.

———. *Global Easts: Remembering-Imagining-Mobilizing*. New York: Columbia University Press, 2022.

———. "'The Good Old Cause' in the New Polish Left Historiography." *Science & Society* 61, no. 4 (1997): 541–49.

———. "Mnemonic Solidarity in the Global Memory Space." *Global-e* 12, no. 4 (2019). https://www.21global.ucsb.edu/global-e/global-e-series/mnemonic-solidarity.

———. "Narody-ofiary i ich megalomania," trans. Marek Darewski. *Więź* 2.616–3.617 (2010): 22–34.

———. "Nationalism, Neo-Nationalism." In *Encyclopedia of Global Studies*, vol. 3., ed. Helmut K. Anheier and Mark Juergensmeyer. London: Sage Publications, 2012.

———. *Opfernationalismus. Erinnerung und Herrschaft in der postkolonialen Welt*, trans. Utku Mogultay. Berlin: Klaus Wagenbach, 2024.

———. "A Postcolonial Reading of the *Sonderweg*: Marxist Historicism Revisited." *Journal of Modern European History* 12, no. 2 (2014): 280–94.

———. "Second World War in Global Memory Space." In *Cambridge History of Second World War*, ed. Michael Geyer and Adam Tooze. Cambridge: Cambridge University Press, 2015.

———. "Transnational Memory Activism and the Performative Nationalism." In *Handbook of Memory Activism*, ed. Yifat Gutman and Jenny Wüstenberg. Oxford: Oxford University Press, 2021.

———. "Transnational Memory Formation: Memory-History-Culture." In *The Routledge Companion to World Literature and World History*, ed. May Hawas. New York: Routledge, 2018.

———. "Triple Victimhood: On the Mnemonic Confluence of the Holocaust, Stalinist Crime, and Colonial Genocide." *Journal of Genocide Research* (2020). https://doi.org/10.1080/14623528.202 0.1750822.

———. "Victimhood Nationalism and History Reconciliation in East Asia." *History Compass* 8, no. 1 (2010): 1–10.

———."Victimhood Nationalism in Contested Memories—National Mourning and Global Accountability." In *Memory in a Global Age: Discourses, Practices, and Trajectories*, ed. Aleida Assmann and Sebastian Conrad. Basingstoke, UK: Palgrave Macmillan, 2010.

Lim, Jie-Hyun, and Karen Petrone, eds. *Gender Politics and Mass Dictatorship: Global Perspectives*. New York: Palgrave Macmillan, 2011.

Lim, Jie-Hyun, and Eve Rosenhaft, eds. *Mnemonic Solidarity-Global Interventions*. Basingstoke, UK: Palgrave Macmillan, 2020.

Lim, Jie-Hyun, Barbara Walker, and Peter Lambert, eds. *Mass Dictatorship and Memory as Ever-Present Past*. Basingstoke, UK: Palgrave Macmillan, 2014.

Lipski, Jan Józef. "Ojciec Kolbe i, Mały Dziennik." *Tygodnik Powszechny* 38, no. 1182 (1971).

Loeffler, James. "Becoming Cleopatra: The Forgotten Zionism of Raphael Lemkin." *Journal of Genocide Research* 19, no. 3 (2017): 34–60.

Lu, David John, and Howard John Waitzkin. *Agony of Choice: Matsuoka Yōsuke and the Rise and Fall of the Japanese Empire, 1880–1946*. Lanham, Md.: Lexington Books, 2002.

Łuczewski, Michał. *Kapitał moralny. Polityki historyczne w późnej nowoczesności*. Kraków: Ośrodek Myśli Politycznej, 2017.

Lukas, Richard C. *Forgotten Holocaust: The Poles Under German Occupation*. Rev. ed. New York: Hippocrene Books, 2005.

Machcewicz, Paweł. "In the Shadow of Jedwabne." In *Thou Shalt Not Kill: Poles on Jedwabne*, ed. Jacek Borkowicz and Israel Gutman. Warsaw: Więź, 2001.

———. *The War That Never Ends: The Museum of the Second World War in Gdańsk*. Berlin: De Gruyter, 2019.

Machcewicz, Paweł, and Krzysztof Persak, eds. *Wokół Jedwabnego: Studia*, vol. 1. Warsaw: Instytut Pamięci Narodowej, 2002.

Maclelland, Gwyn. "Guilt, Persecution, and Resurrection in Nagasaki: Atomic Memories and the Urakami Catholic Community." *Social Science Japan Journal* 18, no. 2 (2015): 233–40.

MacMillan, Margaret. *Dangerous Games: The Uses and Abuses of History*. New York: Modern Library, 2008.

Madajczyk, Piotr. "S. Gawlitta, 'Aus dem Geist des Konzils! Aus der Sorge der Nachbarn!' Der Briefwechsel der polnischen und deutschen Bischöfe von 1965 und seine Kontexte." *Kwartalnik Historyczny* 125, no. 2 (2018): 184–89.

Madley, Benjamin. "From Africa to Auschwitz: How German South West Africa Incubated Ideas and Methods Adopted and Developed by the Nazis in Eastern Europe." *European History Quarterly* 35, no. 3 (2005): 429–64.

Madras, Ronald. "John Paul, St. Maximilian, and Anti-Semitism." In *Martyrs of Charity*, part 2. Washington, D.C.: St. Maximilian Kolbe Foundation, 1989.

Maier, Charles. *The Unmasterable Past: History, Holocaust and German National Identity.* 2d ed. Cambridge, Mass.: Harvard University Press, 1997.
Maksidi, Ussama. "Atonement at the Expense of Another." *The New Fascism Syllabus.* June 12, 2021. https://newfascismsyllabus.com/opinions/the-catechism-debate/atonement-at-the-expense-of-another/.
Mallet, Robert. "Foreword." In *Totalitarian Movements and Political Religions* 1, no. 1 (2000).
Mann, Michael. *The Dark Side of Democracy: Explaining Ethnic Cleansing.* Cambridge: Cambridge University Press, 2005.
Manne, Robert. "In Denial: The Stolen Generations and the Right." *Australian Quarterly Essay* 1 (2001).
Markiewicz, Tadek, and Keren Sharvit. "When Victimhood Goes to War? Israel and Victim Claims." *Political Psychology* 42, no. 1 (2021): 111–26.
Materski, Wojciech, and Tomasz Szarota, eds. *Polska 1939–1945. Straty osobowe i ofiary represji pod dwiema okupacjami.* Warsaw: Instytut Pamięci Narodowej, 2009.
Matyjaszek, Konrad. "You Need to Speak Polish: Antony Polonsky Interviewed by Konrad Matyjaszek." *Studia Litteraria et Historica* 6 (2017): 1–35.
Mayblin, Lucy, Aneta Piekut, and Gill Valentine. "'Other' Posts in 'Other' Places: Poland Through Postcolonial Lens?" *Sociology* 50, no. 1 (2016): 60–76.
Mazower, Mark. "The Cold War and the Appropriation of Memory: Greece After Liberation." In *The Politics of Retribution in Europe: World War II and Its Aftermath,* ed. István Deák, Jan T. Gross, and Tony Judt. Princeton, N.J.: Princeton University Press, 2000.
———. *Dark Continent: Europe's Twentieth Century.* London: Allen Lane, 1998.
McFadden, Bernice L. *The Book of Harlan.* New York: Akashic Books, 2016.
Merari, Ariel, et al. "Making Palestinian Martyrdom Operations/Suicide Attacks Interview with Would-Be Perpetrators and Organizers." *Terrorism and Political Violence* 22, no. 1 (2009): 102–19.
Michael, George. "Mahmoud Ahmadinejad's Sponsorship of Holocaust Denial." *Totalitarian Movements and Political Religions* 8, nos. 3–4 (2007): 667–71.
Michlik, Joanna B. "'At the Crossroads': Jedwabne and Polish Historiography of the Holocaust." *Dapim: Studies on the Holocaust* 31, no. 3 (2017): 296–306.
Michnik, Adam. "Nationalism," *Social Research* 58, no. 4 (1991): 757–63.
———. "Poles and Jews: How Deep the Guilt?" In *The Neighbors Responded: The Controversy Over the Jedwabne Massacre in Poland,* ed. Antony Polonsky and Joanna Michlic. Princeton, N.J.: Princeton University Press, 2004.
Miles, William F. S. "Indigenization of the Holocaust and the Tehran Holocaust Conference: Iranian Aberration or Third World Trend?" *Human Rights Review* 10, no. 4 (2009): 505–19.
———. "Third World Views of the Holocaust." *Journal of Genocide Research* 6, no. 3 (2004): 371–93.
Mishra, Pankaj. *From the Ruins of Empire: The Intellectuals Who Remade Asia.* London: Allen Lane, 2012.
Mitchell, Timothy, ed. *Questions of Modernity.* Minneapolis: University of Minnesota Press, 2000.
Moeller, Robert G. "Responses to Alon Confino." *Cultural Analysis* 4 (2005): 66–72.

———. "War Stories: The Search for a Usable Past in the Federal Republic of Germany." *American Historical Review* 101, no. 4 (1996): 1008–48.

———. *War Stories: The Search for a Usable Past in the Federal Republic of Germany*. Berkeley: University of California Press, 2001.

Molden, Berthold. "Resistant Pasts Versus Mnemonic Hegemony: On the Power Relations of Collective Memory." *Memory Studies* 9, no. 2 (2016): 125–42.

———. "Vietnam, the New Left, and the Holocaust: How the Cold War Changed Discourse on Genocide." In *Memory in a Global Age: Discourses, Practices and Trajectories*, ed. Aleida Assmann and Sebastian Conrad. Basingstoke, UK: Palgrave Macmillan, 2010.

Morozov, Viatcheslav. "Subaltern Empire? Toward a Postcolonial Approach to Russian Foreign Policy." *Problems of Post-Communism* 60, no. 6 (2013): 16–28.

Morris-Suzuki, Tessa. *The Past Within Us: Media, Memory, History*. New York: Verso, 2005.

Morrison, Toni. *The Source of Self-Regard: Selected Essays, Speeches, and Meditations*. New York: Knopf 2019.

Moses, A. Dirk. "Conceptual Blockages and Definitional Dilemmas in the 'Racial Century': Genocides of Indigenous Peoples and the Holocaust." *Patterns of Prejudice* 36, no. 4 (2020): 7–36.

———. "Der Katechismus der Deutschen" *Geschichte der Gegenwart*. Online ed. May 23, 2021.

———, ed. *Empire, Colony, Genocide*. New York: Berghan Books, 2008.

———. "Genocide and the Terror of History." *Parallax* 17, no. 4 (2011): 90–108.

———. "The Holocaust and World History." In *The Holocaust and Historical Methodology*, ed. Dan Stone. New York: Berghahn Books, 2012.

Mosse, George L. *Fallen Soldiers: Reshaping the Memory of the World Wars*. Oxford: Oxford University Press, 1990.

———. *The Fascist Revolution: Toward a General Theory of Fascism*. New York: Howard Fertig, 1999.

———. *The Nationalization of the Masses: Political Symbolism and Mass Movements in Germany from the Napoleonic Wars Through the Third Reich*. New York: Howard Fertig, 1975.

Motyka, Grzegorz. *Wołyń '43; Ludobójcza czystka—fakty, analogie, polityka historyczna*. Kraków: Wydawnictwo Literackie, 2016.

Moyn, Samuel. *Christian Human Rights*. Philadephia: University of Pennsylvania Press, 2015.

———. *The Last Utopia: Human Rights in History*. Cambridge, Mass.: Harvard University Press, 2010.

Musiał, Bogdan. *Stalins Beutezug: die Plünderung Deutschlands und der Aufstieg der Sowjetuni on zur Wehrmacht*. Berlin: List, 2011.

Najarian, James. "Gnawing at History: The Rhetoric of Holocaust Denial." *Midwest Quarterly* 39, no. 1 (1997): 74–89.

Nandy, Ashis. *The Intimate Enemy: Loss and Recovery of Self Under Colonialism*. Delhi: Oxford University Press, 1983.

Niven, Bill, ed. *Germans as Victims*. Basingstoke, UK: Palgrave Macmillan, 2006.

Northrop, Douglas, ed. *A Companion to World History*. Chichester, UK: Wiley-Blackwell, 2012.

Novick, Peter. *The Holocaust and Collective Memory*. London: Bloomsbury, 2001.

Nowak, Jerzy Robert. *Myśli o Polsce i Polakach*. Warsaw: Wydawnictwo Unia, 1993.
Noy, Chaim. "Memory, Media, and Museum Audience's Discourse of Remembering." *Critical Discourse Studies* 15, no. 1 (2018): 19–38.
Nozaki, Yoshiko. *War Memory, Nationalism and Education in Postwar Japan, 1945–2007: The Japanese History Textbook Controversy and Ienaga Saburo's Court Challenge*. London: Routledge, 2008.
O'Brien, Melanie. "'Don't Kill Them, Let's Choose Them as Wives': The Development of the Crimes of Forced Marriage, Sexual Slavery and Enforced Prostitution in International Criminal Law." *International Journal of Human Rights* 20, no. 3 (2016): 386–406.
Ohnuki-Tierney, Emiko, *Kamikaze. Cherry Blossoms and Nationalisms: The Militarization of Aesthetics in Japanese History*. Chicago: University of Chicago Press, 2002.
Olejnek, Tadeusz. *Wieluń. Polska Guernica*. Wieluń, Pol.: BWTN, 2004.
Onishi, Yuichiro. "The New Negro of the Pacific: How African Americans Forged Cross-Racial Solidarity with Japan, 1917–1922." *Journal of African American History* 92, no. 2 (2007): 191–213.
Oron, Yahir. *Jewish-Israeli Identity*. Tel Aviv: Sifriat Poalim, 1992.
Orr, James J. *The Victim as Hero: Ideologies of Peace and National Identity in Postwar Japan*. Honolulu: University of Hawaii Press, 2001.
Orzełek, Ariel. "U genezy Chrześcijańskiego Stowarzyszenia Społecznego. Powstanie i rozpad pierwszego zespołu redakcyjnego tygodnika 'Za i Przeciw.'" *Kwartalnik Historyczny* 126, no. 4 (2019): 721–63.
Pakier, Małgorzata, and Joanna Wawrzyniak, eds. *Memory and Change in Europe: Eastern Perspectives*. New York: Berghahn Books, 2016.
Pappe, Ilan. "Critique and Agenda: the Post-Zionist Scholars in Israel." *History and Memory* 7, no. 1 (1995): 66–90.
Paul, Christa. *Zwangsprostitution. Staatlich errichtete Bordelle im Nationalsozialismus*. Berlin: Edition Hentrich, 1994.
Paxton, Robert O. *The Anatomy of Fascism*. New York: Knopf, 2004.
Pedahzur, Ami, Arie Perliger, and Leonard Weinberg. "Altruism and Fatalism: The Characteristics of Palestinian Suicide Terrorists." *Deviant Behavior* 24, no. 4 (2003): 405–23.
Pękala, Urszula. "The Abuse of Forgiveness in Dealing with Legacies of Violence." In *Forgiveness: Philosophy, Psychology and the Arts*, ed. Tim McKenry and Charlotte B. Thingholm. Oxfordshire: Inter-Disciplinary Press, 2013.
———. "Asymetrie pojednania. Pojednanie niemiecko-polskie i niemiecko-francuskie po II wojnie światowej." In *Perspektywy dialogu: Studia na temat niemiecko-polskich procesów transferowych w przestrzeni religijnej*, ed. Aleksandra Chylewska-Tölle. Słubice, Pol.: Collegium Polonicum, 2016.
Pergher, Roberta, et al. "Scholarly Forum on the Holocaust and Genocide." *Dapim: Studies on the Holocaust* 27, no. 1 (2013): 40–73.
Piotrowski, Tadeusz. *Poland's Holocaust: Ethnic Strife, Collaboration with Occupying Forces and Genocide in the Second Republic, 1918–1947*. Jefferson, N.C.: McFarland, 1998.
Piskorski, Jan M., ed. *Historiographical Approaches to Medieval Colonization of East Central Europe*. New York: Columbia University Press, 2002.

Polonsky, Antony, and Joanna Michlic, eds. *The Neighbors Responded: The Controversy Over the Jedwabne Massacre in Poland*. Princeton, N.J.: Princeton University Press, 2004.
——, ed. *My Brother's Keeper? Recent Polish Debates on the Holocaust*. London: Routledge, 1990.
Popescu, Diana I., and Tanja Schult, eds. *Revisiting Holocaust Representation in the Post-Witness Era*. Basingstoke, UK: Palgrave Macmillan, 2015.
Pötzl, Norbert F. "Versöhnen oder Verhöhnen: Dauerstreitum die Stiftung 'Flucht, Vertreibung, Versöhnung.'" In *Die Deutschen im Osten Europas: Eroberer, Siedler, Vertriebene*, ed. Annette Großbongardt, Uwe Klußmann, and Norbert F. Pötz. Munich: Deutsche Verlagsanstalt, 2011.
Prekerowa, Teresa. "The Just and the Passive." in *My Brother's Keeper? Recent Polish Debates on the Holocaust*, ed. Antony Polonsky. London: Routledge, 1990.
Ram, Uri. "Zionist Historiography and the Invention of Modern Jewish Nationhood: The Case of Ben Zion Dinur." *History and Memory* 7, no. 1 (1995): 91–124.
Renan, Ernest. *Qu'est-ce qu'une nation?* Paris: Calmann Lévy, 1882.
Ricoeur, Paul. *Memory, History, Forgetting*, trans. Kathleen Blamey and David Pellauer. Chicago: University of Chicago Press, 2004.
Risch, William Jay. "What the Far Right Does Not Tell Us About the Maidan." *Kritika: Explorations in Russian and Eurasian History* 16, no. 1 (2015): 137–44.
Röger, Maren. "News Media and Historical Remembrance: Reporting on the Expulsion of Germans in Polish and German Magazines." In *Mediation, Remediation, and the Dynamics of Cultural Memory*, ed. Astrid Erll and Ann Rigney. Berlin: Walter de Gruyter, 2009.
Rosenfeld, Alvin H. "Popularization and Memory: The Case of Anne Frank." In *Lessons and Legacies. The Meaning of the Holocaust in a Changing World*, ed. Peter Hayes. Evanston, Ill.: Northwestern University Press, 1991.
Rossoliński-Liebe, Grzegorz. "Debating, Obfuscating and Disciplining the Holocaust: Post-Soviet Historical Discourses on the OUN–UPA and Other Nationalist Movements." *East European Jewish Affairs* 42, no. 3 (2012): 199–241.
Rothberg, Michael. "Between Auschwitz and Algeria: Multidirectional Memory and the Counter Public Witness." *Critical Inquiry* 33, no. 1 (2006): 158–84.
——. "Comparing Comparisons: From the 'Historikerstreit to the Mbembe Affair," *Geschichte der Gegenwart*. Online ed. September 23. 2020.
——. "From Gaza to Warsaw: Mapping Multidirectional Memory." *Criticism* 53, no. 4 (2011): 523–48.
——. *Implicated Subject: Beyond Victims and Perpetrators*. Stanford, Calif.: Stanford University Press, 2019.
——. *Multidirectional Memory: Remembering the Holocaust in the Age of Decolonization*. Stanford, Calif.: Stanford University Press, 2009.
——. "On the Mbembe Affair: The Specters of Comparison." *Goethe Institut Latitude: Rethinking Power Relations for a Decolonized and Non-racial World* (2020). https://www.goet he.de/prj/lat/en/dis/21864662.html/
Rothberg, Michael, and Yasemin Yildiz. "Memory Citizenship: Migrant Archives of Holocaust Remembrance in Contemporary Germany." *Parallax* 17, no. 4 (2011): 32–48.

Rummel, R. J. *Statistics of Democide*. Honolulu: University of Hawaii Press, 1997. https://www.hawaii.edu/powerkills/SOD.CHAP3.HTM.

Rymsza, Marek. "Dyskusja: czy to nasza sprawa?" *Więź* 4, no. 662 (2015).

Sadako, Kurihara. "The Literature of Auschwitz and Hiroshima: Thoughts on Reading Lawrence Langer's The Holocaust and the Literary Imagination." *Holocaust and Genocide Studies* 7, no. 1 (1993): 77–106.

Sakai, Naoki. *The End of Pax Americana: The Loss of Empire and Hikikomori Nationalism*. Durham, N.C.: Duke University Press, 2021.

———. *Translation and Subjectivity: On 'Japan' and Cultural Nationalism*. Minneapolis: University of Minnesota Press, 1997.

Sakamoto, Rumi. "The Women's International War Crimes Tribunal on Japan's Military Sexual Slavery: A Legal and Feminist Approach to the 'Comfort Women' Issue." *New Zealand Journal of Asian Studies* 3, no. 1 (2001): 49–58.

Salmonowicz, Stanisław. "The Deep Roots and Long Life of Stereotype." In *My Brother's Keeper? Recent Polish Debates on the Holocaust*, ed. Antony Polonsky. London: Routledge, 1990.

Salter, Michael. "Countering Holocaust Denial in Relation to the Nuremberg Trials." In *Holocaust and Genocide Denial: A Contextual Perspective*, ed. Paul Behrens, Nicholas Terry, and Olaf Jensen. New York: Routledge, 2017.

Sand, Jordan. "Subaltern Imperialists: The New Historiography of the Japanese Empire." *Past and Present* 225, no. 1 (2014): 273–88.

Schaffer, Kay, and Sidonie Smith. "Venues of Storytelling: The Circulation of Testimony in Human Rights Campaigns." *Life Writing* 1, no. 2 (2004): 3–26.

Schischkoff, Georgi. *Die gesteuerte Vermassung*. Meisenheim am Glan, Ger.: Anton Hain, 1964.

Seaton, Philip A. *Japan's Contested War Memories: The Memory Rifts in Historical Consciousness of World War II*. London: Routledge, 2007.

Sebald, W. G. *Luftkrieg und Literatur. Mit einem Essay zu Alfred Andersch*. Munich: Carl Hanser, 1999.

Segev, Tom. *The Seventh Million: The Israelis and the Holocaust*, trans. Haim Watzman. New York: Owl Book, 2000.

Seidl, Claudius "War der Holocaust eine koloniale Tat?" *FAZ*. March 1. 2021.

Sereny, Gitta. *The German Trauma: Experiences and Reflections, 1938–2001*. London: Penguin Books, 2001.

Seydewitz, Max. *Die unbesiegbare Stadt. Zerstung und Wiederaufbau von Dresden*. Berlin: Kongress Verla, 1956.

Siła-Nowicki, Władysław. "A Reply to Jan Błoński." In *My Brother's Keeper? Recent Polish Debates on the Holocaust*, ed. Antony Polonsky. London: Routledge, 1990.

Simon, Joshua. *The Ideology of Creole Revolution: Imperialism and Independence in American and Latin American Political Thought*. Cambridge: Cambridge University Press, 2019.

Sindbæk Andersen, Tea, and Barbara Törnquist-Plewa, eds. *Disputed Memory: Emotions and Memory Politics in Central, Eastern and South-Eastern Europe*. Berlin: Walter de Gruyter, 2016.

Sivakumaran, Sandesh. "Lost in Translation: UN Responses to Sexual Violence Against Men and Boys in Situations of Armed Conflict." *International Review of the Red Cross* 92, no. 877 (2010): 259–77.

———. "Sexual Violence Against Men in Armed Conflict." *European Journal of International Law* 18, no. 2 (2007): 253–76.

Smelser, Ronald, and Edward J. Davies II. *The Myth of the Eastern Front: The Nazi-Soviet War in American Popular Culture*. Cambridge: Cambridge University Press, 2008.

Smith, Anthony D. ed. *Nationalist Movements*. London: Palgrave Macmillan, 1976.

Snyder, Timothy. *Bloodlands: Europe Between Hitler and Stalin*. New York: Basic Books, 2010.

Soh, C. Sarah. *The Comfort Women: Sexual Violence and Postcolonial Memory in Korea and Japan*. Chicago: University of Chicago Press, 2020.

Sontag, Susan, and Allan Kaprow. "An Art of Radical Juxtaposition." *The Second Coming Magazine* (January 1965): 20–24.

Southhard, Susan. *Nagasaki: Life After Nuclear War*. New York: Penguin Books, 2016.

Stack, Steven. "Emile Durkheim and Altruistic Suicide." *Archives of Suicide Research* 8, no. 1 (2004): 9–22.

Stearns, Peter N., and Carol Z. Stearns. "Emotionology: Clarifying the History of Emotions and Emotional Standards." *American Historical Review* 90, no. 4 (1985): 813–36.

Steinlauf, Michael C. *Bondage to the Dead: Poland and the Memory of the Holocaust*. Syracuse, N.Y.: Syracuse University Press, 1997.

———. "Teaching About the Holocaust in Poland." In *Contested Memories: Poles and Jews During the Holocaust and Its Aftermath*, ed. Joshua D. Zimmerman. New Brunswick, N.J.: Rutgers University Press, 2003.

Sternhell, Zeev. *The Founding Myths of Israel: Nationalism, Socialism, and the Making of the Jewish State*, trans. David Maisel. Princeton, N.J.: Princeton University Press, 2009.

Sternhell, Zeev, with Mario Sznajder and Maia Asheri. *The Birth of Fascist Ideology: From Cultural Rebellion to Political Revolution*, trans. David Maisel. Princeton, N.J.: Princeton University Press, 1994.

Stola, Dariusz. "Fighting Against the Shadows: The 'Anti-Zionist' Campaign of 1968." In *Anti-Semitism and Its Opponents in Modern Poland*, ed. Robert Blobaum. Ithaca, N.Y.: Cornell University Press, 2005.

———. *Kampania antysyjonistyczna w Polsce 1967–1968*. Warsaw: ISP PAN, 2000.

Stone, Dan, ed. *The Historiography of Genocide*. Basingstoke, UK: Palgrave Macmillan, 2010.

———. "The Historiography of Genocide: Beyond 'Uniqueness and Ethnic Competition.'" *Rethinking History* 8, no. 1 (2004): 127–42.

———, ed. *The Holocaust and Historical Methodology*. New York: Berghahn Books, 2012.

Sturken, Marita. "Absent Images of Memory: Remembering and Reenacting the Japanese Internment." In *Perilous Memories: The Asia-Pacific War(s)*, ed. Takeshi Fujitani, Geoffrey M. White, and Lisa Yoneyama. Durham, N.C.: Duke University Press, 2001.

Subotić, Jelena. *Yellow Star, Red Star: Holocaust Remembrance After Communism*. Ithaca, N.Y.: Cornell University Press, 2019.

Sunseri, Thaddeus. "Exploiting the Urwald: German Post colonial Forestry in Poland and Central Africa, 1900–1960." *Past & Present* 214, no. 1 (2012): 305–42.

Surmann, Jan. "Zwischen Restitution und Erinnerung. Die US-Restitutionspolitik am Ende des 20. Jahrhunderts und die Auflosung der Tripartite Gold Commission." In *Universalisierung des Holocaust? Erinnerungskultur und Geschichtspolitik in internationaler Perspektive, Beitrage zur Geschichte des Nationalsozialismus*, vol. 24, ed. Moisel Eckel. Göttingen, Ger.: Wallstein, 2008.

Svetlana, Alexievich. *The Unwomanly Face of War: An Oral History of Women in World War II*, trans. Richard Pevear. New York: Random House, 2017.

Szaynok, Bozena. "The Impact of the Holocaust on Jewish Attitudes in Postwar Poland." In *Contested Memories: Poles and Jews During the Holocaust and Its Aftermath*, ed. Joshua D. Zimmerman. New Brunswick, N.J.: Rutgers University Press, 2003.

——. "The Jewish Pogrom in Kielce, July 1946: New Evidence." *Intermarium* 1, no. 3 (2016). https://ciaotest.cc.columbia.edu/olj/int/int_0103a.html.

Sznaider, Natan. "The Summer of Discontent: Achille Mbembe in Germany." *Journal of Genocide Research* (2020): 1–8. https://doi.org/10.1080/14623528.2020.1847862.

Takenaka, Akiko. "Mobilizing Death: Bodies and Spirits of the Modern Japanese Military Dead." In *The Palgrave Handbook of Mass Dictatorship*, ed. Paul Corner and Jie-Hyun Lim. London: Palgrave Macmillan, 2016.

——. *Yasukuni Shrine: History, Memory, and Japan's Unending Postwar*. Honolulu: University of Hawai'i Press, 2015.

Taylor, Telford. *Nuremberg and Vietnam: An American Tragedy*. Chicago: Quadrangle Books, 1970.

Tanaka, Stefan. *Japan's Orient: Rendering Pasts Into History*. Berkeley: University of California Press, 1993.

Tetsuro, Konishi. "The Original Manuscript of Takashi Nagai's Funeral Address at a Mass for the Victims of the Nagasaki Atomic Bomb." *Journal of Nagasaki University of Foreign Studies* 18, no. 18 (2014): 55–68.

Tetsuya, Takahashi. "The Emperor Shōwa Standing at Ground Zero: On the (Re-)configuration of a National Memory of the Japanese People." *Japan Forum* 15, no. 1 (2003): 3–14.

Tischner, Józef. *Pomoc w rachunku sumienia*. Kraków: Znak, 2002.

Todorov, Tzvetan. *Facing the Extreme: Moral Life in the Concentration Camps*, trans. Arthur Denner and Abigail Pollak. London: Weidenfeld & Nicolson, 1999.

——. "Totalitarianism: Between Religion and Science." *Totalitarian Movements and Political Religions* 2, no. 1 (2001): 28–42.

Tonini, Carla. "The Jews in Poland After the Second World War: Most Recent Contributions of Polish Historiography." *Quest—Issues in Contemporary Jewish History. Journal of Fondazione CDEC* 1 (2010): 61–62.

Traverso, Enzo. *The Origins of Nazi Violence*, trans. Janet Lloyd. New York: New Press, 2003.

Turowicz, Jerzy. "Ethical Problems of the Holocaust: Discussion Held at International Conference on the History and Culture of Polish Jewry in Jerusalem on Monday, 1 February 1988." In *My Brother's Keeper? Recent Polish Debates on the Holocaust*, ed. Antony Polonsky. London: Routledge, 1990.

Ulbricht, Walter. "Warum Nationale Front des demokratischen Deutschlands?" In *Zur Geschichte des Deutschen Arbeiterbewegung: Aus Reden und Aufsätzen*, vol. 3. Berlin: Dietz Verlag, 1954.

Valkenier, Elizabeth K. "The Rise and Decline of Official Marxist Historiography in Poland, 1945–1983." *Slavic Review* 44, no. 4 (1985): 663–80.

Valmet, Aro. "Occupied Identities: National Narratives in Baltic Museums of Occupations." *Journal of Baltic Studies* 42, no. 2 (2011): 189–211.

Vidal-Naquet, Pierre. *Assassins of Memory: Essays on the Denial of the Holocaust*. New York: Columbia University Press, 1992.

von Ankum, Katharina. "Victims, Memory, History: Antifascism, and the Question of National Identity in East German Narratives After 1990." *History and Memory* 7, no. 2 (1995): 41–69.

von Benda-Beckmann, Bas. *A German Catastrophe?: German Historians and the Allied Bombings, 1945–2010*. Amsterdam: Amsterdam University Press, 2010.

Waldstein, Maxim K. "Observing *Imperium*: A Postcolonial Reading of Ryszard Kapuściński's Account of Soviet and Post-Soviet Russia." *Social Identities* 8, no. 3 (2002): 481–99.

Walicki, Andrzej. *Trzy patriotyzmy*. Warsaw: Res Publica, 1991.

Warschawski, Michel. *On the Border*, trans. Levi Laub. Cambridge, Mass.: South End Press, 2005.

Watt, Lori. *When Empire Comes Home: Repatriation and Reintegration in Postwar Japan*. Cambridge, Mass: Harvard University Press, 2009.

Wawrzyniak, Joanna. *Veterans. Victims and Memory: The Politics of the Second World War in Communist Poland*, trans. Simon Lewis. Frankfurt am Main: Peter Lang, 2015.

Weinbaum, Lawrence. *The Struggle for Memory in Poland: Auschwitz, Jedwabne, and Beyond*. Jerusalem: Institute of the World Jewish Congress, 2011.

Weinberg, Werner. *Self-Portrait of a Holocaust Survivor*. Jefferson, N.C.: McFarland, 1985.

Welch, Steven R. "Commemorating 'Heroes of a Special Kind': Deserter Monuments in Germany." *Journal of Contemporary History* 47, no. 2 (2012): 370–401.

Werner, Michael and Bénédicte Zimmermann. "Beyond Comparison: Histoire Croisée and the Challenge of Reflexivity." *History and Theory* 45, no. 1 (2006): 30–50.

White, Hayden. *Figural Realism: Studies in the Mimesis Effect*. Baltimore, Md.: Johns Hopkins University Press, 1999.

Wieliński, Bartosz T. "'Polska nie chce uchodźców, bo nie rozliczyła się ze zbrodni na Żydach.' Oburzenie po tekście Grossa." *Gazeta Wyborcza*. September 15, 2015.

Wiesel, Elie. "Freedom of Conscience: A Jewish Commentary." *Journal of Ecumenical Studies* 14, no. 4 (1977): 638–49.

Wiesenthal, Simon. *The Sunflower: On the Possibilities and Limits of Forgiveness*. New York: Schocken Books, 1997.

Wieviorka, Annette. *The Era of the Witness*, trans. Jared Stark. Ithaca, N.Y.: Cornell University Press, 2006.

Wigura, Karolina. "Alternative Historical Narrative: 'Polish Bishops' Appeal to Their German Colleagues' of 18 November 1965." *East European Politics and Societies and Cultures* 27, no. 3 (2013): 400–412.

———. *Wina Narodów: Przebaczenie jako strategia prowadzenia polityki*. Gdańsk, Pol.: Scholar, 2011.

Wimmer, Andreas, and Nina Glick Schiller. "Methodological Nationalism and Beyond: Nation-State Building, Migration, and Sociology." *Global Networks* 2, no. 4 (2002): 301–34.

Winstone, Martin. *The Dark Heart of Hitler's Europe: Nazi Rule in Poland Under the General Government*. London: Tauris, 2015.

Winter, Jay. *Sites of Memory, Sites of Mourning: The Greatest War in European Cultural History*. Cambridge: Cambridge University Press, 1998.

Wogenstein, Sebastian. "Negative Symbiosis? Israel, Germany, and Austria in Contemporary Germanophone Literature." *Prooftexts: A Journal of Jewish Literary History* 33, no. 1 (2013): 105–32.

Wojtyła, Kardynał Karol. "Znak Naszej Epoki." *Tygodnik Powszechny* 42, no. 1186 (1971).

Wolf, Joan B. " 'Anne Frank Is Dead, Long Live Anne Frank': The Six-Day War and the Holocaust in French Public Discourse." *History & Memory* 11, no. 1 (1999): 104–40.

Wolff, Larry. *Inventing Eastern Europe: The Map of Civilization on the Mind of the Enlightenment*. Stanford, Calif.: Stanford University Press, 1994.

Wolpe, Rebecca. "From Slavery to Freedom: Abolitionist Expressions in Maskilic Sea Adventures." *AJS Review* 36, no. 1 (2012): 43–70.

Wóycicki, Kazimierz, ed. *Ofiary czy Współwinni: nazizm i sowietyzm w świadomości historycznej*. Warsaw: Volumen, 1997.

Wüllner, Fritz. *Die NS-Militarjustiz und das Elend der Geschichtsschreibung: ein grundlegender Forschungsbericht*. 2d ed. Baden-Baden, Ger.: Nomos, 1997.

X, Malcolm. *The Autobiography of Malcolm X*. New York: Grove Press, 1966.

Yang, Daqing. "The Challenges of the Nanjing Massacre: Reflections on Historical Inquiry." In *The Nanjing Massacre in History and Historiography*, ed. Joshua Fogel. Berkeley: University of California Press, 2000.

———. "The Malleable and the Contested: The Nanjing Massacre in Postwar China and Japan." In *Perilous Memories: The Asia-Pacific War(s)*, ed. Takeshi Fujitani, Geoffrey M. White, and Lisa Yoneyama. Durham, N.C.: Duke University Press, 2001.

Yoneyama, Lisa.. *Cold War Ruins: Transpacific Critique of American Justice and Japanese War Crimes*. Durham, N.C.: Duke University Press, 2016.

———. *Hiroshima Traces: Time, Space, and the Dialectics of Memory*. Berkeley: University of California Press, 1999.

Yoshida, Takashi. "A Battle Over History: The Nanjing Massacre in Japan." In *The Nanjing Massacre in History and Historiography*, ed. Joshua Fogel. Berkeley: University of California Press, 2000.

Young, Lung-Chang. "Altruistic Suicide: A Subjective Approach." *Sociological Bulletin* 21, no. 2 (1972): 103–21.

Zehfuss, Maja. *Wounds of Memory: The Politics of War in Germany*. Cambridge: Cambridge University Press, 2007.

Zertal, Idith. *From Catastrophe to Power: Holocaust Survivors and the Emergence of Israel*. Berkeley: University of California Press, 1998.

———. *Israel's Holocaust and the Politics of Nationhood*, trans. Chaya Galai. Cambridge: Cambridge University Press, 2005.

Zerubavel, Yael. "The Death of Memory and the Memory of Death: Masada and the Holocaust as Historical Metaphors." *Representations* 45 (1994): 72–100.

Ziemer, Klaus, ed. *Memory and Politics of Cultural Heritage in Poland and Germany*. Warsaw: Cardinal Stefan Wyszyński University in Warsaw, 2015.

Zimmerer, Jürgen. "Die Geburt des Ostlandes aus dem Geiste des Kolonialismus: Die nationalsozialistische Eroberungs- und Beherrschungspolitik in (post-)kolonialer Perspektive." *Sozial Geschichte* 19, no. 1 (2004): 10–43.

Zimmerer, J., and M. Rothberg. "Erinnerungskultur: Enttabuisiert den Vergleich!" *Die Zeit*, no. 14. Online ed. March 31. 2021.

Zimmerman, Joshua D., ed. *Contested Memories: Poles and Jews During the Holocaust and Its Aftermath*. New Brunswick, N.J.: Rutgers University Press, 2003.

Ziółkowski, Marek. "Memory and Forgetting after Communism." *Polish Sociological Review* 137, no. 1 (2002): 7–24.

Žižek, Slavoj. *The Parallax View*. Cambridge, Mass.: MIT Press, 2006.

Zubrzycki, Geneviève. *The Crosses of Auschwitz: Nationalism and Religion in Post-Communist Poland*. Chicago: University of Chicago Press, 2006.

Zwigenberg, Ran. *Hiroshima: The Origins of Global Memory Culture*. Cambridge: Cambridge University Press, 2014.

———. "Never Again: Hiroshima, Auschwitz and the Politics of Commemoration." *Asia-Pacific Journal* 13, no. 3 (2015): 1–14.

ONLINE SOURCES

"[국경일 노래와 가사] 제헌절 노래 (정인보 작사, 박태준 작곡)." 건시스템 커뮤니케이션즈 커뮤니티. https://www.gunsys.com/tn/board.php?board=lovesongboard&page=1&category=1&comman d=body&no=112.

"[기념일 노래와 가사] 현충일 노래 (조지훈 작사, 임원식 작곡)." 건시스템 커뮤니케이션즈 커뮤니티. https://www.gunsys.com/tn/board.php?board=lovesongboard&category=1&command=body& no=92.

"독후감—안네의 일기." 좋은글. http://joungul.co.kr/after/after1/%EB%8F%85%ED%9B%84%EA%B0%90_52984.asp.

"안네의 일기 (안네 프랑크 저)." 티스토리. https://bookbugs.tistory.com/entry/%EC%95%88%EB%8 4%A4%EC%9D%98-%EC%9D%BC%EA%B8%B0-%EC%95%88%EB%84%A4-%ED%94%84B%9E%91%ED%81%AC-%EC%A0%80.

"『안네의 일기』 어린이 독후감대회 참여작." Yes24. http://www.yes24.com/Product/Goods/1418754.

"안네의일기 줄거리 독후감." 네이버블로그. https://m.blog.naver.com/PostView.nhn?blogId=sbbamt ol&logNo=220064081996&proxyReferer=https:%2F%2Fwww.google.com%2F.

"비디오 함께한 지일본 일주 (3 일차)—독가스님 오루노시나에 남겨신 선은." 네이버블로그. https://blog.naver.com/jcjw1234/221558239896.

BIBLIOGRAPHY 417

"히로시마 여행-오쿠노시마(토끼섬, 독가스섬)." 네이버블로그. https://blog.naver.com/jbm993
/221543 384914.

"[일본] 히로시마 토끼섬 오쿠노시마 (大久野島)." 네이버블로그. https://blog.naver.com
/xjvmgksrldnj/221627795080.

"히로시마 토끼섬(오쿠노시마)." 네이버카페. https://cafe.naver.com/sarangkeeper/100529.

"주요사업—추도 순례." 일제강제동원피해자지원재단 홈페이지. https://www.ilje.or.kr/service
/body/list/.

"키워드검색—'만보산사건.'" 네이버 뉴스 라이브러리. https://newslibrary.naver.com/search
/searchByKeyword.nhn#%7B%22mode%22%3A1%2C%22sort%22%3A0%2C%22trans%2
2%3A%22 1%22%2C%22pageSize%22%3A10%2C%22keyword%22%3A%22%EB%A7%8C%
EB%B3%B4%E C%82%B0%EC%82%AC%EA%B1%B4%22%2C%22status%22%3A%22succ
ess%22%2C%22start Index%22%3A1%2C%22page%22%3A8%2C%22startDate%22%3A
%221920-03-05%22%2C%22 endDate%22%3A%221999-12-31%22%7D.

ホロコースト記念館. http://www.hecjpn.org/index.html.

"常設展示." 広島平和記念資料館. http://hpmmuseum.jp/modules/exhibition/index.php?action
=Fac ilityView&facility_id=1&lang=jpn.

"広島平和記念資料館 tiらのメッセージ." 広島平和記念資料館. http://hpmmuseum.jp/modules
/exhibition/index.php?action=CornerView&corner_id=4&lang=jpn.

"平和記念公園の建設." 広島平和記念資料館. http://hpmmuseum.jp/modules/exhibition/index
.php? action=ItemView&item_id=101&lang=jpn.

"Adolf Berman. Wgłównym nurcie historii. Żydowski Instytut Historyczny im. Emanuela Ringe lbluma." *Jewish Historical Institute Blog.* https://web.archive.org/web/20161005115834
/http://www.jhi.pl/blog/2013-10-17-adolf-berman-w-glownym-nurcie-historii.

"Apostolic Pilgrimage to Poland. Holy Mass at the Concentration Camp. Homily of His Holiness John Paul II." *Libreria Editrice Vaticana.* https://w2.vatican.va/content/john-paul
-ii/e n/homilies/1979/documents/hf_jp-ii_hom_19790607_polonia-brzezinka.html.

"Auschwitz-Birkenau: Auschwitz Convent." Jewish Virtual Library. https://www.jewish
virtuallibrary.org/auschwitz-convent.

"Avantgarde der Versöhnung: Über den Briefwechsel der Bischöfe und die Ostdenkschrift des EKD von 1965." Magazin Dialog. https://www.dialogmagazin.eu/leseprobe-ausgabe
-72-73-briefwechsel-bischoefe.html.

"Benjamin (Ben) Meed Describes the Burning of the Warsaw Ghetto During the 1943 Ghetto Uprising." United States Holocaust Memorial Museum. https://encyclopedia.ushmm.org
/c ontent/en/oral-history/benjamin-ben-meed-describes-the-burning-of-the-warsaw
-ghet to-during-the-1943-ghetto-uprising?parent=en%2F3636.

"Community Reviews of *The Book of Haralan.* 2016." Goodreads. https://www.goodreads
.com/book/show/22642465-the-book-of-harlan.

"Compilation of Korean News Articles on Comfort Women Survivors and Holocaust Survivor s' Meetings." KACE 시민참여센터. http://kace.org/2011/12/21/compilation-of-news
-articles-on-comfort-women-survivors-and-holocaust-survivors%27-meeting/.

"Customer Reviews of *Fear.* 2007." https://www.amazon.com/-/ko/product-reviews
/0812967461/ref=acr_dp_hist_1?ie=UTF8&filterByStar=one_star&reviewerType=all
_reviews#r eviews-filter-bar.

"Customer Reviews of *Neighbors*. 2002." https://www.amazon.com/Neighbors-Destruction-Jewish-Community-Jedwabne/product-reviews/0142002402/ref=cm_cr_getr_d_paging_btm_next_2?ie=UTF8&showViewpoints=0&filterBy=addOneStar&filterByStar=one_star&pageNumber=2.

"Customer Reviews of *So Far from the Bamboo Grove*. 2008." https://www.amazon.com/-/ko/Bamboo-Grove-Yoko-Kawashima-Watkins/product-reviews/0688131158/ref=cm_cr_arp_d_viewpnt_rgt?ie=UTF8&reviewerType=all_reviews&pageNumber=1&filterByStar=critical.

Denkmal für die Verfolgten der NS-Militärjustiz in Wien. https://deserteursdenkmal.at/wordpress/home/.

"Die Antwort der deutschen Bischöfe vom 5. Dezember 1965." *Zentrum für Dialog und Gebet in Oświęcim*. http://cdim.pl/1965-11-18-botschaft-der-polnischen-an-die-deutschen-bisch-fe,2942.

"Facebook Page of Mesto Bardejov." https://www.facebook.com/mestobardejovofficial/photos/pcb.4688961001154123/4688957987821091.

"Glendale Government Library, Art & Culture Department ReflectSpace." City of Glendale. http://www.glendaleca.gov/government/departments/library-arts-culture/central-library-grand-re-opening-may-1-2017/reflectspace.

"I Am My Brother's Keeper: A Tribute to the Righteous Among the Nations. Paying the Ultimate Price. Jozef and Wiktoria Ulma." Yad Vashem. https://www.yadvashem.org/yv/en/exhibitions/righteous/ulma.asp.

"Information About the Prisoners of War of the Japanese 1939–1945." *Forces War Records*. https://www.forces-war-records.co.uk/prisoners-of-war-of-the-japanese-1939–1945.

Nikkei for Civil Rights and Redress. http://www.ncrr-la.org/about.html.

Northwestern California Genocide Project. https://nwgenocide.omeka.net/.

"Odezwa "Protest!" konspiracyjnego Frontu Odrodzenia Polski pióra Zofii Kossak-Szczuckiej, sierpień 1942 r." *Żydów w Polsce*. http://www.zydziwpolsce.edu.pl/biblioteka/zrodla/r3_5d.html.

"Petition to Remove Monument and Not Support Any International Harassment Related Issue Against People Japan." White House. https://petitions.whitehouse.gov/petition/remove-monument-and-not-support-any-international-harassment-related-issue-against-people-japan/FPfs7p0Q.

"Thucydides, *History of the Peloponnesian War*, 2.42." Perseus Digital Library. http://www.perseus.tufts.edu/hopper/text?doc=Thuc.+2.42&fromdoc=Perseus%3Atext%3A1999.01.0200.

"Winds of Peace Newsletters." MQI Vietnam: Madison Quakers, Inc. http://www.mqivietnam.org/archives.

"Wojciech Materski and Tomasz Szarota, eds. "Polska 1939–1945. Straty osobowe i ofiary represji pod dwiema okupacjami." Institute of National Remembrance (IPN), Warsaw. https://web.archive.org/web/20120323161233/http://niniwa2.cba.pl/polska_1939_1945.htm.

INDEX

Abe, Shinzō, 107, 236, 313–14
Abel, 22, 36. *See also* Cain
Abe Shintaro, 106–7
absolutist pacifism, 157–58, 159–60
accountability, 81, 96, 158, 175, 184; colonialism relation to, 192; for Nazism, 143–44; Treaty on Basic Relations Between Japan and the Republic of Korea and, 300
accusatory denialism, 249–50, 251, 253, 255
Adenauer, Konrad, 145, 165, 350n12
ADL. *See* Anti-Defamation League
Adorno, Theodor, 265
affective memory, 6, 8–9, 67, 127, 139, 320n26
African National Congress, 94
Agamben, Giorgio, 271
Agent Orange, 119, 215
Agnew, Harold, 353n64
Ahmadinejad, Mahmoud, 244
Ahn Dongwon, 191–92
Air and Space Museum, 158
AJC. *See* American Jewish Committee
AK. *See* Armia Krajowa
Akçam, Taner, 105
Alexievich, Svetlana, 269, 273

Algeria, France relation to, 102–3
Algerian National Liberation Army, 100, 103
altruistic suicide, 330n3
Amanpour, Christiane, 363n104
American Jewish Committee (AJC), 206
Anatomy of Nazism, The, 206
Andersch, Alfred, 75
Anderson, Benedict, 60
Anielewicz, Mordechai, 207, 208
Anne Frank House, 95–96, 305
Anne Frank Rose Garden (Fukuyama), 130
Anpo protests, 112
anti-Apartheid activists, 94–95
Anti-Chinese Riots, 202
Anti-Defamation League (ADL), 206
antisemitism, 33, 95, 180, 281, 304–5, 306; *E'tatism* relation to, 99; in France, 189, 358n17; in Germany, 92; Holocaust relation to, 219; Israel relation to, 245; Kielce pogrom and, 182–84; of Kolbe, 223, 234–36, 237–39, 240, 313; Kossak-Szczucka relation to, 185–86; in *Mały Dziennik*, 128; among Muslims, 244–45; in Poland, 23–24, 34, 40, 122, 126, 184–85, 357n12; in PZPR, 359n33; *Sonderweg* and, 313; of Stalin, 9; Stalinism and, 207

antiwar movement: in East Asia, 100; in Japan, 101–2
Apartheid, 94, 238, 314–15; Holocaust compared to, 305, 310; Nazism compared to, 95–96
"Aporia of Auschwitz, The," 8, 271
Apotheosis of the Fallen, The, 59
Arab League, 145
Arafat, Yasser, 211
Arendt, Hannah, x, 142–44, 181–82, 315–16
Armenian Genocide, 88–89, 105, 326n27
Armia Krajowa (AK), 97
Arnold, Agnieszka, 36, 38
Aron, Raymond, 211
Asahi Shimbun, 73–74, 100–101, 228–29, 239
Asante, Amma, 96–97
Ashkenazi Jews, 94, 210–11
Asiacentrism, 118
Asian Exclusion Act (1924), 133
Asian Relations Conference, 192
Asia-Pacific War, 27, 68, 101, 148, 248, 263; atrocities in, 107–8, 150; death toll in, 178, 325n21; forced labor in, 135; funeral rites in, 66–67; in history textbooks, 110; Liberal Democratic Party on, 155–56; sexual violence in, 85, 91; war crimes in, 131
Asiatic Bolshevism, 17
Assmann, Aleida, 373n52
Assmann, Jan, 12–13
Atlanta Race Riot, 92
atrocities, 7; in Asia-Pacific War, 107–8, 150; in Vietnam War, 100–101
Auschwitz-Birkenau State Museum, 111
Auschwitz concentration camp, 112, 120, 247, 270–71, 327n44; Austria relation to, 174; Catholics relation to, 123–28; Holocaust denialism relation to, 248; Nagasaki relation to, 19, 219–20, 222, 239, 241; photographs of, 273–74; PZPR relation to, 121–22
Auschwitz Lies, 211
Australia, German Consulate in, 94

Austria, 73, 173–74
Austrian Veterans' Association, 73
Axis powers, 171–72; memory cultures of, 151; Western imperialism relation to, 4

Ballhausplatz, 73
Bandera, Stepan, 218–19
Bandung regime, 2
Bantustans, 95
Bar, Joachim, 235
Bardoń, Karol, 181
Bartov, Omer, 261
Batavia War Crimes Trials, 337n25
Bauman, Zygmunt, 18, 104, 160, 304, 317n5; global memory formation and, 319n21; on hereditary victimhood, 40; on shame, 35–36
BDS. *See* Boycott, Divestment, and Sanctions
BdV. *See* Federation of Expellees
Begin, Menachem, 211–12
Beheiren, 101–2
Belarus, 325n19
Belgrade, 157–58
Bells of Nagasaki, The (Nagai), 221–22, 365n27
Beneš, Edvard, 163
Ben-Gurion, David, 204–5, 210–11, 350n12
Bensberger Kreis, 296–97
Berberyusz, Ewa, 32
Bereza Kartuska, 309
Bergen-Belsen concentration camp, 144
Bergen County Justice Center, Memorial Island in, 9–10
Berman, Adolf, 25, 186, 324n16
Berman, Jakub, 24–25, 186, 324n16
Beyrak, Nathan, 268
Bialik, Haim Nahman, 204
"Biedni Polacy patrzą na getto," 21–22, 29
Bienkowski, Oliver, 189
Bikila, Abebe, 150
Bikont, Anna, 37, 179

Birobidzhan, Jewish Autonomous Region in, 135
Black Lives Matter movement, 6
Black nationalism, 2
Blair, Tony, 175
Bloch, Marc, 266, 317n2
Błoński, Jan, 21–22, 29–30, 33–34, 37, 326n29
Blue Deer school, 53
Böll, Heinrich, 75
Bolshevism, 9, 17, 98, 120–21
Bomba, Abraham, 23
Bonn, Hans, 115, 352n42
Book of Harlan, The (McFadden), 96
Bosnia, 85, 87
Bosnian War, 86
Boston, Massachusetts, Korean Consulate General in, ix–x
Boston Globe, ix
Bourbon dynasty, 60
Boycott, Divestment, and Sanctions (BDS), 306
Brandeis University, 207
Brandt, Willy, 167, 289
Brexit, 2
Bridge on the River Kwai, The, 193
Browning, Christopher, 256, 319n21
Bruce, John Edward, 134
Bruno, Giordano, 30–33
Buber, Martin, 266
Buchenwald concentration camp, 96, 143, 144
Buergenthal, Thomas, 140
Bungei Shunju, 223
burnt offering, 51
Buruma, Ian, 77, 148
Busan, Noguchi detachment in, 193–94, 196
Byelorussian Soviet Socialist Republic, 180
Byron, 53

Cain, 22, 28, 36
Cambodia, Khmer Rouge of, 163
Camil, Mustafa, 132

"Campo di Fiori," 30–33
Canaan Farm, 136
capitalism, xi, 16; Holocaust relation to, 9, 357n9; Nazism relation to, 146, 147, 176
Carmelite convent, 123–25, 127, 239, 346n42
Catholic Club, 233
Catholicism, 287–88, 293, 297; colonialism relation to, 230–31; East Asia relation to, 299–303; forgiveness and, 279, 280, 281, 284, 298; Japan relation to, 224–27, 299–303; Jews relation to, 238; Nagasaki relation to, 221; Nazis relation to, 291; PZPR relation to, 283. *See also* Polish Catholic Church
Catholics, 185, 187; Auschwitz relation to, 123–28; PAX, 113–14; in Poland, 22, 39–40, 235–36
CDU. *See* Christian Democratic Union
censorship, 160; of history textbooks, 107–9
CENTOS, 324n16
Césaire, Aimé, 310–11
"Chair for the Study of Resistance During the Holocaust," 94
Chang, Iris, 101
Charter of German Expellees, 164–65
Chechenia, 309–10
China, 43, 160, 171, 199–200; memory politics in, 188–89; Nanjing Massacre relation to, 101
Chirac, Jacques, 331n22
Chon Kwangyong, 180
Chosun Ilbo, 42, 135, 199, 200, 202
Christian Democratic Union (CDU), 144, 145–46, 164
Christianity, 59, 64; colonialism relation to, 290–91; cult of the fallen soldiers and, 62–63; forgiveness relation to, 294–95; in Japan, 223–27, 230–31. *See also* Catholicism
Christian Social Association, 113
Christian Socialist Party (CSU), 164
Chui, Mathieu Ngudjolo, 87
Chun Doo-Hwan, 253, 256–57

Churchill, Ward, 103
Churchill, Winston, 173
Church of West Germany, 164–65
civil religion, 59, 64, 72, 80, 208, 330n13; in Japan, 237; of Nazis, 71
civil rights: of Jews, 345n29; in U.S., 100
Cold War, 5, 9; global memory culture relation to, 16–17; global memory formation and, 239; Hiroshima-Auschwitz Peace March relation to, 114–16; Jewish commies relation to, 206–7; memory politics of, 140; post–Cold War, 4, 9, 16, 17, 124, 168, 175, 284, 307; red textbooks and, 108
collective guilt, 45, 98, 165, 181–82, 262, 293; collective innocence relation to, 203–4
collective innocence, 19, 165, 181–82, 293; collective guilt relation to, 203–4; in Korea, 196, 199, 202, 203; in Poland, 186–88, 189–90
collective memory, 6, 12, 13, 63, 176, 311; in Germany, 144; in Korea, 27, 196; national identity and, 320n25; in Poland, 22, 28, 189–91
colonial genocide, xi–xii, 98–99, 103–4, 304
colonialism, 11, 93–94, 99, 119, 361n65; accountability relation to, 192; Catholicism relation to, 230–31; Christianity relation to, 290–91; grassroots memories of, 16–17; hereditary victimhood relation to, 40–41; of Japan, x, 42–43, 108, 109, 167; Poland relation to, 309–10; *Sonderweg* relation to, 176; Western, 232, 313
Columbus, Christopher, 103
Comfort Women, 45, 86, 247, 272, 321n38, 338n40; Batavia War Crimes Trials and, 337n25; denialism of, 90, 248, 249, 257, 259, 260, 262; globalization and, 5; Hiroshima-Auschwitz Peace March relation to, 117; Kupferberg Holocaust Center relation to, 138; Memorial Island and, 9–10; memory war and, 6; mnemonic solidarity for, 89–91; Park Young-Shim, 254–55; sexual violence and, 49; suffering of, 274–75; UN Human Rights Council and, 88; WIWCT relation to, 84–85
Commemoration of the Koreans Deceased in War Catastrophe, 27
Commentary, 142–43
Committee for Investigation of Damage Inflicted by Forced Mobilization During the Period of Resistance Against Japan and Aid for Victims of Forced International Migration, 197
communism, 9, 24, 100, 127; Jews relation to, 28; in Korea, 140; Laudański brothers' relation to, 180
Communist Party, 16, 113–14. *See also* Polish United Workers' Communist Party
Communist Party of Germany (KPD), 145–46
Communist Party USA, 206
Condor Legion, 169
Confederation of Independent Poland, 126
Conference on Nazi Gold, 79
Confessions of St. Augustine, The, 280
conscientious objectors, 334n74
conspiracy theories, 201–2, 236, 249, 253, 259–60; Kielce pogrom and, 250–51, 252
Constantine Bae Ki Hyun, 301
Convention on the Prevention and Punishment of the Crime of Genocide, 93–94
Cooper, William, 94
Corfu, Greece, 23
Corradini, Enrico, 64
cosmopolitanization, of Holocaust, 11, 128, 137
Council of Constance, 290
Crabwalk (Grass), 166–67, 168–69. *See also* Gustloff, Wilhelm
Creole nationalism, 2, 48
Croatia, 217

Croce, Benedetto, 172
CSU. *See* Christian Socialist Party
Cuban Missile Crisis, 112
cultural memory, 12, 13–14, 45, 54, 57, 221; hereditary victimhood as, 40–41, 204; of Holocaust, 208–9, 211, 212; imagination relation to, 247; in Poland, 28, 190–91; victims in, 58, 268–69; of West Germany, 162–63. *See also* memory cultures
Cyrankiewicz, Józef, 122
Czechoslovakia, 163
Czech Revolutionary Guards, 163–64

Dahn, Daniela, 145
Daily News, 194
dark tourism, 161
death toll: in Asia-Pacific War, 178, 325n21; in Dresden, 153; of *hikiagesha*, 166; of Japanese POWs, 171; in Poland, 24–27; at POW camps, 194
Declaration of the Rights of Man and of the Citizen, 78
Declaration on the Elimination of Violence against Women, 86
deep memory, xi, 20, 270–71, 273. *See also* intellectual memory
Delbo, Charlotte, 102–3, 270
Demjanjuk, John, 359n37
democratization, 57–58, 59, 69, 70
denialism, x, 189–90, 250, 253, 255, 371n30; of Comfort Women, 90, 248, 249, 257, 259, 260, 262; genocide relation to, 19–20, 246, 248, 257; Holocaust, 244–46, 248, 308; of Kielce pogrom, 189–90; memory cultures and, 251–52; positivistic, 255–56, 258–60, 264, 269
Denialist International, 244, 247
De-Nur, Yehiel, 209
Der Standard, 174
deserters, 71–72; monuments to, 73, 74–75
Destruction of Dresden, The (Irving), 152
detention camps, 163
"Determination Toward Truth," 299–300

deterritorialization (of memory), 15, 19, 77, 106, 119, 123, 136, 141. *See also* reterritorialization (of memory)
Deutsch, Lorenz, 305
Deutsche Welle, 130
Diary of Anne Frank, The, 46
Diary of a Young Girl, The (Frank), 94–95, 129; Korea relation to, 134
Die Welt, 292–93, 297, 308
digital capitalism, 16
Dik, Ayzi-Meyer, 93
Dinur, Yehiel, 266, 267, 272
Discours sur le colonialisme (Césaire), 310–11
disenchantment (*Entzauberung*), 55
Dollfuss, Engelbert, 173–74
Dong-A Ilbo, 106–7, 200
Don't Fence Me In, 216
Döpfner, Julius, 285–86, 296
Do the Right Thing, 89
Dresden, 26, 146, 151, 152–54; Hiroshima relation to, 115, 352n42
Du Bois, W. E. B., 91–92, 132, 133–34
Duda, Andrzej, 187
Duke, David, 244–45
Duras, Marguerite, 102
Durkheim, Émile, 330n3
Dziennik Łódźki, 112
Dziennik Polski, 111

East Asia: antiwar movement in, 100; Catholicism relation to, 299–303; funeral rites in, 55; global memory formation in, 109–10; memory cultures of, 49; memory regime in, 16–18; memory war in, xi, 20; political religion in, 76; Western imperialism in, 132. *See also* Japan; Korea
East Asia History Forum for Criticism and Solidarity, 40
Eastern borderland (*kresy*), 309
Eastern history (*Toyoshi*), 3
Eastern studies (*Ostforschung*), 3
"East Europeans Have No Shame," 308–9

East Germany, 145, 146, 151–52, 162, 168; Nazism relation to, 147, 282–83
Ebert, Roger, 22
Eichmann trial, 102, 211, 266–67, 269, 272, 363n94; grassroots memories and, 209–10
EKD. See Evangelical Church in Germany
Emma, 91
Encyclopedia of the Holocaust, 212
Endō Shūsaku, 228–30, 234, 238, 239, 241
Engelking, Barbara, 190
Enlightenment, 331n18
Enola Gay, 158
entangled memories, xiii, 4, 7, 9–10, 14–15, 17, 91, 109, 214, 307, 320n23, 320n31
Entzauberung (disenchantment), 55, 61–62, 333n44
Esprit, 238
Estonia, National Day of Mourning in, 218
E'tatism, 99
Eurocentrism, 20, 104, 304–5; Holocaust relation to, 310, 312–13, 314; Mnemonic, 5, 20, 80, 304–8, 312–15
European Union, 168
Evangelical Church in Germany (EKD), 286–88
Evans, Richard, 371n24, 371n30

fallen soldiers, cult of the, 59, 60, 61, 64–65, 67–68, 75; Christianity and, 62–63; memory cultures and, 74
Fanon, Franz, 102, 238, 316
fascism, 59, 104, 217, 313; East Germany relation to, 146; political religion relation to, 63; victims of, 172–73, 176–77
Father Kolbe of Nagasaki (Tōmei), 228
fatherland, 53, 59, 64, 72–73
Faurisson, Robert, 245
FDP. See Free Democratic Party
Fear (Gross), 251
Federation of Expellees (BdV), 164–65, 292
Feldjägerkorps, 71
feudalism, 176

Fifteen Years' War, 100
Final Solution, 205
Finlay, Ian Hamilton, 73
First International Conference on the Holocaust and Genocide, 321n35
First World War. See World War I
Fogliano Redipuglia War Memorial, 59
forced labor, 69, 81–83, 135, 193
Forced Labor Convention, 86
forced migrants, 7, 162, 197
forced mobilization, 69, 71, 83, 197, 336n14
forced prostitution, 90–91
Foreign Press Club, 287
forgiveness, 20, 129, 278, 293, 296; Catholicism and, 279, 280, 281, 284, 298; Christianity relation to, 294–95; memory politics relation to, 276–77, 280–81
Fortunoff Archive, 268
Forverts, 93
Foundation Act, 81
Foundation for the Victims of Forced Mobilization Under the Japanese Occupation, 69
Fragments (Wilkomirski), 271
France, 26, 28, 56, 60, 100, 102–3; antisemitism in, 189, 358n17; Germany relation to, 295, 354n78
Francis (Pope), 243
Frank, Anne, 94–96, 130–31, 223, 347n55, 348n66; Anne Frank House, 95–96, 305; Anne Frank Rose Garden in Fukuyama, 130; forgiveness and, 129
Frank, Otto, 96, 130, 346n53
Frankl, Viktor, 131
Frankowski, Jan, 113–14
Fraser, Nancy, 315
Frederick the Great (Friedrich der Grosse), 290–91
Free Democratic Party (FDP), 305
Freemasonry, 236; Masonic Mafia, 237–38
French Indochina, 117
French Revolution, 56, 59, 78, 80
Friedrich, Jörg, 154–55

INDEX 425

Friedrich Ebert Foundation, 83
Front for the Rebirth of Poland (Front Odrodzenia Polski), 185
Fujioka Nobukatsu, 257
Fujio Masayuki, 108, 150, 251n33
Fujiwara, Tei, 47
Fukuda Takeo, 106–7
Fukushima nuclear acccident, 241, 352n38
Fukuyama Holocaust Education Center, 129–31, 346n53
funeral rites, 55, 62, 66–67
Fushosa Publishing, 109

Gajowniczek, Franciszek, 219, 233, 237
Gallic male nationalism, 2
Gance, Abel, 62
Gandhi, Mohandas, 132
Gazeta Wyborcza, 178–79
Geneva Convention, 193
genocide, 80, 140, 155, 183, 221; Armenian, 88–89, 105, 326n27; colonial, xi–xiii, 98–99, 103–4, 304; Convention on the Prevention and Punishment of the Crime of, 93–94; denialism relation to, 19–20, 246, 248, 257; Rwandan, 85; sexual violence relation to, 87; in Srebrenica, 247
German Consulate, in Australia, 94
German expellees, 161–65, 168, 286–87, 295–96; suffering of, 166–67, 169, 291–93
German Foundation Act, 81
German-Soviet Pact, 39
Germany, 3, 63, 129, 325n20, 325n23; antisemitism in, 92; collective memory in, 144; France relation to, 295, 354n78; immigrants in, 105–6; Israel relation to, 97–98, 145–46, 308, 350nn12–13; memory cultures in, xi–xii, 75, 98, 165–66, 174–75, 262; memory war in, 305–6; mnemonic solidarity in, 104; Namibia relation to, 98–99; national identity of, 2, 175; Poland relation to, 377n35; *Sonderweg* in, 17, 177–78, 313; suffering in, 142–43; Treaty on the Final Settlement concerning, 81–82. *See also* East Germany; West Germany
Gerstenmaier, Eugen, 287
Gessen, Masha, 315–16
Ghetto Fighters' Museum, 213
Gimborski, Cesaro, 163
Girard, René, 226
Glemp, Józef, 125
Glendale, California, 88–90
globalization, 1–2, 106; of Holocaust, 141, 267; of memory, 4–5, 6–7, 9, 58, 69, 77–78, 80, 304, 312
global memory culture, 4, 11, 77–78, 83–85; Cold War relation to, 16–17; Holocaust relation to, 80
global memory formation, 7–11, 99–100, 243, 266, 305, 319n15; Bauman and, 319n21; Cold War and, 239; denialism in, 19–20; in East Asia, 109–10; Holocaust in, 341n73; mnemonic solidarity in, 316; reterritorialization and, 15; social formation compared to, 5–6; suffering relation to, 165, 214–15
Gluck, Carol, 13, 86
Goebbels, Joseph, 212
Gomułka, Władysław, 288
Gorbachev, Mikhail, 22–23
Göring, Hermann, 212
Gotōda Masaharu, 342n89
Grabowski, Jan, 190, 307–8
Graf, Jürgen, 245
Grass, Günter, 71, 73–74, 144, 166–67, 168–69
grassroots memories, 13, 16–17, 22, 198–99, 242; Eichmann trial and, 209–10
Grbavica, 91
Great East Japan Earthquake, 241–42, 352n38
Greater East Asia Co-Prosperity Sphere, 110, 159, 192, 199
Great Escape, The, 96–97
Great Kanto earthquake, 109–10, 183, 300

Great Vietnamese Famine, 258
Greco-Roman Mediterranean civilization, 331n18
Greece, 23, 100
Greek War of Independence, 53
Greniuch, Tomasz, 190, 367n60
Gross, Jan, 39, 187–88, 248, 251, 264–65, 266; "East Europeans Have No Shame" of, 308–9; *Neighbors* of, 36–38, 80–81, 250, 261, 327n49
Gross, John, 237
Guardian, 315–16
Guernica, 154, 160, 169
guilty conscience, 33, 35, 38–39
Gustloff, Wilhelm, 168–69
Gwangju Uprising, 54, 139, 252–53, 256
Gwangsoo Series, 252–53
Gyunggi Middle School, 68–69

Ha'avara, 205–6
Hallasan, 139
Halwachs, Maurice, 12–13
Hamas, 315–16
Hartoonian, Harry, 326n27
Hausner, Gideon, 209, 266
Havel, Václav, 22–23
Hayashi Fusao, 132–33
Heatley, Basil, 150
Heinemann, Gustav, 287
Heldengedenktag, 349n8
Heldenplatz, 73
hereditary victimhood, 2, 52, 211, 213, 317n5; as cultural memory, 40–41, 204; in Poland, xi–xii, 18, 38
heroes, 120, 206; victims as, 57–58
heroic nationalism, 57–58, 76, 136–37, 139–40
Herrenvolk ("master race"), 96
Heschel, Abraham Joshua, 276–77, 279
Heydrich, Reinhard, 212, 246
hikiagesha, 43, 44–45, 166, 171, 249
hikikomori nationalism, 2
Hilberg, Raul, 265–66, 372n45

Himmler, Heinrich, 103, 205, 212, 246, 247–48, 256
Hirohito (Emperor), 84, 263
Hiroshima, 26, 152, 160, 203, 243; Dresden relation to, 115, 352n42; memory politics in, 228; Sino-Japanese War and, 157; Soviet Union relation to, 156; white supremacy relation to, 155
Hiroshima-Auschwitz Peace March, 19, 111–13, 117, 118; Cold War relation to, 114–16
Hiroshima on August 6 (Exhibition), 156–57
Hiroshima Peace Memorial Museum, 156–57, 159
Hiroshima Peace Park, 159, 243
Historikerstreit (historians' dispute), 16, 81, 98, 306, 307–8, 314
Historikerstreit (Nolte), 218
history textbooks, 215–16; censorship of, 107–9; Nanjing Massacre in, 108, 109–10, 342n84
Hitler, Adolf, 163, 205, 212, 310, 357n15; Austria relation to, 73; positivistic denialism relation to, 256
Ho Feng-Shan, 188–89
Holocaust, 5, 87, 111–12, 304, 341n73; accountability for, 81, 175; antisemitism relation to, 219; Apartheid compared to, 305, 310; Armenian Genocide relation to, 105; Bolshevism relation to, 98; capitalism relation to, 9, 357n9; Catholics relation to, 185; cosmopolitanization of, 11, 128, 137; cultural memory of, 208–9, 211, 212; education on, 79–80, 137; Eurocentrism relation to, 310, 312–13, 314; German expellees compared to, 165; globalization of, 141, 267; in global memory formation, 341n73; guilty conscience about, 38–39; immigrants relation to, 104–5; Israel relation to, 120, 204; LGBT victims of, 189; memory activists relation to, 311–12, 313; memory cultures and, xi–xii, 99; memory politics relation to, 140, 218; mnemonic solidarity relation to, 213; Nanjing

Massacre compared to, 131–32; Poland relation to, 33–34, 36; positivistic denialism relation to, 256; sexual violence in, 91; shame relation to, 35–36; *So Far from the Bamboo Grove* relation to, 137–38; South Korea relation to, 136–37, 139; Stockholm International Forum on the, 77–78; transatlantic slave trade compared to, 97; Vietnam War compared to, 100, 215, 315; Zionists relation to, 40, 207
Holocaust denialism, 244–46, 248, 308
Holocaust Deniers International, 245
Holocaust Survivors Film Archive Project, 270
Holodomor, 325n19
homosexual violence, 87–88
Honda Katsuichi, 100–101
Hondo Shuntaro, 230–32
Horkheimer, Max, 206
Horowitz, Irene, 261
human rights, 10–11, 43, 57, 80, 267–68, 306; cultural memory relation to, 57; North Korea relation to, 321n38; WIWCT relation to, 85
"human zoo" (*Völkerschau*), 97
Hurwitz, Leo, 363n94
Hussein, Saddam, 341n73
Husseini, Amin al-, 212
Hyeyeon Jun Monica, 89

ICTR. *See* International Criminal Tribunal for Rwanda
ICTY. *See* International Criminal Tribunal for the former Yugoslavia
Ida, 37–38
Ienaga Saburo trial, 259
imagination, 1, 247
immigrants, 10, 104–6
imperialism, 2–3, 100, 116, 152, 297; of Japan, 27, 117–18, 202; victims of, 197; Western, 4, 108, 132, 147, 148, 156
Imperial Rule Assistance, in Japan, 175
Im Won-sik, 53

Index Expurgatorius, 306
Indonesian National Armed Forces, 199
Inoue Hisashi, 226
Institut d'Histoire du Temps Présent, 322n43
Institute of History, at Polish Academy of Sciences, 37
Institute of National Remembrance (IPN, Poland), 25, 190, 251, 327n49, 367n60
intellectual memory, 270–71. *See also* deep memory
Internal Security Agency, of Poland, 297
International Court of Justice, 140
International Criminal Court, 86, 87
International Criminal Tribunal for Rwanda (ICTR), 85–86
International Criminal Tribunal for the former Yugoslavia (ICTY), 85–86
International Institute for Holocaust Research, 94
International Labor Organization, 86
International League of Darker Peoples, 134
International March of the Living, 126
International Sociological Association, 92
internment camps, 88, 216
Investigative Committee for Past Events, 256–57
IPN. *See* Institute of National Remembrance
Iranian Revolution, 245
Irving, David, 152–53, 245, 256, 371n24
Irving v. Lipstadt, 259, 267
Irwin-Zarecka, Iwona, 122
Ishimaru, Dota, 133
Ishiwara Kanji, 133
Islamophobia, 88, 308, 310
Israel, 40, 207–8, 213, 245, 321n35; Germany relation to, 97–98, 145–46, 308, 350nn12–13; hereditary victimhood in, xi–xii, 18; heroic nationalism of, 136–37, 139–40; Holocaust relation to, 120, 204; Jewish diasporic victims relation to, 204–5, 210; Palestine relation to, 2, 11, 305, 312, 314–16; South Korea relation to, 135–36

Israeli Declaration of Independence, 209, 306
Italy, xi–xii, 2, 63, 173

J'accuse, 62
Jacobin regime, in Poland, 59–60
Jagiellonian University, 112
Jaksch, Wenzel, 297
Jang Soo-eob, 196
Janowska concentration camp, 277
Japan, 46, 64–65, 75–76, 82–83, 175–76, 313–14; absolutist pacifism in, 157–58, 159–60; antiwar movement in, 101–2; capitalism relation to, 176; Catholicism relation to, 224–27, 299–303; Christianity in, 223–27, 230–31; civil religion in, 237; colonialism of, x, 42–43, 108, 109, 167; Comfort Women denialism in, 90; forced mobilization in, 71; grassroots memories of, 242; history textbooks in, 107–10; Holocaust Education Center in, 129–31; imperialism of, 27, 117–18, 202; Imperial Rule Assistance in, 175; Japan Catholic Council for Justice and Peace, 300; Japanese Catholic Church, 303; Japanese Catholic Council, 301; Jewel Voice Broadcast, 226; Korea relation to, ix–x, 2–3, 44, 107, 134, 254, 336n14, 338n40; Liberal Democratic Party of, 155–56, 342n84; Manila relation to, 221–22; memory cultures in, xi–xii, 109, 131, 147–49, 155, 220, 223, 231, 262, 263; #MeToo movement in, 260; Ministry of Health of, 166; neighboring countries clause of, 342n89; Okunoshima Poison Gas Museum relation to, 161; Peace Constitution, 149; Poland relation to, 19, 343n8; POW camps of, 194; *So Far from the Bamboo Grove* in, 47–48; Soviet Union relation to, 44–45; U.S. relation to, 112, 114, 132–33, 149–50; Western imperialism relation to, 108, 148
Japanese-American National Museum, 216
Japanese Ministry of Health, Labor, and Welfare, 43–44

Japanese National Language textbook, 234
Japanese POWs, 170–72
Japanese Red Cross Film Festival, 239
Japanese Society of History Textbook Reform, 43
Japan Self-Defense Force, 150
Japan-U.S. War, The (Ishimaru), 133
Jasenovac Committee of the Holy Assembly of Bishops of the Serbian Orthodox Church, 216–17
Jasenovac extermination camp, 216
Jasna Góra, 289
Jaspers, Karl, 266
Jastrzębowski, Jerzy, 34–35
Jedwabne pogrom, 36–37, 80–81, 181, 187, 261, 265; denialism of, 189, 250; Laudański brothers relation to, 178–79, 197–98; Nazis relation to, 38–39
Jee Man-won, 252–53
Jeju *halmangs*, 273
Jeju uprising, 139
Jeong Chan, 139, 349n77
Jerusalem Post, 83
Jesus Christ, 58–59, 326n25
Jewel Voice Broadcast, 226
Jewish Americans, 9, 120–21
Jewish Autonomous Region, in Birobidzhan, 135
Jewish commies (Żydokomuna), 28, 39, 126, 178, 179, 180; Cold War relation to, 206–7
Jewish diasporic victims, 204–5, 210
Jewish Historical Institute, 366n30
Jewish Life, 92
Jews, 2, 91–94, 174, 180, 207, 210–11; Catholicism relation to, 238; civil rights of, 345n29; communism relation to, 28; in Poland, 21–23, 28–29, 33
Jihadists, suicide missions of, 52–53
Jogiches, Leon, 123
John Paul II (Pope), 123, 125, 239, 243, 286; Kolbe relation to, 368n63. *See also* Wojtyła, Karol
Jo Jihun, 53

Jo Moon-sang, 196
Joongang Ilbo, 203
Joseon, 135, 198–99, 200, 202, 361n65; Manchuria compared to, 201; prison camps at, 194, 195
Joseon National Maritime Youth Corps, 69
Józefów, Poland, 170
Judeocide, in Poland, 182–83
Jungkook, 67

Kaesŏng, 70
Kalinowski, Józef, 183
Kałków-Godów, 240
Kamei Shizuka, 109
Kamikaze Special Attack Units, 67, 70, 160
Kamiński, Janusz, 275
Kapitan Lee (Chon), 180
Karta, Neturei, 244
Katanga, Germain, 87
Kathrada, Ahmed, 94–95
Katsuya Taiji, 300
Katyn Forest, 343n8
Kaunas, Lithuania, 188
Kawakami Hajime, 64
Kawashima-Watkins, Yoko, ix–xi, 41–42, 46, 166–67; Unit 731 relation to, 254, 255; VANK relation to, 45. See also *So Far from the Bamboo Grove*
Keller, Helen, 222
Kemal, Mustafa, 132
Kerama Islands, 237
Kershaw, Ian, 327n44
Kfar Kassem, 212
Khmer Rouge, 163
Khomeini, Ayatollah, 245
Kielce pogrom, 29, 182–84, 200; conspiracy theories and, 250–51, 252; denialism of, 189–90; PZPR relation to, 201
Kierkegaard, Søren, 53
Kim Chul-soo, 198
Kim Hak-soon, 85
Kim Han-sang, 274
Kim Il Sung, 75–76, 202–3

Kim Seongnae, 273
Kim Yong-ki, 136
King, Martin Luther, Jr., 140
Kiseki (Sono), 233
Kishida (prime minister), 171
Klein, Felix, 97
Kobla, Rosalia, 238
Koch, Ilse, 96
Koh Hwang Kyung, 192
Kohl, Helmut, 175, 284
Kołakowski, Leszek, 81
Kolbe, Maksymilian, 124, 127–28, 219, 220–22, 228; antisemitism of, 223, 234–36, 237–39, 240, 313; Great East Japan Earthquake relation to, 241–42; John Paul II relation to, 368n63; Nagai and, 365n20; Polish Catholic Church relation to, 286; Sono relation to, 233–34; Western colonialism relation to, 232; *A Woman's Life* relation to, 229–30, 231
Kolbe Museum of Seibo no Kishi, 241–42
Kominek, Bolesław, 35, 281–82, 285–89, 291
Komitet Obrony Robotników, 21
Komiyama, 107
Kono Yohei, 342n89
Korea, 41, 192–93, 314, 325n21, 328n64; Catholicism relation to, 299–303; China relation to, 199–200; collective innocence in, 196, 199, 202, 203; collective memory in, 27, 196; communism in, 140; cult of the fallen soldiers in, 67–68; hereditary victimhood in, xi–xii; Japan relation to, ix–x, 2–3, 44, 107, 134, 254, 336n14, 338n40; Korean Bishops' Conference, 301; Korean Catholic Church, 302–3; Korean Consulate General, in Boston, ix–x; Korean Council for Justice and Remembrance for the Issues of Military Sexual Slavery by Japan, 274; Korean language, 51–52; memory cultures in, 135, 138–39, 199, 201, 272; reparations relation to, 82–83; "Song of Memorial Day" in, 53–54; Vietnam War relation to, 106. *See also* North Korea; South Korea

Korea Herald, xi, 48
Korean American Civic Empowerment, 138
Korean Americans, xi, 49, 88, 138; *So Far from the Bamboo Grove* relation to, 41–42, 45–46, 47, 48
Korean War, 68–69, 70
Kossak-Szczucka, Zofia, 185–86
KPD. *See* Communist Party of Germany
Kraków Academy, 290
Krasiński Square, 30–31
kresy (Eastern borderland), 309
Kristallnacht, 94, 152, 248
Ku Klux Klan, 92, 244
Kuksa (National history), 3
Kupferberg Holocaust Center, 138
Kure, 160
Kurihara Sadako, 119, 159
Kuroita Katsumi, 65–66, 333n57
Kurokawa Umekichi, 66–67
Kuwahara Hideaki, 113
Kuźnica, 184
Kwaśniewski, Aleksander, 39
Kwon Heon-Ik, 273
Kyunghyang Shinmun, 82–83

laïcité conflicts, 64
Lamsdorf/Łambinowice camp, 163
Land (토지, novel), 201
Landscape of Memory, 89
Lanzmann, Claude, 22–23, 28, 37, 122–23
Laub, Dori, 270–71
Laudański brothers, 182, 189, 190, 359n37; communism relation to, 180; Jedwabne pogrom relation to, 178–79, 197–98
Lausanne movement, 294
Law and Justice Party (PiS), 187, 190, 324n6, 328n60
League of Nations, 150, 200, 326n25
Lebanon, 212
Lee Hak-Rae, 195–97
Lee Long-Soo, 255
Lee Myung-bak, 54
Lee San-ha, 139

Lee Yong-soo, 272, 274
Lemkin, Raphael, 93–94, 221
Lenin Steelworks, 112
Lepper, Andrzej, 357n15
Les Belles Lettres, 102
Les Larmes de Jacqueline, 195–96
Les Temps Modernes, 102
Levi, Primo, 102, 227, 279
LGBT victims, 189
Life for Life (Życie za życie, film), 239
Life of Father Kolbe, The, 239
Lipski, Jan Józef, 99, 234–35
London, 154
London Agreement on German External Debts (1953), 81
long-distance nationalism, 18, 49
Lourdes water, 220
Łuczak, Czesław, 25
Łuczewski, Michał, 333n44
Ludwików Steelworks, 183
Luksemburg, Róża (Luxemburg, Rosa), 123
Lytton Report, 150, 200

Maas, Heiko, 307–8
Macharski, Franciszek, 124–25
Magdeburg, 290
Magee, John G., 258
Magnus, Albert, 315
Maidan Revolution, 218–19
Makdisi, Ussama, 306–7
Mały Dziennik, 128, 234–35
Manchukuo, 44, 133–34, 188, 202–3
Manchuria, x, 44, 150, 170–71, 199–200; Joseon compared to, 201. *See also* Wanpaoshan incident
Manchurian Incident, 133
Mandela, Nelson, 95, 305
Manila, 221–22
Mann, Michael, 104
Man's Search for Meaning (Frankl), 131
Mao Zedong, 101
March 1st Movement, 301
"Marching for Our Beloved," 54

INDEX 431

Marco Polo (Bungei), 223
Marshall Plan, 146
Märtyrer, 51
martyrs, 18, 50, 56, 222, 332n34; Kolbe as, 234, 237, 239–40, 242; *męczennik*, 51; sacrifice relation to, 52–53; for secular religion, 60–61; socialist, 146; war dead as, 59
Martyrs' and Heroes Remembrance Law (1959), 208
Maruyama Masao, 175–76
Marxism, 61
Masaaki, Noda, 171
Masada, 208
masochistic history, 328n60
Masonic Mafia, 237–38
Massachusetts Department of Elementary and Secondary Education, ix, 328n64
"master race" (*Herrenvolk*), 96
Matsuoka Yosuke, 133, 150, 326n25
Mauthausen Memorial, 90–91
Mazowiecki, Tadeusz, 284
Mbembe, Achille, 97, 305, 306, 307, 310, 314
McCarthyism, 363n94
McDonald, Gabrielle Kirk, 86
McFadden, Bernice, 96
McFadden, Harlan, 96
męczennik, 51
media representation, 263–64
Meiji Restoration, 65, 118, 132
Memorandum of Tübingen, 288
Memorial Island, in Bergen County Justice Center, 9–10
memory activists, 4, 16, 75, 125, 138, 305; Holocaust relation to, 311–12, 313; WIWCT relation to, 83–84
memory cultures, 10, 14, 16, 48, 73, 173; of Axis powers, 151; in Croatia, 217; cult of the fallen soldiers and, 74; denialism and, 251–52; of East Asia, 49; Eurocentrism in, 104; of France, 103; in Germany, xi–xii, 75, 98, 165–66, 174–75, 262; *Historikerstreit* in, 98; Holocaust

and, xi–xii, 99; in Japan, xi–xii, 109, 131, 147–49, 155, 220, 223, 231, 262, 263; in Korea, 135, 138–39, 199, 201, 272; in Nagasaki, 222–23; in Poland, 37, 80–81, 123, 181, 240, 293, 310–11; reparations relation to, 82; in U.S., 215–16, 315; in West Germany, 167, 289; of Zionists, 208. *See also* global memory culture
memory diplomacy, 128, 308
"Memory Keepers," 155
memory politics, 8, 14, 139, 168, 216–17, 274; in China, 188–89; of Cold War, 140; forgiveness relation to, 276–77, 280–81; Gwangju Uprising and, 256; in Hiroshima, 228; Holocaust relation to, 140, 218; in Israel, 213; of Poland, 180; in Urakami *hansai* theory, 226–27
memory regime, xiii, 7–8; in East Asia, 16–18
memory war, 11, 18, 128, 269; Comfort Women and, 6; in Germany, 305–6; Xi, 20
Mengele, Josef, 255
Mercier (Cardinal), 332n34
metamemory, 13
#MeToo movement, 90, 260
Mexico City Olympics (1968), 150
Michelet, Jules, 61
Michnik, Adam, 179, 184
Mickiewicz, Adam, 28
Militia Immaculatae, 221, 236
Miłosz, Czesław, 29–30, 32–33
Ministry of Health, of Japan, 166
Misuzu Shobo, 131
Mitsubishi Heavy Industries, 160
Mitterand, François, 22–23
Miyazawa Kiichi, 342n89
mnemonic solidarity, 20, 102; for Comfort Women, 89–91; in Germany, 104; in global memory formation, 316; Holocaust relation to, 213
Moczar, Mieczysław, 24, 121
Modern Film Association, 239
Mohammed V, 189

Molotov-Ribbentrop Pact, 179–80, 188, 218
monuments, 60, 66, 325n20; to A-Bomb Hiroshima/Nagasaki, 116, 118; to Auschwitz, 123; Civil War in U.S.A, 158; to Comfort Women, 10, 88, 320n30; to deserters, 73, 74–75; Gwangju, 253; Morocco, 189
Moon Tae-bok, 197
Morawiecki, Mateusz, 187
Morita Shogo, 131
Morocco, 189
Morrison, Toni, 93
Moscow Conference, 173
Moses, Dirk, 307
Mosse, George, 76
Mujahideen, 341n73
Murayama Tomiichi, 342n89
Museum of Genocide Victims, 217
Museum of Modern Art, in Warsaw, 112
Museum of the Second World War (Gdańsk), 189
Musiał, Bogdan, 261–62, 372n35
Muslim Public Affairs Council, 88
Muslims, 104–6, 341n73; antisemitism among, 244–45
Mussolini, Benito, 173
Muta Kazue, 90
My Brother's Keeper, 22
Mỹ Lai massacre, 119, 215, 315

Nagai Takashi, 219–22, 223–26, 227, 241, 365n21, 365n27; Kolbe and, 365n20
Nagasaki, 119, 155, 160; Auschwitz relation to, 19, 219–20, 222, 225, 239, 241; Catholicism relation to, 221; global memory formation and, 243; *Joongang Ilbo* relation to, 203; Kolbe in, 219, 230; memory cultures in, 222–23; survivor's guilt and, 227–28
Nagasaki Bell, 365n27
Nagasaki Peace Park, 115–16
Nagasaki Shimbun, 366n39
Nakasone administration, 109

Namibia, 98–99; Herero and Nama, 4, 99
Nanjing Massacre, 85, 87, 189, 251n33, 321n38; China relation to, 101; denialism of, 248, 258; Hiroshima-Auschwitz Peace March relation to, 117; in history textbooks, 108, 109–10, 342n84; Holocaust compared to, 131–32; Wanpaoshan incident compared to, 200
narrative template of victimhood nationalism, 2, 13, 14, 16, 97, 246
Naruhara Akira, 45
National Basic Issues Society, 109
National Day of Mourning, in Estonia, 218
National history (*Kuksa*), 3
national identity, 19; collective memory and, 320n25; of Germany, 2, 175; in Israel, 204; of Poland, 328n60
nationalism. *See specific topics*
nationalization, 72, 106
National Museum of Japanese Forced Mobilization, 194–95, 336n14
National Radical Camp (Obóz Narodowo-Radykalny, ONR), 190, 235, 367n60
national self-determination, 2
National Showa Memorial Museum, 148
NATO countries, 9, 79, 157–58
Nausėda, Gitanas, 291
Nazis, 78–79, 172, 184, 189, 190, 263–64; Austria relation to, 73, 173–74; Catholicism relation to, 291; civil religion of, 71; conscientious deserters relation to, 334n74; German expellees relation to, 286–87; Ha'avara relation to, 205–6; human rights relation to, 43; Jedwabne pogrom relation to, 38–39; North Korea compared to, 140. *See also* Holocaust
Nazism, 22, 189, 219, 314; accountability for, 143–44; Apartheid compared to, 95–96; capitalism relation to, 146, 147, 176; *Crabwalk* relation to, 168–69; East Germany relation to, 147, 282–83; as secular religion, 333n53; Stalinism relation to, 98, 198, 218, 306

INDEX 433

Nazism in South Africa, 95–96, 305
NCRR. *See* Nikkei for the Civil Rights and Redress
necropolitics, 65, 66
"Negro and the Warsaw Ghetto, The," 91
Nehru, Jawaharlal, 132
neighboring countries clause, 342n89
Neighbors (Gross), 36–38, 80–81, 250, 261, 327n49
neo-Nazis, 168
Netanyahu, Benjamin, 212, 312, 363n104
Netherlands, 26, 129
Neumann, Franz, 372n45
New Dong-A, 253
New Eastern Policy (Ostpolitik), of SPD, 289, 378n53
Newstown, 252
New Village Movement, 136
New York Times, 22, 237
Nigerian Civil War, 341n73
Night Watch, The, 183
Nikkei for the Civil Rights and Redress (NCRR), 88–89
Nissenbaum, Isaac, 57
Nixon, Richard, 256
NKWD. *See* Soviet secret police
Noguchi detachment, 193–94, 196
Nolte, Ernst, 98, 218, 306, 314
nomenklatura (ruling elites), 24, 28
Nonlinear Histories, 89–90
Nonreturned Act, 43–44
North Africa, 189
North Korea, 75–76, 171, 202–3, 252–53; human rights relation to, 321n38; Nazis compared to, 140
Nuremberg and Vietnam, 100
Nuremberg Laws, 95
Nuremberg Trials, 87, 100, 163, 173
Nyokodo, 221–22

Oath of the Japanese Imperial Subjects, 75
Oblak, Tadeusz K., 233

Obóz Narodowo-Radykalny (ONR). *See* National Radical Camp
O'Brown, Agbola, 97
Observateur, 102
Occidentalism, of Poland, 3
Ochab, Edward, 114
Oder-Neisse line, 283–84, 285, 291, 297; German expellees relation to, 295–96; *Ostdenkschrift* and, 286, 288
Oedipus, 61
Oe Kenzaburo, 73–74, 237
official memories, 8, 13, 74, 197, 200, 258
ofiara, 51
ofiara całopalna, 51
Oh Ki-young, 200
Okawa Shumei, 133
Okinawa, 237
Okinawa Notes (Oe), 237
Okunoshima, 160–61
Okunoshima Poison Gas Museum, 161
Opfer, 51, 330n2
Opfertod, 51
oral history, 268
Order of the White Eagle, 186
Oriental History, 118
Orientalism, 118, 175, 309; of Germany, 3
Osaka Peace Museum, 343n8
Oshagan, Anahid, 89–90
Oshagan, Ara, 89–90
Ostdenkschrift, 286–89, 296
Ostforschung (Eastern studies), 3
Ostpolitik, 289
Otsuka Makoto, 130–31, 346n53
Otto, Karl, 96
Otto the Great, 289
Oura Cathedral, 229, 231–32
Oura Saint Kolbe Memorial Museum, 241–42
Oyadomari Josei, 150
Ozaki Tōmei, 228, 230, 366n39

Pacific Comrades Association, 69
Paczkowski, Andrzej, 326n29

Pal, Radhabinod, 156
Palestine, 72, 135, 205–6; Israel relation to, 2, 11, 305, 312, 314–16
Palestine Post, 205
Palestinian Intifada, 213
Panthéon, 60
Papon, Maurice, 102
Paris Massacre, 102
Park Chung-hee, 136, 139
Park Namjoo, 243
Park Young-Shim, 254–55, 274
particular path (*Sonderweg*), 17, 176–77, 313
Partition, 28
Parzyński, Elijasz, 34–35
patriarchy, 87, 260
Paul, Christa, 91
Paul VI (Pope), 292
Pawlikowski, Paweł, 37–38
PAX, 113–14
Pax Christi-Bewegung, 286
Peace Constitution (Japan), 149
Peace of Westphalia, 1–2
Pearl Harbor, 221, 353n64
Peasant Party (Stronnictwo Chłopskie) convention, 183–84
pedagogika wstydu, 328n60
Pericles, 331n15
Perilous Kinship (Şenocak), 105
perpetrators, 19, 43, 165–66; forgiveness relation to, 280–81; of Kielce pogrom, 182–83; positivistic denialism of, 269; victims relation to, 169, 178, 181–82, 198
Perry (Commodore), 2–3
Petitjean (Father), 231, 232
phenomenology, of memory, 6
"Philosophy for Palestine," 315
photographs, 262–63, 273–74, 275
Piasecki, Bolesław, 114, 181
Pietà, 63
Pięta, Stanisław, 111–12
"pile of gold," 78–79
Piłsudski, Józef, 233
Piotrowski, Tadeusz, 25

PiS. *See* Law and Justice Party
Poalej Syjon, 324n16
Poland, 2, 25, 27, 127, 162–63, 325n20; antisemitism in, 23–24, 34, 40, 122, 126, 184–85, 357n12; Catholics in, 22, 39–40, 235–36; collective innocence in, 186–88, 189–90; collective memory in, 22, 28, 189–91; colonialism relation to, 309–10; German expellees relation to, 161, 165; Germany relation to, 377n35; hereditary victimhood in, xi–xii, 18, 38; Holocaust relation to, 33–34, 36; Jacobin regime in, 59–60; Japan relation to, 19, 343n8; Jews in, 21–23, 28–29, 33; Józefów, 170; Judeocide in, 182–83; memory cultures in, 37, 80–81, 123, 181, 240, 293, 310–11; memory politics of, 180; national identity of, 328n60; Occidentalism of, 3; People's Poland, 24; reparations for, 325n23; in Russo-Japanese War, 231; Stalinism relation to, 22, 38–39, 381n20; Ukraine relation to, 284–85; Warsaw, 26, 30–31, 112; West Germany relation to, 282–84, 285–90, 291–93, 296–98, 375n9
Polar Film, 263–64
Polish Academy of Sciences, Institute of History at, 37
Polish Catholic Church, 187, 240, 281–82, 283, 286, 302. *See also* Catholicism
Polish Council to Aid Jews. *See* Żegota
Polish Galicja, 92
Polish Intelligence Agency, 295
Polish Ministry of Finance, 25
Polish Socialist Party (PPS), 183
Polish Underground State, Jews relation to, 180
Polish United Workers' Communist Party (PZPR), 121–22, 282, 287, 289, 324n6; antisemitism in, 359n33; Catholicism relation to, 283; Kielce pogrom relation to, 201; Secret Police of, 180
Polish War Reparations Bureau, 24–25, 27
Polish Workers' Party (PPR), 183

political regime change, xiii, 7–8, 17–18
political religion, 54, 330n13, 333n44; in East Asia, 76; fascism relation to, 63; fatherland relation to, 72–73; sacrifice relation to, 55; State Shinto as, 64–65
Politik der Feindschaft (Mbembe), 97
Polonsky, Anthony, 326n29
Pomerania, 291
Ponnier, Matthias, 263
Ponticelli, Lazare, 331n22
"Poor Christian Looks at the Ghetto, A," 29–30
Popiełuszko, Jerzy, 240–41
positivistic denialism, 255–56, 258, 264, 269; conspiracy theories' relation to, 259–60
postcolonial(-ism), 2, 4, 5, 11, 17, 20, 40, 41, 67
postcommunist, 4, 38, 217–19, 308, 310–11
Pot, Pol, 341n73
Potsdam Conference, 162
POW camps, 144, 191–93; war crimes in, 194–97
PPR. *See* Polish Workers' Party
PPS. *See* Polish Socialist Party
Prague Declaration, 312
Preston, Paul, 341n73
prison camps: at Joseon, 194, 195; in West Germany, 169–70. *See also* POW camps
Prison of Robben Island, 94
pro domino mori, 60
proletarian internationalism, 9, 24–25, 113, 121, 167–68
pro patria mori, 60
Protocols of the Elders of Zion, The, 236
Putin, Vladimir, 219
PZPR. *See* Polish United Workers' Communist Party

al-Qaeda, 160
Qian Xiuling, 188–89
Queensborough Community College, 138
Quisling regime, of Norway, 184

Rabe, John, 189
Rafu Shimpo, 89
Ranam, 46. *See also So Far from the Bamboo Grove*
Rape of Nanjing, 85, 101
Ratzinger, Joseph, 378n53
Ravensbrück, 91
Rebirth, 184
Red Purge, The, 166
red textbooks, in Japan, 108
reenchantment (*Wiederzauberung*), 55
ReflectSpace, 89–90
Remembrance, Responsibility and Future Foundation, 81, 82–83
Renan, Ernest, 54, 320n26
reparations, 75, 83, 325n23; memory cultures relation to, 82
Reserve Police Battalion 101, 170
reterritorialization (of memory), 11, 15, 19, 119, 123, 136, 141, 306, 311, 316. *See also* deterritorialization (of memory)
"Rhineland Mongrel," 96–97
Richthofen, Wolfram Freiherr von, 154
Ricoeur, Paul, 6, 294
Righteous Among the Nations, 186, 187
Rikidōzan, 150–51
rituals, 18, 54, 55, 59; for war dead, 61, 65, 67–68
Romantic nationalism, 2
Rome, 30–32
Rome Statute, 86
Roosevelt, Franklin, 148, 158–59
Rosenberg spy case, 9, 206
Rosenfeld, Netty, 358n17
Rotem, Simha, 32
Rothberg, Michael, 15, 104, 306
Rousseau, Jean-Jacques, 59
Ruhr Triennial Arts Festival, 97
ruling elites (*nomenklatura*), 24, 28
Russell, Bertrand, 100
Russell Tribunal, 83, 100
Russia, 63, 309–10
Russo, Henry, 322n43

Russo-Japanese War, 64, 65, 132; Poland in, 231
Rwanda, 85–86
Rwandan genocide, 85
Rycerz Niepokalanej, 235

sacer, 52
sacrifice, 56, 61, 70, 223–27; by forced mobilization, 83; martyrs relation to, 52–53; political religion relation to, 55; sublimation of, 50; victims relation to, 51–52; in *A Woman's Life*, 229–30
Sanacja regime, 309
Sankei Shimbun, 236
Sapieha, Adam Stefan, 251
Sartre, Jean-Paul, 100
Sasaki Sadako, 347n55
Sato Gyotsu, 112, 116–17, 119
"savonette," 363n90
SCAP. *See* Supreme Commander for the Allied Powers
Schadenfreude, 143
Schatz, Adam, 316
Schindler's List, 275
School of Servants of God Ulma Family, 187
screen memory, 28, 155, 216, 223, 311; in China, 188–89
SDKP. *See* Social Democracy of the Kingdom of Poland
Sealey, John, 96–97
Sebald, Winfried G., 154
Second Alien Land Law (1920), 133
Secret Police, of PZPR, 180
secular ideologies, 50
secular religion, 58; martyrs for, 60–61; Nazism as, 333n53
SED. *See* Socialist Unity Party
Seebohm, Hans-Christoph, 165
Seibo no Kishi, 220, 231, 232, 239, 365n21; Kolbe Museum of, 241–42
Şenocak, Zafer, 105
Seoul National Cemetery, 67
Seoul Women's University, 192

Sephardi Jews, 94, 210
Sepoy Rebellion, 132
Serbia, 216–17, 311
Sereny, Gitta, 333n53
Sergius (Father), 232
7th Cavalry Regiment, 103
sexual violence, 5, 45, 161; in Asia-Pacific War, 85, 91; Comfort Women and, 49; genocide relation to, 87; *hikiagesha* and, 166; in Rwanda, 85–86
Seydewitz, Max, 152
Shaltiel, David, 204–5
shame: Holocaust relation to, 35–36; war dead relation to, 74
Shoah, 22–24, 27–28, 37, 122–23
Shokonsha, 65
Shokun!, 155
Shot at Dawn, 75
Siberia, POW camps in, 194
Siła-Nowicki, Władysław, 34
Silesia, 291
Simon Wiesenthal Center, 341n73
Sinanyan, Zareh, 88–89
Sinograph, 52
Sino-Japanese War, 65, 117–18; atrocities in, 101; Hiroshima and, 157
Sinuiju Student Protest, 70
Six-Day War, 135–36, 211
Slánský, Rudolf, 207
Slawson, John, 206
Śliwiński, Krzysztof, 126
Slovak Jewish Memory Restoration project, 268
Smithsonian Museum, 158
Smoloar, Aleksander, 308–9
Sobibor Extermination Camp, 359n37
Social and Cultural Association of Jews, 28
Social Democracy of the Kingdom of Poland (SDKP), 123
Social Democratic Party (SPD), 287, 288–89, 378n53
social formation, global memory formation compared to, 5–6

INDEX   437

socialist martyrs, 146
Socialist Unity Party (SED), 146
"Society of Enmity, The," 305
Society to Make New History Textbooks, 109, 148
So Far from the Bamboo Grove (Kawashima-Watkins), ix–xi, 41–43, 166–67, 169, 251, 328n64; *hikiagesha* in, 44–45; Holocaust relation to, 137–38; in Japan, 47–48; VANK relation to, 46–47
solidarity, 11; mnemonic, 20, 89–91, 102, 104, 213, 316
Solidarność, 21
Somuncu, Serdar, 105
Sonderweg (particular path), 17, 176–77, 313
"Song of Constitution Day," 53–54
"Song of Memorial Day," 53–54
Song of Sorrows (Jung), 139
Sono Ayako, 233–34, 235–37, 238
South Africa. *See* Apartheid
South Korea, 41–42, 108–9, 135–36, 140, 202–3; Holocaust relation to, 136–37, 139; war dead relation to, 69–70
Soviet-Jewish Occupation, 39
Soviet secret police (NKWD), 39–40, 179–80, 181, 250–51
Soviet Union, 26, 39, 71–72, 112, 288, 291; Dresden relation to, 152–53; Hiroshima relation to, 156; Japanese POWs in, 170–72; Japan relation to, 44–45
Spanish Civil War, 154, 169, 341n73
SPD. *See* Social Democratic Party
Special Court for Sierra Leone, 87
Spence, Donald, 271
Spiegel, 174, 307
Spielberg, Steven, 275
Srebrenica, 247
Stalin, Joseph, 9, 153; Order No. 227 of, 72
Stalingrad, 154–55
Stalinism, 147, 189, 207; Gulag, 4, 218, 304; Nazism relation to, 98, 198, 218, 306; Poland relation to, 22, 38–39, 381n20

Stalins Beutezug, 372n35
Stalin's Order No. 227, 72
Stangl, Franz, 333n53
"Statement in Commemoration of the Hundredth Anniversary of the March 1st Movement," 301
State Shinto, 64–65, 130
Stearns, Peter, 373n52
Steele, Brent J., 320n25
Stein, Edith, 124, 127–28, 239
Stern, 174
Sternhell, Zeev, 104, 208
Stockholm Declaration, 18, 79–80
Stockholm International Forum on the Holocaust, 77–78
Stola, Dariusz, 326n29
Stolen Generations, 248
"Strength Through Joy" program, 169
Studia Zachodnie (Western studies), 3
sublimation, 50, 55–56, 62, 227
Suez Canal crisis, 212
suffering, 19, 54, 56–57, 58, 320n26, 330n2; of Comfort Women, 274–75; at Dresden, 154; of German expellees, 166–67, 169, 291–93; in Germany, 142–43; global memory formation relation to, 165, 214–15; of Japanese POWs, 171; in *So Far from the Bamboo Grove*, 45–46
Suga Yoshihide, 203
Sugihara Chiune, 188
suicide, 70, 72, 208, 237, 330n3; of Jihadists, 52–53
Sukarno, Achmed, 199
Sunflower, The (Wiesenthal), 277–79
Sunobe Ryojo, 107
Sun Yat-Sen, 132
Supreme Commander for the Allied Powers (SCAP), 149, 175
survivor's guilt, 62, 182, 227–28
suspicion-based denialism, 249
Suzuki Zenko, 107
Świtoń, Kazimierz, 126
Switzerland, 66

System Club, 252
Sznaider, Natan, 97–98, 306

Tagore, Rabindranath, 132
Taiping Rebellion, 132
Taiwan, 262
Takahashi Shinji, 365n27
Tange Kenzo, 159
Taylor, Charles, 87
Taylor, Telford, 100
Tehran, Iran, 244
Tehran Times, 245
Tell, Wilhelm, 66
testimonies, 12, 266, 267–68, 270–71
Teutonic Order, 290–91, 295
Thai-Burma Death Railway, The (special exhibition), 195
Thailand-Burma Railway, 193, 195
Third Reich Private, The (film), 263–64
Third World, 2, 208, 311
Those Who Became War Criminals (permanent exhibition), 194
Tlaib, Rashida, 315
Tochinoki Hot Springs, 365n20
Todorov, Tzvetan, 76
Tokashiki Islands, 237
TOK FM, 38
Tokyo Olympics (1964), 150, 159
Tokyo Trials, 87, 150, 175
Tombs of the Unknown Soldiers, 74
Toyoshi (Eastern history), 3
Toyotomi Hideyoshi, 224
transatlantic slave trade, 5, 93, 97, 304
transnational denialism, 262
transnational history, 319n12
Travel to India (Koh), 192
Treatise of Japan-U.S. War, The, 133
Treaty of San Francisco, 192
Treaty of Zgorzelec/Görlitz, 162
Treaty on Basic Relations Between Japan and the Republic of Korea, 83, 300
Treaty on the Final Settlement concerning Germany, 81–82

Treblinka death camp, 23, 154, 212, 245, 333n53
Treece, Patricia, 237
Tribute to the Army and Nav,, A, 60
Trump, Donald, 363n104
Trumpism, 2
Trybuna Ludu, 297
Tsuburaya Kokichi, 150
Tsuruga, 188
Tucholsky, Kurt, 74–75
Tulsa Race Massacre, 315, 361n62
Turner, Alfred, 94
Turowicz, Jerzy, 21
Tutsi women, 85
Twenty-Six Martyrs Museum, 222
Tych, Feliks, 366n30
Tygodnik Powszechny, 21, 234–35

Uighur internment camps, 188
Ukraine, 218–19, 284–85, 325n19
Ulbricht, Walter, 146
Ulma, Józef, 186–87, 189
Ulma, Wiktoria, 186–87, 189
Ulma Family Museum of Poles Saving Jews in World War II: Amendment to the Act on the Institute of National Remembrance in the, 187–88
Umsiedler, 297
Uncle Tom's Cabin (Stowe), 93
UN Genocide Convention, 103
Ungváry, Krisztián, 261
UN Human Rights Council, Comfort Women and, 88
Unit 731, 46, 254, 255, 348n66
United Nations Economic and Social Council, 27
United States (U.S.), x–xi, 47, 93, 146, 207, 312; civil rights in, 100; colonial genocide in, 103; Islamophobia in, 88; Japan relation to, 112, 114, 132–33, 149–50; memory cultures in, 215–16, 315
Universal Declaration of Human Rights, 97–98, 306
"Unknown Deserter," 75

Unknown Soldiers, 60
UN Peacekeeping Forces, 87
UN Report of the Special Rapporteur on Cultural Rights, 10
UN Special Rapporteur on Sexual Slavery, 84
Un'yō incident, 2–3
Urakami Cathedral, 221, 222; Urakami *hansai* theory, 223–25, 226–27
U.S. *See* United States
U.S.-Japan Security Treaty, 114
Ustasha, 216–17

Valley of Crosses, at Carmelite convent, 127
VANK. *See* Voluntary Agency Network of Korea
Velshi, Ali, 314–15
vernacular memories, 8–9, 13, 38, 259, 289
Vertriebene, 151, 164, 165, 289, 297
Vichy France, 189
victimhood. *See specific topics*
victims, 50, 69, 78, 103–4, 189, 271–72; in cultural memory, 58, 268–69; of fascism, 171–72, 176–77; forgiveness relation to, 280–81; as heroes, 57–58; of imperialism, 197; Jewish diasporic, 204–5, 210; perpetrators relation to, 169, 178, 181–82, 198; sacrifice relation to, 51–52; survivor's guilt of, 182
Vietnam War, xi, 102, 106, 119; atrocities in, 100–101; Holocaust compared to, 100, 215, 315. *See also* Mỹ Lai massacre
Villot (Cardinal), 332n34
Visegrád Group, 187
Viseur-Seller, Patricia, 86
Volhynia massacre, 219
Völkerschau ("human zoo"), 97
Volkstrauertag, 349n8
Voluntary Agency Network of Korea (VANK), 45, 46–47, 254–55
Vorster, Balthazar J., 95

Wadani, Richard, 72
Wadi Salib, 210

Waffen-SS, 75
Wałęsa, Lech, 126
Wanpaoshan incident, 199–201, 202, 203, 361n62
war crimes, 131, 194–97
war dead, 57, 63, 331n15, 349n8; funeral rites for, 62; Jesus Christ relation to, 58–59; rituals for, 61, 65, 67–68; shame relation to, 74; South Korea relation to, 69–70; sublimation of, 55–56. *See also* Yasukuni Shrine
War of Annihilation, 260–61, 262–63
Warsaw, Poland, 26, 30–31, 112
Warsaw ghetto, 91–92, 97, 122, 185, 207, 324n16; Rotem and, 32
Warsaw Pact, 9
Warsaw Uprising, 186
Warschawski, Michel, 363n90
Wasersztajn, Szmuel, 179, 250, 261, 264–65
Washington Post, 237
Wawel Royal Castle, 112
WCC. *See* World Council of Churches
Weber, Mark, 245
Weber, Max, 333n44
Wehrmacht, 334n74
Wehrmacht deserters, 73
Weidauer, Walter, 152
Weinberg, Werner, 204
Weiss, Avraham, 124, 125, 127, 128, 346n42
Western colonialism, 232, 313
Western imperialism, 4, 132, 146, 156; Japan relation to, 108, 148
Western Institute, 343n8
Western studies (*Studia Zachodnie*), 3
West Germany, 144–46, 161–65, 206–7; Dresden relation to, 153–54; memory cultures in, 167, 289; Poland relation to, 282–84, 285–90, 291–93, 296–98, 375n9; prison camps in, 169–70
Where Hands Touch, 96–97
Where Is My Elder Son Cain, 36
"white Australia policy," 94
"white Pacific," 148

"White Rose," 292
white supremacy, 155, 244–45
Wiederzauberung (reenchantment), 55
Wielka Encyklopedia Powszechna PWN, 121
Wieluń, 154, 160
Wiesel, Elie, 130, 321n35
Wiesenthal, Simon, 277–79
Wilhelm Gustloff, 167–68. See also *Crabwalk*
Wilkomirski, Binjamin, 271
Wilson, Woodrow, 2
Winowska, Maria, 233, 236
Wirsching, Andreas, 307–8
WIWCT. *See* Women's International War Crimes Tribunal on Japan's Military Sexual Slavery
Włodkowic, Paweł, 290
Wojnarowska, Cezaryna, 123
Wojtyła, Karol, 235, 286, 368n63. *See also* John Paul II
Wolf, Christa, 145
Woman's Life, A (Endō), 228–31, 239
Women's International War Crimes Tribunal on Japan's Military Sexual Slavery (WIWCT), 18–19, 83–85
Women's Society of Saint Paul of Japan, 239
Working Group for Asia and the Far East, at United Nations Economic and Social Council, 27
World Conference on Human Rights (1993), 86
World Council of Churches (WCC), 294
World Heritage Site, 128
World Jewish Congress, 79
World Trade Center, 160
World War I, 2, 59, 60, 75, 233
World War II, 7, 88, 187–88, 216. *See also* Holocaust
World Zionist Congress, 212
Wounded Knee Massacre, 103
Wrocław, 286, 287–88

Wyka, Kazimierz, 184
Wyszyński, Stefan, 281, 283, 296, 298

Xavier, Francisco, 222
Xi Jinping, 189

Yad Mordechai, 208, 321n35
Yad Vashem, 94, 186, 187, 208, 366n30
Yale University, 268, 270
Yamada Kan, 226
Yamahata Yosuke, 263
Yang Chil-seong, 199
Yasukuni Circus, 65
Yasukuni Shrine, 64, 65–66, 68, 70, 74, 342n89; Fukuda Takeo at, 106–7; Yushukan Museum at, 148, 158–59
Yildiz, Yasemin, 104
Yom HaShoah, 207–8
Yonehara Mari, 170
Yonhap News, 41–42
Yoshida, Akio, 346n53
Yoshida Akio, 347n58
Yoshida Yutaka, 325n21
Young Ireland, 2
Young Italy, 2
Young Turks, 2
Youth European Forum, 285
Yugoslavia, 85–86, 157–58, 216–17, 223
Yugoslav Wars, 5, 91, 217
Yushukan Museum, 148, 158–59

Zaremba, Marcin, 308–9
Żegota (Polish Council to Aid Jews), 185–86
Zgorzelec Treaty, 283
Zionists, 204–5, 208, 210–11; Holocaust relation to, 40, 207
Žižek, Slavoj, 243
Znak, 287
Zündel, Ernst, 245
Zwigenberg, Ran, 112
Żydokomuna. *See* Jewish commies

GPSR Authorized Representative: Easy Access System Europe, Mustamäe tee 50, 10621 Tallinn, Estonia, gpsr.requests@easproject.com

www.ingramcontent.com/pod-product-compliance
Lightning Source LLC
Chambersburg PA
CBHW022024290426
44109CB00014B/738